LEARNSMART ADVANTAGE WORKS

More C students earn B's

*Study: 690 students / 6 institutions

Without LearnSmart

Over 20%
more students pass the class with LearnSmart

*A&P Research Study

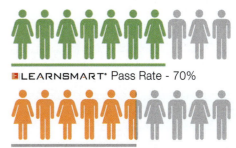

LEARNSMART® Pass Rate - 70%

Without LearnSmart Pass Rate - 57%

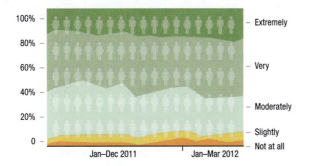

Jan–Dec 2011   Jan–Mar 2012

100%
80%
60%
40%
20%
0

— Extremely
— Very
— Moderately
— Slightly
— Not at all

More than 60%
of all students agreed LearnSmart was a very or extremely helpful learning tool

*Based on 750,000 student survey responses

> **AVAILABLE** *ON-THE-GO*

fundamentals of
Human Resource Management

fundamentals of
Human Resource Management

SIXTH EDITION

Raymond A. Noe
The Ohio State University

John R. Hollenbeck
Michigan State University

Barry Gerhart
University of Wisconsin–Madison

Patrick M. Wright
University of South Carolina

McGraw Hill Education

FUNDAMENTALS OF HUMAN RESOURCE MANAGEMENT, SIXTH EDITION

Published by McGraw-Hill Education, 2 Penn Plaza, New York, NY 10121. Copyright © 2016 by McGraw-Hill Education. All rights reserved. Printed in the United States of America. Previous editions © 2014, 2011, and 2009. No part of this publication may be reproduced or distributed in any form or by any means, or stored in a database or retrieval system, without the prior written consent of McGraw-Hill Education, including, but not limited to, in any network or other electronic storage or transmission, or broadcast for distance learning.

Some ancillaries, including electronic and print components, may not be available to customers outside the United States.

This book is printed on acid-free paper.

3 4 5 6 7 8 9 DOW 21 20 19 18 17 16

ISBN 978-0-07-771836-7
MHID 0-07-771836-4

Senior Vice President, Products & Markets: *Kurt L. Strand*
Vice President, General Manager, Products & Markets: *Michael Ryan*
Vice President, Content Design & Delivery: *Kimberly Meriwether David*
Brand Manager: *Anke Weeks*
Product Developer: *Jane Beck*
Marketing Manager: *Michael Gedatus*
Director of Development: *Ann Torbert*
Director, Content Design & Delivery: *Terri Schiesl*
Executive Program Manager: *Faye M. Herrig*
Content Project Managers: *Jessica Portz, Danielle Clement, Judi David*
Buyer: *Debra R. Sylvester*
Design: *Studio Montage, St. Louis, MO*
Content Licensing Specialists: *Keri Johnson, Ann Marie Jannette*
Cover Image: *Dimitri Otis/Getty Images*
Compositor: *MPS Limited*
Typeface: *10/12 Janson Text Lt Std*
Printer: *R. R. Donnelley*

All credits appearing on page or at the end of the book are considered to be an extension of the copyright page.

Library of Congress Cataloging-in-Publication Data

Noe, Raymond A.
  Fundamentals of human resource management / Raymond A. Noe, John R.
Hollenbeck, Barry Gerhart, Patrick M. Wright.—Sixth edition.
    pages cm
  ISBN 978-0-07-771836-7 (alk. paper)
1. Personnel management. I. Title.
  HF5549.F86 2016
  658.3--dc23

                                              2014041580

The Internet addresses listed in the text were accurate at the time of publication. The inclusion of a website does not indicate an endorsement by the authors or McGraw-Hill Education, and McGraw-Hill Education does not guarantee the accuracy of the information presented at these sites.

www.mhhe.com

About the Authors

Raymond A. Noe is the Robert and Anne Hoyt Designated Professor of Management at The Ohio State University. He was previously a professor in the Department of Management at Michigan State University and the Industrial Relations Center of the Carlson School of Management, University of Minnesota. He received his BS in psychology from The Ohio State University and his MA and PhD in psychology from Michigan State University. Professor Noe conducts research and teaches undergraduate as well as MBA and PhD students in human resource management, managerial skills, quantitative methods, human resource information systems, training, employee development, and organizational behavior. He has published articles in the *Academy of Management Annals, Academy of Management Journal, Academy of Management Review, Journal of Applied Psychology, Journal of Vocational Behavior,* and *Personnel Psychology*. Professor Noe is currently on the editorial boards of several journals including *Personnel Psychology, Journal of Applied Psychology*, and *Journal of Organizational Behavior*. Professor Noe has received awards for his teaching and research excellence, including the Ernest J. McCormick Award for Distinguished Early Career Contribution from the Society for Industrial and Organizational Psychology. He is also a fellow of the Society of Industrial and Organizational Psychology.

John R. Hollenbeck holds the positions of University Distinguished Professor at Michigan State University and Eli Broad Professor of Management at the Eli Broad Graduate School of Business Administration. Dr. Hollenbeck received his PhD in Management from New York University in 1984. He served as the acting editor at *Organizational Behavior and Human Decision Processes* in 1995, the associate editor of *Decision Sciences* from 1999 to 2004, and the editor of *Personnel Psychology* from 1996 to 2002. He has published over 90 articles and book chapters on the topics of team decision making and work motivation. According to the Institute for Scientific Information, this body of work has been cited over 3,000 times by other researchers. Dr. Hollenbeck has been awarded fellowship status in both the Academy of Management and the American Psychological Association, and was recognized with the Career Achievement Award by the HR Division of the Academy of Management (2011) and the Early Career Award by the Society of Industrial and Organizational Psychology (1992). At Michigan State, Dr. Hollenbeck has won several teaching awards including the Michigan State Distinguished Faculty Award, the Michigan State Teacher-Scholar Award, and the Broad MBA Most Outstanding Faculty Member.

Barry Gerhart is Professor of Management and Human Resources and the Bruce R. Ellig Distinguished Chair in Pay and Organizational Effectiveness, School of Business, University of Wisconsin-Madison. He has also served as department chair or area coordinator at Cornell, Vanderbilt, and Wisconsin. His research interests include compensation, human resource strategy, international human resources, and employee retention. Professor Gerhart received his BS in psychology from Bowling Green State University and his PhD in industrial relations from the University of Wisconsin-Madison. His research has been published in a variety of outlets, including the *Academy of Management Annals*, *Academy of Management Journal*, *Annual Review of Psychology*, *International Journal of Human Resource Management*, *Journal of Applied Psychology*, *Management and Organization Review*, and *Personnel Psychology*. He has co-authored two books in the area of compensation. He serves on the editorial boards of journals such as the *Academy of Management Journal*, *Industrial and Labor Relations Review*, *International Journal of Human Resource Management*, *Journal of Applied Psychology*, *Journal of World Business*, *Management & Organization Review*, and *Personnel Psychology*. Professor Gerhart is a past recipient of the Heneman Career Achievement Award, the Scholarly Achievement Award, and of the International Human Resource Management Scholarly Research Award, all from the Human Resources Division, Academy of Management. He is a Fellow of the Academy of Management, the American Psychological Association, and the Society for Industrial and Organizational Psychology.

Patrick M. Wright is the Thomas C. Vandiver Bicentennial Chair in the Darla Moore School of Business at the University of South Carolina. Prior to joining USC, he served on the faculties at Cornell University, Texas A&M University, and the University of Notre Dame.

Professor Wright teaches, conducts research, and consults in the area of Strategic Human Resource Management (SHRM), particularly focusing on how firms use people as a source of competitive advantage and the changing nature of the Chief HR Officer role. For the past eight years he has been studying the CHRO role through a series of confidential interviews, public podcasts, small discussion groups, and conducting the HR@Moore Survey of Chief HR Officers. In addition, he is the faculty leader for the Cornell ILR Executive Education/NAHR program, "The Chief HR Officer: Strategies for Success," aimed at developing potential successors to the CHRO role. He served as the lead editor on the recently released book, *The Chief HR Officer: Defining the New Role of Human Resource Leaders*, published by John Wiley and Sons.

He has published more than 60 research articles in journals as well as more than 20 chapters in books and edited volumes. He is the Incoming Editor at the *Journal of Management*. He has coedited a special issue of *Research in Personnel and Human Resources Management* titled "Strategic Human Resource Management in the 21st Century" and guest edited a special issue of *Human Resource Management Review* titled "Research in Strategic HRM for the 21st Century."

He has conducted programs and consulted for a number of large organizations, including Comcast, Royal Dutch Shell, Kennametal, Astra-Zeneca, BT, and BP. He currently serves as a member on the Board of Directors for the National Academy of Human Resources (NAHR). He is a former board member of HRPS, SHRM Foundation, and World at Work (formerly American Compensation Association). In 2011, 2012, and 2013 he was named by *HRM Magazine* as one of the 20 "Most Influential Thought Leaders in HR."

Preface

Managing human resources is a critical component of any company's overall mission to provide value to customers, shareholders, employees, and the community in which it does business. Value includes profits as well as employee growth and satisfaction, creation of new jobs, contributions to community programs, and protection of the environment. All aspects of human resource management, including acquiring, preparing, developing, and compensating employees, can help companies meet their daily challenges, create value, and provide competitive advantages in the global marketplace. In addition, effective human resource management requires an awareness of broader contextual issues affecting business, such as the economy, legislation, and globalization.

Both the media and academic research show that effective HRM practices result in greater value for shareholders and employees. For example, the human resource practices at companies such as Google, SAS, The Boston Consulting Group, Edward Jones, and Quicken Loans helped them earn recognition on *Fortune* magazine's recent list of "The Top 100 Companies to Work For." This publicity creates a positive vibe for these companies, helping them attract talented new employees, motivate and retain current employees, and make their products and services more desirable to consumers.

Our Approach: Engage, Focus, and Apply

Following graduation, most students will find themselves working in businesses or not-for-profit organizations. Regardless of position or career aspirations, their role in directly managing other employees or understanding human resource management practices is critical for ensuring both company and personal success. As a result, *Fundamentals of Human Resource Management*, Sixth Edition, focuses on human resource issues and how HR is used at work. *Fundamentals* is applicable to both HR majors and students from other majors or colleges who are taking an HR course as an elective or a requirement.

Our approach to teaching human resource management involves *engaging* students in learning through the use of real-world examples and best practices; *focusing* them on important HR issues and concepts; and *applying* what they have learned through chapter features and end-of-chapter exercises and cases. Students not only learn about best practices but are actively engaged through the use of cases and decision making. As a result, students will be able to take what they have learned in the course and apply it to solving HRM problems they will encounter on the job.

As described in the guided tour of the book that follows, each chapter includes several different pedagogical features. "Best Practices" provides examples of companies whose HR activities work well. "HR Oops!" highlights HRM issues that have been handled poorly. "Did You Know?" offers interesting statistics about chapter topics and how they play out in real-world companies. "HRM Social" demonstrates how social media and the Internet can be useful in managing HR activities in any organization. "Thinking Ethically" confronts students with issues that occur in managing human resources. For this new edition, we have added questions to each of the features to assist students with critical thinking and to spark classroom discussions.

Fundamentals also assists students with learning "How to" perform HR activities, such as writing effective HR policies, being strategic about equal employment opportunities, and making the most of HR analytics. These are all work situations students are likely to encounter as part of their professional careers. The end-of-chapter cases focus on corporate sustainability ("Taking Responsibility"), managing the workforce ("Managing Talent"), and HR activities in small organizations ("HR in Small Business").

Organization of the Sixth Edition

Based on user and reviewer feedback, we have made several changes to the chapter organization for the Sixth Edition. The chapter on developing human resources now concludes Part 2, and the chapter on creating and maintaining high-performance organizations has been moved up to open Part 3. We believe these changes will help strengthen the discussion of key concepts.

Part 1 (Chapters 1–4) discusses the environmental forces that companies face in trying to manage human resources effectively. These forces include economic, technological, and social trends; employment laws; and work design. Employers typically have more control over work design than trends and equal employment laws, but all of these factors influence how companies attract, retain, and motivate human resources. Chapter 1 discusses why HRM is a critical component to an organization's overall success. The chapter introduces HRM practices and the roles and responsibilities of HR professionals and other managers in managing human resources.

Some of the major trends discussed in Chapter 2 include how workers continue to look for employment as the U.S. economy recovers from recession and how the recovery has motivated employees to look for new jobs and career opportunities. The chapter also highlights the greater availability of new and less expensive technologies for HRM, including social media and the Internet; the growth of HRM on a global scale as more U.S. companies expand beyond national borders; the types of skills needed for today's jobs; and the importance of aligning HRM with a company's overall strategy to gain competitive advantage. Chapter 3 provides an overview of the major laws affecting employees and the ways organizations can develop HR practices that comply with the laws. Chapter 4 highlights how jobs and work systems determine the knowledge, skills, and abilities that employees need to perform their jobs and influence employees' motivation, satisfaction, and safety at work. The chapter also discusses the process of analyzing and designing jobs.

Part 2 (Chapters 5–8) deals with acquiring, training, and developing human resources. Chapter 5 discusses how to develop a human resources plan. It emphasizes the strengths and weaknesses of different options for dealing with shortages and excesses of human resources, including outsourcing, use of contract workers, and downsizing. Strategies for recruiting talented employees are highlighted, including use of electronic recruiting sources such as social media and online job sites.

Chapter 6 emphasizes that employee selection is a process that starts with screening applications and résumés and concludes with a job offer. The chapter takes a look at the most widely used methods for minimizing mistakes in choosing employees, including employment tests and candidate interviews. Selection method standards, such as reliability and validity, are discussed in understandable terms. Chapter 7 covers the features of effective training systems. Effective training includes not only creating a good learning environment but also hiring managers who encourage employees to use training content in their jobs and hiring employees who are motivated and ready to learn. Concluding Part 2, Chapter 8 demonstrates how assessment, job experiences, formal courses, and mentoring relationships can be used to develop employees for future success.

Part 3 (Chapters 9–11) focuses on assessing and improving performance. Chapter 9 sets the tone for this section of the book by discussing the important role of HRM in creating and maintaining an organization that achieves a high level of performance for employees, managers, customers, shareholders, and community. The chapter describes high-performance work systems and the conditions that contribute to high performance. Chapter 10 examines the strengths and weaknesses of different performance management systems. Chapter 11 discusses how to maximize employee engagement and productivity and retain valuable employees as well as how to fairly and humanely separate employees when the need arises because of poor performance or economic conditions.

Part 4 (Chapters 12–14) covers rewarding and compensating human resources, including how to design pay structures, recognize good performers, and provide benefits. Chapter 12 discusses how managers weigh the importance and costs of pay to develop a compensation structure and levels of pay for each job given the worth of the jobs, legal requirements, and employee judgments about the fairness of pay levels. Chapter 13 covers the advantages and disadvantages of different types of incentive pay, including merit pay, gainsharing, and stock ownership. Chapter 14 highlights the contents of employee benefits packages, the ways organizations administer benefits, and what companies can do to help employees understand the value of benefits and control benefits costs.

Part 5 (Chapters 15–16) covers other HR topics including collective bargaining and labor relations and managing human resources on a global basis. Chapter 15 explores HR activities as they pertain to employees who belong to unions or who are seeking to join unions. Traditional issues in labor–management relations such as union membership and contract negotiations are discussed. The chapter also highlights new approaches to labor relations, the growing role of employee empowerment, and the shrinking size of union membership.

Concluding Part 5, Chapter 16 focuses on HR activities in international settings, including planning, selecting, training, and compensating employees who work overseas. The chapter also explores how cultural differences among countries and workers affect decisions about human resources.

New Features and Content Changes

In addition to all new or revised chapter pedagogy, the Sixth Edition of *Fundamentals* contains the following features:

- **New Format for Chapter Summaries:** To help students learn chapter content, the Chapter Summary has been revamped to highlight key points in a bulleted list format for each chapter learning objective.

- **Review Questions Keyed to Learning Objectives:** As a way of pinpointing key concepts, the chapter review questions now tie in to specific chapter learning objectives for quick student reference.

- **Key Terms in Discussion Order:** To assist students in learning important chapter topics, key terms are now listed in discussion order rather than alphabetical order at the end of the chapter. The key terms and definitions are also listed in the end-of-book glossary for additional study.
- **HR in Small Business:** A case has been added to each chapter that highlights some of the HR challenges faced by small businesses.

The following content changes help students and instructors keep current on important HR trends and topics:

- Chapter 1 addresses the new chapter reorganization in Figure 1.1 and Table 1.3. It also discusses a recent trend in which some companies are doing away with separate HR departments, encouraging managers and other employees to handle HR issues as they arise. Table 1.2 has been updated to list the top qualities employers look for in potential employees. Figure 1.3 has been revised to reflect the competencies and example behaviors defined by the Society of Human Resource Management (SHRM). Figure 1.6 has been updated to reflect current median salaries for HRM positions.

- Chapter 2 provides updated workforce statistics, including projections for number of workers over the next several years, as well as a discussion on various age and ethnic groups within the workforce. Chapter figures have been revised to reflect current labor force data. Other trends discussed include which occupations are expected to gain the most jobs in the coming decade. A new section on the trends in cost control and the impact of the Affordable Care Act is touched on and revisited later in the benefits chapter (Chapter 14). New sections on declining union membership and reshoring of jobs back to the United States have been added.

- Chapter 3 has been updated to include a discussion on the Lilly Ledbetter Fair Pay Act and its impact on pay discrimination and employment law. Chapter figures have been updated to reflect current statistics on age discrimination, disability complaints filed under ADA, types of charges filed with the EEOC, and rates of occupational injuries and illnesses. A section has been added about how to keep emergency response workers safe as they aid victims of disasters.

- Chapter 4 includes a new discussion on analyzing teamwork and an updated discussion on the growing trend among companies to encourage telework arrangements with workers.

- Chapter 5's discussion on downsizing, reducing hours, and outsourcing includes new company examples that help students understand how real-world companies deal with the ups and downs of everyday business and decisions relating to human resources.

- Chapter 6 has several topics that have been updated, including the importance of hiring workers who will fit in well with a company's culture; how the legalization of marijuana may impact drug testing as part of the employee selection process; and how companies are changing their approach to subjectivity when it comes to interviewing job candidates.

- In the training chapter (Chapter 7), new examples explore how some companies are thinking differently about training strategies, employing virtual reality, simulations, teamwork exercises, and social media for learning reinforcement and employee motivation.

- Chapter 8 focuses on development and includes an updated section on the use of assessment tools, including the DiSC assessment tool.
- Chapter 9 provides an updated discussion of how HRM practices can contribute to high performance of any organization, including job design, recruitment and selection, training, performance management, and compensation.
- Chapter 10 includes a new discussion on how managers should adjust their approach to performance feedback to the level of performance demonstrated by individual employees.
- Chapter 11 provides an expanded discussion on implementing strategies to ensure a company's discipline system follows procedures consistent for all employees.
- Chapter 12's discussion about earnings data for women, men, and minorities has been updated, as well as the discussion about HRM salaries in various parts of the country. The chapter also contains current statistics about CEO pay and compensation.
- Chapter 13 focuses on recognizing employee contributions with pay, including new real-world examples about how businesses are rethinking their approach to performance bonuses, tying them to company performance, and the increased use of retention bonuses for executives and other key employees as part of company mergers and acquisitions.
- Chapter 14 includes updated data on employee benefits as a percentage of total compensation, Social Security information, and taxes paid by employers and employees. The section on health care benefits, including updates about the Patient Protection and Affordable Care Act, has been revised to include current information and requirements.
- Chapter 15 has been updated with current trends and statistics in union membership. Content on work stoppages and lockouts has been added. New sections focus on increased cooperation between unions and management and highlight several nonunion representation systems currently being used by companies across the country.
- Concluding the Sixth Edition, Chapter 16 highlights trends in managing human resources globally, including the issue of labor relations in various countries, which may impact a company's ability to be successful on foreign soil.

The author team believes that the focused, engaging, and applied approach of *Fundamentals* distinguishes it from other books that have similar coverage of HR topics. The book has timely coverage of important HR issues, is easy to read, has many features that grab the students' attention, and gets students actively involved in learning.

We would like to thank those of you who have adopted previous editions of *Fundamentals*, and we hope that you will continue to use upcoming editions. For those of you considering *Fundamentals* for adoption, we believe that our approach makes *Fundamentals* your text of choice for human resource management.

Acknowledgments

The Sixth Edition of *Fundamentals of Human Resource Management* would not have been possible without the staff of McGraw-Hill Education. Despite the uncertainty surrounding the reorganization at McGraw-Hill, Mike Ablassmeir and Anke Weekes, the editors who worked on this edition of *Fundamentals*, deserve kudos for their laser focus on ensuring that we continue to improve the book based on the ideas of both adopters and students. Also, we appreciate that they gave us creative license to use new cases and examples in the chapter pedagogy and text to keep *Fundamentals* interesting and current. John Weimeister, our former editor, helped us develop the vision for the book and gave us the resources we needed to develop a top-of-the-line HRM teaching package. Jane Beck's valuable insights and organizational skills kept the author team on deadline and made the book more visually appealing than the authors could have ever done on their own. We would also like to thank Cate Rzasa who worked diligently to make sure that the book was interesting, practical, and readable and remained true to findings of human resource management research. We also thank Michael Gedatus for his marketing efforts for this new edition.

We would like to extend our sincere appreciation to all of the professors who gave of their time to offer their suggestions and insightful comments that helped us to develop and shape this new edition:

Glenda Barrett
University of Maryland, University College

Marian Canada
Ivy Tech Community College

Jeanie Douglas
Columbia College

Joseph Eppolito
Syracuse University

Betty Fair
Georgia College and State University

Amy Falink
University of Minnesota

Lisa Foeman
University of Maryland, University College

Deborah Good
University of Pittsburgh

Jonathon Halbesleben
University of Alabama, Birmingham

Tanya Hubanks
Chippewa Valley Technical College

Roy Johnson
Iowa State University

Chris McChesney
Indian River State College

Garry McDaniel
Franklin University

Liliana Meneses
University of Maryland, University College

Barbara Minsky
Troy State University, Dothan

Richard Murdock
Utah Valley University

Dan Nehring
Morehead State University

James Phillips
Northeastern State University

David Ripley
University of Maryland, University College

Rudy Soliz
Houston Community College

Gary Stroud
Franklin University

Gary Thurgood
Texas A&M University, College Station

Sheng Wang
University of Nevada, Las Vegas

Donna Wyatt
University of Maryland, University College

Joy Young
University of South Carolina, Columbia

Our supplement authors deserve thanks for helping us create a first-rate teaching package. Joyce LeMay of Bethel University wrote the newly custom-designed *Instructor's Manual* and Dr. Connie Sitterly authored the new PowerPoint presentation.

We would also like to thank the professors who gave of their time to review the previous editions through various stages of development.

Michelle Alarcon, Esq.
Hawaii Pacific University

Dr. Minnette A. Bumpus
University of the District of Columbia

Brennan Carr
Long Beach City College/El Camino College

Tom Comstock
Gannon University

Susie S. Cox
McNeese State University

Juan J. DelaCruz
Lehman College—CUNY

AnnMarie DiSienna
Dominican College

Lorrie Ferraro
Northeastern University

Carla Flores
Ball State University

Linette P. Fox
Johnson C. Smith University

Britt Hastey
UCLA, Chapman University, and Los Angeles City College

Kim Hester
Arkansas State University

Samira B. Hussein
Johnson County Community College

Joseph V. Ippolito
Brevard College

Adonis "Sporty" Jeralds
The University of South Carolina–Columbia

Guy Lochiatto
Mass Bay Community College

Liliana Meneses
University of Maryland University College

Kelly Mollica
The University of Memphis

Tami Moser
Southern Oklahoma State University

Richard J. Wagner
University of Wisconsin–Whitewater

Brandon L. Young
Embry-Riddle Aeronautical University

Raymond A. Noe
John R. Hollenbeck
Barry Gerhart
Patrick M. Wright

fundamentals of **human**
resource
management

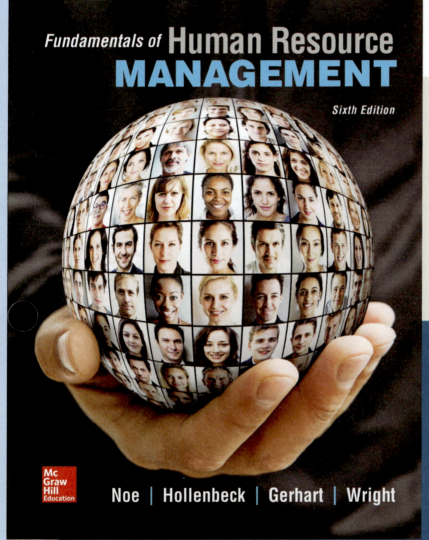

engaging.
focused.
applied.

The sixth edition of
*Fundamentals of Human
Resource Management*
continues to offer students
a brief introduction to
HRM that is rich with
examples and engaging in
its application.

**Please take a moment to
page through some of
the highlights of this new
edition.**

Features

Students who want to learn more about how human resource management is used in the everyday work environment will find that the sixth edition is engaging, focused, and applied, giving them the HRM knowledge they need to succeed.

WHAT DO I NEED TO KNOW?

Assurance of learning:

- Learning objectives open each chapter.
- Learning objectives are referenced in the page margins where the relevant discussion begins and are referenced in each Review and Discussion Question at the end of the chapter.
- The chapter summary is written around the same learning objectives and is provided in an easy-to-read bulleted list format.
- Instructor testing questions are tagged to the appropriate objective they cover.

2 Trends in Human Resource Management

What Do I Need to Know?
After reading this chapter, you should be able to:

LO 2-1 Describe trends in the labor force composition and how they affect human resource management.

LO 2-2 Summarize areas in which human resource management can support the goal of creating a high-performance work system.

LO 2-3 Define employee empowerment, and explain its role in the modern organization.

LO 2-4 Identify ways HR professionals can support organizational strategies for growth, quality, and efficiency.

LO 2-5 Summarize ways in which human resource management can support organizations expanding internationally.

LO 2-6 Discuss how technological developments are affecting human resource management.

LO 2-7 Explain how the nature of the employment relationship is changing.

LO 2-8 Discuss how the need for flexibility affects human resource management.

Introduction

Business experts point out that if you want your company to gain an advantage over competitors, you have to do something differently. Some managers are taking a hard look at human resources management, asking if it needs to be a department at all. At the consulting firm LRN Corporation, management decided to eliminate the human resources department. Their idea was that if all managers were responsible for managing talent, they would make those decisions in a way that directly served their group's performance. Beam, the maker of spirits such as Maker's Mark bourbon and Jim Beam whiskey, made its line managers responsible for hiring, training, and making compensation decisions. They are advised by a small group of "business partners," who consult with the line managers on HR questions.

Is this the end of human resource management? Probably not. The typical company today is maintaining the size of its human resource department and even spending a little more on the function. At LRN, current and former employees have said line managers sometimes struggle with making HR decisions. For example, a line manager needs time to figure out how to define a job and set a salary range for it, which slows down the whole hiring process. At Beam, the HR business partners are playing a more strategic role than a traditional HR staffer focused on routine processes.

 HR Oops!

Less Helpful than a Search Engine?

A lot of managers are disappointed in the support they get from their HR teams, according to a survey by the Hay Group, a global consulting firm. The survey questioned line managers and HR directors in China, the United Kingdom, and the United States about their working relationships. The results suggest that those relationships are often strained.

HR directors reported being challenged by cutbacks in their department. One-third said they spend 21% to 50% of their time responding to inquiries from managers, and three-fourths said line managers want immediate responses. For their part, 41% of line managers in the United States said the HR department is too slow in responding, and 47% said they could make decisions better and faster if they had more information from the department. An embarrassing 29% rated Google above the HR department for providing pertinent information.

Hay's consultants suggest that human resource managers need to focus on how they can empower line managers by providing them with easy access to relevant information.

Questions

1. Suggest one way that HR managers might improve their helpfulness to line managers

2. Suggest one way that line managers can improve communications with HR managers, so they get the support they need.

Sources: Laurence Doe, "Relationship between Line Managers and HR under Increasing Strain, Hay Group Finds," *HR Magazine (UK)*, November 21, 2013, http://www.hrmagazine.co.uk; Hay Group, "More Managers Turn to Google for HR Information," *Business Wire*, November 20, 2013, http://www.businesswire.com; Philip Spriet, "'Power On': From Passing the Buck to Activating the Line," Hay Group Blog, October 16, 2013, http://blog.haygroup.com.

 UPDATED!

 HR Oops!

Engage students through examples of companies whose HR departments have fallen short. Discussion questions at the end of each feature encourage student analysis of the situation. Examples include "Few Companies Are Prepared for Future Talent Needs," "401(k) Plans Are a Missed Opportunity for Many," and "Cross-Cultural Management Mishaps."

Best Practices

Engage students through examples of companies whose HR departments are working well. Examples include "Morton Salt's Prize-Winning Safety Program," "Employees Are Quicken Loans' Most Valuable Asset," and "Machinists and Steelworkers Unions Help Harley-Davidson Get Lean."

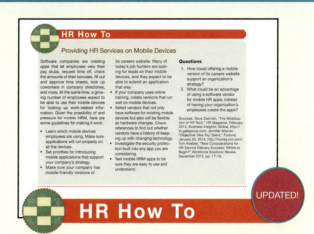

HR How To

Engage students through specific steps to create HRM programs and tackle common challenges. Examples include "Writing Effective HR Policies," "Providing HR Services on Mobile Devices," and "Complying with the Affordable Care Act."

HRM Social

Engage students through examples of how HR departments use social media as part of their daily activities. Examples include "The Discrimination Risk of Using Social Media in Hiring," "Salary Talk Is Trending," and "Social Support for Getting Healthy."

Did You Know?

Engage students through interesting statistics related to chapter topics. Examples include "Half of U.S. Employees Interested in Changing Jobs," "Selection Decisions Affect the Bottom Line," and "Employers Stress Merit Pay to Retain Workers."

Features

Focused on ethics. Reviewers indicate that the Thinking Ethically feature, which confronts students in each chapter with an ethical issue regarding managing human resources, is a highlight. This feature has been updated throughout the text.

Apply the concepts in each chapter through comprehensive review and discussion questions, which are now keyed to chapter learning objectives.

Apply concepts in each chapter through three cases that focus on corporate sustainability, talent management, and HR in small business. These cases can be used as the basis for class lectures, and the questions provided at the end of each case are suitable for assignments or discussion.

Results-Driven Support

Across the country, instructors and students continue to raise an important question: How can Human Resource Management courses further support students throughout the learning process to shape future business leaders? While there is no one solution, we see the impact of new learning technologies and innovative study tools that not only fully engage students in course material but also inform instructors of the students' skill and comprehension levels.

Interactive learning tools, including those offered through McGraw-Hill *Connect*, are being implemented to increase teaching effectiveness and learning efficiency in thousands of colleges and universities. By facilitating a stronger connection with the course and incorporating the latest technologies—such as McGraw-Hill LearnSmart, an adaptive learning program—these tools enable students to succeed in their college careers, which will ultimately increase the percentage of students completing their postsecondary degrees and create the business leaders of the future.

McGraw-Hill Connect

Connect is an all-digital teaching and learning environment designed from the ground up to work with the way instructors and students think, teach, and learn. As a digital teaching, assignment, and assessment platform, *Connect* strengthens the link among faculty, students, and coursework, helping everyone accomplish more in less time.

LearnSmart

THE SMARTEST WAY TO GET FROM B TO A

LearnSmart is the most widely used and intelligent adaptive learning resource. It is proven to strengthen memory recall, improve course retention, and boost grades by distinguishing between what students know and what they don't know and honing in on the concepts that they are most likely to forget. LearnSmart continuously adapts to each student's needs by building an individual learning path. As a result, students study smarter and retain more knowledge.

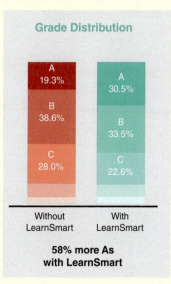

Grade Distribution

Without LearnSmart
A 19.3%
B 38.6%
C 28.0%

With LearnSmart
A 30.5%
B 33.5%
C 22.6%

58% more As with LearnSmart

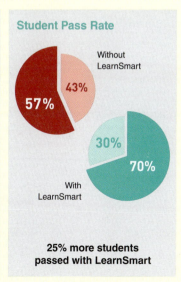

Student Pass Rate

Without LearnSmart 43%
With LearnSmart 57%
30%
70%

25% more students passed with LearnSmart

SmartBook

A REVOLUTION IN READING

Fueled by LearnSmart, SmartBook is the first and only adaptive reading experience available today. SmartBook personalizes content for each student in a continuously adapting reading experience. Reading is no longer a passive and linear experience, but an engaging and dynamic one where students are more likely to master and retain important concepts, coming to class better prepared.

LearnSmart Achieve

EXCEL IN YOUR CLASS

Accelerate student success with LearnSmart Achieve™—the first and only adaptive study experience that pinpoints individual student knowledge gaps and provides targeted, interactive help at the moment of need.

Interactive Applications

A HIGHER LEVEL OF LEARNING

These *exercises* require students to APPLY what they have learned in a real-world scenario. These online exercises will help students assess their understanding of the concepts.

Media Rich eBook

Connect provides students with a cost-saving alternative to the traditional textbook. A seamless integration of a media rich eBook features the following:

- A web-optimized eBook, allowing for anytime, anywhere online access to the textbook.
- Powerful search function to pinpoint and connect key concepts in a snap.
- Highlighting and note-taking capabilities as well as access to shared instructors' notations.

The Best Instructor Support on the Market

 McGraw-Hill strengthens the link between faculty, students, and coursework, helping everyone accomplish more in less time.

Efficient Administrative Capabilities

Connect offers you, the instructor, auto-gradable material in an effort to facilitate teaching and learning.

Reviewing Homework	Giving Tests or Quizzes	Grading
60 minutes without Connect → 15 minutes with Connect	60 minutes without Connect → 0 minutes with Connect	60 minutes without Connect → 12 minutes with Connect

Student Progress Tracking

Connect keeps instructors informed about how each student, section, and class is performing, allowing for more productive use of lecture and office hours. The progress tracking function enables instructors to:

- View scored work immediately and track individual or group performance with assignment and grade reports.
- Access an instant view of student or class performance relative to learning objectives.
- Collect data and generate reports required by many accreditation organizations, such as AACSB.

Actionable Data

Connect Insight is a powerful data analytics tool that allows instructors to leverage aggregated information about their courses and students to provide a more personalized teaching and learning experience.

> *Connect* and LearnSmart allow students to present course material to students in more ways than just the explanations they hear from me directly. Because of this, students are processing the material in new ways, requiring them to think. I now have more students asking questions in class because the more we think, the more we question.
>
> *Instructor at Hinds Community College*

Connect Instructor Library

Connect's instructor library serves as a one-stop, secure site for essential course materials, allowing you to save prep time before class. The instructor resources found in the library include:

- **Instructor's Manual:** The custom-designed Instructor's Manual includes chapter summaries, learning objectives, an extended chapter outline, key terms, description of text boxes, discussion questions, summary of end-of-chapter cases, and additional activities.

- **Test Bank:** The Test Bank has been revised and updated to reflect the content of the Sixth Edition of the book. Each chapter includes multiple-choice, true/false, and essay questions.

- **EZ Test:** McGraw-Hill's EZ Test is a flexible and easy-to-use electronic testing program. The program allows instructors to create tests from book-specific items. It accommodates a wide range of question types and instructors may add their own questions. Multiple versions of the test can be created and any test can be exported for use with course management systems such as BlackBoard, D2L, or Moodle. The program is available for Windows and Macintosh environments.

- **PowerPoint:** The slides include lecture material, additional content to expand concepts in the text, and discussion questions, and the PowerPoint slides also include detailed teaching notes.

- **Videos:** Human Resource Management Video DVD, volume 3, offers video clips on HRM issues for each chapter of this edition. You'll find a new video produced by the SHRM Foundation entitled "Once the Deal Is Done: Making Mergers Work." Three new videos specifically address employee benefits: "GM Cuts Benefits and Pay," "Sulphur Springs Teachers," and "Google Employees' Perks." Other new videos available for this edition include "E-Learning English" for the chapter on employee development and "Recession Job Growth" for the chapter on HR planning recruitment. Two new videos specifically address recession-related HR issues: "Some Workers Willing to Sacrifice to Avoid Layoffs" and "Stretched Small Business Owners Forced to Lay Off Employees." Other notable videos available for this edition include "Johnson & Johnson eUniversity" for the chapter on training and "Hollywood Labor Unions" for the chapter on collective bargaining and labor relations.

Video Library DVDs

McGraw-Hill offers the most comprehensive video support for the Human Resource Management classroom through course library video DVDs. This discipline has library volume DVDs tailored to integrate and visually reinforce chapter concepts. The library volume DVD contains more than 40 clips! The rich video material, organized by topic, comes from sources such as PBS, NBC, BBC, SHRM, and McGraw-Hill. Video cases and video guides are provided for some clips.

Destination CEO Videos

These video clips feature CEOs on a variety of topics. Accompanying each clip are multiple-choice questions and discussion questions to use in the classroom or assign as a quiz.

Create

Instructors can now tailor their teaching resources to match the way they teach! With McGraw-Hill Create, **www. mcgrawhillcreate.com,** instructors can easily rearrange chapters, combine material from other content sources, and quickly upload and integrate their own content, like course syllabi or teaching notes. Find the right content in Create by searching through thousands of leading McGraw-Hill textbooks. Arrange the material to fit your teaching style. Order a Create book and receive a complimentary print review copy in three to five business days or a complimentary electronic review copy via e-mail within one hour. Go to **www.mcgrawhillcreate. com** today and register.

Binder-Ready Loose-Leaf Text (ISBN 9781259304415)

This full-featured text is provided as an option to the price-sensitive student. It is a four-color text that's three-hole punched and made available at a discount to students. It is also available in a package with Connect.

Tegrity Campus

Tegrity makes class time available 24/7 by automatically capturing every lecture in a searchable format for students to review when they study and complete assignments. With a simple one-click start-and-stop process, you capture all computer screens and corresponding audio. Students can replay any part of any class with easy-to-use browser-based viewing on a PC or Mac. Educators know that the more students can see, hear, and experience class resources, the better they learn. In fact, studies prove it. With patented Tegrity "search anything" technology, students instantly recall key class moments for replay online or on iPods and mobile devices. Instructors can help turn all their students' study time into learning moments immediately supported by their lecture. To learn more about Tegrity, watch a two-minute Flash demo at **http://tegritycampus.mhhe.com.**

Blackboard® Partnership

McGraw-Hill Education and Blackboard have teamed up to simplify your life. Now you and your students can access *Connect* and Create right from within your Blackboard course—all with one single sign-on. The grade books are seamless, so when a student completes an integrated *Connect* assignment, the grade for that assignment automatically (and instantly) feeds your Blackboard grade center. Learn more at **www.domorenow.com.**

McGraw-Hill Campus™

 Campus

McGraw-Hill Campus is a new one-stop teaching and learning experience available to users of any learning management system. This institutional service allows faculty and students to enjoy single sign-on (SSO) access to all McGraw-Hill Higher Education materials, including the award-winning McGraw-Hill *Connect* platform, from directly within the institution's website. With McGraw-Hill Campus, faculty receive instant access to teaching materials (e.g., eBooks, test banks, PowerPoint slides, animations, learning objects, etc.), allowing them to browse, search, and use any instructor ancillary content in our vast library at no additional cost to instructor or students.

Course Design and Delivery

In addition, students enjoy SSO access to a variety of free content (e.g., quizzes, flash cards, narrated presentations, etc.) and subscription-based products (e.g., McGraw-Hill *Connect*). With McGraw-Hill Campus enabled, faculty and students will never need to create another account to access McGraw-Hill products and services. Learn more at **www.mhcampus.com.**

Assurance of Learning Ready

Many educational institutions today focus on the notion of *assurance of learning*, an important element of some accreditation standards. *Fundamentals of Human Resource Management* is designed specifically to support instructors' assurance of learning initiatives with a simple yet powerful solution. Each test bank question maps to a specific chapter learning objective listed in the text. Instructors can use our test bank software, EZ Test and EZ Test Online, to easily query for learning objectives that directly relate to the learning outcomes for their course. Instructors can then use the reporting features of EZ Test to aggregate student results in similar fashion, making the collection and presentation of assurance of learning data simple and easy.

AACSB Tagging

McGraw-Hill Education is a proud corporate member of AACSB International. Understanding the importance and value of AACSB accreditation, *Fundamentals of Human Resource Management* recognizes the curricula guidelines detailed in the AACSB standards for business accreditation by connecting selected questions in the text and the test bank to the six general knowledge and skill guidelines in the AACSB standards. The statements contained in *Fundamentals of Human Resource Management* are provided only as a guide for the users of this textbook. The AACSB leaves content coverage and assessment within the purview of individual schools, the mission of the school, and the faculty. While the *Fundamentals of Human Resource Management* teaching package makes no claim of any specific AACSB qualification or evaluation, we have labeled selected questions according to the six general knowledge and skills areas.

McGraw-Hill Customer Experience Group Contact Information

At McGraw-Hill Education, we understand that getting the most from new technology can be challenging. That's why our services don't stop after you purchase our products. You can e-mail our Product Specialists 24 hours a day to get product training online. Or you can search our knowledge bank of Frequently Asked Questions on our support website. For Customer Support, call **800-331-5094** or visit **www.mhhe.com/support.** One of our Technical Support Analysts will be able to assist you in a timely fashion.

Brief Contents

Contents

PART 4

Compensating Human Resources 365

The Human Resource Environment

PART ONE

1

Managing Human Resources

What Do I Need to Know?

After reading this chapter, you should be able to:

LO 1-1 Define human resource management, and explain how HRM contributes to an organization's performance.

LO 1-2 Identify the responsibilities of human resource departments.

LO 1-3 Summarize the types of skills needed for human resource management.

LO 1-4 Explain the role of supervisors in human resource management.

LO 1-5 Discuss ethical issues in human resource management.

LO 1-6 Describe typical careers in human resource management.

Introduction

Sarah Koustrup calls her position at National Hospitality Services (NHS) in Fargo, North Dakota, "a job with a lot of meaning." NHS, which operates more than a dozen hotels, hired Koustrup to be its director of human resources. In that role, Koustrup puts into action the chief executive's vision of a company treating its employees well so they in turn will treat customers well. She works directly with the CEO and has input on all areas of the business.

Josephine Simmons also believes her work matters. Simmons, another director of human resources, works for SatCom Marketing in Brooklyn Park, Minnesota. The telemarketing firm hired her to build a human resources department from the ground up. SatCom's chief executive also wanted Simmons to improve the company's culture, a challenge that requires skills in creating enthusiasm about change.

Koustrup and Simmons are enthusiastic about their function: finding great people and creating the conditions that enable those people to help a company succeed in its mission. The significance of this work helps explain why, in a recent pair of surveys, human resources professionals were more likely than employees overall to say they are satisfied with their current job. Workers in this field also appreciate the variety in the skills they use and projects they tackle.[1]

The challenges and professional rewards that Sarah Koustrup and Josephine Simmons experience are important dimensions of **human resource management (HRM),** the policies, practices, and systems that influence employees' behavior, attitudes, and performance. Many companies refer to HRM as involving "people practices." Figure 1.1 emphasizes that there are several important HRM practices that should support the organization's business strategy: analyzing work and designing jobs, determining how many employees with specific knowledge and skills are needed (human resource planning), attracting potential employees (recruiting), choosing employees (selection), teaching employees how to perform their jobs and preparing them for the future (training and development), evaluating their performance (performance management), rewarding employees (compensation), and creating a positive work environment (employee relations). An organization performs best when all of these practices are managed well. At companies with effective HRM, employees and customers tend to be more satisfied, and the companies tend to be more innovative, have greater productivity, and develop a more favorable reputation in the community.[2]

In this chapter, we introduce the scope of human resource management. We begin by discussing why human resource management is an essential element of an organization's success. We then turn to the elements of managing human resources: the roles and skills needed for effective human resource management. Next, the chapter describes how all managers, not just human resource professionals, participate in the activities related to human resource management. The following section of the chapter addresses some of the ethical issues that arise with regard to human resource management. We then provide an overview of careers in human resource management. The chapter concludes by highlighting the HRM practices covered in the remainder of this book.

Human Resource Management (HRM)
The policies, practices, and systems that influence employees' behavior, attitudes, and performance.

LO 1-1 Define human resource management, and explain how HRM contributes to an organization's performance.

Human Resources and Company Performance

Managers and economists traditionally have seen human resource management as a necessary expense, rather than as a source of value to their organizations. Economic value is usually associated with *capital*—cash, equipment, technology, and facilities. However, research has demonstrated that HRM practices can be valuable.[3] Decisions such as whom to hire, what to pay, what training to offer, and how to evaluate

Figure 1.1
Human Resource Management Practices

Strategic HRM

Analysis and design of work | HR planning | Recruiting | Selection | Training and development | Performance management | Compensation | Employee relations → **Company Performance**

employee performance directly affect employees' motivation and ability to provide goods and services that customers value. Companies that attempt to increase their competitiveness by investing in new technology and promoting quality throughout the organization also invest in state-of-the-art staffing, training, and compensation practices.[4]

The concept of "human resource management" implies that employees are *resources* of the employer. As a type of resource, **human capital** means the organization's employees, described in terms of their training, experience, judgment, intelligence, relationships, and insight—the employee characteristics that can add economic value to the organization. In other words, whether it manufactures automobiles or forecasts the weather, for an organization to succeed at what it does, it needs employees with certain qualities, such as particular kinds of training and experience. This view means employees in today's organizations are not interchangeable, easily replaced parts of a system but the source of the company's success or failure. By influencing *who* works for the organization and *how* those people work, human resource management therefore contributes to basic measures of an organization's performance, such as quality, profitability, and customer satisfaction. Figure 1.2 shows this relationship.

In the United States, low-price retailers are notorious for the ways they keep labor costs down. They pay low wages, limit employees to part-time status (providing little or no employee benefits), and make last-minute adjustments to schedules so staffing is minimal when store traffic is light. Retailing expert Zeynep Ton has studied retailers that invest more in employees—paying higher wages and offering full-time schedules, greater training, and more opportunity for advancement. Ton has found that these stores tend to enjoy higher sales and greater profitability. At Costco, for example, employees earn about 40% more than at the company's main competitor, Sam's Club, and most store managers are promoted from within. Costco's sales per square foot are almost double those of Sam's Club, and its rating in the American Customer Satisfaction Index is comparable to that of the prestigious Nordstrom chain. The QuikTrip chain of convenience stores trains employees to handle a wide variety of tasks, from brewing coffee to ordering merchandise and cleaning restrooms. Instead of sending employees home when traffic is slow, QuikTrip expects them to handle tasks other

Human Capital

An organization's employees, described in terms of their training, experience, judgment, intelligence, relationships, and insight.

Figure 1.2

Impact of Human Resource Management

than selling. Employees have predictable schedules, stay busy throughout their shift, and sell 66% more per square foot than the average convenience store. In these and other chains that see employees as more than just an expense, retailers are outperforming their competitors.[5]

Human resource management is critical to the success of organizations because human capital has certain qualities that make it valuable. In terms of business strategy, an organization can succeed if it has a *sustainable competitive advantage* (is better than competitors at something and can hold that advantage over a sustained period of time). Therefore, we can conclude that organizations need the kind of resources that will give them such an advantage. Human resources have these necessary qualities:

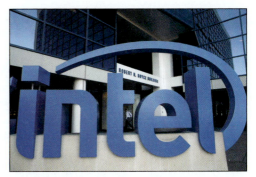

At Intel, the company's focus is on keeping employees loyal, trained, and compensated. In turn, there is a low turnover rate and a high degree of customer satisfaction.

- Human resources are *valuable*. High-quality employees provide a needed service as they perform many critical functions.
- Human resources are *rare* in the sense that a person with high levels of the needed skills and knowledge is not common. An organization may spend months looking for a talented and experienced manager or technician.
- Human resources *cannot be imitated*. To imitate human resources at a high-performing competitor, you would have to figure out which employees are providing the advantage and how. Then you would have to recruit people who can do precisely the same thing and set up the systems that enable those people to imitate your competitor.
- Human resources have *no good substitutes*. When people are well trained and highly motivated, they learn, develop their abilities, and care about customers. It is difficult to imagine another resource that can match committed and talented employees.

These qualities imply that human resources have enormous potential. An organization realizes this potential through the ways it practices human resource management.

Effective management of human resources can form the foundation of a *high-performance work system*—an organization in which technology, organizational structure, people, and processes work together seamlessly to give an organization an advantage in the competitive environment. As technology changes the ways organizations manufacture, transport, communicate, and keep track of information, human resource management must ensure that the organization has the right kinds of people to meet the new challenges. High-performance work systems also have been essential in making organizations strong enough to weather the storm of the recent recession and remain profitable as the economy slowly begins to expand again. Maintaining a high-performance work system may include development of training programs, recruitment of people with new skill sets, and establishment of rewards for such behaviors as teamwork, flexibility, and learning. In the next chapter, we will see some of the changes that human resource managers are planning for, and Chapter 9 examines high-performance work systems in greater detail.

Responsibilities of Human Resource Departments

In all but the smallest organizations, a human resource department is responsible for the functions of human resource management. On average, an organization has one or two full-time HR staff persons for every hundred employees on the payroll.[6] One way

LO 1-2 Identify the responsibilities of human resource departments.

to define the responsibilities of HR departments is to think of HR as a business within the company with three product lines[7]:

1. *Administrative services and transactions*—Handling administrative tasks (for example, hiring employees and answering questions about benefits) efficiently and with a commitment to quality. This requires expertise in the particular tasks.
2. *Business partner services*—Developing effective HR systems that help the organization meet its goals for attracting, keeping, and developing people with the skills it needs. For the systems to be effective, HR people must understand the business so it can understand what the business needs.
3. *Strategic partner*—Contributing to the company's strategy through an understanding of its existing and needed human resources and ways HR practices can give the company a competitive advantage. For strategic ideas to be effective, HR people must understand the business, its industry, and its competitors.

Another way to think of HR responsibilities is in terms of specific activities. Table 1.1 details the responsibilities of human resource departments. These responsibilities include the practices introduced in Figure 1.1 plus two areas of responsibility that support those practices: (1) establishing and administering personnel policies and (2) ensuring compliance with labor laws.

Although the human resource department has responsibility for these areas, many of the tasks may be performed by supervisors or others inside or outside the organization. No two human resource departments have precisely the same roles because of differences in organization sizes and characteristics of the workforce, the industry, and management's values. In some companies, the HR department handles all the activities listed in Table 1.1. In others, it may share the roles and duties with managers of other departments such as finance, operations, or information

Table 1.1

Responsibilities of HR Departments

FUNCTION	RESPONSIBILITIES
Analysis and design of work	Work analysis; job design; job descriptions
Recruitment and selection	Recruiting; job postings; interviewing; testing; coordinating use of temporary labor
Training and development	Orientation; skills training; career development programs
Performance management	Performance measures; preparation and administration of performance appraisals; discipline
Compensation and benefits	Wage and salary administration; incentive pay; insurance; vacation leave administration; retirement plans; profit sharing; stock plans
Employee relations	Attitude surveys; labor relations; employee handbooks; company publications; labor law compliance; relocation and outplacement services
Personnel policies	Policy creation; policy communication
Employee data and information systems	Record keeping; HR information systems; workforce analytics
Compliance with laws	Policies to ensure lawful behavior; reporting; posting information; safety inspections; accessibility accommodations
Support for strategy	Human resource planning and forecasting; talent management; change management

Sources: Bureau of Labor Statistics, "Human Resources Managers," *Occupational Outlook Handbook, 2014–2015*, January 8, 2014, http://www.bls.gov/ooh; SHRM-BNA Survey No. 66, "Policy and Practice Forum: Human Resource Activities, Budgets, and Staffs, 2000–2001," *Bulletin to Management,* Bureau of National Affairs Policy and Practice Series (Washington, DC: Bureau of National Affairs, June 28, 2001).

technology. In some companies, the HR department actively advises top management. In others, the department responds to top-level management decisions and implements staffing, training, and compensation activities in light of company strategy and policies. And, in a recent trend, some companies are doing away with their HR departments altogether, preferring to flatten their organizational structure and to encourage department managers and other employees to handle HR issues as they arise.[8]

Home Depot and other retail stores use in-store kiosks similar to the Career Center shown here to recruit applicants for employment.

Let's take an overview of the HR functions and some of the options available for carrying them out. Human resource management involves both the selection of which options to use and the activities involved with using those options. Later chapters of the book will explore each function in greater detail.

Analyzing and Designing Jobs

To produce their given product or service (or set of products or services), companies require that a number of tasks be performed. The tasks are grouped together in various combinations to form jobs. Ideally, the tasks should be grouped in ways that help the organization operate efficiently and obtain people with the right qualifications to do the jobs well. This function involves the activities of job analysis and job design. **Job analysis** is the process of getting detailed information about jobs. **Job design** is the process of defining the way work will be performed and the tasks that a given job requires.

In general, jobs can vary from having a narrow range of simple tasks to having a broad array of complex tasks requiring multiple skills. At one extreme is a worker on an assembly line at a poultry-processing facility; at the other extreme is a doctor in an emergency room. In the past, many companies have emphasized the use of narrowly defined jobs to increase efficiency. With many simple jobs, a company can easily find workers who can quickly be trained to perform the jobs at relatively low pay. However, greater concern for innovation and quality has shifted the trend to using more broadly defined jobs. Also, as we will see in Chapters 2 and 4, some organizations assign work even more broadly, to teams instead of individuals.

Job Analysis
The process of getting detailed information about jobs.

Job Design
The process of defining the way work will be performed and the tasks that a given job requires.

Recruiting and Hiring Employees

Based on job analysis and design, an organization can determine the kinds of employees it needs. With this knowledge, it carries out the function of recruiting and hiring employees. **Recruitment** is the process through which the organization seeks applicants for potential employment. **Selection** refers to the process by which the organization attempts to identify applicants with the necessary knowledge, skills, abilities, and other characteristics that will help the organization achieve its goals. An organization makes selection decisions in order to add employees to its workforce, as well as to transfer existing employees to new positions.

Approaches to recruiting and selection involve a variety of alternatives. Some organizations may actively recruit from many external sources, such as Internet job postings, online social networks, and college recruiting events. Other organizations may rely heavily on promotions from within, applicants referred by current employees, and the availability of in-house people with the necessary skills.

Recruitment
The process through which the organization seeks applicants for potential employment.

Selection
The process by which the organization attempts to identify applicants with the necessary knowledge, skills, abilities, and other characteristics that will help the organization achieve its goals.

1. Teamwork skills
2. Decision making, problem solving
3. Planning, prioritizing tasks
4. Verbal communication skills
5. Gathering/processing information

Source: Based on National Association of Colleges and Employers, "The Candidate Skills/Qualities Employers Want," news release, October 10, 2013, http://www.naceweb.org.

At some organizations the selection process may focus on specific skills, such as experience with a particular programming language or type of equipment. At other organizations, selection may focus on general abilities, such as the ability to work as part of a team or find creative solutions. The focus an organization favors will affect many choices, from the way the organization measures ability, to the questions it asks in interviews, to the places it recruits. Table 1.2 lists the top five qualities that employers say they are looking for in job candidates.

Training and Developing Employees

Although organizations base hiring decisions on candidates' existing qualifications, most organizations provide ways for their employees to broaden or deepen their knowledge, skills, and abilities. To do this, organizations provide for employee training and development. **Training** is a planned effort to enable employees to learn job-related knowledge, skills, and behavior. For example, many organizations offer safety training to teach employees safe work habits. **Development** involves acquiring knowledge, skills, and behaviors that improve employees' ability to meet the challenges of a variety of new or existing jobs, including the client and customer demands of those jobs. Development programs often focus on preparing employees for management responsibility. Likewise, if a company plans to set up teams to manufacture products, it might offer a development program to help employees learn the ins and outs of effective teamwork.

Decisions related to training and development include whether the organization will emphasize enabling employees to perform their current jobs, preparing them for future jobs, or both. An organization may offer programs to a few employees in whom the organization wants to invest, or it may have a philosophy of investing in the training of all its workers. Some organizations, especially large ones, may have extensive formal training programs, including classroom sessions and training programs online. Other organizations may prefer a simpler, more flexible approach of encouraging employees to participate in outside training and development programs as needs are identified. For an example of a company where decisions about training and other HR practices are aimed at success in a tumultuous global environment, see the "Best Practices" box.

Managing Performance

Managing human resources includes keeping track of how well employees are performing relative to objectives such as job descriptions and goals for a particular position. The process of ensuring that employees' activities and outputs match the organization's goals is called **performance management.** The activities of performance management include specifying the tasks and outcomes of a job that contribute to the

Training
A planned effort to enable employees to learn job-related knowledge, skills, and behavior.

Development
The acquisition of knowledge, skills, and behaviors that improve an employee's ability to meet changes in job requirements and in customer demands.

Performance Management
The process of ensuring that employees' activities and outputs match the organization's goals.

How Abbott Laboratories Creates a Healthy Business

Anant Jain left a job at a consumer goods company to work for the finance department of Abbott Laboratories. It was a step that would propel him up the management ranks. Abbott paid for Jain to earn an MBA, including the skills necessary for making financial forecasts. Before long, Jain was ready to move to Dubai in the United Arab Emirates to take charge of financial planning for the Middle Eastern region.

Jain's story is hardly unique. Abbott's business strategy is based on hiring talented people and helping them develop their careers as they gain skills that increase their value to the company. When new employees join Abbott, the human resources department helps them set short-term goals and map out a career path. Reviews of employees' performance consider whether the employees are on track. Further development comes from a combination of on-the-job learning, training programs, and support from mentors.

Jain was hired by Abbott's subsidiary in India, but the commitment to employee growth and development is part of Abbott's global strategy. The company operates in more than 150 countries. Its industry—medical devices and (outside the United States) pharmaceuticals—undergoes constant change from innovation and regulation. To stay at the forefront of knowledge while remaining profitable in a turbulent industry, Abbott needs a special kind of employee who is flexible, open to change, and committed to excellence. Along with careful hiring and commitment to training, Abbott recruits and retains talent with efforts such as a mentoring program, surveys of employees, and in the United States, aid in translating veterans' military skills into career-related skills relevant to the civilian sector.

Questions

1. How could a company such as Abbott benefit from sending an employee to school to study finance or another business subject?
2. How do you think hiring and training could work hand-in-hand to help a company such as Abbott meet its business objectives?

Sources: Company website, "Careers and Opportunities," http://www.abbott.com, accessed April 8, 2014; Abbott India Ltd., "About Us," http://www.abbott.co.in, accessed April 8, 2014; Suprotip Ghosh, "What the Doctor Ordered," *Business Today*, August 4, 2013, pp. 78, 80.

---

organization's success. Then various measures are used to compare the employee's performance over some time period with the desired performance. Often, rewards—the topic of the next section—are developed to encourage good performance.

The human resource department may be responsible for developing or obtaining questionnaires and other devices for measuring performance. The performance measures may emphasize observable behaviors (for example, answering the phone by the second ring), outcomes (number of customer complaints and compliments), or both. When the person evaluating performance is not familiar with the details of the job, outcomes tend to be easier to evaluate than specific behaviors.[9] The evaluation may focus on the short term or long term and on individual employees or groups. Typically, the person who completes the evaluation is the employee's supervisor. Often employees also evaluate their own performance, and in some organizations, peers and subordinates participate, too.

Planning and Administering Pay and Benefits

The pay and benefits that employees earn play an important role in motivating them. This is especially true when rewards such as bonuses are linked to the individual's or group's achievements. Decisions about pay and benefits can also support other aspects of an organization's strategy. For example, a company that wants to provide an

One reason W.L. Gore is repeatedly named one of the 100 Best Companies to Work For in the United States is the company's unusual corporate hierarchy that dispenses with titles in favor of small teams and direct communication among employees. How do you think this boosts morale in the workplace?

exceptional level of service or be exceptionally innovative might pay significantly more than competitors in order to attract and keep the best employees. At other companies, a low-cost strategy requires knowledge of industry norms, so that the company does not spend more than it must.

Planning pay and benefits involves many decisions, often complex and based on knowledge of a multitude of legal requirements. An important decision is how much to offer in salary or wages, as opposed to bonuses, commissions, and other performance-related pay. Other decisions involve which benefits to offer, from retirement plans to various kinds of insurance to time off with pay. All such decisions have implications for the organization's bottom line, as well as for employee motivation.

Administering pay and benefits is another big responsibility. Organizations need systems for keeping track of each employee's earnings and benefits. Employees need information about their health plan, retirement plan, and other benefits. Keeping track of this involves extensive record keeping and reporting to management, employees, the government, and others.

Maintaining Positive Employee Relations

Organizations often depend on human resource professionals to help them maintain positive relations with employees. This function includes preparing and distributing employee handbooks that detail company policies and, in large organizations, company publications such as a monthly newsletter or a website on the organization's intranet. Preparing these communications may be a regular task for the human resource department.

The human resource department can also expect to handle certain kinds of communications from individual employees. Employees turn to the HR department for answers to questions about benefits and company policy. If employees feel they have been discriminated against, see safety hazards, or have other problems and are dissatisfied with their supervisor's response, they may turn to the HR department for help. Members of the department should be prepared to address such problems.

In organizations where employees belong to a union, employee relations entail additional responsibilities. The organization periodically conducts collective bargaining to negotiate an employment contract with union members. The HR department maintains communication with union representatives to ensure that problems are resolved as they arise.

Establishing and Administering Personnel Policies

All the human resource activities described so far require fair and consistent decisions, and most require substantial record keeping. Organizations depend on their HR department to help establish policies related to hiring, discipline, promotions, and benefits. For example, with a policy in place that an intoxicated worker will be immediately terminated, the company can handle such a situation more fairly and objectively than if it addressed such incidents on a case-by-case basis. The company depends on its HR professionals to help develop and then communicate the policy to every employee,

HR How To

Writing Effective HR Policies

Effective policies make it clear to employees what the organization requires. Policies should be easily understandable and relevant to employees. To write effective policies, apply the following guidelines:

- Decide whether a policy is needed for a situation. For example, does the law require a policy? Does behavior by employees or managers suggest that they need guidance? What would lead to better outcomes—a consistent standard or flexibility?
- Find out whether any legal requirements affect the policy. For example, hiring and promotion decisions must meet legal requirements for avoiding discrimination.
- Consult with experts to be sure the needs of the situation are

clear. Experts might include employees, managers, and the company's legal advisers.
- Be specific about the policy's purpose, the people it applies to, and the actions to take or avoid. Avoid jargon, and define any terms employees may not fully understand.
- Imagine scenarios where the policy might come into play. Make sure the way the policy applies in each situation is clear and appropriate, revising it if necessary.
- Tell where employees can ask questions or look up answers.

Questions

1. Why do you think it is important to tell employees the purpose of a policy?
2. Suppose some employees are coming to work dressed in a

way that distracts others. How could writing a dress code policy help in this situation? If you were a manager, would you rather handle the situation by referring to a policy or discussing a specific employee's clothing choices? Why?

Sources: HR Council for the Nonprofit Sector, "HR Policies and Employment Legislation," *HR Toolkit*, http://hrcouncil.ca, accessed April 8, 2014; Susan M. Heathfield, "How to Write a Policy," About.com Human Resources, http://humanresources.about.com, accessed April 8, 2014; Susan M. Heathfield, "How to Develop a Policy," About.com Human Resources, http://humanresources.about.com, accessed April 8, 2014; Suzanne Lucas, "Policies Never Solve People Problems," *Inc.*, August 28, 2013, http://www.inc.com.

so that everyone knows its importance. If anyone violates the rule, a supervisor can quickly intervene—confident that the employee knew the consequences and that any other employee would be treated the same way. Not only do such policies promote fair decision making, but they also promote other objectives, such as workplace safety and customer service.

Developing fair and effective policies requires strong decision-making skills, the ability to think ethically, and a broad understanding of business activities that will be covered by the policies. For more ideas on writing HR policies, see "HR How To." In addition, for employees to comply with policies, they have to know and understand the policies. Therefore, human resource management requires the ability to communicate through a variety of channels. Human resource personnel may teach policies by giving presentations at meetings, posting documents online, writing e-mail messages, setting up social-media pages for employees, and in many other ways.

Managing and Using Human Resource Data

All aspects of human resource management require careful and discreet record keeping, from processing job applications, to performance appraisals, benefits enrollment, and government-mandated reports. Handling records about employees requires accuracy as well as sensitivity to employee privacy. Whether the organization keeps records in file cabinets or on a sophisticated computer information system, it must have methods for ensuring accuracy and for balancing privacy concerns with easy access for those who need information and are authorized to see it.

Thanks to computer tools, employee-related information is not just an administrative responsibility; it also can be the basis for knowledge that gives organizations an edge over their competitors. Data about employees can show, for example, which of the company's talent has the most promise for future leadership, what kinds of employees tend to perform best in particular positions, and in which departments the need for hiring will be most pressing. To use the data for answering questions such as these, many organizations have set up human resource information systems. They may engage in **workforce analytics,** which is the use of quantitative tools and scientific methods to analyze data from human resource databases and other sources to make evidence-based decisions that support business goals. Chapter 2 will take a closer look at how developments in technology are enabling more sophisticated analysis of employee data to support decision making.

Workforce Analytics
The use of quantitative tools and scientific methods to analyze data from human resource databases and other sources to make evidence-based decisions that support business goals.

Ensuring Compliance with Labor Laws

As we will discuss in later chapters, especially Chapter 3, the government has many laws and regulations concerning the treatment of employees. These laws govern such matters as equal employment opportunity, employee safety and health, employee pay and benefits, employee privacy, and job security. Government requirements include filing reports and displaying posters, as well as avoiding unlawful behavior. Most managers depend on human resource professionals to help them keep track of these requirements.

Ensuring compliance with laws requires that human resource personnel keep watch over a rapidly changing legal landscape. For example, the increased use of and access to electronic databases by employees and employers suggest that in the near future legislation will be needed to protect employee privacy rights. Currently, no federal laws outline how to use employee databases in such a way as to protect employees' privacy while also meeting employers' and society's concern for security.

Lawsuits that will continue to influence HRM practices concern job security. Because companies are forced to close facilities and lay off employees because of economic or competitive conditions, cases dealing with the illegal discharge of employees have increased. The issue of "employment at will"—that is, the principle that an employer may terminate employment at any time without notice—will be debated. As the age of the overall workforce increases, as described in the next chapter, the number of cases dealing with age discrimination in layoffs, promotions, and benefits will likely rise. Employers will need to review work rules, recruitment practices, and performance evaluation systems, revising them if necessary to ensure that they do not falsely communicate employment agreements the company does not intend to honor (such as lifetime employment) or discriminate on the basis of age.

Supporting the Organization's Strategy

At one time, human resource management was primarily an administrative function. The HR department focused on filling out forms and processing paperwork. As more organizations have come to appreciate the significance of highly skilled human resources, however, many HR departments have taken on a more active role in supporting the organization's strategy. As a result, today's HR professionals need to understand the organization's business operations, project how business trends might affect the business, reinforce positive aspects of the organization's culture, develop talent for present and future needs, craft effective HR strategies, and make a case for them to top

HR Oops!

"Talent Management Sounds Great, but . . ."

"We don't have time for it." At least, that seems to be the thinking at many companies.

Many managers agree that it sounds wise to plan for the kinds of people needed to carry out the organization's strategy, just as they would plan for every other resource. And it makes sense that managers would set goals for and measure the success of employee selection, training, performance feedback, and retention.

However, when the consulting firm Right Management surveyed hundreds of managers, the researchers found that only 12% have established and implemented a strategy for talent management.

Companies are much more likely to treat HR activities as separate processes disconnected from business objectives. In spite of that, about half the managers claimed that their company's leaders consider talent management a top priority. Even worse off may be the companies where 38% of managers said talent management is not a priority.

Questions

1. Why do you suppose half the managers say talent management is important at their company but only 12% say their company is doing it? In other words, what is missing when people fail to do what they say is important?
2. How might a company that uses talent management gain an advantage over a competitor that treats HR tasks as unrelated activities?

Sources: Toni Hodges DeTuncq and Lynn Schmidt, "Examining Integrated Talent Management," *T+D*, September 2013, pp. 31–35; Bloomberg BNA, "Study Finds Little Consensus on Talent Management," *Report on Salary Surveys*, March 1, 2013, http://news.bna. com; Right Management, "The Struggle over Talent Management Strategy," *Research Highlights*, 2012, http://www. right.com.

---

management. Evidence for greater involvement in strategy comes from interviews with finance and HR executives who say they are more interested than ever in collaborating to strengthen their companies.[10] Finance leaders can see that employees are a major budget item, so they want to make sure they are getting the best value for that expense. HR leaders, for their part, are learning to appreciate the importance of using quantitative tools to measure performance.

An important element of this responsibility is **human resource planning,** identifying the numbers and types of employees the organization will require in order to meet its objectives. Using these estimates, the human resource department helps the organization forecast its needs for hiring, training, and reassigning employees. Planning also may show that the organization will need fewer employees to meet anticipated needs. In that situation, human resource planning includes how to handle or avoid layoffs. Human resource planning provides important information for **talent management**— a systematic, planned effort to attract, retain, develop, and motivate highly skilled employees and managers. When managers are clear about the kinds of people they will need to achieve the organization's goals, talent management combines recruiting, selection, training, and motivational practices to meet those needs. Approaching these tasks in terms of talent management is one way HR managers are making the link to organizational strategy. At Zeno Group, a Chicago public relations firm, CFO Tony Blasco has collaborated with the HR manager to identify people to hire as future strategic needs arise. Together, says Blasco, they are planning for how future hires will "further our ambitious growth goals."[11] Unfortunately, as described in the "HR Oops!" box, this commitment to talent management has yet to catch on at many organizations.

As part of its strategic role, one of the key contributions HR can make is to engage in evidence-based HR. **Evidence-based HR** refers to demonstrating that human resource practices have a positive influence on the company's profits or key stakeholders

Human Resource Planning
Identifying the numbers and types of employees the organization will require to meet its objectives.

Talent Management
A systematic, planned effort to attract, retain, develop, and motivate highly skilled employees and managers.

Evidence-Based HR
Collecting and using data to show that human resource practices have a positive influence on the company's bottom line or key stakeholders.

(employees, customers, community, shareholders). This practice helps show that the money invested in HR programs is justified and that HRM is contributing to the company's goals and objectives. For example, data collected on the relationship between HR practices and productivity, turnover, accidents, employee attitudes, and medical costs may show that HR functions are as important to the business as finance, accounting, and marketing.

Often, an organization's strategy requires some type of change—for example, adding, moving, or closing facilities; applying new technology; or entering markets in other regions or countries. Common reactions to change include fear, anger, and confusion. The organization may turn to its human resource department for help in managing the change process. Skilled human resource professionals can apply knowledge of human behavior, along with performance management tools, to help the organization manage change constructively.

Another strategic challenge tackled by a growing number of companies is how to seek profits in ways that communities, customers, and suppliers will support over the long run. This concern is called **sustainability**—broadly defined as an organization's ability to profit without depleting its resources, including employees, natural resources, and the support of the surrounding community. Success at sustainability comes from meeting the needs of the organization's **stakeholders,** all the parties who have an interest in the organization's success. Typically, an organization's stakeholders include shareholders, the community, customers, and employees. Sustainable organizations meet their needs by minimizing their environmental impact, providing high-quality products and services, ensuring workplace safety, offering fair compensation, and delivering an adequate return to investors. Sustainability delivers a strategic advantage when it boosts the organization's image with customers, opens access to new markets, and helps attract and retain talented employees. In an organization with a sustainable strategy, HR departments focus on employee development and empowerment rather than short-term costs, on long-term planning rather than smooth turnover and outsourcing, and on justice and fairness over short-term profits.[12] At IBM, human resource management sustainably addresses the company's global presence and drive for innovation in several ways. Diversity training helps people work productively in teams regardless of ethnicity, gender, or other differences. Global Enablement Teams address employee development needs in various regions by sending employees from highly developed nations to mentor employees in developing nations; the mentors teach business skills while learning about these high-potential markets. And IBM's Smarter Planet projects to lower resource use and pollution attract talented innovators; job candidates are excited about the chance to be part of this effort.[13]

Sustainability
An organization's ability to profit without depleting its resources, including employees, natural resources, and the support of the surrounding community.

Stakeholders
The parties with an interest in the company's success (typically, shareholders, the community, customers, and employees).

LO 1-3 Summarize the types of skills needed for human resource management.

Skills of HRM Professionals

With such varied responsibilities, the human resource department needs to bring together a large pool of skills. The Society of Human Resource Management (SHRM) has defined sets of behaviors and skills associated with success, grouping these into nine categories it calls *HR success competencies:* relationship management, ethical practice, HR expertise, business acumen, critical evaluation, diversity and inclusion, leadership and navigation, consultation, and communication.[14] Figure 1.3 describes the competencies and provides example behaviors that HR professionals should demonstrate as part of their growth and development.[15] Members of the HR department need to be:

1. *Credible activists*—Are so well respected in the organization that they can influence the positions taken by managers. HR professionals who are competent in this area

Figure 1.3

Competencies and Example Behaviors for HR Professionals

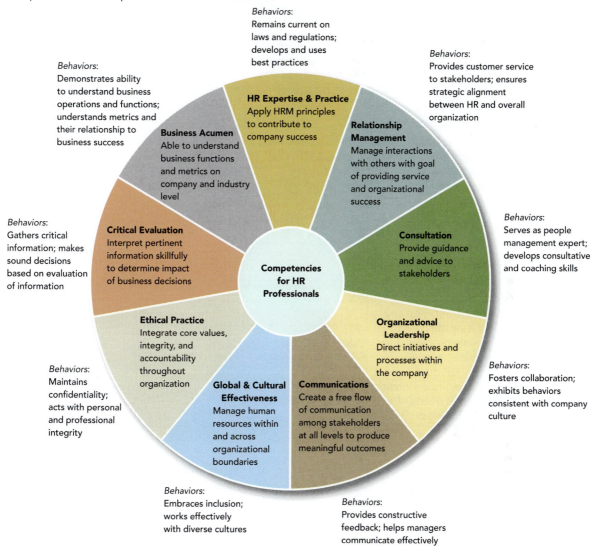

Source: Based on Society for Human Resource Management, "SHRM Elements for HR Success," www.shrm.org, accessed May 13, 2014.

have the most influence over the organization's success, but to build this competency, they have to gain credibility by mastering all the others.

2. *Cultural and change steward*—Understands the organization's culture and helping to build and strengthen or change that culture by identifying and expressing its values through words and actions.

3. *Talent manager/organizational designer*—Knows the ways that people join the organization and move to different positions within it. To do this effectively requires knowledge of how the organization is structured and how that structure might be adjusted to help it meet its goals for developing and using employees' talents.

4. *Strategic architect*—Requires awareness of business trends and an understanding of how they might affect the business, as well as opportunities and threats they might present.

CEO and CFO Relationships with HRM

Executives want HR leaders to play a key role in strategic planning, according to a survey of chief executive officers and chief financial officers in the United States and Europe. But while over half of CEOs think HR is fulfilling that role, few CFOs agree. This is partly because the financial officers want to measure hard numbers, and many HR executives are not delivering that quantitative view of performance.

Question

What skills or competencies could help HR managers build stronger relationships with chief financial officers?

Sources: IBM, "Essential Partnerships for HR," IBM and Oracle, http://www.ibm.com, accessed April 8, 2014; "New Study Details Ways Human Resources Executives Can Take a Bigger Role in Driving Growth," *Market Wired*,

February 11, 2013, http://www.marketwired.com; IBM and Oracle, "CFO Perspectives: How HR Can Take On a Bigger Role in Driving Growth," *Economist Intelligence Unit*, 2012, http://www.oracle.com

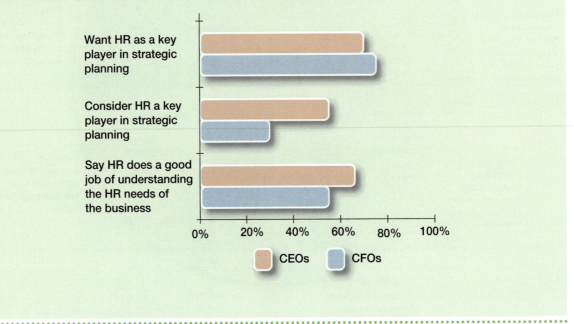

A person with this capability spots ways effective management of human resources can help the company seize opportunities and confront threats to the business.

5. *Business allies*—Know how the business makes money, who its customers are, and why customers buy what the company sells.

6. *Operational executors*—At the most basic level carry out particular HR functions such as handling the selection, training, or compensation of employees and communicating through a variety of media. All of the other HR skills require some ability as operational executor, because this is the level at which policies and transactions deliver results by legally, ethically, and efficiently acquiring, developing, motivating, and deploying human resources.

All of these competencies require interpersonal skills. Successful HR professionals must be able to share information, build relationships, and influence persons inside and outside the company. The "Did You Know?" box suggests some of the challenges involved.

HR Responsibilities of Supervisors

LO 1-4 Explain the role of supervisors in human resource management.

Although many organizations have human resource departments, HR activities are by no means limited to the specialists who staff those departments. In large organizations, HR departments advise and support the activities of the other departments. In small organizations, there may be an HR specialist, but many HR activities are carried out by line supervisors. Either way, non-HR managers need to be familiar with the basics of HRM and their role in managing human resources.

At a start-up company, the first supervisors are the company's founders. Not all founders recognize their HR responsibilities, but those who do have a powerful advantage. When Rusty George first founded his marketing firm, Rusty George Creative, in Tacoma, Washington, hiring was just something he did to keep up with rising demand. As he signed on law firms, museums, and other clients, he added staff to take care of them. Then the economy took a dive, and all the clients decided to do without the firm's services. George had no way to continue paying all 17 of his employees. He laid off 9 of them. When business started to build again, George knew he had to be more methodical about hiring. He now analyzes all the costs associated with a new hire, including parking spaces, equipment, and even coffee. Then he looks at the additional revenue a particular position can generate. Only when those numbers show that a new hire will be profitable does George start contacting candidates who have submitted their résumés. Based on a painful lesson, George has learned to align his hiring practices with his business requirements.[16]

As we will see in later chapters, supervisors typically have responsibilities related to all the HR functions. Figure 1.4 shows some HR responsibilities that supervisors are likely to be involved in. Organizations depend on supervisors to help them determine what kinds of work need to be done (job analysis and design) and how many employees are needed (HR planning). Supervisors typically interview job candidates and participate in the decisions about which candidates to hire. Many organizations expect supervisors to train employees in some or all aspects of the employees' jobs. Supervisors conduct performance appraisals and may recommend pay increases. And, of course, supervisors play a key role in employee relations because they are most often the voice of management for their employees, representing the company on a day-to-day basis. In all these activities, supervisors can participate in HRM by taking into consideration the ways that decisions and policies will affect their employees. Understanding the principles of communication, motivation, and other elements of human behavior can help supervisors inspire the best from the organization's human resources.

Help define jobs

Motivate, with support from pay, benefits, and other rewards

Forecast HR needs

Communicate policies

Provide training

Recommend pay increases and promotions

Appraise performance

Interview (and select) candidates

Figure 1.4

Supervisors' Involvement in HRM: Common Areas of Involvement

LO 1-5 Discuss
ethical issues in human
resource management.

Ethics
The fundamental princi-
ples of right and wrong.

Ethics in Human Resource Management

Whenever people's actions affect one another, ethical issues arise, and business decisions are no exception. **Ethics** refers to fundamental principles of right and wrong;
ethical behavior is behavior that is consistent with those principles. Business decisions,
including HRM decisions, should be ethical, but the evidence suggests that is not
always what happens. Recent surveys indicate that the general public and managers
do not have positive perceptions of the ethical conduct of U.S. businesses. For example, in a Gallup poll on honesty and ethics in 21 professions, only 18% of Americans
rated business executives high or very high; close to twice as many rated them low or
very low. And within organizations, a recent survey of workers found that 45% had
witnessed some form of unethical conduct at their workplace.[17]

Many ethical issues in the workplace involve human resource management. The recent financial crisis, in which the investment bank Lehman Brothers collapsed, insurance
giant AIG survived only with a massive infusion of government funds, and many observers
feared that money for loans would dry up altogether, had many causes. Among these, some
people believe, were ethical lapses related to compensation and other HR policies.

Employee Rights

In the context of ethical human resource management, HR managers must view employees as having basic rights. Such a view reflects ethical principles embodied in the
U.S. Constitution and Bill of Rights. A widely adopted understanding of human rights,
based on the work of the philosopher Immanuel Kant, as well as the tradition of the
Enlightenment, assumes that in a moral universe, every person has certain basic rights:

- *Right of free consent*—People have the right to be treated only as they knowingly
  and willingly consent to be treated. An example that applies to employees would be
  that employees should know the nature of the job they are being hired to do; the
  employer should not deceive them.
- *Right of privacy*—People have the right to do as they wish in their private lives, and
  they have the right to control what they reveal about private activities. One way an
  employer respects this right is by keeping employees' personal records confidential.
- *Right of freedom of conscience*—People have the right to refuse to do what violates
  their moral beliefs, as long as these beliefs reflect commonly accepted norms. A
  supervisor who demands that an employee do something that is unsafe or envi-
  ronmentally damaging may be violating this right if the task conflicts with the employee's values. (Such behavior could be illegal as well as unethical.)
- *Right of freedom of speech*—People have the right to criticize an organization's ethics
  if they do so in good conscience and their criticism does not violate the rights of
  individuals in the organization. Many organizations address this right by offering
  hot lines or policies and procedures designed to handle complaints from employees.
- *Right to due process*—If people believe their rights are being violated, they have the
  right to a fair and impartial hearing. As we will see in Chapter 3, Congress has addressed this right in some circumstances by establishing agencies to hear complaints
  when employees believe their employer has not provided a fair hearing. For example, the Equal Employment Opportunity Commission may prosecute complaints of
  discrimination if it believes the employer did not fairly handle the problem.

One way to think about ethics in business is that the morally correct action is the one
that minimizes encroachments on and avoids violations of these rights.

Organizations often face situations in which the rights of employees are affected.
In particular, the right of privacy of health information has received much attention

in recent years. Computerized record keeping and computer networks have greatly increased the ways people can gain (authorized or unauthorized) access to records about individuals. Health-related records can be particularly sensitive. HRM responsibilities include the ever-growing challenge of maintaining confidentiality and security of employees' health information as required by the Health Insurance Portability and Accountability Act (HIPAA).

Standards for Ethical Behavior

Ethical, successful companies act according to four principles.[18] First, in their relationships with customers, vendors, and clients, ethical and successful companies emphasize mutual benefits. Second, employees assume responsibility for the actions of the company. Third, such companies have a sense of purpose or vision that employees value and use in their day-to-day work. Finally, they emphasize fairness; that is, another person's interests count as much as their own.

Executives at 3M realized the company needed to recommit to principles such as these when the company was trying for a comeback after several difficult years. In an effort to improve profits, past leadership had focused on cutting costs, and 3M's reputation as an innovator suffered from neglect. When George W. Buckley took the chief executive's job, 3M intended to refocus employees on growth and innovation. This would require changes in employees' actions and mind-sets. Angela S. Lalor, 3M's senior vice president of human resources, explained to the leadership team that successful change on that scale would require a high level of employee trust. In particular, employees would need to feel they trusted their immediate supervisors. So the company's HR professionals focused on creating plans to build trusting relationships by ensuring that supervisors treated employees fairly. The company also sought to engage employees by ensuring they were aware of and connected to its efforts to operate sustainably by reducing pollution, providing grants for community projects, and promoting employee health. Since 3M launched the effort, employee surveys have shown higher levels of trust in managers and engagement with the company. The company's financial performance improved as well.[19]

For human resource practices to be considered ethical, they must satisfy the three basic standards summarized in Figure 1.5.[20] First, HRM practices must result in the greatest good for the largest number of people. Second, employment practices must

Figure 1.5

Standards for Identifying Ethical Practices

Greatest good for greatest number

Fair and equitable

Ethical Alternative

Respect for basic human rights

respect basic human rights of privacy, due process, consent, and free speech. Third, managers must treat employees and customers equitably and fairly. At 3M, the human resources department helped supervisors treat employees fairly by educating the supervisors in what kinds of conduct employees consider fair—for example, communicating in ways that are honest, open, and realistic. The training also emphasized the importance of listening carefully to employees and asking questions rather than dictating solutions. HR staffers provided supervisors with information about how 3M establishes pay rates so the supervisors themselves can share the information with employees and demonstrate that the decisions are based on fair criteria.[21]

LO 1-6 Describe typical careers in human resource management.

Careers in Human Resource Management

There are many different types of jobs in the HRM profession. Figure 1.6 shows selected HRM positions and their salaries. The salaries vary depending on education and experience, as well as the type of industry in which the person works. As you can see from Figure 1.6, some positions involve work in specialized areas of HRM such as recruiting, compensation, or employee benefits. Usually, HR generalists make between $50,000 and $80,000, depending on their experience and education level. Generalists usually perform the full range of HRM activities, including recruiting, training, compensation, and employee relations.

The vast majority of HRM professionals have a college degree, and many also have completed postgraduate work. The typical field of study is business (especially human resources or industrial relations), but some HRM professionals have degrees in the

Figure 1.6

Median Salaries for HRM Positions

Source: Data from Salary Wizard, Salary.com, http://swz.salary.com, accessed April 8, 2014.

HRM Social

SHRM's Social-Media Presence

Members of the Society of Human Resource Management can connect with the organization's resources and with one another online, thanks to several applications of social media:

- SHRM has a Twitter account (http://twitter.com/shrm), so members can sign up for the group's Twitter feed.
- At the SHRM website, the SHRM Blog (http://blog.shrm.org) gives members a place to read the organization's latest thoughts and get involved in the conversation by reading and posting comments.
- Also at the website, SHRM has established its own members-only social network called SHRM Connect (http://community .shrm.org). Those who join the network can meet other SHRM members online and trade ideas. SHRM's features include search capabilities and e-mail alerts so members can look up and be aware of discussions on topics of interest.
- Another way to participate in member discussions at the website is to visit HR Talk (http://shrm.org/hrtalk), a discussion forum where members can post questions and answers in various HR subject areas.
- SHRM has a members-only group on LinkedIn, the careers networking site. The SHRM Group has more than 2,000 members.

Questions

1. Do you use Twitter or LinkedIn? Would you be interested in seeing career-related information in social media such as these?
2. How might participating in online discussion groups help you in your career?

Sources: Based on Henry G. Jackson, "Embracing Social Media," *HR Magazine,* December 2011, p. 10; Society for Human Resource Management, "SHRM Membership: Do More with More," member benefits guide, http://www.shrm.org, accessed April 8, 2014; SHRM, "HR Talk," https://www.shrm.org, accessed April 8, 2014; SHRM, "SHRM Connect," http://community.shrm.org/home, accessed April 8, 2014; "SHRM Group," LinkedIn, http://www.linkedin.com, accessed April 8, 2014.

social sciences (economics or psychology), the humanities, and law programs. Those who have completed graduate work have master's degrees in HR management, business management, or a similar field. This is important because to be successful in HR, you need to speak the same language as people in the other business functions. You have to have credibility as a business leader, so you must be able to understand finance and to build a business case for HR activities.

HR professionals can increase their career opportunities by taking advantage of training and development programs. These may include taking courses toward a master's degree, accepting assignments to spend time observing, or "shadowing," a manager in another department, or taking a position in another department to learn more about the business. When Michael Brady was a district HR manager for Walmart, he would travel with the operations manager for his region. Each manager was interested in learning more about the other's perspective on the business, and they eventually learned enough to help one another spot issues to address. Marian M. Graddick-Weir started her HR career as a generalist at AT&T. Her supervisor asked her to serve as chief of staff to the company's vice chairman. The position was heavy on clerical duties but gave Graddick-Weir access to the kinds of decisions and conversations that take place at the highest level of the organization. Graddick-Weir paid attention and then took that knowledge with her when she returned to the HR department. Today she is executive vice president of human resources at Merck & Co.[22]

Some HRM professionals have a professional certification in HRM, but many more are members of professional associations. The primary professional organization for HRM is the Society for Human Resource Management (SHRM). SHRM is the world's largest human resource management association, with more than 250,000 professional

Table 1.3

Topics Covered in This Book

I.   The Human Resource Environment
1. Managing Human Resources
2. Trends in Human Resource Management
3. Providing Equal Employment Opportunity and a Safe Workplace
4. Analyzing Work and Designing Jobs

II. Acquiring, Training, and Developing Human Resources
5. Planning for and Recruiting Human Resources
6. Selecting Employees and Placing Them in Jobs
7. Training Employees
8. Developing Employees for Future Success

III. Assessing and Improving Performance
9. Creating and Maintaining High-Performance Organizations
10. Managing Employees' Performance
11. Separating and Retaining Employees

IV. Compensating Human Resources
12. Establishing a Pay Structure
13. Recognizing Employee Contributions with Pay
14. Providing Employee Benefits

V.   Meeting Other HR Goals
15. Collective Bargaining and Labor Relations
16. Managing Human Resources Globally

and student members throughout the world. SHRM provides education and information services, conferences and seminars, government and media representation, and online services and publications (such as *HR Magazine*). You can visit SHRM's website to see their services at **www.shrm.org**. SHRM also connects with members through various social-media tools, as described in "HRM Social."

Organization of This Book

This chapter has provided an overview of human resource management to give you a sense of its scope. In this book, the topics are organized according to the broad areas of human resource management shown in Table 1.3. The numbers in the table refer to the part and chapter numbers.

The remaining chapters in Part 1 discuss aspects of the human resource environment: trends shaping the field (Chapter 2), legal requirements (Chapter 3), and the work to be done by the organization, which is the basis for designing jobs (Chapter 4). Part 2 explores the responsibilities involved in acquiring and equipping human resources for current and future positions: HR planning and recruiting (Chapter 5), selection and placement of employees (Chapter 6), training (Chapter 7), and developing (Chapter 8). Part 3 turns to the assessment and improvement of performance through creation of high-performance organizations (Chapter 9), performance management (Chapter 10), and appropriate handling of employee separation when the organization determines it no longer wants or needs certain employees (Chapter 11). Part 4 addresses topics related to compensation: pay structure (Chapter 12), pay to recognize performance (Chapter 13), and benefits (Chapter 14). Part 5 explores special topics faced by HR managers today: human resource management in organizations where employees have or are seeking union representation (Chapter 15) and international human resource management (Chapter 16).

Along with examples highlighting how HRM helps a company maintain high performance, the chapters offer various other features to help you connect the principles to real-world situations. "Best Practices" boxes tell success stories related to the chapter's topic. "HR Oops!" boxes identify situations gone wrong and invite you to find better alternatives. "HR How To" boxes provide details about how to carry out a practice in each HR area. "Did You Know?" boxes are snapshots of interesting statistics related to chapter topics. Many chapters also include an "HRM Social" box identifying ways that human resource professionals are applying social media to help their organizations excel in the fast-changing modern world.

THINKING ETHICALLY

HOW SHOULD AN EMPLOYER WEIGH CONFLICTING VALUES?

One of the largest relief organizations in the United States recently struggled with HR policy. As a religious (Christian)-based organization, it may use religion as the basis for employment standards. This organization has developed policies in an employee conduct manual intended to ensure that employees demonstrate the beliefs and morals of its founders' faith. Among those requirements is "abstinence before marriage and fidelity in marriage."

The problem for the organization's board of directors was that some states—including Washington, where it is headquartered—have made same-sex marriage legal, so the organization could potentially receive job applications from people who have married a partner of the same sex. To respect the values of employees and donors who hold traditional religious views, the organization had been denying them employment.

The board decided that religious views in the United States had become diverse enough that it should begin to allow people in same-sex marriages to work for the organization. However, when the board announced the decision, many donors became upset; by some reports, about 2,000 child sponsorships were ended. The board quickly reversed its decision. The organization's president expressed regret for not having consulted more with its community of supporters.

The organization tries to set high ethical standards for its employees. Neither the decision to allow hiring of workers in same-sex marriages nor the reversal of that decision violated the law as it applies to a religious-based organization. However, it did create embarrassing publicity for an organization that was trying to broaden its appeal and keep the focus on charity.

Questions

1. In this situation, whose rights were affected? What basic rights were at stake?
2. How well do you think the organization applied standards for ethical behavior? Why?

Sources: Sarah Pulliam Bailey, "Analysis: World Vision's Gay Marriage Flip-Flop Reflects Evangelical Angst as Culture Shifts," *Salt Lake Tribune*, March 28, 2014, http://www.sltrib.com; Joel Connelly, "World Vision, in Reversal, Won't Hire Christians in Same-Sex Marriages," *Seattle Post-Intelligencer*, March 26, 2014, http://blog.seattlepi.com; Sarah Pulliam Bailey, "World Vision to Recognize Employees' Same-Sex Marriages," *Washington Post*, March 25, 2014, http://www.washingtonpost.com.

SUMMARY

LO 1-1 Define human resource management, and explain how HRM contributes to an organization's performance.

- Human resource management consists of an organization's policies, practices, and systems that influence employees' behavior, attitudes, and performance.
- HRM influences who works for an organization and how.
- Well-managed human resources can be a source of sustainable competitive advantage by contributing to quality, profits, and customer satisfaction.

LO 1-2 Identify the responsibilities of human resource departments.

- Analyze and design jobs.
- Recruit and select employees.
- Equip employees by training and developing them.
- Through performance management, ensure that employees' activities and outputs match the organization's goals.
- Plan and administer pay and employee benefits.

- Engage in employee relations—for example, communications and collective bargaining.
- Establish and administer personnel policies and keep records.
- Help ensure compliance with labor laws.
- Support the development and execution of corporate strategy.

LO 1-3 Summarize the types of skills needed for human resource management.

- Communication, negotiation, and team development skills.
- Decision-making skills based on HR knowledge and company business.
- Leadership skills for managing conflict and change.
- Technical skills including knowledge of current techniques, applicable laws, and computer systems.

LO 1-4 Explain the role of supervisors in human resource management.

- Help analyze work.
- Interview job candidates and participate in selection decisions.
- Provide employee training.
- Conduct performance appraisals.

- Recommend pay increases.
- Represent the company to their employees.

LO 1-5 Discuss ethical issues in human resource management.

- Should make decisions that result in the greatest good for the largest number of people.
- Should respect basic rights of privacy, due process, consent, and free speech.
- Should treat others equitably and fairly.
- Should recognize ethical issues that arise in areas such as employee privacy, protection of employee safety, and fairness in employment practices.

LO 1-6 Describe typical careers in human resource management.

- Careers may involve specialized work (e.g., recruiting, training, or labor relations).
- Others may be generalists, performing a range of activities.
- A college degree in business or social sciences usually is required.
- People skills must be balanced with attention to details of law and knowledge of business.

KEY TERMS

human resource management (HRM), 3
human capital, 4
job analysis, 7
job design, 7
recruitment, 7

selection, 7
training, 8
development, 8
performance management, 8
workforce analytics, 12
human resource planning, 13

talent management, 13
evidence-based HR, 13
sustainability, 14
stakeholders, 14
ethics, 18

REVIEW AND DISCUSSION QUESTIONS

1. How can human resource management contribute to a company's success? (*LO 1.1*)
2. Imagine that a small manufacturing company decides to invest in a materials resource planning (MRP) system. This is a computerized information system that improves efficiency by automating such work as planning needs for resources, ordering materials, and scheduling work on the shop floor. The company hopes that with the new MRP system, it can grow by quickly and efficiently processing small orders for a variety of products. Which of the human resource functions are likely to be affected by this change? How

can human resource management help the organization carry out this change successfully? (*LO 1.2*)
3. What skills are important for success in human resource management? Which of these skills are already strengths of yours? Which would you like to develop? (*LO 1.3*)
4. Traditionally, human resource management practices were developed and administered by the company's human resource department. Line managers are now playing a major role in developing and implementing HRM practices. Why do you think non-HR managers are becoming more involved? (*LO 1.4*)

5. If you were to start a business, which aspects of human resource management would you want to entrust to specialists? Why? (*LO 1.3*)
6. Why do all managers and supervisors need knowledge and skills related to human resource management? (*LO 1.4*)
7. Federal law requires that employers not discriminate on the basis of a person's race, sex, national origin, or age over 40. Is this also an ethical requirement? A competitive requirement? Explain. (*LO 1.5*)
8. When a restaurant employee slipped on spilled soup and fell, requiring the evening off to recover, the owner realized that workplace safety was an issue to which she had not devoted much time. A friend warned the owner that if she started creating a lot of safety rules and procedures, she would lose her focus on customers and might jeopardize the future of the restaurant. The safety problem is beginning to feel like an ethical dilemma. Suggest some ways the restaurant owner might address this dilemma. What aspects of human resource management are involved? (*LO 1.5*)
9. Does a career in human resource management, based on this chapter's description, appeal to you? Why or why not? (*LO 1.6*)

TAKING RESPONSIBILITY

How "Good Things Happen to" Costco

Talking to a reporter, Costco's chief executive, Craig Jelinek, had a habit of stating the conditions in which "good things will happen to you." To summarize his retail company's strategy, Jelinek said, "As long as you continue to take care of the customer, take care of employees, and keep your expenses in line, good things are going to happen to you." Indeed, good things *have* happened to Costco, which stands out from other retailers for remaining profitable and avoiding layoffs during the Great Recession and beyond.

Although Costco has an online presence, the company is mainly a chain of warehouse stores that charge consumers a membership fee to enjoy rock-bottom prices. By ordering in bulk packages, displaying goods on pallets and steel shelving, and setting markups just a sliver over costs, Costco lures shoppers with low prices. It makes most of its profits from selling memberships. Consumers like the arrangement: the renewal rate is nearly 90%.

Costco's commitment to shaving expenses carries over to its plain headquarters but not to the way it treats employees. Since the 1980s, Costco has increased pay rates every three years, keeping compensation above industry norms. Even during the financial crisis in 2009, Costco announced raises. On average, a Costco worker earns $20.89 an hour, compared with $12.67 for an hourly employee working full-time for Walmart, which runs Costco's chief competitor, Sam's Club. In addition, Costco reported that 88% of its employees had company-sponsored health insurance plans, compared with Walmart's statement saying "more than half" of employees were covered. Costco also has resisted layoffs. For example, as other companies downsized store workforces and installed self-checkout lanes, Costco determined that its employees were more efficient and better suited to its customer service goals.

These decisions assume that satisfied employees will build a stronger company by being more committed to the organization and less likely to quit. Costco has a low rate of employee turnover (the percentage who quit each year): 5% among employees with at least a year on the job, or about one-fourth the industry average. The company therefore spends less to recruit and train new employees, and employees have more experience they can apply to providing great service. Costco also uses store employees as its main source of management talent. It pays tuition for hourly workers to pursue their education and move up the corporate ladder.

Costco's executives credit the treatment of employees with helping the company thrive. Its sales and stock price have been surging over the past few years. The company has been expanding in Europe and Asia, where it hopes its commitment to employee well-being will serve the company equally well.

Questions

1. In what ways does Costco meet the criteria for a "sustainable" organization?
2. What would you describe as Costco's basic strategy as a retailer? How do its human resource practices support that strategy?

Sources: Elizabeth A. Harris, "Walmart Will Lay Off 2,300 Sam's Club Workers," *New York Times*, January 24, 2014, www.nytimes.com; Caroline Fairchild, "Bulking Up Abroad," *Fortune*, January 16, 2014, http://money.cnn.com; Brad Stone, "Costco CEO Craig Jelinek Leads the Cheapest, Happiest Company in the World," *Bloomberg Businessweek*, June 6, 2013, www.businessweek.com; Anne Fisher, "A Blueprint for Creating Better Jobs—and Bigger Profits," *Fortune*, December 12, 2013, http://management.fortune.cnn.com.

MANAGING TALENT

Ingersoll Rand's Problem-Solving Approach to HRM

When Craig Mundy joined Ingersoll Rand as a human resources executive, he brought a business perspective. His approach was welcome at the company, which makes transportation and building products in support of a mission to create "comfortable, sustainable and efficient environments." The business's perspective is one of solving problems. In construction, for example, beyond selling heating and ventilation systems, it aims to improve air quality and comfort while reducing energy consumption. Likewise, in looking at its own operations, Ingersoll Rand has harnessed employee creativity to improve energy efficiency.

In contrast, Mundy knew that the focus of human resource management has often been on tasks more than on solutions. At a previous employer, Mundy had managed business projects. There, the company's HR staff was not always as helpful as he would have wished. Applying the experience, he came to Ingersoll Rand with determination to solve business problems.

Mundy started by identifying the strategic priorities of his business unit. He learned, for example, that Ingersoll Rand was seeking growth in countries with developing economies, a goal that required excellent country-level management. Mundy had the HR team determine how many country managers the company would need, when the need for each would arise, and what qualities make someone an excellent country manager. This information formed the basis of goals for supporting international growth. To achieve the goals, the HR team evaluated talent inside and outside the company and set up ways to help employees acquire the needed skills.

Mundy developed this approach into a Talent Solutions framework for addressing challenges facing each business area. He learned that one region had a problem with high turnover among sales representatives. Managers had tried to handle the problem by improving the process for recruiting new sales reps, but the high turnover continued. Applying the Talent Solutions framework, the HR team analyzed the pattern of turnover. The analysts found that turnover was highest after salespeople had been on the job about two and a half years, and that this was the point at which they were just becoming productive. The HR team decided to focus on helping salespeople become productive faster, so their jobs would become more rewarding faster. The team studied the entire process of hiring, training, and retaining employees and set goals for improvement in each stage of the process. Before long, salespeople were more engaged, delivered better results, and were less likely to quit.

Mundy's focus on business problems and solutions has improved Ingersoll Rand's performance. It also has reshaped the way Ingersoll Rand's business managers think about human resource management. Today they see Mundy's group as a strategic partner.

Questions

1. What important HRM skills has Craig Mundy applied to his role at Ingersoll Rand?
2. How do talent management and evidence-based HR support Mundy's efforts to offer solutions?

Sources: Ingersoll Rand, "Our Culture," http://company.ingersollrand.com, accessed April 8, 2014; Ingersoll Rand, "Ingersoll Rand Recognized as One of the Achievers 50 Most Engaged Workplaces in the United States," news release, January 20, 2014, http://investor.shareholder.com/ir; Ingersoll Rand, "Ingersoll Rand Changes Segment Reporting to Align with Reorganization Following Expected Security Spin," news release, November 6, 2013, http://investor.shareholder.com/ir; Marc Major, "One Step Forward: Driving Sustainability at Ingersoll Rand," *EHS Today*, June 2013, pp. 45–49; J. Craig Mundy, "Be a Strategic Performance Consultant," *HR Magazine*, March 2013.

HR IN SMALL BUSINESS

Managing HR at a Services Firm

Susan K. Dubin describes herself as someone who enjoys helping others and making her company a positive place to work. Those attitudes have provided a strong basis for her successful career in human resource management. In two different companies, Dubin took on responsibilities for payroll, training, and employee relations. As she built her experience, she established a strong working relationship with Danone Simpson, an insurance agent.

Dubin was impressed with what she saw as Simpson's "commitment to client services." So when Simpson prepared to open her own insurance services business, Dubin was interested in signing on. For several years now, Dubin has been HR director for Montage Insurance Solutions (formerly Danone Simpson Insurance Services), which operates from offices in Woodland Hills, California. She also answers questions from clients who call the agency's HR hotline.

Dubin sees herself as contributing to the fastgrowing company's success. For example, she looks for the best deals in benefits programs in order to have room in her budget for the little things that contribute to an employee-friendly workplace: monthly luncheons, raffle prizes, and break rooms. That's a priority, Dubin says, because employees who are "happy at work" are "more productive, so everybody wins." Simpson sees that balance between nurturing and practicality in Dubin. According to Simpson, Dubin is supportive but also firm in enforcing standards: "She doesn't put up with any nonsense . . . but does it in a wonderful way."

Perhaps the Careers page of the company's website puts it best. Besides promoting the agency as an "honest and hardworking team," it says simply, "Please be advised that our organization cares about its employees."

Questions

1. Based on the description in this case, how well would you say Susan Dubin appreciates the scope of human resource management? What, if any, additional skills of an HR professional would you encourage her to develop?

2. Look up descriptions of HR jobs by searching under "human resources" in the latest edition of the Bureau of Labor Statistics' *Occupational Outlook Handbook* (available online at www.bls.gov/OCO/). What position in the handbook best matches Dubin's job, as described in this case?

3. How would you expect Dubin's job in a small services company to be different from a similar position in a large manufacturing company?

Source: Montage Insurance Solutions corporate website, http://www.montageinsurance.com, accessed April 16, 2014; Susan Dubin, "How HR Inspires Me," Montage Blog, http://www.montageinsurance.com, accessed April 16, 2014; Mark R. Madler, "Valley's Top Human Resources Professionals: Susan K. Dubin," *San Fernando Valley Business Journal*, April 13, 2009, Business & Company Resource Center, http://galenet.galegroup.com.

NOTES

1. Adrienne Fox, "The Joy of Work in HR," *HR Magazine*, January 2014, https://www.shrm.org.
2. A. S. Tsui and L. R. Gomez-Mejia, "Evaluating Human Resource Effectiveness," in *Human Resource Management: Evolving Rules and Responsibilities*, ed. L. Dyer (Washington, DC: BNA Books, 1988), pp. 1187–227; M. A. Hitt, B. W. Keats, and S. M. DeMarie, "Navigating in the New Competitive Landscape: Building Strategic Flexibility and Competitive Advantage in the 21st Century," *Academy of Management Executive* 12, no. 4 (1998), pp. 22–42; J. T. Delaney and M. A. Huselid, "The Impact of Human Resource Management Practices on Perceptions of Organizational Performance," *Academy of Management Journal* 39 (1996), pp. 949–69.
3. W. F. Cascio, *Costing Human Resources: The Financial Impact of Behavior in Organizations*, 3rd ed. (Boston: PWS-Kent, 1991).
4. S. A. Snell and J. W. Dean, "Integrated Manufacturing and Human Resource Management: A Human Capital Perspective," *Academy of Management Journal* 35 (1992), pp. 467–504; M. A. Youndt, S. Snell, J. W. Dean Jr., and D. P. Lepak, "Human Resource Management, Manufacturing Strategy, and Firm Performance," *Academy of Management Journal* 39 (1996), pp. 836–66.
5. Zeynep Ton, "Why Good Jobs Are Good for Retailers," *Harvard Business Review*, January–February 2012, pp. 124–31; Brad Stone, "Costco CEO Craig Jelinek Leads the Cheapest, Happiest Company in the World," *Bloomberg Businessweek*, June 6, 2013, http://www.businessweek.com; Anne Fisher, "A Blueprint for Creating Better Jobs—and Bigger Profits," *Fortune*, December 12, 2013, http://management.fortune.cnn.com.
6. Steve Wexler, "How Many HR Employees Do You Have—and Should You Have—in Your Organization?" Institute for Corporate Productivity, May 21, 2010, http://www.i4cp.com; Eric Krell, "Is HR Doing More with Less? Or Is It Undergoing a Transformation?" *HR Magazine*, September 2013, www.shrm.org.
7. E. E. Lawler, "From Human Resource Management to Organizational Effectiveness," *Human Resource Management* 44 (2005), pp. 165–69.
8. Lauren Weber and Rachel Feintzeig, "Companies Say No to Having an HR Department," *The Wall Street Journal*, April 9, 2014, http://online.wsj.com.
9. S. Snell, "Control Theory in Strategic Human Resource Management: The Mediating Effect of Administrative Information," *Academy of Management Journal* 35 (1992), pp. 292–327.
10. Joanne Sammer, "A Marriage of Necessity," *HR Magazine*, October 2011, pp. 58–62.
11. Ibid., p. 61.
12. Wendy S. Becker, "Are You Leading a Socially Responsible and Sustainable Human Resource Function?" *People & Strategy*, March 2011, pp. 18–23.
13. Brad Power, "IBM Focuses HR on Change," *Bloomberg Businessweek*, January 10, 2012, http://www.businessweek.com.
14. Society for Human Resource Management, "Competencies: Model," www.shrm.org, accessed April 2, 2014.
15. Robert J. Grossman, "New Competencies for HR," *HR Magazine*, June 2007, pp. 58–62.
16. Wendy Kaufman, "A Single Hire Is a Big Deal to a Small Business," National Public Radio, October 10, 2011, http://www.npr.org.
17. Jeffrey M. Jones, "Record 64% Rate Honesty, Ethics of Members of Congress Low," Gallup, December 12, 2011,

http://www.gallup.com; Corruption Currents, "Survey Sees Less Misconduct but More Reporting and Retaliation," *The Wall Street Journal*, January 5, 2012, http://blogs.wsj.com.

18. M. Pastin, *The Hard Problems of Management: Gaining the Ethics Edge* (San Francisco: Jossey-Bass, 1986); T. Thomas, J. Schermerhorn Jr., and J. Dienhart, "Strategic Leadership of Ethical Behavior in Business," *Academy of Management Executive* 18 (2004), pp. 56–66.

19. Benjamin Schneider and Karen B. Paul, "In the Company We Trust," *HR Magazine*, January 2011, Business & Company Resource Center, http://galenet.galegroup.com.

20. G. F. Cavanaugh, D. Moberg, and M. Velasquez, "The Ethics of Organizational Politics," *Academy of Management Review* 6 (1981), pp. 363–74.

21. Schneider and Paul, "In the Company We Trust."

22. Adrienne Fox, "Paths to the Top," *HR Magazine*, November 2011, pp. 30–35.

2

Trends in Human Resource Management

What Do I Need to Know?

After reading this chapter, you should be able to:

LO 2-1 Describe trends in the labor force composition and how they affect human resource management.

LO 2-2 Summarize areas in which human resource management can support the goal of creating a high-performance work system.

LO 2-3 Define employee empowerment, and explain its role in the modern organization.

LO 2-4 Identify ways HR professionals can support organizational strategies for growth, quality, and efficiency.

LO 2-5 Summarize ways in which human resource management can support organizations expanding internationally.

LO 2-6 Discuss how technological developments are affecting human resource management.

LO 2-7 Explain how the nature of the employment relationship is changing.

LO 2-8 Discuss how the need for flexibility affects human resource management.

Introduction

Business experts point out that if you want your company to gain an advantage over competitors, you have to do something differently. Some managers are taking a hard look at human resources management, asking if it needs to be a department at all. At the consulting firm LRN Corporation, management decided to eliminate the human resources department. Their idea was that if all managers were responsible for managing talent, they would make those decisions in a way that directly served their group's performance. Beam, the maker of spirits such as Maker's Mark bourbon and Jim Beam whiskey, made its line managers responsible for hiring, training, and making compensation decisions. They are advised by a small group of "business partners," who consult with the line managers on HR questions.[1]

Is this the end of human resource management? Probably not. The typical company today is maintaining the size of its human resource department and even spending a little more on the function.[2] At LRN, current and former employees have said line managers sometimes struggle with making HR decisions. For example, a line manager needs time to figure out how to define a job and set a salary range for it, which slows down the whole hiring process. At Beam, the HR business partners are playing a more strategic role than a traditional HR staffer focused on routine processes.

However, these changes may be a sign that today's businesses are impatient with the status quo. It is no longer enough to manage human resources a certain way because other companies do it that way. Rather, HR managers and employees are valuable to the extent they are willing to understand the organization in business terms, including the financial, accounting, and analytic tools that managers use to measure their success.[3]

LO 2-1 Describe trends in the labor force composition and how they affect human resource management.

Despite the hard look that managers are directing at human resource management, organizations depend on this work more than ever. Even with a slow pace of economic growth, many employers report that recruiting the specific kinds of talent they need is getting harder. The skills required within industries often are changing as technology advances, so current employees need training as much as ever. Rising costs of benefits, especially health insurance, have demanded creativity in planning compensation packages. The difficult economy has made it essential for organizations to find ways for their employees to work more efficiently—getting more done faster and placing lighter demands on natural resources, all without sacrificing quality and customer service. These efficiency improvements can only come from creative thinking by highly motivated and well-trained workers. Addressing all of these challenges and other trends in today's business climate requires more innovative human resource management than ever.

This chapter describes major trends that are affecting human resource management. It begins with an examination of the modern labor force, including trends that are determining who will participate in the workforce of the future. Next is an exploration of the ways HRM can support a number of trends in organizational strategy, from efforts to maintain high-performance work systems to changes in the organization's size and structure. Often, growth includes the use of human resources on a global scale, as more and more organizations hire immigrants or open operations overseas. The chapter then turns to major changes in technology, especially the role of the Internet. As we will explain, the Internet is changing organizations themselves, as well as providing new ways to carry out human resource management. Finally, we explore the changing nature of the employment relationship, in which careers and jobs are becoming more flexible.

Change in the Labor Force

Internal Labor Force
An organization's workers (its employees and the people who have contracts to work at the organization).

External Labor Market
Individuals who are actively seeking employment.

The term *labor force* is a general way to refer to all the people willing and able to work. For an organization, the **internal labor force** consists of the organization's workers—its employees and the people who have contracts to work at the organization. This internal labor force has been drawn from the organization's **external labor market,** that is, individuals who are actively seeking employment. The number and kinds of people in the external labor market determine the kinds of human resources available to an organization (and their cost). Human resource professionals need to be aware of trends in the composition of the external labor market because these trends affect the organization's options for creating a well-skilled, motivated internal labor force.

An Aging Workforce

In the United States, the Bureau of Labor Statistics (BLS), an agency of the Department of Labor, tracks changes in the composition of the U.S. labor force and forecasts employment trends. The BLS has projected that from 2012 to 2022, the total U.S. civilian labor force will grow from 155 million to 163 million workers.[4] This 5.5% increase is noticeably lower than the more than 13% increase experienced during the 1990s.

Some of the expected change involves the distribution of workers by age. From 2012 to 2022, the fastest-growing age group is expected to be workers 55 and older. The 25- to 44-year-old group will increase its numbers only slightly, so its share of the total workforce will fall. And young workers between the ages of 16 and 24 will actually be fewer in number. This combination of trends will cause the overall workforce to age. Figure 2.1 shows the change in age distribution, as forecast by the Bureau of Labor Statistics between 2012 and 2022. By 2022, all baby boomers will be at least 55 years old, swelling the ranks of workers nearing retirement.[5] Human resource professionals will therefore spend much of their time on concerns related to planning retirement, retraining older workers, and motivating workers whose careers have plateaued. Organizations will struggle with ways to control the rising costs of health care and other benefits, and many of tomorrow's managers will supervise employees much older than themselves. At the same time, organizations will have to find ways to attract, retain, and prepare the youth labor force.

Today's older generation includes many people who are in no hurry to retire. They may enjoy making a contribution at work, have ambitious plans for which they want to earn money, or simply be among the many who have inadequate savings for full retirement. Therefore, older workers often want to be allowed to gradually move toward retirement by working part-time or taking temporary assignments. Scripps Health helps its employees gradually transition to full retirement. Employees are allowed to reduce their work hours gradually while maintaining their health insurance. Employees who work at least 16 hours a week are eligible for training programs and flextime. Atlantic Health System allows retirees to take part-time jobs, per diem jobs (billing for each day worked), and temporary assignments. Retired employees have returned to work as consultants and contract workers, and some have telecommuting arrangements (working from home). Many of these assignments give older employees a chance to act as mentors to their younger colleagues.[6]

With older workers continuing to hold jobs at least part-time, today's workplaces often bring together employees representing three or four generations. This creates a

As more and more of the workforce reaches retirement age, some companies have set up mentoring programs between older and younger workers so that knowledge is not lost but passed on. How does the company benefit from these mentoring programs?

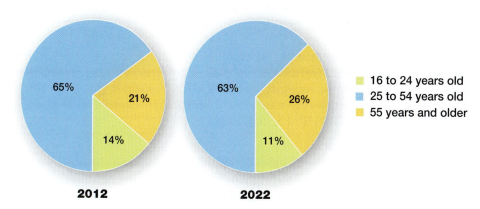

Figure 2.1
Age Distribution of U.S. Labor Force, 2012 and 2022

2012: 65% (25 to 54 years old), 21% (55 years and older), 14% (16 to 24 years old)

2022: 63% (25 to 54 years old), 26% (55 years and older), 11% (16 to 24 years old)

- 16 to 24 years old
- 25 to 54 years old
- 55 years and older

Source: Bureau of Labor Statistics, "Employment Projections, 2012–2022," news release, December 19, 2013, http://www.bls.gov/emp.

HRM Social

What Social-Media Policies Are Suitable across Generations?

Some managers believe organizations need policies restricting employees' access to social media such as Twitter and Facebook. Their belief is based on the assumption that using social media is merely a distraction from doing real work. However, the research evidence for this assumption is mixed—and the impact of social media may vary across generations of workers.

Some studies simply ask employees for their opinions about their access to social media. A survey of Canadian workers found that almost two-thirds have been distracted by social media, e-mail, or Web browsing. One-third reported losing more than an hour a day in checking e-mail and social media, and two-thirds said they would get more done if they were disconnected from the Internet for a set time each day. But in an international survey of information workers, almost half said using social media had *increased* their productivity. The younger the workers, the more likely they were to associate social-media use with greater productivity and to say they could do their jobs even better if their employer would loosen restrictions on the use of social media.

Another study, conducted by the Warwick Business School, in the United Kingdom, measured output instead of opinions. According to the researchers, using social media was associated with greater productivity. The two-year study of employees at a telecommunications company found that they were more productive when they used social media to communicate with customers. The mixed results suggest that a single policy might not apply equally well to all employees.

Questions

1. Thinking about your current job or a job you would like to have, would access to social media help or distract you? Do you think your age plays a role in your opinion? Why?
2. How could human resource management support decisions about creating a policy for using social media?

Sources: Thomson Reuters, "Two-Thirds of Workers Distracted by Emails, Internet, Social Media: Survey," *Canadian HR Reporter*, April 17, 2014, http://www.hrreporter.com; Shea Bennett, "Social Media Increases Office Productivity, but Management Still Resistant, Says Study," *MediaBistro*, June 26, 2013, http://www.mediabistro.com; Bernhard Warner, "When Social Media at Work Don't Create Productivity-Killing Distractions," *Bloomberg Businessweek*, April 1, 2013.

need for understanding the values and work habits that tend to characterize each generation.[7] For example, members of the silent generation (born between 1925 and 1945) tend to value income and employment security and avoid challenging authority. Baby boomers (born between 1946 and 1964) tend to value unexpected rewards, opportunities for learning, and time with management. Members of Generation X (1965–1980) tend to be pragmatic and cynical, and they have well-developed self-management skills. Those born from 1981 to 1995, often called millennials, or Generation Y, are comfortable with the latest technology, and they want to be noticed, respected, and involved. Some generational differences can be addressed through effective human resource management. For example, organizations train managers to provide frequent feedback to members of Generation Y, and they show respect for older generations' hard work and respect for authority by asking them to mentor younger workers. Generational differences also can affect how managers approach policies about social media, as described in the "HRM Social" box.

A Diverse Workforce

Another kind of change affecting the U.S. labor force is that it is growing more diverse in racial, ethnic, and gender terms. As Figure 2.2 shows, the 2022 workforce is expected to be 78% white, 12% African American, and 10% Asian and other minorities. The fastest growing of these categories are Asian and "other groups" because these groups are experiencing immigration and birthrates above the national average. In addition to these racial categories, the ethnic category of Hispanics is growing even faster, and the Hispanic share of the U.S. labor force is expected to reach 19% of the total by 2022.[8] Along with greater racial and ethnic diversity, there is also greater gender diversity. More women today than in the past are in the paid labor force, and the labor force participation rate for men has been slowly declining. During the economic recession and slow recovery, women's labor force participation rate also declined slightly, but between 2012 and 2022, women's share of the labor force is expected to remain steady, at around 47%.[9]

One important source of racial and ethnic diversity is immigration. The U.S. government establishes procedures for foreign nationals to follow if they wish to live and work permanently in the United States, and it sets limits on the number of immigrants who are admitted through these channels. Of the more than 1 million immigrants who come to the United States legally each year, more than 6 out of 10 are relatives of U.S. citizens. Another 14% come on work-related visas, some of which are set aside for workers with exceptional qualifications in science, business, or the arts. (About half of the work-related visas go to the immediate relatives of those coming to the United States to work, allowing workers to bring their spouse and children.) The U.S. government also grants temporary work visas to a limited number of highly educated workers, permitting them to work in the United States for a set period of time but not to remain as immigrants. U.S. law requires employers to verify that any job candidate who is not a U.S. citizen has received permission to work in the United States as an immigrant or with a temporary work permit. (This requirement is discussed in Chapter 6.)

Other foreign-born workers in the United States arrived in this country without meeting the legal requirements for immigration or asylum. These individuals, known as undocumented or illegal immigrants, likely number in the millions. While government policy toward immigrants is a matter of heated public debate, the human resource implications have two practical parts. The first involves the supply of and demand for labor. Many U.S. industries, including meatpacking, construction, farming, and services, rely on immigrants to perform demanding work that may be low paid. In other industries, such as computer software development, employers say they have difficulty finding enough qualified U.S. workers to fill technical jobs. These employers are pressing for immigration laws to allow a greater supply of foreign-born workers.

The other HR concern is the need to comply with laws. In recent years, Immigration and Customs and Enforcement has focused its efforts on auditing employers to ensure they are following proper procedures to avoid employing undocumented immigrants. Businesses that have justified hiring these people on the grounds that they work hard and are needed for the business to continue operating now are facing greater legal risks.[10] Even as some companies are lobbying for changes to immigration laws, the constraints on labor supply force companies to consider a variety of ways to meet their demand for labor, including job redesign (see Chapter 4), higher pay (Chapter 12), and foreign operations (Chapter 16).

The greater diversity of the U.S. labor force challenges employers to create HRM practices that ensure they fully utilize the talents, skills, and values of all employees. As

Figure 2.2

Projected Racial/Ethnic Makeup of the U.S. Workforce, 2022

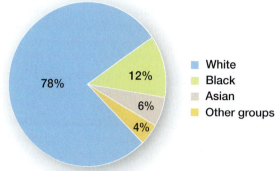

White
Black
Asian
Other groups

Source: Bureau of Labor Statistics, "Employment Projections, 2012–2022," news release, December 19, 2013, http://www.bls.gov/emp.

a result, organizations cannot afford to ignore or discount the potential contributions of women and minorities. Employers will have to ensure that employees and HRM systems are free of bias and value the perspectives and experience that women and minorities can contribute to organizational goals such as product quality and customer service. As we will discuss further in the next chapter, managing cultural diversity involves many different activities. These include creating an organizational culture that values diversity, ensuring that HRM systems are bias-free, encouraging career development for women and minorities, promoting knowledge and acceptance of cultural differences, ensuring involvement in education both within and outside the organization, and dealing with employees' resistance to diversity.[11] Figure 2.3 summarizes ways in which HRM can support the management of diversity for organizational success.

Many U.S. companies have already committed themselves to ensuring that they recognize the diversity of their internal labor force and use it to gain a competitive advantage. In a recent survey of executives at large global corporations, 85% said a "diverse and inclusive workforce" is important for encouraging innovation. Majorities of respondents said their companies have a program to recruit a diverse group of employees (65%) and develop an inclusive workforce (53%).[12]

An organization doesn't have to be a huge global enterprise to benefit from valuing diversity. In Poughkeepsie, New York, the Bridgeway Federal Credit Union has realized that it can best serve the groups in its community by ensuring that its employees are representative of that community. About one-fourth of Bridgeway's members are African American, and about 12% are Hispanics. Many of these members come from low-income households where access to banking services has been limited in the past. To attract and include employees from this community, Bridgeway conducts outreach events in neighborhoods and provides diversity training programs for its employees. With ideas from its diverse employees, Bridgeway has come up with helpful products, such as its Drive Up Savings Account, which provides qualified customers with an auto loan that has a

Figure 2.3

HRM Practices That Support Diversity Management

Source: Based on M. Loden and J. B. Rosener, *Workforce America!* (Homewood, IL: Business One Irwin, 1991).

payment plan in which a part of the monthly payments is directed into a savings plan. When the loan is paid off, Bridgeway rewards the borrowers by giving them a discount on the interest they paid, and the customers find that they have saved up a tidy sum.[13]

Throughout this book, we will show how diversity affects HRM practices. For example, from a staffing perspective, it is important to ensure that tests used to select employees are not unfairly biased against minority groups. From the perspective of work design, employees need flexible schedules that allow them to meet nonwork needs. In terms of training, it is clear that employees must be made aware of the damage that stereotypes can do. With regard to compensation, organizations are providing benefits such as elder care and day care as a way to accommodate the needs of a diverse workforce. As we will see later in the chapter, successfully managing diversity is also critical for companies that compete in international markets.

Skill Deficiencies of the Workforce

The increasing use of computers to do routine tasks has shifted the kinds of skills needed for employees in the U.S. economy. Such qualities as physical strength and mastery of a particular piece of machinery are no longer important for many jobs. More employers are looking for mathematical, verbal, and interpersonal skills, such as the ability to solve math or other problems or reach decisions as part of a team. Often, when organizations are looking for technical skills, they are looking for skills related to computers and using the Internet. Today's employees must be able to handle a variety of responsibilities, interact with customers, and think creatively.

To find such employees, most organizations are looking for educational achievements. A college degree is a basic requirement for many jobs today. Competition for qualified college graduates in many fields is intense. At the other extreme, workers with less education often have to settle for low-paying jobs. Some companies are unable to find qualified employees and instead rely on training to correct skill deficiencies.[14] Other companies team up with universities, community colleges, and high schools to design and teach courses ranging from basic reading to design blueprint reading.

Not all the skills employers want require a college education. The National Association of Manufacturers year after year has reported that the manufacturing companies in the United States have difficulty finding enough people who can operate sophisticated computer-controlled machinery. These jobs rely at least as much on intelligence and teamwork as on physical strength. In some areas, companies and communities have set up apprenticeship and training programs to fix the worker shortage. Some companies are turning to veterans of the wars in Iraq and Afghanistan. These workers have already demonstrated high levels of commitment and teamwork, as well as the ability to make creative use of the resources at hand in difficult situations. Many of them have been trained already by the military in a variety of technical skills. The challenge for employers has been to support these employees in other areas, such as helping them weather the emotional strain of the transition back to civilian life, as well as training them in the technical requirements of their new jobs.[15]

High-Performance Work Systems

Human resource management is playing an important role in helping organizations gain and keep an advantage over competitors by becoming **high-performance work systems.** These are organizations that have the best possible fit between their social system (people and how they interact) and technical system (equipment and processes).[16] As the nature of the workforce and the technology available to organizations have changed,

High-Performance Work Systems
Organizations that have the best possible fit between their social system (people and how they interact) and technical system (equipment and processes).

LO 2-2 Summarize areas in which human resource management can support the goal of creating a high-performance work system.

so have the requirements for creating a high-performance work system. Customers are demanding high quality and customized products, employees are seeking flexible work arrangements, and employers are looking for ways to tap people's creativity and interpersonal skills. Such demands require that organizations make full use of their people's knowledge and skill, and skilled human resource management can help organizations do this.

Among the trends that are occurring in today's high-performance work systems are reliance on knowledge workers, empowerment of employees to make decisions, and use of teamwork. The following sections describe those three trends, and Chapter 9 will explore the ways HRM can support the creation and maintenance of a high-performance work system. HR professionals who keep up with change are well positioned to help create high-performance work systems.

Knowledge Workers

The growth in e-commerce, plus the shift from a manufacturing to a service and information economy, has changed the nature of employees who are most in demand. The Bureau of Labor Statistics forecasts that between 2012 and 2022, most new jobs will be in service occupations, especially health care and social assistance. Construction jobs also are expected to increase, but mostly to replace jobs that were lost during the financial crisis and recession of a few years ago.

The number of service jobs has important implications for human resource management. Research shows that if employees have a favorable view of HRM practices—career opportunities, training, pay, and feedback on performance—they are more likely to provide good service to customers. Therefore, quality HRM for service employees can translate into customer satisfaction.

Besides differences among industries, job growth varies according to the type of job. Table 2.1 lists the 10 occupations expected to gain the most jobs between 2012 and 2022 and the 10 expected to grow at the fastest rate. Occupations with the most jobs are expected to involve health care, sales, food preparation, as well as other services. Many of the fastest-growing occupations also are in the health care field.[17] These and other fast-growing occupations reflect the steadily growing demand for health care and an expected rebound in the construction industry. While some of these jobs and other

Table 2.1

Top 10 Occupations for Job Growth

Source: Bureau of Labor Statistics, "Employment Projections, 2012–2022," news release, December 19, 2013, http://www.bls.gov, Tables 4, 5.

MOST NEW JOBS	FASTEST RATE OF GROWTH
Personal care aides	Industrial-organizational psychologists
Registered nurses	Personal care aides
Retail salespersons	Home health aides
Home health aides	Insulation workers, mechanical
Combined food preparation and serving workers[a]	Interpreters and translators
Nursing assistants	Diagnostic medical sonographers
Secretaries and administrative assistants[b]	Helpers: brickmasons, blockmasons, stonemasons, and tile and marble setters
Customer service representatives	Occupational therapy assistants
Janitors and cleaners[c]	Genetic counselors
Construction laborers	Physical therapist assistants

[a]Includes fast food.
[b]Except legal, medical, and executive.
[c]Except maids and housekeeping cleaners.

fast-growing occupations require a college degree, many of the fast-growing occupations require only on-the-job training. (Exceptions are industrial-organizational psychologists and registered nurses.) This means that many companies' HRM departments will need to provide excellent training as well as hiring.

These high-growth jobs are evidence of another trend: The future U.S. labor market will be both a knowledge economy and a service economy.[18] Along with low-education jobs in services like health care and food preparation, there will be many high-education professional and managerial jobs. To meet these human capital needs, companies are increasingly trying to attract, develop, and retain knowledge workers. **Knowledge workers** are employees whose main contribution to the organization is specialized knowledge, such as knowledge of customers, a process, or a profession. Further complicating that challenge, many of these knowledge workers will have to be "technoservice" workers who not only know a specialized field such as computer programming or engineering, but also must be able to work directly with customers.

Knowledge workers are in a position of power because they own the knowledge that the company needs in order to produce its products and services, and they must share their knowledge and collaborate with others in order for their employer to succeed. An employer cannot simply order these employees to perform tasks. Managers depend on the employees' willingness to share information. Furthermore, skilled knowledge workers have many job opportunities, even in a slow economy. If they choose, they can leave a company and take their knowledge to another employer. Replacing them may be difficult and time consuming.

The idea that only some of an organization's workers are knowledge workers has come under criticism.[19] To the critics, this definition is no longer realistic in a day of computerized information systems and computer-controlled production processes. For the company to excel, everyone must know how their work contributes to the organization's success. At the same time, employees—especially younger generations, which grew up with the Internet—will expect to have wide access to information. From this perspective, successful organizations treat *all* their workers as knowledge workers. They let employees know how well the organization is performing, and they invite ideas about how the organization can do better.

Can the "knowledge worker" label really fit everywhere? Think of the expectations organizations have for the typical computer programmer. These high-in-demand employees expect to be valued for their skills, not the hours they put in or the way they dress. Organizations that successfully recruit and retainer computer programmers give them plenty of freedom to set up their work space and their own schedule. They motivate by assigning tasks that are interesting and challenging and by encouraging friendly collaboration. To some degree, these kinds of measures apply to many employees and many work situations. W. W. Grainger, for example, is not a glamorous company, but it is one that many companies depend on. Grainger distributes an enormous variety of supplies and parts needed by its business customers. Grainger creates an attractive environment for the modern-day version of the knowledge worker by helping to match them up with jobs in which they matter and can excel, even if that means trying out jobs in a variety of departments. Linda Kolbe, the manager of Grainger's e-commerce, started as an administrative assistant and worked her way up, with help from the company's mentoring program. And branch manager Roger Lubert has found that the company is eager to try out his ideas for managing inventory and store operations. The company treats these and other employees as individuals who can both expand their knowledge and apply it to benefit the entire organization.[20]

Knowledge Workers
Employees whose main contribution to the organization is specialized knowledge, such as knowledge of customers, a process, or a profession.

Employee Empowerment

LO 2-3 Define employee empowerment, and explain its role in the modern organization.

To completely benefit from employees' knowledge, organizations need a management style that focuses on developing and empowering employees. **Employee empowerment** means giving employees responsibility and authority to make decisions regarding all aspects of product development or customer service.[21] Employees are then held accountable for products and services. In return, they share the resulting losses and rewards. Employee empowerment can also extend to innovation. Employees at all levels are encouraged to share their ideas for satisfying customers better and operating more efficiently and safely. This is empowering if management actually listens to the ideas, implements valuable ones, and rewards employees for their innovations.

Employee Empowerment
Giving employees responsibility and authority to make decisions regarding all aspects of product development or customer service.

HRM practices such as performance management, training, work design, and compensation are important for ensuring the success of employee empowerment. Jobs must be designed to give employees the necessary latitude for making a variety of decisions. Employees must be properly trained to exert their wider authority and use information resources such as the Internet as well as tools for communicating information. Employees also need feedback to help them evaluate their success. Pay and other rewards should reflect employees' authority and be related to successful handling of their responsibility. In addition, for empowerment to succeed, managers must be trained to link employees to resources within and outside the organization, such as customers, co-workers in other departments, and websites with needed information. Managers must also encourage employees to interact with staff throughout the organization, must ensure that employees receive the information they need, and must reward cooperation. Finally, empowered employees deliver the best results if they are fully engaged in their work. *Employee engagement*—full involvement in one's work and commitment to one's job and company—is associated with higher productivity, better customer service, and lower turnover.[22]

As with the need for knowledge workers, use of employee empowerment shifts the recruiting focus away from technical skills and toward general cognitive and interpersonal skills. Employees who have responsibility for a final product or service must be able to listen to customers, adapt to changing needs, and creatively solve a variety of problems.

Teamwork

Teamwork
The assignment of work to groups of employees with various skills who interact to assemble a product or provide a service.

Modern technology places the information that employees need for improving quality and providing customer service right at the point of sale or production. As a result, the employees engaging in selling and producing must also be able to make decisions about how to do their work. Organizations need to set up work in a way that gives employees the authority and ability to make those decisions. One of the most popular ways to increase employee responsibility and control is to assign work to teams. **Teamwork** is the assignment of work to groups of employees with various skills who interact to assemble a product or provide a service. Work teams often assume many activities traditionally reserved for managers, such as selecting new team members, scheduling work, and coordinating work with customers and other units of the organization. Work teams also contribute to total quality by performing inspection and quality-control activities while the product or service is being completed.

In some organizations, technology is enabling teamwork even when workers are at different locations or work at different times. These organizations use *virtual teams*—teams that rely on communications technology such as videoconferences, e-mail, and cell phones to keep in touch and coordinate activities.

Teamwork can motivate employees by making work more interesting and significant. At organizations that rely on teamwork, labor costs may be lower as well. Spurred by such advantages, a number of companies are reorganizing assembly operations—abandoning the assembly line in favor of operations that combine mass production with jobs in which employees perform multiple tasks, use many skills, control the pace of work, and assemble the entire final product.

Witnessing the resulting improvements, companies in the service sector also have moved toward greater use of teamwork. Teamwork is a necessary component of more and more computer programming tasks. Companies that develop software are increasingly using an

One way companies can increase employee responsibility and control is to assign work to teams.

approach they call *agile*, which involves weaving the development process more tightly into the organization's activities and strategies. In agile software development, self-directed teams of developers and programmers work directly with the business users of the software, using as much face-to-face communication as possible. Rather than devoting endless hours to negotiating contracts and documenting processes, the teams focus on frequently delivering usable components of the software. Throughout the development process the team is open to changing requirements and computer code as a result of their communication with users. Users of agile software development say it increases customer satisfaction and speeds up the time from concept to usable software.[23]

Focus on Strategy

As we saw in Chapter 1, traditional management thinking treated human resource management primarily as an administrative function, but managers today are beginning to see a more central role for HRM. They are looking at HRM as a means to support a company's *strategy*—its plan for meeting broad goals such as profitability, quality, and market share. This strategic role for HRM has evolved gradually. At many organizations, managers still treat HR professionals primarily as experts in designing and delivering HR systems (see the "HR Oops!" box). But at a growing number of organizations, HR professionals are strategic partners with other managers.

This means they use their knowledge of the business and of human resources to help the organization develop strategies and to align HRM policies and practices with those strategies. To do this, human resource managers must focus on the future as well as the present, and on company goals as well as human resource activities. They may, for example, become experts at analyzing the business impact of HR decisions or at developing and keeping the best talent to support business strategy. Organizations do this, for example, when they integrate all the activities involved in talent management with each other and with the organization's other processes to provide the skills the organization needs to pursue its strategy. An integrated approach to talent management includes acquiring talent (recruiting and selection), providing the right opportunities for training and development, measuring performance, and creating compensation plans that reward the needed behaviors. To choose the right talent, provide the right training, and so on, HR professionals need to be in close, ongoing contact with the members of the organization who need the talent. And when the organization modifies its strategy, HR professionals are part of the planning process so they can modify

LO 2-4 Identify ways HR professionals can support organizational strategies for quality, growth, and efficiency.

talent management efforts to support the revised strategy. One organization that does all this is Universal Weather and Aviation, which provides services and support to the owners of private jets. In this market niche, the company does not expect to find people with the precise set of skills it needs; rather, its talent management program emphasizes finding individuals who are a good fit with the organization's culture and then training them in the areas where their skills are weak. Executives are rewarded for achieving talent management objectives that include retaining the best-performing employees and identifying potential successors to fill key positions.[24]

The specific ways in which human resource professionals support the organization's strategy vary according to their level of involvement and the nature of the strategy. Strategic issues include emphasis on quality and decisions about growth and efficiency. Human resource management can support these strategies, including efforts such as quality improvement programs, mergers and acquisitions, and restructuring. Decisions to use reengineering and outsourcing can make an organization more efficient and also give rise to many human resource challenges. International expansion presents a wide variety of HRM challenges and opportunities. Figure 2.4 summarizes these strategic issues facing human resource management.

Mergers and Acquisitions

Often, organizations join forces through mergers (two companies becoming one) and acquisitions (one company buying another). Some mergers and acquisitions result in consolidation within an industry, meaning that two firms in one industry join to hold a greater share of the industry. For example, British Petroleum's acquisition of Amoco Oil represented a consolidation, or a reduction of the number of companies in the oil

Figure 2.4
Business Strategy:
Issues Affecting HRM

industry. Other mergers and acquisitions cross industry lines. In a merger to form Citigroup, Citicorp combined its banking business with Traveler's Group's insurance business. Furthermore, these deals more frequently take the form of global megamergers, or mergers of big companies based in different countries (as in the case of BP-Amoco).

HRM should have a significant role in carrying out a merger or acquisition. Differences between the businesses involved in the deal make conflict inevitable. Training efforts should therefore include development of skills in conflict resolution. Also, HR professionals have to sort out differences in the two companies' practices with regard to compensation, performance appraisal, and other HR systems. Settling on a consistent structure to meet the combined organization's goals may help bring employees together.

High Quality Standards

To compete in today's economy, companies need to provide high-quality products and services. If companies do not adhere to quality standards, they will have difficulty selling their product or service to vendors, suppliers, or customers. Therefore, many organizations have adopted some form of **total quality management (TQM)**—a companywide effort to continually improve the ways people, machines, and systems accomplish work.[25] TQM has several core values[26]:

- Methods and processes are designed to meet the needs of internal and external customers (that is, whomever the process is intended to serve).
- Every employee in the organization receives training in quality.
- Quality is designed into a product or service so that errors are prevented from occurring, rather than being detected and corrected in an error-prone product or service.

Total Quality Management (TQM)
A companywide effort to continually improve the ways people, machines, and systems accomplish work.

- The organization promotes cooperation with vendors, suppliers, and customers to improve quality and hold down costs.
- Managers measure progress with feedback based on data.

Based on these values, the TQM approach provides guidelines for all the organization's activities, including human resource management. To promote quality, organizations need an environment that supports innovation, creativity, and risk taking to meet customer demands. Problem solving should bring together managers, employees, and customers. Employees should communicate with managers about customer needs.

Quality improvement can focus on the HRM function itself. One area where managers are increasingly pressing for improvement is performance management. Business consultants note that many companies have grown dissatisfied with the ways they measure and reward performance, believing that the traditional practices do not yield measurable benefits. George Boué, a human resources executive with the real estate firm Stiles Corporation, says his company has tried to improve the quality of performance management by hiring coaches to help employees figure out how to develop their skills.[27]

Cost Control

Some organizations have a low-cost, low-price strategy. These organizations particularly depend on human resource management to identify ways for limiting costs related to maintaining a qualified, motivated workforce. However, this challenge is relevant in any organization. HR managers contribute to success whenever they help lower costs without compromising quality.

Human resource management supports cost control both by helping the organization use human resources more efficiently and by making HRM processes as efficient as possible. This has become particularly relevant to employee benefits, specifically health insurance.[28] As we will discuss in Chapter 14, the cost of this benefit has grown rapidly, while the Affordable Care Act has introduced a set of employer requirements, which can be expensive. How to manage the costs while meeting the requirements is complicated. Employers need to weigh factors such as legal requirements, the costs and types of plans available, the impact on departments' budgets, and the effect on employee morale and retention, as well as on the ability to recruit new employees. Management relies on well-informed HR managers to identify alternatives and recommend which ones will best support the company's strategy.

Beyond specific issues such as health insurance and the Affordable Care Act, human resource management can support strategic efforts to control costs through downsizing, reengineering, and outsourcing.

Downsizing   As shown in Figure 2.5, the number of employees laid off when organizations downsized soared in 2008 and 2009.[29] Since those years, downsizing has continued, but at a declining rate. The surge in unemployment created a climate of fear for many workers. Even at organizations that were maintaining their workforce, employees tended to worry, and employees who might have otherwise left tended to hold on to their jobs if they could. Therefore, an important challenge for employers was how to maintain a reputation as an employer of choice and how to keep employees engaged in their work and focused on the organization's goals. The way employers meet this challenge will influence how sustainably they can compete, especially as unemployment falls and talented workers see possibilities for work in other organizations.

Figure 2.5

Number of Employees Laid Off during the Past Decade

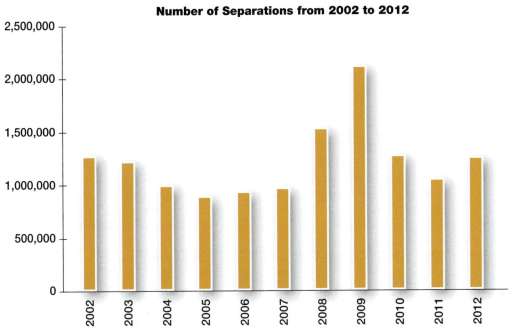

Number of Separations from 2002 to 2012

Sources: Bureau of Labor Statistics, "Extended Mass Layoffs: Fourth Quarter 2011, Annual Totals 2011," news release, February 10, 2012, http://www.bls.gov/mls; Bureau of Labor Statistics, "Mass Layoff Statistics," last updated May 13, 2013, http://data.bls.gov.

Downsizing presents a number of challenges and opportunities for HRM. In terms of challenges, the HRM function must "surgically" reduce the workforce by cutting only the workers who are less valuable in their performance. Achieving this is difficult because the best workers are most able (and often willing) to find alternative employment and may leave voluntarily before the organization lays off anyone. Early-retirement programs are humane, but they essentially reduce the workforce with a "grenade" approach—not distinguishing good from poor performers but rather eliminating an entire group of employees. In fact, contrary to popular belief, research has found that downsizing is associated with negative stock returns and lower profitability following the layoffs. One reason may be that although labor costs fall after a downsizing, sales per employee also tend to fall. Circuit City, for example, tried to save money by laying off its highest-paid salespeople. Customers soon found that they preferred other electronics retailers, and Circuit City went out of business. In contrast, Southwest Airlines, which has never laid off employees—not even after air travel plummeted following the terrorist attacks of September 11, 2001—has outperformed its rivals. Like Southwest's managers, Susan Marvin, president of Marvin Windows, thinks it is illogical to call employees the company's "greatest asset" and then lay them off. Although the recent economic recession has been devastating to the construction business and its suppliers, Marvin has avoided layoffs and let employment decline naturally by not replacing employees who have retired during the lean years. Instead, employees have been doing without bonuses and some employee benefits, and the workweek has been shortened, reducing pay to hourly workers. Susan Marvin is convinced that the impact on morale of everyone pulling together during tough times builds a strong commitment to the organization.[30]

Another HRM challenge is to boost the morale of employees who remain after the reduction; this is discussed in greater detail in Chapter 5. HR professionals should maintain open communication with remaining employees to build their trust and commitment, rather than withholding information.[31] All employees should be informed why the downsizing is necessary, what costs are to be cut, how long the downsizing will last, and what strategies the organization intends to pursue. Finally, HRM can provide downsized employees with outplacement services to help them find new jobs. Such services are ways an organization can show that it cares about its employees, even though it cannot afford to keep all of them on the payroll.

Reengineering   Rapidly changing customer needs and technology have caused many organizations to rethink the way they get work done. For example, when an organization adopts new technology, its existing processes may no longer result in acceptable quality levels, meet customer expectations for speed, or keep costs to profitable levels. Therefore, many organizations have undertaken **reengineering**—a complete review of the organization's critical work processes to make them more efficient and able to deliver higher quality.

Reengineering
A complete review of the organization's critical work processes to make them more efficient and able to deliver higher quality.

Ideally, reengineering involves reviewing all the processes performed by all the organization's major functions, including production, sales, accounting, and human resources. Therefore, reengineering affects human resource management in two ways. First, the way the HR department itself accomplishes its goals may change dramatically. Second, the fundamental change throughout the organization requires the HR department to help design and implement change so that all employees will be committed to the success of the reengineered organization. Employees may need training for their reengineered jobs. The organization may need to redesign the structure of its pay and benefits to make them more appropriate for its new way of operating. It also may need to recruit employees with a new set of skills. Often, reengineering results in employees being laid off or reassigned to new jobs, as the organization's needs change. HR professionals should also help with this transition, as they do for downsizing.

Outsourcing
The practice of having another company (a vendor, third-party provider, or consultant) provide services.

Outsourcing   Many organizations are increasingly outsourcing some of their business activities. **Outsourcing** refers to the practice of having another company (a vendor, third-party provider, or consultant) provide services. For instance, a manufacturing company might outsource its accounting and transportation functions to businesses that specialize in these activities. Outsourcing gives the company access to in-depth expertise and is often more economical as well.

Not only do HR departments help with a transition to outsourcing, but many HR functions are being outsourced. According to a recent survey of human resource managers, about 70% of companies had outsourced at least one HR activity. The functions that were most likely to be outsourced were employee assistance, retirement planning, and outplacement.[32] Goodyear Tire and Rubber Company improved its recruiting and hiring practices by outsourcing these activities to a specialist. The recruiting service provider started by learning about Goodyear's history, culture, and experiences with recruiting. It used Internet technology to streamline the hiring process and track the progress of job candidates throughout that process. After outsourcing this function, Goodyear began making quicker hiring decisions, improved the diversity and quality of employees it hired, and reduced employee turnover.[33] See the "Best Practices" box for another example of HR outsourcing.

Outsourcing Enriches the Bottom Line for Land O'Lakes

Land O'Lakes is an example of a company that has successfully reduced costs by outsourcing human resource activities. Best known for its butter and other dairy products, the company is a food and agriculture cooperative owned by the farmers who participate in the business. The co-op's 10,000 employees work toward a strategy of delivering strong financial performance for its farmer-owners while providing programs and services that help the farmers operate more successfully.

In support of that strategy, Pam Grove, the senior director of benefits and HR operations, led Land O'Lakes to outsource the administration of employee benefits. Management determined that benefits administration was not an activity that contributed to the company's

strategy, and Land O'Lakes already had successfully used an outside firm to administer its 401(k) retirement savings plan. So Grove arranged to have a firm administer its health insurance and pension plans as well.

Outsourcing achieved the basic goal of reducing costs, but that was not the only advantage. Grove freed up time for focusing on strategy-related activities, and she says the outsourcing arrangement also has improved service to employees. When the company tackled health benefit costs by offering a high-deductible health plan, which shifts spending decisions to employees, Grove and her staff visited 100 Land O'Lakes locations to explain the new option. Employee enrollment was double her expectations, helping

the company save millions of dollars while keeping employees satisfied with their benefits.

Questions

1. When does outsourcing make strategic sense for an organization such as Land O'Lakes?
2. How does Grove ensure that a cost-conscious practice such as outsourcing is well received by employees?

Sources: Land O'Lakes Inc., "Company," http://www.landolakesinc .com, accessed April 22, 2014; Land O'Lakes Inc., "Careers," http://www .landolakesinc.com/careers, accessed April 22, 2014; Susan J. Wells, "Benefits Strategies Grow: And HR Leads the Way," *HR Magazine*, March 2013.

Expanding into Global Markets

Companies are finding that to survive they must compete in international markets as well as fend off foreign competitors' attempts to gain ground in the United States. To meet these challenges, U.S. businesses must develop global markets, keep up with competition from overseas, hire from an international labor pool, and prepare employees for global assignments. This global expansion can pose some challenges for human resource management as HR employees learn about the cultural differences that shape the conduct of employees in other parts of the world.

Companies that are successful and widely admired not only operate on a multinational scale, but also have workforces and corporate cultures that reflect their global markets. Yum Brands was quick to seize on the potential of China's massive population: in 1987, its KFC restaurants became the first fast-food chain to enter China, and its Pizza Hut brand was the first pizza chain there in 1990. Today the company has more than 6,000 restaurants in the country with plans to open hundreds more. More than half the company's sales are made in China. Behind the success of this overseas expansion is a willingness to adapt menus to local tastes and develop local management talent.[34]

The Global Workforce For today's and tomorrow's employers, talent comes from a global workforce. Organizations with international operations hire at least some of their employees in the foreign countries where they operate. In fact,

LO 2-5 Summarize ways in which human resource management can support organizations expanding internationally.

regardless of where their customers are located, organizations are looking overseas to hire talented people willing to work for less pay than the U.S. labor market requires. The efforts to hire workers in other countries are common enough that they have spurred the creation of a popular name for the practice: **offshoring.** Just a few years ago, most offshoring involved big manufacturers building factories in countries with lower labor costs. But today it is so easy to send information and software around the world that even start-ups are hiring overseas. During the 2000s, large U.S.-based multinational companies were shrinking their domestic employment while hiring overseas. Even when they made cuts overseas during the last recession, they tended to cut more domestic than foreign workers. The trend was driven by more than labor costs: demand for the companies' products was often growing faster in other parts of the world. More recently, however, the offshoring trend has slowed. Labor costs in popular locations such as China have risen, and some companies have even announced plans for *reshoring*, or reestablishing some of their operations in North America.[35]

Offshoring
Moving operations from the country where a company is headquartered to a country where pay rates are lower but the necessary skills are available.

Hiring in developing nations such as India, Mexico, and Brazil gives employers access to people with potential who are eager to work yet who will accept lower wages than elsewhere in the world. Challenges, however, may include employees' lack of familiarity with technology and corporate practices, as well as political and economic instability in the areas. Important issues that HR experts can help companies weigh include whether workers in the offshore locations can provide the same or better skills, how offshoring will affect motivation and recruitment of employees needed in the United States, and whether managers are well prepared to manage and lead offshore employees. At the same time, as companies based in these parts of the world are developing experienced employees and managers, they are becoming competitors for global talent. Information technology companies based in India, for example, have in recent years increased their hiring of employees in the United States and Europe.[36] This poses a new challenge for U.S. recruiters who may need to improve their tactics and offers if they want to win the war for the best talent.

Even hiring at home may involve selection of employees from other countries. The beginning of the 21st century, like the beginning of the last century, has been a time of significant immigration, with over a million people obtaining permanent resident status in 2012 alone.[37] Figure 2.6 shows the distribution of immigration by continent of origin. The impact of immigration is especially large in some regions of the United States, with the largest immigrant populations being in the cities and suburbs of New York, Los Angeles, Miami, Chicago, and Houston. About 7 out of 10 foreign-born workers are Hispanics and Asians.[38] Employers in tight labor markets—such as those seeking experts in computer science, engineering, and information systems—have been especially likely to recruit international students.

Figure 2.6
Where Immigrants to the United States Came from in 2012

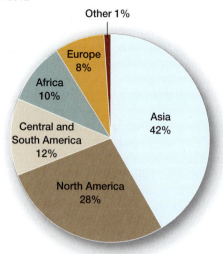

Other 1%

Europe 8%

Africa 10%

Central and South America 12%

North America 28%

Asia 42%

Source: Department of Homeland Security, Office of Immigration Statistics, "U.S. Legal Permanent Residents: 2012," *Annual Flow Report*, March 2013, Table 3, p. 4, www.dhs.gov.

International Assignments   Besides hiring an international workforce, organizations must be prepared to send employees to other countries. This requires HR expertise in selecting employees for international assignments and preparing them for those assignments. Employees who take assignments in other countries are called **expatriates.**

U.S. companies must better prepare employees to work in other countries. The failure rate for U.S. expatriates is greater than that for European and Japanese expatriates.[39] To improve in this area, U.S. companies must carefully select employees to work abroad based on their ability to understand and respect the cultural and business norms of the host country. Qualified candidates also need language skills and technical ability. In Chapter 16, we discuss practices for training employees to understand other cultures.

Expatriates
Employees who take assignments in other countries.

Technological Change in HRM

Advances in computer-related technology have had a major impact on the use of information for managing human resources. Large quantities of employee data (including training records, skills, compensation rates, and benefits usage and cost) can easily be stored on personal computers and manipulated with user-friendly spreadsheets or statistical software. Often these features are combined in a **human resource information system (HRIS),** a computer system used to acquire, store, manipulate, analyze, retrieve, and distribute information related to an organization's human resources.[40] An HRIS can support strategic decision making, help the organization avoid lawsuits, provide data for evaluating programs or policies, and support day-to-day HR decisions. Table 2.2 describes some of the technologies that may be included in an organization's HRIS.

The support of an HRIS can help HR professionals think strategically. As strategies are planned, implemented, and changed, the organization must be constantly prepared to have the right talent in place at all levels. This requires keeping track of an enormous amount of information related to employees' skills, experience, and training needs, as well as the organization's shifting needs for the future. An HRIS can support talent management by integrating data on recruiting, performance management, and

LO 2-6 Discuss how technological developments are affecting human resource management.

Human Resource Information System (HRIS)
A computer system used to acquire, store, manipulate, analyze, retrieve, and distribute information related to an organization's human resources.

TECHNOLOGY	WHAT IT DOES	EXAMPLE
Internet portal	Combines data from several sources into a single site; lets user customize data without programming skills.	A company's manager can track labor costs by work group.
Shared service centers	Consolidate different HR functions into a single location; eliminate redundancy and reduce administrative costs; process all HR transactions at one time.	AlliedSignal combined more than 75 functions, including finance and HR, into a shared service center.
Cloud computing, such as application service providers (ASPs)	Lets companies rent space on a remote computer system and use the system's software to manage its HR activities, including security and upgrades.	KPMG Consulting uses an ASP to host the company's computerized learning program.
Business intelligence	Provides insight into business trends and patterns and helps businesses improve decisions.	Managers use the system to analyze labor costs and productivity among different employee groups.
Data mining	Uses powerful computers to analyze large amounts of data, such as data about employee traits, pay, and performance.	Managers can identify high-potential employees throughout a large organization and offer them development opportunities.

Table 2.2

New Technologies Influencing HRM

The Internet and e-HRM are helpful for employees who work outside the office because they can receive and share information online easily. The benefits of products such as smartphones are enormous, but is it possible to be too accessible?

Electronic Human Resource Management (e-HRM)
The processing and transmission of digitized HR information, especially using computer networking and the Internet.

training. Integrating the data means, for example, that the HRIS user can see how specific kinds of recruiting, hiring, and training decisions relate to performance success. This helps HR professionals identify how to develop the organization's talent and where to recruit new talent so that an ongoing supply of human resources is available to fill new positions or new openings in existing positions.[41]

Electronic Human Resource Management (e-HRM)

Many HRM activities have moved onto the Internet. Electronic HRM applications let employees enroll in and participate in training programs online. Employees can go online to select from items in a benefits package and enroll in the benefits they choose. They can look up answers to HR-related questions and read company news, perhaps downloading it as a podcast. This processing and transmission of digitized HR information is called **electronic human resource management (e-HRM).**

E-HRM has the potential to change all traditional HRM functions. For example, employees in different geographic areas can work together. Use of the Internet lets companies search for talent without geographic limitations. Recruiting can include online job postings, applications, and candidate screening from the company's website or the websites of companies that specialize in online recruiting, such as Monster.com or CareerBuilder. Employees from different geographic locations can all receive the same training over the company's computer network.

Technology trends that are shaping Internet use are also shaping e-HRM. One example, introduced in Chapter 1, is social networking. Table 2.3 identifies some ways that creative organizations are applying social networking tools to human resource management.

Another recent technology trend is *cloud computing*, which generally refers to arrangements in which remote server computers do the user's computing tasks. Thus, an organization that once owned a big mainframe computer to process data for payroll and performance data could contract with a service provider to do the data processing on its computer network and make the results available online. Access to cloud computing makes powerful HRIS tools available even to small organizations with limited computer hardware. Some organizations specialize in offering such services. An example is Workday, which hosts software for human resource management, including workforce planning, job design, analysis of compensation to make sure it is aligned with performance, and assessment of the organization's skills and training needs.[42]

Privacy is an important issue in e-HRM. A great deal of HR information is confidential and not suitable for posting on a website for everyone to see. One solution is to set up e-HRM on an *intranet*, which is a network that uses Internet tools but limits access to authorized users in the organization. With any e-HRM application, however, the organization must ensure that it has sufficient security measures in place to protect employees' privacy.

Table 2.3

HRM Applications for Social Networking

APPLICATION	PURPOSE
Sites for capturing, sharing, storing knowledge	Preserving knowledge that otherwise could be lost when employees retire
Online surveys to gather employees' opinions	Increasing employees' engagement with the jobs and the organization
Networking tools to create online expert communities	Identifying employee expertise and making it available to those who can apply it
Online discussions, such as commenting tools	Promoting creativity and innovation
Sites where users can post links to articles, webinars, training programs, and other information	Reinforcing lessons learned during training and on-the-job experience
Instant messaging and other communication tools to use with mentors and coaches	Providing employee development through mentoring and coaching
Site where the HR department posts job openings and responds to candidates' questions	Identifying and connecting with promising job candidates

Sources: P. Brotherson, "Social Networks Enhance Employee Learning," *T + D,* April 2011, pp. 18–19; T. Bingham and M. Connor, *The New Social Learning* (Alexandria, VA: American Society for Training and Development, 2010); M. Derven, "Social Networking: A Frame for Development," *T + D,* July 2009, pp. 58–63; M. Weinstein, "Are You Linked In?" *Training,* September/October 2010, pp. 30–33.

Sharing of Human Resource Information

Information technology is changing the way HR departments handle record keeping and information sharing. Today, HR employees use technology to automate much of their work in managing employee records and giving employees access to information and enrollment forms for training, benefits, and other programs. As a result, HR employees play a smaller role in maintaining records, and employees now get information through **self-service.** This means employees have online access to information about HR issues such as training, benefits, compensation, and contracts; go online to enroll themselves in programs and services; and provide feedback through online surveys. Today, employees routinely look up workplace policies and information about their benefits online, and they may receive electronic notification when deposits are made directly to their bank accounts.

Self-Service
System in which employees have online access to information about HR issues and go online to enroll themselves in programs and provide feedback through surveys.

Self-service is especially convenient when combined with today's use of mobile computing devices such as smartphones and tablet computers. For example, organizations that use the services of ADP can download a free mobile app that enables employees to look up their payroll and benefits information. Employees can use the app to fill out their time sheet or look up their 401(k) (retirement savings plan) contributions and balance. Employers can use the app to deliver company news or offer a directory with employees' contact information.[43] To read more ideas for providing HR applications on mobile devices, see the "HR How To" box.

A growing number of companies are combining employee self-service with management self-service, such as the ability to go online to authorize pay increases, approve expenses, and transfer employees to new positions. More sophisticated systems extend management applications to decision making in areas such as compensation and performance management. To further support management decisions, the company may create an *HR dashboard,* or a display of how the company is performing on specific HR metrics, such as productivity and absenteeism. For example, Cisco Systems helps with talent management by displaying on its HR dashboard how many of its people move and why.[44] The data can help management identify divisions where the managers are successfully developing new talent.

HR How To

Providing HR Services on Mobile Devices

Software companies are creating apps that let employees view their pay stubs, request time off, check the amounts of their bonuses, fill out and approve time sheets, look up coworkers in company directories, and more. At the same time, a growing number of employees expect to be able to use their mobile devices for looking up work-related information. Given the possibility of and pressure for mobile HRM, here are some guidelines for making it work:

- Learn which mobile devices employees are using. Make sure applications will run properly on all the devices.
- Set priorities for introducing mobile applications that support your company's strategy.
- Make sure your company has mobile-friendly versions of its careers website. Many of today's job hunters are looking for leads on their mobile devices, and they expect to be able to submit an application that way.
- If your company uses online training, create versions that run well on mobile devices.
- Select vendors that not only have software for existing mobile devices but also will be flexible as hardware changes. Check references to find out whether vendors have a history of keeping up with changing technology.
- Investigate the security protection built into any app you are considering.
- Test mobile HRM apps to be sure they are easy to use and understand.

Questions

1. How could offering a mobile version of its careers website support an organization's strategy?
2. What could be an advantage of using a software vendor for mobile HR apps, instead of having your organization's employees create the apps?

Sources: Dave Zielinski, "The Mobilization of HR Tech," *HR Magazine*, February 2014, Business Insights: Global, http://bi.galegroup.com; Jennifer Alsever, "Objective: Hire Top Talent," *Fortune*, January 23, 2014, http://money.cnn.com; Tom Keebler, "New Considerations for HR Service Delivery Success: Where to Begin?" *Workforce Solutions Review*, December 2013, pp. 17–19.

In the age of social networking, information sharing has become far more powerful than simply a means of increasing efficiency through self-service. Creative organizations are enabling information sharing online to permit a free flow of knowledge among the organization's people. Essilor International uses social networking to improve learning in the 40 countries where it makes and sells lenses for use by eye doctors. Trainers share knowledge of what is working best for them: for example, a Thai lens-processing center came up with a game to teach workers to understand lens shapes and then made it available online.[45] A more dramatic application of social networking to human resource management is the talent management at Morning Star, a California tomato processor. Morning Star has no formal hierarchy or job descriptions. Instead, each employee writes a letter describing his or her responsibilities. As the company has grown to hundreds of full-time employees, it began to use a database of the employees' letters. Employees can go into the database to modify their letters, search for employees with needed experience, or offer one another feedback related to the commitments they made in their letters.[46]

Change in the Employment Relationship

LO 2-7 Explain how the nature of the employment relationship is changing.

Technology and the other trends we have described in this chapter require managers at all levels to make rapid changes in response to new opportunities, competitive challenges, and customer demands. These changes are most likely to succeed in flexible, forward-thinking organizations, and the employees who will thrive in such organizations need to be flexible and open to change as well. In this environment, employers and employees have begun to reshape the employment relationship.[47]

A Psychological Contract

We can think of that relationship in terms of a **psychological contract,** a description of what an employee expects to contribute in an employment relationship and what the employer will provide the employee in exchange for those contributions.[48] Unlike a written sales contract, the psychological contract is not formally put into words. Instead, it describes unspoken expectations that are widely held by employers and employees. In the traditional version of this psychological contract, organizations expected their employees to contribute time, effort, skills, abilities, and loyalty. In return, the organizations would provide job security and opportunities for promotion.

Psychological Contract
A description of what an employee expects to contribute in an employment relationship and what the employer will provide the employee in exchange for those contributions.

However, this arrangement is being replaced with a new type of psychological contract. Companies expect employees to take more responsibility for their own careers, from seeking training to balancing work and family. These expectations result in less job security for employees, who can count on working for several companies over the course of a career. In exchange for top performance and working longer hours without job security, employees want companies to provide flexible work schedules, comfortable working conditions, more control over how they accomplish work, training and development opportunities, and financial incentives based on how the organization performs. Employees realize that companies cannot provide employment security, so they want *employability*. This means they want their company to provide training and job experiences to help ensure that they can find other employment opportunities.

In the federal government's most recent survey of employee tenure, workers age 25 and older report they had been working with their present employer for a median of just 4.6 years.[49] Workers 55 and older tend to have a much longer tenure, and so do workers in government jobs. Still, if four and a half years with a company is typical, this amounts to many employers in the course of one's career. In fact, some employees engage in *job hopping*, the intentional practice of changing jobs frequently—say, every year or two (see the "Did You Know?" box).[50] Job hopping can be appealing to an employee as a way to stave off boredom and win some rapid increases in pay and responsibility. Some employees even are able to pick short-term jobs that give them valuable, carefully targeted experiences. However, there are some significant disadvantages. Every time the employee starts with a new employer, the employee needs to learn a new network of contacts and a new set of policies and procedures. This can slow down the employee's ability to learn a career in depth and reduce the employee's value to each employer. Therefore, employers tend to be wary of a job candidate who seems to have a history of job hopping. They may interpret job hopping as evidence of a character flaw such as inability to make a commitment or lack of conscientiousness. Often, employees can enjoy variety, develop skills, and build an interesting career without job hopping by asking for challenging assignments and cultivating a network of professional contacts within their present company.

Declining Union Membership

Another trend affecting the employment relationship has been ongoing for several decades. As we will explore in Chapter 15, the percentage of employees who belong to unions has been declining since the 1980s. Outside of government agencies, fewer U.S. workers today are union members. This trend is consistent with the idea of individual workers taking responsibility for their own careers. Whereas once many workers saw

Did You Know?

Half of U.S. Employees Interested in Changing Jobs

Half of employed workers are looking for a new job or would welcome an offer, according to a U.S. survey by the Jobvite software company. Looking at both employed and unemployed workers, Jobvite found that 71% are actively seeking or open to a new job. Jobvite's CEO notes that workers with mobile devices are looking for jobs "all the time."

Question

What challenges and opportunities do employers face in a climate where half of an organization's employees feel ready to leave?

Sources: Bureau of National Affairs, "Half of Workers Open to or Actively Seeking New Job, Jobvite Survey Finds," *HR Focus*, March 2014, p. 16; Dinah Wisenberg Brin, "Study: Most U.S. Workers Willing to Quit," Society for Human Resource Management, February 25, 2014, http://www.shrm.org; company website, "Jobvite Seeker Nation Study," 2014, http://recruiting.jobvite.com.

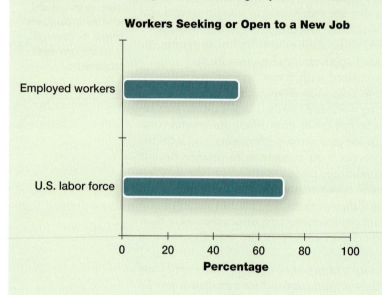

Workers Seeking or Open to a New Job

strength in numbers from joining a union, perhaps workers of the Internet era will prefer using numbers a different way: finding salary data and employer reviews online to negotiate their own career paths.

Flexibility

LO 2-8 Discuss how the need for flexibility affects human resource management.

The psychological contract largely results from the HRM challenge of building a committed, productive workforce in turbulent economic conditions—conditions that offer opportunity for financial success but can also quickly turn sour, making every employee expendable. From the organization's perspective, the key to survival in a fast-changing environment is flexibility. Organizations want to be able to change as fast as customer needs and economic conditions change. Flexibility in human resource management includes flexible staffing levels and flexible work schedules.

Alternative Work Arrangements
Methods of staffing other than the traditional hiring of full-time employees (for example, use of independent contractors, on-call workers, temporary workers, and contract company workers).

Flexible Staffing Levels A flexible workforce is one the organization can quickly reshape and resize to meet its changing needs. To be able to do this without massive hiring and firing campaigns, organizations are using more alternative work arrangements. **Alternative work arrangements** are methods of staffing other than the traditional hiring of full-time employees. There are a variety of methods, with the following being most common:

- *Independent contractors* are self-employed individuals with multiple clients.
- *On-call workers* are persons who work for an organization only when they are needed.
- *Temporary workers* are employed by a temporary agency; client organizations pay the agency for the services of these workers.
- *Contract company workers* are employed directly by a company for a specific time specified in a written contract.

However, employers need to use these options with care. In general, if employers direct workers in the details of how and when they do their jobs, these workers are legally defined as employees, not contractors. In that case, employers must meet the legal requirements for paying the employer's share of Social Security, Medicare, and unemployment insurance.

Recent research suggests that the use of contingent workers has been growing and has surpassed 2 million workers in the United States and one-fourth of total work hours.[51] Employers once mainly relied on contingent workers to fill administrative jobs, but now turn to contingent work arrangements for production workers, technical support, and even some professional tasks, such as graphic design, engineering, and finance. A major reason for the popularity of contingent work arrangements is that paying contractors enables an organization to pay only for completion of specific tasks and therefore to control costs.

More workers in alternative employment relationships are choosing these arrangements, but preferences vary. Most independent contractors and contract workers have this type of arrangement by choice. In contrast, temporary agency workers and on-call workers are likely to prefer traditional full-time employment. There is some debate about whether nontraditional employment relationships are good or bad. Some labor analysts argue that alternative work arrangements are substandard jobs featuring low pay, fear of unemployment, poor health insurance and retirement benefits, and dissatisfying work. Sometimes it is difficult or impossible for organizations to know whether these contract workers, located anywhere in the world, have safe working conditions and are not children. Others claim that these jobs provide flexibility for companies and employees alike. With alternative work arrangements, organizations can more easily modify the number of their employees. Continually adjusting staffing levels is especially cost effective for an organization that has fluctuating demand for its products and services. And when an organization downsizes by laying off temporary and part-time employees, the damage to morale among permanent full-time workers is likely to be less severe.

Flexible Work Schedules   The globalization of the world economy and the development of e-commerce have made the notion of a 40-hour workweek obsolete. As a result, companies need to be staffed 24 hours a day, seven days a week. Employees in manufacturing environments and service call centers are being asked to work 12-hour days or to work afternoon or midnight shifts. Similarly, professional employees face long hours and work demands that spill over into their personal lives. E-mail, texts, and tweets bombard employees with information and work demands. In the car, on vacation, on planes, and even in the bathroom, employees can be interrupted by work demands. More demanding work results in greater employee stress, less satisfied employees, loss of productivity, and higher turnover—all of which are costly for companies.

Multitasking has become a way of life for many employees who need to make the most of every minute. This trend is affecting human resource management and the employees it supports.

Many organizations are taking steps to provide more flexible work schedules, to protect employees' free time, and to more productively use employees' work time. Workers consider flexible schedules a valuable way to ease the pressures and conflicts of trying to balance work and nonwork activities. Employers are using flexible schedules to recruit and retain employees and to increase satisfaction and productivity. For Weatherby Healthcare, this kind of flexibility is a good fit with its corporate strategy of providing superior service by "putting people first." Weatherby, a physician staffing company, helps hospitals and other health care institutions find qualified physicians. Weatherby's employees must be skilled at uncovering its clients' culture, needs, and preferences and also be able to identify thousands of top-quality candidates every year, verify their credentials, and discern which clients would be a match for those candidates. To find and keep employees with the necessary level of people skills, Weatherby hires primarily for personal qualities, provides coaching, and works hard to create a positive atmosphere at work. Then they are allowed freedom to get their work done. Eddie Rodriguez, senior marketing coordinator, says, "No one's chained to their desk here." If workers need a break, they are free to go play table tennis or watch the news in the employee lounge. And if they meet their weekly goals by three o'clock on Friday, they are welcome to get an early start on the weekend.[52]

THINKING ETHICALLY

HOW SHOULD EMPLOYERS PROTECT THEIR DATA ON EMPLOYEES' DEVICES?

One area in which business managers might consult with HR managers involves the treatment of company data on employees' electronic devices. In the past, organizations stored their data on their own hardware. But laptop computers and, more recently, tablet computers and smartphones make it possible for employees to carry around data on these mobile devices. Increasingly often, the devices are not even owned by the company, but by the employees themselves. For example, an employee's smartphone might include business as well as personal contacts in several mobile apps.

The situation is convenient for everyone until something goes wrong: a device is lost, an employee becomes upset with a manager, or the organization lays off some workers. From the standpoint of protecting data, the obvious solution is to remove the data from the devices. So far, no law forbids this. However, it has consequences for the employees. Remotely wiping data from a device will remove all of it, including the user's personal data, such as photos and addresses.

Companies are addressing concerns by crafting security policies for employees who want to use their own devices for work-related tasks such as e-mail. Typically, the policy requires the employee to download a program for mobile device management. If specified conditions arise, such as loss of the device or termination of the employee, the company can use the software to send the device a message that wipes out all the data stored on the device. The company also can give the employee some notice, allowing time to save personal data, but this increases the risk to the company. Some employees have complained about their phones being unexpectedly erased after they left a company. They admit they might have been given a link to terms and conditions but tend not to read the terms of using a program such as company e-mail.

Questions

1. Imagine you work in the human resources department of a company considering a policy to protect its data on employees' mobile devices. In advising on this policy, what rights should you consider?

2. What advice would you give or actions would you take to ensure that the policy is administered fairly and equitably?

Sources: "Using Your Personal Phone for Work Could Cost You," *CBS Miami*, March 26, 2014, http://miami.cbslocal.com; Lauren Weber, "BYOD? Leaving a Job Can Mean Losing Pictures of Grandma," *Wall Street Journal*, January 21, 2014, http://online.wsj.com; Society for Human Resource Management, "Safety and Security Technology: Can an Employer Remotely Wipe/Brick an Employee's Personal Cell Phone?" SHRM Knowledge Center, November 5, 2013, http://www.shrm.org.

SUMMARY

LO 2-1 Describe trends in the labor force composition and how they affect human resource management.

- An organization's internal labor force comes from its external labor market—individuals actively seeking employment.
- In the United States, the labor market is aging and becoming more racially and ethnically diverse, with women representing roughly half of the total.
- To compete for talent, organizations must be flexible enough to meet the needs of older workers and must recruit from a diverse population; establish bias-free HR systems; and help employees understand and appreciate cultural differences.
- Organizations need employees with skills that may be hard to find: decision making, customer service, and teamwork, as well as technical skills.
- To meet this challenge, organizations may hire employees who lack certain skills, then train them for their jobs.

LO 2-2 Summarize areas in which human resource management can support the goal of creating a high-performance work system.

- To find and keep the best possible fit between their social system and technical system, HRM recruits and selects employees with broad skills and strong motivation, especially in organizations that rely on knowledge workers.
- Job design and appropriate systems for assessment and rewards have a central role in supporting employee empowerment and teamwork.

LO 2-3 Define employee empowerment, and explain its role in the modern organization.

- Employee empowerment means giving employees responsibility and authority to make decisions regarding all aspects of product development or customer service. The organization holds employees accountable for products and services, and in exchange, the employees share in the rewards (or losses) that result.
- Selection decisions should provide employees who have the necessary decision-making and interpersonal skills.
- Job design should give employees latitude for decision making.
- Employees should be trained to handle their broad responsibilities.
- Feedback and rewards must be appropriate for the work of empowered employees.
- HRM can also play a role in giving employees access to the information they need.

LO 2-4 Identify ways HR professionals can support organizational strategies for growth, quality, and efficiency.

- HR professionals should be familiar with the organization's strategy and may even play a role in developing the strategy.
- In a merger or acquisition, HRM must lead efforts to manage change with skillful employee relations and meaningful rewards. HR professionals can bring "people issues" to the attention of the managers leading change, provide training in conflict-resolution skills, and apply knowledge of the other organization's culture. HR professionals also must resolve differences between the companies' HR systems, such as benefits packages and performance appraisals.
- For empowering employees to practice total quality management, job design is essential.
- Cost control may focus on a specific issue, such as managing health benefits, or on support for a strategic move such as downsizing, reengineering, or outsourcing.
- To support cost control through downsizing, the HR department can develop voluntary programs to reduce the workforce or can help identify the least valuable employees to lay off. Employee relations can help maintain the morale of employees who remain after a downsizing.
- In reengineering, the HR department can lead in communicating with employees and providing training. It will also have to prepare new approaches for recruiting and appraising employees that are better suited to the reengineered jobs.
- Outsourcing presents similar issues related to job design and employee selection.

LO 2-5 Summarize ways in which human resource management can support organizations expanding internationally.

- Organizations with international operations hire employees in foreign countries where they operate, so they need knowledge of differences in culture and business practices.
- At home, qualified candidates include immigrants, so HRM needs to understand and train employees to deal with differences in cultures, as well as to ensure laws are followed.
- HRM helps organizations select and prepare employees for overseas assignments.
- To support efficiency and growth, HR staff can prepare companies for offshoring, in which operations are moved to countries where wages are lower or demand is growing. HR experts can help organizations determine whether workers in offshore locations can provide the same or better

skills, how offshoring will affect motivation and recruitment of employees needed in the United States, and whether managers are prepared to manage offshore employees.

LO 2-6 Discuss how technological developments are affecting human resource management.

- Information systems for HRM are widely used and often are provided through the Internet.
- Internet applications include searching for talent globally, using online job postings, screening candidates online, providing career-related information on the organization's website, and delivering training online.
- Online information sharing enables employee self-service for many HR needs, from application forms to training modules to information about the details of company policies and benefits.
- Organizations can structure work that involves collaboration among employees at different times and places, so HR professionals must ensure that communications remain effective enough to detect and correct problems when they arise.

LO 2-7 Explain how the nature of the employment relationship is changing.

- The employment relationship takes the form of a "psychological contract" that describes what employees and employers expect from the employment relationship, including unspoken expectations that are widely held.
- In the traditional version, organizations expected their employees to contribute time, effort, skills, abilities, and loyalty in exchange for job security and opportunities for promotion.
- Modern organizations' needs are constantly changing, so organizations require top performance and longer work hours but cannot provide job security. Instead, employees seek flexible work schedules, comfortable working conditions, greater autonomy, opportunities for training and development, and performance-related financial incentives.
- For HRM, the changes require planning for flexible staffing levels.
- For employees, the changes may make job hopping look attractive, but this career strategy often backfires.
- Union membership has been declining, which is consistent with the idea of taking personal responsibility for one's career.

LO 2-8 Discuss how the need for flexibility affects human resource management.

- Organizations seek flexibility in staffing levels through alternatives to the traditional employment relationship—outsourcing and temporary and contract workers. The use of such workers can affect job design and also the motivation of the organization's permanent employees.
- Organizations also may seek flexible work schedules, including shortened workweeks, which can be a way for employees to adjust work hours to meet personal and family needs.
- Organizations also may move employees to different jobs to meet changes in demand.

KEY TERMS

internal labor force, 30
external labor market, 30
high-performance work
   systems, 35
knowledge workers, 37
employee empowerment, 38
teamwork, 38

total quality management
   (TQM), 41
reengineering, 44
outsourcing, 44
offshoring, 46
expatriates, 47

human resource information
   system (HRIS), 47
electronic human resource
   management (e-HRM), 48
self-service, 49
psychological contract, 51
alternative work arrangements, 52

REVIEW AND DISCUSSION QUESTIONS

1. How does each of the following labor force trends affect HRM? *(LO 2-1)*
   a. Aging of the labor force.
   b. Diversity of the labor force.
   c. Skill deficiencies of the labor force.
2. At many organizations, goals include improving people's performance by relying on knowledge workers, empowering employees, and assigning work to teams. How can HRM support these efforts? *(LO 2-2)*
3. How do HRM practices such as performance management and work design encourage employee empowerment? *(LO 2-3)*

4. Merging, downsizing, and reengineering all can radically change the structure of an organization. Choose one of these changes, and describe HRM's role in making the change succeed. If possible, apply your discussion to an actual merger, downsizing, or reengineering effort that has recently occurred. *(LO 2-4)*

5. When an organization decides to operate facilities in other countries, how can HRM practices support this change? *(LO 2-5)*

6. Why do organizations outsource HRM functions? How does outsourcing affect the role of human resource professionals? Would you be more attracted to the role of the HR professional in an organization that outsources many HR activities or in the outside firm that has the contract to provide the HR services? Why? *(LO 2-6)*

7. What HRM functions could an organization provide through self-service? What are some advantages and disadvantages of using self-service for these functions? *(LO 2-6)*

8. How is the employment relationship that is typical of modern organizations different from the relationship of a generation ago? *(LO 2-7)*

9. Discuss several advantages of flexible work schedules. What are some disadvantages? *(LO 2-8)*

TAKING RESPONSIBILITY

Taking Care of People Gives Cisco Systems a Strategic Advantage

Strategic thinking about human resource management and other services has helped Cisco Systems take care of its people and even people beyond the organization. At the same time, it has helped the company, which sells computer networking hardware and services, maintain consistent growth and profitability.

During the recent recession, sales slowed, and Cisco's executives sought more efficient ways to operate. Out of that effort came a plan for restructuring HRM and other services such as purchasing and customer support. Management determined that these services would be delivered on a global scale as part of a Global Business Services unit. That unit, in turn, was divided into groups focused on delivering day-to-day services and others focused on strategic planning. HRM employees were divided, with some assigned to tactics and others to strategy.

The head of tactical HRM is Don McLaughlin, Cisco's vice president of employee experience. Applying his background in manufacturing, McLaughlin took a businesslike approach. He set measurable goals for hiring, training, rewards, communication, and work design, treating Cisco's employees as customers of those services. He measures the time to deliver each service and his customers' satisfaction. While driving down the cost of each service by at least 10%, McLaughlin has maintained or raised customer satisfaction scores. He works closely with the human resource partners assigned to support strategy for each Cisco group around the world. Those HR managers get to know their businesses and create plans for improving the company's talent, leadership, organization, and culture.

One of the regional HR managers is Danielle Monaghan, human resource partner in Cisco's Technical Services Division in San Jose, California. Born in South Africa, Monaghan worked for other technology companies before joining Cisco to manage human resources in Asia. In the Asian assignment, she saw firsthand some of the challenges of recruiting and developing talent in the continent's distinctive cultures. In Japan, for example, she needed to build networks to locate talent, because it is inappropriate to make a job search public. In China, the issues are developing leadership skills and learning to manage the rise of unions. Monaghan's global perspective is now helping Monaghan tackle strategic issues such as workforce planning.

Perhaps one of the company's most distinctive efforts is the Cisco Learning Network, which grew out of the training efforts of Cisco's education services division. The division trains customers and partners, and it saw an online network as a way to reach people around the world with information about how to use the technology Cisco sells. People from high school students through experienced professionals join the network to take classes, study together, and share ideas. As participation has ballooned from 600,000 in the first year to more than 2 million recently, the company added information about careers, job openings, and industry trends. The data created through social networking and the connections to a worldwide community have given Cisco an edge in building its reputation and understanding its labor market.

Questions

1. How has Cisco Systems prepared itself for responding to trends in the labor force?

2. How have Cisco's HR managers balanced concerns for cost and quality?

Sources: Ladan Nikravan, "Cisco: Divide and Conquer," *Talent Management*, February 4, 2014, http://talentmgt.com; John Scorza, "An HR Journey Leads to Insights on Asia," *HR Magazine*, July 2013, Business Insights: Global, http://bi.galegroup.com; Robert Berkman, "How Cisco's Learning Network Became a Social Hub for the IT Industry," *MIT Sloan Management Review*, February 12, 2013, http://sloanreview.mit.edu; "Analysts' Choice: Strong, Steady Cisco Wins Race," *Dow Theory Forecasts*, July 29, 2013, p. 8.

MANAGING TALENT

Netflix Treats Workers "Like Adults"

When Patty McCord talks about human resource management at Netflix, she refers to treating people "like adults." McCord, until recently the company's chief talent officer, means the company hires people who are mature enough to take responsibility and then simply gives them responsibility. The result, McCord insists, is that employees live up to what is expected of them. If not, the company feels free to find someone else. That direct approach makes sense to the knowledge workers who populate the results-oriented, data-respecting world of information technology.

When McCord was at Netflix, she and CEO Reed Hastings settled on five principles that would direct the company's approach to human resource management:

1. *Hire, reward, and keep only "fully formed adults."* For McCord and Hastings, such employees use common sense, address problems openly, and put company interests ahead of their own. People like this need not be managed with endless policies. Rather, the company can trust them to take off time when they need it and spend money appropriately. The employees also are literally adults; Netflix favors hiring experienced workers over recruiting at colleges.
2. *Tell the truth about performance.* Managers are expected to make performance feedback part of their routine conversations with employees. If an employee is no longer working out, managers are supposed to let him or her know directly, offering a good severance package to smooth a dignified path to the exit.
3. *Managers are responsible for creating great teams.* The manager of each group is expected to envision what that group should accomplish and what skills are necessary. If the manager needs different skills than the ones already on the team, the manager is supposed to make changes. To keep workers on the team, Netflix is open about paying salaries in line with the labor market—what employees would be offered if they considered leaving for a competitor.
4. *The company's leaders must create the company culture.* Netflix executives are supposed to model behaviors such as truth-telling and treating people like adults.
5. *HR managers should think of themselves first as businesspeople.* As chief talent manager, McCord focused on the company's financial success and products, not on employee morale. She assumed that if employees, as adults, were able to make Netflix a high-performance organization and be compensated fairly, that would improve morale more than anything.

To put these principles into action, Netflix rewards high-performing employees with fair pay and a flexible schedule. Employees who do not perform up to standards are asked to leave. Rewarding high performance, in fact, makes it easier to allow flexibility and empowerment, because managers do not have to police every action and decision. It also creates an environment in which employees do not assume they have a Netflix job forever. Rather, they are responsible for doing good work and developing the skills that continue to make them valuable to their employer. Netflix's approach to talent helps the company stay agile—perhaps agile enough to withstand the shifting winds of entertainment in the digital age.

Questions

1. How well suited do you think Netflix's principles are to managing the knowledge workers (mainly software engineers) who work for Netflix? Explain.
2. What qualities of Netflix support the idea that it is a high-performance work system? What other qualities would contribute to it being a high-performance work system?

Sources: Patty McCord, "How Netflix Reinvented HR," *Harvard Business Review*, January–February 2014, pp. 71–6; Edward E. Lawler III, "Netflix: We Got It Right!" *Forbes*, June 24, 2013, http://www.forbes.com; Francesca Fenzi, "Three Big Ideas to Steal from Netflix," *Inc.*, February 5, 2013, http://www.inc.com; Robert J. Grossman, "Tough Love at Netflix," *HR Magazine*, April 1, 2010, http://www.shrm.org.

HR IN SMALL BUSINESS

Radio Flyer Rolls Forward

The mid-2000s were a difficult time for Radio Flyer, a private business famous for its little red wagons. After spending hundreds of thousands of dollars to develop what they hoped was a hit, managers realized their idea wouldn't fly, so they killed it. And in the same year, management decided the company could no longer afford to build wagons in the United States.

First, the development flop: Thomas Schlegel, vice president for product development, thought he had a winner with an idea for a collapsible wagon to be called Fold 2 Go Wagon. It would be a fun product that parents could fold up and toss into the back of a minivan for a trip to the park or other outings. The problem was, a collapsing toy that children sit inside is difficult to make both functional and safe. The costs were excessive.

When Schlegel ended the project, he feared his reputation might suffer as well. But CEO Robert Pasin assured Schlegel that failure was acceptable as long as the company could learn from it. The value placed on learning became something that Schlegel capitalized on as his team applied what they learned to the development of a new success, the Twist Trike and a new model of its wagons called the Ultimate Family Wagon. Furthermore, Pasin expanded that one experience into a teaching opportunity. He invites new employees to join him for breakfasts, during which he recalls the incident as a way to reinforce the company's commitment to innovation and learning.

The story of Radio Flyer's need to outsource manufacturing has what some might see as a less-happy ending. Looking at the numbers, management determined that it would have to close its factory in Chicago and lay off about half of its workforce. Manufacturing moved to a factory in China. Pasin describes the effort as "an incredibly difficult time."

The company's effort with its remaining U.S. employees focused on building morale. These efforts include creating ideas for employees to have fun and pursue their passions, with events such as the Radio Flyer Olympics, during which employees compete in silly contests like tricycle races. More seriously, teams of employees tackle issues that they care about. The wellness committee put together a cash benefit that pays employees up to $300 for participating in health-related activities such as weight-loss counseling or running races. Another committee brought together employees concerned about the environment. They assembled a campaign aimed at persuading employees to reduce their carbon footprint.

In caring for the U.S. employees, Radio Flyer hasn't forgotten the ones in China. The company tries to maintain similar levels of benefits and engagement among the four dozen employees in its China office.

Questions

1. How could a human resource manager help Radio Flyer get the maximum benefit from the motivational efforts described in this case?
2. Do you think outsourcing would be harder on employees in a small company such as Radio Flyer than in a large corporation? Why or why not? How could HRM help smooth the transition?
3. What additional developments described in this chapter could help Radio Flyer live out the high value it places on learning and innovation?

Sources: Radio Flyer corporate website, www.radioflyer.com, accessed April 24, 2014; "2013 Best Small Workplaces: #13: Radio Flyer, Inc.," *Great Place to Work*, www.greatplacetowork.com, accessed April 24, 2014; Jessie Scanlon, "Radio Flyer Learns from a Crash," *Bloomberg Businessweek*, October 21, 2010, http://www.businessweek.com.

NOTES

1. Lauren Weber and Rachel Feintzeig, "Companies Say No to Having an HR Department," *The Wall Street Journal*, April 8, 2014, http://online.wsj.com; Todd Henneman, "Is HR at Its Breaking Point?" *Workforce*, March 22, 2013, http://www.workforce.com.
2. Eric Krell, "Is HR Doing More with Less? Or Is It Undergoing a Transformation?" *HR Magazine*, September 2013, Business Insights: Global, http://bi.galegroup.com.
3. Bureau of National Affairs, "2014 Outlook: Screening, Recruiting, ACA Compliance, Talent Management on HR's Agenda," *HR Focus*, February 2014, pp. 1–6.
4. Bureau of Labor Statistics, "Employment Projections, 2012–2022," news release, December 19, 2013, http://www.bls.gov.
5. Ibid.
6. AARP, "Best Employers for Workers over 50: 2011 Winners," September 2011, http://www.aarp.org.
7. A. Fox, "Mixing It Up," *HR Magazine*, May 2011, pp. 22–7; B. Hite, "Employers Rethink How They Give Feedback," *The Wall Street Journal*, October 13, 2008, p. B5; E. White, "Age Is as Age Does: Making the Generation Gap Work for You," *The Wall Street Journal*, June 30, 2008, p. B3.
8. Bureau of Labor Statistics, "Employment Projections, 2012–2022."
9. Ibid.
10. For background, see Randall Monger and James Yankay, "U.S. Legal Permanent Residents: 2012," *Annual Flow Report*, U.S. Department of Homeland Security, Office of Immigration Statistics, March 2013, http://www.dhs.gov; U.S. Citizenship and Immigration Services, "Green Card (Permanent Residence)," http://www.uscis.gov, last updated May 13, 2011; U.S. Department of State, "Temporary Worker Visas," http://travel.state.gov, accessed April 14, 2014; Amy Sherman, "Obama Holds Record for Cracking Down on Employers Who Hire Undocumented Workers, Says Wasserman Schultz," *Politifact*, July 3, 2013, http://www.politifact.com (rating Wasserman Schultz's statement "half true"); Doris Meissner, Donald M. Kerwin, Muzaffar Chishti, and Claire Bergeron, *Immigration Enforcement in the United States: The Rise of a Formidable Machinery* (Washington, DC: Migration Policy Institute, January 2013), p. 6, accessed at http://www.migrationpolicy.org.
11. T. H. Cox and S. Blake, "Managing Cultural Diversity: Implications for Organizational Competitiveness," *The Executive* 5 (1991), pp. 45–56.
12. "Global Diversity and Inclusion: Fostering Innovation through a Diverse Workforce," *Forbes Insights*, July 2011, http://www.forbes.com/forbesinsights.

13. Craig Wolf, "Diversity Helps Bridgeway Grow," *Poughkeepsie (N.Y.) Journal*, January 14, 2012, http://www.poughkeepsie-journal.com.

14. Bureau of National Affairs, "Employers Report Difficulty Finding Qualified Candidates for Certain Positions, Poll Reveals," *HR Focus*, June 2013, p. 7; Lorri Freifeld, "Bridging the Skills Gap," *Training*, April 3, 2013, http://www.trainingmag.com; Bureau of National Affairs, "2014 Outlook," p. 6; K. Frasch, "The Talent-Job Mismatch," *Human Resource Executive*, March 2013, p. 10.

15. James R. Hagerty, "Industry Puts Heat on Schools to Teach Skills Employers Need," *The Wall Street Journal*, June 6, 2011, http://online.wsj.com; Lucia Mutikani, "Veterans Help Manufacturers Plug Skills Gap," Reuters, February 2, 2012, http://www.reuters.com.

16. J. A. Neal and C. L. Tromley, "From Incremental Change to Retrofit: Creating High-Performance Work Systems," *Academy of Management Executive* 9 (1995), pp. 42–54.

17. Bureau of Labor Statistics, "Employment Projections, 2012–2022."

18. M. Hilton, "Skills for Work in the 21st Century: What Does the Research Tell Us?" *Academy of Management Executive*, November 2008, pp. 63–78.

19. Evan Rosen, "Every Worker Is a Knowledge Worker," *Bloomberg Businessweek*, January 11, 2011, http://www.businessweek.com; Joe McKendrick, "These Days, Who Is Not a 'Knowledge Worker'?" *SmartPlanet*, April 12, 2010, http://www.smartplanet.com.

20. Corilyn Shropshire, "Grainger Gives Employees Room to Grow," *Chicago Tribune*, November 15, 2011, http://www.chicagotribune.com. See also Jessica Stillman, "The Perpetually Vexing Problem of Hiring Programmers," *Inc.*, January 5, 2012, http://www.inc.com.

21. T. J. Atchison, "The Employment Relationship: Untied or Re-Tied," *Academy of Management Executive* 5 (1991), pp. 52–62.

22. R. Vance, *Employee Engagement and Commitment* (Alexandria, VA: Society for Human Resource Management, 2006); M. Huselid, "The Impact of Human Resource Management Practices on Turnover, Productivity, and Corporate Financial Performance," *Academy of Management Journal* 38 (1995), pp. 635–72; S. Payne and S. Webber, "Effects of Service Provider Attitudes and Employment Status on Citizenship Behaviors and Customers' Attitudes and Loyalty Behavior," *Journal of Applied Psychology* 91 (2006), pp. 365–68; J. Hartner, F. Schmidt, and T. Hayes, "Business-Unit Level Relationship between Employee Satisfaction, Employee Engagement, and Business Outcomes: A Meta-analysis," *Journal of Applied Psychology* 87 (2002), pp. 268–79.

23. Alex Adamopoulos, "'Agile' Grows Up, Readies to Take Over Your Whole Business," *VentureBeat*, February 9, 2012, http://venturebeat.com; Agile Alliance, "What Is Agile Software Development?" http://www.agilealliance.org, accessed February 10, 2012.

24. Adrienne Fox, "Achieving Integration: Boost Corporate Performance," *HR Magazine*, April 2011, Business & Company Resource Center, http://galenet.galegroup.com.

25. J. R. Jablonski, *Implementing Total Quality Management: An Overview* (San Diego: Pfeiffer, 1991).

26. R. Hodgetts, F. Luthans, and S. Lee, "New Paradigm Organizations: From Total Quality to Learning to World-Class," *Organizational Dynamics*, Winter 1994, pp. 5–19.

27. Bureau of National Affairs, "2014 Outlook," pp. 4–5.

28. Ibid., p. 3; Bureau of National Affairs, "Experts Detail the Evolving Role of HR and Compensation," *Report on Salary Surveys*, July 2013, pp. 8–10; Bureau of National Affairs, "HR in the Middle as Employers Consider Health Care Coverage Options," *Managing Benefits Plans*, March 2014, pp. 5–6.

29. Bureau of Labor Statistics, "Extended Mass Layoffs: Fourth Quarter 2011, Annual Totals 2011," news release, February 10, 2012, http://www.bls.gov/mls; Bureau of Labor Statistics, "Mass Layoff Statistics," last updated May 13, 2013, http://data.bls.gov. In response to budget cuts, the BLS stopped publishing mass layoff statistics after the first quarter of 2013.

30. "Lay Off the Layoffs," *Newsweek*, February 4, 2010, http://www.thedailybeast.com/newsweek; Ryan Bakken, "Marvin: A Window on the Economy," *Grand Forks (ND) Herald*, November 21, 2011, Business & Company Resource Center, http://galenet.galegroup.com.

31. A. Church, "Organizational Downsizing: What Is the Role of the Practitioner?" *Industrial-Organizational Psychologist* 33, no. 1 (1995), pp. 63–74.

32. Dori Meinert, "HR Budgets Show Modest Growth," *HR Magazine*, November 2011, p. 24.

33. The Right Thing, "The Goodyear Tire and Rubber Company Discovers Key to Successful Outsourcing Partnerships," *Workforce Management*, March 2011, p. S2.

34. Yum Brands, "Yum Restaurants China," http://www.yum.com, accessed April 24, 2014; Laurie Burkitt, "Yum Bids to Regain Consumer Confidence in China with New Menu," *Wall Street Journal*, March 27, 2014, http://online.wsj.com; Caitlin Bowling, "China: The Key to Yum Brands Bounce-Back Year," *Louisville Business First*, April 24, 2014, http://www.bizjournals.com/louisville; Reuters, "Yum Brands' China Restaurant Sales Improve, Shares Rise," April 22, 2014, http://www.reuters.com.

35. David Wessel, "Big U.S. Firms Shift Hiring Abroad," *The Wall Street Journal*, April 19, 2011, http://online.wsj.com; David Wessel, "U.S. Firms Keen to Add Foreign Jobs," *The Wall Street Journal*, November 22, 2011, http://online.wsj.com; M. Hess, "Homeward Bound," *Workforce Management*, February 2013, pp. 26–31; Emily Chasan, "Outsourcing Loses Its Luster for U.S. Tech Companies," *The Wall Street Journal*, March 6, 2014, http://blogs.wsj.com.

36. Megha Bahree, "Indian Tech Firms Look to Hire Abroad," *The Wall Street Journal*, November 11, 2011, http://online.wsj.com; Bureau of National Affairs, "2014 Outlook," p. 5.

37. Monger and Yankay, "U.S. Legal Permanent Residents: 2012."

38. Audrey Singer, "Immigrants in 2010 Metropolitan America: A Decade of Change," *State of Metropolitan America*, no. 43, Brookings Institution, October 24, 2011, http://www.brookings.edu; Bureau of Labor Statistics, "Foreign-Born Workers: Labor Force Characteristics, 2012," news release, May 22, 2013, http://www.bls.gov/cps.

39. R. L. Tung, "Expatriate Assignments: Enhancing Success and Minimizing Failure," *Academy of Management Executive* 12, no. 4 (1988), pp. 93–106.

40. M. J. Kavanaugh, H. G. Guetal, and S. I. Tannenbaum, *Human Resource Information Systems: Development and Application* (Boston: PWS-Kent, 1990).

41. Dave Zielinski, "HRIS Features Get More Strategic," *HR Magazine*, December 2011, p. 15.
42. Ed Frauenheim, "Strong to the Core," *Workforce Management*, August 2013, Business Insights: Global, http://bi.galegroup.com.
43. "Payroll as You Go," *Entrepreneur*, October 2011, p. 45.
44. N. Lockwood, *Maximizing Human Capital: Demonstrating HR Value with Key Performance Indicators* (Alexandria, VA: SHRM Research Quarterly, 2006).
45. "Social Technologies on the Front Line: The Management 2.0 M-Prize Winners," *McKinsey Quarterly*, September 2011, http://www.mckinseyquarterly.com.
46. Ibid.
47. J. O'Toole and E. Lawler III, *The New American Workplace* (New York: Palgrave Macmillan, 2006).
48. D. M. Rousseau, "Psychological and Implied Contracts in Organizations," *Employee Rights and Responsibilities Journal* 2 (1989), pp. 121–29.
49. Bureau of Labor Statistics, "Employee Tenure in 2012," news release, September 18, 2012, http://www.bls.gov/cps.
50. Dan Schawbel, "How Job Hopping Can Hurt Your Career," CNN, January 17, 2012, http://articles.cnn.com; Chrissy Scivicque, "How to Stop Job Hopping Once and for All," *Forbes*, January 23, 2012, http://www.forbes.com; Alina Dizik, "The Pros and Cons of Job-Hopping," CNN, July 4, 2011, http://www.cnn.com.
51. Fast Fact, "Temporary Workforce Stronger than Ever," *T + D*, May 2011, p. 21; Kate Lister, "Freelance Nation," *Entrepreneur*, September 2010, pp. 89–97; Pete Fehrenbach, "Temp Help as Labor Force De-volatile-izer," *Industry Week*, October 2013, p. 40.
52. Ed Finkel, "Positive Thinking," *Modern Healthcare*, October 24, 2011, Business & Company Resource Center, http://galenet.galegroup.com; Weatherby Healthcare, "About Us," http://www.weatherbyhealthcare.com, accessed January 25, 2012.

3 Providing Equal Employment Opportunity and a Safe Workplace

What Do I Need to Know?

After reading this chapter, you should be able to:

LO 3-1 Explain how the three branches of government regulate human resource management.

LO 3-2 Summarize the major federal laws requiring equal employment opportunity.

LO 3-3 Identify the federal agencies that enforce equal employment opportunity, and describe the role of each.

LO 3-4 Describe ways employers can avoid illegal discrimination and provide reasonable accommodation.

LO 3-5 Define sexual harassment, and tell how employers can eliminate or minimize it.

LO 3-6 Explain employers' duties under the Occupational Safety and Health Act.

LO 3-7 Describe the role of the Occupational Safety and Health Administration.

LO 3-8 Discuss ways employers promote worker safety and health.

Introduction

When Donald Sterling, then owner of the Los Angeles Clippers basketball team, chided a female friend for bringing her black friends to games, he might have thought the conversation was purely personal. Even when he discovered that the conversation had been recorded and leaked to the media, he might have thought the exposure of blatantly racist remarks was just a personal embarrassment. If he thought so, he soon discovered that he was wrong. Furious Clippers players protested, and Clippers fans threatened to boycott the remaining games of the season.

NBA Commissioner Adam Silver stepped in and investigated. He determined that Sterling's actions were not merely rude but a violation of the NBA's core values. Noting that the NBA has a history of taking "a leadership role in matters of race relations," Silver called Sterling's comments "contrary to the principles of inclusion and respect that form the foundation of our diverse, multicultural and multiethnic league." Silver fined Sterling $2.5 million and barred him from entering any Clippers facility. Sterling's family recently sold the team to former Microsoft CEO, Steve Ballmer.[1] Silver's decision made a point that is relevant outside the world of sports: the leaders of an organization set the tone for the organization. Organizations depend on leaders to model ethical and legal conduct that is consistent with their values, and they depend on employees to follow that good example.

As we saw in Chapter 1, human resource management takes place in the context of the company's goals and society's expectations for how a company should operate. In the United States, the federal government has set some limits on how an organization can practice human resource management. Among these limits are requirements intended to prevent discrimination in hiring and employment practices and to protect the health and safety of workers while they are on the job. Questions about a company's compliance with these requirements can result in lawsuits and negative publicity that often cause serious problems for a company's success and survival. Conversely, a company that skillfully navigates the maze of regulations can gain an advantage over

One way the executive branch communicates information about laws is through websites like Youth Rules!. This site is designed to provide young workers with a safe workplace by making them aware of laws that, for example, restrict the amount of work they can do and the machinery they can operate.

its competitors. A further advantage may go to companies that go beyond mere legal compliance to make fair employment and worker safety important components of the company's business strategy. The NBA commissioner was not required to punish Donald Sterling because of a law; rather, he was maintaining a climate in the professional basketball league that would be favorable to the best players of all races and welcoming to fans of all races and ethnicities. Similarly, an employer that requires employees to treat one another with respect fosters a climate that attracts and keeps talented workers.

This chapter provides an overview of the ways government bodies regulate equal employment opportunity and workplace safety and health. It introduces you to major laws affecting employers in these areas, as well as the agencies charged with enforcing those laws. The chapter also discusses ways organizations can develop practices that ensure they are in compliance with the laws.

One point to make at the outset is that managers often want a list of dos and don'ts that will keep them out of legal trouble. Some managers rely on strict rules such as "Don't ever ask a female applicant if she is married," rather than learning the reasons behind those rules. Clearly, certain practices are illegal or at least inadvisable, and this chapter will provide guidance on avoiding such practices. However, managers who merely focus on how to avoid breaking the law are not thinking about how to be ethical or how to acquire and use human resources in the best way to carry out the company's mission. This chapter introduces ways to think more creatively and constructively about fair employment and workplace safety.

Regulation of Human Resource Management

All three branches of the U.S. government—legislative, executive, and judicial—play an important role in creating a legal environment for human resource management. The legislative branch, which consists of the two houses of Congress, has enacted a

LO 3-1 Explain how the three branches of government regulate human resource management.

number of laws governing human resource activities. Senators and U.S. representatives generally develop these laws in response to perceived societal needs. For example, during the civil rights movement of the early 1960s, Congress enacted Title VII of the Civil Rights Act to ensure that various minority groups received equal opportunities in many areas of life.

The executive branch, including the many regulatory agencies that the president oversees, is responsible for enforcing the laws passed by Congress. Agencies do this through a variety of actions, from drawing up regulations detailing how to abide by the laws to filing suit against alleged violators. Some federal agencies involved in regulating human resource management include the Equal Employment Opportunity Commission and the Occupational Safety and Health Administration. In addition, the president may issue executive orders, which are directives issued solely by the president, without requiring congressional approval. Some executive orders regulate the activities of organizations that have contracts with the federal government. For example, President Lyndon Johnson signed Executive Order 11246, which requires all federal contractors and subcontractors to engage in affirmative-action programs designed to hire and promote women and minorities. (We will explore the topic of affirmative action later in this chapter.)

The judicial branch, the federal court system, influences employment law by interpreting the law and holding trials concerning violations of the law. The U.S. Supreme Court, at the head of the judicial branch, is the court of final appeal. Decisions made by the Supreme Court are binding; they can be overturned only through laws passed by Congress. The Civil Rights Act of 1991 was partly designed to overturn Supreme Court decisions.

Equal Employment Opportunity

LO 3-2 Summarize the major federal laws requiring equal employment opportunity.

Equal Employment Opportunity (EEO)
The condition in which all individuals have an equal chance for employment, regardless of their race, color, religion, sex, age, disability, or national origin.

Among the most significant efforts to regulate human resource management are those aimed at achieving **equal employment opportunity (EEO)**—the condition in which all individuals have an equal chance for employment, regardless of their race, color, religion, sex, age, disability, or national origin. The federal government's efforts to create equal employment opportunity include constitutional amendments, legislation, and executive orders, as well as court decisions that interpret the laws. Table 3.1 summarizes major EEO laws discussed in this chapter. These are U.S. laws; equal employment laws in other countries may differ.

Constitutional Amendments

Two amendments to the U.S. Constitution—the Thirteenth and Fourteenth—have implications for human resource management. The Thirteenth Amendment abolished slavery in the United States. Though you might be hard-pressed to cite an example of race-based slavery in the United States today, the Thirteenth Amendment has been applied in cases where discrimination involved the "badges" (symbols) and "incidents" of slavery.

The Fourteenth Amendment forbids the states from taking life, liberty, or property without due process of law and prevents the states from denying equal protection of the laws. Recently it has been applied to the protection of whites in charges of reverse discrimination. In a case that marked the early stages of a move away from race-based quotas, Alan Bakke alleged that as a white man he had been discriminated against in the selection of entrants to the University of California at Davis medical school.[2] The

Table 3.1

Summary of Major EEO Laws and Regulations

ACT	REQUIREMENTS	COVERS	ENFORCEMENT AGENCY
Thirteenth Amendment	Abolished slavery	All individuals	Court system
Fourteenth Amendment	Provides equal protection for all citizens and requires due process in state action	State actions (e.g., decisions of government organizations)	Court system
Civil Rights Acts (CRAs) of 1866 and 1871 (as amended)	Grants all citizens the right to make, perform, modify, and terminate contracts and enjoy all benefits, terms, and conditions of the contractual relationship	All individuals	Court system
Equal Pay Act of 1963	Requires that men and women performing equal jobs receive equal pay	Employers engaged in interstate commerce	EEOC
Title VII of CRA	Forbids discrimination based on race, color, religion, sex, or national origin	Employers with 15 or more employees working 20 or more weeks per year; labor unions; and employment agencies	EEOC
Age Discrimination in Employment Act of 1967	Prohibits discrimination in employment against individuals 40 years of age and older	Employers with 15 or more employees working 20 or more weeks per year; labor unions; employment agencies; federal government	EEOC
Rehabilitation Act of 1973	Requires affirmative action in the employment of individuals with disabilities	Government agencies; federal contractors and subcontractors with contracts greater than $2,500	OFCCP
Pregnancy Discrimination Act of 1978	Treats discrimination based on pregnancy-related conditions as illegal sex discrimination	All employees covered by Title VII	EEOC
Americans with Disabilities Act of 1990	Prohibits discrimination against individuals with disabilities	Employers with more than 15 employees	EEOC
Executive Order 11246	Requires affirmative action in hiring women and minorities	Federal contractors and subcontractors with contracts greater than $10,000	OFCCP
Civil Rights Act of 1991	Prohibits discrimination (same as Title VII)	Same as Title VII, plus applies Section 1981 to employment discrimination cases	EEOC
Uniformed Services Employment and Reemployment Rights Act of 1994	Requires rehiring of employees who are absent for military service, with training and accommodations as needed	Veterans and members of reserve components	Veterans' Employment and Training Service
Genetic Information Nondiscrimination Act of 2008	Prohibits discrimination because of genetic information	Employers with 15 or more employees	EEOC
Lilly Ledbetter Fair Pay Act of 2009	Allows employees to claim discriminatory compensation within a set time after receiving a discriminatory paycheck	Employees covered by Title VII of CRA, Age Discrimination in Employment Act, and Americans with Disabilities Act	EEOC

university had set aside 16 of the available 100 places for "disadvantaged" applicants who were members of racial minority groups. Under this quota system, Bakke was able to compete for only 84 positions, whereas a minority applicant was able to compete for all 100. The federal court ruled in favor of Bakke, noting that this quota system had violated white individuals' right to equal protection under the law.

An important point regarding the Fourteenth Amendment is that it applies only to the decisions or actions of the government or of private groups whose activities are deemed government actions. Thus, a person could file a claim under the Fourteenth Amendment if he or she had been fired from a state university (a government organization) but not if the person had been fired by a private employer.

Legislation

The periods following the Civil War and during the civil rights movement of the 1960s were times when many voices in society pressed for equal rights for all without regard to a person's race or sex. In response, Congress passed laws designed to provide for equal opportunity. In later years, Congress has passed additional laws that have extended EEO protection more broadly.

Civil Rights Acts of 1866 and 1871 During Reconstruction, Congress passed two Civil Rights Acts to further the Thirteenth Amendment's goal of abolishing slavery. The Civil Rights Act of 1866 granted all persons the same property rights as white citizens, as well as the right to enter into and enforce contracts. Courts have interpreted the latter right as including employment contracts. The Civil Rights Act of 1871 granted all citizens the right to sue in federal court if they feel they have been deprived of some civil right. Although these laws might seem outdated, they are still used because they allow the plaintiff to recover both compensatory and punitive damages (that is, payment to compensate them for their loss plus additional damages to punish the offender).

Equal Pay Act of 1963 Under the Equal Pay Act of 1963, if men and women in an organization are doing equal work, the employer must pay them equally. The act defines *equal* in terms of skill, effort, responsibility, and working conditions. However, the act allows for reasons why men and women performing the same job might be paid differently. If the pay differences result from differences in seniority, merit, quantity or quality of production, or any factor other than sex (such as participating in a training program or working the night shift), then the differences are legal.

Title VII of the Civil Rights Act of 1964 The major law regulating equal employment opportunity in the United States is Title VII of the Civil Rights Act of 1964. Title VII directly resulted from the civil rights movement of the early 1960s, led by such individuals as Dr. Martin Luther King Jr. To ensure that employment opportunities would be based on character or ability rather than on race, Congress wrote and passed Title VII, and President Lyndon Johnson signed it into law in 1964. The law is enforced by the **Equal Employment Opportunity Commission (EEOC)**, an agency of the Department of Justice.

Equal Employment Opportunity Commission (EEOC)
Agency of the Department of Justice charged with enforcing Title VII of the Civil Rights Act of 1964 and other antidiscrimination laws.

Title VII prohibits employers from discriminating against individuals because of their race, color, religion, sex, or national origin. An employer may not use these characteristics as the basis for not hiring someone, for firing someone, or for discriminating against them in the terms of their pay, conditions of employment, or privileges of employment. In addition, an employer may not use these characteristics to limit, segregate, or classify employees or job applicants in any way that would deprive any individual of employment opportunities or otherwise adversely affect his or her status as an employee. The act applies to organizations that employ 15 or more persons working 20 or more weeks a year and that are involved in interstate commerce, as well as state and local governments, employment agencies, and labor organizations.

Title VII also states that employers may not retaliate against employees for either "opposing" a perceived illegal employment practice or "participating in a proceeding" related to an alleged illegal employment practice. *Opposition* refers to expressing to someone through proper channels that you believe an illegal employment act has taken place or is taking place. *Participation in a proceeding* refers to testifying in an investigation, hearing, or court proceeding regarding an illegal employment act. The purpose of this provision is to protect employees from employers' threats and other forms of intimidation aimed at discouraging employees from bringing to light acts they believe to be illegal. Companies that violate this prohibition may be liable for punitive damages.

Age Discrimination in Employment Act (ADEA)

One category of employees not covered by Title VII is older workers. Older workers sometimes are concerned that they will be the targets of discrimination, especially when a company is downsizing. Older workers tend to be paid more, so a company that wants to cut labor costs may save by laying off its oldest workers. To counter such discrimination, Congress in 1967 passed the Age Discrimination in Employment Act (ADEA), which prohibits discrimination against workers who are over the age of 40. Similar to Title VII, the ADEA outlaws hiring, firing, setting compensation rates, or other employment decisions based on a person's age being over 40.

Many firms have offered early-retirement incentives as an alternative or supplement to involuntary layoffs. Because this approach to workforce reduction focuses on older employees, who would be eligible for early retirement, it may be in violation of the ADEA. Early-retirement incentives require that participating employees sign an agreement waiving their rights to sue under the ADEA. Courts have tended to uphold the use of early-retirement incentives and waivers as long as the individuals were not coerced into signing the agreements, the agreements were presented in a way the employees could understand (including technical legal requirements such as the ages of discharged and retained employees in the employee's work unit), and the employees had been given enough time to make a decision.[3] Also, these waivers must meet the basic requirements of a contract, so the employer must offer something of value—for example, payment of a percentage of the employee's salary—in exchange for the employee giving up rights under the waiver.

To defend against claims of discrimination, one practical way is to establish performance-related criteria for layoffs, rather than age- or salary-related criteria. Of course, those criteria must be genuinely performance related. The EEOC recently sued a Michigan manufacturer for apparently manipulating its layoff criteria in order to target the oldest engineers for layoffs. In the first round of layoffs at Hutchinson Sealing Systems, the oldest project engineer was the one who met the criteria. Then the company revised its criteria and laid off two more engineers, again the oldest on the payroll. If the criteria had not been changed, younger engineers would have met the layoff criteria, and the EEOC saw that as evidence of age discrimination.[4]

Figure 3.1

Age Discrimination Complaints, 1999–2013

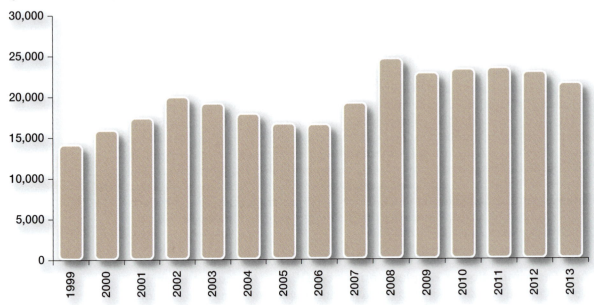

Source: Equal Employment Opportunity Commission, http://www1.eeoc.gov//eeoc/statistics/enforcement/.

Age discrimination complaints make up a large percentage of the complaints filed with the Equal Employment Opportunity Commission, and whenever the economy is slow, the number of complaints grows. For example, as shown in Figure 3.1, the number of age discrimination cases jumped in 2008, when many firms were downsizing, and has fallen slightly as the recovery has proceeded at a slow pace. Another increase in age discrimination claims accompanied the economic slowdown at the beginning of the 2000s.

In today's environment, in which firms are seeking talented individuals to achieve the company's goals, older employees can be a tremendous pool of potential resources. Researchers have found that although muscle power tends to decline with age, older workers tend to offer other important strengths, including conscientiousness and interpersonal skills.[5] Older workers also may have acquired deep knowledge of their work, industry, and employer. Successful companies are finding ways to keep these valuable older workers on the job and contributing. Union Carbide asks retired managers to serve as mentors for its current managers. In Australia, a bank called Westpac has identified knowledgeable older workers, labeled them "sages," and asked them to create a database of what they know about the organization and their work. At Mercy Health Systems, workers approaching retirement are allowed to take leaves of absence with benefits, and retired workers are invited to be part of a temporary workforce that comes back during periods of heavy demand.

Affirmative Action
An organization's active effort to find opportunities to hire or promote people in a particular group.

Vocational Rehabilitation Act of 1973   In 1973, Congress passed the Vocational Rehabilitation Act to enhance employment opportunity for individuals with disabilities. This act covers executive agencies and contractors and subcontractors that receive more than $2,500 annually from the federal government. These organizations must engage in affirmative action for individuals with disabilities. **Affirmative action**

is an organization's active effort to find opportunities to hire or promote people in a particular group. Thus, Congress intended this act to encourage employers to recruit qualified individuals with disabilities and to make reasonable accommodations to all those people to become active members of the labor market. The Department of Labor's Employment Standards Administration enforces this act.

Vietnam Era Veterans' Readjustment Act of 1974   Similar to the Rehabilitation Act, the Vietnam Era Veterans' Readjustment Act of 1974 requires federal contractors and subcontractors to take affirmative action toward employing veterans of the Vietnam War (those serving between August 5, 1964, and May 7, 1975). The Office of Federal Contract Compliance Procedures, discussed later in this chapter, has authority to enforce this act.

Pregnancy Discrimination Act of 1978   An amendment to Title VII of the Civil Rights Act of 1964, the Pregnancy Discrimination Act of 1978 defines discrimination on the basis of pregnancy, childbirth, or related medical conditions to be a form of illegal sex discrimination. According to the EEOC, this means that employers may not treat a female applicant or employee "unfavorably because of pregnancy, childbirth, or a medical condition related to pregnancy or childbirth."[6] For example, an employer may not refuse to hire a woman because she is pregnant. Decisions about work absences or accommodations must be based on the same policies as the organization uses for other disabilities. Benefits, including health insurance, should cover pregnancy and related medical conditions in the same way that it covers other medical conditions.

Americans with Disabilities Act (ADA) of 1990   One of the farthest-reaching acts concerning the management of human resources is the Americans with Disabilities Act. This 1990 law protects individuals with disabilities from being discriminated against in the workplace. It prohibits discrimination based on disability in all employment practices, such as job application procedures, hiring, firing, promotions, compensation, and training. Other employment activities covered by the ADA are employment advertising, recruitment, tenure, layoff, leave, and fringe benefits.

The ADA defines **disability** as a physical or mental impairment that substantially limits one or more major life activities, a record of having such an impairment, or being regarded as having such an impairment. The first part of the definition refers to individuals who have serious disabilities—such as epilepsy, blindness, deafness, or paralysis—that affect their ability to perform major bodily functions and major life activities such as walking, learning (for example, functions of the brain and immune system), caring for oneself, and working. The second part refers to individuals who have a history of disability, such as someone who has had cancer but is currently in remission, someone with a history of mental illness, and someone with a history of heart disease. The third part of the definition, "being regarded as having a disability," refers to people's subjective reactions, as in the case of someone who is severely disfigured; an employer might hesitate to hire such a person on the grounds that people will react negatively to such an employee.[7]

The ADA covers specific physiological disabilities such as cosmetic disfigurement and anatomical loss affecting the body's systems. In addition, it covers mental and psychological disorders such as mental retardation, organic brain syndrome, emotional or mental illness, and learning disabilities. Conditions not covered include obesity, substance abuse, irritability, and poor judgment.[8] Also, if a person needs ordinary

Disability
Under the Americans with Disabilities Act, a physical or mental impairment that substantially limits one or more major life activities, a record of having such an impairment, or being regarded as having such an impairment.

Figure 3.2

Disabilities Associated with Complaints Filed under ADA

Source: Equal Employment Opportunity Commission, "ADA Charge Data by Impairments/ Bases: Receipts, FY1997–FY2013," http://www1.eeoc.gov, accessed April 29, 2014.

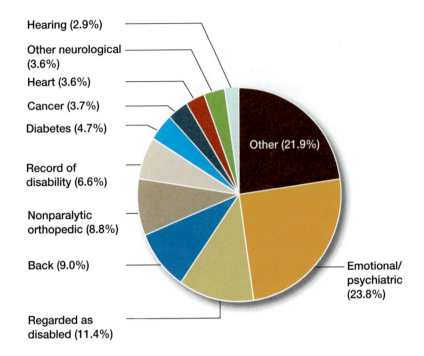

Hearing (2.9%)

Other neurological (3.6%)

Heart (3.6%)

Cancer (3.7%)

Diabetes (4.7%)

Record of disability (6.6%)

Nonparalytic orthopedic (8.8%)

Back (9.0%)

Regarded as disabled (11.4%)

Other (21.9%)

Emotional/ psychiatric (23.8%)

eyeglasses or contact lenses to perform each major life activity with little or no difficulty, the person is not considered disabled under the ADA. (In determining whether an impairment is substantially limiting, mitigating measures, such as medicine, hearing aids, and prosthetics, once could be considered but now must be ignored.) Figure 3.2 shows the types of disabilities associated with complaints filed under the ADA in 2013.

In contrast to other EEO laws, the ADA goes beyond prohibiting discrimination to require that employers take steps to accommodate individuals covered under the act. If a disabled person is selected to perform a job, the employer (perhaps in consultation with the disabled employee) determines what accommodations are necessary for the employee to perform the job. Examples include using ramps and lifts to make facilities accessible, redesigning job procedures, and providing technology such as TDD lines for hearing-impaired employees. Some employers have feared that accommodations under the ADA would be expensive. However, the Department of Labor has found that two-thirds of accommodations cost less than $500, and many of these cost nothing.[9] As technology advances, the cost of many technologies has been falling. In addition, the federal government has created a tax credit, the Work Opportunity Tax Credit, of up to $2,400 for each qualified disabled worker hired. That means accommodating disabled workers can lower an employer's income taxes.

Civil Rights Act of 1991   In 1991 Congress broadened the relief available to victims of discrimination by passing a Civil Rights Act (CRA 1991). CRA 1991 amends Title VII of the Civil Rights Act of 1964, as well as the Civil Rights Act of 1866, the Americans with Disabilities Act, and the Age Discrimination in Employment Act of 1967. One major change in EEO law under CRA 1991 has been the addition of compensatory and punitive damages in cases of discrimination under Title VII and the Americans with Disabilities Act. Before CRA 1991, Title VII limited damage claims to *equitable relief,* which courts have defined to include back pay, lost benefits, front pay in some cases, and attorney's fees and costs. CRA 1991 allows judges to award

EMPLOYER SIZE	DAMAGE LIMIT
14 to 100 employees	$ 50,000
101 to 200 employees	100,000
201 to 500 employees	200,000
More than 500 employees	300,000

Table 3.2

Maximum Punitive Damages Allowed under the Civil Rights Act of 1991

compensatory and punitive damages when the plaintiff proves the discrimination was intentional or reckless. Compensatory damages include such things as future monetary loss, emotional pain, suffering, and loss of enjoyment of life. Punitive damages are a punishment; by requiring violators to pay the plaintiff an amount beyond the actual losses suffered, the courts try to discourage employers from discriminating.

Recognizing that one or a few discrimination cases could put an organization out of business, and so harm many innocent employees, Congress has limited the amount of punitive damages. As shown in Table 3.2, the amount of damages depends on the size of the organization charged with discrimination. The limits range from $50,000 per violation at a small company (14 to 100 employees) to $300,000 at a company with more than 500 employees. A company has to pay punitive damages only if it discriminated intentionally or with malice or reckless indifference to the employee's federally protected rights.

Uniformed Services Employment and Reemployment Rights Act of 1994

When members of the armed services were called up following the terrorist attacks of September 2001, a 1994 employment law—the Uniformed Services Employment and Reemployment Rights Act (USERRA)—assumed new significance. Under this law, employers must reemploy workers who left jobs to fulfill military duties for up to five years. When service members return from active duty, the employer must reemploy them in the job they would have held if they had not left to serve in the military, providing them with the same seniority, status, and pay rate they would have earned if their employment had not been interrupted. Disabled veterans also have up to two years to recover from injuries received during their service or training, and employers must make reasonable accommodations for a remaining disability.

Service members also have duties under USERRA. Before leaving for duty, they are to give their employers notice, if possible. After their service, the law sets time limits for applying to be reemployed. Depending on the length of service, these limits range from approximately 2 to 90 days. Veterans with complaints under USERRA can obtain assistance from the Veterans' Employment and Training Service of the Department of Labor.

Genetic Information Nondiscrimination Act of 2008

Thanks to the decoding of the human genome and developments in the fields of genetics and medicine, researchers can now identify more and more genes associated with risks for

Aric Miller, an Army reservist sergeant, was deployed for service with the 363rd military police unit in Iraq for over a year. When he returned to the states, he was able to resume his job as an elementary school teacher thanks to the 1994 Uniformed Services Employment and Reemployment Rights Act. The act requires employers to reemploy service members in the job they would have held if they had not left to serve in the military. Why is this act important?

developing particular diseases or disorders. While learning that you are at risk of, say, colon cancer may be a useful motivator to take precautions, the information opens up some risks as well. For example, what if companies began using genetic screening to identify and avoid hiring job candidates who are at risk of developing costly diseases? Concerns such as this prompted Congress to pass the Genetic Information Nondiscrimination Act (GINA) of 2008.

Under GINA's requirements, companies with 15 or more employees may not use genetic information in making decisions related to the terms, conditions, or privileges of employment—for example, decisions to hire, promote, or lay off a worker. This genetic information includes information about a person's genetic tests, genetic tests of the person's family members, and family medical histories. Furthermore, employers may not intentionally obtain this information, except in certain limited situations (such as an employee voluntarily participating in a wellness program or requesting time off to care for a sick relative). If companies do acquire such information, they must keep the information confidential. The law also forbids harassment of any employee because of that person's genetic information.

Lilly Ledbetter Fair Pay Act of 2009   In reaction to a Supreme Court decision overturning an EEOC policy that defined the time frame when employees may file a complaint, Congress passed the Lilly Ledbetter Fair Pay Act. The act covers discrimination in pay; that is, when an individual receives different pay than his or her coworkers, and the difference is due to race, color, religion, sex, national origin, age, or disability. Named after the worker whose pay discrimination complaint did not withstand the Supreme Court's ruling, the act made the EEOC's policy a federal law. It provides three ways to determine the time period within which an employee may file a complaint: counting from (1) when the employer's decision or other discriminatory practice happened; (2) when the person became subject to the decision or practice; or (3) when the compensation was affected by the decision or practice, including each time the employee received a discriminatory level of compensation from the employer.

Executive Orders

Two executive orders that directly affect human resource management are Executive Order 11246, issued by Lyndon Johnson, and Executive Order 11478, issued by Richard Nixon. Executive Order 11246 prohibits federal contractors and subcontractors from discriminating based on race, color, religion, sex, or national origin. In addition, employers whose contracts meet minimum size requirements must engage in affirmative action to ensure against discrimination. Those receiving more than $10,000 from the federal government must take affirmative action, and those with contracts exceeding $50,000 must develop a written affirmative-action plan for each of their establishments. This plan must be in place within 120 days of the beginning of the contract. This executive order is enforced by the Office of Federal Contract Compliance Procedures.

Executive Order 11478 requires the federal government to base all its employment policies on merit and fitness. It specifies that race, color, sex, religion, and national origin may not be considered. Along with the government, the act covers all contractors and subcontractors doing at least $10,000 worth of business with the federal government. The U.S. Office of Personnel Management is in charge of ensuring that the government is in compliance, and the relevant government agencies are responsible for ensuring the compliance of contractors and subcontractors.

The Government's Role in Providing for Equal Employment Opportunity

LO 3-3 Identify the federal agencies that enforce equal employment opportunity, and describe the role of each.

At a minimum, equal employment opportunity requires that employers comply with EEO laws. To enforce those laws, the executive branch of the federal government uses the Equal Employment Opportunity Commission and the Office of Federal Contract Compliance Programs.

Equal Employment Opportunity Commission (EEOC)

The Equal Employment Opportunity Commission (EEOC) is responsible for enforcing most of the EEO laws, including Title VII, the Equal Pay Act, and the Americans with Disabilities Act. To do this, the EEOC investigates and resolves complaints about discrimination, gathers information, and issues guidelines. As described in "HR How To," the EEOC has tried to increase its effectiveness by setting priorities where it believes its enforcement will have the most impact.

When individuals believe they have been discriminated against, they may file a complaint with the EEOC or a similar state agency. They must file the complaint within 180 days of the incident. The meaning of an "incident" for this purpose is defined by law. For example, the Lilly Ledbetter Fair Pay Act establishes that for determining pay discrimination, an incident can be receiving a paycheck. Figure 3.3 illustrates the number of charges filed with the EEOC for different types of discrimination in 2013.

Figure 3.3

Types of Charges Filed with the EEOC

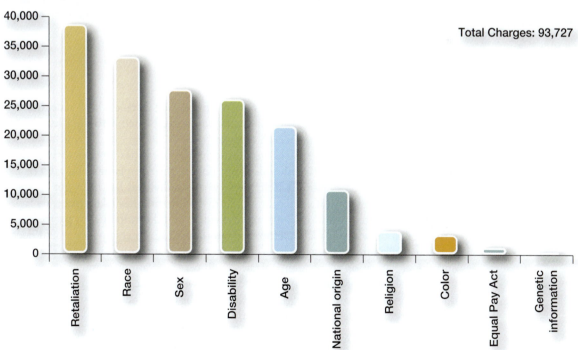

Source: Equal Employment Opportunity Commission, "Charge Statistics FY 1997 through FY 2013," http://www1.eeoc.gov, accessed April 29, 2014.

Being Strategic about EEO

Recently, the Equal Employment Opportunity Commission announced that it would be more strategic about how it carries out its mission. Employers may find it useful to be equally strategic in compliance.

The EEOC established six areas that would be priorities because they have the greatest potential to reduce and deter employment discrimination. The six areas are (1) eliminating barriers in recruitment and hiring; (2) protecting immigrant, migrant, and other workers considered vulnerable; (3) addressing emerging issues, such as accommodating workers with disabilities and preventing discrimination against gay and lesbian employees, which could take the form of sex discrimination; (4) enforcing equal pay laws; (5) preserving access to the legal system by targeting retaliation; and (6) preventing harassment.

Employers must, of course, obey *all* the EEO laws. But the commission's focus on these concerns suggest that employers can have the most impact on compliance and reduce legal problems by ensuring that the organization is performing well in the same six areas. Employers should:

- Review all of their selection methods to be sure none of them discriminates unintentionally.
- Ensure all employees know how to avoid harassing or segregating groups of workers, such as immigrants or gay and lesbian employees.
- Train all supervisors and HR decision makers in avoiding discrimination and retaliation.
- Keep complete records of performance reviews and pay decisions to ensure that pay gaps are due to performance differences.

Questions

1. Suppose you are an HR manager in a U.S. company. How would you explain to your company's business managers the importance of the EEOC's strategic priorities?
2. How would you suggest that your department apply these priorities in planning its management training programs?

Sources: Nicole Saleem, "National Priorities: The EEOC's Four Year Plan," *101 Practice Series* (American Bar Association Young Lawyers Division), http://www.americanbar.org, accessed April 30, 2014; Andrea Davis, "EEOC Goes CSI," *Employee Benefit News*, April 15, 2013, pp. 8, 10; Lydell C. Bridgeford, "Q&A: Key Takeaways from EEOC's Strategic Enforcement Plan," *Bloomberg BNA Labor & Employment Blog*, January 7, 2013, http://www.bna.com; Equal Employment Opportunity Commission, "EEOC Approves Strategic Enforcement Plan," news release, December 18, 2012, http://www1.eeoc.gov.

Many individuals file more than one type of charge (for instance, both race discrimination and retaliation), so the total number of complaints filed with the EEOC is less than the total of the amounts in each category.

After the EEOC receives a charge of discrimination, it has 60 days to investigate the complaint. If the EEOC either does not believe the complaint to be valid or fails to complete the investigation within 60 days, the individual has the right to sue in federal court. If the EEOC determines that discrimination has taken place, its representatives will attempt to work with the individual and the employer to try to achieve a reconciliation without a lawsuit. Sometimes the EEOC enters into a consent decree with the discriminating organization. This decree is an agreement between the agency and the organization that the organization will cease certain discriminatory practices and possibly institute additional affirmative-action practices to rectify its history of discrimination. A settlement with the EEOC can be costly, including such remedies as back pay, reinstatement of the employee, and promotions.

If the attempt at a settlement fails, the EEOC has two options. It may issue a "right to sue" letter to the alleged victim. This letter certifies that the agency has investigated the victim's allegations and found them to be valid. The EEOC's other option, which it uses less often, is to aid the alleged victim in bringing suit in federal court.

The EEOC also monitors organizations' hiring practices. Each year organizations that are government contractors or subcontractors or have 100 or more employees must file an Employer Information Report (EEO-1) with the EEOC. The **EEO-1 report** is an online questionnaire requesting the number of employees in each job category (such as managers, professionals, and laborers), broken down by their status as male or female, Hispanic or non-Hispanic, and members of various racial groups. The EEOC analyzes those reports to identify patterns of discrimination, which the agency can then attack through class-action lawsuits. Employers must display EEOC posters detailing employment rights. These posters must be in prominent and accessible locations—for example, in a company's cafeteria or near its time clock. Also, employers should retain copies of documents related to employment decisions—recruitment letters, announcements of jobs, completed job applications, selections for training, and so on. Employers must keep these records for at least six months or until a complaint is resolved, whichever is later.

Besides resolving complaints and suing alleged violators, the EEOC issues guidelines designed to help employers determine when their decisions violate the laws enforced by the EEOC. These guidelines are not laws themselves. However, the courts give great consideration to them when hearing employment discrimination cases. For example, the ***Uniform Guidelines on Employee Selection Procedures*** is a set of guidelines issued by the EEOC and other government agencies. The guidelines identify ways an organization should develop and administer its system for selecting employees so as not to violate Title VII. The courts often refer to the *Uniform Guidelines* to determine whether a company has engaged in discriminatory conduct. Similarly, in the *Federal Register*, the EEOC has published guidelines providing details about what the agency will consider illegal and legal in the treatment of disabled individuals under the Americans with Disabilities Act.

Office of Federal Contract Compliance Programs (OFCCP)

The **Office of Federal Contract Compliance Programs (OFCCP)** is the agency responsible for enforcing the executive orders that cover companies doing business with the federal government. As we stated earlier in the chapter, businesses with contracts for more than $50,000 may not discriminate in employment based on race, color, religion, national origin, or sex, and they must have a written affirmative-action plan on file. This plan must include three basic components:

1. *Utilization analysis*—A comparison of the race, sex, and ethnic composition of the employer's workforce with that of the available labor supply. The percentages in the employer's workforce should not be greatly lower than the percentages in the labor supply.
2. *Goals and timetables*—The percentages of women and minorities the organization seeks to employ in each job group, and the dates by which the percentages are to be attained. These are meant to be more flexible than quotas, requiring only that the employer have goals and be seeking to achieve the goals.
3. *Action steps*—A plan for how the organization will meet its goals. Besides working toward its goals for hiring women and minorities, the company must take affirmative steps toward hiring Vietnam veterans and individuals with disabilities.

Each year, the OFCCP audits government contractors to ensure they are actively pursuing the goals in their plans. The OFCCP examines the plan and conducts on-site visits to examine how individual employees perceive the company's affirmative-action policies.

EEO-1 Report
The EEOC's Employer Information Report, which counts employees sorted by job category, sex, ethnicity, and race.

Uniform Guidelines on Employee Selection Procedures
Guidelines issued by the EEOC and other agencies to identify how an organization should develop and administer its system for selecting employees so as not to violate antidiscrimination laws.

Office of Federal Contract Compliance Programs (OFCCP)
The agency responsible for enforcing the executive orders that cover companies doing business with the federal government.

If the agency finds that a contractor or subcontractor is not complying with the requirements, it has several options. It may notify the EEOC (if there is evidence of a violation of Title VII), advise the Department of Justice to begin criminal proceedings, request that the Secretary of Labor cancel or suspend any current contracts with the company, and forbid the firm from bidding on future contracts. For a company that depends on the federal government for a sizable share of its business, that last penalty is severe.

LO 3-4 Describe ways employers can avoid illegal discrimination and provide reasonable accommodation.

Businesses' Role in Providing for Equal Employment Opportunity

Rare is the business owner or manager who wants to wait for the government to identify that the business has failed to provide for equal employment opportunity. Instead, out of motives ranging from concern for fairness to the desire to avoid costly lawsuits and settlements, most companies recognize the importance of complying with these laws. Often, management depends on the expertise of human resource professionals to help in identifying how to comply. These professionals can help organizations take steps to avoid discrimination and provide reasonable accommodation.

Avoiding Discrimination

How would you know if you had been discriminated against? Decisions about human resources are so complex that discrimination is often difficult to identify and prove. However, legal scholars and court rulings have arrived at some ways to show evidence of discrimination.

Disparate Treatment
Differing treatment of individuals, where the differences are based on the individuals' race, color, religion, sex, national origin, age, or disability status.

Disparate Treatment   One potential sign of discrimination is **disparate treatment**—differing treatment of individuals, where the differences are based on the individuals' race, color, religion, sex, national origin, age, or disability status. For example, disparate treatment would include hiring or promoting one person over an equally qualified person because of the individual's race. Or suppose a company fails to hire women with school-age children (claiming the women will be frequently absent) but hires men with school-age children. In that situation, the women are victims of disparate treatment, because they are being treated differently based on their sex. To sustain a claim of discrimination based on disparate treatment, the women would have to prove that the employer intended to discriminate.

To avoid disparate treatment, companies can evaluate the questions and investigations they use in making employment decisions. These should be applied equally. For example, if the company investigates conviction records of job applicants, it should investigate them for all applicants, not just for applicants from certain racial groups. Companies may want to avoid some types of questions altogether. For example, questions about marital status can cause problems, because interviewers may unfairly make different assumptions about men and women. (Common stereotypes about women have been that a married woman is less flexible or more likely to get pregnant than a single woman, in contrast to the assumption that a married man is more stable and committed to his work.)

Evaluating interview questions and decision criteria to make sure they are job related is especially important given that bias is not always intentional or even conscious. Researchers have conducted studies finding differences between what people *say* about how they evaluate others and how people actually *act* on their attitudes. Duke University business professor Ashleigh Shelby Rosette has found various ways to uncover how individuals evaluate the performance of others.[10] In a recent study, she and colleagues compared the way sports reporters interpreted the performance of college quarterbacks—the leaders of football teams. The researchers found that when teams with a white quarterback performed well, the commentators more often gave credit to the intelligence of the quarterback. When the winning teams had a black quarterback, the announcers were more likely to praise the athletic strengths of the quarterback. When teams with a black quarterback lost, the announcers blamed the quarterback's decision making. In prior research, Rosette has found similar patterns in commentary about the leadership of corporations. In describing successful companies led by black managers, analysts more often credit the managers for their good sense of humor or speaking ability or even point to a favorable market rather than crediting the leaders for their intelligence. Notice that the pattern is not to say people consciously think the black leaders lack intelligence; rather, the association between the leader and intelligence simply is not made. These results suggest that even when we doubt we have biases, it may be helpful to use decision-making tools that keep the focus on the most important criteria.

Is disparate treatment ever legal? The courts have held that in some situations, a factor such as sex or religion may be a **bona fide occupational qualification (BFOQ),** that is, a necessary (not merely preferred) qualification for performing a job. A typical example is a job that includes handing out towels in a locker room. Requiring that employees who perform this job in the women's locker room be female is a BFOQ. However, it is very difficult to think of many jobs where criteria such as sex and religion are BFOQs. In a widely publicized case from the 1990s, Johnson Controls, a manufacturer of car batteries, instituted a "fetal protection" policy that excluded women of childbearing age from jobs that would expose them to lead, which can cause birth defects. Johnson Controls argued that the policy was intended to provide a safe work place and that sex was a BFOQ for jobs that involved exposure to lead. However, the Supreme Court disagreed, ruling that BFOQs are limited to policies directly related to a worker's ability to do the job.[11]

Bona Fide Occupational Qualification (BFOQ)
A necessary (not merely preferred) qualification for performing a job.

Disparate Impact   Another way to assess potential discrimination is by identifying **disparate impact**—a condition in which employment practices are seemingly neutral yet disproportionately exclude a protected group from employment opportunities. In other words, the company's employment practices lack obvious discriminatory content, but they affect one group differently than others. Examples of employment practices that might result in disparate impact include pay, hiring, promotions, or training. In the area of hiring, for example, many companies encourage their employees to refer friends and family members for open positions. These referrals can produce a pool of well-qualified candidates who would be a good fit with the organization's culture and highly motivated to work with people they already know. However, given people's tendency to associate with others like themselves, this practice also can have an unintentional disparate impact on groups not already well represented at the employer. Organizations that encourage employee referrals therefore should combine the program with other kinds of recruitment and make sure that every group in the organization is equally encouraged to participate in the referral program.[12] For another example of disparate impact, see "HRM Social."

A commonly used test of disparate impact is the **four-fifths rule**, which finds evidence of potential discrimination if the hiring rate for a minority group is less than four-fifths the hiring rate for the majority group. Keep in mind that this rule of thumb

Disparate Impact
A condition in which employment practices are seemingly neutral yet disproportionately exclude a protected group from employment opportunities.

Four-Fifths Rule
Rule of thumb that provides (or shows) evidence of potential discrimination if an organization's hiring rate for a minority group is less than four-fifths the hiring rate for the majority group.

HRM Social

The Discrimination Risk of Using Social Media in Hiring

At many organizations, the people who make hiring decisions conduct an online search of social media to learn more about candidates. The objective is to gain greater insight into people's character and spot red flags that a person might behave unprofessionally. However, some recent research at Carnegie Mellon University suggests that screening candidates with social media contributes to discriminatory hiring decisions.

The study was an experiment in which the researchers created fictional résumés and social-media profiles and sent the résumés to U.S. businesses that had advertised job openings. All the résumés listed the same qualifications under different names, but the social media hinted that applicants were either Christian or Muslim or that they were either gay or straight. The companies were more likely to call the applicants with the Christian-sounding profiles than the ones

who seemed to be Muslim. Broken down geographically, the difference was statistically significant in some states. The researchers did not find a difference in response rates related to sexual orientation.

The Equal Employment Opportunity Commission has recognized concerns about whether use of social media promotes discriminatory employment decisions. It recently held a meeting to gather information about the issue. Panelists described the need for caution—that employers must be sure the information they gather is related to job qualifications. They also suggested that employers consider using a third-party company to conduct background checks on social media. That agency would report only the job-related information obtained from the background check and omit protected information, such as an employee's religion, health, and pregnancy status.

Questions

1. Explain how the Carnegie Mellon study is an example of disparate impact.
2. For the employee characteristics protected by EEO laws, which could you avoid revealing on a social-media career site such as LinkedIn? Which would be difficult or impossible to avoid disclosing?

Sources: Jon Hyman, "EEOC Holds Public Meeting on Social Media in the Workplace," *Workforce*, March 13, 2014, http://www.workforce.com; Equal Employment Opportunity Commission, "Social Media Is Part of Today's Workplace but Its Use May Raise Employment Discrimination Concerns," news release, March 12, 2014, http://www1.eeoc.gov; Jennifer Valentino-DeVries, "Bosses May Use Social Media to Discriminate against Job Seekers," *Wall Street Journal*, November 20, 2013, http://online.wsj.com.

---

compares *rates* of hiring, not numbers of employees hired. Figure 3.4 illustrates how to apply the four-fifths rule.

If the four-fifths rule is not satisfied, it provides evidence of potential discrimination. To avoid declarations of practicing illegally, an organization must show that the disparate impact caused by the practice is based on a "business necessity." This is accomplished by showing that the employment practice is related to a legitimate business need or goal. Of course, it is ultimately up to the court to decide if the evidence provided by the organization shows a real business necessity or is illegal. The court will also consider if other practices could have been used that would have met the business need or goal but not resulted in discrimination.

An important distinction between disparate treatment and disparate impact is the role of the employer's intent. Proving disparate treatment in court requires showing that the employer intended the disparate treatment, but a plaintiff need not show intent in the case of disparate impact. It is enough to show that the result of the treatment was unequal. For example, the requirements for some jobs, such as firefighters or pilots, have sometimes included a minimum height. Although the intent may be to identify people who can perform the jobs, an unintended result may be disparate impact on groups that are shorter than average. Women tend to

Example: A new hotel has to hire employees to fill 100 positions. Out of 300 total applicants, 200 are black and the remaining 100 are white. The hotel hires 40 of the black applicants and 60 of the white applicants.

Figure 3.4

Applying the Four-Fifths Rule

Step 1: Find the Rates

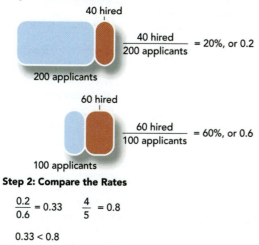

40 hired

200 applicants

$$\frac{40 \text{ hired}}{200 \text{ applicants}} = 20\%, \text{ or } 0.2$$

60 hired

100 applicants

$$\frac{60 \text{ hired}}{100 \text{ applicants}} = 60\%, \text{ or } 0.6$$

Step 2: Compare the Rates

$$\frac{0.2}{0.6} = 0.33 \qquad \frac{4}{5} = 0.8$$

$$0.33 < 0.8$$

The four-fifths requirement is not satisfied, providing evidence of potential discrimination.

be shorter than men, and people of Asian ancestry tend to be shorter than people of European ancestry.

One way employers can avoid disparate impact is to be sure that employment decisions are really based on relevant, valid measurements. If a job requires a certain amount of strength and stamina, the employer would want measures of strength and stamina, not simply individuals' height and weight. The latter numbers are easier to obtain but more likely to result in charges of discrimination. Assessing validity of a measure can be a highly technical exercise requiring the use of statistics. The essence of such an assessment is to show that test scores or other measurements are significantly related to job performance. Some employers are also distancing themselves from information that could be seen as producing a disparate impact. For example, many employers are investigating candidates by looking up their social-media profiles. This raises the possibility that candidates for hiring or promotion could say the company passes them over because of information revealed about, say, their religion or ethnic background. Therefore, some companies hire an outside researcher to check profiles and report only information related to the person's job-related qualifications.[13]

Many employers also address the challenge of disparate impact by analyzing their pay data to look for patterns that could signal unintended discrimination. If they find such patterns, they face difficult decisions about how to correct any inequities. An obvious but possibly expensive option is to increase the lower-paid employees' pay so it is comparable to pay for the higher-paid group. If these pay increases are difficult to afford, the employer could phase in the change gradually. Another way to handle the issue is to keep detailed performance records, because they may explain any pay differences. Finally, to make a pay gap less likely in the future, employers can ensure that lower-paid employees are getting enough training, experience, and support to reach their full potential and earn raises.[14]

HR Oops!

Lack of Rewards May Explain "Leaky Pipeline"

At the biggest U.S. companies, evidence shows increasing levels of diversity among nonmanagement employees. But when researchers measure the percentage of women and minorities at each level of the organization, they find less and less diversity as they move up the hierarchy. In other words, the talent pipeline is leaking women and minorities.

One reason may be that although companies say they want to promote diversity and inclusion, they do not actually reward managers for their performance in this area. According to a poll of executives by Korn Ferry, a recruiting agency, 96% agree that "having a diverse and inclusive workforce can improve employee engagement and business performance." Almost three-quarters said their company has a strategy for promoting diversity and inclusion. However, only about half said their performance appraisals measure how well they promote diversity. Less than one-fourth said any part of their bonus pay is tied to performance on diversity.

Learning to work with people who are different from oneself can take extra energy and insight. Executives are under daily pressure to deliver results. If they are not rewarded for helping diverse employees navigate their career paths—or punished for failing to do so—they might well consider that promoting employees like themselves is the path of least resistance.

Questions

1. How might a bonus related to diversity affect the ways executives promote, train, and develop their employees?
2. What issues of fairness would you need to consider in tying part of an executive's bonus to performance on diversity?

Sources: Dennis McCafferty, "How Diversity Delivers on ROI, Employee Engagement," *CIO Insight,* December 3, 2013, http://www.cioinsight.com; Andrew McIlvaine, "Engaging the C-Suite," *HRE Online,* November 20, 2013, http://www.hreonline.com; Anne Fisher, "Could Bonuses Lead to More Diversity at the Top?" *Fortune,* October 30, 2013, http://management.fortune.cnn.com.

EEO Policy   Employers can also avoid discrimination and defend against claims of discrimination by establishing and enforcing an EEO policy. The policy should define and prohibit unlawful behaviors, as well as provide procedures for making and investigating complaints. The policy also should require that employees at all levels engage in fair conduct and respectful language. Derogatory language can support a court claim of discrimination.

Affirmative Action and Reverse Discrimination   In the search for ways to avoid discrimination, some organizations have used affirmative-action programs, usually to increase the representation of minorities. In its original form, affirmative action was meant as taking extra effort to attract and retain minority employees. These efforts have included extensively recruiting minority candidates on college campuses, advertising in minority-oriented publications, and providing educational and training opportunities to minorities. Such efforts have helped to increase diversity among entry-level employees. Although as the "HR Oops!" box describes, other efforts are needed to promote diversity at the top. Over the years, however, many organizations have resorted to quotas, or numerical goals for the proportion of certain minority groups, to ensure that their workforce mirrors the proportions of the labor market. Sometimes these organizations act voluntarily; in other cases, the quotas are imposed by the courts or the EEOC.

Whatever the reasons for these hiring programs, by increasing the proportion of minority or female candidates hired or promoted, they necessarily reduce the proportion of white or male candidates hired or promoted. In many cases, white and/or male individuals have fought against affirmative action and quotas, alleging what is called *reverse discrimination*. In other words, the organizations are allegedly discriminating against white males by preferring women and minorities. Affirmative action remains controversial in the United States. Surveys have found that Americans are least likely to favor affirmative action when programs use quotas.[15]

Besides going beyond EEO laws to actively recruit women and minorities, some companies go beyond the USERRA's requirement to reemploy workers returning from military service. These companies actively seek returning veterans to hire. In doing so, they are addressing a pressing need in U.S. society. Recent figures show that the unemployment rate for veterans of the wars in Iraq and Afghanistan was recently 9%, which is higher than the overall U.S. rate.[16]

Providing Reasonable Accommodation

Especially in situations involving religion and individuals with disabilities, equal employment opportunity may require that an employer make **reasonable accommodation**. In employment law, this term refers to an employer's obligation to do something to enable an otherwise qualified person to perform a job. Accommodations for an employee's religion often involve decisions about what kinds of clothing to permit or require. Imperial Security ran afoul of discrimination laws when it would not allow a Muslim security guard to wear a *khimar*, a covering for her hair, ears, and neck. When the employee arrived for her first day on the job, she was asked to remove the *khimar*. When she said she couldn't because her religion required it, the company fired her. In contrast, Belk, a retailer, requested that an employee wear a Santa hat and holiday apron during the weeks leading up to Christmas. The employee, a Jehovah's Witness, explained that her religion does not permit her to celebrate holidays, so she would not wear the items. Her company also fired her for not complying with its dress requirements. In both cases, the EEOC filed a lawsuit against the employer and eventually settled for tens of thousands of dollars.[17]

In the context of religion, this principle recognizes that for some individuals, religious observations and practices may present a conflict with work duties, dress codes, or company practices. For example, some religions require head coverings, or individuals might need time off to observe the sabbath or other holy days, when the company might have them scheduled to work. When the employee has a legitimate religious belief requiring accommodation, the employee should demonstrate this need to the employer. Assuming that it would not present an undue hardship, employers are required to accommodate such religious practices. They may have to adjust schedules so that employees do not have to work on days when their religion forbids it, or they may have to alter dress or grooming requirements.

For employees with disabilities, reasonable accommodations also vary according to the individuals' needs. As shown in Figure 3.5, employers may restructure jobs, make facilities in the workplace more accessible, modify equipment, or reassign an employee to a job that the person can perform. In some situations, a disabled individual may provide his or her own accommodation, which the employer allows, as in the case of a blind worker who brings a guide dog to work.

If accommodating a disability would require significant expense or difficulty, however, the employer may be exempt from the reasonable accommodation requirement (although the employer may have to defend this position in court). An accommodation is considered "reasonable" if it does not impose an undue hardship on the employer, such as an expense that is large in relation to a company's resources.

Reasonable Accommodation
An employer's obligation to do something to enable an otherwise qualified person to perform a job.

Figure 3.5

Examples of Reasonable Accommodations under the ADA

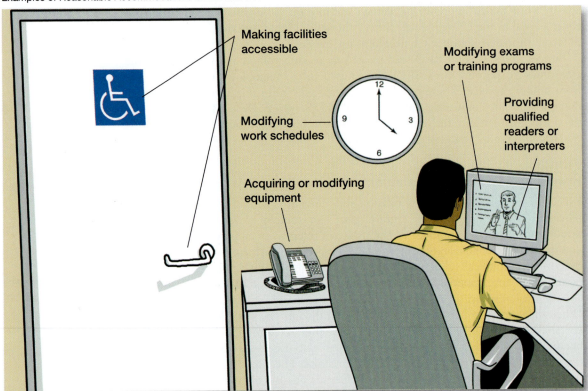

Note: Reasonable accommodations do *not* include hiring an unqualified person, lowering quality standards, or compromising co-workers' safety.

Source: Based on Equal Employment Opportunity Commission, "The ADA: Your Responsibilities as an Employer," modified August 1, 2008, www .eeoc.gov.

LO 3-5 Define sexual harassment, and tell how employers can eliminate or minimize it

Sexual Harassment
Unwelcome sexual advances as defined by the EEOC.

Preventing Sexual Harassment

Based on Title VII's prohibition of sex discrimination, the EEOC defines sexual harassment of employees as unlawful employment discrimination. **Sexual harassment** refers to unwelcome sexual advances. The EEOC has defined the types of behavior and the situations under which this behavior constitutes sexual harassment:

Unwelcome sexual advances, requests for sexual favors, and other verbal or physical contact of a sexual nature constitute sexual harassment when

1. Submission to such conduct is made either explicitly or implicitly a term or condition of an individual's employment,
2. Submission to or rejection of such conduct by an individual is used as the basis for employment decisions affecting such individual, or
3. Such conduct has the purpose or effect of unreasonably interfering with an individual's work performance or creating an intimidating, hostile, or offensive working environment.[18]

Under these guidelines, preventing sexual discrimination includes managing the workplace in a way that does not permit anybody to threaten or intimidate employees through sexual behavior.

In general, the most obvious examples of sexual harassment involve *quid pro quo harassment*, meaning that a person makes a benefit (or punishment) contingent on an employee's submitting to (or rejecting) sexual advances. For example, a manager who promises a raise to an employee who will participate in sexual activities is engaging in quid pro quo harassment. Likewise, it would be sexual harassment to threaten to reassign someone to a less-desirable job if that person refuses sexual favors.

A more subtle, and possibly more pervasive, form of sexual harassment is to create or permit a "hostile working environment." This occurs when someone's behavior in the workplace creates an environment in which it is difficult for someone of a particular sex to work. Common complaints in sexual harassment lawsuits include claims that harassers ran their fingers through the plaintiffs' hair, made suggestive remarks, touched intimate body parts, posted pictures with sexual content in the workplace, and used sexually explicit language or told sex-related jokes. The reason that these behaviors are considered discrimination is that they treat individuals differently based on their sex.

Although a large majority of sexual harassment complaints received by the EEOC involve women being harassed by men, a growing share of sexual harassment claims have been filed by men. Some of the men claimed that they were harassed by women, but same-sex harassment also occurs and is illegal. In one case, a teenager working at McDonald's eventually overcame his embarrassment and reported that a male manager was making sexual comments and had started grabbing him. Three other employees also came forward and filed a complaint with the EEOC. The restaurant settled the lawsuit for $90,000.[19]

To ensure a workplace free from sexual harassment, organizations can follow some important steps. First, the organization can develop a policy statement making it very clear that sexual harassment will not be tolerated in the workplace. Second, all employees, new and old, can be trained to identify inappropriate workplace behavior. In addition, the organization can develop a mechanism for reporting sexual harassment in a way that encourages people to speak out. Finally, management can prepare to act promptly to discipline those who engage in sexual harassment, as well as to protect the victims of sexual harassment.

Valuing Diversity

As we mentioned in Chapter 2, the United States is a diverse nation, and becoming more so. In addition, many U.S. companies have customers and operations in more than one country. Managers differ in how they approach the challenges related to this diversity. Some define a diverse workforce as a competitive advantage that brings them a wider pool of talent and greater insight into the needs and behaviors of their diverse customers. These organizations say they have a policy of *valuing diversity*.

The practice of valuing diversity has no single form; it is not written into law or business theory. Organizations that value diversity may practice some form of affirmative action, discussed earlier. They may have policies stating their value of understanding and respecting differences. Organizations may try to hire, reward, and promote employees who demonstrate respect for others. They may sponsor training programs designed to teach employees about differences among groups. Whatever their form, these efforts are intended to make each individual feel respected. Also, these actions can support equal employment opportunity by cultivating an environment in which individuals feel welcome and able to do their best.

Valuing diversity, especially in support of an organization's mission and strategy, need not be limited to the categories protected by law. For example, many

Organizations that value diversity may try to hire, reward, and promote employees who demonstrate respect for others.

organizations see workers struggling to meet the demands of family and career, so they provide family-friendly benefits and policies, as described in Chapter 14. Managers and human resource professionals also are concerned about learning how to treat transgender employees respectfully and appropriately. Transgender individuals who are transitioning to the opposite sex would typically change their names. This change involves administrative decisions for a human resource department. Some of these—for example, changing e-mail addresses and business cards—are a simple matter of calling employees by the names they wish to use. Typically, organizations already do this when, for example, Rebecca Jones wants to be known as Becky or Paul John Smith wants to be known as P. J. If company policies are too rigid to allow this kind of personal decision, the needs of the transgender employee may prompt a review of the policies. Other aspects of the change must meet legal requirements; for example, the name on tax documents must match the name on the employee's Social Security card, so changing those documents must wait for a legal name change. Even so, employers can respect diversity by demanding no more documentation for name changes in this situation than in other types of name changes (for example, for a woman who wishes to change her name after getting married).[20]

LO 3-6 Explain employers' duties under the Occupational Safety and Health Act

Occupational Safety and Health Act (OSH Act)
U.S. law authorizing the federal government to establish and enforce occupational safety and health standards for all places of employment engaging in interstate commerce.

Occupational Safety and Health Act (OSH Act)

Like equal employment opportunity, the protection of employee safety and health is regulated by the government. Through the 1960s, workplace safety was primarily an issue between workers and employers. By 1970, however, roughly 15,000 work-related fatalities occurred every year. That year, Congress enacted the **Occupational Safety and Health Act (OSH Act)**, the most comprehensive U.S. law regarding worker safety. The OSH Act authorized the federal government to establish and enforce occupational safety and health standards for all places of employment engaging in interstate commerce.

The OSH Act divided enforcement responsibilities between the Department of Labor and the Department of Health. Under the Department of Labor, the **Occupational Safety and Health Administration (OSHA)** is responsible for inspecting employers, applying safety and health standards, and levying fines for violation. The Department of Health is responsible for conducting research to determine the criteria for specific operations or occupations and for training employers to comply with the act. Much of the research is conducted by the National Institute for Occupational Safety and Health (NIOSH).

General and Specific Duties

The main provision of the OSH Act states that each employer has a general duty to furnish each employee a place of employment free from recognized hazards that cause or are likely to cause death or serious physical harm. This is called the act's *general-duty clause.* Employers also must keep records of work-related injuries and illnesses and post an annual summary of these records from February 1 to April 30 in the following year. Figure 3.6 shows a sample of OSHA's Form 300A, the annual summary that must be posted, even if no injuries or illnesses occurred.

The act also grants specific rights; for example, employees have the right to:

- Request an inspection
- Have a representative present at an inspection
- Have dangerous substances identified
- Be promptly informed about exposure to hazards and be given access to accurate records regarding exposure
- Have employer violations posted at the work site

Although OSHA regulations have a (sometimes justifiable) reputation for being complex, a company can get started in meeting these requirements by visiting OSHA's website (**www.osha .gov**) and looking up resources such as the agency's *Small Business Handbook* and its step-by-step guide called "Compliance Assistance Quick Start."

The Department of Labor recognizes many specific types of hazards, and employers must comply with all the occupational safety and health standards published by NIOSH. One area of concern is the illnesses and injuries experienced by emergency response workers who are putting aside concern for themselves as they aid victims of a disaster. The General Accounting Office and Rand Corporation noted that the health of workers responding to the World Trade Center attacks in 2001 was not sufficiently addressed. Despite attempts to learn from the experience, problems occurred again following Hurricane Katrina and the *Deepwater Horizon* oil spill in the Gulf of Mexico. In an effort to improve planning for how to monitor the health and safety of emergency response workers, NIOSH partnered with other federal agencies to develop a set of guidelines for protecting these workers. The guidelines include efforts ahead of emergencies, such as

Occupational Safety and Health Administration (OSHA)
Labor Department agency responsible for inspecting employers, applying safety and health standards, and levying fines for violation.

OSHA is responsible for inspecting businesses, applying safety and health standards, and levying fines for violations. OSHA regulations prohibit notifying employers of inspections in advance.

Figure 3.6
OSHA Form 300A: Summary of Work-Related Injuries and Illnesses

OSHA's Form 300A (Rev. 01/2004)

Summary of Work-Related Injuries and Illnesses

Year 20___

U.S. Department of Labor
Occupational Safety and Health Administration

Form approved OMB no. 1218-0176

All establishments covered by Part 1904 must complete this Summary page, even if no work-related injuries or illnesses occurred during the year. Remember to review the Log to verify that the entries are complete and accurate before completing this summary.

Using the Log, count the individual entries you made for each category. Then write the totals below, making sure you've added the entries from every page of the Log. If you had no cases, write "0."

Employees, former employees, and their representatives have the right to review the OSHA Form 300 in its entirety. They also have limited access to the OSHA Form 301 or its equivalent. See 29 CFR Part 1904.35, in OSHA's recordkeeping rule, for further details on the access provisions for these forms.

Number of Cases

Total number of deaths	Total number of cases with days away from work	Total number of cases with job transfer or restriction	Total number of other recordable cases
(G)	(H)	(I)	(J)

Number of Days

Total number of days away from work	Total number of days of job transfer or restriction
(K)	(L)

Injury and Illness Types

Total number of . . .
(M)
(1) Injuries _____ (4) Poisonings _____
(2) Skin disorders _____ (5) Hearing loss _____
(3) Respiratory conditions _____ (6) All other illnesses _____

Post this Summary page from February 1 to April 30 of the year following the year covered by the form.

Public reporting burden for this collection of information is estimated to average 58 minutes per response, including time to review the instructions, search and gather the data needed, and complete and review the collection of information. Persons are not required to respond to the collection of information unless it displays a currently valid OMB control number. If you have any comments about these estimates or any other aspects of this data collection, contact: US Department of Labor, OSHA Office of Statistical Analysis, Room N-3644, 200 Constitution Avenue, NW, Washington, DC 20210. Do not send the completed forms to this office.

Establishment information

Your establishment name _____

Street _____

City _____ State _____ ZIP _____

Industry description (e.g., Manufacture of motor truck trailers) _____

Standard Industrial Classification (SIC), if known (e.g., 3715) _ _ _ _

OR

North American Industrial Classification (NAICS), if known (e.g., 336212) _ _ _ _ _ _

Employment information (If you don't have these figures, see the Worksheet on the back of this page to estimate.)

Annual average number of employees _____

Total hours worked by all employees last year _____

Sign here

Knowingly falsifying this document may result in a fine.

I certify that I have examined this document and that to the best of my knowledge the entries are true, accurate, and complete.

_____ Company executive Title _____

( ) _____ / /
Phone Date

Source: Occupational Safety and Health Administration, "Injury & Illness Recordkeeping Forms," accessed at https://www.osha.gov.

health screening and safety training of emergency responders, as well as requirements for during and after deployment.[21]

Although NIOSH publishes numerous standards, it is impossible for regulators to anticipate all possible hazards that could occur in the workplace. Thus, the general-duty clause requires employers to be constantly alert for potential sources of harm in the workplace (as defined by the standard of what a reasonably prudent person would do) and to correct them. Information about hazards can come from employees or from outside researchers. The union-backed Center for Construction Research and Training sponsored research into the safety problems related to constructing energy-efficient buildings. The study found that workers in "green" construction faced greater risks of falling and were exposed to new risks from building innovations such as rooftop gardens and facilities for treating wastewater. Employers need to make these construction sites safer through measures such as better fall protection and more use of prefabrication.[22]

Enforcement of the OSH Act

LO 3-7 Describe the role of the Occupational Safety and Health Administration.

To enforce the OSH Act, the Occupational Safety and Health Administration conducts inspections. OSHA compliance officers typically arrive at a workplace unannounced; for obvious reasons, OSHA regulations prohibit notifying employers of inspections in advance. After presenting credentials, the compliance officer tells the employer the reasons for the inspection and describes, in a general way, the procedures necessary to conduct the investigation.

An OSHA inspection has four major components. First, the compliance officer reviews the company's records of deaths, injuries, and illnesses. OSHA requires this kind of record keeping at all firms with 11 or more full- or part-time employees. Next, the officer—typically accompanied by a representative of the employer (and perhaps by a representative of the employees)—conducts a "walkaround" tour of the employer's premises. On this tour, the officer notes any conditions that may violate specific published standards or the less specific general-duty clause. The third component of the inspection, employee interviews, may take place during the tour. At this time, anyone who is aware of a violation can bring it to the officer's attention. Finally, in a closing conference, the compliance officer discusses the findings with the employer, noting any violations.

Following an inspection, OSHA gives the employer a reasonable time frame within which to correct the violations identified. If a violation could cause serious injury or death, the officer may seek a restraining order from a U.S. District Court. The restraining order compels the employer to correct the problem immediately. In addition, if an OSHA violation results in citations, the employer must post each citation in a prominent place near the location of the violation.

Besides correcting violations identified during the inspection, employers may have to pay fines. These fines range from $20,000 for violations that result in death of an employee to $1,000 for less-serious violations. Other penalties include criminal charges for falsifying records that are subject to OSHA inspection or for warning an employer of an OSHA inspection without permission from the Department of Labor.

Employee Rights and Responsibilities

Although the OSH Act makes employers responsible for protecting workers from safety and health hazards, employees have responsibilities as well. They have to follow

OSHA's safety rules and regulations governing employee behavior. Employees also have a duty to report hazardous conditions.

Along with those responsibilities go certain rights. Employees may file a complaint and request an OSHA inspection of the workplace, and their employers may not retaliate against them for complaining. Employees also have a right to receive information about any hazardous chemicals they handle in the course of their jobs. OSHA's Hazard Communication Standard and many states' **right-to-know laws** require employers to provide employees with information about the health risks associated with exposure to substances considered hazardous. State right-to-know laws may be more stringent than federal standards, so organizations should obtain requirements from their state's health and safety agency, as well as from OSHA.

Under OSHA's Hazard Communication Standard, organizations must have **material safety data sheets (MSDSs)** for chemicals that employees are exposed to. An MSDS is a form that details the hazards associated with a chemical; the chemical's producer or importer is responsible for identifying these hazards and detailing them on the form. Employers must also ensure that all containers of hazardous chemicals are labeled with information about the hazards, and they must train employees in safe handling of the chemicals. Office workers who encounter a chemical infrequently (such as a secretary who occasionally changes the toner in a copier) are not covered by these requirements. In the case of a copy machine, the Hazard Communication Standard would apply to someone whose job involves spending a large part of the day servicing or operating such equipment.

Right-to-Know Laws
State laws that require employers to provide employees with information about the health risks associated with exposure to substances considered hazardous.

Material Safety Data Sheets (MSDSs)
Forms on which chemical manufacturers and importers identify the hazards of their chemicals.

Impact of the OSH Act

The OSH Act has unquestionably succeeded in raising the level of awareness of occupational safety. Yet legislation alone cannot solve all the problems of work site safety. Indeed, the rate of occupational illnesses more than doubled between 1985 and 1990, according to the Bureau of Labor Statistics, while the rate of injuries rose by about 8 percent. However, as depicted in Figure 3.7, the combined rate of injuries and illnesses has showed a steady downward trend since then, and illnesses remain a small share of the total, at around 5%.[23] A more troubling trend is an increase in the number of claims of retaliation against employees who report injuries. The data do not indicate whether more employers are actually retaliating, however, or more employees are learning that the law forbids retaliation.[24]

Many industrial accidents are a product of unsafe behaviors, not unsafe working conditions. Because the act does not directly regulate employee behavior, little behavior change can be expected unless employees are convinced of the standards' importance.[25]

Conforming to the law alone does not necessarily guarantee their employees will be safe, so many employers go beyond the letter of the law. In the next section we examine various kinds of employer-initiated safety awareness programs that comply with OSHA requirements and, in some cases, exceed them.

LO 3-8 Discuss ways employers promote worker safety and health.

Employer-Sponsored Safety and Health Programs

Many employers establish safety awareness programs to go beyond mere compliance with the OSH Act and attempt to instill an emphasis on safety. The "Best Practices" box provides an example. A safety awareness program has three primary components: identifying and communicating hazards, reinforcing safe practices, and promoting safety internationally.

Figure 3.7

Rates of Occupational Injuries and Illnesses

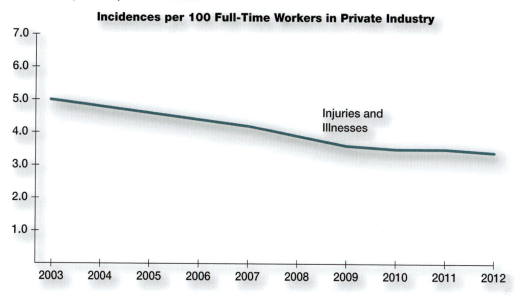

Note: Data do not include fatal work-related injuries and illnesses.

Source: Bureau of Labor Statistics, "Employer-Reported Workplace Injuries and Illnesses, 2012," news release, November 7, 2013, http://www.bls.gov.

Identifying and Communicating Job Hazards

Employees, supervisors, and other knowledgeable sources need to sit down and discuss potential problems related to safety. One method for doing this is the **job hazard analysis technique**.[26] With this technique, each job is broken down into basic elements, and each of these is rated for its potential for harm or injury. If there is agreement that some job element has high hazard potential, the group isolates the element and considers possible technological or behavior changes to reduce or eliminate the hazard. This method poses some special challenges for high-tech companies, where workers may be exposed to materials and conditions that are not yet well understood. An example is nanotechnology, which involves applications of extremely tiny products. Masks and other traditional protective equipment do not necessarily prevent nanoparticles from entering the body, and their impact on health is not known. Some exposures may be harmless, but researchers are only beginning to learn their impact.[27]

Another means of isolating unsafe job elements is to study past accidents. The **technic of operations review (TOR)** is an analysis method for determining which specific element of a job led to a past accident.[28] The first step in a TOR analysis is to establish the facts surrounding the incident. To accomplish this, all members of the work group involved in the accident give their initial impressions of what happened. The group must then, through discussion, come to an agreement on the single, systematic failure that most likely contributed to the incident, as well as two or three major secondary factors that contributed to it.

McShane Construction Company combined job analysis with mobile computing technology when it signed on with Field ID to provide the software for its

Job Hazard Analysis Technique
Safety promotion technique that involves breaking down a job into basic elements, then rating each element for its potential for harm or injury.

Technic of Operations Review (TOR)
Method of promoting safety by determining which specific element of a job led to a past accident.

Best Practices

Morton Salt's Prize-Winning Safety Program

Many of Morton Salt's employees work in one of the most dangerous industries: mining. Even so, the company recently earned a spot on *EHS Today* magazine's list of America's safest companies. The honor was no accident. The company makes safety one of its sustainability goals and actively promotes employee involvement in safe practices.

Morton's safety program involves four main efforts. First, the company directs employees to report to a supervisor any "near misses," or hazards that could cause an accident if ignored. Morton has learned that the more near-miss reports it receives (and responds to), the fewer accidents occur, so it strives for 750 reports each quarter.

The second safety effort is an annual Safety Day held at each facility. Production stops so employees can participate in team building and safety training exercises, with a break for lunch hosted by top managers. Third, Morton invites safety suggestions, which it posts online and distributes via e-mail. Prizes go to employees whose ideas are selected as the best.

Finally, the company participates in OSHA's Voluntary Protection Program (VPP). OSHA approves an application to this program only if the company has demonstrated that it has established corporate-level systems for managing health and safety, implements them effectively, and uses control processes to evaluate each facility's performance at maintaining worker safety and health. Many VPP-certified organizations are federal agencies; Morton was the seventh business to be certified, and as of this writing, only five businesses currently participate.

While VPP certification and a place on *EHS Today*'s list are certainly honors to appreciate, the real accomplishment is the well-being of Morton's employees. Morton periodically celebrates this accomplishment with events for employees whose facilities have passed safety milestones. For example, the facility in Grand Saline, Texas, recently held a banquet to celebrate a million work hours without an accident, and an event in Rittman, Ohio, celebrated that facility's achievement of nine million accident-free hours.

Questions

1. How does Morton Salt's safety program surpass the requirements of the OSH Act?
2. How might a human resource manager at Morton Salt support the company's efforts to promote worker health and safety?

Sources: Morton Salt, "Sustainability," http://www.mortonsalt.com, accessed April 30, 2014; Occupational Safety and Health Administration, "Voluntary Protection Programs: VPP Corporate," https://www.osha.gov, accessed April 30, 2014; "Morton Salt Honors Employees," *Grand Saline (TX) Sun*, March 8, 2014, http://www.grandsalinesun.com; "America's Safest Companies 2013 Protect Workers, Production and Property," *EHS Today*, November 2013, pp. 35–43; "Morton Salt Achieves Prestigious OSHA Award," *Amboy Guardian*, October 4, 2013, http://www.amboyguardian.com; Morton Salt, "More than Nine Million Reasons to Celebrate at Morton Salt," news release, December 13, 2011, http://www.mortonsalt.com.

safety inspections. When safety inspectors visit construction sites, they use a mobile device to scan a bar code or read a radio frequency identification (RFID) tag on each piece of equipment. The code calls up a checklist of safety measures for that equipment, and the inspector simply checks off or scores the items one by one. The mobile device then transmits the inspection data to a Field ID database, where information can easily be retrieved if the company ever needs to study the cause of an accident.[29]

To communicate with employees about job hazards, managers should talk directly with their employees about safety. Memos also are important because the written communication helps establish a "paper trail" that can later document a history of the employer's concern regarding the job hazard. Posters, especially if placed near the hazard, serve as a constant reminder, reinforcing other messages.

In communicating risk, managers should recognize that different groups of individuals may constitute different audiences. Safety trainer Michael Topf often encounters workplaces where employees speak more than one language. In those situations, Topf says, it is important to provide bilingual training and signs. But English skills alone do not guarantee that safety messages will be understood. Supervisors and trainers need to use vocabulary and examples that employees will understand, and they need to ask for feedback in a culturally appropriate way. For example, in some cultures, employees will think it is improper to speak up if they see a problem. It is therefore important for managers to promote many opportunities for communication.[30] Human resource managers can support this effort by providing opportunities for supervisors to learn about the values and communication styles of the cultures represented at work.

Safety concerns and safety training needs also vary by age group. According to the Bureau of Labor Statistics, injuries and illnesses requiring time off from work occurred at the highest rate among workers between the ages of 45 and 54; workers aged 55 to 64 were the next highest group. However, patterns vary according to type of injury. The Centers for Disease Control and Prevention found the highest rates of falls leading to a doctor visit occurring among people older than 75, with the next highest rate being among teenagers. Thus, safety training needs to address the needs of all age groups. Older workers may have more appreciation of the need for safety, as they have experienced the impact of wear and tear on their bodies and perhaps have seen people injured on the job. Younger workers will expect training to be fast-paced and engaging, and if possible, to incorporate technology. One trainer addressed the needs of multiple generations in a session on fall protection. The group reviewed a few slides of background information, then engaged in discussions of actual workplace conditions and planned how to protect workers. Finally, the group tried on the safety equipment required for their jobs.[31]

Reinforcing Safe Practices

To ensure safe behaviors, employers should not only define how to work safely but reinforce the desired behavior. One common technique for reinforcing safe practices is implementing a safety incentive program to reward workers for their support of and commitment to safety goals. Such programs start by focusing on monthly or quarterly goals or by encouraging suggestions for improving safety. Possible goals might include good housekeeping practices, adherence to safety rules, and proper use of protective equipment. Later, the program expands to include more wide-ranging, long-term goals. Typically, the employer distributes prizes in highly public forums, such as company or department meetings. Surprisingly, one of the most obvious ways to reinforce behavior often does not occur: when employees report unsafe conditions or behavior, the employer should take action to correct the problem. This response signals that the organization is serious when it says it values safety. In a recent survey of employees, most said their organization had a policy that encouraged reporting safety concerns, but many said they did not bother because they had come to expect a negative reaction or no response at all.[32]

Besides focusing on specific jobs, organizations can target particular types of injuries or disabilities, especially those for which employees may be at risk. For example, Prevent Blindness America estimates that more than 2,000 eye injuries occur every day in occupational settings.[33] Organizations can prevent such injuries through a

Top 10 Causes of Workplace Injuries

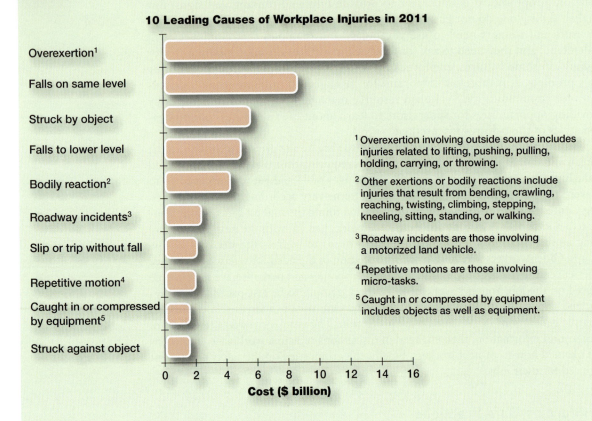

10 Leading Causes of Workplace Injuries in 2011

Causes (top to bottom):
- Overexertion[1]
- Falls on same level
- Struck by object
- Falls to lower level
- Bodily reaction[2]
- Roadway incidents[3]
- Slip or trip without fall
- Repetitive motion[4]
- Caught in or compressed by equipment[5]
- Struck against object

X-axis: Cost ($ billion) — 0, 2, 4, 6, 8, 10, 12, 14, 16

[1] Overexertion involving outside source includes injuries related to lifting, pushing, pulling, holding, carrying, or throwing.

[2] Other exertions or bodily reactions include injuries that result from bending, crawling, reaching, twisting, climbing, stepping, kneeling, sitting, standing, or walking.

[3] Roadway incidents are those involving a motorized land vehicle.

[4] Repetitive motions are those involving micro-tasks.

[5] Caught in or compressed by equipment includes objects as well as equipment.

Every year, Liberty Mutual conducts research it calls the Workplace Safety Index. In 2011, the most recent year for which data is available, serious work-related injuries cost employers more than $55 billion. The leading cause was overexertion (for example, excessive lifting, pushing, carrying, or throwing), followed by falls on the same level (rather than from a height, such as a ladder) and being struck by an object or equipment.

Question

Think about your current job, your most recent job, or the job you would like to have. Which of the categories of injuries shown in the graph are most likely to occur on that job? (Don't assume injuries never occur in office jobs!)

Sources: Liberty Mutual, "2013 Liberty Mutual Workplace Safety Index," http://www.libertymutualgroup.com, accessed April 29, 2014; Langdon Dement, "Employee Injuries Cost US Companies in Excess of a Billion Dollars a Week," *EHS Safety News America*, March 14, 2014, http://ehssafetynews.wordpress.com; Liberty Mutual Research Institute for Safety, "Ten Leading Causes of Disabling Workplace Injuries: 2013 Workplace Safety Index," *From Research to Reality*, Winter 2013–14, pp. 6–7.

combination of job analysis, written policies, safety training, protective eyewear, rewards and sanctions for safe and unsafe behavior, and management support for the safety effort. Similar practices for preventing other types of injuries are available in trade publications, through the National Safety Council, and on the website of the Occupational Safety and Health Administration (**www.osha.gov**).

Promoting Safety Internationally

Given the increasing focus on international management, organizations also need to consider how to ensure the safety of their employees regardless of the nation in which they operate. Cultural differences may make this more difficult than it seems. For example, a study examined the impact of one standardized corporationwide safety policy on employees in three different countries: the United States, France, and Argentina. The results of this study indicate that employees in the three countries interpreted the policy differently because of cultural differences. The individualistic, control-oriented culture of the United States stressed the role of top management in ensuring safety in a top-down fashion. However, this policy failed to work in Argentina, where the culture is more "collectivist" (emphasizing the group). Argentine employees tend to feel that safety is everyone's joint concern, so the safety programs needed to be defined from the bottom of the organization up.[34]

Another challenge in promoting safety internationally is that laws, enforcement practices, and political climates vary from country to country. With the extensive use of offshoring, described in Chapter 2, many companies have operations in countries where labor standards are far less strict than U.S. standards. Managers and employees in these countries may not think the company is serious about protecting workers' health and safety. In that case, strong communication and oversight will be necessary if the company intends to adhere to the ethical principle of valuing its foreign workers' safety as much as the safety of its U.S. workers.

Overseas experience also can provide insights for improving safety at home as well as abroad. Liberty Mutual's Center for Injury Epidemiology (CIE) noticed that during harvest season in Vietnam, people who worked both in agricultural and industrial jobs were injured at far higher rates than those who worked only in one position. The CIE applied that insight to the U.S. workforce and investigated accident rates among employees holding two jobs at the same time. The researchers found much higher accident rates for these workers, both on and off the job. Possible reasons include that they may be less experienced, under more stress, or more poorly trained than employees holding one job.[35] Given that many employers today are hiring people to work part-time, they should consider that these workers may try to hold two jobs and be at greater risk of injury. Training programs and incentives should take that risk into account—for example, with more flexible schedules for safety training.

THINKING ETHICALLY

IS DISCRIMINATION AGAINST THE UNEMPLOYED ETHICAL?

Imagine that your job includes identifying qualified applicants to fill job openings at your company. As you compare two résumés, you see that the applicants' experiences are similar, except that one applicant was working until a month ago, while the other's last job ended a year ago. How will you choose between them?

Reports and some research suggest that some companies are more likely to choose the candidate who was employed until recently. Some job advertisements have even specified that the company will not consider the long-term unemployed. Practical thinking may be behind the practice: if you assume that someone who has been out of work for a long time has been job hunting, you might suspect that other employers have found reasons not to hire him or her. It seems efficient not to repeat the process of uncovering those problems, whatever they might be.

In most states, the practice is legal, despite some efforts to pass laws against it. At the same time, however, it creates conditions that strike many people as unfair and even cruel to those who are already struggling. Following the severe recession of a few years ago, the short-term unemployment rate has returned to levels experienced before the recession. But for those out of work for at least 27 weeks, the unemployment rate is more than twice as high. Working-age men have been hit disproportionately hard, as job losses were severest in male-dominated industries, especially in jobs requiring less than a college education. The share of men no longer even trying to find jobs has been growing, which has implications for society as a whole.

In response to these concerns, volunteers with the Society for Human Resource Management have developed guidelines to encourage hiring policies that do not discriminate "based solely on their unemployment status." The Obama administration urged businesses to pledge not to discriminate against the unemployed, and several hundred have signed the pledge, including Apple, Gap, General Motors, and Walt Disney Company.

Questions

1. If an employer's hiring policies give preference to those who are already employed, what is the impact on (1) the company's performance; (2) workers seeking jobs; and (3) the communities where a company operates? Based on the impact of these policies, would you say they are ethical? Why or why not?
2. Apply the ethical value of fairness to these policies: is it fair to discriminate against the long-term unemployed? Is it fair not to let employers choose employees with a track record of holding a job? What hiring policy best achieves fairness?

Sources: Lisa Guerin, "Discrimination against the Unemployed," Nolo Legal Topics, http://www.nolo.com, accessed April 29, 2014; Mark Peters and David Wessel, "More Men in Prime Working Ages Don't Have Jobs," *Wall Street Journal*, February 5, 2014, http://online.wsj.com; Kathleen Hennessey, "CEOs Pledge Not to Discriminate against Long-Term Unemployed," *Los Angeles Times*, January 31, 2014, http://articles.latimes.com; Bill Leonard, "Obama Urges Employers to Hire the Long-Term Unemployed," *HR News* (Society for Human Resource Management), January 31, 2014, http://www.shrm.org; Matthew Yglesias, "Statistical Discrimination against the Long-Term Unemployed," *Slate*, April 23, 2013, http://www.slate.com.

SUMMARY

LO 3-1 Explain how the three branches of government regulate human resource management.

- The legislative branch develops laws such as those governing equal employment opportunity and worker safety and health.
- The executive branch establishes agencies such as the Equal Employment Opportunity Commission and Occupational Safety and Health Administration to enforce the laws by publishing regulations, filing lawsuits, and performing other activities. The president may also issue executive orders, such as requirements for federal contractors.
- The judicial branch hears cases related to employment law and interprets the law.

LO 3-2 Summarize the major federal laws requiring equal employment opportunity.

- The Civil Rights Acts of 1866 and 1871 grant all persons equal property rights, contract rights, and the right to sue in federal court if they have been deprived of civil rights.
- The Equal Pay Act of 1963 requires equal pay for men and women who are doing work that is equal in terms of skill, effort, responsibility, and working conditions.

- Title VII of the Civil Rights Act of 1964 prohibits employment discrimination on the basis of race, color, religion, sex, or national origin.
- The Age Discrimination in Employment Act prohibits employment discrimination against persons older than 40.
- The Vocational Rehabilitation Act of 1973 requires that federal contractors engage in affirmative action in the employment of persons with disabilities.
- The Vietnam Era Veterans' Readjustment Act of 1974 requires affirmative action in employment of veterans who served during the Vietnam War.
- The Pregnancy Discrimination Act of 1978 treats discrimination based on pregnancy-related conditions as illegal sex discrimination.
- The Americans with Disabilities Act of 1990 requires reasonable accommodations for qualified workers with disabilities.
- The Civil Rights Act of 1991 provides for compensatory and punitive damages in cases of discrimination.
- The Uniformed Services Employment and Reemployment Rights Act of 1994 requires that

employers reemploy service members who left jobs to fulfill military duties.

- The Genetic Information Nondiscrimination Act (GINA) of 2008 forbids employers from using genetic information in making decisions related to the terms, conditions, or privileges of employment.
- Lilly Ledbetter Fair Pay Act of 2009 allows employees to claim discriminatory compensation within a set time after receiving a discriminatory paycheck.

LO 3-3 Identify the federal agencies that enforce equal employment opportunity, and describe the role of each.

- The Equal Employment Opportunity Commission is responsible for enforcing most of the EEO laws, including Title VII and the Americans with Disabilities Act. It investigates and resolves complaints, gathers information, and issues guidelines.
- The Office of Federal Contract Compliance Procedures is responsible for enforcing executive orders that call for affirmative action by companies that do business with the federal government. It monitors affirmative-action plans and takes action against companies that fail to comply.

LO 3-4 Describe ways employers can avoid illegal discrimination and provide reasonable accommodation.

- Employers can avoid discrimination by avoiding disparate treatment of job applicants and employees, as well as policies that result in disparate impact.
- Companies can develop and enforce an EEO policy coupled with policies and practices that demonstrate a high value placed on diversity.
- Affirmative action may correct past discrimination, but quota-based activities can result in charges of reverse discrimination.
- To provide reasonable accommodation, companies should recognize needs based on individuals' religion or disabilities. Accommodations could include adjusting schedules or dress codes, making the workplace more accessible, or restructuring jobs.

LO 3-5 Define sexual harassment, and tell how employers can eliminate or minimize it.

- Sexual harassment is unwelcome sexual advances and related behavior that makes submitting to the conduct a term of employment or the basis for

employment decisions or that interferes with an individual's work performance or creates a work environment that is intimidating, hostile, or offensive.

- Organizations can prevent sexual harassment by developing a policy that defines and forbids it, training employees to recognize and avoid this behavior, and providing a means for employees to complain and be protected.

LO 3-6 Explain employers' duties under the Occupational Safety and Health Act.

- Under the Occupational Safety and Health Act, employers have a general duty to provide employees a place of employment free from recognized safety and health hazards.
- They must inform employees about hazardous substances.
- They must maintain and post records of accidents and illnesses.
- They must comply with NIOSH standards about specific occupational hazards.

LO 3-7 Describe the role of the Occupational Safety and Health Administration.

- The Occupational Safety and Health Administration publishes regulations and conducts inspections.
- If OSHA finds violations, it discusses them with the employer and monitors the employer's response in correcting the violation.

LO 3-8 Discuss ways employers promote worker safety and health.

- Besides complying with OSHA regulations, employers often establish safety awareness programs designed to instill an emphasis on safety.
- They may identify and communicate hazards through the job hazard analysis technique or the technic of operations review.
- They may adapt communications and training to the needs of different employees, such as differences in experience levels or cultural differences from one country to another.
- Employers may also establish incentive programs to reward safe behavior.

KEY TERMS

equal employment opportunity (EEO), 64
Equal Employment Opportunity Commission (EEOC), 66

affirmative action, 68
disability, 69
EEO-1 report, 75

Uniform Guidelines on Employee Selection Procedures, 75

Office of Federal Contract
    Compliance Programs
    (OFCCP), 75
disparate treatment, 76
bona fide occupational qualification
    (BFOQ), 77
disparate impact, 77

four-fifths rule, 77
reasonable accommodation, 81
sexual harassment, 82
Occupational Safety and Health
    Act (OSH Act), 84
Occupational Safety and Health
    Administration (OSHA), 85

right-to-know laws, 88
material safety data sheets
    (MSDSs), 88
job hazard analysis technique, 89
technic of operations review
    (TOR), 89

REVIEW AND DISCUSSION QUESTIONS

1. What is the role of each branch of the federal government with regard to equal employment opportunity? *(LO 3-1)*
2. For each of the following situations, identify one or more constitutional amendments, laws, or executive orders that might apply. *(LO 3-2)*
   a. A veteran of the Vietnam conflict experiences lower-back pain after sitting for extended periods of time. He has applied for promotion to a supervisory position that has traditionally involved spending most of the workday behind a desk.
   b. One of two female workers on a road construction crew complains to her supervisor that she feels uncomfortable during breaks, because the other employees routinely tell off-color jokes.
   c. A manager at an architectural firm receives a call from the local newspaper. The reporter wonders how the firm wishes to respond to calls from two of its employees alleging racial discrimination. About half of the firm's employees (including all of its partners and most of its architects) are white. One of the firm's clients is the federal government.

3. For each situation in the preceding question, what actions, if any, should the organization take? *(LO 3-4)*
4. The Americans with Disabilities Act requires that employers make reasonable accommodations for individuals with disabilities. How might this requirement affect law enforcement officers and firefighters? *(LO 3-4)*
5. To identify instances of sexual harassment, the courts may use a "reasonable woman" standard of what constitutes offensive behavior. This standard is based on the idea that women and men have different ideas of what behavior is appropriate. What are the implications of this distinction? Do you think this distinction is helpful or harmful? Why? *(LO 3-5)*
6. Given that the "reasonable woman" standard referred to in Question 5 is based on women's ideas of what is appropriate, how might an organization with mostly male employees identify and avoid behavior that could be found to be sexual harassment? *(LO 3-5)*
7. What are an organization's basic duties under the Occupational Safety and Health Act? *(LO 3-6)*
8. OSHA penalties are aimed at employers, rather than employees. How does this affect employee safety? *(LO 3-7)*
9. How can organizations motivate employees to promote safety and health in the workplace? *(LO 3-8)*
10. For each of the following occupations, identify at least one possible hazard and at least one action employers could take to minimize the risk of an injury or illness related to that hazard. *(LO 3-8)*
    a. Worker in a fast-food restaurant
    b. Computer programmer
    c. Truck driver
    d. House painter

TAKING RESPONSIBILITY

Keeping Sprint's Subcontractors Safe

Recently, a worker on a Sprint communication tower in North Carolina fell about 200 feet to his death after unsuccessfully trying to attach his safety harness to the tower. The same month, in Oregon, a worker at a Sprint tower was critically injured when the aerial lift he was in tipped over. A few months after that, a man working on a Sprint cell network installed on a water tower in Maryland fell 180 feet and died.

Sadly, those incidents were not isolated but part of a larger pattern of accidents affecting communication tower workers. In 2008, after 18 tower workers were killed in accidents, the Occupational Safety and Health Administration called this industry the most dangerous in the United States, because it had the highest rate of accidents. The industry is small, with only about 10,000 workers. The rate dropped the following year but spiked again in 2013 as cell phone service providers pushed hard to upgrade their networks faster than the competition. Sprint, for example, has been engaged in an ambitious program to upgrade all of its 38,000 towers. Of the 19 fatal accidents reported to OSHA, 17 involved towers for mobile-phone networks; 4 of these involved Sprint sites.

OSHA responded by investigating the accidents and trying to change what it considers an ineffective approach to safety in the industry. The agency announced that as it studies accident data, it will identify which mobile networks were involved, regardless of whether the workers were employees or contractors. OSHA is concerned that because carriers usually line up contractors to work on their towers, company management is not invested enough in the workers' safety. The agency sent all businesses in the industry a letter indicating they could be held accountable if they do not insist in their contracts that workers follow safe procedures. It also directed businesses to consider safety criteria in choosing contractors. In addition, OSHA assigned its employees to inspect all worksites they encounter involving communication towers, because tower work is too short-term for problems to be caught with random inspections.

Initial reports suggest that what pushed aside concern for safety was the industry's ambitious drive to improve networks. Workers reportedly have been on the job for 12 to 16 hours at a time, rarely taking a day off to rest. Employees acknowledge that they are responsible for following safety rules, but some point out the difficulty of taking all precautions while under pressure to work fast. Investigators have found evidence of poor safety training, improper equipment, and intense time pressure. OSHA inspections reveal that workers often are not properly protected from falling. The National Association of Tower Erectors (NATE), a trade association, shares OSHA's concern. NATE has developed safety guidelines and checklists, which it encourages its members to use as part of creating a culture of safety. One NATE member, U.S. Cellular, has been requiring that all tower contractors be members of NATE, as a way to ensure they are well qualified to operate safely.

Sprint insists that safety is a top priority. The company says it requires contractors to have a written safety program and put someone in charge of safety at each worksite. Sprint has stepped up its efforts to ensure that workers, even those employed by contractors, are safe. The company hired PICS Auditing to review its contractors' safety performance, including accident rates, training programs, and the content of their safety manuals.

Questions

1. What responsibility do you think Sprint has to the employees of subcontractors working on its communication towers? How well is it meeting that responsibility?
2. Beyond the steps Sprint says it has taken, what else could it do to meet or exceed OSHA requirements to protect worker safety at its communication towers?

Sources: Liz Day, "Feds to Look Harder at Cell Carriers When Tower Climbers Die," *Frontline*, April 1, 2014, http://www.pbs.org; David Michaels, letter to communication tower industry employers, Occupational Health and Safety Administration, February 10, 2014, https://www.osha.gov; Glenn Bischoff, "It's Been a Tough Year for Tower Safety," *Urgent Communications*, September 19, 2013, http://urgentcomm.com; Phil Goldstein, "Spike in Cell Tower Worker Deaths Prompts Fresh Concern," *Fierce Wireless*, August 22, 2013, http://www.fiercewireless.com; Ryan Knutson, "A New Spate of Deaths in the Wireless Industry," *Wall Street Journal*, August 21, 2013, http://online.wsj.com; Occupational Safety and Health Administration, "Communication Towers," Safety and Health Topics, https://www.osha.gov.

MANAGING TALENT

Walmart's Struggle to Manage Diversity and Safety on a Grand Scale

Walmart drew national attention when it announced an initiative it calls the Veterans Welcome Home Commitment. Under that policy, any veteran who has been honorably discharged from the U.S. military and applies to work at Walmart within 12 months of being discharged is guaranteed a job, assuming he or she passes a drug test and background check. The company said it expected to hire more than 100,000 veterans over five years under the program. Walmart U.S. chief executive Bill Simon pointed out that this serves a practical as well as patriotic purpose: "Veterans have a record of performance under pressure," as well as being "quick learners" and "team players."

For Walmart, hiring veterans is just one way it lives out its mission of "Making better possible." That includes helping shoppers save money, but also enabling people to work in a fair and honest environment. The company teaches four beliefs: service to customers, respect for individuals, striving for excellence, and acting with integrity. At its headquarters, respect for others is expressed in a festive environment at an annual Cultural World Fair, where employees representing different ethnic backgrounds share food and the arts with one another. Employees in the corporate offices also can find sympathetic colleagues by joining resource groups such as UNITY, the African American resource group, and Pride, a group for lesbian, gay, bisexual, and transgender employees and their allies.

These principles, as well as policies such as hiring veterans, have a large impact, because Walmart operates on a massive scale. The company employs 2.2 million people in more than two dozen countries around the world. Principles such as valuing diversity affect more than a million workers in the United States alone. In the case of hiring veterans, the 20,000 veterans hired per year is a huge number but account for only about 4% of Walmart's new U.S. employees. The disadvantage is that spreading a value such as equal opportunity is difficult to do in such a large organization, where many personnel decisions are made at the individual-store level.

Evidence for the difficulty comes from the variety of complaints made to the Equal Employment Opportunity Commission, as well as the resulting lawsuits and settlements. In one recent settlement, Walmart paid more than $360,000 after store managers failed to stop an employee from sexually harassing an intellectually disabled coworker for several years. In another, the company paid $87,500 after a store refused to hire a brother and sister whose mother previously had charged the company with sex discrimination. The EEOC found that the store's decision was retaliation against the mother. In yet another case, the EEOC sued Wal-Mart Stores of Texas for violating the Age Discrimination in Employment Act for harassing and eventually firing a 54-year-old manager who had requested accommodation for his diabetes. And the agency recently sued Wal-Mart Stores East when the management of a Maryland store refused to authorize a saliva drug test for a job applicant who had end-stage renal disease and therefore could not take a urine test.

These complaints are a contrast from corporate policy and publicity. Walmart notes that more than half of the promotions granted to hourly workers in its stores go to women. At headquarters, the company recently announced a 40 percent increase in the number of women holding top executive positions. For human resource managers, the question is how to build on these successes and help spread fair employment practices throughout the entire organization.

Questions

1. In what ways is Walmart trying to meet legal requirements for equal employment opportunity? In what ways do its actions exceed legal requirements?
2. What could Walmart's HR managers do to help the company improve its performance in complying with EEO laws?

Sources: Walmart, "Working at Walmart," http://careers.walmart.com, accessed April 29, 2014; Equal Employment Opportunity Commission (EEOC), "Wal-Mart to Pay $363,419 to Settle EEOC Sexual Harassment and Retaliation Suit," news release, March 25, 2014, http://www1.eeoc.gov; EEOC, "EEOC Sues Wal-Mart Stores East for Disability Discrimination," news release, March 21, 2014, http://www1.eeoc.gov; Kevin McGuinness, "EEOC Sues Wal-Mart for Age Discrimination," *PlanSponsor*, March 12, 2014, http://www.plansponsor.com; EEOC, "Wal-Mart to Pay $87,500 to Settle EEOC Suit for Unlawful Retaliation," news release, January 27, 2014, http://www1.eeoc.gov; "Leadership Team Shows Diversity," MMR, December 9, 2013, Business Insights: Global, http://bi.galegroup.com; Kim Souza, "Wal-Mart's Home Office Celebrates Diversity," *City Wire*, September 19, 2013, http://www.thecitywire.com; Saabira Chaudhuri, "Wal-Mart Unveils Plans to Offer Jobs to Veterans; Boost Domestic Sourcing by $50 Billion," *Wall Street Journal*, January 16, 2013, http://online.wsj.com; Christopher Matthews, "Is Walmart's Buy American/Hire Veterans Initiative Anything More Than a PR Stunt?" *Time*, January 15, 2013, http://business.time.com; James Dao, "Wal-Mart Plans to Hire Any Veteran Who Wants a Job," *New York Times*, January 14, 2013, http://www.nytimes.com.

HR IN SMALL BUSINESS

Company Fails Fair-Employment Test

Companies have to comply with federal as well as state and local laws. One company that didn't was Professional Neurological Services (PNS), which was cited by the Chicago Commission on Human Relations when it discriminated against an employee because she is a parent. Chicago is one of a few cities that prohibit this type of discrimination.

The difficulties began with employee Dena Lockwood as soon as she was interviewing for a sales position with PNS. The interviewer noticed that Lockwood made a reference to her children, and he asked her if her responsibilities as a parent would "prevent her from working 70 hours a week." Lockwood said no, but the job offer she received suggests that the interviewer had his doubts. According to Lockwood's later complaint, female sales reps without children routinely were paid a $45,000 base salary plus a 10% commission. Lockwood was offered $25,000 plus the 10% commission. Lockwood negotiated and eventually accepted $45,000 plus 5%, with a promise to increase the commission rate to

10% when she reached sales of $300,000. She was also offered five vacation days a year; when she objected, she was told not to worry.

Lockwood worked hard and eventually reached her sales goal. Then the company raised the requirement for the higher commission rate, and the situation took a turn for the worse. Lockwood's daughter woke up one morning with pink-eye, a highly contagious ailment. Lockwood called in to reschedule a meeting for that day, but her manager told her not to bother; she was being fired. When Lockwood asked why, the manager said "it just wasn't working out."

She went to the Chicago Human Relations Commission for help. The commission investigated and could find no evidence of performance-related problems that would justify her dismissal. Instead, the commission found that Lockwood was a victim of "blatant" discrimination against employees with children and awarded her $213,000 plus attorney's fees—a hefty fine for a

company with fewer than 50 employees. PNS stated that it would appeal the decision.

Questions

1. Why do you think "parental discrimination" was the grounds for this complaint instead of a federally protected class? Could you make a case for discrimination on the basis of sex? Why or why not?
2. How could Professional Neurological Services have avoided this problem?
3. Imagine that the company has called you in to help it hold down human resources costs, including costs of lawsuits such as this one. What advice would you give? How can the company avoid discrimination and still build an efficient workforce?

Sources: Courtney Rubin, "Single Mother Wins $200,000 in Job Bias Case," *Inc.*, January 25, 2010, www.inc.com; Ameet Sachdev, "She Took a Day Off to Care for Sick Child, Got Fired," *Chicago Tribune*, January 24, 2010, NewsBank, http://infoweb.newsbank.com.

NOTES

1. Michael Martinez and Lindy Hall, "Steve Ballmer Now Owns NBA's Clippers for Record $2 Billion," *CNN*, August 12, 2014, http://www.cnn.com; Ben Bolch, "Donald Sterling Sanctioned: Adam Silver Moves to Eject Clippers Owner," *Los Angeles Times*, April 29, 2014, http://www.latimes.com; "Full Transcript of Adam Silver on Donald Sterling Ban," *USA Today*, April 29, 2014, http://www.usatoday.com; Ashby Jones, "NBA's Decision against Clippers' Owner: Is It Legal?" *Wall Street Journal*, April 29, 2014, http://blogs.wsj.com.
2. *Bakke v. Regents of the University of California*, 17 F.E.P.C. 1000 (1978).
3. Equal Employment Opportunity Commission, "Understanding Waivers of Discrimination Claims in Employee Severance Agreements," http://www.eeoc.gov, accessed February 14, 2012; Equal Employment Opportunity Commission, "Age Discrimination," http://www1.eeoc.gov, accessed February 14, 2012.
4. Equal Employment Opportunity Commission, "EEOC Sues Hutchinson Sealing Systems for Age Discrimination," news release, January 20, 2012, http://www1.eeoc.gov.
5. "Age Shall Not Wither Them," *The Economist*, April 9, 2011, EBSCOhost, http://web.ebscohost.com.
6. Equal Employment Opportunity Commission, "Pregnancy Discrimination," http://www1.eeoc.gov, accessed February 14, 2012.
7. Equal Employment Opportunity Commission, "Facts about the Americans with Disabilities Act," http://www1.eeoc.gov//eeoc/publications/, accessed March 3, 2010; Equal Employment Opportunity Commission, "Notice Concerning the Americans with Disabilities Act (ADA) Amendments Act of 2008," http://www1.eeoc.gov, accessed February 14, 2012.
8. Equal Employment Opportunity Commission, "Questions and Answers for Small Businesses: The Final Rule Implementing the ADA Amendments Act of 2008," http://www1.eeoc.gov, accessed February 20, 2012, University of New Hampshire Human Resources, "Americans with Disabilities Act, as Amended 2008 (ADAAA)," http://www.unh.edu/hr/ada.htm, accessed February 20, 2012.
9. Jenell L. S. Wittmer and Leslie Wilson, "Turning Diversity into Dollars: A Business Case for Hiring People with Disabilities," *T + D*, February 2010, pp. 58–61; Office of Disability Employment Policy, "Disability Employment Policy Resources by Topic," http://www.dol.gov/odep/, accessed February 20, 2012.
10. Melissa Korn, "Race Influences How Leaders Are Assessed," *The Wall Street Journal*, January 3, 2012, http://online.wsj.com; Katherine W. Phillips, "Transparent Barriers," *Kellogg Insight* (Kellogg School of Management), November 2008, http://insight.kellogg.northwestern.edu.
11. *UAW v. Johnson Controls, Inc.*, 499 U.S. 187 (1991).
12. Karen Burke, "Referrals and Diversity, Transgender Name Changes, Termination Meeting Pay," *HR Magazine*, November 2011, pp. 27–8.
13. Anne Fisher, "Checking Out Job Applicants on Facebook? Better Ask a Lawyer," *Fortune*, March 2, 2011, http://management.fortune.cnn.com.
14. Bureau of National Affairs, "HR Pros Believe Gender Pay Gaps Exist—but What to Do about It?" *Report on Salary Surveys*, April 2011, pp. 1–8; Joann S. Lublin, "Coaching Urged for Women," *Wall Street Journal*, April 4, 2011, http://online.wsj.com; Conor Dougherty, "Strides by Women, Still a Wage Gap," *Wall Street Journal*, March 1, 2011, http://online.wsj.com.
15. D. Kravitz and J. Platania, "Attitudes and Beliefs about Affirmative Action: Effects of Target and of Respondent Sex and Ethnicity," *Journal of Applied Psychology* 78 (1993), pp. 928–38.
16. Bureau of Labor Statistics, "Employment Situation of Veterans, 2013," news release, March 20, 2014, http://www.bls.gov.

17. Equal Employment Opportunity Commission, "Imperial Security Will Pay $50,000 to Settle EEOC Religious Discrimination Lawsuit," news release, November 23, 2011, http://www1.eeoc.gov; Equal Employment Opportunity Commission, "Belk, Inc. to Pay $55,000 to Settle EEOC Religious Discrimination Suit," news release, March 16, 2011, http://www1.eeoc.gov.

18. EEOC guideline based on the Civil Rights Act of 1964, Title VII.

19. Dana Mattioli, "More Men Make Harassment Claims," *The Wall Street Journal*, March 23, 2010, http://online.wsj.com; Equal Employment Opportunity Commission, "Sexual Harassment Charges: EEOC and FEPAs Combined, FY1997–FY2011," http://www1.eeoc.gov, accessed February 15, 2012.

20. Burke, "Referrals and Diversity," p. 28.

21. John A. Decker, Renée Funk, and D. Gayle DeBord, "Conducting Responder Health Research and Biomonitoring during and following Disasters," *NIOSH Science Blog*, October 18, 2013, http://blogs.cdc.gov; Centers for Disease Control and Prevention, "Emergency Responder Health Monitoring and Surveillance (ERHMS)," last updated July 31, 2012, http://www.cdc.gov/niosh.

22. Laura Walter, "'Green' Construction Workers May Face Additional Safety Risks," *EHS Today*, November 30, 2011, http://www.ehstoday.com.

23. Bureau of Labor Statistics, "Employer-Reported Workplace Injuries and Illnesses, 2012," news release, November 7, 2013, http://www.bls.gov.

24. James R. Hagerty, "Workplace Injuries Drop, but Claims of Employer Retaliation Rise," *Wall Street Journal*, July 22, 2013, http://online.wsj.com.

25. J. Roughton, "Managing a Safety Program through Job Hazard Analysis," *Professional Safety* 37 (1992), pp. 28–31.

26. Roughton, "Managing a Safety Program"; "The Basics of Job Hazard Analysis," *Safety Compliance Letter*, September 2013, Business Insights: Global, http://bi.galegroup.com.

27. Duncan Graham-Rowe, "Is Nanotechnology Safe in the Workplace?" *Guardian*, February 13, 2012, http://www.guardian.co.uk; Jennifer L. Topmiller and Kevin H. Dunn, "Controlling Exposures to Workers Who Make or Use Nanomaterials," *NIOSH Science Blog*, December 9, 2013, http://blogs.cdc.gov.

28. R. G. Hallock and D. A. Weaver, "Controlling Losses and Enhancing Management Systems with TOR Analysis," *Professional Safety* 35 (1990), pp. 24–6.

29. Field ID, "McShane Construction Selects Field ID to Enhance Worksite Safety and Quality Assurance," news release, October 11, 2011, http://www.fieldid.com; Field ID, "What Is Field ID?" http://www.fieldid.com, accessed February 21, 2012.

30. Jill Jusko, "Meeting the Safety Challenge of a Diverse Workforce," *Industry Week*, December 2011, p. 14.

31. Anthony Geise, "The Barriers to Effective Safety Training: Finding Training Techniques That Bridge Generation Gaps," *EHS Today*, October 2011, pp. 72–6; Bureau of Labor Statistics, "Nonfatal Occupational Injuries and Illnesses Requiring Days Away from Work, 2010," news release, November 9, 2011, http://www.bls.gov; Centers for Disease Control and Prevention, "QuickStats: Rate of Nonfatal, Medically Consulted Fall Injury Episodes, by Age Group," *Morbidity and Mortality Weekly*, February 3, 2012, http://www.cdc.gov.

32. Phillip Ragain, Ron Ragain, Michael Allen, and Mike Allen, "A Study of Safety Intervention: The Causes and Consequences of Employees' Silence," *EHS Today*, July 2011, pp. 36–8.

33. Prevent Blindness America, "Eye Safety at Work," http://www.preventblindness.org, accessed April 29, 2014; American Optometric Association, "Protecting Your Eyes at Work," Patients and Public: Caring for Your Vision, http://www.aoa.org, accessed April 29, 2014.

34. M. Janssens, J. M. Brett, and F. J. Smith, "Confirmatory Cross-Cultural Research: Testing the Viability of a Corporation-wide Safety Policy," *Academy of Management Journal* 38 (1995), pp. 364–82.

35. Liberty Mutual Research Institute for Safety (RIS), "Multiple Job Holding: Present-Day Reality Raises New Questions," *From Research to Reality*, Winter 2013–14, p. 3; RIS, "Research Focus: Does Multiple Job Holding Increase Risk of Injury?" *From Research to Reality*, Winter 2013–14, pp. 4–5.

Analyzing Work and Designing Jobs

What Do I Need to Know?

After reading this chapter, you should be able to:

LO 4-1 Summarize the elements of work flow analysis.

LO 4-2 Describe how work flow is related to an organization's structure.

LO 4-3 Define the elements of a job analysis, and discuss their significance for human resource management.

LO 4-4 Tell how to obtain information for a job analysis.

LO 4-5 Summarize recent trends in job analysis.

LO 4-6 Describe methods for designing a job so that it can be done efficiently.

LO 4-7 Identify approaches to designing a job to make it motivating.

LO 4-8 Explain how organizations apply ergonomics to design safe jobs.

LO 4-8 Discuss how organizations can plan for the mental demands of a job.

Introduction

As workers master new technology, they are sometimes surprised to find that old ways of doing business still matter. An example is using the telephone. So much communication has shifted to texting and sending e-mail that many people who grew up with mobile devices feel uncomfortable about picking up the phone and talking. Patty Baxter noticed this in the sales office of her company, Metro Guide Publishing. The room used to be filled with the chatter of employees asking businesspeople to buy ads, but they had switched to the more comfortable task of sending out e-mails to potential clients. However, this new approach didn't work as well. E-mail was less effective for building customer relationships, and employees sometimes misinterpreted prospects' needs and intentions. Baxter hired a trainer to build her employees' telephone skills and confidence. She also modified their jobs by providing scripts for voice messages and adding the requirement that they keep records of the way they contact each client.

The trainer that Baxter hired for Metro Guide is not alone in noticing that more employees are uncomfortable with using the phone. A trainer at a utility company recently recalled teaching an employee the technical features of a desktop telephone—for example, the dial tone and absence of a Send button. But at least as important as knowing devices' technical features is skill at using one's voice, both on and off the phone. Recent research supports the idea that a person's tone of voice affects the impression he or she makes. When subjects are asked to rate people based on recordings of their voices, they form negative opinions of people who speak in breathy, rough, strained, or weak tones. Another habit that creates a negative impression is ending sentences in a rising voice, as if asking a question. Fortunately for individuals with these speaking styles, clear and pleasant speech is a skill people can learn.[1]

Metro Guide Publishing earns money by selling ads to local businesses, so it needs strong relationships with many different companies. That need gives rise to knowledge of the kinds of skills and work habits employees must provide, such as the ability to speak and listen well over the phone. Consideration of such elements is at the heart of analyzing work, whether in a start-up enterprise, a multinational corporation, or a government agency.

This chapter discusses the analysis and design of work and, in doing so, lays out some considerations that go into making informed decisions about how to create and link jobs. The chapter begins with a look at the big-picture issues related to analyzing work flow and organizational structure. The discussion then turns to the more specific issues of analyzing and designing jobs. Traditionally, job analysis has emphasized the study of existing jobs in order to make decisions such as employee selection, training, and compensation. In contrast, job design has emphasized making jobs more efficient or more motivating. However, as this chapter shows, the two activities are interrelated.

LO 4-1 Summarize the elements of work flow analysis.

Work Flow Design
The process of analyzing the tasks necessary for the production of a product or service.

Job
A set of related duties.

Position
The set of duties (job) performed by a particular person.

Work Flow in Organizations

Informed decisions about jobs take place in the context of the organization's overall work flow. Through the process of **work flow design**, managers analyze the tasks needed to produce a product or service. With this information, they assign these tasks to specific jobs and positions. (A **job** is a set of related duties. A **position** is the set of duties performed by one person. A school has many teaching *positions;* the person filling each of those positions is performing the *job* of teacher.) Basing these decisions on work flow design can lead to better results than the more traditional practice of looking at jobs individually.

Work Flow Analysis

Before designing its work flow, the organization's planners need to analyze what work needs to be done. Figure 4.1 shows the elements of a work flow analysis. For each type of work, such as producing a product line or providing a support service (accounting, legal support, and so on), the analysis identifies the output of the process, the activities involved, and the three categories of inputs (materials and information, equipment, and human resources).

Outputs are the products of any work unit, say, a department or team. Outputs may be tangible, as in the case of a restaurant meal or finished part. They may be intangible, such as building security or an answered question about employee benefits. In identifying the outputs of particular work units, work flow analysis considers both quantity and quality. Thinking in terms of these outputs gives HRM professionals a clearer view of how to increase each work unit's effectiveness.

Work flow analysis next considers the *work processes* used to generate the outputs identified. Work processes are the activities that a work unit's members engage in to produce a given output. They are described in terms of operating procedures for every task performed by each employee at each stage of the process. Specifying the processes

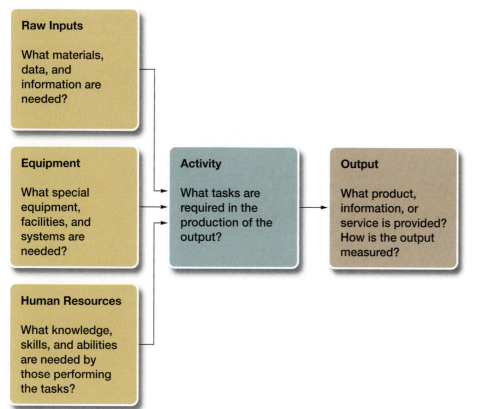

Figure 4.1
Developing a Work Flow Analysis

helps HRM professionals design efficient work systems by clarifying which tasks are necessary. Knowledge of work processes also can guide staffing changes when work is automated, outsourced, or restructured.

Finally, work flow analysis identifies the *inputs* required to carry out the work processes. As shown in Figure 4.1, inputs fall into three categories: raw inputs (materials and information), equipment, and human resources (knowledge, skills, and abilities). In the advertising industry, for example, technology has changed the relative importance of inputs. The stars of the ad business used to be the creative minds who dreamed up messages for television ads that would get people talking (and buying). But as consumers turn their attention to digital media, ad agencies need people who understand the latest in social media and who can not only generate a stream of messages but also can measure the reactions streaming back from consumers. Data and skill in analyzing data are today's hotly demanded inputs for advertising.[2] Another way to understand the importance of identifying inputs is to consider what can go wrong. The "HR Oops!" box illustrates that if an organization's outputs fall short of goals, HR managers might find that the cause is a failure in planning for inputs.

Work Flow Design and an Organization's Structure

Work flow takes place in the context of an organization's structure. It requires the cooperation of individuals and groups. Ideally, the organization's structure brings together the people who must collaborate to create the desired outputs efficiently. The structure may do this in a way that is highly centralized (that is, with authority

LO 4-2 Describe how work flow is related to an organization's structure.

Workers Often Don't Have What They Need to Succeed

Work flow analysis spells out the human and other resources needed for carrying out well-defined tasks that will meet objectives. Success requires the right people with access to resources including equipment and information. However, research suggests that some of these inputs may be missing at many organizations.

In a survey of more than 500 U.S. workers in different industries, At-Task, a maker of project management software, found that large numbers of workers are struggling to meet objectives on time—if they even know what their objectives are. According to AtTask, 60% of the workers said they are completely overwhelmed or barely meeting deadlines.

Responses to other questions in the survey point to some possible causes. One-third of the workers said they are unable to turn in assignments on time because some resources they need are not available. Even more (about 50%) say their organizations do not have enough people to get all the necessary tasks finished unless people work overtime. More than a third of them say they are only somewhat, a little, or not clear about desired outputs— how their work is measured or how their supervisor defines success.

Questions

1. What consequences might an organization expect to result

from the conditions described by the AtTask survey?
2. How might an organization use work flow analysis to prevent some of these problems?

Sources: AtTask, "2013 AtTask State of Work Survey: Executive Summary," http://www.attask.com, accessed May 6, 2014; Dennis McCafferty, "Projects Suffer from Lack of Staffing, Resources," *CIO Insight*, December 19, 2013, http://www.cioinsight.com; AtTask, "AtTask Survey: Workers Overwhelmed by Deadlines Blame Lack of Focus and Constant Interruptions," news release, November 14, 2013, http://www.attask.com.

concentrated in a few people at the top of the organization) or decentralized (with authority spread among many people). The organization may group jobs according to functions (for example, welding, painting, packaging), or it may set up divisions to focus on products or customer groups.

Although there are an infinite number of ways to combine the elements of an organization's structure, we can make some general observations about structure and work design. If the structure is strongly based on function, workers tend to have low authority and to work alone at highly specialized jobs. Jobs that involve teamwork or broad responsibility tend to require a structure based on divisions other than functions. When the goal is to empower employees, companies then need to set up structures and jobs that enable broad responsibility, such as jobs that involve employees in serving a particular group of customers or producing a particular product, rather than performing a narrowly defined function. The organization's structure also affects managers' jobs. Managing a division responsible for a product or customer group tends to require more experience and cognitive (thinking) ability than managing a department that handles a particular function. In contrast, managing a functional department requires skill in managing conflicts and aligning employees' efforts with higher-level goals, because these employees tend to identify heavily with their department or profession.[3]

Work design often emphasizes the analysis and design of jobs, as described in the remainder of this chapter. Although all of these approaches can succeed, each focuses on one isolated job at a time. These approaches do not necessarily consider how that single job fits into the overall work flow or structure of the organization. To use these techniques effectively, human resource personnel should also understand their organization as a whole.

For example, Procter & Gamble traditionally gives each product division a great deal of control over its activities. Thus, research and development for a product line was the responsibility of the division controlling that line. But when consumers responded to difficult economic times by spending less on P&G's brand-name consumer goods, each division tightened its research budget to the point that the company overall was not spending enough to develop new ideas. The company's top leaders decided to restructure work by making R&D a corporate-wide function so they could concentrate resources on ideas that would have the most impact on the company's overall performance.[4]

Job Analysis

To achieve high-quality performance, organizations have to understand and match job requirements and people. This understanding requires **job analysis**, the process of getting detailed information about jobs. Analyzing jobs and understanding what is required to carry out a job provide essential knowledge for staffing, training, performance appraisal, and many other HR activities. For instance, a supervisor's evaluation of an employee's work should be based on performance relative to job requirements. In very small organizations, line managers may perform a job analysis, but usually the work is done by a human resource professional. A large company may have a compensation management department that includes job analysts (also called personnel analysts). Organizations may also contract with firms that provide this service.

Job Descriptions

An essential part of job analysis is the creation of job descriptions. A **job description** is a list of the tasks, duties, and responsibilities (TDRs) that a job entails. TDRs are observable actions. For example, a news photographer's job requires the jobholder to use a camera to take photographs. If you were to observe someone in that position for a day, you would almost certainly see some pictures being taken. When a manager attempts to evaluate job performance, it is most important to have detailed information about the work performed in the job (that is, the TDRs). This information makes it possible to determine how well an individual is meeting each job requirement.

A job description typically has the format shown in Figure 4.2. It includes the job title, a brief description of the TDRs, and a list of the essential duties with detailed specifications of the tasks involved in carrying out each duty. Although organizations may modify this format according to their particular needs, all job descriptions within an organization should follow the same format. This helps the organization make consistent decisions about such matters as pay and promotions. It also helps the organization show that it makes human resource decisions fairly.

Whenever the organization creates a new job, it needs a new job description. Preparation of a job description begins with gathering information about the job from people already performing the task, the position's supervisor, or the managers creating the position. Based on that information, the writer of the job description identifies the essential duties of the job, including mental and physical tasks and any methods and resources required. Job descriptions should then be reviewed periodically

LO 4-3 Define the elements of a job analysis, and discuss their significance for human resource management.

Job Analysis
The process of getting detailed information about jobs.

Job Description
A list of the tasks, duties, and responsibilities (TDRs) that a particular job entails.

Careful job analysis makes it possible to define what a person in a certain position does and what qualifications are needed for the job. Firefighters use specific equipment to extinguish fires, require physical strength to do their jobs, and must possess the ability to make decisions under pressure.

Figure 4.2

Sample Job Description

Source: Union Pacific,
"Union Pacific Careers:
Train Crew," https://
up.jobs/train-crew.html,
accessed May 7, 2014.

TRAIN CREW/SERVICE AT UNION PACIFIC

OVERVIEW

When you work on a Union Pacific train crew, you're working at the very heart of our railroad. Train crew employees are responsible for serving our customers by providing the safe, on-time, and on-plan movement of freight trains.

JOB DESCRIPTION

In this entry-level position, you'll start as a Switchperson or Brakeperson, working as on-the-ground traffic control. You don't need any previous railroad experience; we provide all training. These jobs directly lead to becoming a Conductor and a Locomotive Engineer, where you will have a rare opportunity to work on board a moving locomotive. The Conductor is responsible for the train, the freight and the crew. The Locomotive Engineer actually operates the locomotive.

DUTIES

You will work outdoors in all weather conditions and frequently at elevations more than 12 feet above the ground. You must wear personal protective equipment, such as safety glasses and safety boots. You will frequently carry loads and regularly step on and off equipment and work from ladders. You will use and interpret hand signals and sounds, use computers, count train cars, and follow posted regulations.

MAJOR TASKS AND RESPONSIBILITIES

You won't work a standard 40-hour workweek. Train crews are always on call, even on weekends and holidays. You'll travel with our trains, sometimes spending a day or more away from your home terminal.

(say, once a year) and updated if necessary. Performance appraisals can provide a good opportunity for updating job descriptions, as the employee and supervisor compare what the employee has been doing against the details of the job description.

Organizations should give each newly hired employee a copy of his or her job description. This helps the employee to understand what is expected, but it shouldn't be presented as limiting the employee's commitment to quality and customer satisfaction. Ideally, employees will want to go above and beyond the listed duties when the situation and their abilities call for that. Many job descriptions include the phrase *and other duties as requested* as a way to remind employees not to tell their supervisor, "But that's not part of my job."

Job Specification

A list of the knowledge, skills, abilities, and other characteristics (KSAOs) that an individual must have to perform a particular job.

Job Specifications

Whereas the job description focuses on the activities involved in carrying out a job, a **job specification** looks at the qualities or requirements the person performing the job must possess. It is a list of the knowledge, skills, abilities, and other characteristics (KSAOs) that an individual must have to perform the job. *Knowledge* refers to

Figure 4.3
Sample Job
Specifications

Source: Union Pacific,
"Union Pacific Careers:
Train Crew," https://
up.jobs/train-crew.html,
accessed May 7, 2014.

TRAIN CREW/SERVICE AT UNION PACIFIC

REQUIREMENTS

You must be at least 18 years old. You must speak and read English because you'll be asked to follow posted bulletins, regulations, rule books, timetables, switch lists, etc. You must pass a reading comprehension test (see sample) to be considered for an interview.

JOB REQUIREMENTS

You must be able to use a computer keyboard, and you must be able to count and compare numbers. (You might, for example, be asked to count the cars on a train during switching.)

You must be able to solve problems quickly and react to changing conditions on the job.

You must have strong vision and hearing, including the ability to: see and read hand signals from near and far; distinguish between colors; visually judge the speed and distance of moving objects; see at night; and recognize changes in sounds.

You must also be physically strong: able to push, pull, lift, and carry up to 25 pounds frequently; up to 50 pounds occasionally; and up to 83 pounds infrequently. You'll need good balance to regularly step on and off equipment and work from ladders to perform various tasks. And you must be able to walk, sit, stand, and stoop comfortably.

---

factual or procedural information that is necessary for successfully performing a task. For example, this course is providing you with knowledge in how to manage human resources. A *skill* is an individual's level of proficiency at performing a particular task—that is, the capability to perform it well. With knowledge and experience, you could acquire skill in the task of preparing job specifications. *Ability*, in contrast to skill, refers to a more general enduring capability that an individual possesses. A person might have the ability to cooperate with others or to write clearly and precisely. Finally, *other characteristics* might be personality traits such as someone's persistence or motivation to achieve. Some jobs also have legal requirements, such as licensing or certification. Figure 4.3 is a set of sample job specifications for the job description in Figure 4.2.

In developing job specifications, it is important to consider all of the elements of KSAOs. As with writing a job description, the information can come from a combination of people performing the job, people supervising or planning for the job, and trained job analysts. A study by ACT's Workforce Development Division interviewed manufacturing supervisors to learn what they do each day and what skills they rely on. The researchers learned that the supervisors spend much of their day monitoring their employees to make sure the workplace is safe, product quality is maintained, and work processes are optimal. Also, they rely heavily on their technical knowledge of the work processes they supervise.[5] Based on this information, job specifications for a

HR How To

Identifying Relevant KSAOs

Without strong support from human resource management, organizations may be tempted to use shortcuts for defining job specifications. They might guess, say, that someone who has a business degree and two years' experience in a similar job would be well qualified for an administrative position. Hiring experts, however, have identified some ways to pinpoint the relevant knowledge, skills, abilities, and other criteria directly related to success in a job:

- Rather than assuming education provides all necessary job skills, tie specifications to the actual skills needed for successful job performance. For example, research by the ACT testing organization found that most people with a college degree have the reading and math skills needed for entry-level jobs in accounting and auditing. But fewer than half have the necessary level of skill in locating information (for example, interpreting graphs and tables). Job specifications should identify these skills, so companies can test for them.

- Set standards high enough that candidates who meet the specifications will do more than just barely complete the work. Rather, write specifications for an employee who can *succeed* in the job. This requires previous creation of a job description that defines successful performance.

- Use performance data. Especially when many people in the organization perform similar jobs, the company's performance data can become a treasure trove for identifying the behaviors and KSAOs associated with success. Google, for example, is famous for analyzing employee performance data on a company-wide level to see what kinds of behaviors are associated with better outcomes. The company then makes ability to perform in those effective ways part of its job specifications. Among other measures, the company has found that an applicant's school grades are less important than learning ability and intellectual skills. Applicants for technical jobs also must demonstrate skill in writing software code.

Questions

1. Why do you think many companies include education level and years of experience in their job specifications?
2. Suppose you are writing job specifications for the position of production supervisor. Suggest a few ways to identify KSAOs for that position.

Sources: Google company website, "How We Hire," Careers, http://www.google.com, accessed May 6, 2014; Thomas L. Friedman, "How to Get a Job at Google," *New York Times*, February 22, 2014, http://www.nytimes.com; Melissa Murer Corrigan, "Measure Work Readiness for Tomorrow's Jobs," *Chief Learning Officer*, October 2013, pp. 44–6; Brad Remillard, "Traditional Job Descriptions Don't Attract Top Talent," *Supervision*, February 2013, pp. 6–7.

manufacturing supervisor would include skill in observing how people work, as well as in-depth knowledge of manufacturing processes and tools.

In contrast to tasks, duties, and responsibilities, KSAOs are characteristics of people and are not directly observable. They are observable only when individuals are carrying out the TDRs of the job—and afterward, if they can show the product of their labor. Thus, if someone applied for a job as a news photographer, you could not simply look at the individual to determine whether he or she can spot and take effective photographs. However, you could draw conclusions later about the person's skills by looking at examples of his or her photographs. Similarly, many employers specify educational requirements. Meeting these requirements is treated as an indication that a person has some desired level of knowledge and skills.

Accurate information about KSAOs is especially important for making decisions about who will fill a job. A manager attempting to fill a position needs information about the characteristics required and about the characteristics of each applicant. Interviews and selection decisions should therefore focus on KSAOs. For more guidelines on writing KSAOs, see "HR How To."

Sources of Job Information

LO 4-4 Tell how to obtain information for a job analysis.

Information for analyzing an existing job often comes from incumbents, that is, people who currently hold that position in the organization. They are a logical source of information because they are most acquainted with the details of the job. Incumbents should be able to provide very accurate information.

A drawback of relying solely on incumbents' information is that they may have an incentive to exaggerate what they do in order to appear more valuable to the organization. Information from incumbents should therefore be supplemented with information from observers, such as supervisors, who look for a match between what incumbents are doing and what they are supposed to do. Research suggests that supervisors may provide the most accurate estimates of the importance of job duties, while incumbents may be more accurate in reporting information about the actual time spent performing job tasks and safety-related risk factors.[6] For analyzing skill levels, the best source may be external job analysts who have more experience rating a wide range of jobs.[7]

The government also provides background information for analyzing jobs. In the 1930s, the U.S. Department of Labor created the *Dictionary of Occupational Titles (DOT)* as a vehicle for helping the new public employment system link the demand for skills and the supply of skills in the U.S. workforce. The *DOT* described over 12,000 jobs, as well as some of the requirements of successful job holders. This system served the United States well for over 60 years, but it became clear to Labor Department officials that jobs in the new economy were so different that the *DOT* no longer served its purpose. The Labor Department therefore introduced a new system, called the Occupational Information Network (O*NET).

Instead of relying on fixed job titles and narrow task descriptions, the O*NET uses a common language that generalizes across jobs to describe the abilities, work styles, work activities, and work context required for 1,000 broadly defined occupations. Users can visit O*NET OnLine (**http://www.onetonline .org**) to review jobs' tasks, work styles and context, and requirements including skills, training, and experience. ManpowerGroup, a staffing services agency, uses O*NET's information on skills to match individuals more precisely to jobs it has been hired to fill. Piedmont Natural Gas uses O*NET to conduct job analyses and match job applicants' skills and preferences to the requirements of available positions. The effort has helped reduce turnover among Piedmont's entry-level workers.[8] Furthermore, although the O*NET was developed to analyze jobs in the U.S. economy, research suggests that its ratings tend to be the same for jobs located in other countries.[9]

O*NET OnLine provides job seekers with detailed descriptions of many broadly defined occupations.

Position Analysis Questionnaire

After gathering information, the job analyst uses the information to analyze the job. One of the broadest and best-researched instruments for analyzing jobs is the

Position Analysis Questionnaire (PAQ)
A standardized job analysis questionnaire containing 194 questions about work behaviors, work conditions, and job characteristics that apply to a wide variety of jobs.

Position Analysis Questionnaire (PAQ). This is a standardized job analysis questionnaire containing 194 items that represent work behaviors, work conditions, and job characteristics that apply to a wide variety of jobs. The questionnaire organizes these items into six sections concerning different aspects of the job:

1. *Information input*—Where and how a worker gets information needed to perform the job.
2. *Mental processes*—The reasoning, decision making, planning, and information-processing activities involved in performing the job.
3. *Work output*—The physical activities, tools, and devices used by the worker to perform the job.
4. *Relationships with other persons*—The relationships with other people required in performing the job.
5. *Job context*—The physical and social contexts where the work is performed.
6. *Other characteristics*—The activities, conditions, and characteristics other than those previously described that are relevant to the job.

The person analyzing a job determines whether each item on the questionnaire applies to the job being analyzed. The analyst rates each item on six scales: extent of use, amount of time, importance to the job, possibility of occurrence, applicability, and special code (special rating scales used with a particular item). The PAQ headquarters uses a computer to score the questionnaire and generate a report that describes the scores on the job dimensions.

Using the PAQ provides an organization with information that helps in comparing jobs, even when they are dissimilar. The PAQ also has the advantage that it considers the whole work process, from inputs through outputs. However, the person who fills out the questionnaire must have college-level reading skills, and the PAQ is meant to be completed only by job analysts trained in this method. In fact, the ratings of job incumbents tend to be less reliable than ratings by supervisors and trained analysts.[10] Also, the descriptions in the PAQ reports are rather abstract, so the reports may not be useful for writing job descriptions or redesigning jobs.

Fleishman Job Analysis System

Fleishman Job Analysis System
Job analysis technique that asks subject-matter experts to evaluate a job in terms of the abilities required to perform the job.

To gather information about worker requirements, the **Fleishman Job Analysis System** asks subject-matter experts (typically job incumbents) to evaluate a job in terms of the abilities required to perform the job. The survey is based on 52 categories of abilities, ranging from written comprehension to deductive reasoning, manual dexterity, stamina, and originality. The person completing the survey indicates which point on the scale represents the level of the ability required for performing the job being analyzed. For example, consider the ability, "written comprehension." Written comprehension includes understanding written English words, sentences, and paragraphs. It is different from oral comprehension (listen and understand spoken English words and sentences) and oral expression (speak English words and sentences so others can understand). The phrase for the highest point on the seven-point scale is "requires understanding of complex or detailed information in writing containing unusual words and phrases and involves fine distinctions in meaning among words." The phrase for the lowest point on the scale is "requires written understanding of short, simple written information containing common words and phrases."[11]

When the survey has been completed in all 52 categories, the results provide a picture of the ability requirements of a job. Such information is especially useful for employee selection, training, and career development.

Analyzing Teamwork

Work design increasingly relies on teams to accomplish an organization's objectives, so HR managers often must identify the best ways to handle jobs that are highly interdependent. Just as there are standardized instruments for assessing the nature of a job, there are standard ways to measure the nature of teams. Three dimensions are most critical [12]:

1. *Skill differentiation*—The degree to which team members have specialized knowledge or functional capacities.
2. *Authority differentiation*—The allocation of decision-making authority among individuals, subgroups, and the team as a whole.
3. *Temporal (time) stability*—The length of time over which team members must work together.

Importance of Job Analysis

Job analysis is so important to HR managers that it has been called the building block of everything that personnel does.[13] The fact is that almost every human resource management program requires some type of information that is gleaned from job analysis [14]:

- *Work redesign*—Often an organization seeks to redesign work to make it more efficient or to improve quality. The redesign requires detailed information about the existing job(s). In addition, preparing the redesign is similar to analyzing a job that does not yet exist.
- *Human resource planning*—As planners analyze human resource needs and how to meet those needs, they must have accurate information about the levels of skill required in various jobs, so that they can tell what kinds of human resources will be needed.
- *Selection*—To identify the most qualified applicants for various positions, decision makers need to know what tasks the individuals must perform, as well as the necessary knowledge, skills, and abilities.
- *Training*—Almost every employee hired by an organization will require training. Any training program requires knowledge of the tasks performed in a job so that the training is related to the necessary knowledge and skills.
- *Performance appraisal*—An accurate performance appraisal requires information about how well each employee is performing in order to reward employees who perform well and to improve their performance if it is below standard. Job analysis helps in identifying the behaviors and the results associated with effective performance.
- *Career planning*—Matching an individual's skills and aspirations with career opportunities requires that those in charge of career planning know the skill requirements of the various jobs. This allows them to guide individuals into jobs in which they will succeed and be satisfied.
- *Job evaluation*—The process of job evaluation involves assessing the relative dollar value of each job to the organization in order to set up fair pay structures. If employees do not believe pay structures are fair, they will become dissatisfied and may quit, or they will not see much benefit in striving for promotions. To put dollar values on jobs, it is necessary to get information about different jobs and compare them.

Job analysis is also important from a legal standpoint. As we saw in Chapter 3, the government imposes requirements related to equal employment opportunity. Detailed, accurate, objective job specifications help decision makers comply with these regulations by keeping the focus on tasks and abilities. These documents also provide evidence of efforts made to engage in fair employment practices. For

With Good Analysis, Work Isn't *Just* a Game

Job analysis can support one of the hot trends in business, called *gamification*. To gamify work, organizations use elements of games designed to yield better results, and they apply them to jobs to enable stronger performance. For example, they observe how runners and cyclists are motivated when they can share their routes and mileage with their friends on social media, or how teams of players collaborate to defeat an enemy in an online game. A "leaderboard" displaying a list of the top scorers also is a widely used tool to motivate players to improve and earn a place on the list.

Employers can easily create a leader board of top salespeople, ask employees to post their progress on a team project, or award badges for completing training modules. But when a gamification effort is just a matter of adding playful features to the company's internal website, employees may ignore it. Well-planned gamification helps employees achieve goals that are relevant

to their own and their organization's success. This is where job analysis comes in, by pinpointing what employees should be accomplishing and what skills and resources they need. Gamification works when it aligns with job requirements and the learning of relevant skills.

In the United Kingdom, for example, the Department of Work and Pensions (DWP) wanted its employees to become more active in developing useful ideas for innovation. To gamify this aspect of employees' jobs, the company set up a collaboration site on its internal network. Employees are encouraged to submit ideas and vote on the ideas they think are most valuable. As ideas earn votes, they move up a leaderboard, and the company acts on them. Coming up with an idea that wins votes is exciting; seeing it move up the leaderboard is even more motivating; and of course, seeing it make a change for the better is the best prize of all.

Questions

1. Suppose you are a human resource manager at a company that is going to gamify the job of its salespeople. How would job analysis help you advise the team on which behaviors to reward?

2. In the same scenario, how would job analysis help you advise the team on which kinds of rewards to incorporate?

Sources: Brian Burke, "Why Gamification's Not a Game," *CIO Journal*, May 6, 2014, http://blogs.wsj.com; Farhad Manjoo, "High Definition: The 'Gamification' of the Office Approaches," *Wall Street Journal*, January 12, 2014, http://online.wsj.com; Meghan M. Biro, "Five Ways Leaders Win at Gamification Technology," *Forbes*, September 15, 2013, http://www.forbes.com; Cliff Saran, "A Business Case for Gameplay at Work," *Computer Weekly*, August 20–26, 2013, pp. 19–22.

example, to enforce the Americans with Disabilities Act, the Equal Employment Opportunity Commission may look at job descriptions to identify the essential functions of a job and determine whether a disabled person could have performed those functions with reasonable accommodations. Likewise, lists of duties in different jobs could be compared to evaluate claims under the Equal Pay Act. However, job descriptions and job specifications are not a substitute for fair employment practices.

Besides helping human resource professionals, job analysis helps supervisors and other managers carry out their duties. Data from job analysis can help managers identify the types of work in their units, as well as provide information about the work flow process, so that managers can evaluate whether work is done in the most efficient way. Job analysis information also supports managers as they make hiring decisions, review performance, and recommend rewards. For an example of this, see "HRM Social."

LO 4-5 Summarize recent trends in job analysis.

Competency Models

These traditional approaches to job analysis are too limited for some HRM needs, however. When human resource management is actively engaged in talent management

Table 4.1

Example of Competencies and a Competency Model

PROJECT MANAGER COMPETENCIES	PROFICIENCY RATINGS
Organizational & Planning Skills Ability to establish priorities on projects and schedule activities to achieve results.	**1—Below Expectations:** Unable to perform basic tasks. **2—Meets Expectations:** Understands basic principles and performs routine tasks with reliable results; works with minimal supervision or assistance. **3—Exceeds Expectations:** Performs complex and multiple tasks; can coach, teach, or lead others.
Communications Ability to build credibility and trust through open and direct communications with internal and external customers.	**1—Below Expectations:** Unable to perform basic tasks. **2—Meets Expectations:** Understands basic principles and performs routine tasks with reliable results; works with minimal supervision or assistance. **3—Exceeds Expectations:** Performs complex and multiple tasks; can coach, teach, or lead others.
Financial & Quantitative Skills Ability to analyze financial information accurately and set financial goals that have a positive impact on company's bottom line and fiscal objectives.	**1—Below Expectations:** Unable to perform basic tasks. **2—Meets Expectations:** Understands basic principles and performs routine tasks with reliable results; works with minimal supervision or assistance. **3—Exceeds Expectations:** Performs complex and multiple tasks; can coach, teach, or lead others.

Source: Based on R. J. Mirabile, "Everything You Wanted to Know about Competency Modeling," *Training and Development* (August 1997): pp. 73–77.

as a way to support strategy, organizations need to think beyond skills for particular jobs. They must identify the capabilities they need to acquire and develop in order to promote the organization's success. For this purpose, organizations develop competency models.

A **competency** is an area of personal capability that enables employees to perform their work successfully.[15] For example, success in a job or career path might require leadership strength, skill in coaching others, and the ability to bring out the best in each member of a diverse team of employees. A competency model identifies and describes all the competencies required for success in a particular occupation or set of jobs. Organizations may create competency models for occupational groups, levels of the organization, or even the entire organization. A competency model might require that all middle managers or all members of the organization be able to act with integrity, value diversity, and commit themselves to delighting customers. Table 4.1 shows an example of a competency model for a project manager. The left side of the table lists competencies required for a project manager (organizational & planning skills; communications; and financial & quantitative skills). The right side of the table shows behaviors that might be used to determine a project manager's level of proficiency for each competency. As in these examples, competency models focus more on how people work, whereas job analysis focuses more on work tasks and outcomes.

Competency models help HR professionals ensure that all aspects of talent management are aligned with the organization's strategy. Looking at the competencies needed for a particular occupational group, department, or the organization as a whole shows which candidates will be the best to fill open positions. Not only can the organization select those who can carry out a particular job today, but it can spot those with competencies they can develop further to assume greater responsibility in the future. Competency models for a career path or for success in

Competency
An area of personal capability that enables employees to perform their work successfully.

management show the organization which competencies to emphasize in plans for development of high-potential employees. And competency models identify the important capabilities to measure in performance evaluations and to reward with pay and promotions.

Trends in Job Analysis

As we noted in the earlier discussion of work flow analysis, organizations have been appreciating the need to analyze jobs in the context of the organization's structure and strategy. In addition, organizations are recognizing that today's workplace must be adaptable and is constantly subject to change. Thus, although we tend to think of "jobs" as something stable, they actually tend to change and evolve over time. Those who occupy or manage jobs often make minor adjustments to match personal preferences or changing conditions.[16] Indeed, although errors in job analysis can have many sources, most inaccuracy is likely to result from job descriptions being outdated. For this reason, job analysis must not only define jobs when they are created, but also detect changes in jobs as time passes.

With global competitive pressure and economic downturns, one corporate change that has affected many organizations is downsizing. Research suggests that successful downsizing efforts almost always entail changes in the nature of jobs, not just their number. Jobs that have survived the downsizing of the most recent recession tend to have a broader scope of responsibilities coupled with less supervision.[17]

These changes in the nature of work and the expanded use of "project-based" organizational structures require the type of broader understanding that comes from an analysis of work flows. Because the work can change rapidly and it is impossible to rewrite job descriptions every week, job descriptions and specifications need to be flexible. At the same time, legal requirements (as discussed in Chapter 3) may discourage organizations from writing flexible job descriptions. This means organizations must balance the need for flexibility with the need for legal documentation. This presents one of the major challenges to be faced by HRM departments in the next decade. Many professionals are meeting this challenge with a greater emphasis on careful job design.

LO 4-6 Describe methods for designing a job so that it can be done efficiently.

Job Design

Although job analysis, as just described, is important for an understanding of existing jobs, organizations also must plan for new jobs and periodically consider whether they should revise existing jobs. When an organization is expanding, supervisors and human resource professionals must help plan for new or growing work units. When an organization is trying to improve quality or efficiency, a review of work units and processes may require a fresh look at how jobs are designed.

Job Design
The process of defining how work will be performed and what tasks will be required in a given job.

These situations call for **job design**, the process of defining how work will be performed and what tasks will be required in a given job, or *job redesign*, a similar process that involves changing an existing job design. To design jobs effectively, a person must thoroughly understand the job itself (through job analysis) and its place in the larger work unit's work flow process (through work flow analysis). Having a detailed knowledge of the tasks performed in the work unit and in the job, a manager then has many alternative ways to design a job. As shown in Figure 4.4, the available approaches emphasize different aspects of the job: the mechanics of

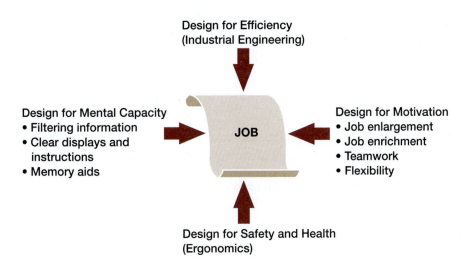

Figure 4.4
Approaches to Job Design

doing a job efficiently, the job's impact on motivation, the use of safe work practices, and the mental demands of the job.

Designing Efficient Jobs

If workers perform tasks as efficiently as possible, not only does the organization benefit from lower costs and greater output per worker, but workers should be less fatigued. This point of view has for years formed the basis of classical **industrial engineering**, which looks for the simplest way to structure work in order to maximize efficiency. Typically, applying industrial engineering to a job reduces the complexity of the work, making it so simple that almost anyone can be trained quickly and easily to perform the job. Such jobs tend to be highly specialized and repetitive.

Industrial Engineering
The study of jobs to find the simplest way to structure work in order to maximize efficiency.

In practice, the scientific method traditionally seeks the "one best way" to perform a job by performing time-and-motion studies to identify the most efficient movements for workers to make. Once the engineers have identified the most efficient sequence of motions, the organization should select workers based on their ability to do the job, then train them in the details of the "one best way" to perform that job. The company also should offer pay structured to motivate workers to do their best. (Chapters 12 and 13 discuss pay and pay structures.) For an example of a company using data analytics to improve efficiency, see "Best Practices."

Industrial engineering provides measurable and practical benefits. However, a focus on efficiency alone can create jobs that are so simple and repetitive that workers get bored. Workers performing these jobs may feel their work is meaningless. Hence, most organizations combine industrial engineering with other approaches to job design.

Designing Jobs That Motivate

LO 4-7 Identify approaches to designing a job to make it motivating.

Especially when organizations must compete for employees, depend on skilled knowledge workers, or need a workforce that cares about customer satisfaction, a pure focus on efficiency will not achieve human resource objectives. Employers also need to ensure that workers have a positive attitude toward their jobs so that they show up at work with enthusiasm, commitment, and creativity. To improve job satisfaction, organizations need to design jobs that take into account factors that make jobs motivating and satisfying for employees.

Big Data for High Efficiency at UPS

United Parcel Service is the world's largest package-shipping company, so saving a tiny bit of gasoline on every truck route can generate enormous savings, both in expenses and in impact on the environment. For example, reducing each route by one mile per day for a year can save the company $50 million. Thus, efficiency is a major factor in work design. UPS keeps improving its ability to gather, analyze, and apply data to making every aspect of package handling use fewer resources. Some of its requirements are as detailed as requiring drivers to hook their truck keys over one finger instead of stashing them in a pocket.

Recently, the company announced that it would begin using a system called Orion (for On-Road Integrated Optimization and Navigation) for its 55,000 drivers in the United States. The Orion system gathers data from customers, vehicles, and drivers' handheld computers. It analyzes the data—even times for pickup and delivery when customers have special requests—and designs routes for each driver to use the minimum time and fuel, driving the minimum distance.

According to UPS, Orion is expected to save the company more than 1.5 million gallons of fuel and eliminate 14,000 metric tons of carbon dioxide emissions in its first year. The company hopes that Orion will eventually do even more to improve outcomes—for example, updating routes when accidents or construction sites cause traffic congestion.

With results like these, it is easy to see why UPS invested years to develop the Orion system. The challenge for managers is to find drivers who are willing to commit to a system in which their every turn is planned by a computer and to keep those jobs engaging.

Questions

1. What benefits does UPS derive from using Orion to help it make drivers' work more efficient?
2. What challenges does the system pose for drivers and their managers?

Sources: Thomas H. Davenport, "Big Brown Finds Big Money from Big Data," *Wall Street Journal,* April 9, 2014, http://blogs.wsj.com; Richard Waters, "Big Data Sparks Cultural Changes," *Financial Times,* March 25, 2014, http://www.ft.com; Mary Schlangenstein, "UPS Crunches Data to Make Routes More Efficient, Save Gas," *Bloomberg News,* October 30, 2013, http://www.bloomberg.com.

A model that shows how to make jobs more motivating is the Job Characteristics Model, developed by Richard Hackman and Greg Oldham. This model describes jobs in terms of five characteristics[18]:

1. *Skill variety*—The extent to which a job requires a variety of skills to carry out the tasks involved.
2. *Task identity*—The degree to which a job requires completing a "whole" piece of work from beginning to end (for example, building an entire component or resolving a customer's complaint).
3. *Task significance*—The extent to which the job has an important impact on the lives of other people.
4. *Autonomy*—The degree to which the job allows an individual to make decisions about the way the work will be carried out.
5. *Feedback*—The extent to which a person receives clear information about performance effectiveness from the work itself.

As shown in Figure 4.5, the more of each of these characteristics a job has, the more motivating the job will be, according to the Job Characteristics Model. The model predicts that a person with such a job will be more satisfied and will produce more and better work. An example of such a job is that of senior analyst at Internet Identity (IID), which combats a kind of online scam known as phishing. Suppose a scam artist

Figure 4.5
Characteristics of a Motivating Job

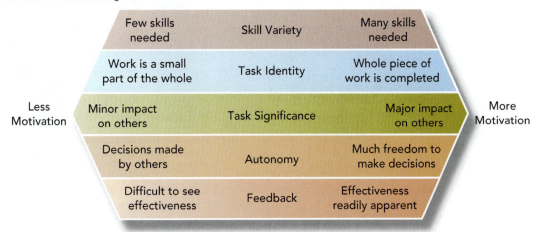

uses the name of a major bank and pretends to represent the bank in messages that ask its customers to visit a Web page and enter their account number. The bank hires IID to find where the phony Web pages are hosted and have them taken down; senior analysts such as Kyle Paris do that detective work. Paris evaluates client requests, analyzes e-mail, studies computer code to identify suspicious practices, and uses detective skills to identify website owners. He directly contacts owners, who may be located anywhere in the world, so he may use a service to translate their conversations. He needs skill in persuasion, because the people hosting the site usually do not even know about the scammers' page and may not see a need to act. Paris also employs people skills to build relationships with clients and Internet service providers. While skill variety and task identity make Paris's work interesting, he especially values his significant role in helping to make the Internet safer for its users.[19] In contrast to his experience, employees in a job that rates low on these characteristics would not find it very motivating.

Applications of the job characteristics approach to job design include job enlargement, job enrichment, self-managing work teams, flexible work schedules, and telework. In applying these methods, HR managers should keep in mind that individual differences among workers will affect how much they are motivated by job characteristics and able to do their best work.[20] For example, someone who thrives in a highly structured environment might not actually be motivated by autonomy and would be a better fit for a job where a supervisor makes most decisions.

Job Enlargement   In a job design, **job enlargement** refers to broadening the types of tasks performed. The objective of job enlargement is to make jobs less repetitive and more interesting. Jobs also become enlarged when organizations add new goals or ask fewer workers to accomplish work that had been spread among more people. In those situations, the challenge is to avoid crossing the line from interesting jobs into jobs that burn out employees. In Minnesota, school principals have been asked to stretch beyond their administrative tasks such as staffing, budgeting, and ensuring building security to take responsibility for student success and teacher development. These goals emphasize the basic purpose that likely drew many principals to careers in education. However, the new goals require many additional hours to observe and

Job Enlargement
Broadening the types of tasks performed in a job.

evaluate teachers. Schools that can afford it are adding behavior specialists and administration managers to help principals keep schools running as they focus on their new priorities.[21]

Nordstrom empowers its employees to resolve customer problems, which can enhance their job experience.

Job Extension

Enlarging jobs by combining several relatively simple jobs to form a job with a wider range of tasks.

Organizations that use job enlargement to make jobs more motivational employ techniques such as job extension and job rotation. **Job extension** is enlarging jobs by combining several relatively simple jobs to form a job with a wider range of tasks. An example might be combining the jobs of receptionist, typist, and file clerk into jobs containing all three kinds of work. This approach to job enlargement is relatively simple, but if all the tasks are dull, workers will not necessarily be more motivated by the redesigned job.

Job Rotation

Enlarging jobs by moving employees among several different jobs.

Job rotation does not actually redesign the jobs themselves, but moves employees among several different jobs. This approach to job enlargement is common among production teams. During the course of a week, a team member may carry out each of the jobs handled by the team. Team members might assemble components one day and pack products into cases another day. As with job extension, the enlarged jobs may still consist of repetitious activities, but with greater variation among those activities.

Job Enrichment

Empowering workers by adding more decision-making authority to jobs.

Job Enrichment   The idea of **job enrichment**, or empowering workers by adding more decision-making authority to their jobs, comes from the work of Frederick Herzberg. According to Herzberg's two-factor theory, individuals are motivated more by the intrinsic aspects of work (for example, the meaningfulness of a job) than by extrinsic rewards, such as pay. Herzberg identified five factors he associated with motivating jobs: achievement, recognition, growth, responsibility, and performance of the entire job. Thus, ways to enrich a manufacturing job might include giving employees authority to stop production when quality standards are not being met and having each employee perform several tasks to complete a particular stage of the process, rather than dividing up the tasks among the employees. For a salesperson in a store, job enrichment might involve the authority to resolve customer problems, including the authority to decide whether to issue refunds or replace merchandise.

In practice, however, it is important to note that not every worker responds positively to enriched jobs. These jobs are best suited to workers who are flexible and responsive to others; for these workers, enriched jobs can dramatically improve motivation.[22]

Self-Managing Work Teams   Instead of merely enriching individual jobs, some organizations empower employees by designing work to be done by self-managing work teams. As described in Chapter 2, these teams have authority for an entire work process or segment. Team members typically have authority to schedule work, hire team members, resolve problems related to the team's performance, and perform other duties traditionally handled by management. Teamwork can give a job such motivating characteristics as autonomy, skill variety, and task identity.

Because team members' responsibilities are great, their jobs usually are defined broadly and include sharing of work assignments. Team members may, at one time or another, perform every duty of the team. The challenge for the organization is to provide enough training so that the team members can learn the necessary skills. Another approach, when teams are responsible for particular work processes or customers, is to assign the team responsibility for the process or customer, then let the team decide which members will carry out which tasks.

A study of work teams at a large financial services company found that the right job design was associated with effective teamwork.[23] In particular, when teams are self-managed and team members are highly involved in decision making, teams are more productive, employees more satisfied, and managers are more pleased with performance. Teams also tend to do better when each team member performs a variety of tasks and when team members view their effort as significant.

Flexible Work Schedules   One way in which an organization can give employees some say in how their work is structured is to offer flexible work schedules. Depending on the requirements of the organization and the individual jobs, organizations may be able to be flexible about when employees work. As introduced in Chapter 2, types of flexibility include flextime and job sharing. Figure 4.6 illustrates alternatives to the traditional 40-hour workweek.

Flextime is a scheduling policy in which full-time employees may choose starting and ending times within guidelines specified by the organization. The flextime policy

Flextime
A scheduling policy in which full-time employees may choose starting and ending times within guidelines specified by the organization.

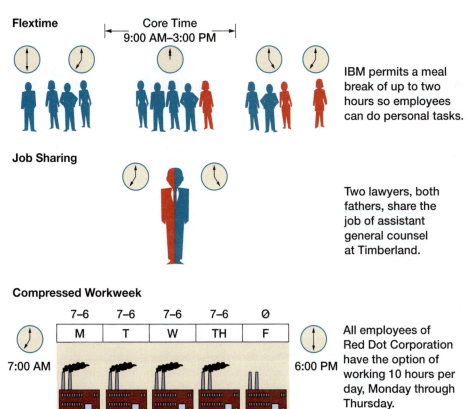

Figure 4.6
Alternatives to the 8-to-5 Job

Flextime

Core Time
9:00 AM–3:00 PM

IBM permits a meal break of up to two hours so employees can do personal tasks.

Job Sharing

Two lawyers, both fathers, share the job of assistant general counsel at Timberland.

Compressed Workweek

7–6	7–6	7–6	7–6	0
M	T	W	TH	F

7:00 AM   6:00 PM

All employees of Red Dot Corporation have the option of working 10 hours per day, Monday through Thursday.

may require that employees be at work between certain hours, say, 10:00 am and 3:00 pm. Employees work additional hours before or after this period in order to work the full day. One employee might arrive early in the morning in order to leave at 3:00 pm to pick up children after school. Another employee might be a night owl who prefers to arrive at 10:00 am and work until 6:00, 7:00, or even later in the evening. A flextime policy also may enable workers to adjust a particular day's hours in order to make time for doctor's appointments, children's activities, hobbies, or volunteer work. A work schedule that allows time for community and family interests can be extremely motivating for some employees.

Job Sharing

A work option in which two part-time employees carry out the tasks associated with a single job.

Job sharing is a work option in which two part-time employees carry out the tasks associated with a single job. Such arrangements can enable an organization to attract or retain valued employees who want more time to attend school or to care for family members. The job requirements in such an arrangement include the ability to work cooperatively and coordinate the details of one's job with another person.

Although not strictly a form of flexibility for all individual employees, another scheduling alternative is the *compressed workweek*. A compressed workweek is a schedule in which full-time workers complete their weekly hours in fewer than five days. For example, instead of working eight hours a day for five days, the employees could complete 40 hours of work in four 10-hour days. This alternative is most common, but some companies use other alternatives, such as scheduling 80 hours over nine days (with a three-day weekend every other week) or reducing the workweek from 40 to 38 or 36 hours. Employees may appreciate the extra days available for leisure, family, or volunteer activities. An organization might even use this schedule to offer a kind of flexibility—for example, letting workers vote whether they want a compressed workweek during the summer months. This type of schedule has a couple of drawbacks, however. One is that employees may become exhausted on the longer workdays. Another is that if the arrangement involves working more than 40 hours during a week, the Fair Labor Standards Act requires the payment of overtime wages to nonsupervisory employees.

Telework   Flexibility can extend to work locations as well as work schedules. Before the Industrial Revolution, most people worked either close to or inside their own homes. Mass production technologies changed all this, separating work life from home life, as people began to travel to centrally located factories and offices. Today, however, skyrocketing prices for office space, combined with drastically reduced prices for portable communication and computing devices, seem ready to reverse this trend. The broad term for doing one's work away from a centrally located office is *telework*, or telecommuting.

For employers, advantages of telework include less need for office space and the ability to offer greater flexibility to employees who are disabled or need to be available for children or elderly relatives. The employees using telework arrangements may have fewer absences from work than employees with similar demands who must commute to work. Telecommuting can also support a strategy of corporate social responsibility because these employees do not produce the greenhouse gas emissions that result from commuting by car. Telework is easiest to implement for people in managerial, professional, or sales jobs, especially those that involve working and communicating on a computer. A telework arrangement is generally difficult to set up for manufacturing workers. The Census Bureau has found telework to be most common

Did You Know?

Occasional Telework Dominates Flexibility Options

In a survey by the Families and Work Institute and the Society for Human Resource Management, most companies said they provide flexible work arrangements. However, the most common kinds of flexibility are limited—letting employees adjust their quitting time or control when they take breaks. Among the flexible work schedules and places discussed in the chapter, telework on an occasional basis is the most common option.

Question

What advantages of telework might make it the most widely used form of flexibility?

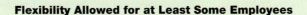

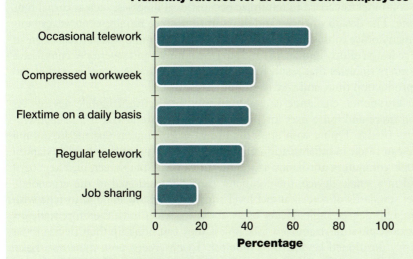

Flexibility Allowed for at Least Some Employees

- Occasional telework
- Compressed workweek
- Flextime on a daily basis
- Regular telework
- Job sharing

Percentage (0 20 40 60 80 100)

Sources: Lauren Weber, "Employers Are Getting More Flexible—Up to a Point," *Wall Street Journal,* April 29, 2014, http://blogs.wsj.com; Sarah Halzack, "A Not-So-Flexible Definition of Flexible Work," *Washington Post,* May 1, 2014, http://www.washingtonpost.com; Kenneth Matos and Ellen Galinsky, "2014 National Study of Employers," Families and Work Institute and Society for Human Resource Management, accessed at http://www.whenworkworks.org.

among management and business professionals, with the fastest growth occurring in computer, engineering, and science jobs. A Chinese website called Ctrip conducted an experiment. It invited its call center workers to choose telework and then compared workers' results over nine months. Productivity was higher among the workers who chose to work at home, presumably because they had fewer distractions but also because they tended to use some of the time saved on commuting to work longer hours. The company also noted that certain categories of workers, such as those who are younger, tended to want to be together at the office, rather than teleworking.[24]

Given the possible benefits, it is not surprising that telework has been a rising trend. In a survey conducted by the Families and Work Institute with the Society for Human Resource Management, the use of telework grew between 2008 and 2014.[25] In fact, as shown in the "Did You Know?" box, the organization found that occasional telework is available at two-thirds of companies.

Designing Ergonomic Jobs

The way people use their bodies when they work—whether toting heavy furniture onto a moving van or sitting quietly before a computer screen—affects their physical well-being and may affect how well and how long they can work. The study of the

LO 4-8 Explain how organizations apply ergonomics to design safe jobs.

Ergonomics
The study of the interface between individuals' physiology and the characteristics of the physical work environment.

interface between individuals' physiology and the characteristics of the physical work environment is called **ergonomics**. The goal of ergonomics is to minimize physical strain on the worker by structuring the physical work environment around the way the human body works. Ergonomics therefore focuses on outcomes such as reducing physical fatigue, aches and pains, and health complaints. Ergonomic research includes the context in which work takes place, such as the lighting, space, and hours worked.[26]

Ergonomic job design has been applied in redesigning equipment used in jobs that are physically demanding. Such redesign is often aimed at reducing the physical demands of certain jobs so that anyone can perform them. In addition, many interventions focus on redesigning machines and technology—for instance, adjusting the height of a computer keyboard to minimize occupational illnesses, such as carpal tunnel syndrome. The design of chairs and desks to fit posture requirements is very important in many office jobs. One study found that having employees participate in an ergonomic redesign effort significantly reduced the number and severity of cumulative trauma disorders (injuries that result from performing the same movement over and over), lost production time, and restricted-duty days.[27]

A recent ergonomic challenge comes from the popularity of mobile devices. As workers find more and more uses for these devices, they are at risk from repetitive-stress injuries (RSIs). Typing with one's thumbs to send frequent text messages on a smartphone can result in inflammation of the tendons that move the thumbs. Laptop and notebook computers are handy to carry, but because the screen and keyboard are attached in a single device, the computer can't be positioned to the ergonomically correct standards of screen at eye level and keyboard low enough to type with arms bent at a 90-degree angle. Heavy users of these devices must therefore trade off eyestrain against physical strain to wrists, unless they can hook up their device to an extra, properly positioned keyboard or monitor. Touchscreens pose their own risks. They are typically part of a flat device such as a smartphone or tablet computer, and these are difficult to position for optimal viewing and typing. Using vertically oriented touchscreens causes even more muscle strain than tapping on a screen lying flat. In addition, because touchscreens usually lack the tactile feedback of pressing keys on a keyboard, users tend to strike them with more force than they use on real keys. Attaching a supplemental keyboard addresses this potential source of strain. When using mobile devices or any computer, workers can protect themselves by taking frequent breaks and paying attention to their posture while they work.[28]

The Occupational Safety and Health Administration has a "four-pronged" strategy for encouraging ergonomic job design. The first prong is to issue guidelines (rather than regulations) for specific industries. As of 2012, these guidelines have been issued for the nursing home, grocery store, and poultry-processing industries, and shipyards. Second, OSHA enforces violations of its requirement that employers have a general duty to protect workers from hazards, including ergonomic hazards. Third, OSHA works with industry groups to advise employers in those industries. And finally, OSHA established a National Advisory Committee on Ergonomics to define needs for further research. You can learn more about OSHA's guidelines at the agency's website, **www .osha.gov**.

LO 4-9 Discuss how organizations can plan for the mental demands of a job.

Designing Jobs That Meet Mental Capabilities and Limitations

Just as the human body has capabilities and limitations, addressed by ergonomics, the mind, too, has capabilities and limitations. Besides hiring people with certain mental skills, organizations can design jobs so that they can be accurately and safely performed given the way the brain processes information. Generally, this means reducing the information-processing requirements of a job. In these simpler jobs, workers may be less likely to make mistakes or have accidents. Of course, the simpler jobs also may be less motivating. Research has found that challenging jobs tend to fatigue and dissatisfy workers when they feel little control over their situation, lack social support, and feel motivated mainly to avoid errors. In contrast, they may enjoy the challenges of a difficult job where they have some control and social support, especially if they enjoy learning and are unafraid of making mistakes.[29] Because of this drawback to simplifying jobs, it can be most ben-

Technological advances can sometimes increase job demands. Some employees may be required to juggle information from several sources at once, which may distract them from their primary job task.

eficial to simplify jobs where employees will most appreciate having the mental demands reduced (as in a job that is extremely challenging) or where the costs of errors are severe (as in the job of a surgeon or air-traffic controller).

There are several ways to simplify a job's mental demands. One is to limit the amount of information and memorization that the job requires. Organizations can also provide adequate lighting, easy-to-understand gauges and displays, simple-to-operate equipment, and clear instructions. For project management, teamwork, and work done by employees in different locations, organizations may provide software that helps with tracking progress. Often, employees try to simplify some of the mental demands of their own jobs by creating checklists, charts, or other aids. Finally, every job requires some degree of thinking, remembering, and paying attention, so for every job, organizations need to evaluate whether their employees can handle the job's mental demands.

Changes in technology sometimes reduce job demands and errors, but in some cases, technology has made the problem worse. Some employees try to juggle information from several sources at once—say, talking on a cell phone while typing, surfing the web for information during a team member's business presentation, or repeatedly stopping work on a project to check e-mail or Twitter feeds. In these cases, the cell phone, handheld computer, and e-mail or tweets are distracting the employees from their primary task. They may convey important information, but they also break the employee's train of thought, reducing performance and increasing the likelihood of errors. Research by a firm called Basex, which specializes in the knowledge economy, found that a big part of the information overload problem is recovery time, that is, the time it takes a person's thinking to switch back from an interruption to the task at hand. The Basex researchers found that recovery time is from 10 to 20 times the length of the interruption. For example, after a 30-second pause to check a Twitter feed, the recovery time could be five minutes or longer.[30]

Organizations probably can't design interruption-free jobs, and few employees would want to isolate themselves entirely from the information and relationships available online. But employers can design jobs that empower workers to manage their time—for example, allowing them to schedule blocks of time when they concentrate on work and do not answer phone calls, e-mails, or text messages. Some employees set aside one or two periods during the day when they will open their e-mail programs, read messages, and respond to the messages immediately. As a vice president at United

Health Group, Kyle McDowell has autonomy to structure his day to be as effective as possible. His tactic is to keep mornings free of meetings and other interruptions so he can spend time focusing on strategic goals.[31]

Information-processing errors also are greater in situations in which one person hands off information to another. Such transmission problems have become a major concern in the field of medicine because critical information is routinely shared among nurses, doctors, and medical technicians, as well as between hospital employees changing shifts. Problems during shift changes are especially likely as a result of fatigue and burnout among employees with stressful jobs.[32] A study of handoffs at Yale–New Haven Hospital found that the information conveyed was often informal, incomplete, and vague. One-fourth of the studied handoffs led to errors in the care given to patients afterward. Pediatrician Ted Sectish has conducted a pilot program to improve information-sharing during handoffs. After he trained young doctors in teamwork, set up computerized summaries of patients, and established a structure for what information to convey, medical errors fell by 40%.[33]

THINKING ETHICALLY

HOW CAN YOU ETHICALLY DESIGN A DANGEROUS JOB?

The most popular professional sport in the United States is football, but the future of the National Football League (NFL) is uncertain. Behind the doubts about football's future is new scientific evidence suggesting that injuries sustained by football players are more serious than had previously been thought. Winning a game requires aggressive play, including head collisions. Sometimes the result is a major concussion, known to be serious. But scientists have observed a link between taking less-severe hits day in and day out and a condition called chronic traumatic encephalopathy (CTE). With CTE, the brain's repeated contact with the skull causes the formation of abnormal protein tangles. People with CTE suffer from headaches, memory loss, episodes of anger, and suicidal tendencies.

A group of players and their families have sued the NFL for covering up the dangers of concussions in the past. They say the league formed a committee to investigate the consequences of these injuries but downplayed the long-term dangers it learned about. The plaintiffs are seeking a settlement of $5 billion to be paid out over 25 years. One of the lawyers points out that for a business earning $9 billion a year, it could be seen as reasonable to compensate former players who are disabled by brain injuries sustained on the job.

Meanwhile, the NFL has tried modifying players' jobs by creating new rules for the game. The rules include requiring knee pads to reduce knee-to-head collisions

and moving kick-offs up five yards to reduce the number of returns. Another change is that players will have fewer full-contact workouts during the preseason. In addition, when players experience symptoms associated with concussions, they may not return to play or practice until they have been cleared by a neurologist who is not affiliated with their team. These changes may reduce the injuries to players, but some players are concerned the changes will make the game less appealing to fans.

Questions

1. How do the basic human rights defined in Chapter 1—free consent, privacy, freedom of conscience, freedom of speech, and due process—apply to professional football players and the safety risks described here?

2. Will making football players' jobs safe achieve the ethical goal of the greatest good for the greatest number of people? Why or why not? Is there an ethical level of safety in football?

Sources: William Weinbaum and Steve Delsohn, "Dorsett, Others Show Signs of CTE," *ESPN Outside the Lines,* April 5, 2014, http://espn.go.com; Joseph Serna, "Study Finds Chronic Brain Damage in Former NFL Players," *Los Angeles Times,* January 22, 2013, http://articles.latimes.com; Paul M. Barrett, "Pain Point," *Bloomberg Businessweek,* January 13, 2013, http://www.businessweek.com; Mark Fainaru-Wade, Jim Avila, and Steve Fainaru, "Doctors: Junior Seau's Brain Had CTE," *Outside the Lines,* ESPN, January 11, 2013, http://espn.go.com.

SUMMARY

LO 4-1 Summarize the elements of work flow analysis.

- First, the analysis identifies the amount and quality of a work unit's outputs (products, parts of products, or services).
- Next, the analyst determines the work processes required to produce the outputs, breaking down tasks into those performed by each person.
- Finally, the work flow analysis identifies the inputs used to carry out the processes.

LO 4-2 Describe how work flow is related to an organization's structure.

- Within an organization, units and individuals must cooperate to create outputs, and the organization's structure brings people together for this purpose.
- The structure may be centralized or decentralized.
- People may be grouped according to function or into divisions focusing on particular products or customer groups.
- A functional structure is most appropriate for people who perform highly specialized jobs and hold relatively little authority.
- Employee empowerment and teamwork succeed best in a divisional structure.

LO 4-3 Define the elements of a job analysis, and discuss their significance for human resource management.

- Job analysis is the process of getting detailed information about jobs. It includes preparation of job descriptions and job specifications.
- A job description lists the tasks, duties, and responsibilities of a job.
- Job specifications look at the qualities needed in a person performing the job. They list the knowledge, skills, abilities, and other characteristics that are required for successful performance of a job.
- Job analysis provides a foundation for carrying out many HRM responsibilities, including work redesign, human resource planning, employee selection and training, performance appraisal, career planning, and job evaluation to determine pay scales.

LO 4-4 Tell how to obtain information for a job analysis.

- Information for analyzing an existing job often comes from incumbents and their supervisors.
- The Labor Department publishes general background information about jobs in the *Dictionary of*

Occupational Titles and Occupational Information Network (O*NET).
- Job analysts, employees, and managers may complete a Position Analysis Questionnaire or fill out a survey for the Fleishman Job Analysis System.
- In the case of teamwork, there are standard ways to measure the nature of teams, such as looking at three critical dimensions: skill differentiation, authority differentiation, and temporal (time) stability.

LO 4-5 Summarize recent trends in job analysis.

- To broaden traditional approaches to job analysis in support of talent management, organizations develop competency models. A competency model identifies and describes all the competencies, or personal capabilities, required for success in a particular occupation or set of jobs.
- Because today's workplace requires a high degree of adaptability, job tasks and requirements are subject to constant change. For example, as some organizations downsize, they are defining jobs more broadly, with less supervision of those positions.
- Organizations are also adopting project-based structures and teamwork, which also require flexibility and the ability to handle broad responsibilities.

LO 4-6 Describe methods for designing a job so that it can be done efficiently.

- The basic technique for designing efficient jobs is industrial engineering, which looks for the simplest way to structure work to maximize efficiency.
- Through methods such as time-and-motion studies, the industrial engineer creates jobs that are relatively simple and typically repetitive.
- These jobs may bore workers because they are so simple.

LO 4-7 Identify approaches to designing a job to make it motivating.

- According to the Job Characteristics Model, jobs are more motivating if they have greater skill variety, task identity, task significance, autonomy, and feedback about performance effectiveness.
- Ways to create such jobs include job enlargement (through job extension or job rotation) and job enrichment.

- Self-managing work teams also offer greater skill variety and task identity.
- Flexible work schedules and telework offer greater autonomy.

LO 4-8 Explain how organizations apply ergonomics to design safe jobs.

- The goal of ergonomics is to minimize physical strain on the worker by structuring the physical work environment around the way the human body works.
- Ergonomic design may involve (1) modifying equipment to reduce the physical demands of performing certain jobs or (2) redesigning the jobs themselves to reduce strain.
- Ergonomic design may target work practices associated with injuries.

LO 4-9 Discuss how organizations can plan for the mental demands of a job.

- Employers may seek to reduce mental as well as physical strain.
- The job design may limit the amount of information and memorization involved.
- Adequate lighting, easy-to-read gauges and displays, simple-to-operate equipment, and clear instructions also can minimize mental strain.
- Computer software can simplify jobs—for example, by performing calculations or filtering out spam from important e-mail.
- Organizations can select employees with the necessary abilities to handle a job's mental demands.

KEY TERMS

work flow design, 102
job, 102
position, 102
job analysis, 105
job description, 105
job specification, 106

Position Analysis Questionnaire (PAQ), 110
Fleishman Job Analysis System, 110
competency, 113
job design, 114
industrial engineering, 115
job enlargement, 117

job extension, 118
job rotation, 118
job enrichment, 118
flextime, 119
job sharing, 120
ergonomics, 122

REVIEW AND DISCUSSION QUESTIONS

1. Assume you are the manager of a fast-food restaurant. What are the outputs of your work unit? What are the activities required to produce those outputs? What are the inputs? *(LO 4-1)*
2. Based on Question 1, consider the cashier's job in the restaurant. What are the outputs, activities, and inputs for that job? *(LO 4-1)*
3. Consider the "job" of college student. Perform a job analysis on this job. What tasks are required in the job? What knowledge, skills, and abilities are necessary to perform those tasks? Prepare a job description based on your analysis. *(LO 4-3)*
4. Discuss how the following trends are changing the skill requirements for managerial jobs in the United States. *(LO 4-5)*
   a. Increasing use of social media
   b. Increasing international competition
   c. Increasing work-family conflicts
5. Suppose you have taken a job as a trainer in a large bank that has created competency models for all its positions. How could the competency models help you succeed in your career at the bank? How could the competency models help you develop the bank's employees? *(LO 4-5)*
6. Consider the job of a customer service representative who fields telephone calls from customers of a retailer that sells online and through catalogs. What measures can an employer take to design this job to make it efficient? What might be some drawbacks or challenges of designing this job for efficiency? *(LO 4-6)*
7. How might the job in Question 6 be designed to make it more motivating? How well would these considerations apply to the cashier's job in Question 2? *(LO 4-7)*
8. What ergonomic considerations might apply to each of the following jobs? For each job, what kinds

of costs would result from addressing ergonomics? What costs might result from failing to address ergonomics? *(LO 4-8)*
a. A computer programmer.
b. A UPS delivery person.
c. A child care worker.
9. Modern electronics have eliminated the need for a store's cashiers to calculate change due on a purchase. How does this development modify the job description for a cashier? If you were a store manager, how would it affect the skills

and qualities of job candidates you would want to hire? Does this change in mental processing requirements affect what you would expect from a cashier? How? *(LO 4-9)*
10. Consider a job you hold now or have held recently. Would you want this job to be redesigned to place more emphasis on efficiency, motivation, ergonomics, or mental processing? What changes would you want, and why? (Or why do you not want the job to be redesigned?) *(LO 4-9)*

TAKING RESPONSIBILITY

How Google Searches for the Right Job Requirements

Each year, around 2.5 million people apply to work at Google—about 60 résumés for every current employee. What makes the company so attractive? Google is famous for perks such as free food and on-site recreation, but these are just the most obvious signs of a philosophy of valuing employees. Google's leaders are committed to designing jobs that are highly motivating—partly to do what is right but also to unleash creativity.

Decisions about job design, like other decisions at Google, are driven by data. The company conducts frequent surveys to measure whether employees are satisfied with a variety of personnel decisions, such as how compensation is structured or how they feel about a new workspace. It shares the results with employees and uses attitude and performance measures to identify decisions associated with high performance.

Jobs at Google are motivating for several reasons. First, the company defines its mission in exciting terms. Software engineers, for example, do not just create programs or systems; they help "develop the next-generation technologies that change how millions interact." Employees have great control over their time: they can negotiate work hours with their supervisor or take breaks to work out, get a massage, or take a nap whenever they need to recharge. Every employee may devote up to 20 percent of each workweek to a project he or she chooses, within or beyond the employee's job description. Google also offers flexibility related to the differences in how people do their best thinking and working. It creates workspaces for diversity, with areas to meet and talk as well as areas for quiet concentration and spaces for exercise. To support hiring of people who thrive with flexibility, job specifications include versatility, strong

ambition, problem-solving skills, and ability to work on teams.

When Google applies data to managers' jobs, it looks for the behaviors associated with motivated workers. Job descriptions may be as specific as detailing actions to take on an employee's first day. These actions, according to Laszlo Bock, the head of People Operations at Google, are associated with 15 percent greater productivity months later.

Google applies its concern for employee well-being to ergonomics. The main concern in an office setting is that hours behind a desk can be unhealthy. The health risks increase further when employees are snacking and gaining weight. Here, as in other areas, solutions focus on choices, with the company nudging employees toward healthy options. While all snacks are free, the healthiest options are displayed most prominently. For ergonomics, employees may choose adjustable sit-stand desks or treadmill desks, so they can spend time out of their chairs.

Questions
1. What elements of motivating jobs has Google put into place, according to this description? Name a few other elements that might be appropriate at Google.
2. What are the ergonomic challenges of jobs at Google? How does the company give workers flexibility in meeting those challenges?

Sources: Google company website, "Software Engineering," Careers, http://www.google.com, accessed May 7, 2014; Christopher Coleman, as told to Venessa Wong, "How to Create a Workplace People Never Want to Leave," *Bloomberg Businessweek*, April 11, 2013, http://www.businessweek.com; Mark C. Crowley, "Not a Happy Accident: How Google Deliberately Designs Workplace Satisfaction," *Fast Company*, March 21, 2013, http://www.fastcompany.com; James B. Stewart, "Looking for a Lesson in Google's Perks," *New York Times*, March 15, 2013, http://www.nytimes.com; John Blackstone, "Inside Google's Workplaces, from Perks to Nap Pods," *CBS News*, January 22, 2013, http://www.cbsnews.com.

MANAGING TALENT

Amazon's Warehouse Jobs: Good or Grueling Work?

As the economy slowly recovers, one concern is that many jobs being created are not "good" jobs—that is, they offer low pay and little prospect for career advancement. However, online retailer Amazon is adding jobs it says are good. With sales steadily increasing, Amazon keeps adding distribution centers to store, sort, and ship merchandise. In each new distribution center, it needs employees. Recently, the company announced it would add 5,000 full-time employees to fill orders in its distribution centers.

Amazon said these fulfillment jobs are "not your typical warehouse jobs," with the difference being the scale of operations. A typical Amazon fulfillment center occupies a million square feet. The job description includes operating a forklift and moving heavy boxes to pick, pack, and ship orders. Job specifications include the ability to put in 12-hour days of walking, bending, and reaching in a facility where temperatures may range between 60 and 90 degrees. Applicants also must be at least 18 years old, have a high school diploma or the equivalent, and be able to read directions in English.

In exchange for hard work, Amazon says it pays 30 percent more than the average worker earns in a retail store. With the average retail wage near $10 per hour, that puts Amazon's pay at about $13 per hour. In addition, full-time employees receive health insurance, a retirement savings plan, shares of the company's stock, and tuition reimbursement up to $3,000 per year.

While working in an Amazon warehouse might pay more than working in the warehouse behind a brick-and-mortar store, managers realize that the strenuous work may not seem like a good job to everyone who tries it. The company therefore has borrowed an idea from Zappos, a business it acquired: it will pay fulfillment center employees to quit. An employee who

decides within the first year that he or she doesn't want to stay at Amazon will receive $2,000 in severance pay. The amount increases by a thousand dollars a year until the fourth year, when employees who quit will receive $5,000. The goal of the program, which has the slogan "Please Don't Take This Offer," is to ensure that all employees are satisfied and committed to their work.

It also may be a way for Amazon to address complaints expressed by some workers in its distribution centers. For example, some employees have filed complaints with the federal government that high temperatures have created unsafe conditions and contributed to injuries resulting in trips to the hospital. Amazon could benefit if employees who find the working conditions too difficult choose to take the severance pay or sign up for tuition reimbursement to learn another kind of work.

Questions

1. Based on the information provided, write a simple work flow analysis listing the inputs, activities, and outputs of an Amazon distribution center.
2. Suppose Amazon hired you as a consultant to help it minimize the cost of severance pay to fulfillment center workers. Suggest a few ways Amazon might consider improving the design of the jobs.

Sources: Mike Davis, "Amazon Warehouse Accepting Applications for Fulfillment Positions," *Times of Trenton (NJ)*, April 22, 2014, http://blog.nj.com; "Would You Take $5,000 to Quit Your Job? Amazon Banks on It," *AirTalk*, April 14, 2014, http://www.scpr.org; Kim Peterson, "Why Amazon Pays Employees $5,000 to Quit," *CBS News*, April 11, 2014, http://www.cbsnews.com; Shannon Mullen, "Is a Job at Amazon a 'Good Job'?" *Marketplace*, July 29, 2013, http://www.marketplace.org; Amazon company website, "Amazon Creates More than 5,000 New Full-Time Jobs across Growing U.S. Fulfillment Network; Hiring Starts Now," news release, July 29, 2013, http://www.amazon.com/pr.

HR IN SMALL BUSINESS

Inclusivity Defines BraunAbility's Products and Its Jobs

Ralph Braun built his company out of his creativity in meeting his own personal needs. Growing up in rural Indiana, Braun had difficulty climbing stairs, and doctors diagnosed him with spinal muscular atrophy. At age 14, Braun needed a wheelchair to get around. He was disappointed but developed his mechanical aptitude, honed by years of helping his uncles fix motorcycles and race cars, and used it to build himself a battery-powered scooter. With the scooter, Braun was able to navigate his way

around a job at an automotive supply factory, where coworkers would ask him to build something similar for their family members and acquaintances. Later, for better transportation to and from the job, Braun figured out how to convert a Dodge van with a lift so he could enter the van on his scooter and drive it from there. Again, people saw the van and asked for something similar. Eventually, Braun took all his earnings from scooters and van conversions and started Save-A-Step Manufacturing, later named BraunAbility, which has become the world's largest maker of wheelchair-accessible vans and wheelchair lifts.

The passion and purposefulness of the company's founder are reflected in the structure of BraunAbility's jobs and work. Recruiting is inclusive, with an especially great appreciation for the potential of disabled workers. Cyndi Garnett, the company's director of human resources, notes that a person with a disability has to go through life solving accessibility problems creatively, so that person is likely to have become a great innovator. Wherever possible, work schedules are tailored to employees' needs. Many employees have flexible schedules, working their choice of eight hours between 7:00 A.M. and 6:00 P.M. Some employees telecommute full-time or part-time. Even production workers, who must coordinate their tasks as vans move from one work station to the next, have flexibility to negotiate arrangements that work for them as a group. They told the company that they wanted just a couple of short breaks during the day instead of a long lunch break, so they could leave earlier. BraunAbility went along with the idea.

As you might expect from a company founded by a creative man, innovation is valued over hierarchy at BraunAbility. Garnett says, "If anyone has an idea, that person is listened to." For example, an employee suggested that, rather than going through the process of safely disposing of leftover paint, workers use it to paint the vehicle floors under the carpet, for a little additional protection of the vehicle. The company readily adopted the suggestion.

Along with feeling respected, workers at BraunAbility feel their work matters to society. In Garnett's words, because the company's vans make it possible to travel independently, employees "know that they're changing the lives of people with disabilities with every product that goes out the door."

Questions

1. In what ways is work at BraunAbility motivating? What other features of motivating work might BraunAbility be able to offer its employees?
2. What place would efficient job design have in a company like BraunAbility? How could BraunAbility improve job efficiency in a way that is consistent with the company's emphasis on inclusiveness and flexibility?
3. Imagine that you work with the HR director at BraunAbility, and she has asked you to suggest some ways to reinforce employees' sense that their jobs have an important positive impact on others. What would you suggest?

Sources: Company website, www.braunability.com, accessed May 14, 2014; "Collaboration, Inclusion Help Create That 'Small-Town' Feeling," white paper, *HR.BLR.com*, January 18, 2010, http://hr.blr.com; "How I Did It: Ralph Braun of BraunAbility," *Inc.*, December 1, 2009, http://www.inc.com; "BraunAbility Launches EntervanXT to Accommodate Needs of Taller Wheelchair and Scooter Users," *Marketing Weekly News*, October 10, 2009, Business & Company Resource Center, http://galenet.galegroup.com.

NOTES

1. Anita Hofschneider, "Bosses Say 'Pick Up the Phone,'" *The Wall Street Journal*, August 27, 2013, http://online.wsj.com; Sue Shellenbarger, "Is This How You Really Talk?" *The Wall Street Journal*, April 23, 2013, http://online.wsj.com.
2. Suzanne Vranica, "Old-School Ad Execs Sweat as Data Geeks Flex Muscle," *The Wall Street Journal*, August 4, 2013, http://online.wsj.com.
3. J. R. Hollenbeck, H. Moon, A. Ellis, et al., "Structural Contingency Theory and Individual Differences: Examination of External and Internal Person-Team Fit," *Journal of Applied Psychology* 87 (2002), pp. 599–606; Sam Grobart, "Hooray for Hierarchy," *Bloomberg Businessweek*, January 14, 2013, p. 74.
4. J. E. Ellis, "At P&G, the Innovation Well Runs Dry," *Bloomberg Businessweek*, September 12, 2012, pp. 24–6.
5. Oliver W. Cummings, "What Do Manufacturing Supervisors Really Do on the Job?" *Industry Week*, February 2010, p. 53.
6. A. O'Reilly, "Skill Requirements: Supervisor-Subordinate Conflict," *Personnel Psychology* 26 (1973), pp. 75–80; J. Hazel, J. Madden, and R. Christal, "Agreement between Worker-Supervisor Descriptions of the Worker's Job," *Journal of Industrial Psychology* 2 (1964), pp. 71–9; A. K. Weyman, "Investigating the Influence of Organizational Role on Perceptions of Risk in Deep Coal Mines," *Journal of Applied Psychology* 88 (2003), pp. 404–12.
7. L. E. Baranowski and L. E. Anderson, "Examining Rater Source Variation in Work Behavior to KSA Linkages," *Personnel Psychology* 58 (2005), pp. 1041–54.
8. National Center for O*NET Development, "O*NET Products at Work," Spring 2011, http://www.onetcenter.org.
9. P. J. Taylor, W. D. Li, K. Shi, and W. C. Borman, "The Transportability of Job Information across Countries," *Personnel Psychology* 61 (2008), pp. 69–111.
10. *PAQ Newsletter*, August 1989; E. C. Dierdorff and M. A. Wilson, "A Meta-analysis of Job Analysis Reliability," *Journal of Applied Psychology* 88 (2003), pp. 635–46.
11. E. Fleishman and M. Reilly, *Handbook of Human Abilities* (Palo Alto, CA: Consulting Psychologists Press, 1992); E. Fleishman and M. Mumford, "Evaluating Classifications of Job Behavior: A Construct Validation of the Ability Requirements Scales," *Personnel Psychology* 44 (1991): 523–75.
12. J. R. Hollenbeck, B. Beersma, and M. E. Schouten, "Beyond Team Types and Taxonomies: A Dimensional Scaling Approach for Team Description," *Academy of Management Review* 37 (2012): 82–108.

13. W. Cascio, *Applied Psychology in Personnel Management*, 4th ed. (Englewood Cliffs, NJ: Prentice Hall, 1991).

14. P. Wright and K. Wexley, "How to Choose the Kind of Job Analysis You Really Need," *Personnel*, May 1985, pp. 51–5.

15. M. Campion, A. Fink, B. Ruggeberg, L. Carr, G. Phillips, and R. Odman, "Doing Competencies Well: Best Practices in Competency Modeling," *Personnel Psychology* 64 (2011): 225–262; R. A. Noe, *Employee Training and Development*, 5e (New York: McGraw-Hill Irwin, 2010); J. Shippmann, R. Ash, M. Battista, L. Carr, L. Eyde, B. Hesketh, J. Kehow, K. Pearlman, and J. Sanchez, "The Practice of Competency Modeling," *Personnel Psychology* 53 (2000): 703–740; A. Lucia and R. Lepsinger, *The Art and Science of Competency Models* (San Francisco: Jossey-Bass, 1999).

16. M. K. Lindell, C. S. Clause, C. J. Brandt, and R. S. Landis, "Relationship between Organizational Context and Job Analysis Ratings," *Journal of Applied Psychology* 83 (1998), pp. 769–76.

17. D. S. DeRue, J. R. Hollenbeck, M. D. Johnson, D. R. Ilgen, and D. K. Jundt, "How Different Team Downsizing Approaches Influence Team-Level Adaptation and Performance," *Academy of Management Journal* 51 (2008), pp. 182–96; Anne Kadet, "'Superjobs': Why You Work More, Enjoy It Less," *The Wall Street Journal*, May 8, 2011, http://online.wsj.com.

18. R. Hackman and G. Oldham, *Work Redesign* (Boston: Addison-Wesley, 1980).

19. Rachel King, "A Day in the Life of an Internet Hall Monitor," *The Wall Street Journal*, April 28, 2014, http://blogs.wsj.com.

20. M. R. Barrick, M. K. Mount, and N. Li, "The Theory of Purposeful Work Behavior: The Role of Personality, Higher-Order Goals, and Job Characteristics," *Academy of Management Review* 38 (2013): 132–53.

21. Alleen Brown, "Twin Cities Principals See Expanding Job Descriptions and Longer Work Hours," *Twin Cities (MN) Daily Planet*, October 30, 2011, http://www.tcdailyplanet.net.

22. F. W. Bond, P. E. Flaxman, and D. Bunce, "The Influence of Psychological Flexibility on Work Redesign: Mediated Moderation of a Work Reorganization Intervention," *Journal of Applied Psychology* 93 (2008), pp. 645–54.

23. M. A. Campion, G. J. Medsker, and A. C. Higgs, "Relations between Work Group Characteristics and Effectiveness: Implications for Designing Effective Work Groups," *Personnel Psychology* 46 (1993), pp. 823–50.

24. Scott Berinato, "To Raise Productivity, Let More Employees Work from Home," *Harvard Business Review*, January–February 2014, pp. 28–9; Neil Shah, "Nearly One in Ten Employees Works from Home," *The Wall Street Journal*, March 5, 2013, http://blogs.wsj.com.

25. Lauren Weber, "Employers Are Getting More Flexible—Up to a Point," *The Wall Street Journal*, April 29, 2014, http://blogs.wsj.com; Kenneth Matos and Ellen Galinsky, "2014 National Study of Employers," Families and Work Institute and Society for Human Resource Management, accessed at http://www.whenworkworks.org.

26. See, for example, S. Sonnentag and F. R. H. Zijistra, "Job Characteristics and Off-the-Job Activities as Predictors of Need for Recovery, Well-Being, and Fatigue," *Journal of Applied Psychology* 91 (2006), pp. 330–50.

27. D. May and C. Schwoerer, "Employee Health by Design: Using Employee Involvement Teams in Ergonomic Job Redesign," *Personnel Psychology* 47 (1994), pp. 861–86.

28. Franklin Tessler, "The Hidden Danger of Touchscreens," *InfoWorld.com*, January 11, 2012, Business & Company Resource Center, http://galenet.galegroup.com.

29. N. W. Van Yperen and M. Hagedoorn, "Do High Job Demands Increase Intrinsic Motivation or Fatigue or Both? The Role of Job Support and Social Control," *Academy of Management Journal* 46 (2003), pp. 339–48; N. W. Van Yperen and O. Janssen, "Fatigued and Dissatisfied or Fatigued but Satisfied? Goal Orientations and Responses to High Job Demands," *Academy of Management Journal* 45 (2002), pp. 1161–71.

30. Jonathan Spira, "Information Overload: None Are Immune," *Information Management*, September/October 2011, p. 32.

31. Alina Dizik, "For Some Executives, Doing Less Means Getting More Done," *The Wall Street Journal*, April 27, 2014, http://online.wsj.com.

32. L. E. LaBlanc, J. J. Hox, W. B. Schaufell, T. W. Taris, and M. C. W. Peters, "Take Care! The Evaluation of a Team-Based Burnout Intervention Program for Oncology Health Care Providers," *Journal of Applied Psychology* 92 (2007), pp. 213–27.

33. Darshak Sanghavi, "The Last of the All-Nighters," *The New York Times Magazine*, August 7, 2011, Business & Company Resource Center, http://galenet.galegroup.com.

Acquiring, Training, and Developing Human Resources

PART TWO

5

Planning for and Recruiting Human Resources

What Do I Need to Know?

After reading this chapter, you should be able to:

LO 5-1 Discuss how to plan for human resources needed to carry out the organization's strategy.

LO 5-2 Determine the labor demand for workers in various job categories.

LO 5-3 Summarize the advantages and disadvantages of ways to eliminate a labor surplus and avoid a labor shortage.

LO 5-4 Describe recruitment policies organizations use to make job vacancies more attractive.

LO 5-5 List and compare sources of job applicants.

LO 5-6 Describe the recruiter's role in the recruitment process, including limits and opportunities.

Introduction

When you interview for a job, you know you should make a good first impression, so you dress appropriately, shake hands, and make eye contact. Employers, too, care about making a good first impression. That was at the top of Lars Schmidt's mind when he joined National Public Radio as its director of talent acquisition. He explored the careers section of NPR's website and realized it was not exactly displaying the best of the organization. While NPR was innovating in the media industry, its website had gone stale—no video, no social media, and a format that did not display well on mobile devices. In a day when people first go online for information, including information about jobs, Schmidt knew that the site was unacceptable. Under Schmidt's direction, NPR updated the site with a better design, links to NPR's presence on social media, and clips of employees telling about NPR's creative culture.

Schmidt also made changes to help NPR reach out to today's mobile generation. He set up a career-related Twitter handle, @nprjobs, for tweets related to job openings and what life is like for the organization's employees. Employees use the hashtag #nprlife when they share thoughts or photos of their work-related activities. Schmidt hopes people interested in radio will follow NPR and develop a positive image of the organization. Evidence suggests that the social-media presence is a plus. For example, one year when NPR had fewer students than usual applying for internships, NPR sent out a tweet that the application deadline would be extended.

Following that one short message, the organization received 140 additional applications yielding 15 qualified new interns. Similarly, it filled a digital-news position when an already-employed worker noticed a tweet about the job and then began following NPR employees on Twitter and Tumblr. This worker liked what she saw of the individuals and NPR's culture, so she applied and was hired.[1]

As this example shows, technology trends have created new opportunities for linking workers and employers. At the same time, changing technological and economic conditions can pose challenges. The explosion in the use of social media and mobile technology has meant stiff competition for workers who understand these technologies. When customer demand rises (or falls), organizations may need more (or fewer) employees. When the labor market changes—say, when more people go to college or when a sizable share of the population retires—the supply of qualified workers may grow, shrink, or change in nature. To prepare for and respond to these challenges, organizations engage in *human resource planning*—defined in Chapter 1 as identifying the numbers and types of employees the organization will require to meet its objectives.

This chapter describes how organizations carry out human resource planning. In the first part of the chapter, we lay out the steps that go into developing and implementing a human resource plan. Throughout each section, we focus especially on recent trends and practices, including downsizing, employing temporary workers, and outsourcing. The remainder of the chapter explores the process of recruiting. We describe the process by which organizations look for people to fill job vacancies and the usual sources of job candidates. Finally, we discuss the role of recruiters.

The Process of Human Resource Planning

Organizations should carry out human resource planning so as to meet business objectives and gain an advantage over competitors. To do this, organizations need a clear idea of the strengths and weaknesses of their existing internal labor force. They also must know what they want to be doing in the future—what size they want the organization to be, what products and services it should be producing, and so on. This knowledge helps them define the number and kinds of employees they will need. Human resource planning compares the present state of the organization with its goals for the future, then identifies what changes it must make in its human resources to meet those goals. The changes may include downsizing, training existing employees in new skills, or hiring new employees.

These activities give a general view of HR planning. They take place in the human resource planning process shown in Figure 5.1. The process consists of three stages: forecasting, goal setting and strategic planning, and program implementation and evaluation. Each of these steps is important, but a recent survey found differences in how well organizations carry out the steps. In particular, most organizations are active in forecasting, but high-performing businesses are much more likely than others to do the work of tying human resource planning to the company's strategy.[2]

Forecasting

The first step in human resource planning is **forecasting**, as shown in the top portion of Figure 5.1. In personnel forecasting, the HR professional tries to determine the supply of and demand for various types of human resources. The primary goal is to predict which areas of the organization will experience labor shortages or surpluses.

LO 5-1 Discuss how to plan for human resources needed to carry out the organization's strategy.

Forecasting
The attempts to determine the supply of and demand for various types of human resources to predict areas within the organization where there will be labor shortages or surpluses.

Figure 5.1

Overview of the Human Resource Planning Process

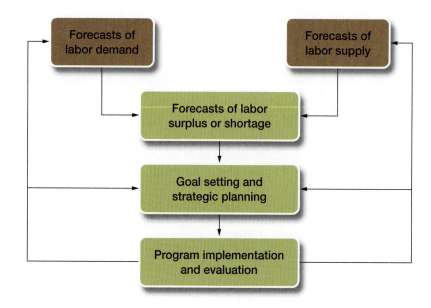

Forecasting supply and demand can use statistical methods or judgment. Statistical methods capture historic trends in a company's demand for labor. Under the right conditions, these methods predict demand and supply more precisely than a human forecaster can using subjective judgment. But many important events in the labor market have no precedent. When such events occur, statistical methods are of little use. To prepare for these situations, the organization must rely on the subjective judgments of experts. Pooling their "best guesses" is an important source of ideas about the future.

LO 5-2 Determine the labor demand for workers in various job categories.

Forecasting the Demand for Labor   Usually, an organization forecasts demand for specific job categories or skill areas. After identifying the relevant job categories or skills, the planner investigates the likely demand for each. The planner must forecast whether the need for people with the necessary skills and experience will increase or decrease. There are several ways of making such forecasts.

At the most sophisticated level, an organization might use **trend analysis**, constructing and applying statistical models that predict labor demand for the next year, given relatively objective statistics from the previous year. These statistics are called **leading indicators**—objective measures that accurately predict future labor demand. They might include measures of the economy (such as sales or inventory levels), actions of competitors, changes in technology, and trends in the composition of the workforce and overall population. For example, ranchers feed corn to their cattle, so an increase in corn prices will cause an increase in the price of beef and a reduction in demand, reducing the need for workers in slaughterhouses. Thus, when a severe drought in 2012 caused corn prices to spike, Cargill forecast a reduction in the need for workers in its beef-processing operations the following year. The company closed a processing plant in Plainview, Texas, ahead of the reduced demand, so it did not have to pay idle workers there.[3]

Statistical planning models are useful when there is a long, stable history that can be used to reliably detect relationships among variables. However, these models

Trend Analysis
Constructing and applying statistical models that predict labor demand for the next year, given relatively objective statistics from the previous year.

Leading Indicators
Objective measures that accurately predict future labor demand.

almost always have to be complemented with subjective judgments of experts. There are simply too many "once-in-a-lifetime" changes to consider, and statistical models cannot capture them.

Determining Labor Supply   Once a company has forecast the demand for labor, it needs an indication of the firm's labor supply. Determining the internal labor supply calls for a detailed analysis of how many people are currently in various job categories or have specific skills within the organization. The planner then modifies this analysis to reflect changes expected in the near future as a result of retirements, promotions, transfers, voluntary turnover, and terminations.

As the average age of many workers in skilled trades grows, the coming demand for workers in many trades is expected to outstrip supply in the United States. There is a potential for employers in some areas to experience a labor shortage because of this. How can HR prepare for this reality? What should be done now to avoid the shortage?

One type of statistical procedure that can be used for this purpose is the analysis of a **transitional matrix**. This is a chart that lists job categories held in one period and shows the proportion of employees in each of those job categories in a future period. It answers two questions: "Where did people who were in each job category go?" and "Where did people now in each job category come from?" Table 5.1 is an example of a transitional matrix.

This example lists job categories for an auto parts manufacturer. The jobs listed at the left were held in 2011; the numbers at the right show what happened to the people in 2014. The numbers represent proportions. For example, .95 means 95% of the people represented by a row in the matrix. The column headings under 2014 refer to the row numbers. The first row is sales managers, so the numbers under column (1) represent people who became sales managers. Reading across the first row, we see that 95 of the people who were sales managers in 2011 are still sales managers in 2014. The other 5% correspond to position (8), "Not in organization," meaning the 5% of employees who are not still sales managers have left the organization. In the second row are sales representatives. Of those who were sales reps in 2011, 5% were promoted to sales manager, 60% are still sales reps, and 35% have left the organization. In row (3), half (50%) of sales apprentices are still in that job, but 20% are now sales reps and 30% have left the organization. This pattern of jobs shows a career path from sales apprentice to sales representative to sales manager. Of course, not everyone is promoted, and some of the people leave instead.

Transitional Matrix A chart that lists job categories held in one period and shows the proportion of employees in each of those job categories in a future period.

Table 5.1

Transitional Matrix: Example for an Auto Parts Manufacturer

2011	2014							
	(1)	(2)	(3)	(4)	(5)	(6)	(7)	(8)
(1) Sales manager	.95							.05
(2) Sales representative	.05	.60						.35
(3) Sales apprentice		.20	.50					.30
(4) Assistant plant manager				.90	.05			.05
(5) Production manager				.10	.75			.15
(6) Production assembler					.10	.80		.10
(7) Clerical							.70	.30
(8) Not in organization	.00	.20	.50	.00	.10	.20	.30	

Reading down the columns provides another kind of information: the sources of employees holding the positions in 2014. In the first column, we see that most sales managers (95%) held that same job three years earlier. The other 5% were promoted from sales representative positions. Skipping over to column (3), half the sales apprentices on the payroll in 2014 held the same job three years before, and the other half were hired from outside the organization. This suggests that the organization fills sales manager positions primarily through promotions, so planning for this job would focus on preparing sales representatives. In contrast, planning to meet the organization's needs for sales apprentices would emphasize recruitment and selection of new employees.

Matrices such as this one are extremely useful for charting historical trends in the company's supply of labor. More important, if conditions remain somewhat constant, they can also be used to plan for the future. For example, if we believe that we are going to have a surplus of labor in the production assembler job category in the next three years, we can plan to avoid layoffs. Still, historical data may not always reliably indicate future trends. Planners need to combine statistical forecasts of labor supply with expert judgments. For example, managers in the organization may see that a new training program will likely increase the number of employees qualified for new openings. Forecasts of labor supply also should take into account the organization's pool of skills. Many organizations include inventories of employees' skills in an HR database. When the organization forecasts that it will need new skills in the future, planners can consult the database to see how many existing employees have those skills.

Besides looking at the labor supply within the organization, the planner should examine trends in the external labor market. The planner should keep abreast of labor market forecasts, including the size of the labor market, the unemployment rate, and the kinds of people who will be in the labor market. For example, we saw in Chapter 2 that the U.S. labor market is aging and that immigration is an important source of new workers. Important sources of data on the external labor market include the *Occupational Outlook Quarterly* and the *Monthly Labor Review*, published by the Labor Department's Bureau of Labor Statistics. Details and news releases are available at the website of the Bureau of Labor Statistics (**www.bls.gov**).

LO 5-3 Summarize the advantages and disadvantages of ways to eliminate a labor surplus and avoid a labor shortage.

Determining Labor Surplus or Shortage   Based on the forecasts for labor demand and supply, the planner can compare the figures to determine whether there will be a shortage or surplus of labor for each job category. Determining expected shortages and surpluses allows the organization to plan how to address these challenges.

Goal Setting and Strategic Planning

The second step in human resource planning is goal setting and strategic planning, as shown in the middle of Figure 5.1. The purpose of setting specific numerical goals is to focus attention on the problem and provide a basis for measuring the organization's success in addressing labor shortages and surpluses. The goals should come directly from the analysis of labor supply and demand. They should include a specific figure indicating what should happen with the job category or skill area and a specific timetable for when the results should be achieved.

For each goal, the organization must choose one or more human resource strategies. A variety of strategies is available for handling expected shortages and surpluses

Table 5.2

HR Strategies for Addressing a Labor Shortage or Surplus

OPTIONS FOR REDUCING A SURPLUS		
OPTION	**SPEED OF RESULTS**	**AMOUNT OF SUFFERING CAUSED**
Downsizing	Fast	High
Pay reductions	Fast	High
Demotions	Fast	High
Transfers	Fast	Moderate
Work sharing	Fast	Moderate
Hiring freeze	Slow	Low
Natural attrition	Slow	Low
Early retirement	Slow	Low
Retraining	Slow	Low
OPTIONS FOR AVOIDING A SHORTAGE		
OPTION	**SPEED OF RESULTS**	**ABILITY TO CHANGE LATER**
Overtime	Fast	High
Temporary employees	Fast	High
Outsourcing	Fast	High
Retrained transfers	Slow	High
Turnover reductions	Slow	Moderate
New external hires	Slow	Low
Technological innovation	Slow	Low

Core Competency
A set of knowledge and skills that make the organization superior to competitors and create value for customers.

of labor. The top of Table 5.2 shows major options for reducing an expected labor surplus, and the bottom of the table lists options for avoiding an expected labor shortage.

This planning stage is critical. The options differ widely in their expense, speed, and effectiveness. Options for reducing a labor surplus cause differing amounts of human suffering. The options for avoiding a labor shortage differ in terms of how easily the organization can undo the change if it no longer faces a labor shortage. For example, an organization probably would not want to handle every expected labor shortage by hiring new employees. The process is relatively slow and involves expenses to find and train new employees. Also, if the shortage becomes a surplus, the organization will have to consider laying off some of the employees. Layoffs involve another set of expenses, such as severance pay, and they are costly in terms of human suffering.

Another consideration in choosing an HR strategy is whether the employees needed will contribute directly to the organization's success. Organizations are most likely to benefit from hiring and retaining employees who provide a **core competency**—that is, a set of knowledge and skills that make the organization superior to competitors and create value for customers. At a store, for example, core competencies include choosing merchandise that shoppers want and providing shoppers with excellent service. For other work that is not a core competency—say, cleaning the store and providing security—the organization may benefit from using HR strategies other than hiring full-time employees.

Organizations try to anticipate labor surpluses far enough ahead that they can freeze hiring and let natural attrition (people leaving on their own) reduce the labor force. Unfortunately for many workers, organizations

Cold Stone Creamery employees give their company the competitive advantage with their "entertainment factor." The company is known to seek out employees who like to perform and then "audition" rather than interview potential employees.

often stay competitive in a fast-changing environment by responding to a labor surplus with downsizing, which delivers fast results. The impact is painful for those who lose jobs, as well as those left behind to carry on without them. To handle a labor shortage, organizations typically hire temporary employees or use outsourcing. Because downsizing, using temporary employees, and outsourcing are most common, we will look at each of these in greater detail in the following sections.

Downsizing

The planned elimination of large numbers of personnel with the goal of enhancing the organization's competitiveness.

Downsizing   As we discussed in Chapter 2, **downsizing** is the planned elimination of large numbers of personnel with the goal of enhancing the organization's competitiveness. The primary reason organizations engage in downsizing is to promote future competitiveness. According to surveys, they do this by meeting four objectives:

1. *Reducing costs*—Labor is a large part of a company's total costs, so downsizing is an attractive place to start cutting costs.
2. *Replacing labor with technology*—Closing outdated factories, automating, or introducing other technological changes reduces the need for labor. Often, the labor savings outweigh the cost of the new technology.
3. *Mergers and acquisitions*—When organizations combine, they often need less bureaucratic overhead, so they lay off managers and some professional staff members.
4. *Moving to more economical locations*—Some organizations move from one area of the United States to another, especially from the Northeast and Midwest to the South and the mountain regions of the West. For example, managers looking for ways to cut costs at H. J. Heinz observed that the facility in Pocatello, Idaho, was no longer mainly processing locally grown potatoes. Rather, in response to shifting consumer demands, it was making products for which 70% of the ingredients came from east of the Mississippi (traveling 1,000 miles or so) and other ingredients were from Denver (almost 600 miles away). Heinz decided to close the Idaho facility and have its Ohio factory handle the production of all frozen foods, because Ohio is more centrally located for both ingredients and customers.[4] Other moves have shifted jobs to other countries, including Mexico, India, and China, where wages are lower.

Although downsizing has an immediate effect on costs, much of the evidence suggests that it hurts long-term organizational effectiveness. This is especially true for certain kinds of companies, such as those that emphasize research and development and where employees have extensive contact with customers.[5] The negative effect of downsizing was especially high among firms that engaged in high-involvement work practices, such as the use of teams and performance-related pay incentives. As a result, the more a company tries to compete through its human resources, the more layoffs hurt productivity.[6]

Why do so many downsizing efforts fail to meet expectations? There seem to be several reasons. First, although the initial cost savings give a temporary boost to profits, the long-term effects of an improperly managed downsizing effort can be negative. Downsizing leads to a loss of talent, and it often disrupts the social networks through which people are creative and flexible.[7] Unless the downsizing is managed well, employees feel confused, demoralized, and even less willing to stay with the organization. Organizations may not take (or even know) the steps that can counter these reactions—for example, demonstrating how they are treating employees fairly, building confidence in the company's plans for a stronger future, and showing the organization's commitment to behaving responsibly with regard to all its stakeholders, including employees, customers, and the community.[8] The "HR Oops!" box illustrates consequences of not taking those steps.

HR Oops!

Trimming More Than Just Fat

Getting lean improves an organization's efficiency and makes it stronger for the long haul. But some organizations are so desperate to cut costs that they don't just get lean, they starve themselves of important human resources.

Some shoppers and business observers think that's what Walmart did during the most recent recession. Since 2008, the start of the recession, the company increased the number of stores by 13% but reduced its workforce by 1.4%. While cuts at headquarters could account for some of the difference between these percentages, it's likely that the impact includes stores trying to operate with fewer employees.

Customers have observed less help available and longer checkout lines. They also complain that overwhelmed employees are unable to keep shelves stocked with merchandise. Walmart's official response is that the percentage of items in stock has actually improved. However, reporters have cited examples of employees saying that the merchandise indeed has been delivered to the store, but they don't have time to move it to the shelves. And in the American Customer Satisfaction Index, a survey of consumer opinions about major corporations, Walmart recently was the lowest-ranked brand of department or discount store—the sixth year it was last or tied for last.

One employee said she was told her store was not allowed to schedule more worker-hours unless it had higher sales. Is this an example of a company that staffs efficiently or one that is starving itself of human resources? Sales at Walmart have been falling, though profits have held steady. Spending less for human resources is one way to limit costs and maintain profits when sales decline. But if customers are leaving to find better service elsewhere, the company could be setting up a downward spiral.

Questions

1. What pros and cons of downsizing do you think apply to this example?
2. Besides reducing the workforce in its stores, how else could a retailer like Walmart respond to a decline in demand?

Sources: Michael Calia, "Wal-Mart Offers Weak Outlook; U.S. Sales Keep Falling," *The Wall Street Journal,* May 15, 2014, http://online.wsj.com; Bill Saporito, "The Trouble Lurking on Walmart's Empty Shelves," *Time,* April 9, 2013, http://business.time.com; Renee Dudley, "Walmart Faces the Cost of Cost-Cutting: Empty Shelves," *Bloomberg Businessweek,* March 28, 2013, http://www.businessweek.com.

Also, many companies wind up rehiring. Downsizing campaigns often eliminate people who turn out to be irreplaceable. In one survey, 80% of the firms that had downsized later replaced some of the very people they had laid off. In one Fortune 100 firm, a bookkeeper making $9 an hour was let go. Later, the company realized she knew many things about the company that no one else knew, so she was hired back as a consultant—for $42 an hour.[9] However, recent trends in employment suggest that companies will not rehire employees for many of the jobs eliminated when they restructure, introduce automation, or move work to lower-cost regions.[10]

Finally, downsizing efforts often fail because employees who survive the purge become self-absorbed and afraid to take risks. Motivation drops because any hope of future promotions—or any future—with the company dies. Many employees start looking for other employment opportunities. The negative publicity associated with a downsizing campaign can also hurt the company's image in the labor market, so it is harder to recruit employees later.

Many problems with downsizing can be reduced with better planning. Instead of slashing jobs across the board, successful downsizing makes surgical strategic cuts that improve the company's competitive position, and management addresses the problem of employees becoming demoralized. During the housing boom of the previous decade, landscaping companies struggled to find enough talented, motivated workers, especially at the supervisory level. When bust followed boom, well-managed landscapers used downsizing as an opportunity to improve quality. Bill Davids of Clarence Davids & Co. was one landscaping manager who selected the least productive employees for layoffs. He then rallied the remaining employees to focus on how to operate more efficiently and keep the business afloat during lean times. Davids told a reporter, "Once [employees] see you're serious and several people have exited, you get the buy-in pretty quick."[11] In fact, for good workers, it can be motivating to be part of a higher-quality, if smaller, team.

Reducing Hours   Given the limitations of downsizing, many organizations are more carefully considering other avenues for eliminating a labor surplus. Among the alternatives listed in Table 5.2, one that is seen as a way to spread the burden more fairly is cutting work hours, generally with a corresponding reduction in pay. Besides the thought that this is a more equitable way to weather a slump in demand, companies choose a reduction in work hours because it is less costly than layoffs requiring severance pay, and it is easier to restore the work hours than to hire new employees after a downsizing effort. When plastics manufacturer Saint-Gobain in Bristol, Rhode Island, experienced a business slowdown, it did not lay off any workers but cut many workers' hours by 40%. The state stepped in and contributed 70% of the lost wages in exchange for the workers' continued employment—less than it would have paid in unemployment compensation. This kind of "work share" program, which helps employers keep experienced employees, has been popular in Europe but is fairly new to the United States.[12]

Early-Retirement Programs   Another popular way to reduce a labor surplus is with an early-retirement program. As we discussed in Chapter 2, the average age of the U.S. workforce is increasing. But even though many baby boomers are reaching traditional retirement age, indications are that this group has no intention of leaving the workforce soon.[13] Reasons include improved health of older people, jobs becoming less physically demanding, concerns about the long-term viability of Social Security and pensions, the recent drop in the value of older workers' retirement assets (especially stock funds and home values), and laws against age discrimination. Under the pressures associated with an aging labor force, many employers try to encourage older workers to leave voluntarily by offering a variety of early-retirement incentives. The more lucrative of these programs succeed by some measures. Research suggests that these programs encourage lower-performing older workers to retire.[14] Sometimes they work so well that too many workers retire.

Many organizations are moving from early-retirement programs to phased-retirement programs. In a *phased-retirement program*, the organization can continue to enjoy the experience of older workers while reducing the number of hours that these employees work, as well as the cost of those employees. This option also can give older employees the economic and psychological benefits of easing into retirement, rather than being thrust entirely into a new way of life.[15]

Employing Temporary and Contract Workers   While downsizing has been a popular way to reduce a labor surplus, the most widespread methods for eliminating a labor shortage are hiring temporary and contract workers and outsourcing work. Employers may arrange to hire a temporary worker through an agency that specializes in linking employers with people who have the necessary skills. The employer pays the agency, which in turn pays the temporary worker. Employers also may contract directly with individuals, often professionals, to provide a particular service.

To use this source of labor effectively, employers need to overcome some disadvantages. In particular, temporary and contract workers may not be as committed to the organization, so if they work directly with customers, that attitude may spill over and affect customer loyalty. Therefore, many organizations try to use permanent employees in key jobs and use temporary and contract workers in ways that clearly supplement—and do not potentially replace—the permanent employees.[16]

Temporary Workers   As we saw in Chapter 2, the federal government estimated that organizations are using over a million temporary workers. Temporary employment is popular with employers because it gives them flexibility they need to operate efficiently when demand for their products changes rapidly. If an employer believes a higher level of demand will persist, it often can hire the temps as permanent workers. Siemens contracts with a temporary employment agency to provide production and warehouse workers for its Rail Systems Division in Sacramento. If Siemens determines a long-term need for additional workers, it selects high-performing temporary employees to put on its payroll.[17]

In addition to flexibility, temporary employment offers lower costs. Using temporary workers frees the employer from many administrative tasks and financial burdens associated with being the "employer of record." The cost of employee benefits, including health care, pension, life insurance, workers' compensation, and unemployment insurance, can account for 40% of payroll expenses for permanent employees. Assuming the agency pays for these benefits, a company using temporary workers may save money even if it pays the agency a higher rate for that worker than the usual wage paid to a permanent employee.

Agencies that provide temporary employees also may handle some of the tasks associated with hiring. Small companies that cannot afford their own testing programs often get employees who have been tested by a temporary agency. Many temporary agencies also train employees before sending them to employers. This reduces employers' training costs and eases the transition for the temporary worker and employer.

Finally, temporary workers may offer value not available from permanent employees. Because the temporary worker has little experience at the employer's organization, this person brings an objective point of view to the organization's problems and procedures. Also, a temporary worker may have a great deal of experience in other organizations that can be applied to the current assignment.

To obtain these benefits, organizations need to overcome the disadvantages associated with temporary workers. For example, tension can develop between temporary and permanent employees. Employers can minimize resentment and ensure that all workers feel valued by not bringing in temporary or contract workers immediately after downsizing and by hiring temporary workers from agencies that provide benefits. In addition, employers must avoid the legal pitfalls associated with temporary employees and contract workers, as described in "HR How To."

Employee or Contractor?   Besides using a temporary employment agency, a company can obtain workers for limited assignments by entering into contracts with them. If the person providing the services is an independent contractor, rather than an employee, the company does not pay employee benefits, such as health insurance and vacations. As with using temporary employees, the savings can be significant, even if the contractor works at a higher rate of pay.

This strategy carries risks, however. If the person providing the service is a contractor and not an employee, the company is not supposed to directly supervise the worker. The company can tell the contractor what criteria the finished assignment should meet but not, for example, where or what hours to work. This distinction is significant, because under federal law, if the company treats the contractor as an employee, the

HR How To

Using Temporary Employees and Contractors

When a company lands a big order, needs to catch up on administrative work, or isn't sure demand will continue at present levels, contingent workers look like the ideal solution. The company can hire workers from a temp agency or negotiate contracts for short-term projects, and when the project ends or demand falls, the company doesn't have to figure out what to do with the workers. In addition, the company may be able to save money because it doesn't have to provide employee benefits or withhold taxes from contract workers' pay.

However, it is not up to the company to decide whether its workers are really independent contractors. The Internal Revenue Service has guidelines for what constitutes an employee and an independent contractor. Here are some tips for how to classify workers:

- Companies can specify what they want a contractor to accomplish. But if the employer tells the workers how to do the work and controls the workers' activities, then the workers are employees, not independent contractors.

- Providing the workers with supplies or tools and reimbursing the workers for the expenses associated with their work tend to be signs that the workers are employees.
- Providing the workers with benefits such as insurance and paid vacation time is a sign that the workers are employees. Usually, temporary workers receive these benefits from an agency that employs them, not from the company that pays the agency for the workers' services.
- If a company hires workers from a temp agency to do work for a long period of time, directly controls what these workers do, and uses them to perform key roles, the government may see the company as an employer or "joint employer" with the temp agency. A company that is a joint employer has to follow labor laws, including those against discrimination (see Chapter 3) and legal requirements for pay (see Chapter 12).
- If a company is not sure whether its workers are employees or independent contractors, it should get professional advice. Companies and workers may ask the IRS

to decide. The way to do this is to file a Form SS-8 requesting a determination from the IRS. The form is available at the IRS website (http://www.irs.gov).

Questions

1. Suppose a small company does not want the headaches of administering benefits programs, so it hires its workers from a temp agency and keeps them on for several years. Would you expect the IRS to agree that these are not employees? Why or why not?
2. Suppose you work in the HR department of a company that wants to hire production workers as independent contractors. What advice would you give management about this idea?

Sources: Internal Revenue Service, "Independent Contractor vs. Employee," Tax Topic 762, last updated March 20, 2014, http://www.irs.gov; Internal Revenue Service, "Independent Contractor (Self-Employed) or Employee?" last updated November 5, 2013, http://www.irs.gov; "Hiring Temporary Employees," *Entrepreneur*, February 25, 2013, http://www.entrepreneur.com.

company has certain legal obligations, described in Part 4, related to matters such as overtime pay and withholding taxes.

When an organization wants to consider using independent contractors as a way to expand its labor force temporarily, human resource professionals can help by alerting the company to the need to verify that the arrangement will meet the legal requirements. A good place to start is with the advice to small businesses at the Internal Revenue Service website (**www.irs.gov**); search for "independent contractor" to find links to information and guidance. In addition, the organization may need to obtain professional legal advice.

Outsourcing   Instead of using a temporary or contract employee to fill a single job, an organization might want a broader set of services. Contracting with another organization to perform a broad set of services is called **outsourcing**. Organizations use outsourcing as a way to operate more efficiently and save money. They choose outsourcing firms that promise to deliver the same or better quality at a lower cost. One reason they can do this is that the outside company specializes in the service and can benefit from economies of scale (the economic principle that producing something in large volume tends to cost less for each additional unit than producing in small volume). This efficiency is often the attraction for outsourcing human resource functions such as payroll. Costs also are lower when the outsourcing firm is located in a part of the world where wages are relatively low. The labor forces of countries such as China, India, Jamaica, and those in Eastern Europe have been creating an abundant supply of labor for unskilled and low-skilled work.

The first uses of outsourcing emphasized manufacturing and routine tasks. However, technological advances in computer networks and transmission have speeded up the outsourcing process and have helped it spread beyond manufacturing areas and low-skilled jobs. For example, newspapers outsource ad creation to Outsourcing USA, a small business in Dallas, Pennsylvania. At Outsourcing USA, employees design advertisements for print, web, and mobile editions of their clients' newspapers. The company offers low costs by specializing in a niche market, focusing relentlessly on efficiency, and hiring recent graduates. Careful supervision and a one-month training program ensure that Outsourcing USA delivers quality work.[18]

Using outsourcing may be a necessary way to operate as efficiently as competitors, but it does pose challenges. Quality-control problems, security violations, and poor customer service have sometimes wiped out the cost savings attributed to lower wages. To ensure success with an outsourcing strategy, companies should follow these guidelines:

- Learn about what the provider can do for the company, not just the costs. Make sure the company has the necessary skills, including an environment that can meet standards for clear communication, on-time shipping, contract enforcement, fair labor practices, and environmental protection. Outsourcing USA finds that its clients prefer buying ad production services from a local company rather than going overseas for potentially lower prices. The Pennsylvania company can offer newspapers in the region faster communications (by being in the same time zone) and greater familiarity with the nuances of American English.[19]
- Do not offshore any work that is proprietary or requires tight security.[20]
- Start small and monitor the work closely, especially in the beginning, when problems are most likely. Indiana's experience offers a cautionary tale with its attempt to outsource the processing of welfare benefits to IBM. While IBM could offer expertise in developing a website and managing the data, it soon became apparent that the company was unfamiliar with some of the challenges of serving the poor. IBM had expected most recipients to sign up online, but most phoned or came into state welfare offices because they were unable to use the Internet or simply more accustomed to handling matters face-to-face. Callers were on hold for hours, and processing fell far behind. Indiana ended up changing the arrangement so that state employees work with clients while IBM handles the back end of the system.[21]
- Look for opportunities to outsource work in areas that promote growth, for example, by partnering with experts who can help the organization tap new markets. Mansfield Sales Partners offers this type of advantage to companies that have a limited sales force or want to test a new market. Such companies can use Mansfield's team of experienced salespeople to introduce their products in markets around the world.[22]

Outsourcing
Contracting with another organization to perform a broad set of services.

Overtime and Expanded Hours Organizations facing a labor shortage may be reluctant to hire employees, even temporary workers, or to commit to an outsourcing arrangement. Especially if the organization expects the shortage to be temporary, it may prefer an arrangement that is simpler and less costly. Under some conditions, these organizations may try to garner more hours from the existing labor force, asking them to go from part-time to full-time status or to work overtime.

A major downside of overtime is that the employer must pay nonmanagement employees one-and-a-half times their normal wages for work done overtime. Even so, employers see overtime pay as preferable to the costs of hiring and training new employees. The preference is especially strong if the organization doubts that the current higher level of demand for its products will last long.

For a short time at least, many workers appreciate the added compensation for working overtime. Over extended periods, however, employees feel stress and frustration from working long hours. Overtime therefore is best suited for short-term labor shortages.

Implementing and Evaluating the HR Plan

For whatever HR strategies are selected, the final stage of human resource planning involves implementing the strategies and evaluating the outcomes. This stage is represented by the bottom part of Figure 5.1. When implementing the HR strategy, the organization must hold some individual accountable for achieving the goals. That person also must have the authority and resources needed to accomplish those goals. It is also important that this person issue regular progress reports, so the organization can be sure that all activities occur on schedule and that the early results are as expected. The "Did You Know?" box reports some of the major challenges managers face during the implementation of an HR plan.

Implementation that ties planning and recruiting to the organization's strategy and to its efforts to develop employees becomes a complete program of talent management. Today's computer systems have made talent management more practical. Companies can tap into databases and use analytic tools to keep track of which skills and knowledge they need, which needs have already been filled, which employees are developing experiences to help them meet future needs, and which sources of talent have met talent needs most efficiently. For example, large warehouses are using labor management systems to staff their facilities in the most efficient way. If the system detects a surge of orders to be picked, it can help managers reassign workers to keep up with the highest-priority tasks and delay low-priority work. The systems also can forecast the number of positions needed to get work done on time. Furthermore, labor management systems are useful for other HR decisions, such as work design and performance measurement.[23]

In evaluating the results, the most obvious step is checking whether the organization has succeeded in avoiding labor shortages or surpluses. Along with measuring these numbers, the evaluation should identify which parts of the planning process contributed to success or failure. For example, consider a company where meeting human resource needs requires that employees continually learn new skills. If there is a gap between needed skills and current skill levels, the evaluation should consider whether the problem lies with failure to forecast the needed skills or with implementation. Are employees signing up for training, and is the right kind of training available?

Did You Know?

The Biggest Hiring Challenges Involve Recruiting

In a survey of more than 700 small business owners, the main hiring challenge was simply finding the right people. More than four out of ten said finding qualified workers is their biggest hiring-related challenge. Almost one-fourth said their biggest challenge is finding employees who are a good fit with their company's culture.

Question

Suppose a new local restaurant has brought you in to advise on how it can gain a competitive advantage over other restaurants in the community. Applying the results of this survey, what would you suggest the restaurant's management focus on doing better?

Sources: Vistage, "Small Business CEO Survey," April 2014, http://www.vistage-index.com; Rhonda Colvin, "April Survey Results: Many Small-Firms Expect to Hire," *The Wall Street Journal*, April 30, 2014, http://online.wsj.com; Vistage, "WSJ/Vistage Small Business CEO Survey," Vistage press center, https://www.vistage.com, accessed May 15, 2014.

Biggest Challenge in Hiring

- Finding qualified workers
- Finding employees who fit culture
- Determining whether to hire based on forecasts
- Competing with larger companies
- Ensuring training pays off
- Other challenges

Applying HR Planning to Affirmative Action

As we discussed in Chapter 3, many organizations have a human resource strategy that includes affirmative action to manage diversity or meet government requirements. Meeting affirmative-action goals requires that employers carry out an additional level of human resource planning aimed at those goals. In other words, besides looking at its overall workforce and needs, the organization looks at the representation of subgroups in its labor force—for example, the proportion of women and minorities.

Affirmative-action plans forecast and monitor the proportion of employees who are members of various protected groups (typically, women and racial or ethnic minorities). The planning looks at the representation of these employees in the organization's job categories and career tracks. The planner can compare the proportion of employees who are in each group with the proportion each group represents in the labor market. For example, the organization might note that in a labor market that is 25% Hispanic, 60% of its customer service personnel are Hispanic. This type of comparison is called a **workforce utilization review**. The organization can use this process to determine whether there is any subgroup whose proportion in the relevant labor market differs substantially from the proportion in the job category.

If the workforce utilization review indicates that some group—for example, African Americans—makes up 35% of the relevant labor market for a job category

Workforce Utilization Review

A comparison of the proportion of employees in protected groups with the proportion that each group represents in the relevant labor market.

but that this same group constitutes only 5% of the employees actually in the job category at the organization, this is evidence of underutilization. That situation could result from problems in selection or from problems in internal movement (promotions or other movement along a career path). One way to diagnose the situation would be to use transitional matrices, such as the matrix shown in Table 5.1 earlier in this chapter.

The steps in a workforce utilization review are identical to the steps in the HR planning process that were shown in Figure 5.1. The organization must assess current utilization patterns, then forecast how they are likely to change in the near future. If these analyses suggest the organization is underutilizing certain groups and if forecasts suggest this pattern is likely to continue, the organization may need to set goals and timetables for changing. The planning process may identify new strategies for recruitment or selection. The organization carries out these HR strategies and evaluates their success.

Recruiting Human Resources

LO 5-4 Describe recruitment policies organizations use to make job vacancies more attractive.

Recruiting
Any activity carried on by the organization with the primary purpose of identifying and attracting potential employees.

As the first part of this chapter shows, it is difficult to always predict exactly how many (if any) new employees the organization will have to hire in a given year in a given job category. The role of human resource recruitment is to build a supply of potential new hires that the organization can draw on if the need arises. In human resource management, **recruiting** consists of any practice or activity carried on by the organization with the primary purpose of identifying and attracting potential employees.[24] It thus creates a buffer between planning and the actual selection of new employees (the topic of the next chapter). The goals of recruiting (encouraging qualified people to apply for jobs) and selection (deciding which candidates would be the best fit) are different enough that they are most effective when performed separately, rather than combined as in a job interview that also involves selling candidates on the company.[25]

Because of differences in companies' strategies, they may assign different degrees of importance to recruiting.[26] In general, however, all companies have to make decisions in three areas of recruiting: personnel policies, recruitment sources, and the characteristics and behavior of the recruiter. As shown in Figure 5.2, these

Figure 5.2
Three Aspects of Recruiting

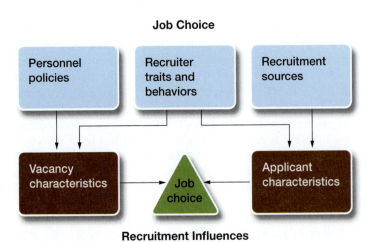

Job Choice

Recruitment Influences

aspects of recruiting have different effects on whom the organization ultimately hires. Personnel policies influence the characteristics of the positions to be filled. Recruitment sources influence the kinds of job applicants an organization reaches. And the nature and behavior of the recruiter affect the characteristics of both the vacancies and the applicants. Ultimately, an applicant's decision to accept a job offer—and the organization's decision to make the offer—depend on the match between vacancy characteristics and applicant characteristics.

The remainder of this chapter explores these three aspects of recruiting: personnel policies, recruitment sources, and recruiter traits and behaviors.

Personnel Policies

An organization's *personnel policies* are its decisions about how it will carry out human resource management, including how it will fill job vacancies. These policies influence the nature of the positions that are vacant. According to the research on recruitment, it is clear that characteristics of the vacancy are more important than recruiters or recruiting sources for predicting job choice. Several personnel policies are especially relevant to recruitment:

- *Internal versus external recruiting*—Organizations with policies to "promote from within" try to fill upper-level vacancies by recruiting candidates internally—that is, finding candidates who already work for the organization. Opportunities for advancement make a job more attractive to applicants and employees. Decisions about internal versus external recruiting affect the nature of jobs, recruitment sources, and the nature of applicants, as we will describe later in the chapter.

- *Lead-the-market pay strategies*—Pay is an important job characteristic for almost all applicants. Organizations have a recruiting advantage if their policy is to take a "lead-the-market" approach to pay—that is, pay more than the current market wages for a job. Higher pay can also make up for a job's less desirable features, such as working on a night shift or in dangerous conditions. Organizations that compete for applicants based on pay may use bonuses, stock options, and other forms of pay besides wages and salaries. Chapters 12 and 13 will take a closer look at these and other decisions about pay.

- *Employment-at-will policies*—Within the laws of the state where they are operating, employers have latitude to set polices about their rights in an employment relationship. A widespread policy follows the principle of **employment at will**, which holds that if there is no specific employment contract saying otherwise, the employer or employee may end an employment relationship at any time. An alternative is to establish extensive **due-process policies**, which formally lay out the steps an employee may take to appeal an employer's decision to terminate that employee. An organization's lawyers may advise the company to ensure that all recruitment documents say the employment is "at will" to protect the company from lawsuits about wrongful charge. Management must decide how to weigh any legal advantages against the impact on recruitment. Job applicants are more attracted to organizations with due-process policies, which imply greater job security and concern for protecting employees, than to organizations with employment-at-will policies.[27]

- *Image advertising*—Besides advertising specific job openings, as discussed in the next section, organizations may advertise themselves as a good place to work in general. Advertising designed to create a generally favorable impression of the organization is called *image advertising*. Image advertising is particularly

Employment at Will
Employment principle that if there is no specific employment contract saying otherwise, the employer or employee may end an employment relationship at any time, regardless of cause.

Due-Process Policies
Policies that formally lay out the steps an employee may take to appeal the employer's decision to terminate that employee.

important for organizations in highly competitive labor markets that perceive themselves as having a bad image.[28] Research suggests that the image of an organization's brand—for example, innovative, dynamic, or fun—influences the degree to which a person feels attracted to the organization.[29] This attraction is especially true if the person's own traits seem to match those of the organization. Also, job applicants seem to be particularly sensitive to issues of diversity and inclusion in image advertising, so organizations should ensure that their image advertisements reflect the broad nature of the labor market from which they intend to recruit.[30]

Recruitment Sources

Another critical element of an organization's recruitment strategy is its decisions about where to look for applicants. The total labor market is enormous and spread over the entire globe. As a practical matter, an organization will draw from a small fraction of that total market. The methods the organization chooses for communicating its labor needs and the audiences it targets will determine the size and nature of the labor market the organization taps to fill its vacant positions.[31] A person who responds to a job advertisement on the Internet is likely to be different from a person responding to a sign hanging outside a factory. Each of the major sources from which organizations draw recruits has advantages and disadvantages. For an example of a company that weighs these carefully, see the "Best Practices" box.

LO 5-5 List and compare sources of job applicants.

Job Posting
The process of communicating information about a job vacancy on company bulletin boards, in employee publications, on corporate intranets, and anywhere else the organization communicates with employees.

Internal Sources

As we discussed with regard to personnel policies, an organization may emphasize internal or external sources of job applicants. Internal sources are employees who currently hold other positions in the organization. Organizations recruit existing employees through **job posting**, or communicating information about the vacancy on company bulletin boards, in employee publications, on corporate intranets, and anywhere else the organization communicates with employees. Managers also may identify candidates to recommend for vacancies. Policies that emphasize promotions and even lateral moves to achieve broader career experience can give applicants a favorable impression of the organization's jobs. The use of internal sources also affects what kinds of people the organization recruits.

For the employer, relying on internal sources offers several advantages.[32] First, it generates applicants who are well known to the organization. In addition, these applicants are relatively knowledgeable about the organization's vacancies, which minimizes the possibility they will have unrealistic expectations about the job. Finally, filling vacancies through internal recruiting is generally cheaper and faster than looking outside the organization.

One company that has benefited from a strong internal hiring system is Intercontinental Hotels Group. Intercontinental has been opening about one new hotel every day. These expansion plans are driving a need for hundreds of thousands of new employees, but the company wants to fill as many positions as possible from inside the organization. Internal recruiting supports the organization's strategy of staffing with people who are so dedicated to the brand that this attitude shows up in exceptional customer service. People already working at the company are most likely to have developed the desired level of commitment. To match employees with open positions, the company runs a Careers Week twice a year. During Careers Week, Intercontinental encourages its employees to create a profile in the company's online

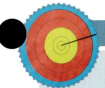

Best Practices

Sources of Talent for Advanced Technology Services

In providing its clients with hard-to-find skills, Advanced Technology Services (ATS) helps them with a recruiting problem—and also has to tackle the problem itself. Based in Peoria, Illinois, ATS provides machinery repair and maintenance services to clients' factories. Clients can focus on designing, making, and selling products, while ATS keeps the factories humming.

This service is valuable because skilled and reliable machinists and maintenance technicians have become hard to find. The offshoring trend of the past few decades scared many young people away from manufacturing careers, and people with math and technical skills were urged to pursue college degrees instead of vocational training. Many of the skilled workers who remain are nearing retirement. Manufacturers complain they cannot find qualified workers and lack the resources to train employees who might learn the necessary skills.

Instead, addressing that need for labor is the main focus of ATS. The

company fills its demand for labor by recruiting from several sources. First, the company is committed to hiring military veterans. The company finds many who have done mechanical and maintenance work and who have good self-discipline. These qualities enable them to learn the skills for maintaining particular kinds of civilian machinery.

ATS also watches for factory closings. When these operations shut down, ATS recruiters move in with an opportunity to apply. This effort can provide experienced workers.

Finally, ATS collaborates with high schools and community colleges where it operates. It identifies needed skills, such as the ability to use computer controls, and it encourages the schools to teach these skills. When it finds candidates with technical interests and factory experience but without the specific skills needed, it brings them aboard at an entry level and connects them to training at area schools.

This combination of recruiting methods is positioning ATS for growth at a time when manufacturers are moving operations back to the United States.

Questions

1. How does ATS's approach to recruitment make it valuable to its clients?
2. Why is it important for ATS to recruit and train young workers instead of only hiring experienced employees from factories that are closing?

Sources: Advanced Technology Services website, http://www.advancedtech.com, accessed May 15, 2014; James R. Hagerty, "Skilled Worker Supplier Fuels U.S. Manufacturing Revival," *The Wall Street Journal*, May 13, 2014, http://online.wsj.com; Amit Chowdhry, "Peoria Based Advanced Technology Services Helps Improve Manufacturing Productivity," *Forbes*, August 21, 2013, http://www.forbes.com.

talent management system. So far, 5,000 employees in 89 countries have created profiles that include preferences for the locations and functions in which they would like to work. When Intercontinental has an opening, it can easily search the profiles to find candidates who might be interested and well qualified. Using the talent management system, Intercontinental is filling 84% of general manager positions and 26% of corporate jobs with current employees. The initiative has lowered recruiting costs, increased employee loyalty, and boosted productivity and profitability.[33]

External Sources

Despite the advantages of internal recruitment, organizations often have good reasons to recruit externally.[34] For entry-level positions and perhaps for specialized upper-level positions, the organization has no internal recruits from which to draw. Also, bringing in outsiders may expose the organization to new ideas or new ways of doing business. An organization that uses only internal recruitment can wind up with a workforce whose members all think alike and therefore may be poorly suited to innovation.[35]

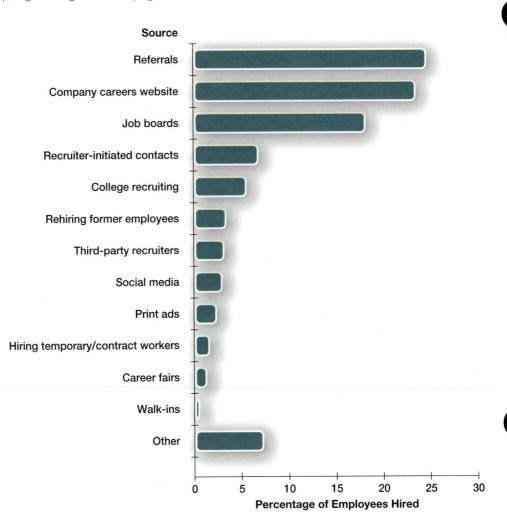

Figure 5.3
External Recruiting
Sources

Source: Based on Gerry
Crispin and Mark Mehler,
"Sources of Hire 2013:
Perception Is Reality,"
CareerXroads, March
2013, http://www
.careerxroads.com.

And finally, companies that are able to grow during a slow economy can gain a competitive edge by hiring the best talent when other organizations are forced to avoid hiring, freeze pay increases, or even lay off talented people. So organizations often recruit through direct applicants and referrals, advertisements, employment agencies, schools, and websites. Figure 5.3 shows which of these sources are used most among large companies surveyed.

Direct Applicants
People who apply for
a vacancy without
prompting from the
organization.

Referrals
People who apply for a
vacancy because some-
one in the organization
prompted them to do so.

Direct Applicants and Referrals Even without a formal effort to reach job applicants, an organization may hear from candidates through direct applicants and referrals. **Direct applicants** are people who apply for a vacancy without prompting from the organization. **Referrals** are people who apply because someone in the organization prompted them to do so. According to the survey results shown in Figure 5.3, the largest share (roughly one-fourth) of new employees hired by large companies came from referrals, and almost as many (23.4%) came from direct applications made at the careers section of the employer's website.[36] These two sources of recruits share some characteristics that make them excellent pools from which to draw.

One advantage is that many direct applicants are to some extent already "sold" on the organization. Most have done some research and concluded there is enough fit between themselves and the vacant position to warrant submitting an application, a process called *self-selection*, which, when it works, eases the pressure on the organization's recruiting and selection systems. A form of aided self-selection occurs with referrals. Many job seekers look to friends, relatives, and acquaintances to help find employment. Using these social networks not only helps the job seeker but also simplifies recruitment for employers.[37] Current employees (who are familiar with the vacancy as well as the person they are referring) decide that there is a fit between the person and the vacancy, so they convince the person to apply for the job.

An additional benefit of using such sources is that it costs much less than formal recruiting efforts. Considering these combined benefits, referrals and direct applications are among the best sources of new hires. Some employers offer current employees financial incentives for referring applicants who are hired and perform acceptably on the job (for example, if they stay 180 days). Others, including the accounting firm Ernst & Young, have set goals to increase the percentage of new employees who result from referrals; Ernst & Young's target is 50%. In support of that goal, applicants referred by employees move through Ernst & Young's selection process faster, partly because designated HR employees give their applications special attention. Ernst & Young's preference for referrals is data-driven: employees who were referred have a track record of superior performance, longer employment, and a shorter time to get up to speed.[38]

The major downside of referrals is that they limit the likelihood of exposing the organization to fresh viewpoints. People tend to refer others who are like themselves. Furthermore, sometimes referrals contribute to hiring practices that are or that appear unfair, an example being **nepotism**, or the hiring of relatives. Employees may resent the hiring and rapid promotion of "the boss's son" or "the boss's daughter," or even the boss's friend.

Nepotism
The practice of hiring relatives.

Electronic Recruiting

Few employers can fill all their vacant positions through direct applications and referrals, so most need to advertise openings. Most often today, that means posting information online. Online recruiting generally involves posting career information at company websites to address people who are interested in the particular company and posting paid advertisements at career services to attract people who are searching for jobs. Job boards such as Monster and CareerBuilder are widely used, but they can generate an unmanageable flood of applications from unqualified workers. Ads on a company's careers web page, in contrast, may generate too little notice, especially at a company that is not large or famous. Employers therefore may advertise on an industry or professional group's website, or they may select specialized niche boards, such as Dice.com's job listings for information technology professionals. In addition, companies are increasingly finding candidates through social media, as described in "HRM Social."

On any of these sites, employers are competing for attention amid the flood of online information. Research by The Ladders, a jobs website, found that workers spend less than a minute and a half reading a job ad before deciding whether to apply. In that context, gaining the interest of

Career pages on corporate websites have become the second most common source of job applicants after personal referrals.

Social Networks Can Also Be Career Networks

Listing job openings online is an easy way to let potential employees know about positions. But the ease of searching and responding to the ads means companies have been swamped with hundreds or thousands of résumés, often from individuals without the necessary qualifications. Employers therefore are trying to maintain more control over the search process.

Many are turning to social media. Most often they use the career-focused LinkedIn network. LinkedIn profiles emphasize work experience, skills, and interests. The site hosts discussion groups related to particular careers and industries. Employers can post job openings addressed to members of selected groups. Also, by joining the groups, they can read comments and identify participants who offer valuable ideas. Using an app created by software company Taleo, LinkedIn members can enter their profile data on job applications and give recruiters access to their profiles.

Employers often go beyond LinkedIn's free services and buy the site's "talent solutions" for human resource management. These products include the Recruiter tool, which can search member profiles to identify individuals with desired characteristics. For selected candidates, recruiters can send e-mail and invite them to connect and get better acquainted. The Recruiter tool also uses specified characteristics to suggest candidates to recruiters. Other tools can organize recruiters' information and plans. Organizations also may create a career page on LinkedIn to describe themselves using keywords candidates might use, highlight job listings, and tailor messages according to visitors' own profiles.

Most basically, of course, recruiters can use their own contacts on social-networking sites. Recruiters should be active wherever candidates are active, whether on LinkedIn, Facebook, Twitter, or industry or professional networks. They can ask their own contacts to suggest people to fill key openings. LinkedIn is popular because it offers such a variety of ways to identify, learn about, and interact with potential candidates. Recruiters for Klarna, an online payments company in Sweden, are encouraged to use LinkedIn because of members' detailed résumés and the site's large membership (more than 230 million), including people who are not actively searching for a job but might be a perfect fit. According to Linked-In's data, about 60% of members are not actively looking but would be open to considering an offer.

Questions

1. Based on this description, what are some advantages of finding a candidate with social media rather than posting jobs on the company's website?
2. Based on this description, would you want to post a profile for yourself on LinkedIn? Why or why not?

Sources: LinkedIn, "Recruiting Solutions on LinkedIn," http://business.linkedin.com, accessed May 15, 2014; Rachel King, "LinkedIn Revamps Recruiter Tools as It Approaches 'Mobile Moment,'" *ZDNet*, April 10, 2014, http://www.zdnet.com; Sarah Halzack, "How LinkedIn Has Changed the Way You Might Get Your Next Job," *Washington Post,* August 4, 2013, http://www.washingtonpost.com; Evelyn M. Rusli, "LinkedIn: The Ugly Duckling of Social Media," *The Wall Street Journal,* February 27, 2013, http://online.wsj.com.

qualified workers requires straightforward, simple job descriptions that highlight what is meaningful about the position. For example, in an ad for health care workers, Sodexo USA says these employees have "a tremendous impact on patient satisfaction."[39]

Most large companies and many smaller ones make career information available at their websites. To make that information easier to find, they may register a domain name with a ".jobs" extension, such as **www.starbucks.jobs** for a link to information about careers at Starbucks and **www.att.jobs** for information about careers at AT&T. To be an effective recruiting tool, corporate career information should move beyond generalities, offering descriptions of open positions and an easy way to submit a résumé. One of the best features of this kind of electronic recruiting is the ability to target and attract job candidates whose values match the organization's values and whose skills match the job requirements.[40] Candidates also appreciate an e-mail response that the company has received the résumé—especially a response that gives a timetable about further communications from the company.

Accepting applications at the company website is not so successful for smaller and less well-known organizations because fewer people are likely to visit the website. These organizations may get better results by going to the websites that are set up to attract job seekers, such as Monster, Yahoo HotJobs, and CareerBuilder, which attract a vast array of applicants. At these sites, job seekers submit standardized résumés. Employers can search the site's database for résumés that include specified key terms, and they can also submit information about their job opportunities, so that job seekers can search that information by key term. With both employers and job seekers submitting information to and conducting searches on them, these sites offer an efficient way to find matches between job seekers and job vacancies. However, a drawback is that the big job websites can provide too many leads of inferior quality because they are so huge and serve all job seekers and employers, not a select segment.

Because of this limitation of the large websites, smaller, more tailored websites called "niche boards" focus on certain industries, occupations, or geographic areas. **Telecommcareers.net**, for example, is a site devoted to, as the name implies, the telecommunications industry. **CIO.com**, a companion site to *CIO Magazine*, specializes in openings for chief information officers.

Advertisements in Newspapers and Magazines   Although computer search tools have made electronic job listings the most popular way to advertise a job opening, some recruiters still follow the traditional route and advertise open positions in newspapers or magazines. When the goal is to find people who know the local community, advertising in a local newspaper can reach that audience. Similarly, when the goal is to find people in a specialized field, advertising in a trade, professional, or industry publication can reach the right subset of job candidates.

Advertising can be expensive, so it is especially important that the ads be well written. The person designing a job advertisement needs to answer two questions:

What do we need to say?
To whom do we need to say it?

With respect to the first question, an ad should give readers enough information to evaluate the job and its requirements, so they can make a well-informed judgment about their qualifications. Providing enough information may require long advertisements, which cost more. The employer should evaluate the additional costs against the costs of providing too little information: Vague ads generate a huge number of applicants, including many who are not reasonably qualified or would not accept the job if they learned more about it. Reviewing all these applications to eliminate unsuitable applicants is expensive. In practice, the people who write job advertisements tend to overstate the skills and experience required, perhaps generating too few qualified candidates.

Specifying whom to reach with the message helps the advertiser decide where to place the ad. Ads placed in the classified section of local newspapers are relatively inexpensive yet reach many people in a specific geographic area who are currently looking for work (or at least interested enough to be reading the classifieds). On the downside, this medium offers little ability to target skill levels. Typically, many of the people reading classified ads are either over- or underqualified for the position. Also, people who are not looking for work rarely read the classifieds. These people may include candidates the organization could lure from their current employers. For reaching a specific part of the labor market, including certain skill levels and more people who are employed, the organization may get better results from advertising in professional or industry journals. Some employers also advertise on television— particularly cable television.[41]

Public Employment Agencies   The Social Security Act of 1935 requires that everyone receiving unemployment compensation be registered with a local state employment office. These state employment offices work with the U.S. Employment Service (USES) to try to ensure that unemployed individuals eventually get off state aid and back on employer payrolls. To accomplish this, agencies collect information from the unemployed people about their skills and experience.

Employers can register their job vacancies with their local state employment office, and the agency will try to find someone suitable, using its computerized inventory of local unemployed individuals. The agency refers candidates to the employer at no charge. The organization can interview or test them to see if they are suitable for its vacancies. Besides offering access to job candidates at low cost, public employment agencies can be a useful resource for meeting certain diversity objectives. Laws often mandate that the agencies maintain specialized "desks" for minorities, disabled individuals, and war veterans. Employers that feel they currently are underutilizing any of these subgroups of the labor force may find the agencies to be an excellent source.

Government-run employment agencies also may partner with nonprofit groups to meet the needs of a community. In California's Alameda and Contra Costa Counties, several agencies have cooperated to form EastBay Works. This organization is dedicated to bringing together employers and workers in the two counties. EastBay Works offers a variety of recruiting tools at its website. Employers can post job openings, research the local labor market, and set up a search tool to identify candidates who have skills the employer is looking for. Job seekers can visit the site to hunt for jobs, set up a search tool that finds jobs related to the skills in their profile, assess their existing skills, and arrange for training in skills that employers want.[42]

Private Employment Agencies   In contrast to public employment agencies, which primarily serve the blue-collar labor market, private employment agencies provide much the same service for the white-collar labor market. Workers interested in finding a job can sign up with a private employment agency whether or not they are currently unemployed. Another difference between the two types of agencies is that private agencies charge the employers for providing referrals. Therefore, using a private employment agency is more expensive than using a public agency, but the private agency is a more suitable source for certain kinds of applicants.

For managers or professionals, an employer may use the services of a type of private agency called an *executive search firm (ESF)*. People often call these agencies "headhunters" because, unlike other employment agencies, they find new jobs for people almost exclusively already employed. For job candidates, dealing with executive search firms can be sensitive. Typically, executives do not want to advertise their availability, because it could trigger a negative reaction from their current employer. ESFs serve as a buffer, providing confidentiality between the employer and the recruit. That benefit may give an employer access to candidates it cannot recruit in other, more direct ways. The advantages of using a private firm are most evident in recruiting top executives. For middle-management jobs, the trend is for companies to hire their own recruiters to tap social media and other business networks.[43]

Colleges and Universities   Most colleges and universities have placement services that seek to help their graduates obtain employment. On-campus interviewing is the most important source of recruits for entry-level professional and managerial vacancies. Organizations tend to focus especially on colleges that have strong reputations in areas for which they have critical needs—say, chemical engineering or public accounting. Bain & Co., a consulting firm, recruits on about 15 U.S. campuses each year and may hire up to 40 students at one school for positions and interns and full-time employees. It chooses schools to visit based on their size, reputation, and whether it has succeeded in finding good employees at the school in the past.[44]

Many employers have found that successfully competing for the best students requires more than just signing up prospective graduates for interview slots. One of the best ways to establish a stronger presence on a campus is with a college internship program. Internship programs give an organization early access to potential applicants and let the organization assess their capabilities directly. Internships also give applicants firsthand experience with the employer, so both parties can make well-informed choices about fit when it comes time to consider long-term commitment.[45] Google calls internships "one of the primary ways we find full-time hires." In a recent year, the company hired 1,000 engineering interns.[46]

One of the best ways for a company to establish a stronger presence on a campus is with a college internship program. Embassy Suites is one company that participates in such a program. How does this benefit the company and the students at the same time?

Another way of increasing the employer's presence on campus is to participate in university job fairs. In general, a job fair is an event where many employers gather for a short time to meet large numbers of potential job applicants. Although job fairs can be held anywhere (such as at a hotel or convention center), campuses are ideal locations because of the many well-educated, yet unemployed, individuals who are there. Job fairs are an inexpensive means of generating an on-campus presence. They can even provide one-on-one dialogue with potential recruits—dialogue that would be impossible through less interactive media, such as newspaper ads.

Evaluating the Quality of a Source

In general, there are few rules that say what recruitment source is best for a given job vacancy. Therefore, it is wise for employers to monitor the quality of all their recruitment sources. One way to do this is to develop and compare **yield ratios** for each source.[47] A yield ratio expresses the percentage of applicants who successfully move from one stage of the recruitment and selection process to the next. For example, the organization could find the number of candidates interviewed as a percentage of the total number of résumés generated by a given source (that is, number of interviews divided by number of résumés). A high yield ratio (large percentage) means that the source is an effective way to find candidates to interview. By comparing the yield ratios of different recruitment sources, HR professionals can determine which source is the best or most efficient for the type of vacancy.

Another measure of recruitment success is the **cost per hire**. To compute this amount, find the cost of using a particular recruitment source for a particular type of vacancy. Then divide that cost by the number of people hired to fill that type of vacancy. A low cost per hire means that the recruitment source is efficient; it delivers qualified candidates at minimal cost.

To see how HR professionals use these measures, look at the examples in Table 5.3. This table shows the results for a hypothetical organization that used six kinds of recruitment sources to fill a number of vacancies. For each recruitment source, the table shows four yield ratios and the cost per hire. To fill these jobs, the best two sources of recruits were local universities and employee referral programs. Online job board ads generated the largest number of recruits (7,000 résumés). However, only 350 were judged acceptable, of which a little more than half accepted employment offers, for a cumulative yield ratio of 200/7,000, or 3%. Recruiting at renowned universities generated highly qualified applicants,

Yield Ratio
A ratio that expresses the percentage of applicants who successfully move from one stage of the recruitment and selection process to the next.

Cost per Hire
The total amount of money spent to fill a job vacancy. The number is computed by finding the cost of using a particular recruitment source and dividing that cost by the number of people hired to fill that type of vacancy.

Table 5.3

Results of a Hypothetical Recruiting Effort

	RECRUITING SOURCE					
	LOCAL UNIVERSITY	**RENOWNED UNIVERSITY**	**EMPLOYEE REFERRALS**	**NEWSPAPER AD**	**ONLINE JOB BOARD AD**	**EXECUTIVE SEARCH FIRMS**
Résumés generated	200	400	50	500	7,000	20
Interview offers accepted	175	100	45	400	500	20
Yield ratio	87%	25%	90%	80%	7%	100%
Applicants judged acceptable	100	95	40	50	350	19
Yield ratio	57%	95%	89%	12%	70%	95%
Accept employment offers	90	10	35	25	200	15
Yield ratio	90%	11%	88%	50%	57%	79%
Cumulative yield ratio	90/200	10/400	35/50	25/500	200/7,000	15/20
	45%	3%	70%	5%	3%	75%
Cost	$30,000	$50,000	$15,000	$20,000	$5,000	$90,000
Cost per hire	$333	$5,000	$428	$800	$25	$6,000

but relatively few of them ultimately accepted positions with the organization. Executive search firms produced the highest cumulative yield ratio. These generated only 20 applicants, but all of them accepted interview offers, most were judged acceptable, and 79% of these acceptable candidates took jobs with the organization. However, notice the cost per hire. The executive search firms charged $90,000 for finding these 15 employees, resulting in the largest cost per hire. In contrast, local universities provided modest yield ratios at the lowest cost per hire. Employee referrals provided excellent yield ratios at a slightly higher cost.

The cost per hire is not simply related to the type of recruiting method. These costs also tend to vary by industry and organization size. A recent survey found that the median cost per hire at companies with more than 10,000 employees was $1,949; small companies paid far more for each hire, a median of $3,665. One reason for this difference is that small companies have fewer recruiters in-house, so they are likelier to hire outsiders at a higher cost. Comparing industries, manufacturers paid the highest cost per hire, because finding individuals with knowledge of the relevant equipment or software is more difficult than finding employees with standard kinds of certification, as in the case of nurses.[48] At any employer, however, recruiters' challenge is to identify the particular methods that will yield the best candidates as efficiently as possible.

LO 5-6 Describe the recruiter's role in the recruitment process, including limits and opportunities.

Recruiter Traits and Behaviors

As we showed in Figure 5.2, the third influence on recruitment outcomes is the recruiter, including this person's characteristics and the way he or she behaves. The recruiter affects the nature of both the job vacancy and the applicants generated. However, the recruiter often becomes involved late in the recruitment process. In many cases, by the time a recruiter meets some applicants, they have already made up their minds about what they desire in a job, what the vacant job has to offer, and their likelihood of receiving a job offer.[49]

Many applicants approach the recruiter with some skepticism. Knowing it is the recruiter's job to sell them on a vacancy, some applicants discount what the recruiter says in light of what they have heard from other sources, such as friends, magazine articles, and professors. When candidates are already familiar with the company through knowing about its products, the recruiter's impact is especially weak.[50] For these and other reasons, recruiters' characteristics and behaviors seem to have limited impact on applicants' job choices.

Characteristics of the Recruiter

Most organizations must choose whether their recruiters are specialists in human resources or are experts at particular jobs (that is, those who currently hold the same kinds of jobs or supervise people who hold the jobs). According to some studies, applicants perceive HR specialists as less credible and are less attracted to jobs when recruiters are HR specialists.[51] The evidence does not completely discount a positive role for personnel specialists in recruiting. It does indicate, however, that these specialists need to take extra steps to ensure that applicants perceive them as knowledgeable and credible.

In general, applicants respond positively to recruiters whom they perceive as warm and informative. "Warm" means the recruiter seems to care about the applicant and to be enthusiastic about the applicant's potential to contribute to the organization. "Informative" means the recruiter provides the kind of information the applicant is seeking. The evidence of impact of other characteristics of recruiters—including their age, sex, and race—is complex and inconsistent.[52]

Behavior of the Recruiter

Recruiters affect results not only by providing plenty of information, but by providing the right kind of information. Perhaps the most-researched aspect of recruiting is the level of realism in the recruiter's message. Because the recruiter's job is to attract candidates, recruiters may feel pressure to exaggerate the positive qualities of the vacancy and to downplay its negative qualities. Applicants are highly sensitive to negative information. The highest-quality applicants may be less willing to pursue jobs when this type of information comes out.[53] But if the recruiter goes too far in a positive direction, the candidate can be misled and lured into taking a job that has been misrepresented. Then unmet expectations can contribute to a high turnover rate. When recruiters describe jobs unrealistically, people who take those jobs may come to believe that the employer is deceitful.[54]

Many studies have looked at how well **realistic job previews**—background information about jobs' positive and negative qualities—can get around this problem and help organizations minimize turnover among new employees. On the whole, the research suggests that realistic job previews have a weak and inconsistent effect on turnover.[55] Although realistic job previews have only a weak association with reduced turnover, the cost of the effort is low, and they are relatively easy to implement. Consequently, employers should consider using them as a way to reduce turnover among new hires.[56]

Realistic Job Preview
Background information about a job's positive and negative qualities.

Finally, for affecting whether people choose to take a job, but even more so, whether they stick with a job, the recruiter seems less important than an organization's personnel policies that directly affect the job's features (pay, security, advancement opportunities, and so on).

Enhancing the Recruiter's Impact

Nevertheless, although recruiters are probably not the most important influence on people's job choices, this does not mean recruiters cannot have an impact. Most recruiters receive little training.[57] If we were to determine what does matter to job candidates, perhaps recruiters could be trained in those areas.

Researchers have tried to find the conditions in which recruiters do make a difference. Such research suggests that an organization can take several steps to increase the positive impact that recruiters have on job candidates:

- Recruiters should provide timely feedback. Applicants dislike delays in feedback. They may draw negative conclusions about the organization (for starters, that the organization doesn't care about their application).
- Recruiters should avoid offensive behavior. They should avoid behaving in ways that might convey the wrong impression about the organization.[58] Figure 5.4 quotes

Figure 5.4
Recruits Who Were Offended by Recruiters

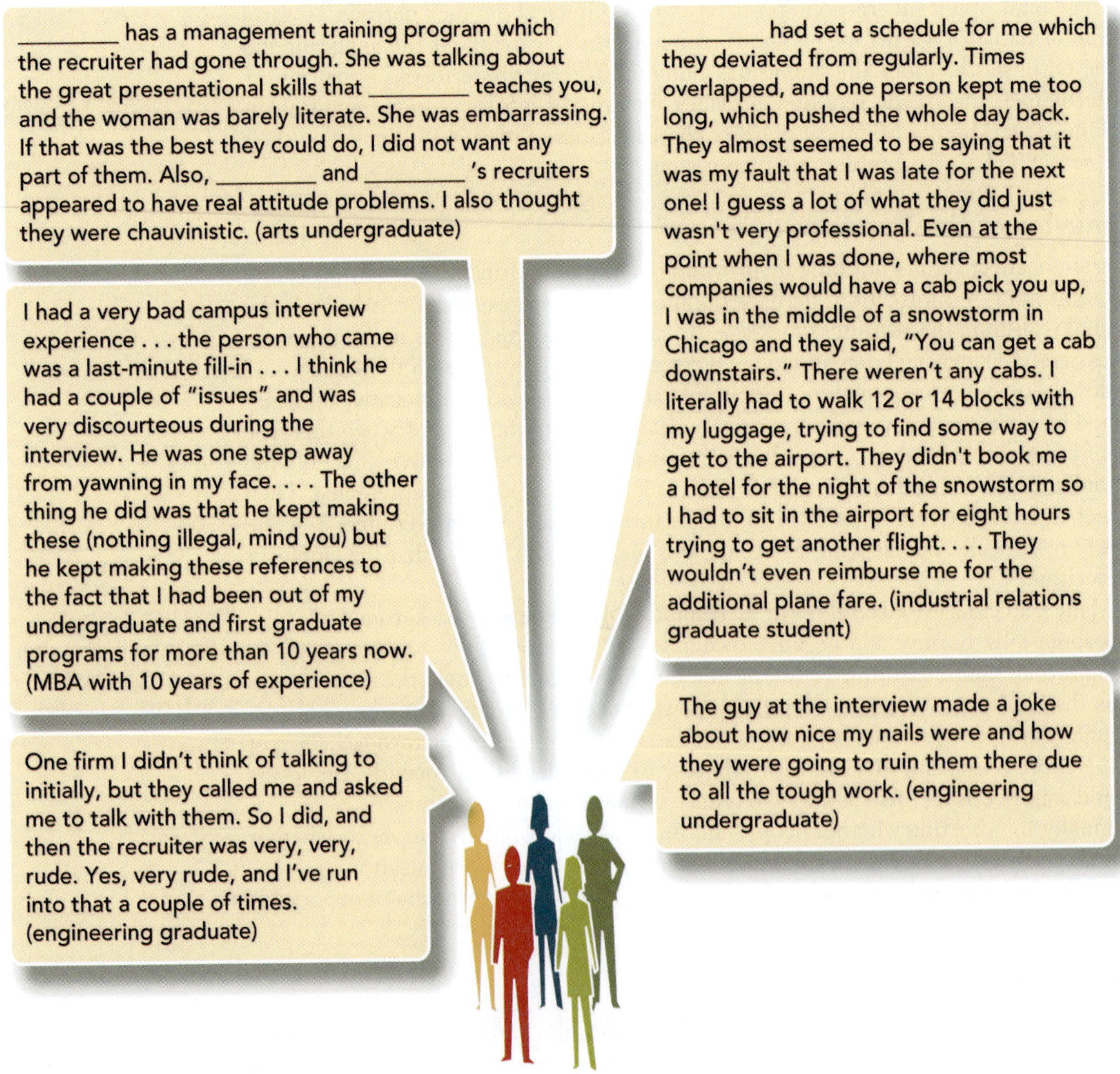

_____ has a management training program which the recruiter had gone through. She was talking about the great presentational skills that _____ teaches you, and the woman was barely literate. She was embarrassing. If that was the best they could do, I did not want any part of them. Also, _____ and _____ 's recruiters appeared to have real attitude problems. I also thought they were chauvinistic. (arts undergraduate)

I had a very bad campus interview experience . . . the person who came was a last-minute fill-in . . . I think he had a couple of "issues" and was very discourteous during the interview. He was one step away from yawning in my face. . . . The other thing he did was that he kept making these (nothing illegal, mind you) but he kept making these references to the fact that I had been out of my undergraduate and first graduate programs for more than 10 years now. (MBA with 10 years of experience)

One firm I didn't think of talking to initially, but they called me and asked me to talk with them. So I did, and then the recruiter was very, very, rude. Yes, very rude, and I've run into that a couple of times. (engineering graduate)

_____ had set a schedule for me which they deviated from regularly. Times overlapped, and one person kept me too long, which pushed the whole day back. They almost seemed to be saying that it was my fault that I was late for the next one! I guess a lot of what they did just wasn't very professional. Even at the point when I was done, where most companies would have a cab pick you up, I was in the middle of a snowstorm in Chicago and they said, "You can get a cab downstairs." There weren't any cabs. I literally had to walk 12 or 14 blocks with my luggage, trying to find some way to get to the airport. They didn't book me a hotel for the night of the snowstorm so I had to sit in the airport for eight hours trying to get another flight. . . . They wouldn't even reimburse me for the additional plane fare. (industrial relations graduate student)

The guy at the interview made a joke about how nice my nails were and how they were going to ruin them there due to all the tough work. (engineering undergraduate)

applicants who felt they had extremely bad experiences with recruiters. Their statements provide examples of behaviors to avoid.

- The organization can recruit with teams rather than individual recruiters. Applicants view job experts as more credible than HR specialists, and a team can include both kinds of recruiters. HR specialists on the team provide knowledge about company policies and procedures.

Through such positive behavior, recruiters can give organizations a better chance of competing for talented human resources. In the next chapter, we will describe how an organization selects the candidates who best meet its needs.

THINKING ETHICALLY

IS SOMETHING WRONG WITH A MUTUAL AGREEMENT NOT TO "STEAL" EMPLOYEES?

In the high-tech industry, recruiting is a war for talent as companies compete for the best engineers and programmers. Presumably, anyone good enough to get hired by Apple or Google would be an asset for another company, so one strategy is to recruit at those and other big-name companies by contacting employees directly and seeing what it would take to lure them away. The aim of this strategy is to get the best people at the expense of competitors, which presumably are left with the second best.

Competing for already-employed workers imposes high costs on employers. They have to pay employees so generously that they would not consider leaving. When recruiting, they have to make even more generous offers. And if many employers are using this recruiting tactic, companies are constantly scrambling to replace workers "stolen" or "poached" by other companies.

Evidence has surfaced that some of the most prominent high-tech firms, including Google, Apple, Intel, and Adobe Systems, may have tried to put a stop to this expensive competition for talent. Correspondence among some executives and HR employees refers to informal agreements not to recruit one another's employees. At some companies, including Facebook and Palm, however, there is evidence that executives have refused to participate in these arrangements.

The possibility of no-poaching agreements came to light because employees complained the practice was suppressing competition in the labor market. What employers were thinking of as poaching employees, these employees viewed as a chance to seek the best employment opportunities. In response to their allegations, the Justice Department filed a civil lawsuit against several companies, saying they illegally colluded to restrict the free movement of labor and to fix wages. The companies settled by agreeing not to restrict recruiting or hiring in the future, while not admitting to any past wrongdoing. More recently, a group of 64,000 engineers filed an antitrust lawsuit. The parties reached a settlement for about $300 million, which if approved, will give each engineer several thousand dollars after the lawyers are paid.

Questions

1. What has been the financial incentive for high-tech companies to agree not to recruit from one another? If the arrangements had not been challenged in court, would you consider them ethical? Why or why not?
2. Given that the Justice Department has seen these arrangements as possibly violating antitrust laws, what would be the most ethical way to decide whether to recruit employees from other companies?

Sources: David Streitfeld, "Tech Giants Settle Antitrust Hiring Suit," *The New York Times*, April 24, 2014, http://www.nytimes.com; Jeff Elder, "Silicon Valley Tech Giants Discussed Hiring, Say Documents," *The Wall Street Journal*, April 20, 2014, http://online.wsj.com; S. Lynch, "Google and Apple Are Safe from Anti-Poaching Laws, but Not for Long," *Silicon Valley Business Journal Online*, April 5, 2013; M. Wohsten, "Gentlemen's Agreements," *Lansing State Journal*, January 29, 2012, p. 13A.

SUMMARY

LO 5-1 Discuss how to plan for human resources needed to carry out the organization's strategy.

- The first step in human resource planning is personnel forecasting. Through trend analysis and good judgment, the planner tries to determine the supply of and demand for various human resources.
- Based on whether a surplus or a shortage is expected, the planner sets goals and creates a strategy for achieving those goals.
- The organization then implements its HR strategy and evaluates the results.

LO 5-2 Determine the labor demand for workers in various job categories.

- The planner can look at leading indicators, assuming trends will continue in the future.
- Multiple regression can convert several leading indicators into a single prediction of labor needs.
- Analysis of a transitional matrix can help the planner identify which job categories can be filled internally and where high turnover is likely.

LO 5-3 Summarize the advantages and disadvantages of ways to eliminate a labor surplus and avoid a labor shortage.

- To reduce a surplus, downsizing, pay reductions, and demotions deliver fast results but at a high cost in human suffering that may hurt surviving employees' motivation and future recruiting. Also, the organization may lose some of its best employees.
- Transferring employees and requiring them to share work are also fast methods, and the consequences in human suffering are less severe.
- A hiring freeze or natural attrition is slow to take effect but avoids the pain of layoffs.
- Early-retirement packages may unfortunately induce the best employees to leave and may be slow to implement; however, they, too, are less painful than layoffs.
- Retraining can improve the organization's overall pool of human resources and maintain high morale, but it is relatively slow and costly.
- To avoid a labor shortage, requiring overtime is the easiest and fastest strategy, which can easily be changed if conditions change. However, overtime may exhaust workers and can hurt morale.
- Using temporary employees and outsourcing do not build an in-house pool of talent, but they quickly and easily modify staffing levels.

- Transferring and retraining employees require investment of time and money, but can enhance the quality of the organization's human resources; however, this may backfire if a labor surplus develops.
- Hiring new employees is slow and expensive, but strengthens the organization if labor needs are expected to expand for the long term. Hiring is difficult to reverse if conditions change.
- Using technology as a substitute for labor can be slow to implement and costly, but it may improve the organization's long-term performance. New technology also is difficult to reverse.

LO 5-4 Describe recruitment policies organizations use to make job vacancies more attractive.

- Internal recruiting (promotions from within) generally makes job vacancies more attractive because candidates see opportunities for growth and advancement.
- Lead-the-market pay strategies make jobs economically desirable.
- Due-process policies signal that employers are concerned about employee rights.
- Image advertising can give candidates the impression that the organization is a good place to work.

LO 5-5 List and compare sources of job applicants.

- Internal sources, promoted through job postings, generate applicants who are familiar to the organization and motivate other employees by demonstrating opportunities for advancement. However, internal sources are usually insufficient for all of an organization's labor needs.
- Direct applicants and referrals tend to be inexpensive and to generate applicants who have self-selected; this source risks charges of unfairness, especially in cases of nepotism.
- Electronic recruiting gives organizations access to a global labor market, tends to be inexpensive, and allows convenient searching of databases.
- Newspaper and magazine advertising reaches a wide audience and may generate many applications, although many are likely to be unsuitable.
- Public employment agencies are inexpensive and typically have screened applicants.
- Private employment agencies charge fees but may provide many services.
- Another inexpensive channel is schools and colleges, which may give the employer access to top-notch entrants to the labor market.

LO 5-6 Describe the recruiter's role in the recruitment process, including limits and opportunities.

- Through their behavior and other characteristics, recruiters influence the nature of the job vacancy and the kinds of applicants generated.
- Applicants tend to perceive job experts as more credible than recruiters who are HR specialists.
- Applicants tend to react more favorably to recruiters who are warm and informative.

- Recruiters should not mislead candidates. Realistic job previews have only a weak association with reduced turnover, but given their low cost and ease of implementation, employers should consider using them.
- Recruiters can improve their impact by providing timely feedback, avoiding behavior that contributes to a negative impression of the organization, and teaming up with job experts.

KEY TERMS

forecasting, 133
trend analysis, 134
leading indicators, 134
transitional matrix, 135
core competency, 137
downsizing, 138

outsourcing, 143
workforce utilization review, 145
recruiting, 146
employment at will, 147
due-process policies, 147
job posting, 148

direct applicants, 150
referrals, 150
nepotism, 151
yield ratio, 155
cost per hire, 155
realistic job preview, 157

REVIEW AND DISCUSSION QUESTIONS

1. Suppose an organization expects a labor shortage to develop in key job areas over the next few years. Recommend general responses the organization could make in each of the following areas: *(LO 5-1)*
   a. Recruitment
   b. Training
   c. Compensation (pay and employee benefits)
2. Review the sample transitional matrix shown in Table 5.1. What jobs experience the greatest turnover (employees leaving the organization)? How might an organization with this combination of jobs reduce the turnover? *(LO 5-2)*
3. In the same transitional matrix, which jobs seem to rely the most on internal recruitment? Which seem to rely most on external recruitment? Why? *(LO 5-2)*
4. Why do organizations combine statistical and judgmental forecasts of labor demand, rather than relying on statistics or judgment alone? Give an example of a situation in which each type of forecast would be inaccurate. *(LO 5-3)*
5. Some organizations have detailed affirmative-action plans, complete with goals and timetables, for women and minorities, yet have no formal human resource plan for the organization as a whole. Why might this be the case? What does this practice

suggest about the role of human resource management in these organizations? *(LO 5-1)*
6. Give an example of a personnel policy that would help attract a larger pool of job candidates. Give an example of a personnel policy that would likely reduce the pool of candidates. Would you expect these policies to influence the quality as well as the number of applicants? Why or why not? *(LO 5-4)*
7. Discuss the relative merits of internal versus external recruitment. Give an example of a situation in which each of these approaches might be particularly effective. *(LO 5-4)*
8. List the jobs you have held. How were you recruited for each of these? From the organization's perspective, what were some pros and cons of recruiting you through these methods? *(LO 5-4)*
9. Recruiting people for jobs that require international assignments is increasingly important for many organizations. Where might an organization go to recruit people interested in such assignments? *(LO 5-5)*
10. A large share of HR professionals have rated e-cruiting as their best source of new talent. What qualities of electronic recruiting do you think contribute to this opinion? *(LO 5-5)*
11. How can organizations improve the effectiveness of their recruiters? *(LO 5-6)*

TAKING RESPONSIBILITY

SAP's Inclusive Approach to Recruiting

Headquartered in Germany, SAP makes software that businesses use to keep the enterprise running smoothly and efficiently. Its 65,000 employees work in more than 130 countries. Given that the company sells complex business systems rather than famous consumer products, recruiting includes educating workers about the company.

SAP's recruiting strategy is based on the idea that its human resources are a source of competitive advantage. Co-CEO Bill McDermott has said SAP is constantly recruiting "young, brilliant minds" and training people, because "sustainability is much more than natural resources. It's also people resources." SAP cultivates the image of a leader in innovation. The careers page of its website says, "We respect the individuality of our employees," and represents this with a transparent process linking each applicant to any relevant openings. Candidates also may set up a "job agent" to send notifications of new openings meeting specified criteria, read "Advice Bytes" stories from employees, and sign up to follow SAP on Twitter.

Where SAP's idea of sustainable human resources really stands out, however, is in an initiative to recruit workers with autism. These workers have trouble finding jobs because they struggle with social tasks like interviewing and networking. For SAP, however, hiring people with autism is not just a matter of accommodating people with disabilities, but one of identifying an often-overlooked group of workers who bring value to the table. The autism spectrum includes a wide range of conditions from high functioning to severe, and some individuals are not only able to work but gifted in some areas. For example, their thinking patterns may be highly structured, and they may pay careful attention to details. For some jobs, such as writing manuals and debugging software, these ways of thinking are exactly what SAP needs. The company therefore has a target that by 2020, up to 1% of its workforce will be employees with autism.

SAP tested its recruitment of workers with autism in Germany and India; based on the pilot program's success, it rolled out the effort to Ireland, Canada, and the United States. A Danish training and consulting firm called Specialisterne screens candidates. Those who pass the screening are referred to SAP. After SAP selects employees, it provides adaptation training to help them adjust to working on teams, and it assigns them to a mentor. In exchange for this extra effort, the company sees a competitive advantage. Luisa Delgado, a member of SAP's executive board, put it this way: "Only by employing people who think differently and spark innovation will SAP be prepared to handle the challenges of the 21st century."

Questions

1. What recruiting methods described here support SAP's need for talented workers who help the company innovate?
2. Suggest a few other recruiting methods that would help SAP remain a strong, innovative company.

Sources: SAP careers page, http://www.careersatsap.com, accessed May 15, 2014; Shirley S. Wang, "How Autism Can Help You Land a Job," *The Wall Street Journal*, March 27, 2014, http://online.wsj.com; Rob Preston, "SAP CEO Envisions Younger, Greener, Cloudier Company," *InformationWeek*, November 25, 2013, http://www.informationweek.com; Katie Moisse, "Tech Giant Sees 'Competitive Advantage' in Autistic Workforce," *ABC News*, May 22, 2013, http://abcnews.go.com; Dave Smith, "SAP Recruits Autism Employees to 'Spark Innovation,'" *International Business Times*, May 22, 2013, http://www.ibtimes.com.

MANAGING TALENT

Boeing's High-Flying Approach to HR Planning and Recruitment

As the world's biggest aerospace company, Boeing is well acquainted with the industry's major human resource challenge: identifying, attracting, and keeping enough skilled workers. Across manufacturing, the demand for engineers is intense, but it is especially so in aerospace. Engineers flocked to aerospace companies during the space race, but more recently, Internet companies are the main attraction. Consequently, the average age for aeronautical engineers is 47, compared with 42 for U.S. workers overall. In other words, many are approaching retirement. Compounding the problem, Boeing is in the defense business, so it faces legal limits on the number of non-U.S. citizens it may hire.

To meet the challenge, Boeing has dedicated years to establishing a systematic approach to talent management linked to strategy. The system begins with the establishment of priorities. HR executives talk to business leaders about anticipated workforce needs. They divide the workforce into segments and identify which are most critical to success and where the current skills of the workforce do not meet those critical needs. They use predictive models to forecast business trends and workforce demographics. They analyze all this information to identify the changes needed to fill in the gaps in Boeing's workforce. Then, to apply the results of this analysis, Boeing's HR team plans how to make the necessary changes through a combination of three tactics: promotions within the company, transfers of employees into positions where they can be developed to meet future needs, and recruitment of employees outside Boeing.

A key aspect of recruitment is reaching out to entry-level engineers on college and university campuses. Boeing has intensified these efforts and is matching other companies' practice of making job offers earlier during students' senior years. During recruitment, students interview with several different managers and tour company facilities, so they understand the company and its culture and opportunities. Then, to ensure that the reality of working for Boeing lives up to the image portrayed during recruitment, Boeing has a workforce development program that plans career growth opportunities as carefully as the company plans hiring.

Recruiting efforts alone cannot meet Boeing's needs unless schools are preparing individuals for technology-related jobs. Therefore, Boeing also enters into partnerships with schools. As analysis of workforce needs uncovers important emerging skills, Boeing helps school leaders plan how to teach those skills. Supporting university research projects bolsters the company's innovative image on campus. Boeing has also set up a Higher Education Integration Board, which identifies needs for continuing education, evaluates the quality of employees hired from specific schools, and sets strategy for future recruiting and research efforts.

Questions

1. To meet labor shortages within the company, Boeing starts with promotions and transfers. What advantages might it experience from filling positions with current employees?

2. Besides the external recruitment sources described here, what other sources would you recommend for Boeing? Why?

Sources: Claire Zillman, "America's Defense Industry Is Going Gray," *Fortune*, November 14, 2013, http://management.fortune.cnn.com; PricewaterhouseCoopers, "The Right Stuff," *Keyword*, July 2013, http://www.pwc.com; Kathleen Koster, "Talent Management: Establishing a Flight Plan," *Employee Benefit News*, April 1, 2013, Business Insights: Global, http://bi.galegroup.com; Agence France-Presse, "Boeing and Airbus 'Fight like Hell,' for Aerospace Engineers," *Industry Week*, June 26, 2012, http://www.industryweek.com.

HR IN SMALL BUSINESS

For Personal Financial Advisors, a Small Staffing Plan with a Big Impact

Robert J. Reed has been a financial planner since 1978 and received his Certified Financial Planner designation in 1981. In 1999, he hired Lucy Banquer, a former legal secretary, to work as his assistant and the only employee at his firm, Personal Financial Advisors LLC in Covington, Louisiana. At that point, human resource planning wasn't on Reed's radar at all.

But around 2005, Reed began to act on a desire to have a more complete plan for his firm's growth. He determined that he wanted the business to grow from about $400,000 in annual revenues to become a million-dollar firm by 2012. That was a realistic goal, but not one he could achieve with only the support of Banquer. Although Banquer does an excellent job of fielding client phone calls and answering questions, Reed needed to bring in more financial expertise to serve more clients.

Typically, a financial-planning firm like Reed's expands by hiring an entry-level adviser to handle routine tasks while learning on the job until he or she can take on clients independently. But Reed didn't simply take the usual path; he considered what role he wanted for himself in his firm as it grew. Reed realized that the part he excelled at and loved most was managing the investments, not the presentations to clients, and that

he wanted the firm to grow in a way that would free more time for him to spend with his family, not expand his hours to supervise others. As Reed defined the scope of his own desired job, he clarified what he wanted from his next employee: a Certified Financial Planner who had experience plus an interest in all the planning and advising tasks *except* investment management.

With that strategy in mind, Reed began the search for another planner to work with him. After about eight months of recruiting, Reed met Lauren Gadkowski, who was running her own advisory firm in Boston, but preparing to relocate to Baton Rouge to be with her future husband, Lee Lindsay. Reed wanted his new financial planner to operate independently, so he agreed to the idea of her office being in Baton Rouge, about a 45-minute drive from his, and he let her determine how often she would need to visit the Covington office.

Reed stuck to his plan: Lauren Lindsay quickly began working with Reed's larger clients and introduced herself as their main contact with the firm. After sitting in on a few meetings to satisfy himself that he had made a good hiring decision, Reed shifted his efforts to managing the investments. About 10% of the clients indicated they would prefer to maintain their working relationship with Reed. Lindsay took over the remaining 90% as well as the new clients she has brought into the firm since joining it.

Reed's decision to focus on investment management has paid off for Personal Financial Advisors, giving the firm better-than-average performance on its investments even as revenues have climbed. And with Lindsay on board to handle client contact, Reed became able to follow the more traditional path to further growth by hiring an associate financial planner, David Hutchinson, in 2008. In contrast to Lindsay, Hutchinson is still preparing to become a Certified Financial Planner, but he has an educational background in financial planning and experience as an investment broker.

Questions

1. Is a company ever too small for the need to engage in human resource planning? Why or why not? Discuss whether you think Robert Reed planned his hiring strategy at an appropriate time in the firm's growth.

2. Using Table 5.2, review the options for avoiding a labor shortage, and discuss how well the options besides new hires could have worked for Reed to reach his goals for growth. As you do so, consider qualities of a financial-planning business that might be relevant (for example, direct client contact and the need for confidentiality).

3. Suppose that when Reed was seeking to hire a certified financial planner, he asked you for advice on where to recruit this person. Which sources would you suggest, and why?

Sources: Angie Herbers, "Letting Go," *Investment Advisor,* June 2009, pp. 96–97; Personal Financial Advisors, "Why Choose Us?" corporate website, http://www.mypfa.com, accessed May 21, 2014.

NOTES

1. Andrew Lapin, "NPR Talent Leader Schmidt Leaves to Start Recruiting Company," *Current.org,* December 19, 2013, http://www.current.org; Bureau of National Affairs, "To Improve Recruiting, Jazz Up Job Sites and Get Employees Involved," *HR Focus,* December 2013, pp. 13–14; Sarah Halzack, "For Nonprofit NPR, Social Media Is 'a Great Equalizer' When It Comes to Hiring," *Washington Post,* January 6, 2013, http://www.washingtonpost.com.

2. Bureau of National Affairs, "Firm Says High-Performing Employers Do It Differently," *Report on Salary Surveys,* July 2013, pp. 13–14.

3. M. Phillips and S. Singh, "High Corn Prices Ripple through Economy," *Businessweek,* February 4, 2013, pp. 13–14.

4. Annie Gasparro, "Tightfisted New Owners Put Heinz on Diet," *Wall Street Journal,* February 10, 2014, http://online.wsj.com.

5. J. P. Guthrie, "Dumb and Dumber: The Impact of Downsizing on Firm Performance as Moderated by Industry Conditions," *Organization Science* 19 (2008), pp. 108–23; "Lay Off the Layoffs," *Newsweek,* February 4, 2010, http://www.thedailybeast.com/newsweek/.

6. C. D. Zatzick and R. D. Iverson, "High-Involvement Management and Workforce Reduction: Competitive Advantage or Disadvantage?" *Academy of Management Journal* 49 (2006), pp. 999–1015.

7. P. P. Shaw, "Network Destruction: The Structural Implications of Downsizing," *Academy of Management Journal* 43 (2000), pp. 101–12.

8. Brenda Kowske, Kyle Lundby, and Rena Rasch, "Turning 'Survive' into 'Thrive': Managing Survivor Engagement in a Downsized Organization," *People & Strategy* 32, no. (4), (2009), pp. 48–56.

9. W. F. Cascio, "Downsizing: What Do We Know? What Have We Learned?" *Academy of Management Executive* 7 (1993), pp. 95–104.

10. Hagerty, "U.S. Factories Buck Decline"; Scott Kirsner, "The Tech Bust: 10 Years After," *Boston Globe,* February 20, 2011, http://www.boston.com; Bill Saporito and Deirdre Van Dyk, "Where the Jobs Are," *Time,* January 17, 2011, EBSCOhost, http://web.ebscohost.com; Erik Brynjolfsson and Andrew McAfee, "Jobs, Productivity and the Great Decoupling," *The New York Times,* December 11, 2012, http://www.nytimes.com.

11. Dan Jacobs, "Lessons from the Recession," *Landscape Management,* June 2011, pp. S21–S23.

12. L. Woellert, "Half the Hours, Most of the Pay," *Bloomberg Businessweek,* January 31, 2013, pp. 23–24.

13. CareerBuilder, "Retirement May Be a Thing of the Past, New CareerBuilder Survey Finds," news release, February 16, 2012, http://www.careerbuilder.com.

14. S. Kim and D. Feldman, "Healthy, Wealthy, or Wise: Predicting Actual Acceptances of Early Retirement Incentives at Three Points in Time," *Personnel Psychology* 51 (1998), pp. 623–42.

15. Donna Rosato, "Ease Your Way into Retirement," *Money,* February 2012, EBSCOhost, http://web.ebscohost.com.

16. S. A. Johnson and B. E. Ashforth, "Externalization of Employment in a Service Environment: The Role of Organizational and Customer Identification," *Journal of Organizational Behavior* 29 (2008), pp. 287–309; M. Vidal and L. M. Tigges, "Temporary Employment and Strategic Staffing in the Manufacturing Sector," *Industrial Relations* 48 (2009), pp. 55–72.

17. "Where Do You Find New Talent?" *Mass Transit,* September/October 2011, pp. 102–103.

18. Tim Sohn, "Don't Go It Alone," *Editor & Publisher,* April 2011, EBSCOhost, http://web.ebscohost.com.

19. Ibid.

20. A. Tiwana, "Does Firm Modularity Complement Ignorance? A Field Study of Software Outsourcing Alliances," *Strategic Management Journal* 29 (2008), pp. 1241–52.

21. Joel Schectman, "Indiana Says It Is Recovering from Failed Experiment in IT Outsourcing," *The Wall Street Journal*, March 7, 2013, http://blogs.wsj.com.

22. Mansfield Sales Partners, "Sales Outsourcing: Expand Rapidly into New Markets," http://www .mansfieldsp.com, accessed March 3, 2012.

23. Bridget McCrea, "LMS: Optimizing the Human Supply Chain," *Modern Materials Handling*, April 2013, pp. 48–50.

24. A. E. Barber, *Recruiting Employees* (Thousand Oaks, CA: Sage, 1998).

25. C. K. Stevens, "Antecedents of Interview Interactions, Interviewers' Ratings, and Applicants' Reactions," *Personnel Psychology* 51 (1998), pp. 55–85; A. E. Barber, J. R. Hollenbeck, S. L. Tower, and J. M. Phillips, "The Effects of Interview Focus on Recruitment Effectiveness: A Field Experiment," *Journal of Applied Psychology* 79 (1994), pp. 886–96; D. S. Chapman and D. I. Zweig, "Developing a Nomological Network for Interview Structure: Antecedents and Consequences of the Structured Selection Interview," *Personnel Psychology* 58 (2005), pp. 673–702.

26. J. D. Olian and S. L. Rynes, "Organizational Staffing: Integrating Practice with Strategy," *Industrial Relations* 23 (1984), pp. 170–83.

27. M. Leonard, "Challenges to the Termination-at-Will Doctrine," *Personnel Administrator* 28 (1983), pp. 49–56; C. Schowerer and B. Rosen, "Effects of Employment-at-Will Policies and Compensation Policies on Corporate Image and Job Pursuit Intentions," *Journal of Applied Psychology* 74 (1989), pp. 653–56.

28. S. L. Rynes and A. E. Barber, "Applicant Attraction Strategies: An Organizational Perspective," *Academy of Management Review* 15 (1990), pp. 286–310; J. A. Breaugh, *Recruitment: Science and Practice* (Boston: PWS-Kent, 1992), p. 34.

29. J. E. Slaughter, M. J. Zickar, S. Highhouse, and D. C. Mohr, "Personality Trait Inferences about Organizations: Development of a Measure and Assessment of Construct Validity," *Journal of Applied Psychology* 89 (2004), pp. 85–103; D. S. Chapman, K. L. Uggerslev, S. A. Carroll, K. A. Piasentin, and D. A. Jones, "Applicant Attraction to Organizations and Job Choice: A Meta-analytic Review of the Correlates of Recruiting Outcomes," *Journal of Applied Psychology* 90 (2005), pp. 928–44. For a contrasting view, see Mark Ritson, "Employer Branding Can Do Real Harm so Stop It," *Marketing Week*, July 11, 2013, EBSCOhost, http://web.b.ebscohost.com.

30. D. R. Avery, "Reactions to Diversity in Recruitment Advertising—Are Differences in Black and White?" *Journal of Applied Psychology* 88 (2003), pp. 672–79.

31. M. A. Conrad and S. D. Ashworth, "Recruiting Source Effectiveness: A Meta-Analysis and Re-examination of Two Rival Hypotheses," paper presented at the annual meeting of the Society of Industrial/Organizational Psychology, Chicago, 1986.

32. Breaugh, *Recruitment*.

33. Taleo Corporation, "Intercontinental Hotels Group Mobilizes Internal Talent with Taleo in Biggest Ever Recruitment Drive," news release, February 6, 2012, http://ir.taleo.com.

34. Breaugh, *Recruitment*, pp. 113–14.

35. R. S. Schuler and S. E. Jackson, "Linking Competitive Strategies with Human Resource Management Practices," *Academy of Management Executive* 1 (1987), pp. 207–19.

36. Gerry Crispin and Mark Mehler, "Sources of Hire 2013: Perception Is Reality," CareerXroads, March 2013, http://www.careerxroads.com.

37. C. R. Wanberg, R. Kanfer, and J. T. Banas, "Predictors and Outcomes of Networking Intensity among Job Seekers," *Journal of Applied Psychology* 85 (2000), pp. 491–503.

38. Nelson D. Schwartz, "In Hiring, a Friend in Need Is a Prospect, Indeed," *The New York Times*, January 27, 2013, http://www.nytimes.com.

39. Lauren Weber, "Help Wanted—on Writing Job Descriptions," *Wall Street Journal*, October 2, 2013, http://online.wsj.com.

40. B. Dineen and R. A. Noe, "Effects of Customization on Applicant Decisions and Applicant Pool Characteristics in a Web-Based Recruiting Context," *Journal of Applied Psychology* 94 (2009), pp. 224–34.

41. Breaugh, *Recruitment*, p. 87.

42. EastBay Works, "What Is EastBay Works?" http://www.eastbayworks.com, accessed March 3, 2012.

43. Carol Hymowitz and Jeff Green, "Executive Headhunters Squeezed by In-House Recruiters," *Bloomberg Businessweek*, January 17, 2013, http://www.businessweek.com.

44. Melissa Korn, "Companies Size Up Options at Small Schools," *The Wall Street Journal*, March 1, 2012, http://online.wsj.com.

45. Hao Zhao and Robert C. Liden, "Internship: A Recruitment and Selection Perspective," *Journal of Applied Psychology* 96 (2011): 221–229.

46. Jessica E. Vascellaro, "Interns Are Largest Target in Battle for Tech Talent," *The Wall Street Journal*, December 22, 2011, http://online.wsj.com.

47. R. Hawk, *The Recruitment Function* (New York: American Management Association, 1967).

48. Lauren Weber, "For Smaller Firms, Recruiting Costs Add Up," *The Wall Street Journal*, November 28, 2011, http://online.wsj.com.

49. C. K. Stevens, "Effects of Preinterview Beliefs on Applicants' Reactions to Campus Interviews," *Academy of Management Journal* 40 (1997), pp. 947–66.

50. C. Collins, "The Interactive Effects of Recruitment Practices and Product Awareness on Job Seekers' Employer Knowledge and Application Behaviors," *Journal of Applied Psychology* 92 (2007), pp. 180–90.

51. M. S. Taylor and T. J. Bergman, "Organizational Recruitment Activities and Applicants' Reactions at Different Stages of the Recruitment Process," *Personnel Psychology* 40 (1984), pp. 261–85; C. D. Fisher, D. R. Ilgen, and W. D. Hoyer, "Source Credibility, Information Favorability, and Job Offer Acceptance," *Academy of Management Journal* 22 (1979), pp. 94–103.

52. L. M. Graves and G. N. Powell, "The Effect of Sex Similarity on Recruiters' Evaluation of Actual Applicants: A Test of the Similarity-Attraction Paradigm," *Personnel Psychology* 48 (1995), pp. 85–98.

53. R. D. Tretz and T. A. Judge, "Realistic Job Previews: A Test of the Adverse Self-Selection Hypothesis," *Journal of Applied Psychology* 83 (1998), pp. 330–37.

54. P. Hom, R. W. Griffeth, L. E. Palich, and J. S. Bracker, "An Exploratory Investigation into Theoretical Mechanisms Underlying Realistic Job Previews," *Personnel Psychology* 51 (1998), pp. 421–51.

55. G. M. McEvoy and W. F. Cascio, "Strategies for Reducing Employee Turnover: A Meta-Analysis," *Journal of Applied Psychology* 70 (1985), pp. 342–53; S. L. Premack and J. P. Wanous, "A Meta-Analysis of Realistic Job Preview Experiments," *Journal of Applied Psychology* 70 (1985), pp. 706–19.

56. D. R. Earnest, D. G. Allen, and R. S. Landis, "Mechanisms Linking Realistic Job Previews with Turnover: A Meta-Analytic Path Analysis," *Personnel Psychology* 64 (2011), pp. 865–897.

57. R. W. Walters, "It's Time We Become Pros," *Journal of College Placement* 12 (1985), pp. 30–33.

58. S. L. Rynes, R. D. Bretz, and B. Gerhart, "The Importance of Recruitment in Job Choice: A Different Way of Looking," *Personnel Psychology* 44 (1991), pp. 487–522.

6

Selecting Employees and Placing Them in Jobs

What Do I Need to Know?

After reading this chapter, you should be able to:

LO 6-1 Identify the elements of the selection process.

LO 6-2 Define ways to measure the success of a selection method.

LO 6-3 Summarize the government's requirements for employee selection.

LO 6-4 Compare the common methods used for selecting human resources.

LO 6-5 Describe major types of employment tests.

LO 6-6 Discuss how to conduct effective interviews.

LO 6-7 Explain how employers carry out the process of making a selection decision.

Introduction

With all the references to U.S. service members as "heroes" and the calls to "support our troops," you might expect that employers would be lining up to hire veterans. Indeed, the U.S. Chamber of Commerce, an association of businesses, has created a Hiring Our Heroes program offering job fairs and workshops to veterans, and many individual companies make a point of recruiting veterans. Even so, the unemployment rate among post–9/11 veterans persists at several percentage points above the rate for the overall U.S. workforce.

What is keeping companies from hiring more veterans? Survey evidence suggests that one hurdle is employers' fears about injuries such as post-traumatic stress disorder (PTSD). Some—incorrectly—worry that individuals with PTSD will be unable to function in the workplace or that accommodating this disability will be expensive. Some employers also operate on the assumption that the experience of following orders in the military has made veterans uncreative, even though military service more typically requires people to be resourceful and solve problems quickly in a variety of challenging situations. A third challenge is that the tasks performed by a service member may seem unrelated to any civilian jobs. It is usually up to veterans to figure out how to translate their experiences and accomplishments into general terms a civilian employer can appreciate. To help veterans overcome these hurdles, the U.S. Army's Warrior Transition Command recently partnered with the Society for Human Resource Management and recruiting firm Orion International to create educational resources for employers.

Their message is that employers who select qualified veterans will gain workers with an impressive work ethic, self-discipline, and ability to perform under pressure.[1]

Hiring decisions are about finding the people who will be a good fit with the job and the organization. Any organization that appreciates the competitive edge provided by good people must take the utmost care in choosing its members. The organization's decisions about selecting personnel are central to its ability to survive, adapt, and grow. Selection decisions become especially critical when organizations face tight labor markets or must compete for talent with other organizations in the same industry. If a competitor keeps getting the best applicants, the remaining companies must make do with who is left.

This chapter will familiarize you with ways to minimize errors in employee selection and placement. The chapter starts by describing the selection process and how to evaluate possible methods for carrying out that process. It then takes an in-depth look at the most widely used methods: applications and résumés, employment tests, and interviews. The chapter ends by describing the process by which organizations arrive at a final selection decision.

Selection Process

LO 6-1 Identify the elements of the selection process.

Personnel Selection
The process through which organizations make decisions about who will or will not be allowed to join the organization.

Through **personnel selection,** organizations make decisions about who will or will not be allowed to join the organization. Selection begins with the candidates identified through recruitment and with attempts to reduce their number to the individuals best qualified to perform the available jobs. At the end of the process, the selected individuals are placed in jobs with the organization.

The process of selecting employees varies considerably from organization to organization and from job to job. At most organizations, however, selection includes the steps illustrated in Figure 6.1. First, a human resource professional reviews the applications received to see which meet the basic requirements of the job. For candidates who meet the basic requirements, the organization administers tests and reviews work samples to rate the candidates' abilities. Those with the best abilities are invited to the organization for one or more interviews. Often, supervisors and team members are involved in this stage of the process. By this point, the decision makers are beginning to form opinions about which candidates are most desirable. For the top few candidates, the organization should check references and conduct background checks to verify that the organization's information is correct. Then

Figure 6.1
Steps in the Selection Process

supervisors, teams, and other decision makers select a person to receive a job offer. In some cases, the candidate may negotiate with the organization regarding salary, benefits, and the like. If the candidate accepts the job, the organization places him or her in that job.

Nowadays, the ease of applying online coupled with the high unemployment rates of the past few years have made this processing overwhelming for many recruiters. A simple job posting online could generate hundreds of résumés in one day. Many employers are coping by automating much of the selection process with an applicant-tracking system. Typically, the system starts by receiving the data provided in electronically submitted résumés and matching it against the company's selection criteria. The system might find that half the résumés lack necessary keywords, so it sends those applicants a polite "no thank you" e-mail. The applications that survive the automated screening go to a hiring manager, often ranked by how well they meet preset criteria. The manager reviews these applications and selects candidates to contact for a telephone or face-to-face interview and/or testing.

Critics point out that these automated systems may arbitrarily reject highly qualified people who submit a creatively worded résumé rather than simply mimicking the wording of the job posting. Moreover, a recent study by the Talent Board suggests that rejected job applicants have the potential to hurt a company's bottom line. More than 8% of the study's participants said that their job rejection would affect their relationship as customers with the company, the sentiment being "if I'm not good enough to work here I probably don't want to be a customer." Nevertheless, automated systems can make the application process more efficient by speeding up the steps and perhaps allowing applicants to check the status of their applications.[2]

How does an organization decide which of these steps to use and in what order? Some organizations simply repeat a selection process that is familiar. If members of the organization underwent job interviews, *they* conduct job interviews, asking familiar questions. However, what organizations *should* do is to create a selection process in support of its job descriptions. In Chapter 3, we explained that a job description identifies the knowledge, skills, abilities, and other characteristics required for successfully performing a job. The selection process should be set up in such a way that it lets the organization identify people who have the necessary KSAOs. In Winston-Salem, North Carolina, a mortgage company called BB&T bases its growth strategy on excellent customer service. BB&T hires customer-focused loan officers by seeking a combination of cultural fit with the organization and skill in "relationship selling" (selling that builds long-term customer relationships by identifying and meeting customers' needs). First, the BB&T recruiter and hiring manager assess cultural fit by talking to candidates about how they work with customers. If candidates focus on their earnings or express little interest in customers' well-being, BB&T screens them out no matter how skillful they are at closing a deal. Candidates with the necessary attitude are invited to continue with an assessment of their technical skills. Candidates who pass both steps of the initial screening are invited to interview with branch managers. If all the interviewers agree that the candidate is a good fit, BB&T makes an offer. This careful approach to hiring has built a workforce characterized by exceptionally high productivity and low turnover.[3]

For employees who work directly with customers, companies should create a selection process that measures employees' interest in customers and their ability to interact in a positive way.

This kind of strategic approach to selection requires ways to measure the effectiveness of selection tools. From science, we have basic standards for this:

- The method provides *reliable* information.
- The method provides *valid* information.
- The information can be *generalized* to apply to the candidates.
- The method offers *high utility* (practical value).
- The selection criteria are *legal*.

LO 6-2 Define ways to measure the success of a selection method.

Reliability

Reliability
The extent to which a measurement is free from random error.

The **reliability** of a type of measurement indicates how free that measurement is from random error.[4] A reliable measurement therefore generates consistent results. Assuming that a person's intelligence is fairly stable over time, a reliable test of intelligence should generate consistent results if the same person takes the test several times. Organizations that construct intelligence tests should be able to provide (and explain) information about the reliability of their tests.

Usually, this information involves statistics such as *correlation coefficients*. These statistics measure the degree to which two sets of numbers are related. A higher correlation coefficient signifies a stronger relationship. At one extreme, a correlation coefficient of 1.0 means a perfect positive relationship—as one set of numbers goes up, so does the other. If you took the same vision test three days in a row, those scores would probably have nearly a perfect correlation. At the other extreme, a correlation of −1.0 means a perfect negative correlation—when one set of numbers goes up, the other goes down. In the middle, a correlation of 0 means there is no correlation at all. For example, the correlation (or relationship) between weather and intelligence would be at or near 0. A reliable test would be one for which scores by the same person (or people with similar attributes) have a correlation close to 1.0.

Reliability answers one important question—whether you are measuring something accurately—but ignores another question that is as important: Are you measuring something that matters? Think about how this applies at companies that try to identify workers who will fit in well with the company's culture. Often these companies depend on teamwork, social networking, and creativity, and they expect those behaviors to prevail when workers get along well and share similar values. However, efforts to seek cultural fit often translate into favoring the most likable candidates—for example, those who make eye contact, display an interest in others, and tell engaging stories.[5] This approach not only raises questions of reliability—for example, whether making eye contact in a job interview is a reliable measure of a person's behavior on the job over time—it also raises questions about the extent to which being likable really translates into effective teamwork and creative problem solving. Perhaps the prickly member of the team will be the one who opens up a new and valuable line of thinking. As in this example, employers need to consider both the reliability of their selection methods and their validity, defined next.

Validity
The extent to which performance on a measure (such as a test score) is related to what the measure is designed to assess (such as job performance).

Validity

For a selection measure, **validity** describes the extent to which performance on the measure (such as a test score) is related to what the measure is designed to assess (such as job performance). Although we can reliably measure such characteristics as weight and height, these measurements do not provide much information about how a person will perform most kinds of jobs. Thus, for most jobs height and weight provide little validity as selection criteria. One way to determine whether a measure is valid is to compare many people's scores on that measure with their job performance. For example, suppose people who score above 60 words per minute on a keyboarding test consistently get high marks for their performance in data-entry jobs. This observation suggests the keyboarding test is valid for predicting success in that job.

As with reliability, information about the validity of selection methods often uses correlation coefficients. A strong positive (or negative) correlation between a measure and job performance means the measure should be a valid basis for selecting (or rejecting) a candidate. This information is important not only because it helps organizations identify the best employees, but also because organizations can demonstrate fair employment practices by showing that their selection process is valid. The federal government's *Uniform Guidelines on Employee Selection Procedures* accept three ways of measuring validity: criterion-related, content, and construct validity.

Criterion-Related Validity   The first category, **criterion-related validity,** is a measure of validity based on showing a substantial correlation between test scores and job performance scores. In the example in Figure 6.2, a company compares two measures—an intelligence test and college grade point average—with performance as sales representative. In the left graph, which shows the relationship between the intelligence test scores and job performance, the points for the 20 sales reps fall near the 45-degree line. The correlation coefficient is near .90 (for a perfect 1.0, all the points would be on the 45-degree line). In the graph at the right, the points are scattered more widely. The correlation between college GPA and sales reps' performance is much lower. In this hypothetical example, the intelligence test is more valid than GPA for predicting success at this job.

Two kinds of research are possible for arriving at criterion-related validity:

1. **Predictive validation**—This research uses the test scores of all applicants and looks for a relationship between the scores and future performance. The

Criterion-Related Validity
A measure of validity based on showing a substantial correlation between test scores and job performance scores.

Predictive Validation
Research that uses the test scores of all applicants and looks for a relationship between the scores and future performance of the applicants who were hired.

Figure 6.2
Criterion-Related Measurements of a Student's Aptitude

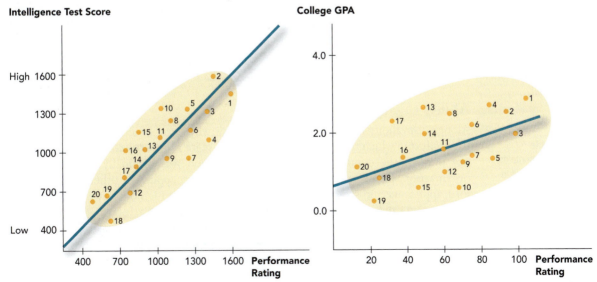

researcher administers the tests, waits a set period of time, and then measures the performance of the applicants who were hired.

2. **Concurrent validation**—This type of research administers a test to people who currently hold a job, then compares their scores to existing measures of job performance. If the people who score highest on the test also do better on the job, the test is assumed to be valid.

Concurrent Validation
Research that consists of administering a test to people who currently hold a job, then comparing their scores to existing measures of job performance.

Predictive validation is more time consuming and difficult, but it is the best measure of validity. Job applicants tend to be more motivated to do well on the tests, and their performance on the tests is not influenced by their firsthand experience with the job. Also, the group studied is more likely to include people who perform poorly on the test—a necessary ingredient to accurately validate a test.[6]

Content Validity
Consistency between the test items or problems and the kinds of situations or problems that occur on the job.

Content and Construct Validity

Another way to show validity is to establish **content validity**—that is, consistency between the test items or problems and the kinds of situations or problems that occur on the job. A test that is "content valid" exposes the job applicant to situations that are likely to occur on the job. It tests whether the applicant has the knowledge, skills, or ability to handle such situations. In the case of a company using tests for selecting a construction superintendent, tests with content validity included organizing a random list of subcontractors into the order they would appear at a construction site and entering a shed to identify construction errors that had intentionally been made for testing purposes.[7] More commonly today, employers use computer role-playing games in which software is created to include situations that occur on the job. The game measures how the candidate reacts to the situations, and then it computes a score based on how closely the candidate's responses match those of an ideal employee.[8]

The usual basis for deciding that a test has content validity is through expert judgment. Experts can rate the test items according to whether they mirror essential functions of the job. Because establishing validity is based on the experts' subjective judgments, content validity is most suitable for measuring behavior that is concrete and observable.

Construct Validity
Consistency between a high score on a test and high level of a construct such as intelligence or leadership ability, as well as between mastery of this construct and successful performance of the job.

For tests that measure abstract qualities such as intelligence or leadership ability, establishment of validity may have to rely on **construct validity.** This involves establishing that tests really do measure intelligence, leadership ability, or other such "constructs," as well as showing that mastery of this construct is associated with successful performance of the job. For example, if you could show that a test measures something called "mechanical ability," and that people with superior mechanical ability perform well as assemblers, then the test has construct validity for the assembler job. Tests that measure a construct usually measure a combination of behaviors thought to be associated with the construct.

Ability to Generalize

Generalizable
Valid in other contexts beyond the context in which the selection method was developed.

Along with validity in general, we need to know whether a selection method is valid in the context in which the organization wants to use it. A **generalizable** method applies not only to the conditions in which the method was originally developed—job, organization, people, time period, and so on. It also applies to other organizations, jobs, applicants, and so on. In other words, is a selection method that was valid in one context also valid in other contexts?

Researchers have studied whether tests of intelligence and thinking skills (called *cognitive ability*) can be generalized. The research has supported the idea that these tests are generalizable across many jobs. However, as jobs become more complex, the validity of many of these tests increases. In other words, they are most valid for complex jobs.[9]

Selection Decisions Affect the Bottom Line

Almost two-thirds (66%) of U.S. employers surveyed by CareerBuilder said their company had experienced negative consequences as a result of selecting someone who was not a good fit or did not perform the job well. Of these respondents, 27% said a poor hiring decision had cost their company more than $50,000. When asked to identify the types of consequences, respondents in the United States most often said productivity suffered.

Question

Do the results of this survey indicate that U.S. companies should spend up to $50,000 to select an employee for every vacant position? Why or why not?

Sources: Rachel Gillett, "Infographic: How Much a Bad Hire Will Actually Cost You," *Fast Company*, April 8, 2014, http://www.fastcompany.com; Adecco, "Hiring Mistakes, the Cost of a Bad Hire," AdeccoUSA blog, June 10, 2013, http://blog.adeccousa.com; Career-Builder, "More Than Half of Companies in the Top Ten World Economies Have Been Affected by a Bad Hire, according to a CareerBuilder Survey," news release, May 8, 2013, http://www.careeerbuilder.com.

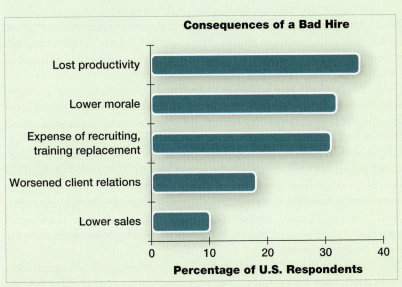

Consequences of a Bad Hire

Practical Value

Not only should selection methods such as tests and interview responses accurately predict how well individuals will perform, but they should also produce information that actually benefits the organization. Being valid, reliable, and generalizable adds value to a method. Another consideration is the cost of using the selection method. Selection procedures such as testing and interviewing cost money. They should cost significantly less than the benefits of hiring the new employees. Methods that provide economic value greater than the cost of using them are said to have **utility.**

The choice of a selection method may differ according to the job being filled. If the job involves providing a product or service of high value to the organization, it is worthwhile to spend more to find a top performer. At a company where salespeople are responsible for closing million-dollar deals, the company will be willing to invest more in selection decisions. At a fast-food restaurant, such an investment will not be worthwhile; the employer will prefer faster, simpler ways to select workers who ring up orders, prepare food, and keep the facility clean. Still, as the "Did You Know?" box illustrates, careless selection decisions are costly in any kind of organization.

Utility
The extent to which something provides economic value greater than its cost.

LO 6-3 Summarize the government's requirements for employee selection.

Legal Standards for Selection

As we discussed in Chapter 3, the U.S. government imposes legal limits on selection decisions. The government requires that the selection process be conducted in a way that avoids discrimination and provides access to employees with disabilities. The laws described in Chapter 3 have many applications to the selection process:

- The Civil Rights Act of 1991 and the Age Discrimination in Employment Act of 1967 place requirements on the choice of selection methods. An employer that uses a neutral-appearing selection method that damages a protected group is obligated to show that there is a business necessity for using that method. For example, if an organization uses a test that eliminates many candidates from minority groups, the organization must show that the test is valid for predicting performance of that job. In this context, good performance does not include "customer preference" or "brand image" as a justification for adverse impact. As we saw in Chapter 3, the courts may view a discriminatory pattern of hiring as evidence that the company is engaged in illegal discrimination.

- The Civil Rights Act of 1991 also prohibits preferential treatment in favor of minority groups. In the case of an organization using a test that tends to reject members of minority groups, the organization may not simply adjust minority applicants' scores upward. Such practices can create an environment that is demotivating to all employees and can lead to government sanctions. In Buffalo, New York, minority firefighters scored poorly on civil service exams, so the city let its list of candidates for promotion expire rather than promote only white firefighters. White firefighters who had been on the list filed a lawsuit claiming they were discriminated against, and they won back pay, benefits, and damages for emotional distress. Their attorney said the situation had created morale problems among firefighters who saw the discriminatory treatment as unfair.[10]

- Equal employment opportunity laws affect the kinds of information an organization may gather on application forms and in interviews. As summarized in Table 6.1, the organization may not ask questions that gather information about a person's protected status, even indirectly. For example, requesting the dates a person attended high school and college could indirectly gather information about an applicant's age.

- The Americans with Disabilities Act (ADA) of 1991 requires employers to make "reasonable accommodation" to disabled individuals and restricts many kinds of questions during the selection process. Under the ADA, preemployment questions may not investigate disabilities, but must focus on job performance. An interviewer may ask, "Can you meet the attendance requirements for this job?" but may not ask, "How many days did you miss work last year because you were sick?" Also, the employer may not, in making hiring decisions, use employment physical exams or other tests that could reveal a psychological or physical disability.

Along with equal employment opportunity, organizations must be concerned about candidates' privacy rights. The information gathered during the selection process may include information that employees consider confidential. Confidentiality is a particular concern when job applicants provide information online. Employers should collect data only at secure websites, and they may have to be understanding if online applicants are reluctant to provide data such as Social Security numbers, which hackers could use for identity theft. For some jobs, background checks look at candidates' credit history. The Fair Credit Reporting Act requires employers to obtain a candidate's consent before using a third party to check the candidate's credit history or

Table 6.1

Permissible and Impermissible Questions for Applications and Interviews

PERMISSIBLE QUESTIONS	IMPERMISSIBLE QUESTIONS
What is your full name? Have you ever worked under a different name? [Ask all candidates.]	What was your maiden name? What's the nationality of your name?
If you are hired, can you show proof of age (to meet a legal age requirement)?	How old are you? How would you feel about working for someone younger than you?
Will you need any reasonable accommodation for this hiring process? Are you able to perform this job, with or without reasonable accommodation?	What is your height? Your weight? Do you have any disabilities? Have you been seriously ill? Please provide a photograph of yourself.
Are you fluent in [language needed for job]? [Statement that employment is subject to verification of applicant's identity and employment eligibility under immigration laws]	What is your ancestry? Are you a citizen of the United States? Where were you born? How did you learn to speak that language?
What schools have you attended? What degrees have you earned? What was your major?	Is that school affiliated with [religious group]? When did you attend high school? [to learn applicant's age]
Can you meet the requirements of the work schedule? [Ask all candidates.]	What is your religion? What religious holidays do you observe?
Can you meet the job requirement to travel overnight several times a month?	What is your marital status? Would you like to be addressed as Mrs., Ms., or Miss? Do you have any children?
Have you ever been convicted of a crime?	Have you ever been arrested?
What organizations or groups do you belong to that you consider relevant to being able to perform this job?	What organizations or groups do you belong to?

Note: This table provides examples and is not intended as a complete listing of permissible and impermissible questions. The examples are based on federal requirements; state laws vary and may affect these examples.

Sources: Equal Employment Opportunity Commission, "Pre-employment Inquiries (General)," Prohibited Employment Policies/Practices, http://www.eeoc.gov, accessed May 20, 2014; Louise Kursmark, "Keep the Interview Legal," Monster Resource Center: Recruiting and Hiring Advice, http://hiring.monster.com, accessed May 20, 2014; Lisa Guerin, "Illegal Interview Questions," Nolo Legal Topics: Employment Law, http://www.nolo.com, accessed May 20, 2014.

references. If the employer then decides to take an adverse action (such as not hiring) based on the report, the employer must give the applicant a copy of the report and summary of the applicant's rights *before* taking the action.

Another legal requirement is that employers hiring people to work in the United States must ensure that anyone they hire is eligible for employment in this country. Under the **Immigration Reform and Control Act of 1986,** employers must verify and maintain records on the legal rights of applicants to work in the United States. They do this by having applicants fill out the U.S. Citizenship and Immigration Services' Form I-9 and present documents showing their identity and eligibility to work. Employers must complete their portion of each Form I-9, check the applicant's documents, and retain the Form I-9 for at least three years. Employers may (and in some cases must) also use the federal government's electronic system for verifying eligibility to work. To use the system, called E-Verify, employers go online (**www.uscis.gov/ e-verify**) to submit information on the applicant's I-9. The system compares it against information in databases of the Social Security Administration and Department of Homeland Security. It then notifies the employer of the candidate's eligibility, usually

Immigration Reform and Control Act of 1986
Federal law requiring employers to verify and maintain records on applicants' legal rights to work in the United States.

within 24 hours. At the same time, assuming a person is eligible to work under the Immigration Reform and Control Act, the law prohibits the employer from discriminating against the person on the basis of national origin or citizenship status.

An important principle of selection is to combine several sources of information about candidates, rather than relying solely on interviews or a single type of testing. The sources should be chosen carefully to relate to the characteristics identified in the job description. When organizations do this, they are increasing the validity of the decision criteria. They are more likely to make hiring decisions that are fair and unbiased. They also are more likely to choose the best candidates.

LO 6-4 Compare the common methods used for selecting human resources.

Job Applications and Résumés

Nearly all employers gather background information on applicants at the beginning of the selection process. The usual ways of gathering background information are by asking applicants to fill out application forms and provide résumés. Organizations also verify the information by checking references and conducting background checks.

Asking job candidates to provide background information is inexpensive. The organization can get reasonably accurate information by combining applications and résumés with background checks and well-designed interviews.[11] A major challenge with applications and résumés is the sheer volume of work they generate for the organization. Human resource departments often are swamped with far more résumés than they can carefully review.

Application Forms

Asking each applicant to fill out an employment application is a low-cost way to gather basic data from many applicants. It also ensures that the organization has certain standard categories of information, such as mailing address and employment history, from each. Figure 6.3 is an example of an application form.

Employers can buy general-purpose application forms from an office supply store, or they can create their own forms to meet unique needs. Either way, employment applications include areas for applicants to provide several types of information:

- *Contact information*—The applicant's name, address, phone number, and e-mail address.
- *Work experience*—Companies the applicant worked for, job titles, and dates of employment.
- *Educational background*—High school, college, and universities attended and degree(s) awarded.
- *Applicant's signature*—Signature following a statement that the applicant has provided true and complete information.

The application form may include other areas for the applicant to provide additional information, such as specific work experiences, technical skills, or memberships in professional or trade groups. Also, including the date on an application is useful for keeping up-to-date records of job applicants. The application form should not request information that could violate equal employment opportunity standards. For example, questions about an applicant's race, marital status, or number of children would be inappropriate.

By reviewing application forms, HR personnel can identify which candidates meet minimum requirements for education and experience. They may be able to rank

Figure 6.3

Sample Job Application Form

APPLICATION FOR EMPLOYMENT
An Equal Opportunity Employer

FIRST NAME	MIDDLE NAME	LAST NAME		SOCIAL SECURITY NUMBER

LOCAL	STREET ADDRESS	CITY AND STATE	ZIP CODE	TELEPHONE

PERMANENT	STREET ADDRESS	CITY AND STATE	ZIP CODE	TELEPHONE

ELECTRONIC MAIL ADDRESS

PLEASE ANSWER ALL ITEMS. IF NOT APPLICABLE, WRITE N/A.

ARE YOU A U.S. CITIZEN OR AUTHORIZED TO BE LEGALLY EMPLOYED ON AN ONGOING BASIS IN THE U.S. BASED ON YOUR VISA OR IMMIGRATION STATUS? ☐ YES ☐ NO

ARE YOU OVER 18 YEARS OF AGE? YES☐ NO ☐

DO YOU CURRENTLY HAVE A NONIMMIGRANT U.S. VISA? ☐ YES ☐ NO IF YES, PLEASE SPECIFY:

DO YOU HAVE ANY RELATIVES EMPLOYED HERE? ☐ NO ☐ YES
IF YES, GIVE NAME, RELATIONSHIP, AND LOCATION WHERE THEY WORK

DO YOU HAVE ANY RELATIVES EMPLOYED BY THE COMPETITION? ☐ NO ☐ YES WHAT COMPANY?

ARE YOU ABLE TO TRAVEL AS REQUIRED FOR THE POSITION SOUGHT? ☐ YES ☐ NO

ARE YOU WILLING TO RELOCATE? ☐ YES ☐ NO

ARE THERE GEOGRAPHICAL AREAS WHICH YOU WOULD PREFER OR REFUSE? ☐ NO ☐ YES IF YES, PLEASE SPECIFY:

HAVE YOU EVER BEEN CONVICTED OR PLED GUILTY TO ANY FELONY OR MISDEMEANOR OTHER THAN FOR A MINOR TRAFFIC VIOLATION? ☐ NO ☐ YES
IF YES, STATE THE DATE(S) AND LOCATIONS:

WHEN | WHERE | NATURE OF OFFENSE(S)

WORK PREFERENCE

SPECIFIC POSITION FOR WHICH YOU ARE APPLYING | NUMBER OF YEARS OF RELATED EXPERIENCE

LIST COMPUTER SOFTWARE PACKAGES OR PROGRAMMING LANGUAGE SKILLS

STARTING SALARY EXPECTED | DATE AVAILABLE TO START WORK | HOW DID YOU HAPPEN TO APPLY FOR A POSITION HERE?

HAVE YOU EVER WORKED AT, OR APPLIED FOR WORK HERE BEFORE? ☐ NO ☐ YES
IF YES, WHEN? | WHERE?

LIST EMPLOYMENT REFERENCES HERE, IF NOT INCLUDED ON ATTACHED RESUME

TURN OVER

COMPLETE THIS SECTION IF INFORMATION IS NOT INCLUDED ON ATTACHED RESUME

EDUCATION CIRCLE THE HIGHEST GRADE COMPLETED: ELEMENTARY 6 7 8   HIGH SCHOOL 1 2 3 4   COLLEGE 1 2 3 4 5 6 7 8

	NAME(S)	LOCATION(S)		MAJOR FIELDS OF STUDY AND PRINCIPAL PROFESSOR (OR ADVISOR)	GRADUATED 1 2 3 4	GRADE AVERAGE	DEGREE(S) RECEIVED	CLASS RANK __ OUT OF
HIGH SCHOOL					☐ YES ☐ NO			
COLLEGE								OVERALL AND MAJOR GPAS

ACADEMIC HONORS OR OTHER SPECIAL RECOGNITION

FOREIGN LANGUAGES READ | FOREIGN LANGUAGES SPOKEN

HAVE YOU TAKEN THE GMAT, GRE, SAT, OR OTHER ACADEMIC ENTRANCE TEST(S) WITHIN THE LAST TEN YEARS? ☐ YES ☐ NO
IF YES, LIST TEST(S), DATE(S) AND HIGHEST SCORE(S).

	DATE TAKEN	SCORE(S)		
SAT		TOTAL:	ENGLISH:	VERBAL: MATHEMATICAL:
ACT		TOTAL:	MATHEMATICS:	READING: SCIENCE:
GRE (GENERAL TEST)		TOTAL:	VERBAL: QUANTITATIVE:	ANALYTICAL:
GMAT		TOTAL:	VERBAL: MATH:	AWA:
OTHER		TOTAL:		

EMPLOYMENT AND MILITARY RECORD

LIST MOST RECENT FIRST. I AGREE TO FURNISH VERIFICATION IF REQUESTED. ATTACH RESUME. RESPOND BELOW IF INFORMATION IS NOT INCLUDED ON RESUME.

NAME AND ADDRESS OF EMPLOYER	POSITION HELD	PRIMARY RESPONSIBILITIES AND ACCOUNTABILITIES	SALARY		DATES		REASON FOR LEAVING
			START	FINISH	FROM	TO	

ENCIRCLE THOSE EMPLOYERS YOU DO NOT WANT US TO CONTACT
TURN OVER

An HR staff member typically reviews résumés from job applicants to identify candidates who meet basic job requirements, such as education and related work experience.

applicants—for example, giving applicants with 10 years of experience a higher ranking than applicants with 2 years of experience. In this way, the applications enable the organization to narrow the pool of candidates to a number it can afford to test and interview.

Résumés

The usual way that applicants introduce themselves to a potential employer is to submit a résumé. An obvious drawback of this information source is that applicants control the content of the information as well as the way it is presented. This type of information is therefore biased in favor of the applicant and (although this is unethical) may not even be accurate. However, résumés are an inexpensive way to gather information and provide employers with a starting point. Organizations typically use résumés as a basis for deciding which candidates to investigate further.

As with employment applications, an HR staff member reviews the résumés to identify candidates meeting such basic requirements as educational background, related work performed, and types of equipment the person has used. Because résumés are created by the job applicants (or the applicants have at least approved résumés created by someone they hire), they also may provide some insight into how candidates communicate and present themselves. Employers tend to decide against applicants whose résumés are unclear, sloppy, or full of mistakes. On the positive side, résumés may enable applicants to highlight accomplishments that might not show up in the format of an employment application. In a recent trend, applicants can even include a link to an online portfolio of work samples; however, few employers have made checking those portfolios part of the selection process. Some are too pressed for time, while many lack the capability in their HR software or are concerned they will see information, such as photos, that will raise fair-employment concerns.[12] Review of résumés is most valid when the content of the résumés is evaluated in terms of the elements of a job description.

References

Application forms often ask that applicants provide the names of several references. Applicants provide the names and phone numbers of former employers or others who can vouch for their abilities and past job performance. In some situations, the applicant may provide letters of reference written by those people. It is then up to the organization to have someone contact the references to gather information or verify the accuracy of the information provided by the applicant.

As you might expect, references are not an unbiased source of information. Most applicants are careful to choose references who will say something positive. In addition, former employers and others may be afraid that if they express negative opinions, they will be sued. Equally problematic from the standpoint of getting useful information is that some candidates fail to list people who can speak about their work history. On occasion, references barely know the candidate or know him or her only in a social context. A hiring manager in a government office even saw his own name listed as a reference for a candidate the manager had never met. In that case, the visibly uncomfortable worker offered the manager an unconvincing explanation, so the references at least tested the candidate's honesty (and he did not get hired).[13]

Usually the organization checks references after it has determined that the applicant is a finalist for the job. Contacting references for all applicants would be time consuming, and it does pose some burden on the people contacted. Part of that burden is the risk of giving information that is seen as too negative or too positive. If the person who is a reference gives negative information, there is a chance the candidate will claim *defamation*, meaning the person damaged the applicant's reputation by making statements that cannot be proved truthful.[14] At the other extreme, if the person gives a glowing statement about a candidate, and the new employer later learns of misdeeds such as sexual misconduct or workplace violence, the new employer might sue the former employer for misrepresentation.[15]

Because such situations occasionally arise, often with much publicity, people who give references tend to give as little information as possible. Most organizations have policies that the human resource department will handle all requests for references and that they will only verify employment dates and sometimes the employee's final salary. In organizations without such a policy, HR professionals should be careful—and train managers to be careful—to stick to observable, job-related behaviors and to avoid broad opinions that may be misinterpreted. In spite of these drawbacks of references, the risks of not learning about significant problems in a candidate's past outweigh the possibility of getting only a little information. Potential employers should check references. In general, the results of this effort will be most valid if the employer contacts many references (if possible, going beyond the list of names provided by the applicant), speaks with them directly by phone, and listens carefully for clues such as tone of voice.[16]

Background Checks

A background check is a way to verify that applicants are as they represent themselves to be. Unfortunately, not all candidates are open and honest. Liz Crawford, who is responsible for hiring employees at Factory VFX, has seen some notable attempts to deceive her. One candidate handed her a résumé including employment experience at a company Crawford knows well. When she commented on this, the candidate gave her a different résumé and tried to explain that the first one was a "wish résumé" of positions she wished she had held. Another candidate announced at his interview that he had been recommended by a Factory VFX artist. At the end of the interview, Crawford picked up the phone and dialed the artist so they could greet one another—and the embarrassed candidate admitted he didn't actually know the artist.[17] In light of incidents such as these, it's no wonder that many hiring managers are interested in using social media to check employees' backgrounds (see "HRM Social").

Besides checking employment references, many employers also conduct criminal background checks. Some positions are so sensitive that the law may even limit hiring a person with certain kinds of convictions: for example, a person convicted of domestic violence may not hold positions that involve shipping firearms. The use of criminal background checks is a sensitive issue in the United States, however, especially since crackdowns on crime have resulted in many arrests. An additional concern is the disparate impact of considering criminal history. Men are far more likely to have a criminal record than women, and arrests and convictions are far more common among African Americans than whites. The Equal Employment Opportunity Commission has published guidelines that employers who check criminal histories do so consistently; that is, they should conduct the same type

HRM Social

Using Social Media as a Background Check

Searching for a job candidate's name online is so easy that it seems like an obvious way to check the person's background. Public information could show, for example, whether the person really is vice president of marketing at XYZ Corporation or has done something that could later embarrass the employer. Indeed, research indicates that employers are interested. A survey by CareerBuilder found that 39% use social media to research candidates, and a survey by recruiting firm Challenger, Grey and Christmas found even greater use: 22% said they always review social media, and another 38% said they sometimes do so.

Employers need to proceed with caution, however. A particular concern is to avoid discrimination, yet the very nature of social media encourages sharing the kinds of information related to being a member of a protected group. For example, photos and descriptions of activities can tell or suggest a person's age, race, sex, religion, marital status, and disabilities. Employers can try to avoid discrimination by

postponing their search of social media until after they have identified a candidate they want to hire, after which they use social media to rule out specific problems.

An even safer way to use social media is to involve someone who is not the decision maker. The company can use a designated HR employee or contract with a service that specializes in screening job candidates. The service uses criteria from the employer—for example, screening out candidates who show evidence of using illegal drugs, engaging in hate speech, or misrepresenting qualifications. It gathers information about the candidate and reports to the employer only the job-related information gathered. Before using a service such as this or conducting any background check, employers should obtain permission from the candidate.

Finally, a few companies have sought greater insight than what is available publicly by asking candidates for their passwords, so the employer can look at a candidate's private information. Experts advise against this practice, which

is invasive, probably violates the media sites' terms of use, violates some states' laws, and is likely to alienate many good candidates.

Questions

1. How well does searching social media fulfill the requirements of providing reliable, valid, high-utility, and legal information for selection decisions?
2. What would show up in a search of public information about your name? How do you try to represent yourself online?

Sources: Catey Hill, "Your Boss Doesn't Care about Your Facebook, Twitter Profiles," *MarketWatch*, May 19, 2014, http://www.marketwatch.com; Rebecca Weiss, "Social Media's Impact on Hiring, Management and Discipline: What Every Employer Needs to Know," *Lexology*, September 2, 2013, http://www.lexology.com; CareerBuilder, "More Employers Finding Reasons Not to Hire Candidates on Social Media, Finds CareerBuilder Survey," news release, June 27, 2013, http://www.careerbuilder.com; Steve Bates, "Use Social Media Smartly When Hiring," Society for Human Resource Management, *HR Topics and Strategy*, March 19, 2013, http://www.shrm.org.

of background check for all candidates and apply the same standards for acting on the information. However, the EEOC also recommends that employers review the particular details of each situation, including the seriousness of each offense, the amount of time that has passed since conviction or completion of sentence, and the crime's relevance to the job the candidate is applying for.[18]

Another type of background check that has recently drawn greater scrutiny is the use of credit checks. Employers in certain situations, such as processes that involve handling money, are concerned that employees with credit problems will behave less honestly. To avoid hiring such employees, these employers conduct a background check. Also, some employers see good credit as an indicator that a person is responsible. But in a time of high unemployment and many home foreclosures, some people see this type of investigation as unfair to people who are desperately trying to find work: the worse their financial situation, the harder the job search becomes. Under federal law, conducting a credit check is legal if the person consents, but some states ban or are considering bans on the practice.

Employment Tests and Work Samples

When the organization has identified candidates whose applications or résumés indicate they meet basic requirements, the organization continues the selection process with this narrower pool of candidates. Often, the next step is to gather objective data through one or more employment tests. These tests fall into two broad categories:

LO 6-5 Describe major types of employment tests.

1. **Aptitude tests** assess how well a person can learn or acquire skills and abilities. In the realm of employment testing, the best-known aptitude test is the General Aptitude Test Battery (GATB), used by the U.S. Employment Service.
2. **Achievement tests** measure a person's existing knowledge and skills. For example, government agencies conduct civil service examinations to see whether applicants are qualified to perform certain jobs.

Before using any test, organizations should investigate the test's validity and reliability. Besides asking the testing service to provide this information, it is wise to consult more impartial sources of information, such as the ones identified in Table 6.2.

Aptitude Tests
Tests that assess how well a person can learn or acquire skills and abilities.

Achievement Tests
Tests that measure a person's existing knowledge and skills.

Physical Ability Tests

Physical strength and endurance play less of a role in the modern workplace than in the past, thanks to the use of automation and modern technology. Even so, many jobs still require certain physical abilities or psychomotor abilities (those connecting brain and body, as in the case of eye-hand coordination). When these abilities are essential to job performance or avoidance of injury, the organization may use physical ability tests. These evaluate one or more of the following areas of physical ability: muscular tension, muscular power, muscular endurance, cardiovascular endurance, flexibility, balance, and coordination.[19]

Although these tests can accurately predict success at certain kinds of jobs, they also tend to exclude women and people with disabilities. As a result, use of physical ability tests can make the organization vulnerable to charges of discrimination. It is therefore important to be certain that the abilities tested for really are essential to job performance or that the absence of these abilities really does create a safety hazard. See "Best Practices" for an example of an organization that does this.

		Table 6.2
Mental Measurements Yearbook	Descriptions and reviews of tests that are commercially available	**Sources of Information about Employment Tests**
Principles for the Validation and Use of Personnel Selection Procedures (Society for Industrial and Organizational Psychology)	Guide to help organizations evaluate tests	
Standards for Educational and Psychological Tests (American Psychological Association)	Description of standards for testing programs	
Tests: A Comprehensive Reference for Assessments in Psychology, Education, and Business	Descriptions of thousands of tests	
Test Critiques	Reviews of tests, written by professionals in the field	

St. Joseph Health Matches Physical Abilities to Job Requirements

If you visit a hospital and observe the activities there, you will see many employees engaged in physical activities—perhaps lifting patients, pushing carts loaded with meals, reaching for supplies, or moving swiftly but safely down the halls to respond to an emergency. Hiring decisions for these employees need to take into account whether they can safely carry out job-related activities (with or without accommodations).

St. Joseph Health, based in Irvine, California, has taken a thorough and objective approach to meeting the challenge. The regional health system's 24,000 employees serve patients in California, Texas, and New Mexico. The faith-based (Catholic) organization expects its employees to demonstrate the values of dignity, service, excellence, and justice. In the case of hiring decisions, this includes fairly matching people to jobs they can perform

well. That requires clearly defining job functions and tests that demonstrate the ability to perform those functions.

At St. Joseph Health, this effort began several years ago with a process of developing job function descriptions for 1,200 positions. With the help of experienced consultants advised by medical and legal experts, the organization identified appropriate test requirements for these functions. For example, applicants to be security guards must demonstrate the strength to restrain a suspect or run up several flights of stairs carrying a load as heavy as firefighting gear.

St. Joseph Health uses these requirements and tests not only to make better hiring decisions but also to help injured employees assess their need for job accommodations and ability to return to their regular jobs. Since using the objective measurements, the health

system has seen greater morale among supervisors and employees, as well as less time off for recovery from injuries.

Questions

1. Based on the information given, how well do the physical ability tests for St. Joseph Health meet the criteria of validity and utility (practical value)?

2. How can St. Joseph Health ensure that it uses physical ability tests in a nondiscriminatory manner?

Sources: DSI Work Solutions, "DSI Job Function Matching Method and Outcome," http://www.dsiworksolutions.com, accessed May 21, 2014; St. Joseph Health, "Fact Sheet," January 2014, http://www.stjhs.org; Roberto Ceniceros, "Employers Put Job Seekers' Physical Ability to the Test," *Business Insurance*, June 17, 2013, Business Insights: Global, http://bi.galegroup.com.

Cognitive Ability Tests

Cognitive Ability Tests
Tests designed to measure such mental abilities as verbal skills, quantitative skills, and reasoning ability.

Although fewer jobs require muscle power today, brainpower is essential for most jobs. Organizations therefore benefit from people who have strong mental abilities. **Cognitive ability tests**—sometimes called "intelligence tests"—are designed to measure such mental abilities as verbal skills (skill in using written and spoken language), quantitative skills (skill in working with numbers), and reasoning ability (skill in thinking through the answer to a problem). Many jobs require all of these cognitive skills, so employers often get valid information from general tests. Many reliable tests are commercially available. The tests are especially valid for complex jobs and for those requiring adaptability in changing circumstances.[20] Employers should, however, be sure tests are administered with security measures to prevent cheating. This is especially an issue with electronic standardized tests, as there is a demand for test takers to share test questions and answers.[21]

The evidence of validity, coupled with the relatively low cost of these tests, makes them appealing, except for one problem: concern about legal issues. These concerns arise from a historical pattern in which use of the tests has had an adverse impact on African Americans. Some organizations responded with *race norming*, establishing different norms for hiring members of different racial groups. Race norming poses its own problems, not the least of which is the negative reputation it bestows on the minority employees selected using a lower standard. In addition, the Civil Rights Act of 1991 forbids the use of race or sex norming. As a result, organizations that want to base selection decisions on cognitive ability must make difficult decisions about how to measure this ability while avoiding legal problems. One possibility is a concept called *banding*. This concept treats a range of scores as being similar, as when an instructor gives the grade of A to any student whose average test score is at least 90. All applicants within a range of scores, or band, are treated as having the same score. Then within the set of "tied" scores, employers give preference to underrepresented groups. This is a controversial practice, and some have questioned its legality.[22]

Job Performance Tests and Work Samples

Many kinds of jobs require candidates who excel at performing specialized tasks, such as operating a certain machine, handling phone calls from customers, or designing advertising materials. To evaluate candidates for such jobs, the organization may administer tests of the necessary skills. Sometimes the candidates take tests that involve a sample of work, or they may show existing samples of their work. Testing may involve a simulated work environment, a difficult team project, or a complex computer programming puzzle.[23] Examples of job performance tests include tests of keyboarding speed and *in-basket tests*. An in-basket test measures the ability to juggle a variety of demands, as in a manager's job. The candidate is presented with simulated memos and phone messages describing the kinds of problems that confront a person in the job. The candidate has to decide how to respond to these messages and in what order. Examples of jobs for which candidates provide work samples include graphic designers and writers.

Tests for selecting managers may take the form of an **assessment center**—a wide variety of specific selection programs that use multiple selection methods to rate applicants or job incumbents on their management potential. An assessment center typically includes in-basket tests, tests of more general abilities, and personality tests. Combining several assessment methods increases the validity of this approach.

Job performance tests have the advantage of giving applicants a chance to show what they can do, which leads them to feel that the evaluation was fair.[24] The tests also are job specific—that is, tailored to the kind of work done in a specific job. So they have a high level of validity, especially when combined with cognitive ability tests and a highly structured interview.[25] This advantage can become a disadvantage, however, if the organization wants to generalize the results of a test for one job to candidates for other jobs. The tests are more appropriate for identifying candidates who are generally able to solve the problems associated with a job, rather than for identifying which particular skills or traits the individual possesses.[26] Developing different tests for different jobs can become expensive. One way to save money is to prepare computerized tests that can be delivered online to various locations.

Assessment Center
A wide variety of specific selection programs that use multiple selection methods to rate applicants or job incumbents on their management potential.

Personality Inventories

In some situations, employers may also want to know about candidates' personalities. For example, one way that psychologists think about personality is in terms of the "Big Five" traits: extroversion, adjustment, agreeableness, conscientiousness, and

Table 6.3

**Five Major Personality
Dimensions Measured by
Personality Inventories**

1. Extroversion	Sociable, gregarious, assertive, talkative, expressive
2. Adjustment	Emotionally stable, nondepressed, secure, content
3. Agreeableness	Courteous, trusting, good-natured, tolerant, cooperative, forgiving
4. Conscientiousness	Dependable, organized, persevering, thorough, achievement-oriented
5. Inquisitiveness	Curious, imaginative, artistically sensitive, broad-minded, playful

inquisitiveness (explained in Table 6.3). There is evidence that people who score high on conscientiousness tend to excel at work, especially when they also have high cognitive ability.[27] For people-related jobs like sales and management, extroversion and agreeableness also seem to be associated with success.[28] Strong social skills help conscientious people ensure that they get positive recognition for their hard work.[29] However, high scores are less than ideal for some traits in some situations. For example, the best performers often score in the middle of the range on emotional stability. In other words, an employee can be either too nervous or too calm to do the best work.[30]

The usual way to identify a candidate's personality traits is to administer one of the personality tests that are commercially available. The employer pays for the use of the test, and the organization that owns the test then scores the responses and provides a report about the test taker's personality. An organization that provides such tests should be able to discuss the test's validity and reliability. Assuming the tests are valid for the organization's jobs, they have advantages. Administering commercially available personality tests is simple, and these tests have generally not violated equal opportunity employment requirements.[31] On the downside, compared with intelligence tests, people are better at "faking" their answers to a personality test to score higher on

To test tech workers' programming and problem-solving skills, Google sponsors contests called Code Jams at locations around the world. The winners gain fame as well as visibility with Google recruiters. The Code Jams also cement Google's reputation for hiring the best thinkers and offering them exciting challenges.

desirable traits.[32] For example, people tend to score higher on conscientiousness when filling out job-related personality tests than when participating in research projects.[33] Ways to address this problem include using trained interviewers rather than surveys, collecting information about the applicant from several sources, and letting applicants know that several sources will be used.[34]

One trend in favor of personality tests is organizations' greater use of teamwork, where personality conflicts can be a significant problem. Traits such as agreeableness and conscientiousness have been associated with effective teamwork.[35] In addition, an organization might try to select team members with similar traits and values in order to promote a strong culture where people work together harmoniously, or they instead might look for a diversity of personalities and values as a way to promote debate and creativity.

Honesty Tests and Drug Tests

No matter what employees' personalities may be like, organizations want employees to be honest and to behave safely. Some organizations are satisfied to assess these qualities based on judgments from reference checks and interviews. Others investigate these characteristics more directly through the use of honesty tests and drug tests.

The most famous kind of honesty test is the polygraph, the so-called lie detector test. However, in 1988 the passage of the Polygraph Act banned the use of polygraphs for screening job candidates. As a result, testing services have developed paper-and-pencil honesty (or integrity) tests. Generally these tests ask applicants directly about their attitudes toward theft and their own experiences with theft. Much of the research into the validity of these tests has been conducted by the testing companies, which tend to find stronger correlations. However, evidence suggests that honesty tests do have some ability to predict such behavior as theft of the employer's property.[36]

As concerns about substance abuse have grown during recent decades, so has the use of drug testing. As a measure of a person's exposure to drugs, chemical testing has high reliability and validity. However, these tests are controversial for several reasons. Some people are concerned that they invade individuals' privacy. Others object from a legal perspective. When all applicants or employees are subject to testing, whether or not they have shown evidence of drug use, the tests might be an unreasonable search and seizure or a violation of due process. Taking urine and blood samples involves invasive procedures, and accusing someone of drug use is a serious matter. On the positive side, a recent analysis of hiring data suggests that drug tests may provide a correction for discriminatory employment decisions. In states that adopted laws encouraging drug testing, hiring trends for white males were unchanged, but the hiring of black men increased. That change did not occur in states where laws were unfavorable to drug testing. Although the study did not prove (or disprove) discrimination, it does show an influence that is helpful to black males.[37]

Employers considering the use of drug tests should ensure that their drug-testing programs conform to some general rules[38]:

- Administer the tests systematically to all applicants for the same job.
- Use drug testing for jobs that involve safety hazards.
- Have a report of the results sent to the applicant, along with information about how to appeal the results and be retested if appropriate.
- Respect applicants' privacy by conducting tests in an environment that is not intrusive and keeping results confidential.

Even at an organization with these best practices, employers have to keep in mind that drug testing will not uncover all problems with impairment. One recent concern is that much drug abuse today involves legal prescription painkillers rather than substances traditionally tested for. Routine testing for prescription drugs (or possibly even marijuana in states that have legalized medical marijuana) is difficult because the employer has to be careful not to discriminate on the basis of disabilities.

Medical Examinations

Especially for physically demanding jobs, organizations may wish to conduct medical examinations to see that the applicant can meet the job's requirements. Employers may also wish to establish an employee's physical condition at the beginning of employment, so that there is a basis for measuring whether the employee has suffered a work-related disability later on. At the same time, as described in Chapter 3, organizations may not discriminate against individuals with disabilities who could perform a job with reasonable accommodations. Likewise, they may not use a measure of size or strength that discriminates against women, unless those requirements are valid in predicting the ability to perform a job. Furthermore, to protect candidates' privacy, medical exams must be related to job requirements and may not be given until the candidate has received a job offer. Therefore, organizations must be careful in how they use medical examinations. Many organizations make selection decisions first and then conduct the exams to confirm that the employee can handle the job with any reasonable accommodations required. Limiting the use of medical exams in this way also holds down the cost of what tends to be an expensive process.

LO 6-6 Discuss how to conduct effective interviews.

Interviews

Supervisors and team members most often get involved in the selection process at the stage of employment interviews. These interviews bring together job applicants and representatives of the employer to obtain information and evaluate the applicant's qualifications. While the applicant is providing information, he or she is also forming opinions about what it is like to work for the organization. Most organizations use interviewing as part of the selection process. In fact, this method is used more than any other.

Interviewing Techniques

Interview techniques include choices about the type of questions to ask and the number of people who conduct the interview. Several question types are possible:

Nondirective Interview
A selection interview in which the interviewer has great discretion in choosing questions to ask each candidate.

- In a **nondirective interview,** the interviewer has great discretion in choosing questions. The candidate's reply to one question may suggest other questions to ask. Nondirective interviews typically include open-ended questions about the candidate's strengths, weaknesses, career goals, and work experience. Because these interviews give the interviewer wide latitude, their reliability is not great, and some interviewers ask questions that are not valid or even legal.

Structured Interview
A selection interview that consists of a predetermined set of questions for the interviewer to ask.

- A **structured interview** establishes a set of questions for the interviewer to ask. Ideally, the questions are related to job requirements and cover relevant knowledge, skills, and experiences. The interviewer is supposed to avoid asking questions that are not on the list. Although interviewers may object to being restricted, the results may be more valid and reliable than with a nondirective interview.

- A **situational interview** is a structured interview in which the interviewer describes a situation likely to arise on the job and asks the candidate what he or she would do in that situation. This type of interview may have high validity in predicting job performance.[39]
- A **behavior description interview (BDI)** is a structured interview in which the interviewer asks the candidate to describe how he or she handled a type of situation in the past. Questions about candidates' actual experiences tend to have the highest validity.[40]

When interviewing candidates, it's valid to ask about willingness to travel if that is part of the job. Interviewers might ask questions about previous business travel experiences and/or how interviewees handled situations requiring flexibility and self-motivation (qualities that would be an asset in someone who is traveling alone and solving business problems on the road).

The common setup for either a nondirected or structured interview is for an individual (an HR professional or the supervisor for the vacant position) to interview each candidate face to face. However, variations on this approach are possible. In a **panel interview,** several members of the organization meet to interview each candidate. A panel interview gives the candidate a chance to meet more people and see how people interact in that organization. It provides the organization with the judgments of more than one person, to reduce the effect of personal biases in selection decisions. Panel interviews can be especially appropriate in organizations that use teamwork. At the other extreme, some organizations conduct interviews without any interviewers; they use a computerized interviewing process. The candidate sits at a computer and enters replies to the questions presented by the computer. Such a format eliminates a lot of personal bias—along with the opportunity to see how people interact. Therefore, computer interviews are useful for gathering objective data, rather than assessing people skills.

For suggestions on how to apply these techniques to conduct effective job interviews, see "HR How To."

Advantages and Disadvantages of Interviewing

The wide use of interviewing is not surprising. People naturally want to see prospective employees firsthand. As we noted in Chapter 1, the top qualities that employers seek in new hires include communication skills and interpersonal skills. Talking face to face can provide evidence of these skills. Interviews can give insights into candidates' personalities and interpersonal styles. They are more valid, however, when they focus on job knowledge and skill. Interviews also provide a means to check the accuracy of information on the applicant's résumé or job application. Asking applicants to elaborate about their experiences and offer details reduces the likelihood of a candidate being able to invent a work history.[41]

Despite these benefits, interviewing is not necessarily the most accurate basis for making a selection decision. Research has shown that interviews can be unreliable, low in validity,[42] and biased against a number of different groups.[43] Interviews are also costly. They require that at least one person devote time to interviewing each candidate, and the applicants typically have to be brought to one geographic location. Interviews are also subjective, so they place the organization at greater risk of discrimination complaints by applicants who were not hired, especially if those individuals were asked questions not entirely related to the job. The Supreme Court has held that subjective selection methods like interviews must be validated, using methods that provide criterion-related or content validation.[44]

Organizations can avoid some of these pitfalls.[45] Human resource staff should keep the interviews narrow, structured, and standardized. The interview should focus on

Situational Interview
A structured interview in which the interviewer describes a situation likely to arise on the job, then asks the candidate what he or she would do in that situation.

Behavior Description Interview (BDI)
A structured interview in which the interviewer asks the candidate to describe how he or she handled a type of situation in the past.

Panel Interview
Selection interview in which several members of the organization meet to interview each candidate.

Interviewing Job Candidates Effectively

Interviewing job candidates is time consuming, and unfortunately, many companies waste that time with highly subjective, unplanned interviews that fail to reveal much relevant information. Here are some ideas for making the most of the interview process:

- Plan questions ahead of time, based on a job analysis. Be sure the questions are related to the competencies and behaviors related to successful performance of the job. To keep interviews to a reasonable length, prepare about four to six questions for a half-hour interview or eight to 12 questions for a one-hour interview.
- Ask the same specific questions in every interview to fill a given position. If the interview questions are consistent, candidates' responses will be easier to compare.
- Although every interview should cover the same questions, be flexible enough to gather complete and accurate information. If a candidate's response is unclear or incomplete, ask follow-up questions.
- Ask candidates to provide specific examples of job-related activities and accomplishments, rather than generalize. For example, "Tell me about a time when you handled a customer who was upset" will yield better information than "Tell me more about your current job."
- Take notes during the interview. Not only does it provide information for later review, but it sets a professional tone and shows the candidate that you are paying attention.
- Avoid distractions and interruptions. Phone calls can wait until after the interview. Interviewers should demonstrate the same respect they expect to receive from job candidates.

Questions

1. Imagine that you have been asked to interview candidates to work as cashiers in a store. You will meet with them at a table in a conference room. What should you bring to the interview?
2. Your friend suggests that the easiest approach to your task would be to simply say, "Tell me about yourself" and then ask, "Why should we hire you?" and let the candidates do the rest. How would you improve on this idea?

Sources: Alaina Brandenburger, "Hiring: Easy Tips for Conducting an Effective Interview," *CBS Denver,* February 17, 2014, http://denver.cbs.local.com; Chad Brooks, "Seven Tips for Conducting an Effective Job Interview," *Fox Small Business Center,* October 2, 2013, http://smallbusiness.foxbusiness.com; Lauren Weber, "Now Hiring? Tips for Conducting Interviews," *The Wall Street Journal,* December 4, 2012, http://online.wsj.com.

accomplishing a few goals, so that at the end of the interview, the organization has ratings on several observable measures, such as ability to express ideas. The interview should not try to measure abilities and skills—for example, intelligence—that tests can measure better. As noted earlier, situational interviews are especially effective for doing this. Organizations can prevent problems related to subjectivity by training interviewers and using more than one person to conduct interviews. Training typically includes focusing on the recording of observable facts, rather than on making subjective judgments, as well as developing interviewers' awareness of their biases.[46] Using a structured system for taking notes or scoring responses may help limit subjectivity and help the interviewer remember and justify an evaluation later.[47] Finally, to address costs of interviewing, many organizations videotape interviews and send the tapes (rather than the applicants) from department to department.

Amazon addresses subjectivity by bringing together multiple interviewer perspectives. Candidates for jobs at headquarters typically undergo a series of phone and in-person interviews with several Amazon employees. Interviewers include "bar raisers," who are not HR professionals but employees in any area of the company who have demonstrated interviewing skills. A bar raiser is assigned to interview candidates who will work in a department other than the bar raiser's; the idea is that he or she will think of issues that others have missed. This approach to interviewing assumes that the various perspectives on each candidate will result in a more objective selection and that the chosen candidate will succeed in more than one position at Amazon.[48]

Preparing to Interview

Organizations can reap the greatest benefits from interviewing if they prepare carefully. A well-planned interview should be standardized, comfortable for the participants, and focused on the job and the organization. The interviewer should have a quiet place in which to conduct interviews without interruption. This person should be trained in how to ask objective questions, what subject matter to avoid, and how to detect and handle his or her own personal biases or other distractions in order to fairly evaluate candidates.

The interviewer should have enough documents to conduct a complete interview. These should include a list of the questions to be asked in a structured interview, with plenty of space for recording the responses. When the questions are prepared, it is also helpful to determine how the answers will be scored. For example, if questions ask how interviewees would handle certain situations, consider what responses are best in terms of meeting job requirements. If the job requires someone who motivates others, then a response that shows motivating behavior would receive a higher score. The interviewer also should have a copy of the interviewee's employment application and résumé to review before the interview and refer to during the interview. If possible, the interviewer should also have printed information about the organization and the job. Near the beginning of the interview, it is a good idea to go over the job specifications, organizational policies, and so on, so that the interviewee has a clearer understanding of the organization's needs.

The interviewer should schedule enough time to review the job requirements, discuss the interview questions, and give the interviewee a chance to ask questions. To close, the interviewer should thank the candidate for coming and provide information about what to expect—for example, that the organization will contact a few finalists within the next two weeks or that a decision will be made by the end of the week.

Selection Decisions

After reviewing applications, scoring tests, conducting interviews, and checking references, the organization needs to make decisions about which candidates to place in which jobs. In practice, most organizations find more than one qualified candidate to fill an open position. The selection decision typically combines ranking based on objective criteria along with subjective judgments about which candidate will make the greatest contribution.

LO 6-7 Explain how employers carry out the process of making a selection decision.

How Organizations Select Employees

The selection decision should not be a simple matter of whom the supervisor likes best or which candidate will take the lowest offer. Also, observing confidence in job candidates does not necessarily mean they are competent. Rather, the people making the selection should look for the best fit between candidate and position. In general, the person's performance will result from a combination of ability and motivation. Often, the selection is a choice among a few people who possess the basic qualifications. The decision makers therefore have to decide which of those people have the best combination of ability and motivation to fit in the position and in the organization as a whole.

Interview Alarm Bells

When managers or HR professionals select candidates to interview, they are trying to find the best match among candidates with basic qualifications. Sometimes, unfortunately, what happens in an interview signals a troubling lack of motivation or business sense. For example, interviewers are unimpressed with someone who arrives at an interview after making no effort to learn anything about the company or prepare any questions to ask.

Sometimes candidates' behavior demonstrates such poor motivation and lack of judgment that it resembles a bad comedy routine. Interviewers have complained of candidates checking Facebook or wearing headphones during an interview; one even took a phone call about a job at another company. Some make odd statements: one told an interviewer she had taken "too much Valium" beforehand, and

another said his personal hero was himself.

Some memorable incidents reported by interviewers are downright frightening. One applicant had a car accident—hitting the employer's building. Another tried making a secret recording of the interview. And a third applicant, responding to an interviewer's prompt to "impress me," lit the interviewer's newspaper on fire.

Questions

1. With a multiple-hurdle model, interviewing typically comes late in the selection process. Based on what you know about the steps in the process, why do you think the candidates described here made it past the earlier hurdles? (For example, might they have other qualifications, or might there be problems with the process?)

2. In the compensatory model, a high score on one type of assessment can make up for a low score on another. Assuming the candidates described here had low scores on their interviews, can you think of a situation in which a high score on some other measure would make these candidates the best choice for a position? Explain.

Sources: Ryan Caldbeck, "These Five Interview Blunders Will Probably Kill Your Job Prospects," *Entrepreneur*, March 14, 2014, http://www.entrepreneur.com; Adam Auriemma, "Fire, Valium, Dentures: Job Interviews Gone Wild," *The Wall Street Journal*, January 16, 2014, http://blogs.wsj.com; CareerBuilder, "Employers Share Most Memorable Interview Blunders," news release, January 16, 2014, http://www.careerbuilder.com.

Multiple-Hurdle Model
Process of arriving at a selection decision by eliminating some candidates at each stage of the selection process.

Compensatory Model
Process of arriving at a selection decision in which a very high score on one type of assessment can make up for a low score on another.

The usual process for arriving at a selection decision is to gradually narrow the pool of candidates for each job. This approach, called the **multiple-hurdle model,** is based on a process such as the one shown earlier in Figure 6.1. Each stage of the process is a hurdle, and candidates who overcome a hurdle continue to the next stage of the process. For example, the organization reviews applications and/or résumés of all candidates, conducts some tests on those who meet minimum requirements, conducts initial interviews with those who had the highest test scores, follows up with additional interviews or testing, and then selects a candidate from the few who survived this process. Another, more expensive alternative is to take most applicants through all steps of the process and then to review all the scores to find the most desirable candidates. With this alternative, decision makers may use a **compensatory model,** in which a very high score on one type of assessment can make up for a low score on another. Think about how each of those two models would apply if you encountered the candidates described in the "HR Oops!" feature.

Whether the organization uses a multiple-hurdle model or conducts the same assessments on all candidates, the decision maker or makers need criteria for choosing among qualified candidates. An obvious strategy is to select the candidates who score highest on tests and interviews. However, employee performance depends on motivation as well as ability. It is possible that a candidate who scores very high on an ability test might be "overqualified"—that is, the employee might be bored by the job the organization needs to fill, and a less-able employee might actually be a better fit. Similarly, a highly motivated person might learn some kinds of jobs very quickly, potentially outperforming someone who has the necessary skills. Furthermore, some organizations have policies of developing employees for career paths in the organization. Such organizations might place less emphasis on the skills needed for a particular job and more emphasis on hiring candidates who share the organization's values, show that they have the people skills to work with others in the organization, and are able to learn the skills needed for advancement.

Finally, organizations have choices about who will make the decision. Usually a supervisor makes the final decision, often alone. This person may couple knowledge of the job with a judgment about who will fit in best with others in the department. The decision could also be made by a human resource professional using standardized, objective criteria. Especially in organizations that use teamwork, selection decisions may be made by a work team or other panel of decision makers.

Communicating the Decision

The human resource department is often responsible for notifying applicants about the results of the selection process. When a candidate has been selected, the organization should communicate the offer to the candidate. The offer should include the job responsibilities, work schedule, rate of pay, starting date, and other relevant details. If placement in a job requires that the applicant pass a physical examination, the offer should state that contingency. The person communicating the offer should also indicate a date by which the candidate should reply with an acceptance or rejection of the offer. For some jobs, such as management and professional positions, the candidate and organization may negotiate pay, benefits, and work arrangements before they arrive at a final employment agreement.

The person who communicates this decision should keep accurate records of who was contacted, when, and for which position, as well as of the candidate's reply. The HR department and the supervisor also should be in close communication about the job offer. When an applicant accepts a job offer, the HR department must notify the supervisor so that he or she can be prepared for the new employee's arrival.

THINKING ETHICALLY

IS A POLICY OF NOT HIRING SMOKERS ETHICAL?

Over the past several years, hospitals in nearly a dozen states have announced that they will no longer hire workers who smoke. Rather than merely forbidding employees from smoking at work, they make abstinence from smoking a requirement for selection. Some enforce the policy by relying on candidates to tell the truth; others use drug tests.

Reasons given in favor of the decision emphasize economic considerations. For example, when the University of Pennsylvania Health System announced its decision to stop hiring smokers, it claimed that employees who smoke cost the employer an average of $3,391 per year in additional health care costs. It also noted that taking breaks to smoke can be disruptive. Beyond the costs, the health system pointed out that the smell of smoke on employees' clothing can be unpleasant for patients and co-workers. Beyond the hospital's reasoning, others have measured higher costs of employing workers who smoke, for reasons such as greater absenteeism or poorer health while on the job. From a purely economic standpoint, an employer might have to pay more to get enough workers if it hires only nonsmokers, but if these workers are less expensive in other ways, the employer can still be ahead in terms of costs.

Some people have criticized these no-smoker policies as unfair. Critics point out that other off-work behavior also can drive up health costs. They say job requirements can specify the same breaks for all employees, regardless of whether they will use the breaks for smoking. They suggest that it would be more ethical for hospitals to consider hiring smokers and offer support to those who are trying to quit. Another criticism is that if smokers have trouble finding jobs, they might be inclined to lie about it and therefore be less likely to get help quitting. A related concern is whether the policy of refusing to hire individuals is too drastic, compared with other measures such as requiring smokers to pay a greater share of health insurance benefits or offering them a lower wage.

Questions

1. Who is affected by a hospital's decision not to hire smokers? Discuss whether this decision achieves the greatest good for the greatest number of individuals.
2. How well does this policy meet the standard of being fair and equitable? Explain.

Sources: Mark Pauly, "Refusing to Hire Workers Who Smoke: An Economic Perspective," *Knowledge@Wharton*, August 8, 2013, http://knowledge.wharton.upenn.edu; Dave Warner, "Pennsylvania Hospitals' Ban on Hiring Smokers Prompts Debate," Reuters, June 28, 2013, http://www.reuters.com; Arthur Caplan, "Barring Smokers from Hospital Jobs Unfair," *CNN.com*, March 1, 2013, http://www.cnn.com.

SUMMARY

LO 6-1 Identify the elements of the selection process.

- Selection typically begins with a review of candidates' employment applications and résumés.
- The organization administers tests to candidates who meet basic requirements.
- Qualified candidates undergo one or more interviews.
- Organizations check references and conduct background checks to verify the accuracy of information provided by candidates.
- A candidate is selected to fill each vacant position.
- Candidates who accept offers are placed in the positions for which they were selected.

LO 6-2 Define ways to measure the success of a selection method.

- One criterion is reliability, meaning free from random error, so that measurements are consistent.
- A selection method should also be valid, meaning that performance on the measure (such as a test score) is related to what the measure is designed to assess (such as job performance).
- Criterion-related validity shows a correlation between test scores and job performance scores.
- Content validity shows consistency between the test items or problems and the kinds of situations or problems that occur on the job.
- Construct validity establishes that the test actually measures a specified construct, such as intelligence or leadership ability, which is presumed to be associated with success on the job.
- A selection method also should be generalizable, or applicable to more than one specific situation.
- Each selection method should have utility, meaning it provides economic value greater than its cost.

- Selection methods should meet the legal requirements for employment decisions.

LO 6-3 Summarize the government's requirements for employee selection.

- The selection process must be conducted in a way that avoids discrimination and provides access to persons with disabilities.
- Selection methods must be valid for job performance, and scores may not be adjusted to discriminate against or give preference to any group.
- Questions may not gather information about a person's membership in a protected class, such as race, sex, or religion, nor may the employer investigate a person's disability status.
- Employers must respect candidates' privacy rights and ensure that they keep personal information confidential.
- Employers must obtain consent before conducting background checks and notify candidates about adverse decisions made as a result of background checks.

LO 6-4 Compare the common methods used for selecting human resources.

- Nearly all organizations gather information through employment applications and résumés. These methods are inexpensive, and an application form standardizes basic information received from all applicants. The information is not necessarily reliable, because each applicant provides the information. These methods are most valid when evaluated in terms of the criteria in a job description.
- References and background checks help verify the accuracy of applicant-provided information.

- Employment tests and work samples are more objective. To be legal, any test must measure abilities that actually are associated with successful job performance. Employment tests range from general to specific. General-purpose tests are relatively inexpensive and simple to administer. Tests should be selected to be related to successful job performance and avoid charges of discrimination.
- Interviews are widely used to obtain information about a candidate's interpersonal and communication skills and to gather more detailed information about a candidate's background. Structured interviews are more valid than unstructured ones. Situational interviews provide greater validity than general questions. Interviews are costly and may introduce bias into the selection process. Organizations can minimize the drawbacks through preparation and training.

LO 6-5 Describe major types of employment tests.

- Physical ability tests measure strength, endurance, psychomotor abilities, and other physical abilities. They can be accurate but can discriminate and are not always job related.
- Cognitive ability tests, or intelligence tests, tend to be valid, especially for complex jobs and those requiring adaptability. They are a relatively low-cost way to predict job performance but have been challenged as discriminatory.
- Job performance tests tend to be valid but are not always generalizable. Using a wide variety of job performance tests can be expensive.
- Personality tests measure personality traits such as extroversion and adjustment. Research supports their validity for appropriate job situations, especially for individuals who score high on conscientiousness, extroversion, and agreeableness. These tests are relatively simple to administer and generally meet legal requirements.
- Organizations may use paper-and-pencil honesty tests, which can predict certain behaviors, including employee theft. Organizations may not use polygraphs to screen job candidates.

- Organizations may also administer drug tests (if all candidates are tested and drug use can be an on-the-job safety hazard).
- Passing a medical examination may be a condition of employment, but to avoid discrimination against persons with disabilities, organizations usually administer a medical exam only after making a job offer.

LO 6-6 Discuss how to conduct effective interviews.

- Interviews should be narrow, structured, and standardized.
- Interviewers should identify job requirements and create a list of questions related to the requirements.
- Interviewers should be trained to recognize their own personal biases and conduct objective interviews.
- Panel interviews can reduce problems related to interviewer bias.
- Interviewers should put candidates at ease in a comfortable place that is free of distractions. Questions should ask for descriptions of relevant experiences and job-related behaviors.
- The interviewers also should be prepared to provide information about the job and the organization.

LO 6-7 Explain how employers carry out the process of making a selection decision.

- The organization should focus on the objective of finding the person who will be the best fit with the job and organization. This includes an assessment of ability and motivation.
- Decision makers may use a multiple-hurdle model in which each stage of the selection process eliminates some of the candidates from consideration at the following stages. At the final stage, only a few candidates remain, and the selection decision determines which candidate is the best fit.
- An alternative is a compensatory model, in which all candidates are evaluated with all methods. A candidate who scores poorly with one method may be selected if he or she scores very high on another measure.

KEY TERMS

personnel selection, 168
reliability, 170
validity, 170
criterion-related validity, 171
predictive validation, 171

concurrent validation, 172
content validity, 172
construct validity, 172
generalizable, 172
utility, 173

Immigration Reform and Control
   Act of 1986, 175
aptitude tests, 181
achievement tests, 181
cognitive ability tests, 182

REVIEW AND DISCUSSION QUESTIONS

1. What activities are involved in the selection process? Think of the last time you were hired for a job. Which of those activities were used in selecting you? Should the organization that hired you have used other methods as well? *(LO 6-1)*

2. Why should the selection process be adapted to fit the organization's job descriptions? *(LO 6-1)*

3. Choose two of the selection methods identified in this chapter. Describe how you can compare them in terms of reliability, validity, ability to generalize, utility, and compliance with the law. *(LO 6-2)*

4. Why does predictive validation provide better information than concurrent validation? Why is this type of validation more difficult? *(LO 6-2)*

5. How do U.S. laws affect organizations' use of each of the employment tests? Interviews? *(LO 6-3)*

6. Suppose your organization needs to hire several computer programmers, and you are reviewing résumés you obtained from an online service. What kinds of information will you want to gather from the "work experience" portion of these résumés? What kinds of information will you want to gather from the "education" portion of these résumés? What methods would you use for verifying or exploring this information? Why would you use those methods? *(LO 6-4)*

7. For each of the following jobs, select the two kinds of tests you think would be most important to include in the selection process. Explain why you chose those tests. *(LO 6-5)*
   a. City bus driver
   b. Insurance salesperson
   c. Member of a team that sells complex high-tech equipment to manufacturers
   d. Member of a team that makes a component of the equipment in (c)

8. Suppose you are a human resource professional at a large retail chain. You want to improve the company's hiring process by creating standard designs for interviews, so that every time someone is interviewed for a particular job category, that person answers the same questions. You also want to make sure the questions asked are relevant to the job and maintain equal employment opportunity. Think of three questions to include in interviews for each of the following jobs. For each question, state why you think it should be included. *(LO 6-6)*
   a. Cashier at one of the company's stores
   b. Buyer of the stores' teen clothing line
   c. Accounts payable clerk at company headquarters

9. How can organizations improve the quality of their interviewing so that interviews provide valid information? *(LO 6-6)*

10. Some organizations set up a selection process that is long and complex. In some people's opinion, this kind of selection process not only is more valid but also has symbolic value. What can the use of a long, complex selection process symbolize to job seekers? How do you think this would affect the organization's ability to attract the best employees? *(LO 6-7)*

TAKING RESPONSIBILITY

How Gild Aims to Create Golden Opportunities for Underappreciated Workers

No matter how hard employers try to provide equal opportunity, total fairness is difficult. For example, companies that rely on referrals or recruiting at top-ranked schools exclude great workers who did not graduate from the right school or don't know a current employee. Luca Bonmassar and Sheeroy Desai looked at this problem and saw opportunity: big data can objectively identify who possesses specific skills in high-demand fields. So Bonmassar and Desai founded Gild, a San Francisco–based company, and hired Vivienne Ming as its chief scientist. Ming is deeply interested in Gild's mission because she has experienced the assumptions that many humans make. Ming, who holds a doctorate in psychology and computational neuroscience, grew up as a male and underwent gender transition as an adult. When she began living as a woman, changes occurred in the way she was treated—for example, students asked her fewer math-related questions. She sees data as a way to reduce "wasted talent" by limiting bias in employment decisions.

Gild looks for publicly available data about computer programmers. It analyzes the data to create algorithms that identify the best programmers. For millions of computer programmers, it compiles hundreds of variables such as the quality of computer code the individual has written and posted for public use, the number of times someone uses the code, productivity measures for paid projects, the language used in discussing technical issues on discussion boards, and popularity ratings for online advice. Its algorithm computes a score of each person's skill. Employers can use the score in conjunction with other measures to make hiring decisions. Eventually, Gild hopes to create algorithms for other jobs, such as website designer, financial analyst, or graphic designer.

Gild has used its algorithm in its own selection decisions. The company identified the highest-scoring job candidate in Southern California—the owner of a T-shirt business who became fed up with high school, dropped out, taught himself to run a business and write code for its website, and became active on websites where computer programmers trade ideas. Gild interviewed him and hired him for his programming brilliance, acknowledging that it is a challenge for this independent-minded individual to thrive in a corporate environment.

This example points to the main critique of Gild's business. Even if the algorithm accurately measures technical skills, those are not the only requirements for success. A person also has to function well within the organization.

Nevertheless, Ming believes that by expanding the use of big data, Gild is doing good. It creates opportunities for people to advance based on talent. Ming even believes that similar analytics can identify talent in children so that high-potential but underprivileged children can be paired with mentors, creating opportunities in communities where there had previously been little hope.

Questions

1. Review the criteria for a successful selection method: reliable, valid, generalizable, practical, and legal. Evaluate how Gild's algorithm addresses or should address these criteria.

2. Recommend how an employer could use interviews along with Gild's scoring method to arrive at fair hiring decisions.

Sources: Tom Foremski, "Gild Says Its Algorithms Could Be Used to Lift People Out of Poverty," *ZDNet*, April 11, 2014, http://www.zdnet.com; Don Peck, "They're Watching You at Work," *Atlantic*, December 2013, http://www.theatlantic.com; "Algorithm Finds Top Programmers, No Resume Required," *Here and Now*, May 21, 2013, http://hereandnow.wbur.org; Matt Richtel, "How Big Data Is Playing Recruiter for Specialized Workers," *The New York Times*, April 27, 2013, http://www.nytimes.com; Mohana Ravindranath, "Facebook, Amazon Recruiting Programmers Based on Social 'Footprint,'" *Washington Post*, December 14, 2012, http://www.washingtonpost.com.

MANAGING TALENT

Hiring for an Oil Boom

North Dakota is experiencing an oil boom as drilling companies apply fracking technology and horizontal drilling to the Bakken shale formation in the state's western region. The state has surpassed Alaska as the second largest oil producer behind only Texas. Its unemployment rate is under 3%, and in the town of Williston—the fastest-growing small U.S. city—it is below 1%. North Dakota officials recently said 25,000 jobs remain unfilled.

Those vacancies are at the more than 150 oil and gas operators operating in North Dakota, the hundreds of subcontractors providing them with labor, and the services businesses growing to meet demand. The state forecasts a peak of about 60,000 drilling jobs, which by 2025 will fall to 50,000 positions needed for longer-term oil production. Another 20,000 jobs are indirectly related to drilling—for example, the restaurant, retail, and health care jobs needed for a growing community.

Given that just about everyone who wants a job is already working, employers are struggling to fill vacancies. One solution is to lure talent from other states, but many workers are leery of North Dakota's harsh climate, and even those who come discover that housing is scarce and expensive. Furthermore, employees may not stay with a company long. Turnover is high as workers jump from job to job, improving their earnings with each move.

In this environment, employers use a variety of tactics. To limit turnover, they may study résumés for signs that employees are not job hopping. Some companies relax their job specifications. One company, for example, recruited a receptionist to be an HR worker, though she had no experience in the field. Others promote workers to management positions without training them for the responsibility. In contrast, for the high-paying jobs at gas and oil companies, employers screen out inexperienced applicants and select those who have worked in the field, often with subcontractors. Truck drivers, another high-growth occupation, must hold a commercial license. Mechanics servicing wells need clean driving records and technical skills.

Employers must weigh the need to meet qualifications against the need to convince even marginally qualified workers to take (and keep) the job. While job candidates need to sell themselves to employers, companies need to sell themselves to the workers. Some of them buy or build housing for their workers, or they pay a housing allowance because rents in the area are so high. They offer generous pay packages, such as $17 for an entry-level job at Walmart or a signing bonus to work in a restaurant. Unfortunately, attracting pay-focused employees means company workers are likely to be attracted to slightly higher wages somewhere else, once they gain a little job experience.

Questions

1. How could an employer's interviewing methods help the company address the challenges of hiring during a boom when unemployment rates are near zero?

2. If you were advising a North Dakota company about its selection process, would you advise it to relax its selection criteria during the oil boom? Why or why not?

Sources: Associated Press, "North Dakota Desperate for Workers to Fill Empty Jobs," *AOL Jobs,* March 18, 2014, http://jobs.aol.com; Ashe Schow, "Another Hiring Surge in North Dakota Thanks to Shale Oil," *Washington Examiner,* December 31, 2013, http://washingtonexaminer.com; Jessica Holdman, "Oil Service Companies on Hiring Blitz," *Bismarck (ND) Tribune,* December 26, 2013, http://bismarcktribune.com; Dori Meinert, "Hiring Frenzy," *HR Magazine,* June 1, 2013, http://www.shrm.org.

HR IN SMALL BUSINESS

Kinaxis Chooses Sales Reps with Personality

Kinaxis is a software company headquartered in Ottawa, Ontario, that sells to clients around the world. Its specialty is software for supply chain management—all the processes and relationships through which companies obtain supplies as needed and get their products to customers on time and at minimal cost. This is a sophisticated type of product, tailored to a company's specific needs. Therefore, Kinaxis depends on salespeople who understand how businesses work, who listen carefully to identify needs, and who provide excellent customer service to maintain long-term business relationships.

Recently, Bob Dolan, vice president for sales at Kinaxis, needed to hire a sales team to serve clients in North America. The company had just one salesperson serving the continent, and Dolan wanted to add four more. He received about 100 résumés and wanted to select from these. He started by reviewing the résumés against job requirements and selected 20 candidates for a first round of interviews. The interview process helped Dolan cut the list of candidates in half, so he needed another way to narrow his options.

Dolan decided his next step would be personality testing. He hired a firm called Opus Productivity Solutions to administer a test called PDP ProScan to the remaining 10 candidates. In addition, Dolan himself took the test and had his current sales rep do the same. The existing salesperson was doing an excellent job, so the results of his test could help Dolan and Opus pinpoint the characteristics of someone likely to succeed in sales at Kinaxis. Based an analysis of all the results, Opus created a benchmark of traits associated with success in the job.

Representatives from Opus also discussed the test results with each candidate, giving each one a chance to disagree with the scores. No one did. Dolan observed that all the candidates scored high in assertiveness and extroversion—not surprising for people in sales. In addition, two of them scored above the benchmark in conformity and below the benchmark in dominance. Those results suggested to Dolan that these candidates might be so eager to please that they would be quick to give in to whatever customers requested—a pattern that could become costly for the company. Dolan eliminated those two candidates.

That meant Dolan still had eight candidates to fill four positions. He asked each one to give him the names of major accounts he or she had signed up in the previous two years. Four candidates were able to come up with three or four large clients. Those were the candidates Dolan hired.

Since then, Dolan says his experience with personality testing has only reinforced his belief that this selection method helps Kinaxis identify the best candidates. For example, one sales rep had scored low on "pace," indicating that the individual might lack the patience needed for the slow cycles required to close a sale of a complex software system. Dolan hoped the issue could be overcome if he provided enough coaching, but in fact, the sales rep sometimes behaved impatiently, annoying prospects. After three years of trying to help him grow into the job, Dolan laid him off.

The company's commitment to careful selection is expressed on its website: "As a growing and determined company, we're always looking for people eager to push the limits each day of what's possible." Kinaxis was recently named one of Canada's top employers for young people.

Questions

1. What selection methods did Bob Dolan use for hiring salespeople? Did he go about using these methods in the best order? What, if anything, would you change about the order of the methods used?

2. What were the advantages to Kinaxis of using personality tests to help select sales representatives? What were the disadvantages?

3. Given the information gathered from the selection methods, what process did Dolan use to make his selection decision? What improvements can you recommend to this process for decisions to hire sales reps in the future?

Sources: Susan Greco, "Personality Testing for Sales Recruits," *Inc.*, March 1, 2009, www.inc.com; Kinaxis Web site, Corporate Overview and Careers pages, www.kinaxis.com, accessed May 27, 2014.

NOTES

1. Katherine Reynolds Lewis, "Three Reasons Why Companies Don't Hire Veterans," *Fortune*, November 11, 2013, http://management.fortune.cnn.com; J. D. Leipold, "Warrior Transition Command Launches 'Hire a Veteran' Campaign," U.S. Army news archive, November 20, 2012, http://www.army.mil.

2. Lauren Weber, "Angry Job Applicants Can Hurt Bottom Line," *The Wall Street Journal*, March 13, 2012, http://online.wsj.com; Lauren Weber, "Your Résumé vs. Oblivion," *The Wall Street Journal*, January 24, 2012, http://online.wsj.com.

3. Patricia M. Sherlock, "Walking the Walk," *Mortgage Banking*, May 2011, Business & Company Resource Center, http://galenet.galegroup.com.

4. J. C. Nunnally, *Psychometric Theory* (New York: McGraw-Hill, 1978).

5. Sue Shellenbarger, "Why Likability Matters More at Work," *The Wall Street Journal*, March 25, 2014, http://online.wsj.com; Logan Hill, "Only BFFs Need Apply," *Bloomberg Businessweek*, January 7–13, 2013, pp. 63–65.

6. N. Schmitt, R. Z. Gooding, R. A. Noe, and M. Kirsch, "Meta-Analysis of Validity Studies Published between 1964 and 1982 and the Investigation of Study Characteristics," *Personnel Psychology* 37 (1984), pp. 407–22.

7. D. D. Robinson, "Content-Oriented Personnel Selection in a Small Business Setting," *Personnel Psychology* 34 (1981), pp. 77–87.

8. George Anders, "Work: The Games They Make You Play," *Guardian (London)*, October 29, 2011, Business & Company Resource Center, http://galenet.galegroup.com.

9. F. L. Schmidt and J. E. Hunter, "The Future of Criterion-Related Validity," *Personnel Psychology* 33 (1980), pp. 41–60; F. L. Schmidt, J. E. Hunter, and K. Pearlman, "Task Differences as Moderators of Aptitude Test Validity: A Red Herring," *Journal of Applied Psychology* 66 (1982), pp. 166–85; R. L. Gutenberg, R. D. Arvey, H. G. Osburn, and R. P. Jeanneret, "Moderating Effects of Decision-Making/Information Processing Dimensions on Test Validities," *Journal of Applied Psychology* 68 (1983), pp. 600–8.

10. Dan Herbeck, "Firefighters Are Awarded $2.7 Million in Bias Case," *Buffalo (NY) News*, February 9, 2012, Business & Company Resource Center, http://galenet.galegroup.com.

11. T. W. Dougherty, D. B. Turban, and J. C. Callender, "Confirming First Impressions in the Employment Interview: A Field Study of Interviewer Behavior," *Journal of Applied Psychology* 79 (1994), pp. 659–65.

12. Melissa Korn, "Giant Résumés Fail to Impress Employers," *The Wall Street Journal*, February 5, 2014, http://online.wsj.com.

13. Claire Suddath, "Your Résumé: Imaginary Friends as Job References," *Bloomberg Businessweek*, January 14, 2013, http://www.businessweek.com.

14. A. Ryan and M. Lasek, "Negligent Hiring and Defamation: Areas of Liability Related to Preemployment Inquiries," *Personnel Psychology* 44 (1991), pp. 293–319.

15. A. Long, "Addressing the Cloud over Employee References: A Survey of Recently Enacted State Legislation," *William and Mary Law Review* 39 (October 1997), pp. 177–228.

16. Dori Meinert, "Seeing behind the Mask," *HR Magazine*, February 2011, pp. 31–37; Jay Goltz, "Why Checking References Isn't a Waste of Time," *The New York Times*, March 10, 2011, http://boss.blogs.nytimes.com.

17. Sarah E. Needleman, "Big Blunders Job Hunters Make," *The Wall Street Journal*, June 28, 2010, http://online.wsj.com.

18. Equal Employment Opportunity Commission, "Background Checks: What Employers Need to Know," EEOC and Federal Trade Commission, http://www1.eeoc.gov, accessed May 20, 2014; Bureau of National Affairs, "Gray Areas Remain on Background Checks under EEOC Guidance," *HR Focus*, January 2014, pp. 14–15; Scott Thurm, "Employment Checks Fuel Race Complaints," *The Wall Street Journal*, June 11, 2013, http://online.wsj.com.

19. L. C. Buffardi, E. A. Fleishman, R. A. Morath, and P. M. McCarthy, "Relationships between Ability Requirements and Human Errors in Job Tasks," *Journal of Applied Psychology* 85 (2000), pp. 551–64; J. Hogan, "Structure of Physical Performance in Occupational Tasks," *Journal of Applied Psychology* 76 (1991), pp. 495–507.

20. J. F. Salagado, N. Anderson, S. Moscoso, C. Bertuas, and F. De Fruyt, "International Validity Generalization of GMA and Cognitive Abilities: A European Community Meta-analysis," *Personnel Psychology* 56 (2003), pp. 573–605; M. J. Ree, J. A. Earles, and M. S. Teachout, "Predicting Job Performance: Not Much More than g," *Journal of Applied Psychology* 79 (1994), pp. 518–24; L. S. Gottfredson, "The g Factor in Employment," *Journal of Vocational Behavior* 29 (1986), pp. 293–96; J. E. Hunter and

R. H. Hunter, "Validity and Utility of Alternative Predictors of Job Performance," *Psychological Bulletin* 96 (1984), pp. 72–98; Gutenberg et al., "Moderating Effects of Decision-Making/Information Processing Dimensions on Test Validities"; F. L. Schmidt, J. G. Berner, and J. E. Hunter, "Racial Differences in Validity of Employment Tests: Reality or Illusion," *Journal of Applied Psychology* 58 (1974), pp. 5–6; J. A. LePine, J. A. Colquitt, and A. Erez, "Adaptability to Changing Task Contexts: Effects of General Cognitive Ability, Conscientiousness, and Openness to Experience," *Personnel Psychology* 53 (2000), pp. 563–93.

21. Cameron McWhirter, "High-Tech Cheaters Pose Test," *The Wall Street Journal*, June 10, 2013, http://online.wsj.com.

22. D. A. Kravitz and S. L. Klineberg, "Reactions to Versions of Affirmative Action among Whites, Blacks, and Hispanics," *Journal of Applied Psychology* (2000), pp. 597–611.

23. George Anders, "The Rare Find," *Bloomberg Businessweek*, October 17, 2011, EBSCOhost, http://web.ebscohost.com.

24. D. J. Schleiger, V. Venkataramani, F. P. Morgeson, and M. A. Campion, "So You Didn't Get the Job . . . Now What Do You Think? Examining Opportunity to Perform Fairness Perceptions," *Personnel Psychology* 59 (2006), pp. 559–90.

25. F. L. Schmidt and J. E. Hunter, "The Validity and Utility of Selection Methods in Personnel Psychology: Practical and Theoretical Implications of 85 Years of Research Findings," *Psychological Bulletin* 124 (1998), pp. 262–74.

26. W. Arthur, E. A. Day, T. L. McNelly, and P. S. Edens, "Meta-Analysis of the Criterion-Related Validity of Assessment Center Dimensions," *Personnel Psychology* 56 (2003), pp. 125–54; C. E. Lance, T. A. Lambert, A. G. Gewin, F. Lievens, and J. M. Conway, "Revised Estimates of Dimension and Exercise Variance Components in Assessment Center Postexercise Dimension Ratings," *Journal of Applied Psychology* 89 (2004), pp. 377–85.

27. N. M. Dudley, K. A. Orvis, J. E. Lebieki, and J. M. Cortina, "A Meta-analytic Investigation of Conscientiousness in the Prediction of Job Performance: Examining the Intercorrelation and the Incremental Validity of Narrow Traits," *Journal of Applied Psychology* 91 (2006), pp. 40–57; W. S. Dunn, M. K. Mount, M. R. Barrick, and D. S. Ones, "Relative Importance of Personality and General Mental Ability on Managers' Judgments of Applicant Qualifications," *Journal of Applied Psychology* 79 (1995), pp. 500–9; P. M. Wright, K. M. Kacmar, G. C. McMahan, and K. Deleeuw, "$P = f(M \times A)$: Cognitive Ability as a Moderator of the Relationship between Personality and Job Performance," *Journal of Management* 21 (1995), pp. 1129–39.

28. M. Mount, M. R. Barrick, and J. P. Strauss, "Validity of Observer Ratings of the Big Five Personality Factors," *Journal of Applied Psychology* 79 (1994), pp. 272–80.

29. L. A. Witt and G. R. Ferris, "Social Skill as Moderator of the Conscientiousness–Performance Relationship: Convergent Results across Four Studies," *Journal of Applied Psychology* 88 (2003), pp. 809–20.

30. H. Le, I. S. Oh, S. B. Robbins, R. Ilies, E. Holland, and P. Westrick, "Too Much of a Good Thing? Curvilinear Relationship between Personality Traits and Job Performance," *Journal of Applied Psychology* 96 (2011): 113–33.

31. L. Joel, *Every Employee's Guide to the Law* (New York: Pantheon, 1993).

32. N. Schmitt and F. L. Oswald, "The Impact of Corrections for Faking on the Validity of Non-cognitive Measures in Selection Contexts," *Journal of Applied Psychology* (2006), pp. 613–21.

33. S. A. Birkland, T. M. Manson, J. L. Kisamore, M. T. Brannick, and M. A. Smith, "Faking on Personality Measures," *International Journal of Selection and Assessment* 14 (December 2006), pp. 317–35.

34. C. H. Van Iddekinge, P. H. Raymark, and P. L. Roth, "Assessing Personality with a Structured Employment Interview: Construct-Related Validity and Susceptibility to Response Inflation," *Journal of Applied Psychology* 90 (2005), pp. 536–52; R. Mueller-Hanson, E. D. Heggestad, and G. C. Thornton, "Faking and Selection: Considering the Use of Personality from Select-In and Select-Out Perspectives," *Journal of Applied Psychology* 88 (2003), pp. 348–55; N. L. Vasilopoulos, J. M. Cucina, and J. M. McElreath, "Do Warnings of Response Verification Moderate the Relationship between Personality and Cognitive Ability?" *Journal of Applied Psychology* 90 (2005), pp. 306–22; J. A. Shaffer and J. E. Postlewaite, "A Matter of Context: A Meta-analytic Investigation of the Relative Validity of Contextualized and Non-contextualized Personality Measures," *Personnel Psychology* 65 (2012): 445–94.

35. V. Knight, "Personality Tests as Hiring Tools," *The Wall Street Journal*, March 15, 2006, p. B1; G. L. Steward, I. S. Fulmer, and M. R. Barrick, "An Exploration of Member Roles as a Multilevel Linking Mechanism for Individual Traits and Team Outcomes," *Personnel Psychology* 58 (2005), pp. 343–65; M. Mount, R. Ilies, and E. Johnson, "Relationship of Personality Traits and Counterproductive Work Behaviors: The Mediation Effects of Job Satisfaction," *Personnel Psychology* 59 (2006), pp. 591–622.

36. D. S. Ones, C. Viswesvaran, and F. L. Schmidt, "Comprehensive Meta-analysis of Integrity Test Validities: Findings and Implications for Personnel Selection and Theories of Job Performance," *Journal of Applied Psychology* 78 (1993), pp. 679–703; H. J. Bernardin and D. K. Cooke, "Validity of an Honesty Test in Predicting Theft among Convenience Store Employees," *Academy of Management Journal* 36 (1993), pp. 1079–1106; C. H. Van Iddekinge, P. L. Roth, P. H. Raymark, and H. N. Odle-Dusseau, "The Criterion-Related Validity of Integrity Tests: An Updated Meta-analysis," *Journal of Applied Psychology* 97 (2012): 499–530.

37. Abigail K. Wozniak, "Discrimination and the Effects of Drug Testing on Black Employment," NBER Working Paper 20095, May 2014, National Bureau of Economic Research, available at http://www.nber.org. For discussion of the research, see Rebecca J. Rosen, "Racism, Again: Why Drug Tests Are Helping Black Americans Get Jobs," *Atlantic*, May 8, 2014, available at http://finance.yahoo.com; Ben Steverman, "How to Fight Racism with a Drug Test," *Bloomberg News*, May 5, 2014, http://www.bloomberg.com.

38. K. R. Murphy, G. C. Thornton, and D. H. Reynolds, "College Students' Attitudes toward Drug Test Programs," *Personnel Psychology* 43 (1990), pp. 615–31; M. E. Paronto, D. M. Truxillo, T. N. Bauer, and M. C. Leo, "Drug Testing, Drug

Treatment, and Marijuana Use: A Fairness Perspective," *Journal of Applied Psychology* 87 (2002), pp. 1159–66.

39. M. A. McDaniel, F. P. Morgeson, E. G. Finnegan, M. A. Campion, and E. P. Braver man, "Use of Situational Judgment Tests to Predict Job Performance: A Clarification of the Literature," *Journal of Applied Psychology* 86 (2001), pp. 730–40; J. Clavenger, G. M. Perreira, D. Weichmann, N. Schmitt, and V. S. Harvey, "Incremental Validity of Situational Judgment Tests," *Journal of Applied Psychology* 86 (2001), pp. 410–17.

40. M. A. Campion, J. E. Campion, and J. P. Hudson, "Structured Interviewing: A Note of Incremental Validity and Alternative Question Types," *Journal of Applied Psychology* 79 (1994), pp. 998–1002; E. D. Pulakos and N. Schmitt, "Experience-Based and Situational Interview Questions: Studies of Validity," *Personnel Psychology* 48 (1995), pp. 289–308; A. P. J. Ellis, B. J. West, A. M. Ryan, and R. P. DeShon, "The Use of Impression Management Tactics in Structured Interviews: A Function of Question Type?" *Journal of Applied Psychology* 87 (2002), pp. 1200–8.

41. N. Schmitt, F. L. Oswald, B. H. Kim, M. A. Gillespie, L. J. Ramsey, and T. Y Yoo, "The Impact of Elaboration on Socially Desirable Responding and the Validity of Biodata Measures," *Journal of Applied Psychology* 88 (2003), pp. 979–88; N. Schmitt and C. Kunce, "The Effects of Required Elaboration of Answers to Biodata Questions," *Personnel Psychology* 55 (2002), pp. 569–87.

42. Hunter and Hunter, "Validity and Utility of Alternative Predictors of Job Performance."

43. R. Pingitore, B. L. Dugoni, R. S. Tindale, and B. Spring, "Bias against Overweight Job Applicants in a Simulated Interview," *Journal of Applied Psychology* 79 (1994), pp. 184–90.

44. *Watson v. Fort Worth Bank and Trust*, 108 Supreme Court 2791 (1988).

45. M. A. McDaniel, D. L. Whetzel, F. L. Schmidt, and S. D. Maurer, "The Validity of Employment Interviews: A Comprehensive Review and Meta-Analysis," *Journal of Applied Psychology* 79 (1994), pp. 599–616; A. I. Huffcutt and W. A. Arthur, "Hunter and Hunter (1984) Revisited: Interview Validity for Entry-Level Jobs," *Journal of Applied Psychology* 79 (1994), pp. 184–90.

46. Y. Ganzach, A. N. Kluger, and N. Klayman, "Making Decisions from an Interview: Expert Measurement and Mechanical Combination," *Personnel Psychology* 53 (2000), pp. 1–21; G. Stasser and W. Titus, "Effects of Information Load and Percentage of Shared Information on the Dissemination of Unshared Information during Group Discussion," *Journal of Personality and Social Psychology* 53 (1987), pp. 81–93.

47. C. H. Middendorf and T. H. Macan, "Note-Taking in the Interview: Effects on Recall and Judgments," *Journal of Applied Psychology* 87 (2002), pp. 293–303; K. G. Melchers, N. Lienhardt, M. Von Aartburg, and M. Kleinmann, "Is More Structure Really Better? A Comparison of Frame of Reference Training and Descriptively Anchored Rating Scales to Improve Interviewers' Rating Quality," *Personnel Psychology* 64 (2011), pp. 53–87.

48. Greg Bensinger, "Amazon's Current Employees Raise the Bar for New Hires," *The Wall Street Journal*, January 7, 2014, http://online.wsj.com.

7

Training Employees

What Do I Need to Know?

After reading this chapter, you should be able to:

LO 7-1 Discuss how to link training programs to organizational needs.

LO 7-2 Explain how to assess the need for training.

LO 7-3 Explain how to assess employees' readiness for training.

LO 7-4 Describe how to plan an effective training program.

LO 7-5 Compare widely used training methods.

LO 7-6 Summarize how to implement a successful training program.

LO 7-7 Evaluate the success of a training program.

LO 7-8 Describe training methods for employee orientation and diversity management.

Introduction

If you listen to or read the comments of employers, you will often hear about a "skills shortage," especially in manufacturing and high-tech jobs. This worry might seem strange in light of persistently high unemployment, but many companies report difficulty in finding qualified people to fill all their open positions. However, some business experts and even some employers criticize companies for having unrealistic expectations. Employers today are apt to look for workers who have already performed the job requirements elsewhere; in the past, companies were more likely to hire hardworking, intelligent individuals and train them to perform the duties of the job. In the words of Grainger CEO James Ryan, some companies have been "on the sidelines" when it comes to training. They need to "get off the bench" and "take some responsibility in investing in training and education."[1]

One company not loafing on the sidelines is Microsoft. An assessment of sales representatives' performance showed they had excellent technical knowledge of the company's products but had difficulty discussing solutions with Microsoft's business customers. Instead of complaining about a skills gap, Microsoft set up a training program called Pitch Perfect. The program includes online courses that teach skills in identifying customers' needs and showing how Microsoft can meet those needs. Salespeople also pair up for role-playing exercises, which are customized for each group, and they receive coaching from trained Microsoft managers. Thousands of Microsoft sales reps have participated in Pitch Perfect, and they say their communication skills have improved—a result that should translate directly into higher sales.[2]

So that sales employees can contribute better to the company's growth strategy, Microsoft provides them with the right kind of training. **Training** consists of an organization's planned efforts to help employees acquire job-related knowledge, skills, abilities, and behaviors, with the goal of applying these on the job. A training program may range from formal classes to one-on-one mentoring, and it may take place on the job or at remote locations. No matter what its form, training can benefit the organization when it is linked to organizational needs and when it motivates employees.

This chapter describes how to plan and carry out an effective training program. We begin by discussing how to develop effective training in the context of the organization's strategy. Next, we discuss how organizations assess employees' training needs. We then review training methods and the process of evaluating a training program. The chapter concludes by discussing some special applications of training: orientation of new employees and the management of diversity.

Training Linked to Organizational Needs

The nature of the modern business environment makes training more important today than it ever has been. Rapid change, especially in the area of technology, requires that employees continually learn new skills. The new psychological contract, described in Chapter 2, has created the expectation that employees invest in their own career development, which requires learning opportunities. Growing reliance on teamwork creates a demand for the ability to solve problems in teams, an ability that often requires formal training. Finally, the diversity of the U.S. population, coupled with the globalization of business, requires that employees be able to work well with people who are different from them. Successful organizations often take the lead in developing this ability.

With training so essential in modern organizations, it is important to provide training that is effective. An effective training program actually teaches what it is designed to teach, and it teaches skills and behaviors that will help the organization achieve its goals. To achieve those goals, HR professionals approach training through **instructional design**—a process of systematically developing training to meet specified needs.[3]

A complete instructional design process includes the steps shown in Figure 7.1. It begins with an assessment of the needs for training—what the organization requires that its people learn. Next, the organization ensures that employees are ready for training in terms of their attitudes, motivation, basic skills, and work environment. The third step is to plan the training program, including the program's objectives, instructors, and methods. The organization then implements the program. Finally, evaluating the results of the training provides feedback for planning future training programs. For an example of a company that effectively uses this process, see the "Best Practices" box.

Training
An organization's planned efforts to help employees acquire job-related knowledge, skills, abilities, and behaviors, with the goal of applying these on the job.

LO 7-1 Discuss how to link training programs to organizational needs.

Instructional Design
A process of systematically developing training to meet specified needs.

Figure 7.1
Stages of Instructional Design

- Assess needs for training
- Ensure readiness for training
- Plan training program
  - Objectives
  - Trainers
  - Methods
- Implement training program
  - Principles of learning
  - Transfer of training
- Evaluate results of training

Feedback

A Strategic Approach to Learning at ConAgra Foods

ConAgra Foods has a strategic goal to be the fastest-growing food company (in terms of sales and profits) by 2017. The company, whose brands include Chef Boyardee, Healthy Choice, and Hunt's, has been acquiring other businesses, helping it grow to more than 25,000 employees. HR managers on ConAgra's Enterprise Learning team realized they would need a strategy to ensure that the company has the skills needed to support further growth. So ConAgra developed a strategy for sharing training resources among local facilities to meet each employee's individual training needs.

In the sales function, for example, ConAgra has a goal that all of its salespeople will know their product line and customers so well they can serve as trusted advisers. This requires that salespeople understand financial data, specifically how sales of their products contribute to ConAgra's profits. The Enterprise Learning team pinpointed the required skills and knowledge, using that information as the basis for creating a three-stage training program. The first stage is a set of simulations, videos, and reading materials to support classroom training in basic business principles. Next, five sales teams (about 100 participants each) gathered for two-day workshops at which they applied the basic principles, engaging in role-plays to practice what they were learning. To sustain what was learned, managers in the final stage of training set goals for the salespeople and monitored their performance. Since the training, the Enterprise Learning team has measured a substantial improvement in profits among the trained salespeople.

Other training programs target management. For the first layer of management, front-line supervisors, ConAgra established the Foundations of Leadership program. This program addresses how to become a leader of individuals and teams—skills a front-line supervisor may not yet have practiced. The goal for Foundations of Leadership is that supervisors will understand what is involved in being a leader at ConAgra Foods so their groups can deliver better results. Surveys of employees provide feedback used for additional training and efforts to sustain what supervisors have learned. The Enterprise Learning team also measured lower average turnover of employees whose supervisors participated in Foundations of Leadership, saving an estimated $116,100 for every class of 28 supervisors trained. Another program, called Managing Talent for Results, used a board game to teach 500 managers how to improve business results by choosing the best people to fill positions as needs open up.

Questions

1. What were the training objectives for salespeople? How did ConAgra measure the results of training them?
2. Why was there a need to train first-line supervisors? What results of that training program did ConAgra observe?

Sources: ConAgra Foods, careers page, http://www.conagrafoodscareers.com, accessed May 29, 2014; "2013 *Chief Learning Officer* Learning in Practice Awards," *Chief Learning Officer*, December 2013, pp. 33–53; Kris Zilliox, "Strategies for Success," *Training*, November 2013, www.trainingmag.com; Lorri Freifeld, "ConAgra Foods Activates Sales GMs," *Training*, April 1, 2013, http://www.trainingmag.com.

Learning Management System (LMS)
A computer application that automates the administration, development, and delivery of training programs.

To carry out this process more efficiently and effectively, a growing number of organizations are using a **learning management system (LMS)**, a computer application that automates the administration, development, and delivery of a company's training programs.[4] Managers and employees can use the LMS to identify training needs and enroll in courses. LMSs can make training programs more widely available and help companies reduce travel and other costs by providing online training. Administrative tools let managers track course enrollments and program completion. The system can be linked to the organization's performance management system to plan for and manage training needs, training outcomes, and associated rewards together.

Needs Assessment

Instructional design logically should begin with a **needs assessment**, the process of evaluating the organization, individual employees, and employees' tasks to determine what kinds of training, if any, are necessary. As this definition indicates, the needs assessment answers questions in three broad areas[5]:

1. *Organization*—What is the context in which training will occur?
2. *Person*—Who needs training?
3. *Task*—What subjects should the training cover?

The answers to these questions provide the basis for planning an effective training program.

A variety of conditions may prompt an organization to conduct a needs assessment. Management may observe that some employees lack basic skills or are performing poorly. Decisions to produce new products, apply new technology, or design new jobs should prompt a needs assessment because these changes tend to require new skills. The decision to conduct a needs assessment also may be prompted by outside forces, such as customer requests or legal requirements.

The outcome of the needs assessment is a set of decisions about how to address the issues that prompted the needs assessment. These decisions do not necessarily include a training program, because some issues should be resolved through methods other than training. For example, suppose a company uses delivery trucks to transport anesthetic gases to medical facilities, and a driver of one of these trucks mistakenly hooks up the supply line of a mild anesthetic from the truck to the hospital's oxygen system, contaminating the hospital's oxygen supply. This performance problem prompts a needs assessment. Whether or not the hospital decides to provide more training will depend partly on the reasons the driver erred. The driver may have hooked up the supply lines incorrectly because of a lack of knowledge about the appropriate line hookup, anger over a request for a pay raise being denied, or mislabeled valves for connecting the supply lines. Out of these three possibilities, only the lack of knowledge can be corrected through training. Other outcomes of a needs assessment might include plans for better rewards to improve motivation, better hiring decisions, and better safety precautions.

The remainder of this chapter discusses needs assessment and then what the organization should do when assessment indicates a need for training. The possibilities for action include offering existing training programs to more employees; buying or developing new training programs; and improving existing training programs. Before we consider the available training options, let's examine the elements of the needs assessment in more detail.

Organization Analysis

Usually, the needs assessment begins with the **organization analysis**. This is a process for determining the appropriateness of training by evaluating the characteristics of the organization. The organization analysis looks at training needs in light of the organization's strategy, resources available for training, and management's support for training activities.

Training needs will vary depending on whether the organization's strategy is based on growing or shrinking its personnel, whether it is seeking to serve a broad customer base or focusing on the specific needs of a narrow market segment, and various other strategic scenarios. An organization that concentrates on serving a niche market may need to continually update its workforce on a specialized skills

LO 7-2 Explain how to assess the need for training.

Needs Assessment
The process of evaluating the organization, individual employees, and employees' tasks to determine what kinds of training, if any, are necessary.

Organization Analysis
A process for determining the appropriateness of training by evaluating the characteristics of the organization.

Pfizer employees go through a representative training phase which teaches them about different Pfizer products and how to market them. Success at a drug company such as Pfizer depends on the frequent introduction of new medicines and the expertise of sales representatives who tell health care professionals about those products.

set. A company that is cutting costs with a downsizing strategy may need to train employees who will be laid off in job search skills. The employees who remain following the downsizing may need cross-training so that they can handle a wider variety of responsibilities.

Anyone planning a training program must consider whether the organization has the budget, time, and expertise for training. For example, if the company is installing computer-based manufacturing equipment in one of its plants, it can ensure that it has the necessary computer-literate employees in one of three ways. If it has the technical experts on its staff, they can train the employees affected by the change. Or the company may use testing to determine which of its employees are already computer literate and then replace or reassign employees who lack the necessary skills. The third choice is to purchase training from an outside individual or organization.

Even if training fits the organization's strategy and budget, it can be viable only if the organization is willing to support the investment in training. Managers increase the success of training when they support it through such actions as helping trainees see how they can use their newly learned knowledge, skills, and behaviors on the job.[6] Conversely, the managers will be most likely to support training if the people planning it can show that it will solve a significant problem or result in a significant improvement, relative to its cost. Managers appreciate training proposals with specific goals, timetables, budgets, and methods for measuring success.

Person Analysis

A process of determining individuals' needs and readiness for training.

Person Analysis

Following the organizational assessment, needs assessment turns to the remaining areas of analysis: person and task. The **person analysis** is a process for determining individuals' needs and readiness for training. It involves answering several questions:

- Do performance deficiencies result from a lack of knowledge, skill, or ability? (If so, training is appropriate; if not, other solutions are more relevant.)
- Who needs training?
- Are these employees ready for training?

The answers to these questions help the manager identify whether training is appropriate and which employees need training. In certain situations, such as the introduction of a new technology or service, all employees may need training. However, when needs assessment is conducted in response to a performance problem, training is not always the best solution.

The person analysis is therefore critical when training is considered in response to a performance problem. In assessing the need for training, the manager should identify all the variables that can influence performance. The primary variables are the person's ability and skills, his or her attitudes and motivation, the organization's input (including clear directions, necessary resources, and freedom from interference and distractions), performance feedback (including praise and performance standards), and positive consequences to motivate good performance. Of these variables, only ability and skills can be affected by training. Therefore, before planning a training program, it is important to be sure that any performance problem results from a deficiency in knowledge and skills. Otherwise, training dollars will be wasted, because the training is unlikely to have much effect on performance.

The person analysis also should determine whether employees are ready to undergo training. In other words, the employees to receive training not only should require additional knowledge and skill, but must be willing and able to learn. (After our discussion of the needs assessment, we will explore the topic of employee readiness in greater detail.)

Task Analysis

The third area of needs assessment is **task analysis**, the process of identifying the tasks, knowledge, skills, and behaviors that training should emphasize. Usually, task analysis is conducted along with person analysis. Understanding shortcomings in performance usually requires knowledge about the tasks and work environment as well as the employee.

Task Analysis
The process of identifying and analyzing tasks to be trained for.

To carry out the task analysis, the HR professional looks at the conditions in which tasks are performed. These conditions include the equipment and environment of the job, time constraints (for example, deadlines), safety considerations, and performance standards. These observations form the basis for a description of work activities, or the tasks required by the person's job. For a selected job, the analyst interviews employees and their supervisors to prepare a list of tasks performed in that job. Then the analyst validates the list by showing it to employees, supervisors, and other subject-matter experts and asking them to complete a questionnaire about the importance, frequency, and difficulty of the tasks. For each task listed, the subject-matter expert uses a sliding scale (for example, 0 = task never performed to 5 = task often performed) to rate the task's importance, frequency, and difficulty.[7]

The information from these questionnaires is the basis for determining which tasks will be the focus of the training. The person or committee conducting the needs assessment must decide what levels of importance, frequency, and difficulty signal a need for training. Logically, training is most needed for tasks that are important, frequent, and at least moderately difficult. For each of these tasks, the analysts must identify the knowledge, skills, and abilities required to perform the task. This information usually comes from interviews with subject-matter experts, such as employees who currently hold the job.

LO 7-3 Explain how to assess employees' readiness for training.

Readiness for Training

Readiness for Training
A combination of employee characteristics and positive work environment that permit training.

Effective training requires not only a program that addresses real needs, but also a condition of employee readiness. **Readiness for training** is a combination of employee characteristics and positive work environment that permit training. It exists when employees are able and eager to learn and when their organizations encourage learning.

Employee Readiness Characteristics

To be ready to learn, employees need basic learning skills, especially *cognitive ability*, which includes being able to use written and spoken language, solve math problems, and use logic to solve problems. Ideally, the selection process identified job candidates with enough cognitive ability to handle not only the requirements for doing a job, but also the training associated with that job. However, recent forecasts of the skill levels of the U.S. workforce indicate that many companies will have to work with employees who lack basic skills.[8] For example, they may have to provide literacy training or access to classes teaching math skills before some employees can participate in job-related training.

Employees learn more from training programs when they are highly motivated to learn—that is, when they really want to learn the content of the training program.[9] Employees tend to feel this way if they believe they are able to learn, see potential benefits from the training program, are aware of their need to learn, see a fit between the training and their career goals, and have the basic skills needed for participating in the program. Managers can influence a ready attitude in a variety of ways—for example, by providing feedback that encourages employees, establishing rewards for learning, and communicating with employees about the organization's career paths and future needs.

Work Environment

Readiness for training also depends on two broad characteristics of the work environment: situational constraints and social support.[10] *Situational constraints* are the limits on training's effectiveness that arise from the situation or the conditions within the organization. Constraints can include a lack of money for training, lack of time for training or practicing, and failure to provide proper tools and materials for learning or applying the lessons of training. Conversely, trainees are likely to apply what they learn if the organization gives them opportunities to use their new skills and if it rewards them for doing so.[11]

Social support refers to the ways the organization's people encourage training, including giving trainees praise and encouraging words, sharing information about participating in training programs, and expressing positive attitudes toward the organization's training programs. Table 7.1 summarizes some ways in which managers can support training.

Understand the content of the training.
Know how training relates to what you need employees to do.
In performance appraisals, evaluate employees on how they apply training to their jobs.
Support employees' use of training when they return to work.
Ensure that employees have the equipment and technology needed to use training.
Prior to training, discuss with employees how they plan to use training.
Recognize newly trained employees who use training content.
Give employees release time from their work to attend training.
Explain to employees why they have been asked to attend training.
Give employees feedback related to skills or behavior they are trying to develop.
If possible, be a trainer.

Table 7.1

What Managers Should Do to Support Training

Sources: Based on A. Rossett, "That Was a Great Class, but . . ." *Training and Development,* July 1977, p. 21; R. Bates, "Managers as Transfer Agents," In E. Hotiton III and T. Baldwin (eds.), *Improving Learning Transfer in Organizations* (San Francisco: Jossey-Bass, 2003): pp. 243–270.

Support can also come from employees' peers. Readiness for training is greater in an organization where employees share knowledge, encourage one another to learn, and have a positive attitude about carrying the extra load when co-workers are attending classes. Employers foster such attitudes and behavior when they reward learning.

Planning the Training Program

LO 7-4 Describe how to plan an effective training program.

Decisions about training are often the responsibility of a specialist in the organization's training or human resources department. When the needs assessment indicates a need for training and employees are ready to learn, the person responsible for training should plan a training program that directly relates to the needs identified. Planning begins with establishing objectives for the training program. Based on those objectives, the planner decides who will provide the training, what topics the training will cover, what training methods to use, and how to evaluate the training.

Objectives of the Program

Formally establishing objectives for the training program has several benefits. First, a training program based on clear objectives will be more focused and more likely to succeed. In addition, when trainers know the objectives, they can communicate them to the employees participating in the program. Employees learn best when they know what the training is supposed to accomplish. Finally, down the road, establishing objectives provides a basis for measuring whether the program succeeded, as we will discuss later in this chapter.

Effective training objectives have several characteristics:

- They include a statement of what the employee is expected to do, the quality or level of performance that is acceptable, and the conditions under which the employee is to apply what he or she learned (for instance, physical conditions, mental stresses, or equipment failure).[12]
- They include performance standards that are measurable.
- They identify the resources needed to carry out the desired performance or outcome. Successful training requires employees to learn but also employers to provide the necessary resources.

A related issue at the outset is who will participate in the training program. Some training programs are developed for all employees of the organization or all members

Many Companies Outsource Training Tasks

A recent survey of U.S.-based corporations found that over half outsourced at least some of the instruction of training courses. Almost half used contractors to operate or host a learning management system, and 45% used contractors to develop at least some of their custom content. In terms of spending, an average of 8% of companies' training budgets went to contractors.

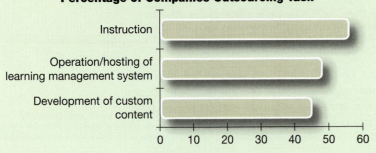

Percentage of Companies Outsourcing Task

Task	
Instruction	
Operation/hosting of learning management system	
Development of custom content	

0   10   20   30   40   50   60

Question

Suppose you need to train office workers on how to use social media without risking your company's reputation or data security.
What are some advantages of company employees developing the course content? What are some advantages of using a firm that specializes in training about information technology?

Source: "2013 Training Industry Report," *Training,* November/December 2013, pp. 22–35.

of a team. Other training programs identify individuals who lack desirable skills or have potential to be promoted, then provide training in the areas of need that are identified for the particular employees. When deciding whom to include in training, the organization has to avoid illegal discrimination. The organization should not—intentionally or unintentionally—exclude members of protected groups, such as women, minorities, and older employees. During the training, all participants should receive equal treatment, such as equal opportunities for practice. In addition, the training program should provide reasonable accommodation for trainees with disabilities. The kinds of accommodations that are appropriate will vary according to the type of training and type of disability. One employee might need an interpreter, whereas another might need to have classroom instruction provided in a location accessible to wheelchairs.

In-House or Contracted Out?

An organization can provide an effective training program, even if it lacks expertise in training. As shown in the "Did You Know?" box, many organizations use outside experts to develop and instruct training courses. Many companies and consultants provide training services to organizations. Community colleges often work with employers to train employees in a variety of skills.

To select a training service, an organization can mail several vendors a *request for proposal (RFP)*, which is a document outlining the type of service needed, the type and number of references needed, the number of employees to be trained, the date by which the training is to be completed, and the date by which proposals should be received. A complete RFP also indicates funding for the project and the process by which the organization will determine its level of satisfaction. Putting together a request for proposal is time consuming but worthwhile because it helps the organization clarify its objectives, compare vendors, and measure results.

Vendors that believe they are able to provide the services outlined in the RFP submit proposals that provide the types of information requested. The organization reviews the proposals to eliminate any vendors that do not meet requirements and to compare the vendors that do qualify. They check references and select a candidate, based on the proposal and the vendor's answers to questions about its experience, work samples, and evidence that its training programs meet objectives.

The cost of purchasing training from a contractor can vary substantially. In general, it is much costlier to purchase specialized training that is tailored to the organization's unique requirements than to participate in a seminar or training course that teaches general skills or knowledge. Preparing a specialized training program can require a significant investment of time for material the consultant won't be able to sell to other clients. Not surprisingly then, companies reduced the amount they spent for outsourcing during the recent recession and have tended to maintain or further cut spending on outside training products and services.[13]

Even in organizations that send employees to outside training programs, someone in the organization may be responsible for coordinating the overall training program. Called *training administration*, this is typically the responsibility of a human resources professional. Training administration includes activities before, during, and after training sessions.

Choice of Training Methods

Whether the organization prepares its own training programs or buys training from other organizations, it is important to verify that the content of the training relates directly to the training objectives. Relevance to the organization's needs and objectives ensures that training money is well spent. Tying training content closely to objectives also improves trainees' learning, because it increases the likelihood that the training will be meaningful and helpful.

After deciding on the goals and content of the training program, planners must decide how the training will be conducted. As we will describe in the next section, a wide variety of methods is available. Training methods fall into the broad categories described in Table 7.2: presentation, hands-on, and group-building methods.

METHOD	TECHNIQUES	APPLICATIONS
Presentation methods: trainees receive information provided by others	Lectures, workbooks, video clips, podcasts, websites	Conveying facts or comparing alternatives
Hands-on methods: trainees are actively involved in trying out skills	On-the-job training, simulations, role-plays, computer games	Teaching specific skills; showing how skills are related to job or how to handle interpersonal issues
Group-building methods: trainees share ideas and experiences, build group identities, learn about interpersonal relationships and the group	Group discussions, experiential programs, team training	Establishing teams or work groups; managing performance of teams or work groups

Table 7.2

Categories of Training Methods

Training programs may use these methods alone or in combination. In general, the methods used should be suitable for the course content and the learning abilities of the participants. The following section explores the options in greater detail.

LO 7-5 Compare widely used training methods.

Training Methods

A wide variety of methods is available for conducting training. Figure 7.2 shows the percentage of training hours delivered to employees by each of several methods: instructor-led classrooms, online self-study, virtual classrooms, social media, mobile devices, and combinations of these methods. Although the share of instruction provided online is growing, classroom training remains the most popular of these methods.[14]

Classroom Instruction

At school, we tend to associate learning with classroom instruction, and that type of training is most widely used in the workplace, too. Classroom instruction typically involves a trainer lecturing a group. Trainers often supplement lectures with slides, discussions, case studies, question-and-answer sessions, and role playing. Actively involving trainees enhances learning.

When the course objectives call for presenting information on a specific topic to many trainees, classroom instruction is one of the least expensive and least time-consuming ways to accomplish that goal. Learning will be more effective if trainers enhance lectures with job-related examples and opportunities for hands-on learning.

Modern technology has expanded the notion of the classroom to classes of trainees scattered in various locations. With *distance learning*, trainees at different locations attend programs online, using their computers to view lectures, participate in discussions, and share documents. Technology applications in distance learning may include videoconferencing, e-mail, instant messaging, document-sharing software, and web cameras. When Steelcase was ready to begin selling its Node chair, a flexible classroom chair with a swivel seat, storage for backpacks, and a customizable work surface, it needed to show its global sales force how adaptable it was to today's classrooms and teaching methods. Steelcase

Figure 7.2

Use of Instructional Methods

Source: "2013 Training Industry Report," *Training,* November/December 2013, pp. 22–35.

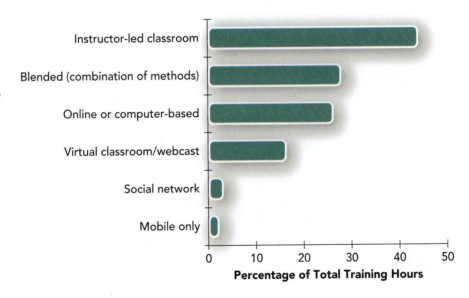

Percentage of Total Training Hours

also had to deliver the training fast, so that the sales reps would be prepared before schools were making their annual purchases for the next academic year. The solution was a virtual classroom, which allowed trainees to see the chair as well as hear the training.[15]

Distance learning provides many of the benefits of classroom training without the cost and time of travel to a shared classroom. The major disadvantage of distance learning is that interaction between the trainer and audience may be limited. To overcome this hurdle, distance learning usually provides a communications link between trainees and trainer. Also, on-site instructors or facilitators should be available to answer questions and moderate question-and-answer sessions.

Audiovisual Training

Presentation methods need not require trainees to attend a class. Trainees can also work independently, using course material in workbooks, on DVDs, or on the Internet. Audiovisual techniques such as overhead transparencies, PowerPoint or other presentation software, and video or audio clips can also supplement classroom instruction.

With modern technology, audiovisual materials can easily be made available on a variety of devices, from desktop computers to the tiny screens of smartphones and MP3 players. Today's mobile devices can display charts, play audio podcasts, and link to video clips. The DoubleTree by Hilton in Bloomington, Illinois, has placed two iPads loaded with training material at its front desk so employees can use them to complete training programs during slow periods. DoubleTree's training lessons are available in a choice of English or Spanish.[16] The "HR How To" box offers ideas for effectively delivering training on iPads and other mobile devices.

Users of audiovisual training often have some control over the presentation. They can review material and may be able to slow down or speed up the lesson. Videos can show situations and equipment that cannot be easily demonstrated in a classroom. Another advantage of audiovisual presentations is that they give trainees a consistent presentation, not affected by an individual trainer's goals and skills. The problems associated with these methods may include their trying to present too much material, poorly written dialogue, overuse of features such as humor or music, and drama that distracts from the key points. A well-written and carefully produced video can overcome these problems.

Computer-Based Training

Although almost all organizations use classroom training, new technologies are gaining in popularity as technology improves and becomes cheaper. With computer-based training, participants receive course materials and instruction distributed over the Internet or on CD-ROM. Often, these materials are interactive, so participants can answer questions and try out techniques, with course materials adjusted according to participants' responses. Online training programs may allow trainees to submit questions via e-mail and to participate in online discussions. Multimedia capabilities enable computers to provide sounds, images, and video presentations, along with text.

Computer-based training is generally less expensive than putting an instructor in a classroom of trainees. The low cost to deliver information gives the company flexibility in scheduling training so that it can fit around work requirements. Training can be delivered in smaller doses so material is easier to remember. Trainees often appreciate the multimedia capabilities, which appeal to several senses, and the chance to learn from experts anywhere in the world. Finally, it is easier to customize computer-based training for individual learners.

HR How To

Developing Training Content for Mobile Devices

Nowadays, workers are already using—or would like to use—a variety of mobile devices, such as smartphones and tablet computers. These devices have the potential to deliver effective training. The following tips can help trainers ensure that mobile learning (m-learning) is well prepared and tailored to users' needs and the company's objectives:

- Learn what devices employees are already using. Also find out what devices your company's information technology policy allows employees to use for work. Some companies allow employees to load company data onto personal devices; others require that employees use company-provided hardware and software.
- Train employees to use the devices on which the training will be provided. Even if employees are using a device to make phone calls or play games, they might not know how to use the company's learning applications.

- Train a few employees in m-learning. Let them be the champions for the new system and perhaps train their co-workers in how to use the system or coach a co-worker who is struggling.
- If the content covers more than trainees will easily use and remember at once, provide tools that make the content easy to search for the relevant subject matter.
- Incorporate analytic tools such as Google Analytics into training software and use it to keep track of how many people are using the content, what hardware and operating system the trainees use, and how long they interact with the training material. This information will provide valuable feedback for improving the m-learning program.
- Test training content on all the kinds of devices the trainees will use. Make sure it works as intended on each kind of

hardware and with the type of network connection that will be available to trainees.

Questions

1. Suppose your company creates an m-learning program, but the analytics tool shows that employees almost never open the content. Which of the tips listed here might the trainers have overlooked?
2. Suppose your company's plan is to provide training on whatever mobile devices employees already bring to work. Which of the guidelines listed will be more difficult because of this plan?

Sources: Nick Floro, "Thinking Mobile First," *Training*, November 2013, www.trainingmag.com; John Coné, "Look Before You Leap into Mobile Learning," *T+D*, June 2013, pp. 40–45; Barry Jass, "Take the Mobile Learning Plunge," *T+D*, February 2013, pp. 29–31.

Current applications of computer-based training can extend its benefits:

E-Learning
Receiving training via the Internet or the organization's intranet.

- **E-learning** involves receiving training via the Internet or the organization's intranet, typically through some combination of web-based training modules, distance learning, and virtual classrooms. E-learning uses electronic networks for delivering and sharing information, and it offers tools and information for helping trainees improve performance. Training programs may include links to other online information resources and to trainees and experts for collaboration on problem solving. The e-learning system may also process enrollments, test and evaluate participants, and monitor progress. Quicken Loans uses e-learning to motivate employees to learn from their peers' best practices in customer service. It created an online contest called "Quicken's Got Talent." Employees who serve customers over the phone can submit recordings of calls they handled well. Trainers pick one submission per day to post on the game. Employees listen to the recordings and rate their co-worker's performance on a scale of 1 to 5. Each month the employee who submitted the top-scoring call receives a prize worth up to $200; winners of the monthly round are eligible for a competition with a $1,000 prize. The e-learning program tracks participation and creates a library of best-practices clips that are available for future learning.[17]

- **Electronic performance support systems (EPSSs)** are computer applications that provide access to skills training, information, and expert advice when a problem occurs on the job.[18] Employees needing guidance can use the EPSS to look up the particular information they need, such as detailed instructions on how to perform an unfamiliar task. Using an EPSS is faster and more relevant than attending classes, even classes offered online. These advantages of an EPSS make it especially appropriate for mobile learning. Xerox, for example, makes performance support videos available on employees' mobile devices. Employees can easily search the learning database to find the relevant content.[19]

The best e-learning combines the advantages of the Internet with the principles of a good learning environment. It takes advantage of the web's dynamic nature and ability to use many positive learning features, including hyperlinks to other training sites and content, control by the trainee, and ability for trainees to collaborate.

On-the-Job Training

Although people often associate training with classrooms, much learning occurs while employees are performing their jobs. **On-the-job training (OJT)** refers to training methods in which a person with job experience and skill guides trainees in practicing job skills at the workplace. This type of training takes various forms, including apprenticeships and internships.

An **apprenticeship** is a work-study training method that teaches job skills through a combination of structured on-the-job training and classroom training. The OJT component of an apprenticeship involves the apprentice assisting a certified tradesperson (a journeyman) at the work site. Typically, the classroom training is provided by local trade schools, high schools, and community colleges. Government requirements for an apprenticeship program vary by occupation, but programs generally range from one to six years. Requirements may be based on a minimum amount of time (often at least 2,000 hours of on-the-job learning), mastery of specified skills following classroom or online instruction plus on-the-job learning, or some combination of the two measures.[20] Some apprenticeship programs are sponsored by individual companies, others by employee unions. As shown in the left column of Table 7.3, most apprenticeship programs are in the skilled trades, such as plumbing, carpentry, and electrical work.

For trainees, a major advantage of apprenticeship is the ability to earn an income while learning a trade. In addition, training through an apprenticeship is usually effective because it involves hands-on learning and extensive practice. Some employers are concerned that an apprenticeship program will require working with a union or that employees who receive such training will leave for a better job. However, unionization is not strongly associated with employer-paid training in most industries, and when an employer provides apprenticeships, employees may in fact feel greater loyalty.[21]

Electronic Performance Support System (EPSS)
Computer application that provides access to skills training, information, and expert advice as needed.

On-the-Job Training (OJT)
Training methods in which a person with job experience and skill guides trainees in practicing job skills at the workplace.

Apprenticeship
A work-study training method that teaches job skills through a combination of on-the-job training and classroom training.

APPRENTICESHIP	INTERNSHIP
Bricklayer	Accountant
Carpenter	Doctor
Electrician	Journalist
Plumber	Lawyer
Nursing assistant	Nurse
Welder	

Table 7.3

Typical Jobs for Apprentices and Interns

Volkswagen partnered with the Tennessee Technology Center of Chattanooga State Community College to create an apprenticeship program in automotive mechatronics. In this three-year program, apprentices receive classroom instruction and on-the-job training in machining, electricity, pneumatics, robotics, automation, programmable logic controls, and computer numeric controls. Volkswagen pays the apprentices for their on-the-job training time, and in return it acquires a workforce with hard-to-find skills in fixing problems in an automated manufacturing facility.[22]

Internship
On-the-job learning sponsored by an educational institution as a component of an academic program.

An **internship** is on-the-job learning sponsored by an educational institution as a component of an academic program. The sponsoring school works with local employers to place students in positions where they can gain experience related to their area of study. Ernst & Young hires interns to prepare them for possible permanent jobs as consultants and accountants if they demonstrate they can lead a project and work with a diverse team. Whirlpool hires interns to test their skills as it prepares them for positions in sales, technology, and human resource management.[23] Many internships prepare students for professions such as those listed in the right column of Table 7.3.

To be effective, OJT programs should include several characteristics:

- The organization should issue a policy statement describing the purpose of OJT and emphasizing the organization's support for it.
- The organization should specify who is accountable for conducting OJT. This accountability should be included in the relevant job descriptions.
- The organization should review OJT practices at companies in similar industries.
- Managers and peers should be trained in OJT principles.
- Employees who conduct OJT should have access to lesson plans, checklists, procedure manuals, training manuals, learning contracts, and progress report forms.
- Before conducting OJT with an employee, the organization should assess the employee's level of basic skills.[24]

Simulations

Simulation
A training method that represents a real-life situation, with trainees making decisions resulting in outcomes that mirror what would happen on the job.

A **simulation** is a training method that represents a real-life situation, with trainees making decisions resulting in outcomes that mirror what would happen on the job. Simulations enable trainees to see the impact of their decisions in an artificial, risk-free environment. They are used for teaching production and process skills as well as management and interpersonal skills. Simulations used in training include call centers stocked with phones and reference materials, as well as mockups of houses used for training cable installers. Airlines purchasing Boeing's latest-model passenger jet, the 787 Dreamliner, are using simulators to train the pilots who will fly it. Although the 787 flight deck is designed with the same layout as the familiar 777, it has a new feature called the head-up display (HUD). When flying conditions are poor, this small see-through screen drops down in pilots' line of vision to provide information to help them navigate. Pilots need to practice with the simulator until they are accustomed to landing the jet while using the HUD.[25]

Simulators must have elements identical to those found in the work environment. The simulator needs to respond exactly as equipment would under the conditions and response given by the trainee. For this reason, simulators are expensive to develop and need constant updating as new information about the work environment becomes available. Still, they are an excellent training method when the risks of a mistake on the job are great. Trainees do not have to be afraid of the impact of wrong decisions when using the simulator, as they would be with on-the-job training. Also, trainees tend to be enthusiastic about this type of learning and to learn quickly, and the lessons are generally related very closely to job performance. Given these benefits, this training method is likely to become more widespread as its development costs fall into a range more companies can afford.[26]

When simulations are conducted online, trainees often participate by creating **avatars**, or computer depictions of themselves, which they manipulate onscreen to play roles as workers or other participants in a job-related situation. Another way to enhance the simulation experience is to use **virtual reality**, a computer-based technology that provides an interactive, three-dimensional learning experience. Using specialized equipment or viewing the virtual model on a computer screen, trainees move through the simulated environment and interact with its components. Devices relay information from the environment to the trainees' senses. For example, audio interfaces, gloves that provide a sense of touch, treadmills, or motion platforms create a realistic but artificial environment. Devices also communicate information about the trainee's movements to a computer.

Here an individual works within a virtual reality training lab during a recent coal mine rescue simulation. Virtual reality is one way to provide an interactive learning experience for workers.

Avatars
Computer depictions of trainees, which the trainees manipulate in an online role-play.

Virtual Reality
A computer-based technology that provides an interactive, three-dimensional learning experience.

Virtual reality is a practical choice for PPD, a business that provides research services to pharmaceutical and biotechnology companies. Its employees are based in offices in 46 countries. Training efficiency is important because time spent traveling to and participating in traveling sessions is time that the employees cannot be billing PPD's clients for services. PPD therefore hired a firm to create a 3D virtual training environment that includes a doctor's office, reception area, and training and conference rooms. Trainers and trainees alike create avatars to participate in this environment online. Not only has this method given employees faster, cheaper access to training, the participants say they prefer it to classroom training and feel more engaged in learning.[27]

Business Games and Case Studies

Training programs use business games and case studies to develop employees' management skills. A case study is a detailed description of a situation that trainees study and discuss. Cases are designed to develop higher-order thinking skills, such as the ability to analyze and evaluate information. They also can be a safe way to encourage trainees to take appropriate risks, by giving them practice in weighing and acting on uncertain outcomes. There are many sources of case studies, including Harvard Business School, the Darden Business School at the University of Virginia, and McGraw-Hill publishing company.

With business games, trainees gather information, analyze it, and make decisions that influence the outcome of the game. To train salespeople in its Winning Major program, Humana assembles teams of five trainees and has each team imagine it is a salesperson for a robotics company. Each team plays three rounds of simulations in which it handles issues from three imaginary clients. The team that generates the most revenue is declared the winner.[28] Games stimulate learning because they actively involve participants and mimic the competitive nature of business. A realistic game may be more meaningful to trainees than presentation techniques such as classroom instruction.

Training with case studies and games requires that participants come together to discuss the cases or the progress of the game. This requires face-to-face or electronic meetings. Also, participants must be willing to be actively involved in analyzing the situation and defending their decisions.

Behavior Modeling

Research suggests that one of the most effective ways to teach interpersonal skills is through behavior modeling.[29] This involves training sessions in which participants observe other people demonstrating the desired behavior, then have opportunities to practice the behavior themselves. For example, a training program could involve several days of four-hour sessions, each focusing on one interpersonal skill, such as communicating or coaching. At the beginning of each session, participants hear the reasons for using the key behaviors; then they watch a video of a model performing the key behaviors. They practice through role-playing and receive feedback about their performance. In addition, they evaluate the performance of the model in the video and discuss how they can apply the behavior on the job.

Experiential Programs

Experiential Programs
Training programs in which participants learn concepts and apply them by simulating behaviors involved and analyzing the activity, connecting it with real-life situations.

To develop teamwork and leadership skills, some organizations enroll their employees in a form of training called **experiential programs**. In experiential programs, participants learn concepts and then apply them by simulating the behaviors involved and analyzing the activity, connecting it with real-life situations.[30] A training company called Pendaran offers its clients a three-day simulation of a golf cart factory at its offices in Ann Arbor, Michigan. The program's goal is to train workers and supervisors to think calmly and creatively under pressure. Some features might sound silly: the characters have fantastic names, workers must wear protective equipment while carrying out tasks simulated on computers, and a toy vacuum represents a forklift. But as staffers bombard the participants with one challenge after another, the trainees come to appreciate the need to plan how they will meet job requirements, rather than simply react to one preventable crisis after another.[31]

Experiential training programs should follow several guidelines. A program should be related to a specific business problem. Participants should feel challenged and move outside their comfort zones but within limits that keep their motivation strong and help them understand the purpose of the program.

Adventure Learning
A teamwork and leadership training program based on the use of challenging, structured outdoor activities.

One form of experiential program, called **adventure learning**, uses challenging, structured outdoor activities, which may include difficult sports such as dogsledding or mountain climbing. Other activities may be structured tasks like climbing walls, completing rope courses, climbing ladders, or making "trust falls" (in which each trainee stands on a table and falls backward into the arms of other group members).

The impact of adventure learning programs has not been rigorously tested, but participants report they gained a greater understanding of themselves and the ways they interact with their co-workers. One key to the success of such programs may be that the organization needs to insist that entire work groups participate together.

One of the most important features of organizations today is teamwork. Experiential programs include team-building exercises like wall climbing and rafting to help build trust and cooperation among employees.

This encourages people to see, discuss, and correct the kinds of behavior that keep the group from performing well.

Before requiring employees to participate in experiential programs, the organization should consider the possible drawbacks. Because these programs are usually physically demanding and often require participants to touch each other, companies face certain risks. Some employees may be injured or may feel that they were sexually harassed or that their privacy was invaded. Also, the Americans with Disabilities Act (discussed in Chapter 3) raises questions about requiring employees with disabilities to participate in physically demanding training experiences.

Team Training

A possible alternative to experiential programs is team training, which coordinates the performance of individuals who work together to achieve a common goal. An organization may benefit from providing such training to groups when group members must share information and group performance depends on the performance of the individual group members. Examples include the military, nuclear power plants, and commercial airlines. In those work settings, much work is performed by crews, groups, or teams. Success depends on individuals' coordinating their activities to make decisions, perhaps in dangerous situations.

Ways to conduct team training include cross-training and coordination training.[32] In **cross-training**, team members understand and practice each other's skills so that they are prepared to step in and take another member's place. In a factory, for example, production workers could be cross-trained to handle all phases of assembly. This enables the company to move them to the positions where they are most needed to complete an order on time.

Cross-Training
Team training in which team members understand and practice each other's skills so that they are prepared to step in and take another member's place.

Coordination Training
Team training that teaches the team how to share information and make decisions to obtain the best team performance.

Coordination training trains the team in how to share information and decisions to obtain the best team performance. This type of training is especially important for commercial aviation and surgical teams. Both of these kinds of teams must monitor different aspects of equipment and the environment, at the same time sharing information to make the most effective decisions regarding patient care or aircraft safety and performance. One way to focus on teamwork behaviors is to have team members participate in an unfamiliar type of project. For example, a group of managers from Thermo Fisher Scientific divided into five teams, each assigned to make one course for the night's dinner. Each team was given the ingredients for a particular dish but not a recipe, and the group members had to figure out how they would solve the problem together. A similar type of learning occurs in a team training program called Dig This, which assigns teams to complete a mission using heavy construction equipment.[33]

Team Leader Training
Training in the skills necessary for effectively leading the organization's teams.

Training may also target the skills needed by the teams' leaders. **Team leader training** refers to training people in the skills necessary for team leadership. For example, the training may be aimed at helping team leaders learn to resolve conflicts or coordinate activities.

Action Learning

Action Learning
Training in which teams get an actual problem, work on solving it and commit to an action plan, and are accountable for carrying it out.

Another form of group building is **action learning**. In this type of training, teams or work groups get an actual problem, work on solving it and commit to an action plan, and are accountable for carrying out the plan. Ideally, the project is one for which the efforts and results will be visible not only to participants but also to others in the organization. The visibility and impact of the task are intended to make participation exciting, relevant, and engaging. At Automatic Data Processing, action learning assigns teams of 10 managers to study a real business problem or opportunity facing the company and present recommendations to senior executives.[34] To heighten learning, organizations can get their best leaders involved as mentors and coaches to the participants.

The effectiveness of action learning has not been formally evaluated. This type of training seems to result in a great deal of learning, however, and employees are able to apply what they learn because action learning involves actual problems the organization is facing. The group approach also helps teams identify behaviors that interfere with problem solving.

LO 7-6 Summarize how to implement a successful training program.

Implementing the Training Program

Learning permanently changes behavior. For employees to acquire knowledge and skills in the training program, the training program must be implemented in a way that applies what is known about how people learn. Equally important, implementation of a training program should enable employees to transfer what they have learned to the workplace—in other words, employees should behave differently as a result of the training.

Principles of Learning

Researchers have identified a number of ways employees learn best.[35] Table 7.4 summarizes ways that training can best encourage learning. In general, effective training communicates learning objectives clearly, presents information in distinctive and memorable ways, and helps trainees link the subject matter to their jobs.

Employees are most likely to learn when training is linked to their current job experiences and tasks.[36] There are a number of ways trainers can make this link. Training

Table 7.4

**Ways That Training Helps
Employees Learn**

TRAINING ACTIVITY	WAYS TO PROVIDE TRAINING ACTIVITY
Communicate the learning objective.	Demonstrate the performance to be expected. Give examples of questions to be answered.
Use distinctive, attention-getting messages.	Emphasize key points. Use pictures, not just words.
Limit the content of training.	Group lengthy material into chunks. Provide a visual image of the course material. Provide opportunities to repeat and practice material.
Guide trainees as they learn.	Use words as reminders about sequence of activities. Use words and pictures to relate concepts to one another and to their context. Prompt trainees to evaluate whether they understand and are using effective tactics to learn the material.
Elaborate on the subject.	Present the material in different contexts and settings. Relate new ideas to previously learned concepts. Practice in a variety of contexts and settings.
Provide memory cues.	Suggest memory aids. Use familiar sounds or rhymes as memory cues.
Transfer course content to the workplace.	Design the learning environment so that it has elements in common with the workplace. Require learners to develop action plans that apply training content to their jobs. Use words that link the course to the workplace.
Provide feedback about performance.	Tell trainees how accurately and quickly they are performing their new skill. Show how trainees have met the objectives of the training.

Sources: Adapted from R. M. Gagne, "Learning Processes and Instruction," *Training Research Journal* 1 (1995/96), pp. 17–28; and Traci Sitzmann, "Self-Regulating Online Course Engagement," *T&D,* March 2010, Business & Company Resource Center, http://galenet.galegroup.com.

sessions should present material using familiar concepts, terms, and examples. As far as possible, the training context—such as the physical setting or the images presented on a computer—should mirror the work environment. Along with physical elements, the context should include emotional elements. In the example of store personnel training to handle upset customers, the physical context is more relevant if it includes trainees acting out scenarios of personnel dealing with unhappy customers. The role-play interaction between trainees adds emotional realism and further enhances learning.

To fully understand and remember the content of the training, employees need a chance to demonstrate and practice what they have learned. Trainers should provide ways to actively involve the trainees, have them practice repeatedly, and have them complete tasks within a time that is appropriate in light of the learning objectives. Practice requires physically carrying out the desired behaviors, not just describing them. Practice sessions could include role-playing interactions, filling out relevant forms, or operating machinery or equipment to be used on the job. The more the trainee practices these activities, the more comfortable he or she will be in applying the skills on the job. People tend to benefit most from practice that occurs over several sessions, rather than one long practice session.[37] For complex tasks, it may be most effective to practice a few skills or behaviors at a time, then combine them in later practice sessions.

Trainees need to understand whether or not they are succeeding. Therefore, training sessions should offer feedback. Effective feedback focuses on specific behaviors and is delivered as soon as possible after the trainees practice or demonstrate what they have learned.[38] One way to do this is to videotape trainees, then show the video while indicating specific behaviors that do or do not match the desired outcomes of the training. Feedback should include praise when trainees show they have learned material, as well as guidance on how to improve.

Well-designed training helps people remember the content. Training programs need to break information into chunks that people can remember. Research suggests that people can attend to no more than four to five items at a time. If a concept or procedure involves more than five items, the training program should deliver information in shorter sessions or chunks.[39] Other ways to make information more memorable include presenting it with visual images and practicing some tasks enough that they become automatic.

Readability

The difficulty level of written materials.

Written materials should have an appropriate reading level. A simple way to assess **readability**—the difficulty level of written materials—is to look at the words being used and at the length of sentences. In general, it is easiest to read short sentences and simple, standard words. If training materials are too difficult to understand, several adjustments can help. The basic approach is to rewrite the material looking for ways to simplify it.

- Substitute simple, concrete words for unfamiliar or abstract words.
- Divide long sentences into two or more short sentences.
- Divide long paragraphs into two or more short paragraphs.
- Add checklists (like this one) and illustrations to clarify the text.

Another approach is to substitute video, hands-on learning, or other nonwritten methods for some of the written material. A longer-term solution is to use tests to identify employees who need training to improve their reading levels and to provide that training first.

Transfer of Training

Transfer of Training

On-the-job use of knowledge, skills, and behaviors learned in training.

Ultimately, the goal of implementation is **transfer of training**, or on-the-job use of knowledge, skills, and behaviors learned in training. Transfer of training requires that employees actually learn the content of the training program. Then, for employees to apply what they learned, certain conditions must be in place: social support, technical support, and self-management.

Social support, as we saw in the discussion of readiness for training, includes support from the organization and from trainees' peers. Before, during, and after implementation, the organization's managers need to emphasize the importance of training, encourage their employees to attend training programs, and point out connections between training content and employees' job requirements. The organization can formally provide peer support by establishing **communities of practice**—groups of employees who work together, learn from each other, and develop a common understanding of how to get work accomplished. It also may assign experienced employees to act as mentors, who provide advice and support to the trainees. Social support has been essential for transfer of training at hospitals teaching doctors to use electronic medical records, which can reduce errors and costs. For example, Good Samaritan Hospital in Vincennes, Indiana, had a tech-savvy radiologist conduct the training. At Deaconess Health System in Evansville, Indiana, the most effective motivation for reluctant physicians came from the doctors who received training early on and who would prod their colleagues to catch up.[40]

Communities of Practice

Groups of employees who work together, learn from each other, and develop a common understanding of how to get work accomplished.

Transfer of training is greater when organizations also provide technical resources that help people acquire and share information. Technical support may come from electronic performance support systems (EPSS), described earlier as a type of

HRM Social

Social Learning with Visual Impact on Pinterest

The Pinterest website does for social media what a bulletin board in the break room does for sharing messages in the workplace or a magnet-covered refrigerator does for sharing artwork and shopping lists in a busy family. It is a place where users set up Pinboards where they post visual expressions and ideas for others to enjoy. Pinterest lets users organize these images according to the topics they select, so the images are searchable by topic.

Training professionals are discovering ways to use Pinterest in support of training objectives. They might pin pictures of ideas for projects or outlines for training courses. They might pin instructional videos or photos. They might get employees excited about participating in training programs by pinning photos of past events. Ahead of an event, they might post graphics containing questions or puzzles for the participants to think about and prepare to discuss. They also can conduct searches on Pinterest to gather fresh ideas for their training programs.

Trainers also can encourage learners to pin items to the training program's Pinboard. For example, if the training includes simulations, games, or experiential learning, participants might have creations they can photograph. Or feedback forms might be made visually interesting for participants to post on the Pinboard. If the training involves a group project, participants can post their ideas on a shared Pinboard.

Consider, for example, how Pinterest could support training of newly hired employees. A company's Pinboard could show photos of employees at work on a typical day. It could include pictures of facilities such as conference rooms and break rooms, to help employees find their way around. It can include links to information such as background about the company, employee contact information, profiles about key employees, and company blogs. Employees can visit Pinterest as an enjoyable and engaging way to get to know their new employer.

Questions

1. How could photos of activities at a team-training event support transfer of training for the members of the team who participated?
2. Besides setting up a Pinterest account, what kinds of technical support would trainers need to provide if they want to use Pinterest to aid transfer of training?

Sources: Kella B. Price, "Using Pinterest as a Training and Development Tool," *T+D,* November 2013, pp. 76–77; Michelle Baker, "Pinterest for Onboarding: Part One," *Phase (Two) Learning,* January 7, 2013, http://phasetwolearning.wordpress.com; Michelle Baker, "Pinterest for Onboarding: Part Two," *Phase (Two) Learning,* January 13, 2013, http://phasetwolearning.wordpress.com.

computer-based training. Knowledge management systems including online and database tools also make it easy for employees to look up information they want to review or consult later.

Organizations are beginning to provide a strong combination of social and technical support for transfer of training by setting up social media applications that promote learning. When participants use social media to share with other employees what they are learning or discuss questions posted by the trainers, it can reinforce lessons and build the whole group's motivation to learn. It also can blur the line between trainer and trainee, as employees share how they are applying principles in practical ways on the job. This expands the total knowledge shared, but it also poses a challenge to the trainers, because they give up some control over the training content.[41] For an example of a social-media tool that trainers are experimenting with, see "HRM Social."

Finally, to ensure transfer of training, an organization's training programs should prepare employees to self-manage their use of new skills and behaviors on the job.[42] To that end, the trainer should have trainees set goals for using skills or behaviors on the job, identify conditions under which they might fail to use the skills and behaviors, and identify the consequences (positive and negative) of using them. Employees should practice monitoring their use of the new skills and behaviors. The trainer should stress that learning to use new skills on the job is naturally difficult and will not necessarily proceed perfectly, but that employees should keep trying. Trainers also should support managers and peers in finding ways to reward employees for applying what they learned.

LO 7-7 Evaluate the success of a training program.

Measuring Results of Training

After a training program ends, or at intervals during an ongoing training program, organizations should ensure that the training is meeting objectives. The stage to prepare for evaluating a training program is when the program is being developed. Along with designing course objectives and content, the planner should identify how to measure achievement of objectives. Depending on the objectives, the evaluation can use one or more of the measures shown in Figure 7.3: trainee satisfaction with the program, knowledge or abilities gained, use of new skills and behavior on the job (transfer of training), and improvements in individual and organizational performance. The usual way to measure whether participants have acquired information is to administer tests on paper or electronically. Trainers or supervisors can observe whether participants demonstrate the desired skills and behaviors. Surveys measure changes in attitude. Changes in company performance have a variety of measures, many of which organizations keep track of for preparing performance appraisals, annual reports, and other routine documents in order to demonstrate the final measure of success shown in Figure 7.3: return on investment.

Evaluation Methods

To measure whether the conditions are in place for transfer of training, the organization can ask employees three questions about specific training-related tasks:

1. Do you perform the task?
2. How many times do you perform the task?
3. To what extent do you perform difficult and challenging learned tasks?

Frequent performance of difficult training-related tasks would signal great opportunity to perform. If there is low opportunity to perform, the organization should conduct further needs assessment and reevaluate readiness to learn. Perhaps the organization does not fully support the training activities in general or the employee's supervisor does not provide opportunities to apply new skills. Lack of transfer can also mean that employees have not learned the course material. The organization might offer a refresher course to give trainees more practice. Another reason for poor transfer of training is that the content of the training may not be important for the employee's job.

Assessment of training also should evaluate training *outcomes*, that is, what (if anything) has changed as a result of the training. The relevant training outcomes are the ones related to the organization's goals for the training and its overall performance. Possible outcomes include the following:

- Information such as facts, techniques, and procedures that trainees can recall after the training.
- Skills that trainees can demonstrate in tests or on the job.

Figure 7.3

Measures of Training Success

- Trainee and supervisor satisfaction with the training program.
- Changes in attitude related to the content of the training (for example, concern for safety or tolerance of diversity).
- Improvements in individual, group, or company performance (for example, greater customer satisfaction, more sales, fewer defects).

Training is a significant part of many organizations' budgets. Therefore, economic measures are an important way to evaluate the success of a training program. Businesses that invest in training want to achieve a high *return on investment*—the monetary benefits of the investment compared to the amount invested, expressed as a percentage. For example, Mayo Clinic provided training for its managers after it discovered that employees were quitting because of dissatisfaction with their managers. After the training, employee turnover rates improved. To determine the return on the investment in the training, Mayo's human resource department calculated that one-third of the employees retained (29 employees) would have left if the training had not occurred. The department calculated the cost of an employee leaving as 75% of average total compensation, or $42,000 per employee. Multiplied by the number of employees ($42,000 times 29), that is equivalent to lowering costs by $609,000. The training cost $125,000, so the company saved $484,000 by providing it. The return on investment would be $484,000 divided by $125,000, or an impressive 387%.[43] Even if some of the estimates were wrong, Mayo's HR department could feel confident in making a case that the training was beneficial.

For any of these methods, the most accurate but most costly way to evaluate the training program is to measure performance, knowledge, or attitudes among all employees before the training and then train only part of the employees. After the training is complete, the performance, knowledge, or attitudes are again measured, and the trained group is compared with the untrained group. A simpler but less accurate way to assess the training is to conduct the pretest and posttest on all trainees, comparing their performance, knowledge, or attitudes before and after the training. This form of measurement does not rule out the possibility that change resulted from something other than training (for example, a change in the compensation system). The simplest approach is to use only a posttest. Use of only a posttest can show if trainees have reached a specified level of competency, knowledge, or skill. Of course, this type of measurement does not enable accurate comparisons, but it may be sufficient, depending on the cost and purpose of the training.

Applying the Evaluation

The purpose of evaluating training is to help with future decisions about the organization's training programs. Using the evaluation, the organization may identify a need to modify the training and gain information about the kinds of changes needed. The organization may decide to expand on successful areas of training and cut back on training that has not delivered significant benefits.

A major producer of packaged foods has identified both successes and needs for improvement after analyzing its training programs. The company began conducting management training for supervisors and treated the first 12 months as a test of the program. After a year, the company determined that turnover rates were much lower among supervisors who had received training. That difference was strongest among more recently hired supervisors and persisted even after the company made statistical adjustments for other possible influences on turnover. The company therefore recommitted to its training goals for supervisors, especially targeting those hired most recently. In contrast,

Training Executives Are Unimpressed with Their Measurement Processes

In a recent survey of more than 200 chief learning officers, roughly three-quarters of them reported a need to improve their company's measurement of training effectiveness. Worse, the numbers have been heading in the wrong direction. In four years of asking this question, the researchers have seen the share of executives who are satisfied with measurement decline, while the dissatisfied share has been rising.

One source of dissatisfaction may be that the most common measurements used at respondents' companies are not directly tied to business success. Most companies measure the amount of training they do: number of courses, number of students, hours of training. A majority of companies also ask participants if they are satisfied with training they participated in. Less than half ask about employee performance or impact of the training on the company's business results.

In this context, training professionals can give their company an edge by linking training programs to business strategy. Ideally, whenever considering a training program, they would start by determining how the company's performance should change as a result of the employees learning new information or skills. They would establish training content to make that performance improvement possible, and they would measure whether the desired results indeed have followed the training program.

Questions

1. Suppose you are a training leader at a manufacturing company, and you have been asked to deliver a report about the value of your department's work. You report the number of training hours provided by your staff and the number of employees trained. How do you think the company's business managers would react to this report?

2. Give examples of a few measures that might be more relevant to these managers.

Sources: Cushing Anderson, "Bad Measurement Affects Training Impact," *Chief Learning Officer*, May 2014, pp. 44–46; James D. Kirkpatrick and Wendy K. Kirkpatrick, "Creating a Post-Training Evaluation Plan," *T+D*, June 2013, pp. 26–28; David Zahn, "No Excuse for Not Measuring Training's Impact," *Connecticut News*, June 10, 2013, http://blog.ctnews.com.

training had a minimal impact on safety performance at the company's facilities. The training department concluded it would have to improve the safety component of the training program or replace it with a new approach to safety training.[44]

Unfortunately—as described in "HR Oops!"—organizations often fail to gain the insights that come from careful evaluation of training. This leaves room for companies that take evaluation seriously to gain an edge over competitors by fully preparing their employees.

LO 7-8 Describe training methods for employee orientation and diversity management.

Applications of Training

Two training applications that have become widespread among U.S. companies are orientation of new employees and training in how to manage workforce diversity.

Orientation of New Employees

Orientation
Training designed to prepare employees to perform their jobs effectively, learn about their organization, and establish work relationships.

Many employees receive their first training during their first days on the job. This training is the organization's **orientation** program—its training designed to prepare employees to perform their job effectively, learn about the organization, and establish work relationships. Organizations provide for orientation because, no matter how realistic the information provided during employment interviews and site visits, people feel shock and surprise when they start a new job.[45] Also, employees need to become familiar with job tasks and learn the details of the organization's practices, policies, and procedures. A well-designed orientation program also can strengthen employees' commitment to the organization by connecting them to co-workers and showing them early on how their work contributes to the company's mission.

The objectives of orientation programs include making new employees familiar with the organization's rules, policies, and procedures. Table 7.5 summarizes the content of a typical orientation program. Such a program provides information about the overall company and about the department in which the new employee will be working. The topics include social as well as technical aspects of the job. Miscellaneous information helps employees from out of town learn about the surrounding community.

While these orientation basics could easily be covered in a classroom setting, some trainers doubt whether that approach adequately engages new employees. For example, when Hyatt Hotels adopted an HR strategy emphasizing teamwork, the company redesigned its orientation program to put the new values in practice from the first day on the job. Each new employee is partnered with a more experienced co-worker, who greets the new employee and teaches about the job and facility. At some hotels, new employees learn their way around by going on a scavenger hunt with their training partner.[46]

Orientation programs may combine various training methods, such as printed and audiovisual materials, classroom instruction, on-the-job training, and e-learning. Decisions about how to conduct the orientation depend on the type of material to be covered and the number of new employees, among other factors.

Diversity Training

In response to Equal Employment Opportunity laws and market forces, many organizations today are concerned about managing diversity—creating an environment that

Table 7.5

Content of a Typical Orientation Program

Company-level information
Company overview (e.g., values, history, mission)
Key policies and procedures
Compensation
Employee benefits and services
Safety and accident prevention
Employee and union relations
Physical facilities
Economic factors
Customer relations
Department-level information
Department functions and philosophy
Job duties and responsibilities
Policies, procedures, rules, and regulations
Performance expectations
Tour of department
Introduction to department employees
Miscellaneous
Community
Housing
Family adjustment

Source: J. L. Schwarz and M. A. Weslowski, "Employee Orientation: What Employers Should Know," *Journal of Contemporary Business Issues,* Fall 1995, p. 48. Used with permission.

Diversity training programs, like the one conducted by Harvard Pilgrim Health Care, are designed to teach employees attitudes and behaviors that support the management of diversity. Why is it important for companies to provide this type of training?

Diversity Training
Training designed to change employee attitudes about diversity and/or develop skills needed to work with a diverse workforce.

allows all employees to contribute to organizational goals and experience personal growth. This kind of environment includes access to jobs as well as fair and positive treatment of all employees. Chapter 3 described how organizations manage diversity by complying with the law. Besides these efforts, many organizations provide training designed to teach employees attitudes and behaviors that support the management of diversity, such as appreciation of cultural differences and avoidance of behaviors that isolate or intimidate others.

Training designed to change employee attitudes about diversity and/or develop skills needed to work with a diverse workforce is called **diversity training**. These programs generally emphasize either attitude awareness and change or behavior change.

Programs that focus on attitudes have objectives to increase participants' awareness of cultural and ethnic differences, as well as differences in personal characteristics and physical characteristics (such as disabilities). These programs are based on the assumption that people who become aware of differences and their stereotypes about those differences will be able to avoid letting stereotypes influence their interactions with people. Many of these programs use video and experiential exercises to increase employees' awareness of the negative emotional and performance effects of stereotypes and resulting behaviors on members of minority groups. A risk of these programs—especially when they define diversity mainly in terms of race, ethnicity, and sex—is that they may alienate white male employees, who conclude that if the company values diversity more, it values them less.[47] Diversity training is more likely to get everyone onboard if it emphasizes respecting and valuing all the organization's employees in order to bring out the best work from everyone to open up the best opportunities for everyone.

Programs that focus on behavior aim at changing the organizational policies and individual behaviors that inhibit employees' personal growth and productivity. Sometimes these programs identify incidents that discourage employees from working up to their potential. Employees work in groups to discuss specific promotion opportunities or management practices that they believe were handled unfairly. Another approach starts with the assumption that all individuals differ in various ways and teaches skills for constructively handling the communication barriers, conflicts, and misunderstandings that necessarily arise when different people try to work together.[48] Trainees may be more positive about receiving this type of training than other kinds of diversity training. Finally, some organizations provide diversity training in the form of *cultural immersion*, sending employees directly into communities where they have to interact with persons from different cultures, races, and nationalities. Participants might talk with community members, work in community organizations, or learn about events that are significant to the community they visit. Sometimes cultural immersion comes with the job. At a large Japanese automaker, Japanese, U.S., and Mexican employees often had to interact but frequently fell victim to misunderstandings. The company hired a training consultant to develop a different classroom training program for each group, focusing on the other groups' cultural expectations and ways to communicate effectively. She also coached employees before they went on international assignments. The training program was well received because it helped employees avoid conflict.[49]

Does diversity training yield improvements in business performance? So far, research has not demonstrated a direct relationship.[50] Training may, however, contribute to the kind of environment in which diversity can enhance performance because people learn from one another's differences. This is most likely when diversity training is part of management's long-term commitment to managing diversity because the company's leaders consider diversity to be an opportunity for employees to learn from one another, work in a supportive environment, and acquire teamwork skills. In other words, successful diversity programs are not merely a training topic but part of an organizational culture that expresses its appreciation for diversity also through other actions, including recruiting, hiring, and developing diverse employees.[51]

Some organizations are getting it right. At the Oregon Center for Nursing, many of the nurses are eager to learn how to provide better care to patients who come from different cultures. The organization hosts online seminars on cultural backgrounds represented in the area, including Latino, Burmese, and Somali/Bantu people. The training also provides general guidelines for identifying relevant cultural differences so that nurses can apply the principles to cultural groups they haven't specifically studied. In contrast, at a big-box retail chain, diversity training had to start by convincing employees of the need for training. The store had launched a strategy calling for improved customer service, and employees were demonstrating that they were learning the lessons taught in sales training programs, but sales were not improving. Research showed that the problem lay with the assumptions salespeople were making: they were operating according to stereotypes about which types of customers would make a purchase, and they were ignoring customers who didn't fit the right profile. The retailer studied purchase data and was able to show salespeople that their assumptions were false. The company developed new training that focused on confronting and correcting the stereotypes. Salespeople began to apply these new lessons, and sales soon began to climb.[52]

THINKING ETHICALLY

INTERNSHIPS: OPPORTUNITY OR EXPLOITATION?

For many college students, an important summer experience is completing an internship and seeing firsthand the career they hope to pursue. The pay might be somewhat below the entry-level rate for a full-time employee, but the interns get practice they hope will aid in their job search after graduation. Some employers, however, do not even pay a low wage; they expect their interns to work for free.

The idea of working for little or no pay has been justified on the grounds that the internship experience is valuable training. Schools that agree may provide course credit for an internship. However, some students

and schools are questioning that argument. Survey data from the National Association of Colleges and Employers showed nearly the same rate of hiring for graduates with no internships and those with unpaid internships. (Students with paid internships on their résumés were hired at a higher rate.)

Employers that want to offer unpaid internships need to meet legal requirements. Under the Fair Labor Standards Act, an unpaid internship must be educational and may not exist for the direct benefit of the employer. In addition, the company may not hire unpaid interns as replacements for paid employees. State laws may impose further requirements. In New York, for example, employers must sacrifice some productivity for the sake of providing training to the interns, and the training should cover skills that apply beyond the particular job at the particular company. For-profit companies that do not meet the requirements for an unpaid internship must pay at least minimum wage plus a higher rate for overtime. In some publicized cases, interns have filed lawsuits against companies they say did not meet those requirements.

At least until recently, unpaid internships were common in some industries, such as fashion, entertainment, and publishing. However, with the negative attention, some employers have pulled back from the practice—either ending their internships or beginning to pay for positions that had been unpaid. Nevertheless, especially in the case of employers that pay interns at least minimum wage, advocates of internship continue to say these programs provide valuable preparation for careers. One way to check whether internships can withstand legal scrutiny is to consider the organization's purpose for creating these programs—whether it is to deliver training or to fill positions inexpensively.

Questions

1. Suppose a publishing company wants to hire an intern to help the company catch up with its paperwork over the summer. Who would be affected by this decision? What would be the benefits or harm to each person?
2. How could a well-designed training program help make this idea meet ethical as well as legal standards?

Sources: J. Corey Asay, "How to Keep Your Unpaid Internship Program Legal," *Lexology*, May 22, 2014, http://www.lexology.com; Gale Scott, "Pressure Rises on Businesses to Pay Interns," *Crain's New York Business*, May 13, 2014, http://www.crainsnewyork.com; Rachel Feintzeig and Melissa Korn, "Colleges, Employers Rethink Internship Policies," *The Wall Street Journal*, April 22, 2014, http://online.wsj.com.

SUMMARY

LO 7-1 Discuss how to link training programs to organizational needs.

- Organizations need to establish training programs that are effective—in other words, programs that (1) teach what they are designed to teach and (2) teach skills and behaviors that will help the organization achieve its goals.
- Organizations create such programs through instructional design.
- The steps in this process are to conduct a needs assessment, ensure readiness for training (including employee characteristics and organizational support), plan a training program, implement the program, and evaluate the results.

LO 7-2 Explain how to assess the need for training.

- Needs assessment consists of an organization analysis, person analysis, and task analysis.
- The organization analysis determines the appropriateness of training by evaluating the characteristics of the organization, including its strategy, resources, and management support.
- The person analysis determines individuals' needs and readiness for training.
- The task analysis identifies the tasks, knowledge, skills, and behaviors that training should emphasize. It is based on examination of the conditions in which tasks are performed, including

equipment and environment of the job, time constraints, safety considerations, and performance standards.

LO 7-3 Explain how to assess employees' readiness for training.

- Readiness for training is a combination of employee characteristics and positive work environment that permit training.
- The necessary employee characteristics include ability to learn the subject matter, favorable attitudes toward the training, and motivation to learn.
- A positive work environment avoids situational constraints such as lack of money and time. In a positive environment, both peers and management support training.

LO 7-4 Describe how to plan an effective training program.

- Planning begins with establishing training objectives, which should define an expected performance or outcome, the desired level of performance, and the conditions under which the performance should occur.
- Based on the objectives, the planner decides who will provide the training, what topics the training will cover, what training methods to use, and how to evaluate the training.

- Even when organizations purchase outside training, someone in the organization, usually a member of the HR department, often is responsible for training administration.
- The training methods selected should be related to the objectives and content of the training program.
- Training methods may include presentation methods, hands-on methods, or group-building methods.

LO 7-5 Compare widely used training methods.

- Classroom instruction is most widely used and is one of the least expensive and least time-consuming ways to present information on a specific topic to many trainees. It also allows for group interaction and may include hands-on practice.
- Audiovisual and computer-based training (often called e-learning) need not require that trainees attend a class, so organizations can reduce time and money spent on training. Computer-based training may be interactive and may provide for group interaction.
- On-the-job training methods such as apprenticeships and internships give trainees firsthand experiences.
- A simulation represents a real-life situation, enabling trainees to see the effects of their decisions without dangerous or expensive consequences.
- Business games and case studies are other methods for practicing decision-making skills. Participants need to come together in one location or collaborate online.
- Behavior modeling gives trainees a chance to observe desired behaviors, so this technique can be effective for teaching interpersonal skills.
- Experiential and adventure learning programs provide an opportunity for group members to interact in challenging circumstances but may exclude members with disabilities.
- Team training focuses a team on achievement of a common goal.
- Action learning offers relevance, because the training focuses on an actual work-related problem.

LO7-6 Summarize how to implement a successful training program.

- Implementation should apply principles of learning and seek transfer of training.
- In general, effective training communicates learning objectives, presents information in distinctive and memorable ways, and helps trainees link the subject matter to their jobs.
- Employees are most likely to learn when training is linked to job experiences and tasks. Employees

learn best when they demonstrate or practice what they have learned and when they receive feedback that helps them improve.

- Trainees remember information better when it is broken into small chunks, presented with visual images, and practiced many times. Written materials should be easily readable by trainees.
- Transfer of training is most likely when there is social support (from managers and peers), technical support, and self-management.

LO 7-7 Evaluate the success of a training program.

- Evaluation of training should look for transfer of training by measuring whether employees are performing the tasks taught in the training program.
- Assessment of training also should evaluate training outcomes, such as change in attitude, ability to perform a new skill, and recall of facts or behaviors taught in the training program.
- Training should result in improvement in the group's or organization's outcomes, such as customer satisfaction or sales. An economic measure of training success is return on investment.

LO 7-8 Describe training methods for employee orientation and diversity management.

- Employee orientation is training designed to prepare employees to perform their job effectively, learn about the organization, and establish work relationships.
- Organizations provide for orientation because, no matter how realistic the information provided during employment interviews and site visits, people feel shock and surprise when they start a new job, and they need to learn the details of how to perform the job.
- A typical orientation program includes information about the overall company and the department in which the new employee will be working, covering social as well as technical aspects of the job.
- Orientation programs may combine several training methods, from printed materials to on-the-job training to e-learning.
- Diversity training is designed to change employee attitudes about diversity and/or develop skills needed to work with a diverse workforce.
- Evidence regarding these programs suggests that diversity training is most effective if it is part of management's long-term commitment to managing diversity as an opportunity for people to learn from one another and acquire teamwork skills.

KEY TERMS

training, 201
instructional design, 201
learning management system (LMS), 202
needs assessment, 203
organization analysis, 203
person analysis, 204
task analysis, 205
readiness for training, 206
e-learning, 212

electronic performance support system (EPSS), 213
on-the-job training (OJT), 213
apprenticeship, 213
internship, 214
simulation, 214
avatars, 215
virtual reality, 215
experiential programs, 216
adventure learning, 216

cross-training, 217
coordination training, 218
team leader training, 218
action learning, 218
readability, 220
transfer of training, 220
communities of practice, 220
orientation, 224
diversity training, 226

REVIEW AND DISCUSSION QUESTIONS

1. "Alicia!" bellowed David to the company's HR specialist, "I've got a problem, and you've got to solve it. I can't get people in this plant to work together as a team. As if I don't have enough trouble with our competitors and our past-due accounts, now I have to put up with running a zoo. You're responsible for seeing that the staff gets along. I want a training proposal on my desk by Monday." Assume you are Alicia. *(LO 7-1)*
    a. Is training the solution to this problem? How can you determine the need for training?
    b. Summarize how you would conduct a needs assessment.
2. How should an organization assess readiness for learning? In Question 1, how do David's comments suggest readiness (or lack of readiness) for learning? *(LO 7-2)*
3. Assume you are the human resource manager of a small seafood company. The general manager has told you that customers have begun complaining about the quality of your company's fresh fish. Currently, training consists of senior fish cleaners showing new employees how to perform the job. Assuming your needs assessment indicates a need for training, how would you plan a training program? What steps should you take in planning the program? *(LO 7-4)*
4. Many organizations turn to e-learning as a less-expensive alternative to classroom training. What are some other advantages of substituting e-learning for classroom training? What are some disadvantages? *(LO 7-5)*
5. Suppose the managers in your organization tend to avoid delegating projects to the people in their groups. As a result, they rarely meet their goals. A training needs analysis indicates that an appropriate

solution is training in management skills. You have identified two outside training programs that are consistent with your goals. One program involves experiential programs, and the other is an interactive computer program. What are the strengths and weaknesses of each technique? Which would you choose? Why? *(LO 7-5)*
6. Consider your current job or a job you recently held. What types of training did you receive for the job? What types of training would you like to receive? Why? *(LO 7-5)*
7. A manufacturing company employs several maintenance employees. When a problem occurs with the equipment, a maintenance employee receives a description of the symptoms and is supposed to locate and fix the source of the problem. The company recently installed a new, complex electronics system. To prepare its maintenance workers, the company provided classroom training. The trainer displayed electrical drawings of system components and posed problems about the system. The trainer would point to a component in a drawing and ask, "What would happen if this component were faulty?" Trainees would study the diagrams, describe the likely symptoms, and discuss how to repair the problem. If you were responsible for this company's training, how would you evaluate the success of this training program? *(LO 7-6)*
8. In Question 7, suppose the maintenance supervisor has complained that trainees are having difficulty trouble shooting problems with the new electronics system. They are spending a great deal of time on problems with the system and coming to the supervisor with frequent questions that show a lack of understanding. The supervisor

is convinced that the employees are motivated to learn the system, and they are well qualified. What do you think might be the problems with the current training program? What recommendations can you make for improving the program? *(LO 7-7)*

9. Who should be involved in orientation of new employees? Why would it not be appropriate to provide employee orientation purely online? *(LO 7-8)*
10. Why do organizations provide diversity training? What kinds of goals are most suitable for such training? *(LO 7-8)*

TAKING RESPONSIBILITY

How MasTec's Training Helps Keep Workers Safe

The top management of MasTec Utility Services Group has defined one of its competitive challenges as finding and keeping the best employees. MasTec works as a contractor for utilities, constructing and maintaining systems for delivering electricity, oil, natural gas, and communications signals. The work is difficult and often dangerous, so a key area of competence is working safely under stressful conditions. A company whose employees work safely not only is more socially responsible, but also operates with lower costs.

Under John Congemi as director of employee development, MasTec set out to develop a "culture of learning," with training programs that would enable workers to be safe as well as skilled at their jobs. When Congemi joined MasTec, he was new to the utility construction industry, so he started by visiting construction sites and meeting with operations managers and safety professionals. This helped him understand workplace challenges, and it built credibility for the training program.

Congemi and his employee development team established three main objectives: (1) develop a curriculum for employee orientation; (2) implement a learning management system (LMS); and (3) start an apprenticeship program for line workers. Each division at MasTec had been following its own approach to orientation, but Congemi's group worked with the company's safety team to identify the skills most important for protecting workers throughout the company. For each skill, the company is developing English- and Spanish-language videos showing workers using the skills in the field.

MasTec's new LMS is designed to improve the efficiency of and access to training. It makes training materials available online, so the company no longer requires a trainer on-site every time an employee needs

to learn a skill. The LMS also will be a more efficient and accurate way to keep track of who is participating in each training program, as well as give employees information about training requirements.

The apprenticeship program links training to promotions and pay increases. Line workers who complete the program earn certificates from MasTec and the U.S. Department of Labor, along with the job title of lineman. The curriculum for this three- to four-year program covers technical skills and safe work practices in installing, maintaining, and removing transmission and distribution systems. To create the training, MasTec worked with a training contractor that specializes in utility construction, so that the program would meet industry standards while applying the lessons to MasTec's operations. The apprenticeship combines on-the-job training with videos and instructor-led classroom training. Supervisors must validate that employees are applying their lessons on the job. At the end of each year, apprentices who have successfully met the year's requirements receive a pay increase, as well as feedback about their progress.

Questions

1. Based on the information given, what issues did Congemi and his employee development group consider that would be part of a needs assessment and readiness for training?
2. What training methods are described in this case? Would you recommend MasTec use other training methods besides these for its line workers? Why or why not?

Sources: MasTec, company website, http://www.mastec.com, accessed May 29, 2014; John Congemi, "Journey to a Culture of Learning," *Training*, January 2014, www.trainingmag.com; John Congemi, "Part 2: MasTec's Apprenticeship Mission," *Training*, March 2014, www.trainingmag.com; John Congemi, "Part 3: MasTec Overhauls Onboarding," *Training*, May 2014, www.trainingmag.com.

MANAGING TALENT

Hewlett-Packard Builds Its Own "University"

When Meg Whitman became CEO of struggling Hewlett-Packard, she was determined to rekindle growth with a strategy of resurrecting and refurbishing HP's reputation for technological excellence. This involves treating employees as assets to be managed so their value to the organization will grow. Whitman charged Tracy Keogh, HP's executive vice president of human resources, with crafting a plan for talent management.

Keogh's approach is to align training activities that bring employees up to speed in their current jobs with development efforts that prepare employees to fill vacancies expected to arise in the future. Previously, HP treated training and development as separate functions. Now it makes them part of a continuous process.

To carry out this process, Keogh had to identify the learning needs of 300,000 employees handling 19 business functions in more than 100 countries. For that massive task, Keogh decided that all learning should take place within one system, named HP University. HP University comprises career paths and learning requirements, as well as physical training centers and online course offerings. At its website, employees identify training needed for a career path, search for resources, and register for courses. The site also gathers data about system usage.

To plan and implement HP University, Keogh's group organized learning content into nine "colleges," such as engineering and sales. They designed an online course catalog and a web portal where users can gather information and sign up for training. After testing their work on groups of employees, they refined the system. Next, they trained the training staff in the use of HP University, so the staffers could train HP's business managers. The system launched in 2012 with about 10,000 courses. During the first week, the site logged

nearly 80,000 visits. By year-end, employees had accessed a course 2.7 million times, representing an 8% growth over the previous year. User comments were full of praise. Based on feedback, Keogh's group began planning additional courses, as well as refinements to the system.

Although HP offers other formats, most courses (84%) involve online learning. For example, to train its sales force, HP hired viaLearning to create games that teach HP's sales strategy and competencies. The company chose "metaphor-based" games, in which demonstrating knowledge helps the learner solve a problem portrayed on the screen, such as winning an Olympics competition or quelling the "storm" of a confused customer. After two to five minutes spent obtaining information, the trainee uses that information to play the game. HP training manager Carol Cohen says the games make learning more interesting, so salespeople are motivated to learn. Cohen also notes that the metaphor format is readily adaptable into different languages and even different content areas.

Questions

1. What aspects of HP University effectively link training to the organization's needs?
2. Hewlett-Packard is a technology company, yet it turned to a contractor to create computerized training games. Evaluate the pros and cons of using a contractor in that situation.

Sources: Hewlett-Packard, "Global Citizenship: HP People," http://www8. hp.com, accessed May 29, 2014; "2013 *Chief Learning Officer* Learning in Practice Awards," *Chief Learning Officer*, December 2013, pp. 33–53; Chuck Battipede, "HP University Supports Company Journey," *T+D*, August 2013, pp. 32–37; Chanin Ballance, "HP Is Playing Learning Games," *Chief Learning Officer*, May 3, 2013, http://www.clomedia.com.

HR IN SMALL BUSINESS

How Nick's Pizza Delivers Training Results

At first glance, Nick's Pizza & Pub sounds as ordinary as a company can be: a pizza restaurant with two locations, each in one of Chicago's northwest suburbs. But when you take a look at the company's performance measures, something special seems to be going on. In an industry where 200% employee turnover and operating profits around $6\frac{1}{2}$% are normal, Nick's has to replace only 20% of its employees each year and enjoys operating profits of 14% or more. These results are

amazing, especially for a business in which 4 out of 10 employees are high school students.

What makes the difference? It could be the culture at Nick's. Rather than hiring expert managers and laying down a lot of rules, Nick's is choosy about who gets hired for every position and then provides them with enough training to operate skillfully and exercise sound judgment. The whole training program emphasizes ways to develop trustworthy, dedicated employees.

Training at Nick's begins with a two-day orientation program. Trainees learn the company's purpose, values, and culture, and they participate in role-playing activities to practice those lessons. Then it's on to skills training, beginning with a course called simply 101. During that four-hour hands-on lesson in the kitchen, all the new employees—regardless of what their future job will be—learn to make a pizza. From there, the trainees divide into work groups for the next level of training. In 201, these groups of trainees embark on longer-term training to be certified in performing a particular job. For example, an employee might train in pizza making for a few weeks until he or she earns a certification as a pizza maker.

Class 201 ends the mandatory training, but Nick's provides incentives for further learning. An employee can participate in additional 201 courses to learn more jobs and earn a pay increase. An employee who earns two more certifications (say, one in salad making and one in sandwich preparation) enjoys a wage increase of 75 cents an hour—and the prestige of exchanging the uniform's tan hat for a red hat. Some employees earn nine certifications, after which their pay rises another $2 an hour, and they get to wear a black hat with their uniform.

Yet another level of training prepares employees to be trainers themselves. This level—301—prepares employees to earn a top skill rating in their areas of certification. Besides these task-oriented skills, the employees receive training in communication and leadership and study a book called *Mastery: The Keys to Success and Long-Term Fulfillment* by George Leonard. Employees who complete these requirements receive a Leadership 301 Passport, which includes a checklist of behaviors they are expected to model for the employees they lead. During the weeks that follow, they watch for situations in which they or others are exhibiting each behavior,

jotting down descriptions of what they witnessed. When the listed behaviors have all been observed and noted, the participants take a course in training, and they finally are ready to be named trainers themselves.

Along with these formal training programs, Nick's provides further on-the-job learning through coaching by managers and trainers. The goal is to provide feedback in the moment, not waiting for performance appraisal meetings. For example, at the end of each shift, trainers will ask trainees to identify one thing they did well that day and one thing they would like to improve. In addition, managers are taught to observe employees' behavior on the job and ask themselves whether what they see would make them want to hire the employee. If yes, the manager is expected to give immediate positive feedback. If no, the manager is expected to coach the employee on how to do better.

Questions

1. To the extent that you can provide details from the information given and a visit to the Nick's Pizza website (www.nickspizzapub.com), prepare a needs assessment for training kitchen staff at Nick's. Remember to include organization, person, and task analyses.

2. How does the work environment support training at Nick's? In what additional ways, besides those described, could the work environment support training?

3. Do you think an outside contractor could provide training for Nick's as effectively as its current methods do? Why or why not? Are there some types or topics of training for which a contractor might be appropriate? If so, which ones?

Sources: Nick's Pizza & Pub corporate website, www.nickspizzapub .com, accessed March 15, 2012; and based on Bo Burlingham, "Lessons from a Blue-Collar Millionaire," *Inc.*, February 2010, www.inc.com.

NOTES

1. Tristan Lejeune, "To Close Skills Gap, Employers Need to 'Get Off the Bench,'" *Employee Benefit News*, April 1, 2013, p. 10; Tanya A. Mulvey and Jennifer Schramm, "Educational Qualifications in Tomorrow's Job Market," *Chief Learning Officer*, December 2013, pp. 66–68.

2. "Microsoft Corporation: Pitch Perfect," *Training*, March 2014, EBSCOhost, http://web.b.ebscohost.com.

3. R. Noe, *Employee Training and Development*, 6th ed. (New York: Irwin/McGraw-Hill, 2013).

4. Ryann K. Ellis, *A Field Guide to Learning Management Systems*, Learning Circuits (American Society for Training & Development, 2009), accessed at http://www.astd.org.

5. Noe, *Employee Training and Development*; E. A. Surface, "Training Needs Assessment: Aligning Learning and

Capability with Performance Requirements and Organizational Objectives," in *The Handbook of Work Analysis: Methods, Systems, Applications and Science of Work Measurement in Organizations*, eds. M. A. Wilson, W. Bennett, S. G. Gibson, and G. M. Alliger (New York: Routledge Academic, 2012), pp. 437–62.

6. J. Z. Rouillier and I. L. Goldstein, "Determinants of the Climate for Transfer of Training" (presented at Society of Industrial/Organizational Psychology meetings, St. Louis, MO, 1991); J. S. Russell, J. R. Terborg, and M. L. Powers, "Organizational Performance and Organizational Level Training and Support," *Personnel Psychology* 38 (1985), pp. 849–63; H. Baumgartel, G. J. Sullivan, and L. E. Dunn, "How Organizational Climate and Personality Affect the

Payoff from Advanced Management Training Sessions," *Kansas Business Review* 5 (1978), pp. 1–10.

7. E. F. Holton III and C. Bailey, "Top-to-Bottom Curriculum Redesign," *Training and Development*, March 1995, pp. 40–44.

8. Eric Spiegel, "Making Science and Math a Priority," *Boston Globe*, December 9, 2011, http://www.boston.com; Lucia Mutikani, "So Many U.S. Manufacturing Jobs, So Few Skilled Workers," Reuters, October 13, 2011, http://www.reuters.com; Steve Hargreaves, "Americans Lacking in Basic Skills," *CNNMoney*, October 29, 2013, http://money.cnn.com.

9. R. A. Noe, "Trainees' Attributes and Attitudes: Neglected Influences on Training Effectiveness," *Academy of Management Review* 11 (1986), pp. 736–49; T. T. Baldwin, R. T. Magjuka, and B. T. Loher, "The Perils of Participation: Effects of Choice on Trainee Motivation and Learning," *Personnel Psychology* 44 (1991), pp. 51–66; S. I. Tannenbaum, J. E. Mathieu, E. Salas, and J. A. Cannon-Bowers, "Meeting Trainees' Expectations: The Influence of Training Fulfillment on the Development of Commitment, Self-Efficacy, and Motivation," *Journal of Applied Psychology* 76 (1991), pp. 759–69.

10. L. H. Peters, E. J. O'Connor, and J. R. Eulberg, "Situational Constraints: Sources, Consequences, and Future Considerations," in *Research in Personnel and Human Resource Management*, eds. K. M. Rowland and G. R. Ferris (Greenwich, CT: JAI Press, 1985), vol. 3, pp. 79–114; E. J. O'Connor, L. H. Peters, A. Pooyan, J. Weekley, B. Frank, and B. Erenkranz, "Situational Constraints' Effects on Performance, Affective Reactions, and Turnover: A Field Replication and Extension," *Journal of Applied Psychology* 69 (1984), pp. 663–72; D. J. Cohen, "What Motivates Trainees?" *Training and Development Journal*, November 1990, pp. 91–93; Russell, Terborg, and Powers, "Organizational Performance."

11. J. B. Tracey, S. I. Trannenbaum, and M. J. Kavanaugh, "Applying Trade Skills on the Job: The Importance of the Work Environment," *Journal of Applied Psychology* 80 (1995), pp. 239–52; P. E. Tesluk, J. L. Farr, J. E. Mathieu, and R. J. Vance, "Generalization of Employee Involvement Training to the Job Setting: Individuals and Situational Effects," *Personnel Psychology* 48 (1995), pp. 607–32; J. K. Ford, M. A. Quinones, D. J. Sego, and J. S. Sorra, "Factors Affecting the Opportunity to Perform Trained Tasks on the Job," *Personnel Psychology* 45 (1992), pp. 511–27.

12. B. Mager, *Preparing Instructional Objectives*, 2nd ed. (Belmont, CA: Lake, 1984); B. J. Smith and B. L. Delahaye, *How to Be an Effective Trainer*, 2nd ed. (New York: Wiley, 1987).

13. "2013 Training Industry Report," *Training*, November/December 2011, pp. 22–35.

14. Ibid., p. 30.

15. Jennifer J. Salopek, "Learning Has a Seat at the Table," *T + D*, October 2011, pp. 49–50.

16. Karina Gonzalez, "iPad a Training Tool at Twin City Hotel," *Pantagraph.com* (Bloomington, IL), March 7, 2012, http://www.pantagraph.com.

17. "Best Practices and Outstanding Initiatives," *Training*, January/February 2011, EBSCOhost, http://web.ebscohost.com.

18. American Society for Training and Development, *Learning Circuits: Glossary*, http://www.astd.org/LC/glossary.

htm, accessed March 16, 2012; Katie Kuehner-Hebert, "Go Mobile?" *Chief Learning Officer*, March 2014, pp. 18–21.

19. Kuehner-Hebert, "Go Mobile?" pp. 19–20.

20. U.S. Department of Labor, Employment and Training Administration (ETA), "At-a-Glance: Three Approaches to Apprenticeship Program Completion, Apprenticeship Final Rule, 29 CFR Part 29," http://www.doleta.gov, accessed March 16, 2012; ETA, "Apprenticeship Final Rule Fact Sheet," http://www.doleta.gov, accessed March 16, 2012; ETA, "At-a-Glance: Electronic Media in Related Instruction, Apprenticeship Final Rule, 29 CFR Part 29," http://www.doleta.gov, accessed March 16, 2012.

21. Lauren Weber, "Apprenticeships Help Create Jobs. So Why Are They in Decline?" *The Wall Street Journal*, April 27, 2014, http://online.wsj.com; C. Jeffrey Waddoups, "Union Coverage and Work-Related Training in the Construction Industry," *Industrial and Labor Relations Review* 67 (2) (April 2014): 532–55.

22. "Apprenticeships Multiply at Volkswagen," *Chattanooga (TN) Times/Free Press*, February 22, 2012, Business & Company Resource Center, http://galenet.galegroup.com; Chattanooga State Community College, "Automotive Mechatronics Program (AMP)," last modified February 17, 2012, http://www.chattanoogastate.edu.

23. Richard Rothschild, "Basic Chemistry? Paid Internships Tend to Yield Full-Time Jobs," *Workforce Management*, August 2011, Business & Company Resource Center, http://galenet.galegroup.com.

24. W. J. Rothwell and H. C. Kanzanas, "Planned OJT Is Productive OJT," *Training and Development Journal*, October 1990, pp. 53–56.

25. Doug Cameron, "Dreamliner's Here: Now Learn to Fly It," *The Wall Street Journal*, November 1, 2011, http://online.wsj.com.

26. T. Sitzmann, "A Meta-analytic Examination of the Instructional Effectiveness of Computer-Based Simulation Games," *Personnel Psychology* 64 (2011): 489–528; C. Cornell, "Better Than the Real Thing?" *Human Resource Executive*, August 2005, pp. 34–37; S. Boehle, "Simulations: The Next Generation of E-Learning," *Training*, January 2005, pp. 22–31.

27. Paul Harris, "Avatars Rule," *T+D*, October 2013, pp. 58–61.

28. Ladan Nikravan, "More than Fun and Games," *Chief Learning Officer*, January 2012, pp. 20–21.

29. G. P. Latham and L. M. Saari, "Application of Social Learning Theory to Training Supervisors through Behavior Modeling," *Journal of Applied Psychology* 64 (1979), pp. 239–46.

30. D. Brown and D. Harvey, *An Experiential Approach to Organizational Development* (Englewood Cliffs, NJ: Prentice Hall, 2000); Larissa Jõgi, review of *The Handbook of Experiential Learning and Management Education*, eds. Michael Reynolds and Russ Vince, *Studies in the Education of Adults* 40, no. 2 (Autumn 2008): pp. 232–234, accessed at OCLC FirstSearch, http://newfirstsearch.oclc.org.

31. Ashlee Vance, "Inside a Job-Training Program That's Just Hellacious Enough to Get Results," *Bloomberg Businessweek*, July 12, 2013, http://www.businessweek.com.

32. J. Cannon-Bowers and C. Bowers, "Team Development and Functioning," in *Handbook of Industrial and Organizational Psychology*, ed. S. Zedeck, volume 1 (Washington, DC: American

Psychological Association, 2011) pp. 597–650; L. Delise, C. Gorman, A. Brooks, J. Rentsch, and D. Steele-Johnson, "The Effects of Team Training on Team Outcomes: A Meta-analysis," *Performance Improvement Quarterly* 22 (2010): 53–80.

33. Toddi Gutner, "For Team-Building Events, a New Ingredient: Fun," *The Wall Street Journal*, April 27, 2014, http://online.wsj.com.

34. "Best Practices and Outstanding Initiatives."

35. C. E. Schneier, "Training and Development Programs: What Learning Theory and Research Have to Offer," *Personnel Journal*, April 1974, pp. 288–93; M. Knowles, "Adult Learning," in *Training and Development Handbook*, 3rd ed., ed. R. L. Craig (New York: McGraw-Hill, 1987), pp. 168–79; B. J. Smith and B. L. Delahaye, *How to Be an Effective Trainer*, 2nd ed. (New York: Wiley, 1987); Traci Sitzmann, "Self-Regulating Online Course Engagement," *T&D*, March 2010, Business & Company Resource Center, http://galenet.galegroup.com.

36. K. A. Smith-Jentsch, F. G. Jentsch, S. C. Payne, and E. Salas, "Can Pretraining Experiences Explain Individual Differences in Learning?" *Journal of Applied Psychology* 81 (1996), pp. 110–16.

37. W. McGehee and P. W. Thayer, *Training in Business and Industry* (New York: Wiley, 1961).

38. R. M. Gagne and K. L. Medsker, *The Condition of Learning* (Fort Worth, TX: Harcourt-Brace, 1996).

39. J. C. Naylor and G. D. Briggs, "The Effects of Task Complexity and Task Organization on the Relative Efficiency of Part and Whole Training Methods," *Journal of Experimental Psychology* 65 (1963), pp. 217–24.

40. Katherine Hobson, "Getting Docs to Use PCs," *The Wall Street Journal*, March 15, 2011, http://online.wsj.com.

41. Kuehner-Hebert, "Go Mobile?" p. 20; Katie Kuehner-Hebert, "Who Controls Your Social Learning?" *Chief Learning Officer*, April 2014, pp. 18–21.

42. R. D. Marx, "Relapse Prevention for Managerial Training: A Model for Maintenance of Behavior Change," *Academy of Management Review* 7 (1982): 433–41; G. P. Latham and C. A. Frayne, "Self-Management Training for Increasing Job Attendance: A Follow-Up and Replication," *Journal of Applied Psychology* 74 (1989): 411–16.

43. D. Sussman, "Strong Medicine Required," *T&D*, November 2005, pp. 34–38.

44. Karie Willyerd and Gene A. Pease, "How Does Social Learning Measure Up?" *T + D*, January 2011, pp. 32–37.

45. M. R. Louis, "Surprise and Sense Making: What Newcomers Experience in Entering Unfamiliar Organizational Settings," *Administrative Science Quarterly* 25 (1980), pp. 226–51; Rachel Emma Silverman, "Companies Try to Make the First Day for New Hires More Fun," *The Wall Street Journal*, May 28, 2013, http://online.wsj.com.

46. Catherine Dunn, "Hyatt's One-Person Welcoming Committee," *Fortune*, March 20, 2014, http://fortune.com.

47. Peter Bregman, "Diversity Training Doesn't Work," *Forbes*, March 12, 2012, http://www.forbes.com.

48. Todd Henneman, "Making the Pieces Fit," *Workforce Management*, August 2011, Business & Company Resource Center, http://galenet.galegroup.com.

49. Mary Beauregard, "Culturally Canny," *T + D*, September 2011, p. 88.

50. T. Kochan, K. Bezrukova, R. Ely, S. Jackson, A. Joshi, K. Jehn, J. Leonard, D. Levine, and D. Thomas, "The Effects of Diversity on Business Performance: Report of the Diversity Research Network," *Human Resource Management* 42 (2003): 8–21; F. Hansen, "Diversity's Business Case Just Doesn't Add Up," *Workforce*, June 2003, pp. 29–32; M. J. Wesson and C. I. Gogus, "Shaking Hands with the Computer: An Examination of Two Methods of Newcomer Socialization," *Journal of Applied Psychology* 90 (2005): 1018–26; R. Anand and M. Winters, "A Retrospective View of Corporate Diversity Training from 1964 to the Present," *Academy of Management Learning and Education* 7 (2008): 356–72.

51. C. T. Schreiber, K. F. Price, and A. Morrison, "Workforce Diversity and the Glass Ceiling: Practices, Barriers, Possibilities," *Human Resource Planning* 16 (1994): 51–69; K. Bezrvkova, K. Jehn, and C. Spell, "Reviewing Diversity Training: Where Have We Been and Where Should We Go?" *Academy of Management Learning and Education* 11(2012): 207–27.

52. Christen McCurdy, "Cultural Competency Training Offered by Oregon Center for Nursing," *The Lund Report*, March 8, 2012, http://www.thelundreport.org; Aaron DeSmet, Monica McGurk, and Elizabeth Schwartz, "Getting More from Your Training Programs," *McKinsey Quarterly*, October 2010, http://www.mckinseyquarterly.com.

Developing Employees for Future Success

What Do I Need to Know?

After reading this chapter, you should be able to:

LO 8-1 Discuss how development is related to training and careers.

LO 8-2 Identify the methods organizations use for employee development.

LO 8-3 Describe how organizations use assessment of personality type, work behaviors, and job performance to plan employee development.

LO 8-4 Explain how job experiences can be used for developing skills.

LO 8-5 Summarize principles of successful mentoring programs.

LO 8-6 Tell how managers and peers develop employees through coaching.

LO 8-7 Identify the steps in the process of career management.

LO 8-8 Discuss how organizations are meeting the challenges of the "glass ceiling," succession planning, and dysfunctional managers.

Introduction

When sports fans want to see or hear who is winning or losing, they often find the coverage they want on one of ESPN's eight cable TV networks, its mobile app, its website, or one of its 300 radio affiliates. Providing up-to-the-minute news about more than 65 sports is a fast-paced business, which creates a human resource challenge: employees are so busy producing and delivering programming that they might feel too pressed for time to consider the next stage of their career. At the same time, employees know they need to keep learning so they can advance and take on more responsibility, while ESPN knows that preparing employees to assume more responsibility is essential for ensuring it has the right talent in place as positions open up.

ESPN meets the challenge with careful planning for employees to develop their skills. The company requires each employee to create an individual development plan (IDP). The IDP helps employees consider where they currently are in their careers, where they want to go in the future, and how they can meet their goals. Employees creating an action plan for their IDP can use ESPN's Leadership GPS, a tool that supports goal setting, choosing activities, and tracking progress toward goals. The company provides several opportunities for development, emphasizing ways to learn on the job, such as shadowing another employee or tackling a challenging new experience. In addition, employees can take business courses taught

by executives through ESPN The University. Employees who demonstrate high potential for leadership also are invited to take part in ESPN Center Court, which rotates them through jobs in several areas of the company and gives them opportunities to interact with top-level managers.[1]

As ESPN realizes and as we noted in Chapter 1, employees' commitment to their organization depends on how their managers treat them. To "win the war for talent," managers must be able to identify high-potential employees, make sure the organization uses the talents of these people, and reassure them of their value so that they do not become dissatisfied and leave the organization. Managers also must be able to listen. Although new employees need strong direction, they expect to be able to think independently and be treated with respect. In all these ways, managers provide for **employee development**—the combination of formal education, job experiences, relationships, and assessment of personality and abilities to help employees prepare for the future of their careers. Human resource management establishes a process for employee development that prepares employees to help the organization meet its goals.

This chapter explores the purpose and activities of employee development. We begin by discussing the relationships among development, training, and career management. Next, we look at development approaches, including formal education, assessment, job experiences, and interpersonal relationships. The chapter emphasizes the types of skills, knowledge, and behaviors that are strengthened by each development method, so employees and their managers can choose appropriate methods when planning for development. The third section of the chapter describes the steps of the career management process, emphasizing the responsibilities of employee and employer at each step of the process. The chapter concludes with a discussion of special challenges related to employee development—the so-called glass ceiling, succession planning, and dysfunctional managers.

Employee Development
The combination of formal education, job experiences, relationships, and assessment of personality and abilities to help employees prepare for the future of their careers.

Training, Development, and Career Management

Organizations and their employees must constantly expand their knowledge, skills, and behavior to meet customer needs and compete in today's demanding and rapidly changing business environment. More and more companies operate internationally, requiring that employees understand different cultures and customs. More companies organize work in terms of projects or customers, rather than specialized functions, so employees need to acquire a broad range of technical and interpersonal skills. Many companies expect employees at all levels to perform roles once reserved for management. Modern organizations are expected to provide development opportunities to employees without regard to their sex, race, ethnic background, or age so that they have equal opportunity for advancement. In this climate, organizations are placing greater emphasis on training and development. To do this, organizations must understand development's relationship to training and career management.

LO 8-1 Discuss how development is related to training and careers.

Development and Training

The definition of development indicates that it is future oriented. Development implies learning that is not necessarily related to the employee's current job.[2] Instead, it prepares employees for other jobs or positions in the organization and increases their ability to move into jobs that may not yet exist.[3] Development also may help employees prepare for changes in responsibilities and requirements in their current jobs, such as changes resulting from new technology, work designs, or customers.

Table 8.1

Training versus Development

	TRAINING	DEVELOPMENT
Focus	Current	Future
Use of work experiences	Low	High
Goal	Preparation for current job	Preparation for changes
Participation	Required	Voluntary

In contrast, training traditionally focuses on helping employees improve performance of their current jobs. Many organizations have focused on linking training programs to business goals. In these organizations, the distinction between training and development is more blurred. Table 8.1 summarizes the traditional differences.

For an example of a company that links training and development to future-oriented business goals, see the "Best Practices" box.

Development for Careers

The concept of a career has changed in recent years. In the traditional view, a career consists of a sequence of positions within an occupation or organization.[4] For example, an academic career might begin with a position as a university's adjunct professor. It continues with appointment to faculty positions as assistant professor, then associate professor, and finally full professor. An engineer might start as a staff engineer, then with greater experience earn promotions to the positions of advisory engineer, senior engineer, and vice president of engineering. In these examples, the career resembles a set of stairs from the bottom of a profession or organization to the top. Especially at organizations where careers progress in this way, development programs need to ensure that employees are prepared to ascend to each new level.

Recently, however, changes such as downsizing and restructuring have become the norm, so the concept of a career has become more fluid. Today's employees are more likely to have a **protean career,** one that frequently changes based on changes in the person's interests, abilities, and values and in the work environment. For example, an engineer might decide to take a sabbatical from her job to become a manager with Engineers without Borders, so she can develop managerial skills and decide whether she likes managing. As in this example, employees in protean careers take responsibility for managing their careers. This practice is consistent with the modern *psychological contract* described in Chapter 2. Employees look for organizations to provide not job security and a career ladder to climb, but instead development opportunities and flexible work arrangements.

To remain marketable, employees must continually develop new skills. Fewer of today's careers involve repetitive tasks, and more rely on an expanding base of knowledge.[5] Jobs are less likely to last a lifetime, so employees have to prepare for newly created positions. Beyond knowing job requirements, employees need to understand the business in which they are working and be able to cultivate valuable relationships with co-workers, managers, suppliers, and customers. They also need to follow trends in their field and industry, so they can apply technology and knowledge that will match emerging priorities and needs. Learning such skills requires useful job experiences as well as effective training programs.

These relationships and experiences often take an employee along a career path that is far different from the traditional steps upward through an organization or profession. Although such careers will not disappear, more employees will follow a spiral career path in which they cross the boundaries between specialties and organizations. As organizations provide for employee development (and as employees take control

Protean Career

A career that frequently changes based on changes in the person's interests, abilities, and values and in the work environment.

Best Practices

How KPMG Develops for the Future

As one of the leading accounting and business advisory firms, KPMG seeks what it calls a "high-performance culture," employing "the best people with the skills and determination to deliver above and beyond." For this, the firm needs people with in-depth, up-to-date knowledge of their profession and clients' industries. The kinds of bright, ambitious people who join a firm like KPMG want careers with room for advancement, which means they will have to develop leadership skills as they gain experience. To meet all of these needs, KPMG's training organization—the KPMG Business School—has established a three-part strategy: understand the marketplace of the future, build the firm of the future, and develop the workforce of the future.

To carry out this future-oriented strategy, the KPMG Business School offers training in job skills and industry trends. This training program focuses on assessments of what skills KPMG will need in its

employees as they move into future roles. For example, instead of promoting employees into their first managerial job and then teaching them management skills, KPMG identifies future managers and teaches them to manage as they prepare for those positions. Top executives visit training sessions to demonstrate the value the firm places on learning. The formal training is backed up with mobile and social-media resources that reinforce learning.

Along with training programs, the company intentionally offers its employees challenging assignments. From the beginning of their career at KPMG, employees have responsibilities that keep them practicing important skills. Many of them take on international assignments or rotate through various positions in the firm to gain a broader perspective.

The firm also matches thousands of employees to experienced mentors. These relationships help the junior employees learn by observing

senior employees, asking them questions, and receiving guidance.

Questions

1. Describe how the activities described here fit the definition of employee development.

2. Suppose KPMG tried to save money by replacing employee development with simply ensuring it has people with the skills needed to fill current positions. What impact do you predict this change would have on KPMG's business performance? Why?

Sources: Company website, "KPMG Campus: High-Performance Culture," http://www.kpmgcampus.com, accessed June 4, 2014; Kate Everson, "KPMG: Building the Firm of the Future," *Chief Learning Officer*, June 2014, pp. 42–43; Lorri Freifeld, "Solving Today's Skill Gaps," *Training*, November 2013, http://www.trainingmag.com; Jennifer Keirn, "2013 Best Places to Work: KPMG," *Inside Business*, September/October 2013, http://ibmag.com.

---

of their own careers), they will need to (1) determine their interests, skills, and weaknesses and (2) seek development experiences involving jobs, relationships, and formal courses. As discussed later in the chapter, organizations can meet these needs through a system for *career management* or *development planning*. Career management helps employees select development activities that prepare them to meet their career goals. It helps employers select development activities in line with their human resource needs.

Approaches to Employee Development

LO 8-2 Identify the methods organizations use for employee development.

The many approaches to employee development fall into four broad categories: formal education, assessment, job experiences, and interpersonal relationships.[6] Figure 8.1 summarizes these four methods. Many organizations combine these approaches.

Formal Education

Organizations may support employee development through a variety of formal educational programs, either at the workplace or off-site. These may include workshops designed specifically for the organization's employees, short courses offered

Figure 8.1
Four Approaches to Employee Development

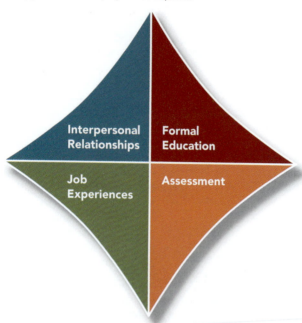

by consultants or universities, university programs offered to employees who live on campus during the program, and executive MBA programs (which enroll managers to meet on weekends or evenings to earn a master's degree in business administration). These programs may involve lectures by business experts, business games and simulations, experiential programs, and meetings with customers. Chapter 7 described most of these training methods, including their pros and cons.

Many companies operate training and development centers that offer seminars and longer-term programs. Among the most famous are General Electric's John F. Welch Leadership Center in Crotonville, New York, and McDonald's Hamburger University in Oak Brook, Illinois. The thousands of restaurant managers and owner-operators who attend Hamburger U each year get classroom training and simulations on how to run a business that delivers consistent service, quality, and cleanliness. They also receive coaching and peer support face-to-face and online. The company's highest-performing executives participate in a nine-month leadership institute at Hamburger U, where they tackle major issues facing the company.[7]

Independent institutions offering executive education include Harvard, the Wharton School of Business, the University of Michigan, and the Center for Creative Leadership. At the University of Virginia, the Darden School of Business offers an executive MBA program in which students attend classes on campus once a month on Thursday through Saturday. The on-campus time provides opportunities for students to collaborate on presentations, simulations, and case studies. The school also brings executive MBA students to campus four times for leadership residencies. During each weeklong residency, the students use workshops, coaching, and reflection to get better at handling their everyday management challenges. Between the times on campus, the students continue their education with independent study, online classes, and tools for virtual meetings and online exams.[8]

LO 8-3 Describe how organizations use assessment of personality type, work behaviors, and job performance to plan employee development.

Another trend in executive education is for employers and the education provider to create short courses with content designed specifically for the audience. Hasbro worked with Dartmouth's Tuck School of Business to create the Hasbro Global Leadership Program. This annual weeklong program covers areas where the toy company's managers needed greater strength: global strategy, emerging markets, personal leadership, ethics, and brand building.[9]

Assessment
Collecting information and providing feedback to employees about their behavior, communication style, or skills.

Assessment

Another way to provide for employee development is **assessment**—collecting information and providing feedback to employees about their behavior, communication style, or skills.[10] Information for assessment may come from the employees, their peers, managers, and customers. The most frequent uses of assessment are to identify employees with managerial potential to measure current managers' strengths and weaknesses. Organizations also use assessment to identify managers with potential to move into higher-level executive positions. Organizations that assign work to teams may use assessment to identify the strengths and weaknesses of individual team members and the effects of the team members' decision-making and communication styles on the team's productivity.

For assessment to support development, the information must be shared with the employee being assessed. Along with that assessment information, the employee needs suggestions for correcting skill weaknesses and for using skills already learned. The suggestions might be to participate in training courses or develop skills through new job experiences. Based on the assessment information and available development opportunities, employees should develop action plans to guide their efforts at self-improvement.

Organizations vary in the methods and sources of information they use in developmental assessment. Many organizations appraise performance. Organizations with sophisticated development systems use psychological tests to measure employees' skills, personality types, and communication styles. They may collect self, peer, and manager ratings of employees' behavior and style of working with others. In a recent survey, business professionals said the tool used most widely in their organization was a type of performance appraisal known as 360-degree assessments, followed by two popular psychological tests (the Myers-Briggs Type Indicator and the DiSC assessment).[11] A less-used but potentially beneficial approach is to send employees to an assessment center for in-depth evaluation of their skills, strengths, and weaknesses. Whether or not they use an assessment center, employers often combine assessment tools for a fuller picture of employees.

Psychological Profiles   When organizations choose assessment tools, they often include some type of questionnaire in which employees answer questions about themselves or select words or statements they agree describe themselves. From the answers, a testing service creates an inventory or profile describing the person's traits or the way the person tends to behave. Two of the most widely used assessments are the ones mentioned in the previous paragraph: the Myers-Briggs Type Indicator and the DiSC assessment.

Myers-Briggs Type Indicator (MBTI) identifies individuals' preferences for source of energy, means of information gathering, way of decision making, and lifestyle. The assessment consists of more than 100 questions about how the person feels or prefers to behave in different situations (such as "Are you usually a good 'mixer' or rather quiet and reserved?"). The results describe these individuals' preferences in the four areas:

> **Myers-Briggs Type Indicator (MBTI)** Psychological test that identifies individuals' preferences for source of energy, means of information gathering, way of decision making, and lifestyle, providing information for team building and leadership development.

1. The *energy* dichotomy indicates where individuals gain interpersonal strength and vitality, measured as their degree of introversion or extroversion. Extroverted types (E) gain energy through interpersonal relationships. Introverted types (I) gain energy by focusing on inner thoughts and feelings.
2. The *information-gathering* dichotomy relates to the preparations individuals make before making decisions. Individuals with a Sensing (S) preference tend to gather the facts and details to prepare for a decision. Intuitive types (N) tend to focus less on the facts and more on possibilities and relationships among them.
3. In *decision making*, individuals differ in the amount of consideration they give to their own and others' values and feelings, as opposed to the hard facts of a situation. Individuals with a Thinking (T) preference try always to be objective in

making decisions. Individuals with a Feeling (F) preference tend to evaluate the impact of the alternatives on others, as well as their own feelings; they are more subjective.

4. The *lifestyle* dichotomy describes an individual's tendency to be either flexible or structured. Individuals with a Judging (J) preference focus on goals, establish deadlines, and prefer to be conclusive. Individuals with a Perceiving (P) preference enjoy surprises, are comfortable with changing a decision, and dislike deadlines.

The alternatives for each of the four dichotomies result in 16 possible combinations. Of course people are likely to be mixtures of these types, but the point of the assessment is that certain types predominate in individuals.

As a result of their psychological types, people develop strengths and weaknesses. For example, individuals who are Introverted, Sensing, Thinking, and Judging (known as ISTJs) tend to be serious, quiet, practical, orderly, and logical. They can organize tasks, be decisive, and follow through on plans and goals. But because they do not have the opposite preferences (Extroversion, Intuition, Feeling, and Perceiving), ISTJs have several weaknesses. They may have difficulty responding to unexpected opportunities, appear to their colleagues to be too task-oriented or impersonal, and make decisions too fast.

Applying this kind of information about employees' preferences or tendencies helps organizations understand the communication, motivation, teamwork, work styles, and leadership of the people in their groups. For example, salespeople or executives who want to communicate better can apply what they learn about their own personality styles and the way other people perceive them. For team development, the MBTI can help teams match team members with assignments based on their preferences and thus improve problem solving.[12] The team could assign brainstorming (idea-generating) tasks to employees with an Intuitive preference and evaluation of the ideas to employees with a Sensing preference.

Research on the validity, reliability, and effectiveness of the MBTI is inconclusive.[13] People who take the MBTI find it a positive experience and say it helps them change their behavior. However, MBTI scores are not necessarily stable over time. Studies in which the MBTI was administered at two different times found that as few as one-fourth of those who took the assessment were classified as exactly the same type the second time. Still, the MBTI is a valuable tool for understanding communication styles and the ways people prefer to interact with others. It is not appropriate for measuring job performance, however, or as the only means of evaluating promotion potential.

DiSC

Brand of assessment tool that identifies individuals' behavioral patterns in terms of dominance, influence, steadiness, and conscientiousness.

The **DiSC** assessment tool is an inventory of behavioral styles based on the work of William Marston, a psychologist who attempted to categorize normal behavior patterns.[14] Over the years, different people have used Marston's model to construct tests to measure versions of Marston's categories; the most widely used instrument, published by Inscape, distinguishes itself with the lowercase *i* in its name. Because there are variations in these inventories, employers should be careful to use a version that has been tested and shown to be valid and reliable.

An employee taking Inscape's DiSC inventory receives a profile report describing his or her behavioral style, preferred environment, and strategies for effectiveness. The style is described in terms of the following categories (which provide the letters for the DiSC acronym):

- *Dominance* means the person emphasizes results and displays confidence. This type of person takes on challenges, sees the big picture, and can be blunt and to the point.

- *Influence* means the person emphasizes relationships and persuasion. This type of person likes to collaborate, dislikes being ignored, and displays optimism and enthusiasm.
- *Steadiness* means the person emphasizes cooperation, sincerity, and dependability. This type of person behaves calmly and with humility, dislikes rushing, and is supportive of others.
- *Conscientiousness* means the person emphasizes quality and accuracy, displaying competency. This type of person worries about mistakes and wants to get the details. He or she favors objective thinking and enjoys working independently.

Assessment Centers   At an **assessment center,** multiple raters or evaluators (assessors) evaluate employees' performance on a number of exercises.[15] An assessment center is usually an off-site location such as a conference center. Usually 6 to 12 employees participate at one time. The primary use of assessment centers is to identify whether employees have the personality characteristics, administrative skills, and interpersonal skills needed for

One way to develop employees is to begin with an assessment that may consist of assigning an activity to a team and seeing who brings what skills and strengths to the team. How can this assessment help employees?

managerial jobs. Organizations also use them to determine whether employees have the skills needed for working in teams. A complete half-day or full-day assessment at an assessment center can cost as much as $20,000, so employers tend to use this method mainly for employees in the highest levels of management.

The types of exercises used in assessment centers include leaderless group discussions, interviews, in-baskets, and role-plays.[16] In a **leaderless group discussion,** a team of five to seven employees is assigned a problem and must work together to solve it within a certain time period. The problem may involve buying and selling supplies, nominating a subordinate for an award, or assembling a product. Interview questions typically cover each employee's work and personal experiences, skill strengths and weaknesses, and career plans. In-basket exercises, discussed as a selection method in Chapter 6, simulate the administrative tasks of a manager's job, using a pile of documents for the employee to handle. In role-plays, the participant takes the part of a manager or employee in a situation involving the skills to be assessed. For example, a participant might be given the role of a manager who must discuss performance problems with an employee, played by someone who works for the assessment center. Other exercises in assessment centers might include interest and aptitude tests to evaluate an employee's vocabulary, general mental ability, and reasoning skills. Personality tests may be used to determine employees' ability to get along with others, tolerance for uncertainty, and other traits related to success as a manager or team member.

The assessors are usually managers who have been trained to look for employee behaviors that are related to the skills being assessed. Typically, each assessor observes and records one or two employees' behaviors in each exercise. The assessors review their notes and rate each employee's level of skills (for example, 5 = high level of leadership skills, 1 = low level of leadership skills). After all the employees have completed the exercises, the assessors discuss their observations of each employee. They compare their ratings and try to agree on each employee's rating for each of the skills.

Assessment Center
Typically an off-site location at which multiple raters or evaluators (assessors) evaluate employees' performance on a number of exercises, usually as they work in a group.

Leaderless Group Discussion
An assessment center exercise in which a team of five to seven employees is assigned a problem and must work together to solve it within a certain time period.

As we mentioned in Chapter 6, research suggests that assessment center ratings are valid for predicting performance, salary level, and career advancement.[17] Assessment centers may also be useful for development because of the feedback that participants receive about their attitudes, skill strengths, and weaknesses.[18]

Performance Appraisals and 360-Degree Feedback   A *performance appraisal*, or formal process for measuring employee performance, is a major component of performance management, which will be described in Chapter 10. This information also can be useful for employee development under certain conditions.[19] The appraisal system must tell employees specifically about their performance problems and ways to improve their performance. Employees must gain a clear understanding of the differences between current performance and expected performance. The appraisal process must identify causes of the performance discrepancy and develop plans for improving performance. Managers must be trained to deliver frequent performance feedback and must monitor employees' progress in carrying out their action plans.

A recent trend in performance appraisals, also discussed in Chapter 10, is *360-degree feedback*—performance measurement by the employee's supervisor, peers, employees, and customers. Often the feedback involves rating the individual in terms of work-related behaviors. For development purposes, the rater would identify an area of behavior as a strength of that employee or an area requiring further development. The results presented to the employee show how he or she was rated on each item and how self-evaluations differ from other raters' evaluations. The individual reviews the results, seeks clarification from the raters, and sets specific development goals based on the strengths and weaknesses identified.[20] Luck Companies, a Virginia miner and supplier of crushed stone, uses 360-degree assessments for all its managers to measure their performance in terms of criteria such as company values and competencies associated with good leadership.[21]

There are several benefits of 360-degree feedback. Organizations collect multiple perspectives of managers' performance, allowing employees to compare their own personal evaluations with the views of others. This method also establishes formal communications about behaviors and skill ratings between employees and their internal and external customers. Several studies have shown that performance improves and behavior changes as a result of participating in upward feedback and 360-degree feedback systems.[22] The change is greatest in people who received lower ratings from others than what they gave themselves. The 360-degree feedback system is most likely to be effective if the rating instrument enables reliable or consistent ratings, assesses behaviors or skills that are job related, and is easy to use. Other ways the organization can make it more likely that 360-degree feedback will yield benefits are to have the assessment results delivered by a trained person and to hold the employees accountable in follow-up meetings with their manager or a coach.[23]

There are potential limitations of 360-degree feedback. This method demands a significant amount of time for raters to complete the evaluations. If raters, especially subordinates or peers, provide negative feedback, some managers might try to identify and punish them. A facilitator is needed to help interpret results. Finally, simply delivering ratings to a manager does not provide ways for the manager to act on the feedback (for example, development planning, meeting with raters, or taking courses). As noted earlier, any form of assessment should be accompanied by suggestions for improvement and development of an action plan.

HR How To

Setting Up Stretch Assignments for Employees

Ideally, a stretch assignment will be a difficult but positive experience in which the employee figures out how to meet the challenge. Here are some principles for achieving that ideal:

- Establish a purpose for each assignment. Have in mind particular skills or competencies the employee would learn in the assignment—for example, understanding the customer's perspective or influencing others in the organization.
- Include one or more of the conditions that make assignments challenging: unfamiliar tasks, greater responsibility, effort to bring about change, work with people in other areas of the organization, and leadership of a diverse group.
- Create a safe context for learning. One approach is to identify the conditions necessary for the employee to succeed and verify that those conditions are

in place. Another approach is to make sure that the assignment is one where a failure will not harm the organization, so failure is tolerated.

- Determine how you will track the employee's progress and measure success. For example, if the employee will develop decision-making skills, prepare to measure how the employee is making decisions, as well as the quality of the decisions.
- Before placing an employee in an assignment, assess the employee's current skills. Use assessment results to match employees with assignments they are prepared to handle.
- Clearly define for the employee the requirements of the stretch assignment. Lay out the expectations for the tasks the employee will perform and the definition of success.
- Assign qualified persons to give support and feedback to employees in stretch assignments.

The support could come from a more experienced mentor or coach. In addition, a group of peers might share knowledge as they learn together.

Questions

1. Which of these principles help ensure that a stretch assignment is not so simple that it is just another routine job responsibility?
2. Which of these principles help ensure that a stretch assignment is not so hard that it generates panic and failure?

Sources: Stu Crandell, "Getting Ready for the Big Jump," *Chief Learning Officer*, July 2013, pp. 34–7; Robert Bullock, "Developing Leaders through On the Job Learning," Scontrino-Powell blog, June 1, 2013, http://www.scontrino-powell.com; Halelly Azulay, "Learning beyond the Comfort Zone," *T+D*, January 2013, Business Insights: Global, http://bi.galegroup.com; Gary Cohen, "Stretch Assignments for High Potential Employees," CO2 Partners blog, May 21, 2012, http://www.co2partners.com.

Job Experiences

Most employee development occurs through **job experiences**[24]—the combination of relationships, problems, demands, tasks, and other features of an employee's jobs. Using job experiences for employee development assumes that development is most likely to occur when the employee's skills and experiences do not entirely match the skills required for the employee's current job. To succeed, employees must stretch their skills. In other words, they must learn new skills, apply their skills and knowledge in new ways, and master new experiences.[25] For example, companies that want to prepare employees to expand overseas markets are assigning them to a variety of international jobs. To read tips for setting up work assignments that stretch employees, see "HR How To."

Most of what we know about development through job experiences comes from a series of studies conducted by the Center for Creative Leadership.[26] These studies asked executives to identify key career events that made a difference in their managerial styles and the lessons they learned from these experiences. The key events included job assignments (such as fixing a failed operation), interpersonal relationships (getting along with supervisors), and types of transitions (situations in which the manager at

LO 8-4 Explain how job experiences can be used for developing skills.

Job Experiences
The combination of relationships, problems, demands, tasks, and other features of an employee's jobs.

first lacked the necessary background). Through job experiences like these, managers learn how to handle common challenges, prove themselves, lead change, handle pressure, and influence others.

The usefulness of job experiences for employee development varies depending on whether the employee views the experiences as positive or negative sources of stress. When employees view job experiences as positive stressors, the experiences challenge them and stimulate learning. When they view job experiences as negative stressors, employees may suffer from high levels of harmful stress. Of the job demands studied, managers were most likely to experience negative stress from creating change and overcoming obstacles (adverse business conditions, lack of management support, lack of personal support, or a difficult boss). Research suggests that all of the job demands except obstacles are related to learning.[27] Organizations should offer job experiences that are most likely to increase learning, and they should consider the consequences of situations that involve negative stress.

Although the research on development through job experiences has focused on managers, line employees also can learn through job experiences. Organizations may, for example, use job experiences to develop skills needed for teamwork, including conflict resolution, data analysis, and customer service. These experiences may occur when forming a team and when employees switch roles within a team.

Various job assignments can provide for employee development. The organization may enlarge the employee's current job or move the employee to different jobs. Lateral moves include job rotation, transfer, or temporary assignment to another organization. The organization may also use downward moves or promotions as a source of job experience. Figure 8.2 summarizes these alternatives.

Job Enlargement   As Chapter 4 stated in the context of job design, *job enlargement* involves adding challenges or new responsibilities to employees' current jobs. Examples include completing a special project, switching roles within a work team, or

Figure 8.2

How Job Experiences Are Used for Employee Development

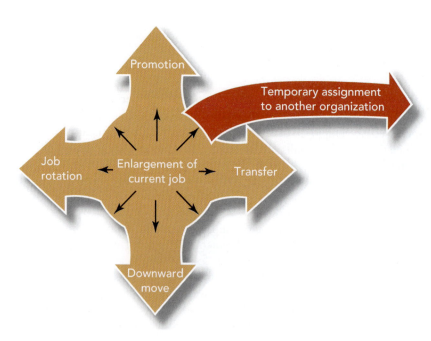

researching new ways to serve customers. An engineering employee might join a task force developing new career paths for technical employees. The work on the project could give the engineer a leadership role through which the engineer learns about the company's career development system while also practicing leadership skills to help the task force reach its goals. In this way, job enlargement not only makes a job more interesting, but also creates an opportunity for employees to develop new skills.

Job Rotation   Another job design technique that can be applied to employee development is *job rotation*, moving employees through a series of job assignments in one or more functional areas. Cummins uses job rotations as the major element of its Engineering Development Program for newly hired engineers with leadership potential. During the five-year program, engineers spend 18 months each in two rotations where they develop basic skills in areas of engineering that are related to the manufacturing company's processes, including electronics and design for applied mechanics. Next is a 12-month rotation into a position that involves working with customer concerns. The final rotation is a 12-month job emphasizing product development. Throughout the program, the engineers are guided by mentors assigned by the company.[28]

Job rotation helps employees gain an appreciation for the company's goals, increases their understanding of different company functions, develops a network of contacts, and improves problem-solving and decision-making skills.[29] Job rotation also helps employees increase their salary and earn promotions faster. However, job rotation poses some problems for employees and the organization. Knowing they will be rotated to another job may give the employees a short-term perspective on problems and their solutions. Employees may feel less satisfied and motivated because they have difficulty developing specialized skills and leave the position too soon to fulfill any challenging assignments. The rotation of employees through a department may hurt productivity and increase the workload of those who remain after employees are rotated out. Job rotation is most likely to succeed when it meets certain conditions:[30]

- The organization establishes and communicates clear policies about which positions are eligible for job rotation. Job rotation for nonmanagement employees as well as managers can be beneficial, depending on the program's objectives.
- Employees and their managers understand and agree on the expectations for the job rotation, including which skills are to be developed.
- Goals for the program support business goals. These might include exposing high-potential employees to a variety of business units, customers, or geographic areas in preparation for management positions or rotating an experienced, talented employee through several business units to mentor or coach employees.
- The rotation schedule is realistic, taking into account how long employees will need to become familiar with their new position, as well as how much time is needed for employees to complete the assignments.
- Top management is committed to the program's success.
- Someone is responsible for measuring whether the program is meeting its goals.

Transfers, Promotions, and Downward Moves   Most companies use upward, downward, and lateral moves as an option for employee development. In a **transfer,** the organization assigns an employee to a position in a different area of the company. Transfers do not necessarily increase job responsibilities or compensation. They are usually lateral moves, that is, moves to a job with a similar level of responsibility. They may involve relocation to another part of the country or even to another country.

Transfer
Assignment of an employee to a position in a different area of the company, usually in a lateral move.

Working outside one's home country is the most important job experience that can develop an employee for a career in the global economy.

Relocation can be stressful because of the demands of moving, especially when family members are affected. People have to find new housing, shopping, health care, and leisure facilities, and they often lack the support of nearby friends and family. These stresses come at the same time the employee must learn the expectations and responsibilities associated with the new position. Because transfers can provoke anxiety, many companies have difficulty getting employees to accept them. Employees most willing to accept transfers tend to be those with high career ambitions and beliefs that the organization offers a promising future and that accepting the transfer will help the company succeed.[31]

A **downward move** occurs when an employee is given less responsibility and authority. The organization may demote an employee because of poor performance or move the employee to a lower-level position in another function so that the employee can develop different skills. The temporary cross-functional move is the most common way to use downward moves for employee development. For example, engineers who want to move into management often take lower-level positions, such as shift supervisor, to develop their management skills.

Many employees have difficulty associating transfers and downward moves with development; these changes may feel more like forms of punishment. Employees often decide to leave an organization rather than accept such a change, and then the organization must bear the costs of replacing those employees. Employees will be more likely to accept transfers and downward moves as development opportunities if the organization provides information about the change and its possible benefits and involves the employee in planning the change. Employees are also more likely to be positive about such a recommendation if the organization provides clear performance objectives and frequent feedback. Employers can encourage an employee to relocate by providing financial assistance with the move, information about the new location and job, and help for family members, such as identifying schools, child care and elder care options, and job search assistance for the employee's spouse.[32]

A **promotion** involves moving an employee into a position with greater challenges, more responsibility, and more authority than in the previous job. Usually promotions include pay increases. Because promotions improve the person's pay, status, and feelings of accomplishment, employees are more willing to accept promotions than lateral or downward moves. Even so, employers can increase the likelihood that employees will accept promotions by providing the same kind of information and assistance that are used to support transfers and downward moves. Organizations can more easily offer promotions if they are profitable and growing. In other conditions, opportunities for promoting employees may be limited.

Temporary Assignments with Other Organizations   In some cases, an employer may benefit from the skills an employee can learn at another organization. The employer may encourage the employee to participate in an **externship**—a full-time temporary position at another organization. Externships are an attractive option for employees in analytical positions, who otherwise might solve the same kinds of problems

Downward Move
Assignment of an employee to a position with less responsibility and authority.

Promotion
Assignment of an employee to a position with greater challenges, more responsibility, and more authority than in the previous job, usually accompanied by a pay increase.

Externship
Employee development through a full-time temporary position at another organization.

over and over, becoming bored as they miss out on exposure to challenging new ideas and techniques. A variation on this approach that may not require a full-time commitment of employees is to encourage skills-based volunteering, in which employees apply and increase their skills by engaging in community service projects. The company pays the employees for the time they spend on the projects, and the employees apply their developing talents to a good cause. For example, employees of United-Health Group participate in projects that help community members manage diabetes and heart disease. Hewlett-Packard employees have coached entrepreneurs in socially conscious start-ups and run "hackathons" where programmers develop apps for non-profits. HP encourages employees to seek leadership roles in their volunteer efforts.[33]

Temporary assignments can include a **sabbatical**—a leave of absence from an organization to renew or develop skills. Employees on sabbatical often receive full pay and benefits. Sabbaticals let employees get away from the day-to-day stresses of their jobs and acquire new skills and perspectives. Sabbaticals also allow employees more time for personal pursuits such as writing a book or spending more time with family members. Universities often give sabbaticals to faculty members; some offer these development opportunities to staff members as well. After Shenandoah University in Winchester, Virginia, made sabbaticals available to employees who had worked there for at least 10 years, a staff member took time off and spent it interviewing alumni. The resulting stories will provide a valuable resource for creating the school's marketing materials. Jenny Lynne Semenza, a librarian at Idaho State University, used a six-month sabbatical to travel between Arizona and Alaska, visiting academic libraries along the way. Semenza gathered ideas for improving ISU's library when she returned to her job.[34] How employees spend their sabbaticals varies from company to company. Some employees may work for a nonprofit service agency; others may study at a college or university or travel and work on special projects in non-U.S. subsidiaries of the company.

Sabbatical
A leave of absence from an organization to renew or develop skills.

Interpersonal Relationships

Employees can also develop skills and increase their knowledge about the organization and its customers by interacting with a more experienced organization member. Increasingly, these interactions are taking place online with social-media tools, as described in "HRM Social." More formally, two types of relationships used for employee development are mentoring and coaching.

LO 8-5 Summarize principles of successful mentoring programs.

Mentors　A **mentor** is an experienced, productive senior employee who helps develop a less-experienced employee, called the *protégé*. Most mentoring relationships develop informally as a result of interests or values shared by the mentor and protégé. According to research, the employees most likely to seek and attract a mentor have certain personality characteristics: emotional stability, ability to adapt their behavior to the situation, and high needs for power and achievement.[35] Mentoring relationships also can develop as part of the organization's planned effort to bring together successful senior employees with less-experienced employees.

One major advantage of formal mentoring programs is that they ensure access to mentors for all employees, regardless of gender or race. A mentoring program also can ensure that high-potential employees are matched with wise, experienced mentors in key areas—and that mentors are hearing the challenges facing employees who have less authority, work directly with customers, or hold positions in other parts of the organization.[36] However, in an artificially created relationship, mentors may have difficulty providing counseling and coaching.[37] One practical way employees can address this shortcoming is to look for more than one mentor, including informal relationships with

Mentor
An experienced, productive senior employee who helps develop a less-experienced employee (a protégé).

Online Support for Career Development

One of the great advantages of social media is the ease of finding and communicating with people who share a common interest. You can locate old friends from high school or join a group discussing a cause or sports team you're passionate about. Applying that technique to careers, employees can join social-media groups whose members work at the same company or in the same profession. Most likely, those groups will include people who have more experience and knowledge in some areas, giving the online relationships potential as a source of career development.

While family and friends certainly can give valuable advice, the main sources of social-media career development will be on career-related sites. These could include a general careers site, such as LinkedIn, which offers millions of groups, or discussion groups on the websites of trade or professional organizations, such as the Society for Human Resource Management. Also, many companies have set up their own social-media tools for employees only. These are especially useful in large companies with operations around the world.

To make the most of any of these sites, employees should think about how to be valuable participants. That includes learning the rules and etiquette. For example, rather than using the site just to get help, one should also offer help. Expressing ideas in a positive manner creates a positive image. And before posting their questions, users should respect participants' time by searching to see if people have already answered that question.

People who become known as polite, helpful, value-adding members of a social-media group do more than gain knowledge from their peers and senior members of the group. They also foster relationships that can lead to more in-depth conversations, both online and offline. Their names are more likely to turn up in searches for candidates to take on stretch assignments or interview for job openings. And when employees take on a stretch assignment that requires assembling a team, those with a strong social-media network have an edge in locating the best people.

Questions

1. Describe a few possible advantages of using social media to offer ideas and advice rather than just asking for help and information.
2. Suppose you work in the HR department of a consumer products company and are interested in making a lateral move to another department as a way to develop your career. Your company has a social-media site where employees can search for co-workers with particular interests, experience, and skills. How might you use that site to plan your lateral move?

Sources: Rich Hein, "How to Use Social Networking to Succeed in Business," *CIO*, June 3, 2014, http://www.cio.com; Rosabeth Moss Kanter, "How to Use Social Media to Advance Your Career," *The Wall Street Journal*, May 12, 2014, http://blogs.wsj.com; Sarah Archer, "Tweet Your Way to a Job: Using Social Media to Develop Your Career," *The Guardian*, March 12, 2014, http://careers.theguardian.com.

interested people outside the organization. Employees also should accept the limits of mentoring relationships. Mentoring is not, for example, a substitute for therapy: a mentor might offer tips for navigating a business presentation, whereas a therapist is a better choice for someone who needs help with persistent anxiety.[38]

Mentoring programs tend to be most successful when they are voluntary and participants understand the details of the program. Rewarding managers for employee development is also important because it signals that mentoring and other development activities are worthwhile. In addition, the organization should carefully select mentors based on their interpersonal and technical skills, train them for the role, and evaluate whether the program has met its objectives.[39]

Mentors and protégés can both benefit from a mentoring relationship. Protégés receive career support, including coaching, protection, sponsorship, challenging assignments, and visibility among the organization's managers. They also receive benefits of a positive relationship—a friend and role model who accepts them, has a positive opinion toward them, and gives them a chance to talk about their worries. Employees with mentors are also more likely to be promoted, earn higher salaries, and have more influence within their organization.[40] Acting as a mentor gives managers a chance to develop their interpersonal skills and increase their feelings that they are contributing something important to the organization. Working with a technically trained protégé on matters such as new research in the field may also increase the mentor's technical knowledge.

So that more employees can benefit from mentoring, some organizations use *group mentoring programs*, which assign four to six protégés to a successful senior employee. A potential advantage of group mentoring is that protégés can learn from each other as well as from the mentor. The leader helps protégés understand the organization, guides them in analyzing their experiences, and helps them clarify career directions. Each member of the group may complete specific assignments, or the group may work together on a problem or issue.

Acting as a mentor gives managers and other experienced employees a chance to develop their interpersonal skills and increase their feelings that they are contributing something important to the organization.

Coaching   A **coach** is a peer or manager who works with an employee to motivate the employee, help him or her develop skills, and provide reinforcement and feedback. Coaches may play one or more of three roles[41]:

1. Working one-on-one with an employee, as when giving feedback.
2. Helping employees learn for themselves—for example, helping them find experts and teaching them to obtain feedback from others
3. Providing resources such as mentors, courses, or job experiences

When ConAgra Foods selected lawyer Colleen Batcheler to be its general counsel, the company's human resource department offered her executive coaching to help prepare for this high-level role. Batcheler met several times with the coaching team, using the assessments and homework they gave her to draw up goals for what she wanted to achieve. For accountability, she met with ConAgra's chief executive and with her staff to review her goals with them. One of Batcheler's goals was to spend more time learning about the strengths of each person on the legal team so she could apply team members' unique qualities in a way that would get the best results for the team overall. Learning to look for personal qualities was difficult at first, but she practiced the behavior until it became second nature. As a result, she is a more effective leader, and her team members are more committed and productive.[42]

Research suggests that coaching helps managers improve by identifying areas for improvement and setting goals.[43] Getting results from a coaching relationship can take at least six months of weekly or monthly meetings. To be effective, a coach generally conducts an assessment, asks questions that challenge the employee to think deeply about his or her goals and motives, helps the employee create an action plan, and follows up regularly to help the employee stay on track. Employees contribute to the success of coaching when they persevere in practicing the behaviors identified in the action plan.[44]

Systems for Career Management

Employee development is most likely to meet the organization's needs if it is part of a human resource system of career management. In practice, organizations' career management systems vary. Some rely heavily on informal relationships, while others

LO 8-6 Tell how managers and peers develop employees through coaching.

Coach
A peer or manager who works with an employee to motivate the employee, help him or her develop skills, and provide reinforcement and feedback.

LO 8-7 Identify the steps in the process of career management.

Figure 8.3

Steps in the Career Management Process

	Data gathering	Feedback	Goal setting	Action planning & Follow-up
Criteria for success	Focus on competencies needed for career success.	Maintain confidentiality.	Involve management and coaches/mentors.	Involve management and coaches/mentors.
	Include a variety of measures.	Focus on specific success factors, strengths, and improvement areas.	Specify competencies and knowledge to be developed.	Measure success and adjust plans as needed.
			Specify developmental methods.	Verify that pace of development is realistic.

are sophisticated programs. As shown in Figure 8.3, a basic career management system involves four steps: data gathering, feedback, goal setting, and action planning and follow-up. Human resource professionals can contribute to the system's success by ensuring that it is linked to other HR practices such as performance management, training, and recruiting. Applied Materials helps employees develop for leadership roles by identifying proven measures of the traits and behaviors of effective leaders. Employees at the high-tech company use assessment tools to identify where they stand in terms of those measures, and they can participate in classroom training and coaching to strengthen leadership skills. The HR department customizes the development program for the needs of particular departments or countries, and it is incorporating the leadership behaviors into its performance measures and performance-based rewards.[45] Unfortunately, not all organizations prepare their employees for leadership roles. See the "HR Oops!" box.

Data Gathering

Self-Assessment
The use of information by employees to determine their career interests, values, aptitudes, behavioral tendencies, and development needs.

In discussing the methods of employee development, we highlighted several assessment tools. Such tools may be applied to data gathering, the first step in the career management process. **Self-assessment** refers to the use of information by employees to determine their career interests, values, aptitudes, and behavioral tendencies. The employee's responsibility is to identify opportunities and personal areas needing improvement. The organization's responsibility is to provide assessment information for identifying strengths, weaknesses, interests, and values.

Self-assessment tools often include psychological tests such as the Myers-Briggs Type Indicator (described earlier in the chapter), the Strong-Campbell Interest Inventory, and the Self-Directed Search. The Strong-Campbell inventory helps employees identify their occupational and job interests. The Self-Directed Search identifies employees' preferences for working in different kinds of environments—sales, counseling,

HR Oops!

Managers Must Look Outside for Development Support

HR departments are failing at developing leaders, according to Herminia Ibarra, a professor of leadership and organizational behavior at the international business school INSEAD. In her experience, organizations provide training to their managers mainly after promoting them to a new position—but in today's economy, those promotions are rare.

Ibarra wondered what managers were relying on to develop leadership skills, so she conducted a survey that asked, "What, if anything, has helped you to become a more effective leader today?" The top answers were an external leadership program (such as attending business school), support from friends and family, and peers or an external network. In other words, the top sources of support were all outside the company. The two lowest-ranked choices were formal training at the managers' company and, at the bottom, their company's human resource management.

Ibarra says the solution is basic: HR managers should be identifying the leadership skills that get results at the organization and then delivering opportunities for employees to develop those skills. Particularly important are stretch assignments, which provide meaningful experiences that prepare people for greater responsibility.

At the same time, managers do not have to wait for HRM to develop their careers for them. Managers who feel stuck in one position can take a look at whom they interact with—typically, the same job-related people, over and over. They can find reasons to contact people in other departments and at other levels of the organization. They can join outside groups, where they can learn what is happening in other organizations and industries. Building relationships in new areas is an effective way to expand one's career prospects.

Questions

1. How might it hurt an organization when HR managers wait to provide leadership education until after employees have been promoted?

2. Suppose you are an HR manager at a company with high turnover among middle managers (that is, many of them quit to work elsewhere). Write a brief argument telling the company's executives why a modest but well-planned investment in leadership development might help the company keep its best managers.

Sources: Herminia Ibarra, "How Companies Are Putting Managers in a Bind," *The Wall Street Journal*, April 27, 2014, http://online.wsj.com; Herminia Ibarra, "How to Break Through a Career Impasse," *Harvard Business Review*, October 10, 2013, http://blogs.hbr.org; Herminia Ibarra, "To Close the Gender Gap, Focus on Assignments," *Harvard Business Review*, May 22, 2012, http://blogs.hbr.org.

and so on. Tests may also help employees identify the relative values they place on work and leisure activities. Self-assessment tools can include exercises such as the one in Figure 8.4. This type of exercise helps an employee consider his or her current career status, future plans, and the fit between the career and the employee's current situation and resources. Some organizations provide counselors to help employees in the self-assessment process and to interpret the results of psychological tests. Completing the self-assessment can help employees identify a development need. Such a need can result from gaps between current skills or interests and the type of work or position the employee has or wants.

Self-assessments play an important role in career development of employees being developed for leadership roles at Tyson Foods, a major processor of chicken, beef, and pork. These employees begin the development process by reading a book called *The Organization Champion* and completing an assessment that measures their skills in being an organization champion. The assessment helps the employees identify their strengths and areas for improvement. Next, the employees participate in a two-day event that includes time to identify their perspectives on life, their skills, what inspires them, and the

Figure 8.4

Sample Self-Assessment Exercise

Step 1: Where am I?
Examine current position of life and career.
Think about your life from past and present to the future. Draw a time line to represent important events.

Step 2: Who am I?
Examine different roles.
Using 3" × 5" cards, write down one answer per card to the question "Who am I?"

Step 3: Where would I like to be, and what would I like to happen?
Begin setting goals.
Consider your life from present to future. Write an autobiography answering these questions:
• What do you want to have accomplished?
• What milestones do you want to achieve?
• What do you want to be remembered for?

Step 4: An ideal year in the future
Identify resources needed.
Consider a one-year period in the future. Answer these questions:
• If you had unlimited resources, what would you do?
• What would the ideal environment look like?
• Does the ideal environment match Step 3?

Step 5: An ideal job
Create current goal.
In the present, think about an ideal job for you with your available resources. Describe your role, resources, and type of training or education needed.

Step 6: Career by objective inventory
Summarize current situation.
• What gets you excited each day?
• What do you do well? What are you known for?
• What do you need to achieve your goals?
• What could interfere with reaching your goals?
• What should you do now to move toward reaching your goals?
• What is your long-term career objective?

Source: Based on J. E. McMahon and S. K. Merman, "Career Development," in *The ASTD Training and Development Handbook,* 4e, edited by R. L. Craig (New York: McGraw-Hill, 1996), pp. 679–697. Reproduced with permission.

unique contributions they make to the company. All of these efforts deliver information the Tyson employees can apply to setting goals for their career development.[46]

Feedback

Feedback

Information employers give employees about their skills and knowledge and where these assets fit into the organization's plans.

In the next step of career management, **feedback,** employees receive information about their skills and knowledge and where these assets fit into the organization's plans. The employee's responsibility is to identify what skills she or he could realistically develop in light of the opportunities available. The organization's responsibility is to communicate the performance evaluation and the opportunities available to the employee, given the organization's long-range plans. Opportunities might include promotions and transfers.

Usually the employer conducts the reality check as part of a performance appraisal or as the feedback stage of performance management. In well-developed career management systems, the manager may hold separate discussions for performance feedback and career development.

Texas electric utility Oncor makes feedback an important part of its career development. Besides conducting 360-degree reviews of employees in its leadership development program, it brings these employees together in groups to work on challenging projects. As they meet to discuss the projects and what they are learning, employees often find that the groups provide the most important source of feedback and motivation because the group members grow so familiar with one another's strengths, concerns, and goals.[47]

Goal Setting

Based on the information from the self-assessment and reality check, the employee sets short- and long-term career objectives. These goals usually involve one or more of the following categories:

- Desired positions, such as becoming sales manager within three years.
- Level of skill to apply—for example, to use one's budgeting skills to improve the unit's cash flow problems.
- Work setting—for example, to move to corporate marketing within two years.
- Skill acquisition, such as learning how to use the company's human resource information system.

As in these examples, the goals should be specific, and they should include a date by which the goal is to be achieved. It is the employee's responsibility to identify the goal and the method of determining her or his progress toward that goal.

Usually the employee discusses the goals with his or her manager. The organization's responsibilities are to ensure that the goal is specific, challenging, and attainable and to help the employee reach the goal. In the Patient Care and Clinical Informatics (PCCI) division of Philips Healthcare, employees take assessments and then engage in regular career discussions to establish goals for where they want to go in PCCI and how they will get there over the next one to five years. These personalized goals can involve lateral moves, enrichment of one's ability to contribute in a current position, or even an exploration of career possibilities, not simply advancement to the next job upward in the company hierarchy. Just six months after PCCI launched this career management program, employees reported feeling much more excited about working there.[48]

Action Planning and Follow-Up

During the final step, employees prepare an action plan for how they will achieve their short- and long-term career goals. The employee is responsible for identifying the steps and timetable to reach the goals. The employer should identify resources needed, including courses, work experiences, and relationships. The employee and the manager should meet in the future to discuss progress toward career goals.

Action plans may involve any one or a combination of the development methods discussed earlier in the chapter—training, assessment, job experiences, or the help of a mentor or coach. The approach used depends on the particular developmental needs and career objectives. For example, suppose the program manager in an information systems department uses feedback from performance appraisals to determine that he needs greater knowledge of project management software. The manager plans to increase that knowledge by reading articles (formal education), meeting with software vendors, and contacting the vendors' customers to ask them

Figure 8.5
Career Development Plan

Name:	**Title:** Product Manager	**Immediate Manager:**

Competencies
Please identify your three greatest strengths and areas for improvement.
Strengths
- Strategic thinking and execution (confidence, command skills, action orientation)
- Results orientation (competence, motivating others, perseverance)
- Spirit for winning (building team spirit, customer focus, respect colleagues)

Areas for Improvement
- Patience (tolerance of people or processes and sensitivity to pacing)
- Written communications (ability to write clearly and succinctly)
- Overly ambitious (too much focus on successful completion of projects rather than developing relationships with individuals involved in the projects)

Career Goals
Please describe your overall career goals.
- **Long-term:** Accept positions of increased responsibility to a level of general manager (or beyond). The areas of specific interest include, but are not limited to, product and brand management, technology and development, strategic planning, and marketing.
- **Short-term:** Continue to improve my skills in marketing and brand management while utilizing my skills in product management, strategic planning, and global relations.

Next Assignments
Identify potential next assignments (including timing) that would help you develop toward your career goals.
- Manager or director level in planning, development, product, or brand management. Timing estimated to be Spring 2016.

Training and Development Needs
List both training and development activities that will either help you develop in your current assignment or provide overall career development.
- Master's degree classes will allow me to practice and improve my written communications skills. The dynamics of my current position, teamwork, and reliance on other individuals allow me to practice patience and to focus on individual team members' needs along with the success of the projects.

Employee _____ **Date** _____
Immediate Manager _____ **Date** _____
Mentor _____ **Date** _____

about the software they have used (job experiences). The manager and his supervisor agree that six months will be the target date for achieving the higher level of knowledge through these activities.

The outcome of action planning often takes the form of a career development plan. Figure 8.5 is an example of a development plan for a product manager. Development plans usually include descriptions of strengths and weaknesses, career goals, and development activities for reaching each goal.

Development-Related Challenges

A well-designed system for employee development can help organizations face three widespread challenges: the glass ceiling, succession planning, and dysfunctional behavior by managers.

The Glass Ceiling

As we mentioned in Chapter 1, women and minorities are rare in the top level of U.S. corporations. Observers of this situation have noted that it looks as if an invisible barrier is keeping women and minorities from reaching the top jobs, a barrier that has come to be known as the **glass ceiling.** A recent examination of the boards of directors of the largest 100 companies based in the United States, Europe, and Asia found that 82% have at least two women on their board of directors, but in a separate analysis of the Fortune 500 (top U.S. companies), women held just 17% of the seats on the board. In other words, most companies have few, if any, women on their boards. Outside the United States, their representation is even lower.[49] For more evidence of the glass ceiling, see "Did You Know?"

The glass ceiling is likely caused by a lack of access to training programs, to appropriate developmental job experiences, and to developmental relationships such as mentoring.[50] With regard to developmental relationships, women and minorities often have trouble finding mentors. They may not participate in the organization's, profession's, or community's "old boys' network." Also, recent evidence finds differences in how women and men pursue advancement and in how executives perceive women's and men's qualifications and ambitions. Female managers tend to find more mentors, but primarily mentors who give advice; their male counterparts find, on average, mentors who are more senior and will sponsor them for key positions. Patterns of promotion suggest that companies are more willing to select men from outside the organization based on their potential, while women do better when they stay with the same company where they can demonstrate a track record of achievements. Consistent with this difference, women who actively promote their achievements tend to advance further in an organization, whereas broadcasting their achievements does not make much difference in their male colleagues' advancement.[51]

Organizations can use development systems to help break through the glass ceiling. Managers making developmental assignments need to carefully consider whether stereotypes are influencing the types of assignments men and women receive. A formal process for regularly identifying development needs and creating action plans can make these decisions more objective.

An organization that is actively trying to eliminate the glass ceiling is Coca-Cola Company, where the effort is part of a commitment to corporate sustainability. The company's chairman, Muhtar Kent, points out that at least two-thirds of the customers who buy the company's products are women. Coca-Cola can best serve these customers, Kent suggests, if it is demographically more like them. Under a program called 2020, Coca-Cola set goals for identifying and developing talented female employees. In the program's first three and a half years, the percentage of women in Coca-Cola's management rose from less than one-quarter of all managers to 40%. The company has a program aimed at developing managers' ability to foster inclusiveness, as well as a Women in Leadership program that selects high-potential female managers for accelerated development.[52]

Succession Planning

Organizations have always had to prepare for the retirement of their leaders, but the need is more intense than ever. The aging of the workforce means that a greater share

LO 8-8 Discuss how organizations are meeting the challenges of the "glass ceiling," succession planning, and dysfunctional managers.

Glass Ceiling
Circumstances resembling an invisible barrier that keep most women and minorities from attaining the top jobs in organizations.

Did You Know?

A Ceiling above a Ceiling

British consulting firm 20-first sees a second glass ceiling for women who have risen to an organization's board of directors. Among the directors, those with the greatest role in making decisions and defining strategy are the members of the executive committee. But especially outside the United States, female directors are much less likely than their male counterparts to serve on their board's executive committee.

Furthermore, of the women who do land a spot, the majority hold staff positions such as head of the legal or HR department, rather than running sales or operations—suggesting that companies are not actively developing women through stretch assignments in line positions.

Question

What do the data presented here suggest to you about how an employee development program could help an organization seeking greater diversity in its leadership?

Sources: Avivah Wittenberg-Cox, "Study: Female Executives Make Progress, but Mostly in Support Functions," *Harvard Business Review*, April 21, 2014, http://blogs.hbr.org; Martha C. White, "Women in Business Leadership: Up Against a Second Glass Ceiling," *NBC News*, April 21, 2014; 20-first, "20-first's 2014 Global Gender Balance Scorecard: Where the World's Top Companies Stand," March 2014, http://20-first.com.

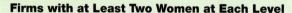

Firms with at Least Two Women at Each Level

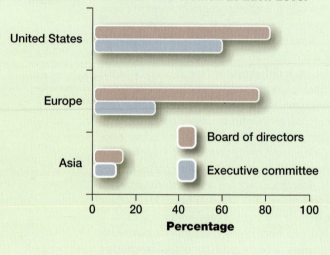

of employees are reaching retirement age. Many organizations are fueling the trend by downsizing through early-retirement programs. As positions at the top of organizations become vacant, many organizations have determined that their middle managers are fewer and often unprepared for top-level responsibility. This situation has raised awareness of the need for **succession planning**—the process of identifying and tracking high-potential employees who will be able to fill top management positions when they become vacant.

Succession planning offers several benefits.[53] It forces senior management to regularly and thoughtfully review the company's leadership talent. It ensures that top-level management talent is available. It provides a set of development experiences that managers must complete to be considered for top management positions, so the organization does not promote managers before they are ready. Succession planning systems also help attract and retain ambitious managerial employees by providing development opportunities.

Succession planning focuses on *high-potential employees*, that is, employees the organization believes can succeed in higher-level business positions such as general manager of a business unit, director of a function (such as marketing or finance), or chief

Succession Planning
The process of identifying and tracking high-potential employees who will be able to fill top management positions when they become vacant.

executive officer.[54] A typical approach to development of high-potential employees is to have them complete an individual development program including education, executive mentoring and coaching, and rotation through job assignments. Job assignments are based on the successful career paths of the managers whom the high-potential employees are preparing to replace. High-potential employees may also receive special assignments, such as making presentations and serving on committees and task forces.

Research shows that an effective program for developing high-potential employees has three stages[55]:

1. *Selection of high-potential employees*—Organizations may select outstanding performers and employees who have completed elite academic programs, such as earning a master's degree in business administration from a prestigious university. They may also use the results of psychological tests such as assessment centers.

2. *Developmental experiences*—As employees participate in developmental experiences, the organization identifies those who succeed in the experiences. The organization looks for employees who continue to show qualities associated with success in top jobs, such as communication skills, leadership talent, and willingness to make sacrifices for the organization. In today's high-performance business environment, these assessments should measure whether participants in the program are demonstrating an ability to lead and delivering results that contribute to the company's success. Employees who display these qualities continue to be considered high-potential employees.

3. *Active involvement with the CEO*—High-potential employees seen by top management as fitting into the organization's culture and having personality characteristics necessary for representing the company become actively involved with the chief executive officer. The CEO exposes these employees to the organization's key people and gives them a greater understanding of the organization's culture. The development of high-potential employees is a slow process. Reaching stage 3 may take 15 to 20 years.

Figure 8.6 breaks this process into eight steps. It begins with identifying the positions to be planned for and the employees to be included in the plan. Planning should also include establishing position requirements and deciding how to measure employees' potential

Figure 8.6
Process for Developing a Succession Plan

Sources: Based on B. Dowell, "Succession Planning," in *Implementing Organizational Interventions,* ed. J. Hedge and E. Pulakos (San Francisco: Jossey-Bass, 2002), pp. 78–109; R. Barnett and S. Davis, "Creating Greater Success in Succession Planning," *Advances in Developing Human Resources* 10 (2008): 721–39.

for being able to fill those requirements. The organization also needs to develop a process for reviewing the existing talent. The next step is to link succession planning with other human resource systems. Then the organization needs a way to provide employees with feedback about career paths available to them and how well they are progressing toward their goals. Finally, measuring the plan's effectiveness provides information for continuing or adjusting future succession plans.

A good example of succession planning is the effort at General Electric. GE insists that there be in place a plan identifying the top candidate to replace each executive in a key position, as well as two or three backup candidates in case something goes wrong with the plan for the top choice. During six-month reviews, GE's board of directors learns about these individuals, so that if someone quickly fills a vacancy, the board is already familiar with that person. For instance, when senior vice president Larry Johnston left GE to become chief executive of Albertsons, the company's board already knew who would replace him. GE was able to announce the new senior vice president at the same time it announced Johnston's departure—in fact, it could also announce other management changes as a series of promotions took place to fill each key vacancy that resulted.[56]

Dysfunctional Managers

A manager who is otherwise competent may engage in some behaviors that make him or her ineffective or even "toxic"—someone who stifles good ideas and drives away employees. These dysfunctional behaviors include insensitivity to others, inability to be a team player, arrogance, poor conflict-management skills, inability to meet business objectives, and inability to adapt to change.[57] For example, a manager who has strong technical knowledge but is abrasive and discourages employees from contributing their ideas is likely to have difficulty motivating employees and may alienate people inside and outside the organization.

When a manager is an otherwise valuable employee and is willing to improve, the organization may try to help him or her change the dysfunctional behavior. The usual ways to provide this type of development include assessment, training, and counseling. Development programs for managers with dysfunctional behavior may also include specialized programs such as one called Individual Coaching for Effectiveness (ICE). The ICE program includes diagnosis, coaching, and support activities tailored to each manager's needs.[58] Psychologists conduct the diagnosis, coach and counsel the manager, and develop action plans for implementing new skills on the job. Research suggests that managers who participate in programs like ICE improve their skills and are less likely to be terminated.[59] One possible conclusion is that organizations can benefit from offering development opportunities to valuable employees with performance problems, not just to star performers.

THINKING ETHICALLY

SHOULD MANAGERS FEEL OBLIGATED TO BE MENTORS?

If mentors play an important role in helping people develop their careers, should managers feel obligated to serve as mentors? It's a delicate question for female managers, given the evidence that women continue to lag behind men in moving through the talent pipeline. Some, hearing about the low rate of women who report ever having had a mentor, want to help correct the imbalance. Managers who have experienced or witnessed other forms of discrimination also might feel committed to mentoring as a way to even out the opportunities for talented workers.

One idea behind this kind of thinking is that the status quo in which some employees are at a disadvantage will never change unless people in charge behave differently. Change requires that someone in power step forward and make a point of helping the ones who have talent but aren't sure how to navigate an unfamiliar business culture. Managers who interpret the situation this way see themselves as the ones who must step forward, often by mentoring.

The question of whether to limit mentoring is tricky because time spent mentoring junior employees benefits the protégés and the employer but not necessarily the mentor. Some consultants say they have observed managers, especially women, taking on so many protégés that they neglect their own career development. These observers suggest that such managers need to think more strategically about which employees to mentor—for example, selecting protégés who excel, contribute to the company, and reflect well on the mentor.

Questions

1. Does committing significant time to mentoring employees necessarily mean that a manager cannot develop his or her own career? Why or why not?
2. Suppose you manage a mentoring program for your employer, and a well-liked manager tells you she receives so many requests to be a mentor that she isn't sure how to handle them fairly. How could you help keep the program fair and equitable?

Sources: Peggy Drexler, "Can Women Succeed without a Mentor?" *Forbes*, March 4, 2014, http://www.forbes.com; Joann S. Lublin, "When Women Mentor Too Much," *The Wall Street Journal*, October 11, 2013, http://online.wsj.com; Barbara Frankel, "Sheryl Sandberg's Message on Mentoring Is Wrong—and Dangerous," *DiversityInc*, March 25, 2013, http://www.diversityinc.com.

SUMMARY

LO8-1 Discuss how development is related to training and careers.

- Employee development is the combination of formal education, job experiences, relationships, and assessment of personality and abilities to help employees prepare for the future of their careers.
- Training is more focused on improving performance in the current job, but training programs may support employee development.
- In modern organizations, the concept of a career is fluid—a protean career that changes along with changes in a person's interests, abilities, and values and changes in the work environment. To plan and prepare for a protean career requires active career management, which includes planning for employee development.

LO8-2 Identify the methods organizations use for employee development.

- Organizations may use formal educational programs at the workplace or off-site, such as workshops, university courses and degree programs, company-sponsored training, or programs offered by independent institutions.
- An assessment process can help employees identify strengths and areas requiring further development. Assessment can help the organization identify employees with managerial potential or identify areas in which teams need to develop.
- Job experiences help employees develop by stretching their skills as they meet new challenges.

- Interpersonal relationships with a more experienced member of the organization—often in the role of mentor or coach—can help employees develop their understanding of the organization and its customers.

LO8-3 Describe how organizations use assessment of personality type, work behaviors, and job performance to plan employee development.

- Organizations collect information and provide feedback to employees about their behavior, communication style, and skills.
- The information may come from the employees, their peers, managers, and customers.
- Many organizations use performance appraisals as a source of assessment information. Appraisals may take the form of 360-degree feedback.
- Some organizations use psychological tests designed for this purpose, including the Myers-Briggs Type Indicator and the DiSC assessment.
- Assessment centers combine a variety of methods to provide assessment information.
- Managers must share the assessments, along with suggestions for improvement.

LO8-4 Explain how job experiences can be used for developing skills.

- Job experiences contribute to development through a combination of relationships, problems, demands, tasks, and other features of an employee's jobs.
- The assumption is that development is most likely to occur when the employee's skills and experiences

do not entirely match the skills required for the employee's current job, so employees must stretch to meet the demands of the new assignment.

- The impact varies according to whether the employee views the experience as a positive or negative source of stress.
- Job experiences that support employee development may include job enlargement, job rotations, transfers, promotions, downward moves, and temporary assignments with other organizations.

LO8-5 Summarize principles of successful mentoring programs.

- A mentor is an experienced, productive senior employee who helps develop a less-experienced employee.
- Although most mentoring relationships develop informally, organizations can link mentoring to development goals by establishing a formal mentoring program. A formal program provides a basis for ensuring that all eligible employees are included.
- Mentoring programs tend to be most successful when they are voluntary and participants understand the details of the program.
- The organization should reward managers for employee development, carefully select mentors based on interpersonal and technical skills, train them for the role, and evaluate whether the program has met its objectives.

LO8-6 Tell how managers and peers develop employees through coaching.

- A coach is a peer or manager who works with an employee to motivate the employee, help him or her develop skills, and provide reinforcement and feedback.
- Coaches should be prepared to take on one or more of three roles: working one-on-one with an employee, helping employees learn for themselves, and providing resources, such as mentors, courses, or job experiences.

LO8-7 Identify the steps in the process of career management.

- The process begins with data gathering. Employees use information to determine their career interests, values, aptitudes, and behavioral tendencies, looking for opportunities and areas needing improvement. Data-gathering tools often include psychological tests or exercises that ask about career status and plans.
- The organization then provides feedback by communicating information about the employee's skills and knowledge and how these fit into the organization's plan.
- The employee sets goals and discusses them with his or her manager, who ensures that the goals are specific, challenging, and attainable.
- Finally, the employee works with his or her manager to create an action plan and follow-up for development activities that will help the employee achieve the goals.

LO8-8 Discuss how organizations are meeting the challenges of the "glass ceiling," succession planning, and dysfunctional managers.

- The glass ceiling is a barrier that has been observed preventing women and other minorities from achieving top jobs in an organization. Development programs can ensure that these employees receive access to development resources, such as coaches, mentors, and developmental job assignments.
- Succession planning ensures that the organization prepares qualified employees to fill management jobs as managers retire. It focuses on applying employee development to high-potential employees. Effective succession planning includes methods for selecting these employees, providing them with developmental experiences, and getting the CEO actively involved with employees who display qualities associated with success as they participate in the developmental activities.
- For dysfunctional managers who have the potential to contribute to the organization, the organization may offer development targeted at correcting the areas of dysfunction. Typically, the process includes collecting information about the manager's personality, skills, and interests; providing feedback, training, and counseling; and ensuring that the manager can apply new, functional behaviors on the job.

KEY TERMS

employee development, 237
protean career, 238
assessment, 240
Myers-Briggs Type
   Indicator (MBTI), 241

DiSC, 242
assessment center, 243
leaderless group discussion, 243
job experiences, 245
transfer, 247

downward move, 248
promotion, 248
externship, 248
sabbatical, 249
mentor, 249

coach, 251
self-assessment, 252

feedback, 254
glass ceiling, 257

succession planning, 258

REVIEW AND DISCUSSION QUESTIONS

1. How does development differ from training? How does development support career management in modern organizations? *(LO 8-1)*

2. What are the four broad categories of development methods? Why might it be beneficial to combine all of these methods into a formal development program? *(LO 8-2)*

3. Recommend a development method for each of the following situations, and explain why you chose that method. *(LO 8-2)*
   a. An employee recently promoted to the job of plant supervisor is having difficulty motivating employees to meet quality standards.
   b. A sales manager annoys salespeople by dictating every detail of their work.
   c. An employee has excellent leadership skills but lacks knowledge of the financial side of business.
   d. An organization is planning to organize its production workers into teams for the first time.

4. A company that markets sophisticated business management software systems uses sales teams to help customers define needs and to create systems that meet those needs. The teams include programmers, salespeople who specialize in client industries, and software designers. Occasionally sales are lost as a result of conflict or communication problems among team members. The company wants to improve the effectiveness of these teams, and it wants to begin with assessment. How can the teams use 360-degree feedback and psychological tests to develop? *(LO 8-3)*

5. In an organization that wants to use work experiences as a method of employee development, what basic options are available? Which of these options would be most attractive to you as an employee? Why? *(LO 8-4)*

6. Many employees are unwilling to relocate because they like their current community and family members prefer not to move. Yet preparation for management requires that employees develop new skills, strengthen areas of weakness, and be exposed to new aspects of the organization's business. How can an organization change an employee's current job to develop management skills? *(LO 8-4)*

7. Many people feel that mentoring relationships should occur naturally, in situations where senior managers feel inclined to play that role. What are some advantages of setting up a formal mentoring program, rather than letting senior managers decide how and whom to help? *(LO 8-5)*

8. What are the three roles of a coach? How is a coach different from a mentor? What are some advantages of using someone outside the organization as a coach? Some disadvantages? *(LO 8-6)*

9. Why should organizations be interested in helping employees plan their careers? What benefits can companies gain? What are the risks? *(LO 8-7)*

10. What are the manager's roles in a career management system? Which role do you think is most difficult for the typical manager? Which is the easiest role? List reasons why managers might resist becoming involved in career management. *(LO 8-7)*

11. What is the glass ceiling? What are the possible consequences to an organization that has a glass ceiling? How can employee development break the glass ceiling? Can succession planning help? Explain. *(LO 8-8)*

12. Why might an organization benefit from giving employee development opportunities to a dysfunctional manager, rather than simply dismissing the manager? Do these reasons apply to nonmanagement employees as well? *(LO 8-8)*

TAKING RESPONSIBILITY

Taking Care of Employees Helps the Patent Office Serve the Public

When David Kappos became director of the U.S. Patent and Trademark Office (USPTO) several years ago, he wanted to strengthen the federal agency's focus on delivering high-quality service. The role of the USPTO's 11,000-plus employees is to review requests for patents and trademarks and to grant all requests that meet the legal requirements. As Kappos understood the agency, this means that the lawyers reviewing the requests will handle them accurately and efficiently, and all the other employees will provide the support necessary to help the lawyers serve the public accurately and efficiently. Furthermore, Kappos determined that to create this service-oriented culture, managers would have to gather input from stakeholders (especially applicants and employees), respond to the input, and develop systems that support employees in their efforts to provide great service.

One of the key systems is employee development. The agency created a leadership development implementation team to plan and administer this program. To ensure that the team would hear from its stakeholders, it includes executives and other decision makers from the agency's departments.

The USPTO offers development programs to all employees, not just managers. Based on the idea that leadership skills are relevant at all levels of the organization, the development team identified five audiences for leadership training: individual leader, aspiring leader, new supervisor, midlevel leader, and senior leader. Applying leadership competencies identified by the Office of Personnel Management, the team identified which skills and content are relevant to each level. In addition, each employee takes a "180-degree" assessment that combines self-assessments with feedback from supervisors or mentors, aimed at identifying existing skills and areas requiring development. Employees use information in the assessment report to identify the development activities that will help them build relevant skills.

Managers not only engage in developing their own careers but also assist in developing the agency's employees, so they receive additional developmental support. All senior managers undergo 360-degree feedback every two years and review the results with an executive coach. Also every two years, the company holds a one-week leadership forum at which all levels of management discuss leadership issues. Bringing together managers across levels helps them understand issues they might not encounter on the job.

Employees appreciate these efforts. In annual employee surveys conducted by the Partnership for Public Service, U.S. government employees rate their job satisfaction and commitment. In 2007, two years before Kappos became director, employee ratings placed the USPTO in 172nd place out of 222 agencies. Since then, the ratings have climbed until, in 2013, the USPTO reached first place—the best place to work in the federal government. Satisfaction with employee development was among the areas of work life that got the most credit.

Questions

1. Besides the approaches to employee development described in the case, how else would you recommend that the USPTO provide for employee development?
2. How could the USPTO strengthen the development program's contribution to achieving the goal of creating a service-oriented culture?

Sources: Jennifer Tokar and John Tindal, "Lessons from the Best," *T+D*, April 2014, pp. 55–58; Partnership for Public Service, "Profiles of Notable Movers," Best Places to Work 2014, http://bestplacestowork.org; David J. Kappos, "Building a Service-Oriented Agency: Lessons from the USPTO," McKinsey Center for Government, April 2014, http://www.mckinsey.com; Danette R. Campbell, "Patent Office Honored as Best Place to Work," *Public Manager*, Summer 2013, Business Insights: Global, http://bi.galegroup.com.

MANAGING TALENT

Procter & Gamble's Succession Management Slip-Up

Consumer products giant Procter & Gamble made headlines recently when CEO Robert McDonald retired and was replaced with former CEO A. G. Lafley. McDonald's retirement was not a surprise, because P&G had struggled to recover since the recent recession dampened sales of P&G's premium brands such as Tide detergent and Pampers diapers. What did surprise observers was that the company brought back a former CEO—implying it had not prepared anyone to move into the CEO's position.

Lafley previously served as CEO from 2000 to 2009, during which time he gained a reputation for promoting innovation and for leading a successful international expansion. He mentored McDonald, who was chief operating officer when Lafley retired. However, McDonald did not hold positions that gave him practice in setting strategy or leading organizational change; he focused on managing operations.

Expectations are that Lafley will stay for a few years and make grooming a replacement one of his main goals. This would be in keeping with Lafley's behavior during his previous tenure as CEO, when he directed the board to begin thinking about his successor just six months after he took the position.

Lafley's return raised questions about why P&G had no one ready to fill McDonald's shoes. Some observers pointed to the departures of several leading executives during McDonald's tenure. Still, at a struggling company, the board of directors (which is responsible for finding a replacement) would know it will need a replacement at the top in the near future.

This failure in succession planning was surprising to many because P&G has been known for its strong development program. Given its vast size and global scope, it offers many opportunities for management development through job experiences, and top executives usually are promoted to their jobs from within the company. P&G's learning team has a mission of developing an employee over 30 or 40 years through formal learning and varied job experiences. Each employee's career development aims at goals spelled out in a development contract agreed upon by the employee and his or her manager. P&G also has a sophisticated computer system for managing its succession planning.

Despite the departures of some key executives, some who remain may have potential to become the next CEO. Examples include Melanie Healey, group president of North America; Deb Henretta, group president of the global beauty care business unit; Martin Riant, group president of global baby care; and David Taylor, group president of global health and grooming. Other possible candidates are executives who left P&G to run other businesses, including Estee Lauder Companies and the private-equity firm Carlyle Group.

Questions

1. Although the board of directors is responsible for filling the CEO position, how could HR managers support the board with a succession management program?
2. Based on the information given, what developmental approaches were part of McDonald's career development? What approaches would you recommend for preparing P&G's next top executives?

Sources: Ladan Nikravan, "Learning Is the Business at Procter & Gamble," *Chief Learning Officer*, June 2014, pp. 30–31; Nadia Damouni, Olivia Oran, and Phil Wahba, "Exclusive: P&G Eyes Alumni Unit Heads as Candidates for CEO Job," *Reuters*, February 13, 2014, http://www.reuters.com; Boris Groysberg and Deborah Bell, "Who's Really Responsible for P&G's Succession Problems?" *Harvard Business Review*, June 3, 2013, http://blogs.hbr.org; Joann S. Lublin, Ellen Byron, and Emily Glazer, "P&G's Lafley Begins New Hunt," *The Wall Street Journal*, May 24, 2013, http://online.wsj.com; Lauren Coleman-Lochner and Carol Hymowitz, "P&G Says A. G. Lafley Rejoins as Chairman, CEO," *Bloomberg News*, May 24, 2013, http://www.bloomberg.com/news.

HR IN SMALL BUSINESS

Employee Sabbatical Benefits Others at Little Tokyo Service Center

The 100 full-time and 50 part-time employees of the Little Tokyo Service Center (LTSC) work to provide a range of social services targeting Asians and Pacific Islanders in Los Angeles County. The organization's focus is on the needs of people in financial difficulty, with physical disabilities, or struggling with language or cultural barriers. Services include counseling, transportation, translation, and consumer education. Emergency care is provided in several different Asian languages plus English and Spanish. LTSC also has sponsored the construction or renovation of community development projects including apartments and community facilities such as child care centers.

LTSC's executive director, Bill Watanabe, says he "really loves" his work, and no wonder, given the organization's importance to the community. Consequently, the thought of taking a sabbatical would not have occurred to him. But several years ago, Watanabe provided a professional reference to a colleague who had applied to the Durfee Foundation for a grant to fund a sabbatical. A staff member at the foundation suggested that Watanabe, too, might benefit from a sabbatical. His initial response was that he didn't need one. After all, he wasn't burning out. But the staff member explained that a sabbatical could help LTSC's people learn to operate more independently. When Watanabe mentioned this to the board of directors, they encouraged him to apply.

With that backing, Watanabe took a three-month sabbatical from LTSC. The first two months were devoted to travel: a tour of Israel and Egypt, a vacation in Tahiti, and a road trip with his brother-in-law. After that, Watanabe stayed put long enough to write an autobiography.

Watanabe found that stepping away for a few months freshened his perspective on LTSC. When he returned, he applied his vision and renewed energy to restructure the agency through a merger of its community services center and its community development corporation, and he accelerated progress on a community organizing project. He also launched more vigorous advocacy to build a community gymnasium in the Little Tokyo neighborhood of Los Angeles, drawing positive attention from politicians and funding sources.

While Watanabe felt personally restored during his time away, he believes the agency benefited, too. In particular, he discovered that his absence provided developmental opportunities for others at LTSC. The agency's deputy director served as interim executive director while Watanabe was away, and two employees reporting to the deputy director shouldered the deputy's responsibilities. One of them has since been promoted. Building on these experiences, the second tier of management at LTSC has taken more direct control of the agency's day-to-day activities, freeing Watanabe to concentrate on broader strategy. Their greater preparation also amounts to a kind of succession planning. According to LTSC's board chairman, "If Bill were to leave tomorrow, the organization would be in very good hands."

Questions

1. Based on the information given, how well did Little Tokyo Service Center follow the career management process described in Figure 8.3? Which elements of that system, if any, were missing?
2. Imagine that LTSC has called you in as a consultant before Watanabe is to start his sabbatical. The agency has asked you to help obtain the maximum developmental benefit from the sabbatical arrangement. How would you recommend that Watanabe,

the board of directors, and the second tier of management proceed?

3. Keeping in mind that an agency like LTSC would have limited funding and just a few senior managers, suggest two additional development activities that are likely to be most beneficial to the organization, and explain why you chose them.

Sources: Deborah S. Linnell and Tim Wolfred, *Creative Disruption: Sabbaticals for Capacity Building and Leadership Development in the Nonprofit Sector* (CompassPoint Nonprofit Services, 2009), p. 8; Little Tokyo Service Center, " About LTSC," corporate website, www.ltsc.org, accessed June 10, 2014.

NOTES

1. F. Kalman, "ESPN's Top Play: Learning," *Chief Learning Officer*, March 2013, pp. 22–25, 47; ESPN careers page, http://espncareers.com.

2. M. London, *Managing the Training Enterprise* (San Francisco: Jossey-Bass, 1989); D. Day, *Developing Leadership Talent* (Alexandria, VA: SHRM Foundation, 2007).

3. R. W. Pace, P. C. Smith, and G. E. Mills, *Human Resource Development* (Englewood Cliffs, NJ: Prentice Hall, 1991); W. Fitzgerald, "Training versus Development," *Training and Development Journal*, May 1992, pp. 81–84; R. A. Noe, S. L. Wilk, E. J. Mullen, and J. E. Wanek, "Employee Development: Issues in Construct Definition and Investigation of Antecedents," in *Improving Training Effectiveness in Work Organizations*, ed. J. K. Ford (Mahwah, NJ: Lawrence Erlbaum, 1997), pp. 153–89.

4. J. H. Greenhaus and G. A. Callanan, *Career Management*, 2nd ed. (Fort Worth, TX: Dryden Press, 1994); D. Hall, *Careers in and out of Organizations* (Thousand Oaks, CA: Sage, 2002).

5. M. B. Arthur, P. H. Claman, and R. J. DeFillippi, "Intelligent Enterprise, Intelligent Careers," *Academy of Management Executive* 9 (1995), pp. 7–20; M. Lazarova and S. Taylor, "Boundaryless Careers, Social Capital, and Knowledge Management: Implications for Organizational Performance," *Journal of Organizational Behavior* 30 (2009): 119–39; D. Feldman and T. Ng, "Careers: Mobility, Embeddedness, and Success," *Journal of Management* 33 (2007): 350–77.

6. R. Noe, *Employee Training and Development*, 6th ed. (New York: McGraw-Hill Irwin, 2013).

7. Pat Galagan, "90,000 Served: Hamburger University Turns 50," *T + D*, April 2011, pp. 46–51; Beth Kowitt, "Why McDonald's Wins in Any Economy," *Fortune*, September 5, 2011, EBSCOhost, http://web.ebscohost.com.

8. University of Virginia Darden School of Business, "MBA for Executives," http://www.darden.virginia.edu, accessed March 30, 2012.

9. Alicia Korney, "From Toys to Talent," *Chief Learning Officer*, September 2011, pp. 48–52.

10. A. Howard and D. W. Bray, *Managerial Lives in Transition: Advancing Age and Changing Times* (New York: Guilford, 1988); J. Bolt, *Executive Development* (New York: Harper Business, 1989); J. R. Hinrichs and G. P. Hollenbeck, "Leadership Development," in *Developing Human Resources* ed. K. N. Wexley (Washington, DC: BNA Books, 1991), pp. 5-221–5-237; Day, *Developing Leadership Talent*.

11. Adrienne Fox, "Organizational and Employee Development Special Report: Upon Further Assessment . . . ," *HR Magazine*, August 2013, http://www.shrm.org.

12. A. Thorne and H. Gough, *Portraits of Type* (Palo Alto, CA: Consulting Psychologists Press, 1993).

13. D. Druckman and R. A. Bjork, eds., *In the Mind's Eye: Enhancing Human Performance* (Washington, DC: National Academy Press, 1991); M. H. McCaulley, "The Myers-Briggs Type Indicator and Leadership," in *Measures of Leadership*, eds. K. E. Clark and M. B. Clark (West Orange, NJ: Leadership Library of America, 1990), pp. 381–418.

14. Inscape Publishing, "DiSC Profile," http://www.discprofile.com, accessed June 5, 2014; Fox, "Organizational and Employee Development Special Report."

15. G. C. Thornton III and W. C. Byham, *Assessment Centers and Managerial Performance* (New York: Academic Press, 1982); L. F. Schoenfeldt and J. A. Steger, "Identification and Development of Management Talent," in *Research in Personnel and Human Resource Management*, eds. K. N. Rowland and G. Ferris (Greenwich, CT: JAI Press, 1989), vol. 7, pp. 151–81; Fox, "Organizational and Employee Development Special Report."

16. Thornton and Byham, *Assessment Centers and Managerial Performance*.

17. P. G. W. Jansen and B. A. M. Stoop, "The Dynamics of Assessment Center Validity: Results of a Seven-Year Study," *Journal of Applied Psychology* 86 (2001), pp. 741–53; D. Chan, "Criterion and Construct Validation of an Assessment Centre," *Journal of Occupational and Organizational Psychology* 69 (1996), pp. 167–81.

18. R. G. Jones and M. D. Whitmore, "Evaluating Developmental Assessment Centers as Interventions," *Personnel Psychology* 48 (1995), pp. 377–88.

19. S. B. Silverman, "Individual Development through Performance Appraisal," in *Developing Human Resources*, pp. 5-120–5-151.

20. J. F. Brett and L. E. Atwater, "360-Degree Feedback: Accuracy, Reactions, and Perceptions of Usefulness," *Journal of Applied Psychology* 86 (2001), pp. 930–42.

21. Fox, "Organizational and Employee Development Special Report."

22. L. Atwater, P. Roush, and A. Fischthal, "The Influence of Up-ward Feedback on Self- and Follower Ratings of Leadership," *Personnel Psychology* 48 (1995), pp. 35–59; J. F. Hazucha, S. A. Hezlett, and R. J. Schneider, "The Impact of 360-Degree Feedback on Management Skill Development," *Human Resource Management* 32 (1993), pp. 325–51; J. W. Smither, M. London, N. Vasilopoulos, R. R. Reilly, R. E. Millsap, and N. Salvemini, "An Examination of the Effects of an Upward Feedback Program over Time," *Personnel Psychology* 48 (1995), pp. 1–34; J. Smither and A. Walker, "Are the Characteristics of Narrative Comments Related to Improvements in Multirater Feedback Ratings over Time?" *Journal of Applied Psychology* 89 (2004), pp. 575–81; J. Smither, M. London, and R. Reilly, "Does Performance Improve Following Multisource Feedback? A Theoretical Model, Meta-analysis, and Review of Empirical Findings," *Personnel Psychology* 58 (2005), pp. 33–66.

23. Center for Creative Leadership, "360-Degree Feedback: Best Practices to Ensure Impact," 2011, http://www.ccl.org, accessed March 30, 2012.

24. M. W. McCall Jr., *High Flyers* (Boston: Harvard Business School Press, 1998).

25. R. S. Snell, "Congenial Ways of Learning: So Near yet So Far," *Journal of Management Development* 9 (1990), pp. 17–23.

26. M. McCall, M. Lombardo, and A. Morrison, *Lessons of Experience* (Lexington, MA: Lexington Books, 1988); M. W. McCall, "Developing Executives through Work Experiences," *Human Resource Planning* 11 (1988), pp. 1–11; M. N. Ruderman, P. J. Ohlott, and C. D. McCauley, "Assessing Opportunities for Leadership Development," in *Measures of Leadership*, pp. 547–62; C. D. McCauley, L. J. Estman, and P. J. Ohlott, "Linking Management Selection and Development through Stretch Assignments," *Human Resource Management* 34 (1995), pp. 93–115.

27. C. D. McCauley, M. N. Ruderman, P. J. Ohlott, and J. E. Morrow, "Assessing the Developmental Components of Managerial Jobs," *Journal of Applied Psychology* 79 (1994), pp. 544–60.

28. Jill Jusko, "Engineering Bench Strength," *Industry Week*, August 2011, p. 18.

29. M. London, *Developing Managers* (San Francisco: Jossey-Bass, 1985); M. A. Camion, L. Cheraskin, and M. J. Stevens, "Career-Related Antecedents and Outcomes of Job Rotation," *Academy of Management Journal* 37 (1994), pp. 1518–42; London, *Managing the Training Enterprise*.

30. Margaret Fiester, "Job Rotation, Total Rewards, Measuring Value," *HR Magazine*, August 2008, Business & Company Resource Center, http://galenet.galegroup.com; "Energize and Enhance Employee Value with Job Rotation," *HR Focus*, January 2008, OCLC FirstSearch, http://newfirstsearch .oclc.org.

31. R. A. Noe, B. D. Steffy, and A. E. Barber, "An Investigation of the Factors Influencing Employees' Willingness to Accept Mobility Opportunities," *Personnel Psychology* 41 (1988), pp. 559–80; S. Gould and L. E. Penley, "A Study of the Correlates of Willingness to Relocate," *Academy of Management Journal* 28 (1984), pp. 472–78; J. Landau and T. H. Hammer, "Clerical Employees' Perceptions of Intraorganizational Career Opportunities," *Academy of Management Journal* 29 (1986), pp. 385–405; M. Brett and A. H. Reilly,

"On the Road Again: Predicting the Job Transfer Decision," *Journal of Applied Psychology* 73 (1988), pp. 614–20.

32. J. M. Brett, "Job Transfer and Well-Being," *Journal of Applied Psychology* 67 (1992), pp. 450–63; F. J. Minor, L. A. Slade, and R. A. Myers, "Career Transitions in Changing Times," in *Contemporary Career Development Issues*, eds. R. F. Morrison and J. Adams (Hillsdale, NJ: Lawrence Erlbaum, 1991), pp. 109–20; C. C. Pinder and K. G. Schroeder, "Time to Proficiency Following Job Transfers," *Academy of Management Journal* 30 (1987), pp. 336–53; Beverly Kaye, "Up Is Not the Only Way . . . Really!" *T + D*, September 2011, pp. 40–45.

33. Bureau of National Affairs, "Companies Encouraging Employees to Use Their Professional Skills," *HR Focus*, April 2013, pp. 5–7.

34. Adrienne Fox, "Make a 'Deal,'" *HR Magazine*, January 2012, Business & Company Resource Center, http://galenet.galegroup.com; "Wandering Librarian," *Library Journal*, March 15, 2012, EBSCOhost, http://web.ebscohost.com.

35. D. B. Turban and T. W. Dougherty, "Role of Protégé Personality in Receipt of Mentoring and Career Success," *Academy of Management Journal* 37 (1994), pp. 688–702; E. A. Fagenson, "Mentoring: Who Needs It? A Comparison of Protégés' and Nonprotégés' Needs for Power, Achievement, Affiliation, and Autonomy," *Journal of Vocational Behavior* 41 (1992), pp. 48–60.

36. A. H. Geiger, "Measures for Mentors," *Training and Development Journal*, February 1992, pp. 65–67; Lynnie Martin and Tyler Robinson, "Why You Should Get on Board the Mentor Ship," *Public Manager*, Winter 2011, pp. 42–45; "The Payoff," *California CPA*, October 2011, p. 12.

37. K. E. Kram, *Mentoring at Work: Developmental Relationships in Organizational Life* (Glenview, IL: Scott-Foresman, 1985); L. L. Phillips-Jones, "Establishing a Formalized Mentoring Program," *Training and Development Journal* 2 (1983), pp. 38–42; K. Kram, "Phases of the Mentoring Relationship," *Academy of Management Journal* 26 (1983), pp. 608–25; G. T. Chao, P. M. Walz, and P. D. Gardner, "Formal and Informal Mentorships: A Comparison of Mentoring Functions and Contrasts with Nonmentored Counterparts," *Personnel Psychology* 45 (1992), pp. 619–36; C. Wanberg, E. Welsh, and S. Hezlett, "Mentoring Research: A Review and Dynamic Process Model," in *Research in Personnel and Human Resources Management*, eds. J. Martocchio and G. Ferris (New York: Elsevier Science, 2003), pp. 39–124.

38. Michele Lent Hirsch, "Mentor Makeover," *Psychology Today*, July/August 2011, EBSCOhost, http://web.ebscohost.com.

39. L. Eby, M. Butts, A. Lockwood, and A. Simon, "Protégés' Negative Mentoring Experiences: Construct Development and Nomological Validation," *Personnel Psychology* 57 (2004), pp. 411–47; R. Emelo, "Conversations with Mentoring Leaders," *T + D*, June 2011, pp. 32–37; M. Weinstein, "Please Don't Go," *Training*, May/June 2011, pp. 38–34; "Training Top 125," *Training*, January/February 2011, pp. 54–93.

40. R. A. Noe, D. B. Greenberger, and S. Wang, "Mentoring: What We Know and Where We Might Go," in *Research in Personnel and Human Resources Management*, eds. G. Ferris and

J. Martocchio (New York: Elsevier Science, 2002), vol. 21, pp. 129–74; T. D. Allen, L. T. Eby, M. L. Poteet, E. Lentz, and L. Lima, "Career Benefits Associated with Mentoring for Protégés: A Meta-Analysis," *Journal of Applied Psychology* 89 (2004), pp. 127–36.

41. D. B. Peterson and M. D. Hicks, *Leader as Coach* (Minneapolis: Personnel Decisions, 1996).

42. Alex Vorro, "Coaching Counsel," *InsideCounsel*, February 2012, Business & Company Resource Center, http://galenet.galegroup.com.

43. J. Smither, M. London, R. Flautt, Y. Vargas, and L. Kucine, "Can Working with an Executive Coach Improve Multisource Ratings over Time? A Quasi-experimental Field Study," *Personnel Psychology* 56 (2003), pp. 23–44.

44. Vorro, "Coaching Counsel."

45. Terri Armstrong Welch, "A Renewed Focus on Leadership," *T+D*, November 2013, pp. 68–69.

46. M. Thompson, "What Makes Tyson's High-Potential Leadership Program Critical to Company Success?" *T + D*, April 2011, pp. 98–100.

47. Debbi Elmer and T. Michael Quinn, "A Culture of Development," *Transmission and Distribution World*, February 2013, EBSCOhost, http://web.b.ebscohost.com.

48. "Ladder Not Required," *T + D*, March 2012, p. 80.

49. Avivah Wittenberg-Cox, "Female Executives Make Progress, but Mostly in Support Functions," *Harvard Business Review*, April 21, 2014, http://blogs.hbr.org; Catalyst, "Quick Take: Women on Boards," Catalyst Knowledge Center, March 3, 2014, http://www.catalyst.org.

50. P. J. Ohlott, M. N. Ruderman, and C. D. McCauley, "Gender Differences in Managers' Developmental Job Experiences," *Academy of Management Journal* 37 (1994), pp. 46–67; L. A. Mainiero, "Getting Anointed for Advancement: The Case of Executive Women," *Academy of Management Executive* 8 (1994), pp. 53–67; P. Tharenov, S. Latimer, and D. Conroy, "How Do You Make It to the Top? An Examination of Influences on Women's and Men's Managerial Advancements," *Academy of Management Journal* 37 (1994), pp. 899–931.

51. R. A. Noe, "Women and Mentoring: A Review and Research Agenda," *Academy of Management Review* 13 (1988), pp. 65–78; B. R. Ragins and J. L. Cotton, "Easier Said than Done: Gender Differences in Perceived Barriers to Gaining a Mentor," *Academy of Management Journal* 34 (1991), pp. 939–51; Joann

S. Lublin, "Female Directors: Why So Few?" *The Wall Street Journal*, December 27, 2011, http://online.wsj.com; Christine Silva and Nancy Carter, "New Research Busts Myths about the Gender Gap," *Harvard Business Review*, October 6, 2011, http://blogs.hbr.org; Catalyst, "Catalyst Study Explodes Myths about Why Women's Careers Lag Men's," news release, October 13, 2011, http://www.catalyst.org; "Too Many Suits," *The Economist*, November 26, 2011, EBSCOhost, http://web.ebscohost.com.

52. Josh Dzieza, "Coke CEO: Promoting Women Is Good Business," *The Daily Beast*, March 9, 2012, http://www.thedailybeast.com; Coca-Cola Company, *As Inclusive as Our Brands*, 2010 U.S. Diversity Stewardship Report, accessed at http://www.thecoca-colacompany.com; Coca-Cola Enterprises Ltd., "Corporate Responsibility Review, 2010/11," http://www.cokecorporateresponsibility.co.uk, accessed March 30, 2012.

53. W. J. Rothwell, *Effective Succession Planning*, 2nd ed. (New York: AMACOM, 2001).

54. B. E. Dowell, "Succession Planning," in *Implementing Organizational Interventions*, eds. J. Hedge and E. D. Pulakos (San Francisco: Jossey-Bass, 2002), pp. 78–109.

55. C. B. Derr, C. Jones, and E. L. Toomey, "Managing High-Potential Employees: Current Practices in Thirty-Three U.S. Corporations," *Human Resource Management* 27 (1988), pp. 273–90; K. M. Nowack, "The Secrets of Succession," *Training and Development* 48 (1994), pp. 49–54; W. J. Rothwell, *Effective Succession Planning*, 4th ed. (New York: AMACOM, 2010).

56. Robert J. Grossman, "Rough Road to Succession," *HR Magazine*, June 2011, pp. 47–51.

57. M. W. McCall Jr. and M. M. Lombardo, "Off the Track: Why and How Successful Executives Get Derailed," *Technical Report*, no. 21 (Greensboro, NC: Center for Creative Leadership, 1983); E. V. Veslo and J. B. Leslie, "Why Executives Derail: Perspectives across Time and Cultures," *Academy of Management Executive* 9 (1995), pp. 62–72.

58. L. W. Hellervik, J. F. Hazucha, and R. J. Schneider, "Behavior Change: Models, Methods, and a Review of Evidence," in *Handbook of Industrial and Organizational Psychology*, 2nd ed., eds. M. D. Dunnette and L. M. Hough (Palo Alto, CA: Consulting Psychologists Press, 1992), vol. 3, pp. 823–99.

59. D. B. Peterson, "Measuring and Evaluating Change in Executive and Managerial Development," paper presented at the annual conference of the Society for Industrial and Organizational Psychology, Miami, 1990.

Assessing and Improving Performance

PART THREE

9

Creating and Maintaining High-Performance Organizations

What Do I Need to Know?

After reading this chapter, you should be able to:

LO 9-1   Define high-performance work systems, and identify the elements of such a system.

LO 9-2   Summarize the outcomes of a high-performance work system.

LO 9-3   Describe the conditions that create a high-performance work system.

LO 9-4   Explain how human resource management can contribute to high performance.

LO 9-5   Discuss the role of HRM technology in high-performance work systems.

LO 9-6   Summarize ways to measure the effectiveness of human resource management.

Introduction

Stories of factory closings and offshoring are so common that people can be forgiven for believing that manufacturing in the United States is doomed. And it was surely a tense time for the employees of General Cable's Jackson, Tennessee, plant a few years ago when the company undertook a study to determine whether it would be feasible to keep the facility open. General Cable, one of the world's largest makers of wire and cable products, operates factories in 26 countries and has a vision of being the most highly regarded and successful company in its industry. If the company's managers did not like the performance they saw in Jackson, they could certainly move production somewhere else.

Instead, management decided to keep the Jackson plant open, but it would have to improve its quality, safety, and efficiency—with no excuses about the severe recession into which the world economy had just plunged. The Jackson facility's managers shut down operations for a day and called all the employees together. They announced a program called All In. Everyone who wanted to stay had to commit to being flexible and learning new skills. Together, they would determine how to exceed expectations for safety and quality. Work was rearranged into production cells, with employees working as teams to make a complete product. Team members were put in charge of their cell's safety, quality, and productivity performance.

The company provided training to equip the employees for their new responsibilities. These changes have driven a 129% increase in productivity, as well as 54% growth in first-pass yield, a measure of production quality. Four years into the new program, General Cable named the Jackson plant its best facility in North America.[1]

The example of General Cable's Jackson facility is a story of a company improving its performance. Measures of business performance include long-term profits, quality, and customer satisfaction. When the Jackson plant improves its safety and productivity, its costs go down, so General Cable is more profitable. Improving the quality of the products made in Jackson contributes to the company's reputation and encourages stronger sales. But performance does not just happen at companies and production facilities. Performance at the company level depends on the performance of each department, each production cell (team), and each employee. Human resource management can contribute to high performance at each of these levels—creating work systems associated with high performance, managing the performance of individual employees (discussed in the next chapter), and maintaining a high-performing workforce through decisions to separate and retain employees (discussed in Chapter 11).

This chapter begins with the basic goal for performance: the creation of *high-performance work systems*. The chapter defines these systems and describes their elements and outcomes. We explain how human resource management can contribute to high performance. Finally, we introduce ways to measure the effectiveness of human resource management.

High-Performance Work Systems

The challenge facing managers today is how to make their organizations into **high-performance work systems,** with the right combination of people, technology, and organizational structure to make full use of resources and opportunities in achieving their organizations' goals. To function as a high-performance work system, each of these elements must fit well with the others in a smoothly functioning whole. Many manufacturers use the latest in processes including flexible manufacturing technology, total quality management, and just-in-time inventory control (meaning parts and supplies are automatically restocked as needed), but of course these processes do not work on their own; they must be run by qualified people. Organizations need to determine what kinds of people fit their needs, and then locate, train, and motivate those special people.[2] According to research, organizations that introduce integrated high-performance work practices usually experience increases in productivity and long-term financial performance.[3]

Creating a high-performance work system contrasts with traditional management practices. In the past, decisions about technology, organizational structure, and human resources were treated as if they were unrelated. An organization might acquire a new information system, restructure jobs, or add an office in another country without considering the impact on its people. More recently, managers have realized that success depends on how well all the elements work together. Consider how Massachusetts General Hospital addressed the information technology (IT) changes that came when the state of Massachusetts introduced health care reform. The hospital had to introduce electronic health records, requiring IT investments at the same time it was improving the organization's overall efficiency. But instead of assuming that efficiency requires layoffs, the hospital brought its IT staff together and invited them to work in teams developing ideas for how to redesign their work to be more efficient and

LO 9-1 Define high-performance work systems, and identify the elements of such a system.

High-Performance Work System
The right combination of people, technology, and organizational structure that makes full use of the organization's resources and opportunities in achieving its goals.

deliver higher-quality service. Physicians spoke to the group about how their work was important to the hospital's mission. Inspired by the mission and the chance to have a say, the teams developed ideas for managing information more efficiently and with a focus on patients' well-being. Those ideas could be carried out within the budget while avoiding layoffs. They also laid the groundwork for an information system that has continued to save the organization money as it has grown in subsequent years.[4]

Elements of a High-Performance Work System

As shown in Figure 9.1, in a high-performance work system, the elements that must work together include organizational structure, task design, people (the selection, training, and development of employees), reward systems, and information systems, and human resource management plays an important role in establishing all these.

Organizational structure is the way the organization groups its people into useful divisions, departments, and reporting relationships. The organization's top management makes most decisions about structure, for instance, how many employees report to each supervisor and whether employees are grouped according to the functions they carry out or the customers they serve. Such decisions affect how well employees coordinate their activities and respond to change. In a high-performance work system, organizational structure promotes cooperation, learning, and continuous improvement.

Task design determines how the details of the organization's necessary activities will be grouped, whether into jobs or team responsibilities. In a high-performance work system, task design makes jobs efficient while encouraging high quality. In Chapter 4, we discussed how to carry out this HRM function through job analysis and job design.

The right *people* are a key element of high-performance work systems. HRM has a significant role in providing people who are well suited and well prepared for their jobs. Human resource personnel help the organization recruit and select people with the needed qualifications. Training, development, and career management ensure that these people are able to perform their current and future jobs with the organization.

Figure 9.1

Elements of a
High-Performance
Work System

Reward systems contribute to high performance by encouraging people to strive for objectives that support the organization's overall goals. Reward systems include the performance measures by which employees are judged, the methods of measuring performance, and the incentive pay and other rewards linked to success. Human resource management plays an important role in developing and administering reward systems, as we will explore in Chapters 12–14.

The final element of high-performance work systems is the organization's *information systems.* Managers make decisions about the types of information to gather and the sources of information. They also must decide who in the organization should have access to the information and how they will make the information available. Modern information systems, including the Internet, have enabled organizations to share information widely.

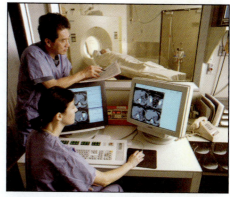

In a high-performance work system, all the elements—people, technology, and organizational structure—work together for success.

HR departments take advantage of this technology to give employees access to information about benefits, training opportunities, job openings, and more, as we will describe later in this chapter.

Outcomes of a High-Performance Work System

Consider the practices of steel minimills in the United States. Some of these mills have strategies based on keeping their costs below competitors' costs; low costs let them operate at a profit while winning customers with low prices. Other steel minimills focus on "differentiation," meaning they set themselves apart in some way other than low price—for example, by offering higher quality or unusual product lines. Research has found that the minimills with cost-related goals tend to have highly centralized structures, so managers can focus on controlling through a tight line of command. These organizations have low employee participation in decisions, relatively low wages and benefits, and pay highly contingent on performance.[5] At minimills that focus on differentiation, structures are more complex and decentralized, so authority is more spread out. These minimills encourage employee participation and have higher wages and more generous benefits. They are high-performance work systems. In general, these differentiator mills enjoy higher productivity, lower scrap rates, and lower employee turnover than the mills that focus on low costs.

Outcomes of a high-performance work system thus include higher productivity and efficiency. These outcomes contribute to higher profits. A high-performance work system may have other outcomes, including high product quality, great customer satisfaction, and low employee turnover. Some of these outcomes meet intermediate goals that lead to higher profits (see Figure 9.2). For example, high quality contributes to customer satisfaction, and customer satisfaction contributes to growth of the business. Likewise, improving productivity lets the organization do more with less, which satisfies price-conscious customers and may help the organization win over customers from its competitors. Other ways to lower cost and improve quality are to reduce absenteeism and turnover, providing the organization with a steady supply of experienced workers. In the previous example of minimills, some employers keep turnover and scrap rates low. Meeting those goals helps the minimills improve productivity, which helps them earn more profits.

In a high-performance work system, the outcomes of each employee and work group contribute to the system's overall high performance. The organization's individuals and

LO 9-2 Summarize the outcomes of a high-performance work system.

Figure 9.2
Outcomes of a High-Performance Work System

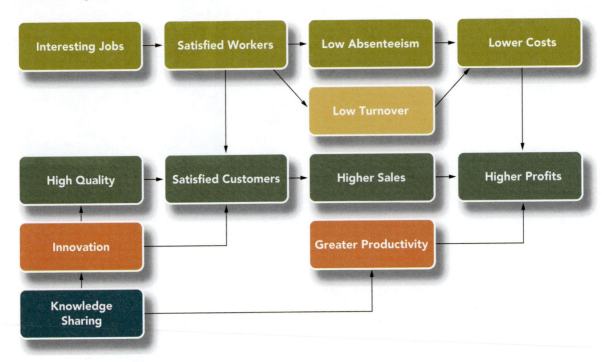

groups work efficiently, provide high-quality goods and services, and so on, and in this way, they contribute to meeting the organization's goals. When the organization adds or changes goals, people are flexible and make changes as needed to meet the new goals.

LO 9-3 Describe the conditions that create a high-performance work system.

Conditions That Contribute to High Performance

Certain conditions underlie the formation of a high-performance work system[6]:

- Teams perform work.
- Employees participate in selection.
- Employees receive formal performance feedback and are actively involved in the performance improvement process.
- Ongoing training is emphasized and rewarded.
- Employees' rewards and compensation relate to the company's financial performance.
- Equipment and work processes are structured, and technology is used to encourage maximum flexibility and interaction among employees.
- Employees participate in planning changes in equipment, layout, and work methods.
- Work design allows employees to use a variety of skills.
- Employees understand how their jobs contribute to the finished product or service.
- Ethical behavior is encouraged.

Practices involving rewards, employee empowerment, and jobs with variety contribute to high performance by giving employees skills, incentives, knowledge, autonomy—and satisfaction, another condition associated with high performance. Ethical behavior is a necessary condition of high performance because it contributes to good long-term relationships with employees, customers, and the public.

Teamwork and Empowerment

As we discussed in Chapter 2, today's organizations empower employees. They expect employees to make more decisions about how they perform their jobs. One of the most popular ways to empower employees is to design work so that it is performed by teams. On a work team, employees bring together various skills and experiences to produce goods or provide services. The organization may

It's important for companies to capture and share the knowledge of workers who have had years to learn their specialty.

charge the team with making decisions traditionally made by managers, such as hiring team members and planning work schedules. Teamwork and empowerment contribute to high performance when they improve job satisfaction and give the organization fuller use of employees' ideas and expertise.

At General Electric's Greenville Airfoils facility in Piedmont, South Carolina, production workers are cross-trained to work on teams. The production teams are involved in the employee selection process, interviewing job candidates and observing them as they participate in games where they work as a team to build a helicopter from blocks. In this way, they choose team members who work together effectively. In addition, the teams are empowered to design their own work processes. Teams have been so effective in improving efficiency that GE lets the teams carry out essentially the same processes in different ways, if that is how they design the work.[7]

For empowerment to succeed, managers must serve in linking and coordinating roles[8] and provide the team with the resources it needs to carry out its work. The manager should help the team and its members interact with employees from other departments or teams and should make sure communication flows in both directions—the manager keeps the team updated on important issues and ensures that the team shares information and resources with others who need them.

Knowledge Sharing

For more than a decade, managers have been interested in creating a **learning organization,** that is, an organization in which the culture values and supports lifelong learning by enabling all employees to continually acquire and share knowledge. The people in a learning organization have resources for training, and they are encouraged to share their knowledge with colleagues. Managers take an active role in identifying training needs and encouraging the sharing of ideas.[9] An organization's information systems, discussed later in this chapter, have an important role in making this learning activity possible. Information systems capture knowledge and make it available even after individual employees who provided the knowledge have left the organization. Ultimately, people are the essential ingredients in a learning organization. They must be committed to learning and willing to share what they have learned.

A learning organization has several key features[10]:

- It engages in **continuous learning,** each employee's and each group's ongoing efforts to gather information and apply the information to their decisions. In many organizations, the process of continuous learning is aimed at improving quality. To engage in continuous learning, employees must understand the entire work system

Learning Organization
An organization that supports lifelong learning by enabling all employees to acquire and share knowledge.

Continuous Learning
Each employee's and each group's ongoing efforts to gather information and apply the information to their decisions in a learning organization.

When Social-Media Tools Support Knowledge Sharing

Given that we use social media to swap status updates, broadcast our ideas, and post content, it seems obvious that social-media sites would be a tool for knowledge sharing. However, some social-media experts have questioned that assumption. They point out some differences between what people do on social media and how organizations need employees to share knowledge. Their insights suggest ways that companies can improve knowledge sharing that occurs via social media.

Perhaps the biggest distinction is that much of the activity on social media involves individuals sharing their own thoughts or ideas with other individuals, whereas knowledge in organizations often is the product or need of groups. Thus, for example, effective knowledge sharing would not be a company vice president writing a blog about customer service. It might be teams of customer service representatives in different geographic areas discussing how they handle angry customers. As they trade ideas, they develop a broader body of knowledge.

Another distinction involves the kinds of content people tend to post.

Typically, people use social media to post their thoughts or links to resources they find interesting. They are pushing content to the people in their networks. However, people tend to gain valuable knowledge when they post questions that pull in ideas from the people in their network. This suggests that organizations can make social media more useful for knowledge sharing if they train and encourage users to approach social media as a resource for soliciting ideas. The sites will be even more useful if employees can search them to look up relevant content.

Ideally, knowledge sharing delivers a complete body of objective, accurate information. However, the knowledge available is only as complete as the people who choose to participate by posting it. Experience shows us that some people in a network will post unverified information or even nonsense. Thus, if organizations want employees to gather information through social media, they need to make the knowledge more complete by treating use of those tools as one of its expectations for employees. Rewards for participation also can help. To protect accuracy,

they should look for sites with well-informed moderators and should appoint moderators for their own sites.

Questions

1. Which sounds more useful for a business: a site where salespeople write stories about their daily experiences or one where salespeople ask for advice on handling challenges? Why?
2. Suppose your company is considering a social-media site as a way for technicians to share tips for repairing equipment. Suggest at least two ways to keep the ideas useful and safe.

Sources: Knoco corporate website, "Knowledge Management Behaviours and Culture," *Knowledge Management Reference,* http://www.knoco.com, accessed June 12, 2014; Nick Milton, "'Social Media Will Destroy the Value in KM'—Discuss," *Knoco Stories,* September 23, 2013, http://www.nickmilton.com; Mark P. McDonald, "Social Media versus Knowledge Management," Gartner, May 9, 2013, http://blogs.gartner.com; Lauren Trees, "Social Media's Role in Knowledge Management," *APQC Blog* (American Productivity and Quality Center), March 11, 2013, http://www.apqc.org.

they participate in, the relationships among jobs, their work units, and the organization as a whole. Employees who continuously learn about their work system are adding to their ability to improve performance.

- Knowledge is *shared.* Therefore, to create a learning organization, one challenge is to shift the focus of training away from merely teaching skills and toward a broader focus on generating and sharing knowledge.[11] In this view, training is an investment in the organization's human resources; it increases employees' value to the organization. Also, training content should be related to the organization's goals. Human resource departments can support the creation of a learning organization by planning training programs that meet these criteria, and they can help create both face-to-face and electronic systems for employee collaboration to create, capture, and share knowledge. Increasingly, this includes giving employees access to social-media tools for knowledge sharing, as described in "HRM Social."

- *Critical, systematic thinking* is widespread. This occurs when organizations encourage employees to see relationships among ideas and to test assumptions and observe the results of their actions. Reward systems can be set up to encourage employees and teams to think in new ways.
- The organization has a *learning culture*—a culture in which learning is rewarded, promoted, and supported by managers and organizational objectives. This culture may be reflected in performance management systems and pay structures that reward employees for gathering and sharing more knowledge. A learning culture creates the conditions in which managers encourage *flexibility* and *experimentation*. The organization should encourage employees to take risks and innovate, which means it cannot be quick to punish ideas that do not work out as intended.
- *Employees are valued.* The organization recognizes that employees are the source of its knowledge. It therefore focuses on ensuring the development and well-being of each employee.

Continuous learning and knowledge sharing can support an environment of employee empowerment. For example, some organizations are giving employees access to software that monitors their productivity on the assumption that if they know data about their performance, they can use the data to improve their own productivity. For example, a program called RescueTime measures how long computer users spend on each website and application, as well as their time away from the computer; TallyZoo lets users enter data—say, time spent on activities and amount of work completed—and create interactive graphs for measuring progress and spotting trends and other patterns. One employee who used tools such as these discovered that he was most productive when he switched tasks periodically, so he set up the software to remind him every 20 minutes to do something different. A programmer who assumed that chatting online was making him less productive tested that assumption and found that time chatting was associated with writing *more* lines of code. Armed with that information, the programmer gave a higher priority to networking with co-workers and customers. Notice in these examples that the workers had latitude to discover how they work best and to control how they applied what they learned.[12]

Job Satisfaction and Employee Engagement

A condition underpinning any high-performance organization is that employees be fully engaged with their work. **Employee engagement** is the degree to which employees are fully involved in their work and the strength of their commitment to their job and company. Being fully engaged tends to require that employees experience their jobs as fulfilling or allowing them to fulfill important values. Research supports the idea that employees' job satisfaction and job performance are related.[13] Higher performance at the individual level should contribute to higher performance for the organization as a whole. Consultants at Gallup have found that the organizations with the most engaged employees have significantly greater customer satisfaction, productivity, and profitability.[14] Aon Hewitt, another major consulting firm, has measured an association between employee engagement and revenue growth. Companies studied by Aon Hewitt cut spending on talent during the 2009 recession and saw engagement drop. As companies began reinvesting in employees, those that saw the biggest surge in employee engagement also reported the strongest growth in revenues.[15] Organizations that want to beat the competition with highly engaged employees have plenty of room to compete; the "Did You Know?" box shows that the majority of U.S. workers are not engaged.

Employee Engagement
The degree to which employees are fully involved in their work and the strength of their job and company commitment.

Three in Ten U.S. Workers Describe Themselves as Engaged

A recent survey by Gallup found that in the United States, 30% of employees are engaged—defined to mean involved in, enthusiastic about, and committed to their work and making a positive contribution to their organization. Another 52% are not engaged, and 18% are actively disengaged, meaning unhappy and unproductive. However, the U.S. workers were more likely than their counterparts in more than 90 other countries to be engaged; the only exceptions were Costa Rica (33% engaged) and Panama (37%).

Question

Suppose you are the HR manager for a chain of restaurants, and you want to propose that your company develop a highly engaged workforce. How could you use this chart to promote your idea to the company's business managers?

Sources: Gallup, "State of the American Workplace," 2013, http://www.gallup.com, accessed June 16, 2014; Steve Crabtree, "Worldwide, 13% of Employees Are Engaged at Work," Gallup, http://www.gallup.com, accessed June 16, 2014; Victor Lipman, "Surprising, Disturbing Facts from the Mother of All Employee Engagement Surveys," *Forbes*, September 23, 2013, http://www.forbes.com.

U.S. Employee Engagement

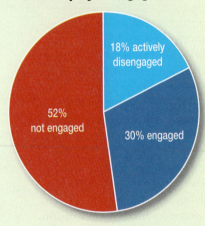

18% actively disengaged

52% not engaged

30% engaged

As we will explore further in Chapter 11, organizations can promote job satisfaction and employee engagement in several ways. They include making jobs more interesting, setting clear and challenging goals, and providing valued rewards that are linked to performance in a performance management system that employees consider fair. Globally, Aon Hewitt has found that the practices that do most to promote employee engagement are opportunities for career progress, recognition for accomplishments, and brand alignment. **Brand alignment** is the process of ensuring that HR policies, practices, and programs support or are congruent with an organization's overall culture or brand, including its products and services. One way to ensure HR policies align with a company's strategic vision is to educate employees about the company's "brand" and their role in bringing that brand to life as part of everyday work activities. Some companies discuss brand alignment as part of employee orientation programs while others develop in-depth training programs about the company's brand and how each employee is an important contributor to the company's overall success. In North America, employers have the most impact on brand alignment by providing career opportunities, using effective performance management systems, and maintaining a positive reputation.[16]

Brand Alignment
The process of ensuring that HR policies, practices, and programs support or are congruent with an organization's overall culture (or brand), products, and services.

Some organizations are moving beyond concern with mere job satisfaction and are trying to foster employees' *passion* for their work. Passionate people are fully engaged with something so that it becomes part of their sense of who they are. Feeling this way about one's work has been called *occupational intimacy*.[17] People experience occupational intimacy when they love their work, when they and their co-workers care about one another, and when they find their work meaningful. Human resource managers have a significant role in creating these conditions. For example, they can select people who care about their work and customers, provide methods for sharing knowledge, design work to make jobs interesting, and establish policies and programs that show concern for employees' needs. Such efforts may become increasingly important as the business world increasingly uses employee empowerment, teamwork, and knowledge sharing to build flexible organizations.[18]

Ethics

In the long run, a high-performance organization meets high ethical standards. Ethics, defined in Chapter 1, establishes fundamental principles for behavior, such as honesty and fairness. Organizations and their employees must meet these standards if they are to maintain positive long-term relationships with their customers and their community.

Ethical behavior is most likely to result from values held by the organization's leaders combined with systems that promote ethical behavior. At Arthur J. Gallagher & Company, an insurance brokerage and risk management firm, a vice president of corporate ethics and sustainability reports directly to the firm's CEO to ensure that ethical conduct is a priority. That vice president, Tom Tropp, travels to the firm's more than 100 offices to discuss its values and listen to employees tell about issues they face. Employees might not expect at first that the company really means what it says, but after Tropp takes employees' concerns back to headquarters and the employees see top management respond, they recognize that the concern for ethics is real. Often, the person in charge of ethics is a lawyer, but Tropp's training is in ethics and philosophy, which helps him think about ethical matters in a deeper way than mere compliance with the law.[19]

A number of organizational systems can promote ethical behavior.[20] These include a written code of ethics that the organization distributes to employees and expects them to use in decision making. This type of guidance can be especially effective if developed with input from employees about situations they encounter. However, standards alone are not enough—the organization should reinforce ethical behavior. For example, performance measures should include ethical standards, and misdeeds should receive swift discipline. The organization should provide channels employees can use to ask questions about ethical behavior or to seek help if they are expected to do something they believe is wrong. Organizations also can provide training in ethical decision making, including training for supervisors in how to handle employees' concerns about ethical matters.

As these examples suggest, ethical behavior is a human resource management concern. The systems that promote ethical behavior include such HRM functions as training, performance management, and discipline policies. A reputation for high ethical standards can also help a company attract workers—and customers—who share those high standards. CA Technologies, which develops management software, includes standards for maintaining an ethical culture among its criteria for managers to receive performance-based pay. The company also provides training to help managers guide their employees in how to handle situations ethically. A chief ethics officer in CA Technologies' legal department meets with managers and focus groups of employees to ensure they understand what the ethical standards are and how the company's legal and ethical resources can help them navigate difficult decisions.[21]

LO 9-4 Explain how human resource management can contribute to high performance.

HRM's Contribution to High Performance

Management of human resources plays a critical role in determining companies' success in meeting the challenges of a rapidly changing, highly competitive environment.[22] The HR practices introduced in Chapter 1 are investments that directly affect employees' motivation and ability to provide products and services that are valued by customers. Table 9.1 lists examples of HRM practices that contribute to high performance.

Research suggests that it is more effective to improve HRM practices as a whole than to focus on one or two isolated practices, such as the organization's pay structure or selection system.[23] Also, to have the intended influence on performance, the HRM practices must fit well with one another and the organization as a whole.[24]

HRM Practices

Let's take a closer look at how the HRM practices can contribute to high performance. Some of these are practices we have introduced already; others will be the subject of later chapters.

Job design can enable the organization to benefit from teamwork and employee empowerment, two of the work conditions associated with high performance. Job design aimed at empowerment includes access to resources such as information technology. The Lowe's chain of home improvement stores wanted to empower its salespeople with more information they need to close sales. So it equipped the salespeople with iPhones that have apps for price scanning, locating items in the store, checking inventory, and looking up competitors' prices. Eventually, the phones also will be able to scan customers' credit cards to complete sales transactions.[25] Lowe's hopes this much access to information will enable its salespeople to initiate conversations with shoppers and walk them through the entire decision process to the closing of a sale.

Recruitment and selection aim at obtaining employees who are enthusiastic about and able to contribute to teamwork, empowerment, and knowledge sharing. Qualities such as creativity and ability to cooperate as part of a team may play a large role in selection decisions. High-performance organizations need selection methods that identify more than technical skills like ability to perform accounting and engineering tasks.

Table 9.1

HRM Practices That Can Help Organizations Achieve High Performance

- HRM practices match organization's goals.
- Individuals and groups share knowledge.
- Work is performed by teams.
- Organization encourages continuous learning.
- Work design permits flexibility in where and when tasks are performed.
- Selection system is job related and legal.
- Performance management system measures customer satisfaction and quality.
- Organization monitors employees' satisfaction.
- Discipline system is progressive.
- Pay systems reward skills and accomplishments.
- Skills and values of a diverse workforce are valued and used.
- Technology reduces time and costs of tasks while preserving quality.

HR Oops!

Few Companies Are Prepared for Future Talent Needs

Compared with organizations that lag behind them, high-performance organizations prioritize succession planning and leadership development, according to the Institute for Corporate Productivity (i4cp). A survey by i4cp ranked companies in terms of scores based on their market share, revenue growth, profitability, and customer satisfaction. The survey found that the top-ranked companies outperformed the low performers most dramatically when it came to preparing for their future talent needs.

However, behind that information is shocking news: less than one-third of respondents say their company is prepared for the future. Even among the top companies, only 27% say they have employees prepared for openings in the executive ranks, and only 18% are ready to fill management positions at lower levels. About one-third (34%) say their organization develops leaders effectively.

If these are the best companies, imagine the room for improvement at the low performers. And imagine the competitive advantage a skilled HR manager could deliver at an organization committed to improving its talent management. For example, i4cp has identified two activities strongly associated with high performance but rarely used: (1) identifying future leaders based on their influence rather than their job title, and (2) taking a strategic approach to workforce planning, tailoring development programs to the competencies forecast to be needed in the future.

Questions

1. What elements of a high-performance work system (see Figure 9.1) would succession planning and employee development contribute to?

2. What outcomes of a high-performance work system (see Figure 9.2) would succession planning and employee development contribute to?

Sources: Institute for Corporate Productivity, "The Top 10 Critical Human Capital Issues: Enabling Sustained Growth through Talent Transparency," http://www.i4cp.com; Claudine Kapel, "Employers Grappling with Lack of Bench Strength," *Canadian HR Reporter*, March 25, 2014, http://www.hrreporter.com; Kevin Martin, "i4cp/AMA Research: Employers Lack Bench Strength to Sustain High Performance," i4cp blog, February 11, 2014, http://www.i4cp.com.

Employers may use group interviews, open-ended questions, and psychological tests to find employees who innovate, share ideas, and take initiative.

When organizations base hiring decisions on qualities like decision-making and teamwork skills, *training* may be required to teach employees the specific skills they need to perform the duties of their job. Extensive training and development also are part of a learning organization, described earlier in this chapter. And when organizations delegate many decisions to work teams, the members of those teams likely will benefit from participating in team development activities that prepare them for their roles as team members. In addition, high-performance organizations are developing their talent to move into positions with greater responsibility—something that the "HR Oops!" box suggests is happening at very few organizations.

Performance management, introduced in Chapter 1 and explored in Chapter 10, ensures that employees' work contributes to achieving the organization's goals. In a high-performance organization, this requires making sure that employees know the organization's goals and what they must do to contribute to goal achievement. A performance management system that meets those requirements applies the process of employee performance, diagrammed in Figure 9.3. Individuals bring a set of skills and abilities to the job, and by applying a set of behaviors to the skills and abilities, they achieve results. The organization's goals should influence each step of that process. The situation also has an influence on every step. For example, an

Figure 9.3

Employee Performance
as a Process

organization's culture might influence how hard individuals try to please customers, and economic conditions might influence how much a salesperson sells, no matter how hard she tries.

This model suggests some guidelines for performance management. First, each aspect of performance management should be related to the organization's goals. Business goals should influence the kinds of employees selected and their training, the requirements of each job, and the measures used for evaluating results. Generally, this means the organization identifies what each department must do to achieve the desired results, then defines how individual employees should contribute to their department's goals. More specifically, the following guidelines describe how to make the performance management system support organizational goals[26]:

- *Define and measure performance in precise terms*—Focus on outcomes that can be defined in terms of how frequently certain behaviors occur. Include criteria that describe ways employees can add value to a product or service (such as through quantity, quality, or timeliness). Include behaviors that go beyond the minimum required to perform a job (such as helping co-workers).
- *Link performance measures to meeting customer needs*—"Customers" may be the organization's external customers, or they may be internal customers (employees receiving services from a co-worker). Service goals for internal customers should be related to satisfying external customers.
- *Measure and correct for the effect of situational constraints*—Monitor economic conditions, the organization's culture, and other influences on performance. Measures of employees' performance should take these influences into account.

Compensation supports high-performance organizations when it is linked in part to performance measures. Chapter 13 will describe methods for doing this. An example is Intel, where part of employees' pay (a bonus) is tied to the achievement of corporate objectives. The percentage of pay that comes as the bonus is greater for employees who hold higher-level positions at Intel, because they have more control over meeting the targets.[27] Compensation also can be tied to performance-related conditions such as successful teamwork or—for a manager—job satisfaction among employees in the manager's department. Furthermore, organizations can increase empowerment and job satisfaction by including employees in decisions about compensation and communicating the basis for pay decisions.[28] Some organizations share financial information with employees or have them participate in setting group goals used as the basis for paying bonuses.

HRM Technology

LO 9-5 Discuss the role of HRM technology in high-performance work systems.

Human resource departments can improve their own and their organization's performance by appropriately using new technology. New technology usually involves *automation and collaboration*—that is, using equipment and information processing to perform activities that had been performed by people and facilitating electronic communication between people. Over the last few decades, automation has improved HRM efficiency by reducing the number of people needed to perform routine tasks. Using automation can free HRM experts to concentrate on ways to determine how human resource management can help the organization meet its goals so technology also can make this function more valuable.[29] For example, information technology provides ways to build and improve systems for knowledge generation and sharing, as part of a learning organization. Among the applications are databases or networking sites where employees can store and share their knowledge, online directories of employee skills and experiences, and online libraries of learning resources, such as technical manuals and employees' reports from seminars and training programs.

HRM Applications

As computers become ever more powerful, new technologies continue to be introduced. In fact, so many HRM applications are developed for use on personal computers that publications serving the profession (such as *HR Magazine* and *Workforce Management*) devote annual issues to reviewing this software. Some of the technologies that have been widely adopted are transaction processing, decision support systems, and expert systems.[30]

Transaction processing refers to computations and calculations involved in reviewing and documenting HRM decisions and practices. It includes documenting decisions and actions associated with employee relocation, training expenses, and enrollments in courses and benefit plans. Transaction processing also includes the activities required to meet government reporting requirements, such as filling out EEO-1 reports, on which employers report information about employees' race and gender by job category. Computers enable companies to perform these tasks more efficiently. Employers can fill out computerized forms and store HRM information in databases (data stored electronically in user-specified categories), so that it is easier to find, sort, and report.

Transaction Processing Computations and calculations involved in reviewing and documenting HRM decisions and practices.

Decision support systems are computer software systems designed to help managers solve problems. They usually include a "what if?" feature that managers can use to enter different assumptions or data and see how the likely outcomes will change. By applying internal data or research results, this type of system can help managers make decisions for human resource planning. The manager can, for example, try out different assumptions about turnover rates to see how those assumptions affect the number of new employees needed. Or the manager can test a range of assumptions about the availability of a certain skill in the labor market, looking at the impact of the assumptions on the success of different recruiting plans. Possible applications for a decision support system include forecasting (discussed in Chapter 5) and succession planning (discussed in Chapter 8).

Decision Support Systems Computer software systems designed to help managers solve problems by showing how results vary when the manager alters assumptions or data.

Expert systems can help with complicated business decisions such as scheduling the optimal number of employees for slow and busy work periods.

Expert Systems

Computer systems that support decision making by incorporating the decision rules used by people who are considered to have expertise in a certain area.

Expert systems are computer systems that incorporate the decision rules used by people who are considered to have expertise in a certain area. The systems help users make decisions by recommending actions based on the decision rules and the information provided by the users. An expert system is designed to recommend the same actions that a human expert would in a similar situation. For example, an expert system could guide an interviewer during the selection process. Some organizations use expert systems to help employees decide how to allocate their money for benefits (when the company offers a set of choices) and help managers schedule the labor needed to complete projects. Expert systems can deliver both high quality and lower costs. By using the decision processes of experts, an expert system helps many people to arrive at decisions that reflect the expert's knowledge. An expert system helps avoid the errors that can result from fatigue and decision-making biases, such as biases in appraising employee performance. An expert system can increase efficiency by enabling fewer or less-skilled employees to do work that otherwise would require many highly skilled employees.

In modern HR departments, transaction processing, decision support systems, and expert systems often are part of a human resource information system. Also, these technologies may be linked to employees through a network such as an intranet. Information systems and networks have been evolving rapidly; the following descriptions provide a basic introduction.

Human Resource Information Systems

A standard feature of a modern HRIS is the use of *relational databases*, which store data in separate files that can be linked by common elements. These common elements are fields identifying the type of data. Commonly used fields for an HR database include name, Social Security number, job status (full- or part-time), hiring date, position, title, rate of pay, citizenship status, job history, job location, mailing address, birth date, and emergency contacts. A relational database lets a user sort the data by any of the fields. For example, depending on how the database is set up, the user might be able to look up tables listing employees by location, rates of pay for various jobs, or employees who have completed certain training courses. This system is far more sophisticated than the old-fashioned method of filing employee data by name, with one file per employee.

The ability to locate and combine many categories of data has a multitude of uses in human resource management. Databases have been developed to track employee benefit costs, training courses, and compensation. The system can meet the needs of line managers as well as the HR department. On an oil rig, for example, management might look up data listing employee names along with safety equipment issued and appropriate skill certification. HR managers at headquarters might look up data on the same employees to gather information about wage rates or training programs needed. Another popular use of an HRIS is applicant tracking, or maintaining and retrieving records of job applicants. This is much faster and easier than trying to sort through stacks of résumés. With relational databases, HR staff can retrieve information about specific applicants or obtain lists of applicants with specific skills, career goals, work history, and employment background. Such information is useful for HR planning, recruitment, succession planning, and career development. Taking the process a step further, the system could store information related to hiring and terminations. By analyzing such data, the HR department could measure the long-term success of its recruiting and selection processes.

One of the most creative developments in HRIS technology is the **HR dashboard,** a display of a series of HR-related indicators, or measures, showing human resource goals and objectives and the progress toward meeting them. Managers with access to the HRIS can look at the HR dashboard for an easy-to-scan review of HR performance. For example, at Cisco Systems, employee development is a priority, so its HR dashboard includes a measure that tracks how many employees move and why.[31] By looking for divisions in which many employees make many lateral and upward moves, Cisco can identify divisions that are actively developing new talent.

HR Dashboard
A display of a series of HR measures, showing human resource goals and objectives and progress toward meeting them.

Human Resource Management Online: E-HRM

During the last decade or so, organizations have seen the advantages of sharing information in computer networks. At the same time, the widespread adoption of the Internet has linked people around the globe. As we discussed in Chapter 2, more and more organizations are engaging in e-HRM, providing HR-related information over the Internet. Because much human resource information is confidential, organizations may do this with an intranet, which uses Internet technology but allows access only to authorized users (such as the organization's employees). For HR professionals, Internet access also offers a way to research new developments, post job openings, trade ideas with colleagues in other organizations, and obtain government documents. In this way, e-HRM combines company-specific information on a secure intranet with links to the resources on the broader Internet. The "Best Practices" box tells how global charity Plan International is realizing benefits such as these.

As Internet use has increasingly taken the form of social-media applications, e-HRM has moved in this direction as well. Generally speaking, social media bring networks of people together to collaborate on projects, solve problems, or socialize. Social-media applications for human resource management include YouTube access to instructional videos, Facebook-style networking sites where employees can share project updates and ideas for improvement, web pages where employees can praise peers' accomplishments and deliver rewards, and crowdsourcing tools for performance appraisals. In terms of job design, social media can promote teamwork by providing an easy means of collaboration, and for recruiting over great distances social media allow virtual job fairs and/or selection interviews. As the use of social media continues to expand, creative minds will devise many other applications that forward-thinking HR professionals can introduce as ways to get employees more fully engaged with the organization and one another.

A benefit of e-HRM is that employees can help themselves to the information they need when they need it, instead of contacting an HR staff person. For example, employees can go online to enroll in or select benefits, submit insurance claims, or fill out employee satisfaction surveys. This can be more convenient for the employees, as well as more economical for the HR department. Adding another kind of convenience, some companies are offering access to online coaching. Employees can look up answers to common problems in databases, post questions for colleagues to

Best Practices

How e-HRM Helps Plan International Respond to Crises with Agility

As a nonprofit aimed to promote development worldwide, Plan International has some tough challenges in talent management. The organization's more than 10,000 employees work throughout the world. Not only are they spread out, but much activity takes place in 50 developing nations of Africa, Asia, and the Americas. Work on projects to promote child welfare and bring these communities better education, water, sanitation, and health may receive funding for a few years, and then the organization needs to send employees to a different project for which donors have provided funds. Also, Plan International's employees help rebuild communities after disasters. From an HRM standpoint, that means sudden, unexpected staffing needs under the worst conditions. In one case, employees were engaged in a disaster recovery and needed a French-speaking accountant. The organization frantically e-mailed its offices around the world, looking for that particular skill set.

To meet these HRM challenges more efficiently, Plan International purchased e-HRM software from a company called SuccessFactors.

The software unites applications for recruiting, hiring, training, compensating, evaluating, and promoting employees. Because data storage and processing are handled remotely via cloud computing, with information available over the Internet, employees in any location with Internet access can use the system. For example, an employee can look up organizational goals, set individual performance goals that align, and keep performance records where they are easy to retrieve. The system also provides a searchable database of job candidates, so the organization can recruit from the database as new needs arise.

One situation where e-HRM proved its value to Plan International was the devastation caused by Typhoon Haiyan, which recently struck the Philippines and destroyed the homes of 800,000 people. The agency needed to quickly locate the employees with the needed combination of language skills and experience in meeting particular kinds of needs, such as education and child protection. By searching its SuccessFactors HR system, Plan International located employees

not only by the skills they originally brought when hired, but also taking into account their learning and development during their time with the organization.

Questions

1. Why might e-HRM be especially valuable when an organization's employees are spread out around the world, rather than in one location?
2. Give an example of how e-HRM improves the efficiency of human resource management for Plan International.

Sources: SAP, "Projects and Solutions: HR Powers Global Growth," *SAP Investor*, Q1 2014, http://www.sap-investor.com; Derek Klobucher, "HR to the Rescue with a Cloud-Based Solution for Speedy Disaster Relief," *SAP Business Trends* (blog), March 19, 2014, http://scn.sap.com; Paul Solman, "Cloud-Based Systems Enable Performance Management," *Financial Times*, November 6, 2013, http://www.ft.com; SuccessFactors, "SuccessFactors Solutions Help Plan International Change More Lives," customer case study, 2013, http://www.successfactors.com.

answer, or contact a professional online. Thanks to the versatility and efficiency of this kind of coaching, employers can offer it to employees at all levels, not just executives or high-potential managers targeted for development.[32]

Most administrative and information-gathering activities in human resource management can be part of e-HRM. For example, online recruiting has become a significant part of the total recruiting effort, as candidates submit résumés online. Employers go online to retrieve suitable résumés from job search sites or retrieve information from forms they post at their own websites. For selection decisions, the organization may have candidates use one of the online testing services available; these services conduct the tests, process the results, and submit reports to employers. Companies can automate aspects of job design, such as schedules, delivery routes, and production layouts. Online appraisal or talent management systems provide data that can help managers spot high performers to reward or types of skills where additional training is a priority. After Comcast installed a computerized talent management system, supervisors caught up with a backlog of performance appraisals, and management became able to find the best employees to groom for promotions.[33] Many types of training can be conducted online, as we discussed in Chapter 7. Herman Miller, which makes office furniture, set up a performance support system that lets its salespeople use their mobile devices to learn about new product features whether they are in the office or out with clients.[34] Online surveys of employee satisfaction can be quick and easy to fill out. Besides providing a way to administer the survey, an intranet is an effective vehicle for communicating the results of the survey and management's planned response.

Many companies use social-media applications as part of their e-HRM strategies to communicate, coach, and train employees.

Not only does e-HRM provide efficient ways to carry out human resource functions, it also poses new challenges to employees and new issues for HR managers to address. The Internet's ability to link people anytime, anywhere has accelerated such trends as globalization, the importance of knowledge sharing, the need for flexibility, and cloud computing. Cloud computing is another recent advance in technology that has several implications for HR practices. **Cloud computing** involves using a network of remote servers hosted on the Internet to store, manage, and process data. These services are offered by data centers around the world (and not within an organization's offices) and are collectively called "the cloud." These services offer the ability to access information that's delivered on demand from any device, anywhere, at any time. Global giant Siemens has a massive cloud computing system for its more than 400,000 employees across 190 countries. In an effort to become more efficient, the company standardized its global recruitment and personnel development processes into a single system via the cloud.[35]

Cloud Computing
The practice of using a network of remote servers hosted on the Internet to store, manage, and process data.

These trends change the work environment for employees. For example, employees in the Internet age are expected to be highly committed but flexible, able to move from job to job. Employees also may be connected to the organization 24/7. In the car, on vacation, in airports, and even in the bathroom, employees with handheld computers can be interrupted by work demands. Organizations depend on their human resource departments to help prepare employees for this changing work world through such activities as training, career development, performance management, and benefits packages that meet the need for flexibility and help employees manage stress.

Effectiveness of Human Resource Management

In recent years, human resource management at some organizations has responded to the quest for total quality management by taking a customer-oriented approach. For an organization's human resource division, "customers" are the organization as a whole and its other divisions. They are customers of HRM because they depend on HRM to provide a variety of services that result in a supply of talented, motivated employees. Taking this customer-oriented approach, human resource management defines its customer groups, customer needs, and the activities required to meet those needs, as shown in Table 9.2. These definitions give an organization a basis for defining goals and measures of success.

LO 9-6 Summarize ways to measure the effectiveness of human resource management.

Table 9.2

Customer-Oriented Perspective of Human Resource Management

WHO ARE OUR CUSTOMERS?	WHAT DO OUR CUSTOMERS NEED?	HOW DO WE MEET CUSTOMER NEEDS?
Line managers	Committed employees	Qualified staffing
Strategic planners	Competent employees	Performance management
Employees		Rewards
		Training and development

Depending on the situation, a number of techniques are available for measuring HRM's effectiveness in meeting its customers' needs. These techniques include reviewing a set of key indicators, measuring the outcomes of specific HRM activity, and measuring the economic value of HRM programs.

Human Resource Management Audits

HRM Audit
A formal review of the outcomes of HRM functions, based on identifying key HRM functions and measures of business performance.

An **HRM audit** is a formal review of the outcomes of HRM functions. To conduct the audit, the HR department identifies key functions and the key measures of business performance and customer satisfaction that would indicate each function is succeeding. Table 9.3 lists examples of these measures for a variety of HRM functions: staffing, compensation, benefits, training, appraisal and development, and overall effectiveness. The audit may also look at any other measure associated with successful management of human resources—for instance, compliance with equal employment opportunity laws, succession planning, maintaining a safe workplace, and positive labor relations. An HRM audit using customer satisfaction measures supports the customer-oriented approach to human resource management.

After identifying performance measures for the HRM audit, the staff carries out the audit by gathering information. The information for the key business indicators is usually available in the organization's documents. Sometimes the HR department has to create new documents for gathering specific types of data. The usual way to measure customer satisfaction is to conduct surveys. Employee attitude surveys, which we will discuss further in Chapter 11, provide information about the satisfaction of these internal customers. Many organizations conduct surveys of top line executives to get a better view of how HRM practices affect the organization's business success. To benefit from the HR profession's best practices, companies also may invite external auditing teams to audit specific HR functions. In New Hampshire, Claremont Savings Bank hired an outside specialist to conduct a comprehensive audit of its HRM practices, focusing on payroll. The auditor showed the bank's HR department how to ensure that its payroll contractor was submitting all the required taxes, and it verified that the correct amounts were being deducted for the benefits each employee had signed up for. Based on this positive experience, Claremont now conducts an external audit every three years, as well as yearly internal audits.[36]

Analyzing the Effect of HRM Programs

HR Analytics
Type of assessment of HRM effectiveness that involves determining the impact of, or the financial cost and benefits of, a program or practice.

Another way to measure HRM effectiveness is the use of **HR analytics.** This process involves measuring a program's success in terms of whether it achieved its objectives and whether it delivered value in an economic sense. For example, if the organization sets up a training program, it should set up goals for that program, such as the training's effects on learning, behavior, and performance improvement (results). The

Table 9.3

Key Measures of Success for an HRM Audit

BUSINESS INDICATORS	CUSTOMER SATISFACTION MEASURES
Staffing	
Average days taken to fill open requisitions	Anticipation of personnel needs
Ratio of acceptances to offers made	Timeliness of referring qualified workers to line supervisors
Ratio of minority/women applicants to representation in local labor market	Treatment of applicants
Per capita requirement costs	Skill in handling terminations
Average years of experience/education of hires per job family	Adaptability to changing labor market conditions
Compensation	
Per capita (average) merit increases	Fairness of existing job evaluation system in assigning grades and salaries
Ratio of recommendations for reclassification to number of employees	Competitiveness in local labor market
Percentage of overtime hours to straight time	Relationship between pay and performance
Ratio of average salary offers to average salary in community	Employee satisfaction with pay
Benefits	
Average unemployment compensation payment (UCP)	Promptness in handling claims
Average workers' compensation payment (WCP)	Fairness and consistency in the application of benefit policies
Benefit cost per payroll dollar	Communication of benefits to employees
Percentage of sick leave to total pay	Assistance provided to line managers in reducing potential for unnecessary claims
Training	
Percentage of employees participating in training programs per job family	Extent to which training programs meet the needs of employees and the company
Percentage of employees receiving tuition refunds	Communication to employees about available training opportunities
Training dollars per employee	Quality of introduction/orientation programs
Employee appraisal and development	
Distribution of performance appraisal ratings	Assistance in identifying management potential
Appropriate psychometric properties of appraisal forms	Organizational development activities provided by HRM department
Overall effectiveness	
Ratio of personnel staff to employee population	Accuracy and clarity of information provided to managers and employees
Turnover rate	Competence and expertise of staff
Absenteeism rate	Working relationship between organizations and HRM department
Ratio of per capita revenues to per capita cost	
Net income per employee	

Source: From Chapter 1.5, "Evaluating Human Resource Effectiveness," by Anne S. Tsui and Luis R. Gomez-Mejia from *Human Resource Management: Evolving Roles & Responsibilities,* edited by Lee Dyer, 1988. Copyright 1988, Society for Human Resource Management, Alexandria, VA. Used with permission. All rights reserved.

analysis would then measure whether the training program achieved the preset goals. To learn more about how to make the most of data analytics using today's powerful computers, see the "HR How To" box.

Wincanton, a trucking and logistics company in the United Kingdom, determined that it needed a more highly skilled workforce to continue winning the competition for customers. For warehouse workers, the company set three levels of learning objectives (two mandatory levels plus an optional level for employees seeking career

HR How To

Making the Most of HR Analytics

HR managers can be a valuable partner in decision making if they know how to use analytical skills and data. Here are some guidelines to follow:

- Hire HR employees with statistical knowledge and analytical skills. This may require recruiting employees who previously specialized in other functions. At the same time, current HR employees lacking skill in this area should consider additional training.

- Talk to business leaders about the talent challenges they face. Identify problems that you could help answer if you had more information, and determine the kinds of data that could give you that missing information. These are situations where data analytics can help.

- Review the assumptions the HR department currently makes. Test those assumptions to see if you can improve your decisions. For example, a financial services company tried to recruit and select the best salespeople by identifying graduates with the best grades from the most prestigious schools. To check its assumption that these were the most effective salespeople, it compared the sales performance of its units with the educational backgrounds of each unit's salespeople. It learned that other factors were more important than educational background. Then, by shifting its hiring decisions, the company added millions to its sales revenue.

- Make a practice of thinking about the business impact of HR activities. Frame them in terms of questions. For example, what is the impact on engineering costs and quality if you hire temporary (contract) workers instead of permanent employees? What is the relationship between managers' participation in leadership training and the performance and employee turnover of the managers' departments? Investigate such questions, implement improvements that the results suggest, and then measure whether the changes are improving the organization's performance. These are steps toward creating a high-performance organization.

Questions

1. How might the use of data analytics improve the quality of decisions that had been based on intuition and experience?

2. What might be the consequence of gathering data without first developing relevant questions to answer with the numbers?

Sources: John Boudreau, "What Is the Future of HR?" *Workforce*, March 28, 2014, http://www.workforce.com; Cliff Stevenson, "Four Ways High-Performing Organizations Are Adapting to the Age of Data," Institute for Corporate Productivity, December 4, 2013, http://www.i4cp.com; Institute for Corporate Productivity, "The Age of Big Data: A Progress Report for Organizations and HR," 2013 preview edition, http://www.i4cp.com; David C. Forman, "Stuck in Neutral," *T+D*, November 2013, pp. 46–50.

---

development). It also let each warehouse set additional performance measures for serving its own set of customers. Two years after launching the training program, Wincanton measured its success in terms of 2,500 warehouse workers trained, a decline in time lost to accidents (down 7.5% in the first year and another 10.3% in the second year), and a 22% increase in the overall score for employee engagement.[37]

The analysis can take an economic approach that measures the dollar value of the program's costs and benefits. Successful programs should deliver value that is greater than the programs' costs. Costs include employees' compensation as well as the costs to administer HRM programs such as training, employee development, or satisfaction surveys. Benefits could include a reduction in the costs associated with employee absenteeism and turnover, as well as improved productivity associated with better selection and training programs.

In general, HR departments should be able to improve their performance through some combination of greater efficiency and greater effectiveness. Greater efficiency means the HR department uses fewer and less-costly resources to perform its functions. Greater effectiveness means that what the HR department does—for example, selecting employees or setting up a performance management system—has a more beneficial effect on employees' and the organization's performance. The computing power available to today's organizations, coupled with people who have skills in HR analytics, enables companies to find more ways than ever to identify practices associated with greater efficiency and effectiveness. For example, organizations can measure patterns in employees' social networks—who is talking to whom, how often—and combine that with performance data. One lesson from such research is that a recruiter's closest friends and colleagues are less useful as a source of leads to qualified job candidates than are people the recruiter communicates with only occasionally. These less-close associates are likelier to have acquaintances who aren't already familiar to the recruiter.[38]

HRM's potential to affect employees' well-being and the organization's performance makes human resource management an exciting field. As we have shown throughout the book, every HRM function calls for decisions that have the potential to help individuals and organizations achieve their goals. For HR managers to fulfill that potential, they must ensure that their decisions are well grounded. The field of human resource management provides tremendous opportunity to future researchers and managers who want to make a difference in many people's lives.

THINKING ETHICALLY

HOW CAN—AND SHOULD—ORGANIZATIONS MEASURE ETHICS PERFORMANCE?

If we accept that ethical conduct is among the conditions that contribute to high performance, then shouldn't organizations be measuring it? Or more broadly, if an organization wants employees to achieve something, the organization needs to establish goals, allocate resources, measure performance, and make corrections if it is falling short. That would apply to ethical conduct as well as other goals such as efficiency and high quality.

An example of this principle contributing to high performance comes from the University of Michigan Health Systems. That organization addressed the problem of reducing medical mistakes and improving patient safety by crafting the Michigan Model, which emphasizes collaboration and transparency. The model is best known for its idea that doctors should freely admit to patients when they have made a mistake and offer an apology. The doctors were relieved to be honest, instead of deferring to the legal system, and the patients were grateful for the honesty and less likely to sue. In addition, the system promotes a culture of problem solving and collaboration instead of blame when mistakes occur, so doctors and hospital employees work together on improving outcomes. The program has made the health system a more desirable place to work and improved the quality of care.

To measure ethics performance, organizations must develop and communicate definitions of their standards

for ethical conduct. For example, employees of the University of Michigan Health Systems would need to know not only that their institute values patient safety but also what they are supposed to do if they see conduct that compromises safety. Systems need to be in place for reporting a problem without retaliation.

One challenge with measuring ethics performance is that some unethical behavior occurs under the radar. For example, if a group of employees mislead a customer in order to close a sale, it is easier for the company to count the value of the sale than to observe the details of the conduct leading up to the sale. For ethical conduct, the company might need indirect measures, such as surveys asking employees whether they have observed unethical conduct and whether they feel able to report that conduct without being punished for it. A model of this type of survey is the National Business Ethics Survey of the Ethics Resource Center. That survey has been observing a declining trend in observed misconduct, but its record low of 41% in 2013 still means that four out of ten employees are witnessing ethics violations such as bribery, health and safety violations, and violations of rules related to compensation and overtime.

Questions

1. How would you expect the measurement of ethical behavior to affect employees' conduct on the job?

2. How could the various HRM practices, such as training and performance management, contribute to achieving an organization's goal of measuring and maintaining high standards for ethical conduct?

Sources: Dov Seidman, "The Transformative Power of Transparency," *The New York Times*, May 23, 2014, http://

dealbook.nytimes.com; Ethics Resource Center, *National Business Ethics Survey of the U.S. Workforce* (Arlington, VA: Ethics Resource Center, 2014), accessed at http://www.ethics.org; Jeffrey Pfeffer, "Measure (and Reward) Ethical Behavior," *Inc.*, March 26, 2013, http://www.inc.com.

SUMMARY

LO 9-1 Define high-performance work systems, and identify the elements of such a system.

- A high-performance work system is the right combination of people, technology, and organizational structure that makes full use of the organization's resources and opportunities in achieving its goals.
- The elements of a high-performance work system are organizational structure, task design, people, reward systems, and information systems. These elements must work together in a smoothly functioning whole.

LO 9-2 Summarize the outcomes of a high-performance work system.

- A high-performance work system achieves the organization's goals, typically including growth, productivity, and high profits.
- On the way to achieving these overall goals, the high-performance work system meets such intermediate goals as high quality, innovation, customer satisfaction, job satisfaction, and reduced absenteeism and turnover.

LO 9-3 Describe the conditions that create a high-performance work system.

- Many conditions contribute to high-performance work systems by giving employees skills, incentives, knowledge, autonomy, and employee satisfaction.
- Teamwork and empowerment can make work more satisfying and provide a means for employees to improve quality and productivity.
- Organizations can improve performance by creating a learning organization in which people constantly learn and share knowledge so that they continually expand their capacity to achieve the results they desire.
- In a high-performance organization, employees experience job satisfaction or even "occupational intimacy."
- For long-run high performance, organizations and employees must be ethical as well.

LO 9-4 Explain how human resource management can contribute to high performance.

- Jobs should be designed to foster teamwork and employee empowerment.
- Recruitment and selection should focus on obtaining employees who have the qualities necessary for teamwork, empowerment, and knowledge sharing.
- When the organization selects for teamwork and decision-making skills, it may have to provide training in specific job tasks. Training also is important because of its role in creating a learning organization.
- The performance management system should be related to the organization's goals, with a focus on meeting internal and external customers' needs.
- Compensation should include links to performance, and employees should be included in decisions about compensation.
- Research suggests that it is more effective to improve HRM practices as a whole than to focus on one or two isolated practices.

LO 9-5 Discuss the role of HRM technology in high-performance work systems.

- Technology can improve the efficiency of the human resource management functions and support knowledge sharing.
- HRM applications involve transaction processing, decision support systems, and expert systems.
- These often are part of a human resource information system using relational databases, which can improve the efficiency of routine tasks and the quality of decisions.
- With Internet technology, organizations can use e-HRM to let all the organization's employees help themselves to the HR information they need whenever they need it.

LO 9-6 Summarize ways to measure the effectiveness of human resource management.

- Taking a customer-oriented approach, HRM can improve quality by defining the internal customers who use its services and determining whether it is meeting those customers' needs.

- One way to do this is with an HRM audit, a formal review of the outcomes of HRM functions. The audit may look at any measure associated with successful management of human resources. Audit information may come from the organization's documents and surveys of customer satisfaction.

- Another way to measure HRM effectiveness is to analyze specific programs or activities. HR analytics can measure success in terms of whether a program met its objectives and whether it delivered value in an economic sense, such as by leading to productivity improvements.

KEY TERMS

high-performance work system, 271

learning organization, 275

continuous learning, 275

employee engagement, 277

brand alignment, 278

transaction processing, 283

decision support systems, 283

expert systems, 284

HR dashboard, 285

cloud computing, 287

HRM audit, 288

HR analytics, 288

REVIEW AND DISCUSSION QUESTIONS

1. What is a high-performance work system? What are its elements? Which of these elements involve human resource management? *(LO 9-1)*

2. As it has become clear that HRM can help create and maintain high-performance work systems, it appears that organizations will need two kinds of human resource professionals. One kind focuses on identifying how HRM can contribute to high performance. The other kind develops expertise in particular HRM functions, such as how to administer a benefits program that complies with legal requirements. Which aspect of HRM is more interesting to you? Why? *(LO 9-2)*

3. How can teamwork, empowerment, knowledge sharing, and job satisfaction contribute to high performance? *(LO 9-3)*

4. If an organization can win customers, employees, or investors through deception, why would

ethical behavior contribute to high performance? *(LO 9-3)*

5. How can an organization promote ethical behavior among its employees? *(LO 9-3)*

6. Summarize how each of the following HR functions can contribute to high performance. *(LO 9-4)*
   a. Job design
   b. Recruitment and selection
   c. Training and development
   d. Performance management
   e. Compensation

7. How can HRM technology make a human resource department more productive? How can technology improve the quality of HRM decisions? *(LO 9-5)*

8. Why should human resource departments measure their effectiveness? What are some ways they can go about measuring effectiveness? *(LO 9-6)*

TAKING RESPONSIBILITY

The Container Store Puts Employees First

Kip Tindell, CEO of the Container Store, clearly envisions what makes his company great. "If you take care of the employees better than anyone else," he says, "they will take care of the customer better than anyone else." Those happy employees and customers will yield the sales and profits that make shareholders happy as well.

Selling only containers for people's belongings seemed rather strange in 1978, when the company started. Talented salespeople were a practical way to make the Container Store exciting and relevant. That requires empowerment—what the Container Store calls allowing employees to "unleash their creative genius." Instead of simply closing sales, employees build strong connections with customers by helping them find solutions to storage problems. In Tindell's words, "We agree on the ends, and then we liberate each employee to choose their means to the ends." That model has yielded strong sales growth year after year.

Supporting the philosophy of putting employees first are several HR practices. The hiring process is intense (as many as eight interviews, including with groups of co-workers) and selective (about 3% of applicants are hired). This effort is aimed at getting a great employee—one who delivers results equal to three employees who are merely good at the job. High standards for selection justify high compensation: pay for salespeople is between one and a half and two times the industry average, and even part-timers are eligible for health insurance.

Training also exceeds industry norms. Full-time employees receive more than 260 hours of training during their first year and another 100 hours during their second year. That compares with 31 hours of training for the average U.S. worker, according to the American Society of Training and Development. Training for Container Store salespeople covers the store's 10,000 products, the company's business philosophy, and ways to make strong connections with customers.

The employees-first philosophy has built a Great Place to Work (designated by the Great Places to Work Institute), a Best Retail Brand (according to Interbrand, a consulting firm in brand management), and one of *Fortune* magazine's 100 Best Companies to Work For. But what about those shareholders? The Container Store was privately held until November 2013, so pleasing outside investors is a new challenge. Following its first year as a publicly traded company, its stock price dropped in response to sales growth failing to generate profits. Investors acknowledge that recent years have been hard on all retailers, so the verdict is still out on whether the Container Store will be a high-performance organization in investors' eyes.

Questions

1. Would you describe the Container Store as a high-performance organization? Why or why not?
2. How could HR managers at the Container Store analyze the effectiveness of HRM to ensure they are helping the company become more profitable? Would your ideas compromise the employees-first policy?

Sources: Susan Thurston, "Indoors or Out, They Excel," *Tampa Bay Times*, April 13, 2014, Business Insights: Global, http://bi.galegroup.com; Interbrand, "Best Retail Brands 2014: The Container Store," http://www. interbrand.com, accessed June 11, 2014; Andria Cheng, "Why the Container Store Stock Is Tanking," *MarketWatch*, January 8, 2014, http://blogs. marketwatch.com; Jessica Rohman, "With an 'Employee-First' Mentality, Everyone Wins: The Container Store," Culture Impact Brief, Great Place to Work Institute, 2013, http://www.greatplacetowork.com.

MANAGING TALENT

Valuing Labor Drives High Performance at HindlePower

HindlePower is a small company with a big idea for success. The Easton, Pennsylvania, manufacturer of battery chargers has just 75 employees, most of whom work in the factory as assemblers. Its president, Bill Hindle, sees those workers not merely as an expense but as a source of value.

That attitude becomes immediately evident when prospective customers visit the facility. At most manufacturers, a manager or salesperson would conduct a factory tour, controlling the experience to present the best face of the company. At HindlePower, employees are the best face of the company, so Bill Hindle simply offers a few safety guidelines and then invites visitors to look around on their own, asking any questions of the workers. More than once, Hindle says, the trust he places in his workers is what seals the deal with customers. They assume that workers in such an environment will be committed to quality.

Another sign of employee empowerment at HindlePower is the absence of time clocks. Employees do not need to punch in and out, and the company has no rules for time off. If family needs arise during business hours, employees are authorized to leave and tend to their families, knowing their colleagues will pitch in to accomplish the required work. According to Hindle, employees have been responsible about making up their time off, to the point that hours in the factory consistently reach 97% to 100% of full-time. In other words, there is essentially nothing to gain from establishing rules and procedures to ensure that employees are on the job for the full 40-hour week.

Seeing workers as a source of value rather than merely a cost also helps HindlePower fill positions with skilled workers. Many manufacturers complain that there is a shortage of workers with the skills needed for modern production systems. However, Hindle has no trouble and says the solution is to be patient and invest in training. HindlePower established a program called the Professional Manufacturing Team, which couples training with worker involvement in designing more efficient processes. The training consists of 25 to 30 courses in a curriculum tailored to each production line. Employees are responsible for completing all of the courses, and when they do, the company considers each one a manufacturing professional. Beyond the training, employee involvement in decision making brings meaningful results. In one case, the workers redesigned a production line so that instead of making 350,000 units a week, it now finishes 500,000.

Over the past decade, HindlePower's well-trained, highly engaged workers have enabled the company to generate average annual revenue growth of 15%, even during the recent recession.

Questions

1. Would you consider HindlePower a high-performance organization? Why or why not?
2. Besides the methods described here, what is one other way an HR manager at HindlePower could contribute to making the company a high-performance organization? How well does your idea fit with Bill Hindle's vision for his company?

Sources: HindlePower, corporate website, http://www.hindlepower.com, accessed June 11, 2014; Pete Fehrenbach, "HindlePower's Pro Shop: Greatness Within," *Industry Week*, June 3, 2014, ProQuest eLibrary, http://elibrary.bigchalk.com; Jill Jusko, "The Value of Labor," *Industry Week*, November 2013, pp. 24–26; Ann Wlazelek, "HindlePower Inc.: Manufacturing without a Time Clock," *Morning Call* (Lehigh Valley, PA), March 4, 2013, http://articles.mcall.com.

HR IN SMALL BUSINESS

Employees Make a Difference at Amy's Ice Creams

One of the bright spots for hungry people in Austin, Texas, is Amy's Ice Creams—its factory on Burnet Road or one of several Amy's stores. Founder Amy Miller, who dropped out of medical school to start the business, figures it is just another way to "make a difference in people's lives," offering customers a fun place to celebrate or cheer up.

Miller had been paying med school with a job at Steve's Ice Cream, but when the company was sold, she thought the new owners were too stodgy, so she opened her own ice cream shop. Given the motivation to strike out on her own, it's not surprising that her goal is to manage her employees in a different way, one that combines informal fun with care for others.

The spirit of fun is defined by the employee selection process Miller invented. When interviewing candidates, Miller hands them a white paper bag with the instruction to "make something creative" and show her later. One applicant used it to make a hot-air balloon. Another put food in a bag, gave it to a homeless person, took a photo of the gift, and put the photo in the bag to return as the creative offering.

Job design also plays up the fun. Amy's prized employees don't just scoop up ice cream but also come up with ways to create a playful atmosphere. The company encourages workers to juggle shakers or give away a scoop of ice cream to a customer who is willing to sing and dance.

While the two painted concrete cows that sit in front of the Amy's factory are an emblem of the company's commitment to fun, its commitment to caring has a more uplifting sign: Amy's Ice Creams funded the construction of a room in a local children's cancer care center. The room resembles an ice cream shop and includes freezers stocked with ice cream—a treat that patients can share with visiting family members.

Service to the community is also connected to employee engagement. At Amy's, the employees choose the charities the company will support. At a prom hosted by Amy's every year, the company selects a King and Queen to honor based on which employees did the most company-sponsored charitable work. In this way, employee rewards are tied to the company's value.

Fun and community service aren't just a way to be nice; they also have made Amy's Ice Creams a company ice cream lovers care to buy from. The company reaps millions of dollars in sales and has expanded the number of locations to meet growing demand in Austin as well as in Houston and San Antonio. Still, it's not just about the revenues. Co-owner (and Amy's husband) Steve Simmons told a reporter, "We never want to be a megacompany. When we don't know employees' names, there's a problem."

Questions

1. Which elements of a high-performance work system (Figure 9.1) does Amy's Ice Creams seem to have?
2. Suppose Amy's hired you as a consultant to evaluate whether the company has an effective HRM function. Which outcomes would you look for? How would you measure them?
3. Generally, a small ice cream shop such as Amy's cannot afford to pay store workers very high wages. How well do you think the company can achieve high employee satisfaction without high pay? What can it

do to foster satisfaction besides the efforts described here? How could e-HRM support these efforts?

Sources: Amy's Ice Creams corporate website, www.amysicecreams.com, accessed June 17, 2014; Janine Popick, "GrowCo.: Growth by Involvement at Amy's Ice Creams," *Inc.*, March 16, 2010, www.inc.com; Renuka Rayasam, "Sweet Success," *Ausin American-Stateman*, September 29, 2005; Business & Company Resource Center, http://galenet.galegroup.com; Michael Malone, "Chain Founder; Amy Miller, Amy's Ice Creams," *Restaurant Business*, March 1, 2003, available at All Business.com, www.allbusiness.com.

NOTES

1. Adrienne Selko, "From Chopping Block to Award Banquet," *Industry Week*, January 2014, pp. 16–17; General Cable, "About Us" and careers page, http://www.generalcable.com, accessed June 12, 2014.

2. S. Snell and J. Dean, "Integrated Manufacturing and Human Resource Management: A Human Capital Perspective," *Academy of Management Journal* 35 (1992), pp. 467–504.

3. M. A. Huselid, "The Impact of Human Resource Management Practices on Turnover, Productivity, and Corporate Financial Performance," *Academy of Management Journal* 38 (1995), pp. 635–72; U.S. Department of Labor, *High-Performance Work Practices and Firm Performance* (Washington, DC: U.S. Government Printing Office, 1993); J. Combs, Y. Liu, A. Hall, and D. Ketchen, "How Much Do High-Performance Work Practices Matter? A Meta-Analysis of Their Effects on Organizational Performance," *Personnel Psychology* 59 (2006), pp. 501–28.

4. Allison Rimm, "Tips for Energizing Your Exhausted Employees," *Harvard Business Review*, November 26, 2013, http://blogs.hbr.org.

5. J. Arthur, "The Link between Business Strategy and Industrial Relations Systems in American Steel Minimills," *Industrial and Labor Relations Review* 45 (1992), pp. 488–506.

6. J. A. Neal and C. L. Tromley, "From Incremental Change to Retrofit: Creating High-Performance Work Systems," *Academy of Management Executive* 9 (1995), pp. 42–54; Huselid, "The Impact of Human Resource Management Practices." For a more recent but similar perspective, see Ehssan Abdallah and Ashish Ahluwalia, "The Keys to Building a High-Performance Culture," *Gallup Business Journal*, December 12, 2013, Business Insights: Global, http://bi.galegroup.com.

7. P. Coy, "A Renaissance in U.S. Manufacturing," *Bloomberg Businessweek*, May 9, 2011, pp. 11–12.

8. D. McCann and C. Margerison, "Managing High-Performance Teams," *Training and Development Journal*, November 1989, pp. 52–60.

9. D. Senge, "The Learning Organization Made Plain and Simple," *Training and Development Journal*, October 1991, pp. 37–44.

10. M. A. Gephart, V. J. Marsick, M. E. Van Buren, and M. S. Spiro, "Learning Organizations Come Alive," *Training and Development* 50 (1996), pp. 34–45.

11. T. T. Baldwin, C. Danielson, and W. Wiggenhorn, "The Evolution of Learning Strategies in Organizations: From Employee Development to Business Redefinition," *Academy of Management Executive* 11 (1997), pp. 47–58; J. J. Martocchio and T. T. Baldwin, "The Evolution of Strategic Organizational Training," in *Research in Personnel and Human Resource Management* 15, ed. G. R. Ferris (Greenwich, CT: JAI Press,

1997), pp. 1–46; "Leveraging HR and Knowledge Management in a Challenging Economy," *HR Magazine*, June 2009, pp. S1–S9.

12. H. James Wilson, "Employees, Measure Yourselves," *The Wall Street Journal*, April 2, 2012, http://online.wsj.com.

13. T. A. Judge, C. J. Thoresen, J. E. Bono, and G. K. Patton, "The Job Satisfaction-Job Performance Relationship: A Qualitative and Quantitative Review," *Psychological Bulletin* 127 (2001), pp. 376–407; R. A. Katzell, D. E. Thompson, and R. A. Guzzo, "How Job Satisfaction and Job Performance Are and Are Not Linked," *Job Satisfaction*, eds. C. J. Cranny, P. C. Smith, and E. F. Stone (New York: Lexington Books, 1992), pp. 195–217.

14. Gallup, "State of the American Workplace," 2013, http://www.gallup.com.

15. Aon Hewitt, "2013 Trends in Global Employee Engagement," 2013, http://www.aon.com.

16. Kathleen Kindle, "Brand Alignment: Getting It Right," http://www.siegelgate.com/blog, accessed May 30, 2012; Aon Hewitt, "Trends in Global Employee Engagement," 2011, http://www.aon.com.

17. P. E. Boverie and M. Kroth, *Transforming Work: The Five Keys to Achieving Trust, Commitment, and Passion in the Workplace* (Cambridge, MA: Perseus, 2001), pp. 71–72, 79.

18. R. P. Gephart Jr., "Introduction to the Brave New Workplace: Organizational Behavior in the Electronic Age," *Journal of Organizational Behavior* 23 (2002), pp. 327–44.

19. Kristin Samuelson, "Secrets of Succeeding with Ethics," *Chicago Tribune*, April 15, 2012, sec. 2, p. 3.

20. Ibid.; Max H. Bazerman and Ann E. Tenbrunsel, "Ethical Breakdowns," *Harvard Business Review*, April 2011, http://hbr.org; Ethics Resource Center, "Why Have a Code of Conduct," May 29, 2009, http://www.ethics.org.

21. Amy Fliegelman Olli, "Aligning Ethics and Compliance with Business Objectives," *Ethisphere*, March 31, 2011, http://ethisphere.com.

22. W. F. Cascio, *Costing Human Resources: The Financial Impact of Behavior in Organizations*, 3rd ed. (Boston: PWS-Kent, 1991); Gergana Markova, "Can Human Resource Management Make a Big Difference in a Small Company?" *International Journal of Strategic Management* 9, no. 2 (2009), pp. 73–80.

23. B. Becker and M. A. Huselid, "High-Performance Work Systems and Firm Performance: A Synthesis of Research and Managerial Implications," in *Research in Personnel and Human Resource Management* 16, ed. G. R. Ferris (Stamford, CT: JAI Press, 1998), pp. 53–101.

24. B. Becker and B. Gerhart, "The Impact of Human Resource Management on Organizational Performance: Progress and Prospects," *Academy of Management Journal* 39 (1996), pp. 779–801.

25. David Hatch, "Can Apple Polish Lowe's Reputation?" *U.S. News & World Report*, May 15, 2012, http://money.usnews.com.

26. H. J. Bernardin, C. M. Hagan, J. S. Kane, and P. Villanova, "Effective Performance Management: A Focus on Precision, Customers, and Situational Constraints," in *Performance Appraisal: State of the Art in Practice*, ed. J. W. Smither (San Francisco: Jossey-Bass, 1998), p. 56.

27. Patrick Darling, "Intel Sets 2020 Environmental Goals," Intel newsroom blog, May 17, 2012, http://newsroom.intel.com; Intel, *2011 Corporate Responsibility Report*, http://www.intel.com, accessed May 18, 2012.

28. L. R. Gomez-Mejia and D. B. Balkin, *Compensation, Organizational Strategy, and Firm Performance* (Cincinnati: South-Western, 1992); G. D. Jenkins and E. E. Lawler III, "Impact of Employee Participation in Pay Plan Development," *Organizational Behavior and Human Performance* 28 (1981), pp. 111–28.

29. S. Shrivastava and J. Shaw, "Liberating HR through Technology," *Human Resource Management* 42, no. 3 (2003), pp. 201–17.

30. R. Broderick and J. W. Boudreau, "Human Resource Management, Information Technology, and the Competitive Edge," *Academy of Management Executive* 6 (1992), pp. 7–17.

31. N. Lockwood, *Maximizing Human Capital: Demonstrating HR Value with Key Performance Indicators* (Alexandria, VA: SHRM Research Quarterly, 2006).

32. Grace Ahrend, Fred Diamond, and Pat Gill Webber, "Virtual Coaching: Using Technology to Boost Performance," *Chief Learning Officer*, July 2010, pp. 44–47.

33. Kim Girard, "A Talent for Talent," *CFO*, May 2011, pp. 27–28.

34. Bob Mosher and Jeremy Smith, "The Case for Performance Support," *Training*, November–December 2011, Business & Company Resource Center, http://galenet.galegroup.com.

35. Matt Charney, "Five Reasons Why Cloud Computing Matters for Recruiting and Hiring," *Monster.com*, http://hiring.monster.com/hr, accessed May 30, 2012; Daniel Shane, "A Human Giant," *Information Age*, http://www.information-age.com, accessed May 30, 2012.

36. Eric Krell, "Auditing Your HR Department," *HR Magazine*, September 2011, http://www.shrm.org.

37. Sean Cusack, "Train to Gain," *Transport and Logistics*, October 2011, pp. 53–56.

38. Steve Lohr, "The Age of Big Data," *The New York Times*, February 11, 2012, http://www.nytimes.com.

10

Managing Employees' Performance

What Do I Need to Know?

After reading this chapter, you should be able to:

LO 10-1 Identify the activities involved in performance management.

LO 10-2 Discuss the purposes of performance management systems.

LO 10-3 Define five criteria for measuring the effectiveness of a performance management system.

LO 10-4 Compare the major methods for measuring performance.

LO 10-5 Describe major sources of performance information in terms of their advantages and disadvantages.

LO 10-6 Define types of rating errors, and explain how to minimize them.

LO 10-7 Explain how to provide performance feedback effectively.

LO 10-8 Summarize ways to produce improvement in unsatisfactory performance.

LO 10-9 Discuss legal and ethical issues that affect performance management.

Introduction

Like other companies, Microsoft wants to identify employees who are doing a great job and reward them generously. It also wants to help employees recognize when they need to improve. For several years, Microsoft did this with a process in which managers rated their employees every year on a scale from 1 to 5. Employees who got the top rating (a 1 on the scale) were in line for extra pay and company stock; employees who received a 5 knew they had to shape up if they wanted a career with the company. Furthermore, the human resources department established a curve. Managers were to place most of their employees near the middle of the range, where pay was set to match the local labor market. They also were expected to single out a few employees to rank at the top and bottom of the curve.

Recently, Microsoft's HR department reconsidered whether this process adequately supported the company's strategic commitment to teamwork and knowledge sharing. In interviews with managers and employees, HR managers found that people were in competition with one another to grab the top ratings rather than thinking of their colleagues as part of a team. So Microsoft changed its practices. Now managers rate performance on each employee's accomplishments, use of coworkers' input, and contribution to coworkers' success. No curve establishes a preset distribution for the ratings. Also, managers provide this feedback more often than the annual reviews, with schedules varying according to the needs of each department. In her announcement of the new methods, the head of human resource management at Microsoft, called this change "an important step in continuing to create the best possible environment for our world-class talent to take on the toughest challenges and do world-changing work."[1]

Rating and discussing employees' performance, as managers do at Microsoft, are elements of performance management. **Performance management** is the process through which managers ensure that employees' activities and outputs contribute to the organization's goals. This process requires knowing what activities and outputs are desired, observing whether they occur, and providing feedback to help employees meet expectations. In the course of providing feedback, managers and employees may identify performance problems and establish ways to resolve those problems.

In this chapter we examine a variety of approaches to performance management. We begin by describing the activities involved in managing performance, then discuss the purpose of carrying out this process. Next, we discuss specific approaches to performance management, including the strengths and weaknesses of each approach. We also look at various sources of performance information. The next section explores the kinds of errors that commonly occur during the assessment of performance, as well as ways to reduce those errors. Then we describe ways of giving performance feedback effectively and intervening when performance must improve. Finally, we summarize legal and ethical issues affecting performance management.

> **Performance Management**
> The process through which managers ensure that employees' activities and outputs contribute to the organization's goals.

The Process of Performance Management

> **LO 10-1** Identify the activities involved in performance management.

Although many employees dread the annual performance appraisal meeting at which a boss picks apart the employee's behaviors from the past year, as we discussed in Chapter 9, performance management can potentially deliver many benefits—to individual employees as well as to the organization as a whole. Effective performance management can tell top performers they are valued, encourage communication between managers and their employees, establish consistent standards for evaluating employees, and help the organization identify its strongest and weakest employees. To meet these objectives, companies must think of effective performance management as a process, not an event.

Figure 10.1 shows the six steps in the performance management process. As shown in the model, feedback and formal performance evaluation are important parts of the process; however, they are not the only critical components. An effective performance management process contributes to the company's overall competitive advantage and must be given visible support by the CEO and other senior managers. This support ensures that the process is consistently used across the company, appraisals are completed on time, and giving and receiving ongoing performance feedback is recognized as an accepted part of the company's culture.

The first two steps of the process involve identifying what the company is trying to accomplish (its goals or objectives) and developing employee goals and actions to achieve these outcomes. Typically the outcomes benefit customers, the employee's peers or team members, and the organization itself. The goals, behaviors, and activities should be measurable and become part of the employee's job description.

Step three in the process—organizational support—involves providing employees with training, necessary resources and tools, and ongoing feedback between the employee and manager, which focuses on accomplishments as well as issues and challenges

Figure 10.1

Steps in the Performance Management Process

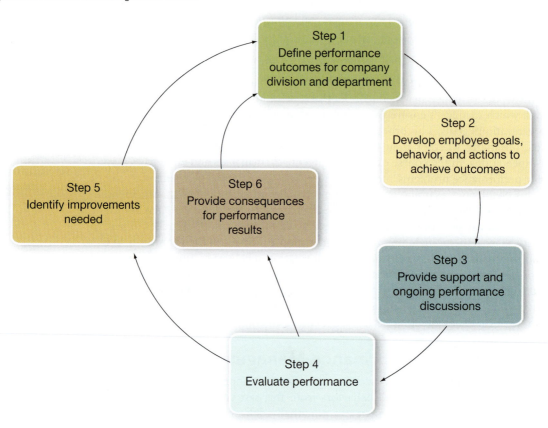

Sources: Based on E. Pulakos, *Performance Management* (Oxford, England: Wiley-Blackwell, 2009); H. Aguinis, "An Expanded View of Performance Management," in J. W. Smith and M. London (eds.), *Performance Management* (San Francisco: Jossey-Bass, 2009), pp. 1–43; J. Russell and L. Russell, "Talk Me Through It: The Next Level of Performance Management," *T + D,* April 2010, pp. 42–48.

that influence performance. For effective performance management, both the manager and the employee have to value feedback and exchange it on a regular basis—not just once or twice a year. Also, the manager needs to make time to provide ongoing feedback to the employee and learn how to give and receive it.

Step four involves evaluating performance; that is, when the manager and employee discuss and compare targeted goals and supporting behavior with actual results. This step includes the annual formal performance review.

The final steps of the performance management process involve both the employee and manager identifying what the employee can do to capitalize on performance strengths and address weaknesses (step 5) and providing consequences for achieving (or failing to achieve) performance outcomes (such as pay increases, bonuses, or action plans) (step 6). This includes identifying training needs; adjusting the type or frequency of feedback the manager provides to the employee; clarifying, adjusting, or modifying performance outcomes; and discussing behaviors or activities that need improvement.

To be effective, the entire performance management process should be reviewed each year to ensure that what is being measured at the employee level aligns strategically with company, division, and departmental goals and objectives.[2]

HR Oops!

"Where Have I Heard That Before?"

More than four out of ten employees hear about the same areas for improvement year after year, according to a survey by the HR training and consulting firm VitalSmarts. The firm asked employees if their latest performance review gave them the same negative feedback as in previous years, and 43 percent said yes. For these employees, being evaluated in prior years was not associated with any improvement in performance.

One explanation may come from another survey finding. Asked whether the review process included planning how to improve their performance, 87 percent said no. They were learning they needed to improve, and then managers were leaving it up to the employees to solve performance problems on their own. These results suggest that managers can be doing much more to develop employees. In that context, the employees who progress will be those who take responsibility for their own development—for example, asking for specific feedback, looking for a mentor, and establishing personal goals to improve.

A manager who takes a very different approach is Dharam Singh, managing director of VCare Project Management in Sydney, Australia. When one of Singh's employees is failing to meet job requirements, Singh has the employee set specific goals for improvement in the problem areas. Singh and the employee collaborate on establishing a plan for how the employee will achieve those goals. Singh also helps the employee understand how falling short of performance targets affects the firm as a whole.

Questions

1. If employees' poor performance is unchanged year after year, what does this say about how effectively performance management is serving its *strategic* and *developmental* purposes? How would the *administrative* purpose of performance management apply in this situation?

2. Which purpose(s) of performance management is Singh fulfilling, according to the description given? Explain your choice(s).

Sources: VitalSmarts, "Avoiding a Déjà Vu Performance Review," research summary, http://www.vitalsmarts.com, accessed June 20, 2014; VitalSmarts, "Avoiding a Déjà Vu Performance Review," survey data, http://www.vitalsmarts.com, accessed June 20, 2014; Matt Schur, "Upon Further Review," *PM Network*, March 2014, pp. 38–43; Ann Pace, "Preventing Poor Performance Déjà Vu," *T + D*, April 2013, p. 14.

Purposes of Performance Management

LO 10-2 Discuss the purposes of performance management systems.

Organizations establish performance management systems to meet three broad purposes: strategic, administrative, and developmental. As you read the "HR Oops!" box and the rest of this section, think about which purposes of performance management the companies and managers should be meeting more effectively.

Strategic purpose means effective performance management helps the organization achieve its business objectives. It does this by helping to link employees' behavior with the organization's goals. Performance management starts with defining what the organization expects from each employee. It measures each employee's performance to identify where those expectations are and are not being met. This enables the organization to take corrective action, such as training, incentives, or discipline. Performance management can achieve its strategic purpose only when measurements are truly linked to the organization's goals and when the goals and feedback about performance are communicated to employees. At wireless provider Sprint, employees are appraised in terms of three to five criteria, each linked to one of the company's strategic objectives for improving the customer experience, strengthening the brand, or increasing profits. Employees in Sprint's call centers and retail stores can go online to review their individual objectives and check their progress toward achieving them.[3]

The *administrative purpose* of a performance management system refers to the ways in which organizations use the system to provide information for day-to-day decisions about salary, benefits, and recognition programs. Performance management can also support decision making related to employee retention, termination for poor behavior, and hiring or layoffs. Because performance management supports these administrative decisions, the information in a performance appraisal can have a great impact on the future of individual employees. Managers recognize this, which is the reason they may feel uncomfortable conducting performance appraisals when the appraisal information is negative and, therefore, likely to lead to a layoff, disappointing pay increase, or other negative outcome.

Finally, performance management has a *developmental purpose*, meaning that it serves as a basis for developing employees' knowledge and skills. Even employees who are meeting expectations can become more valuable when they hear and discuss performance feedback. Effective performance feedback makes employees aware of their strengths and of the areas in which they can improve. For performance feedback to serve a developmental purpose, managers should adjust their approach to the level of performance. For a high-performing employee, the manager should open up a conversation about the employee's ambitions and the organization's developmental opportunities, so the employee sees an inviting career path. Employees who are falling short in some areas will require an effort to uncover the source of poor performance. Even among employees meeting standards, managers should identify areas for future growth. For this, one employee might need additional training while another needs encouragement or more challenging goals.[4]

Criteria for Effective Performance Management

LO 10-3 Define five criteria for measuring the effectiveness of a performance management system.

In Chapter 6, we saw that there are many ways to predict performance of a job candidate. Similarly, there are many ways to measure the performance of an employee. For performance management to achieve its goals, its methods for measuring performance must be good. Selecting these measures is a critical part of planning a performance management system. Several criteria determine the effectiveness of performance measures:

- *Fit with strategy*—A performance management system should aim at achieving employee behavior and attitudes that support the organization's strategy, goals, and culture. If a company emphasizes customer service, then its performance management system should define the kinds of behavior that contribute to good customer service. Performance appraisals should measure whether employees are engaging in those behaviors. Feedback should help employees improve in those areas. When an organization's strategy changes, human resource personnel should help managers assess how the performance management system should change to serve the new strategy.
- *Validity*—As we discussed in Chapter 6, *validity* is the extent to which a measurement tool actually measures what it is intended to measure. In the case of performance appraisal, validity refers to whether the appraisal measures all the relevant aspects of performance and omits irrelevant aspects of performance. Figure 10.2 shows two sets of information. The circle on the left represents all the information in a performance appraisal; the circle on the right represents all relevant measures of job performance. The overlap of the circles contains the valid information. Information that is gathered but irrelevant is "contamination." Comparing salespeople based on how many calls they make to customers could be a contaminated measure. Making a lot of calls does not necessarily improve sales or customer satisfaction,

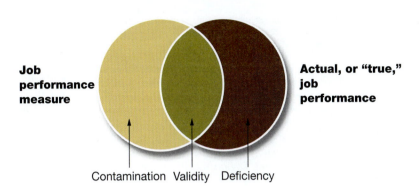

Figure 10.2
Contamination and
Deficiency of a Job
Performance Measure

unless every salesperson makes only well-planned calls. Information that is not gathered but is relevant represents a deficiency of the performance measure. For example, suppose a company measures whether employees have good attendance records but not whether they work efficiently. This limited performance appraisal is unlikely to provide a full picture of employees' contribution to the company. Performance measures should minimize both contamination and deficiency.

- *Reliability*—With regard to a performance measure, reliability describes the consistency of the results that the performance measure will deliver. *Interrater reliability* is consistency of results when more than one person measures performance. Simply asking a supervisor to rate an employee's performance on a scale of 1 to 5 would likely have low interrater reliability; the rating will differ depending on who is scoring the employees. *Test-retest reliability* refers to consistency of results over time. If a performance measure lacks test-retest reliability, determining whether an employee's performance has truly changed over time will be impossible.

- *Acceptability*—Whether or not a measure is valid and reliable, it must meet the practical standard of being acceptable to the people who use it. For example, the people who use a performance measure must believe that it is not too time consuming. Likewise, if employees believe the measure is unfair, they will not use the feedback as a basis for improving their performance.

- *Specific feedback*—A performance measure should specifically tell employees what is expected of them and how they can meet those expectations. Being specific helps performance management meet the goals of supporting strategy and developing employees. If a measure does not specify what an employee must do to help the organization achieve its goals, it does not support the strategy. If the measure fails to point out employees' performance problems, they will not know how to improve.

For an example of a company that sets effective standards for performance management, see the "Best Practices" box.

Methods for Measuring Performance

Organizations have developed a wide variety of methods for measuring performance. Some methods rank each employee to compare employees' performance. Other methods break down the evaluation into ratings of individual attributes, behaviors, or results. Many organizations use a measurement system that includes a variety of the preceding measures, as in the case of applying total quality management to performance management. Table 10.1 compares these methods in terms of our criteria for effective performance management.

LO 10-4 Compare the major methods for measuring performance.

Best Practices

A Goal-Oriented System of Performance Management

Until recently, Minneapolis-based Medtronic had a performance management system with many of the features employees complain about. Managers assigned each employee a rating on a scale of 1 to 5, and a company-imposed curve told the managers how many employees the managers could include in each category. Managers spent a lot of time trying to figure out a fair way to decide that some employees were a "3" and others a "2," even if their impact on the department was essentially the same. On top of that, the performance measurement took place in a system separate from the company's efforts at employee development and rewards.

In her role as chief talent officer at Medtronic, Caroline Stockdale wanted a system that would better support Medtronic's strategy. As a developer and maker of medical devices, the company needed performance management that encouraged innovation and knowledge sharing, not competition for a higher rating. Also, in a dynamic industry, employees needed frequent feedback to help them stay on track toward goals.

In response to these challenges, Stockdale launched a "performance acceleration" system in which employees meet with their managers four times a year. During these feedback sessions, they focus not on ratings, but on each employee's performance goals. The manager fills out a one-page summary of the employee's progress toward the goals. They discuss what employees should start doing, stop doing, and continue doing. In addition, annual reviews provide the documents needed to fill administrative requirements.

Stockdale says focusing on goals instead of scores helps employees understand what they are doing well and need to do better. She also says the quarterly meetings force managers and employees to identify more specific, practical goals, because it is easier to plan activities for just 12 weeks at a time. Quarterly feedback creates more opportunities to observe and praise accomplishments. According to surveys of employee engagement, Medtronic's employees are more satisfied with the new system, and HR analytics show that managers now are more strategic about targeting the biggest rewards to those who contribute the most.

Questions

1. Evaluate how well Medtronic's performance acceleration system, as it is described here, meets the standards for validity and reliability.
2. How does it rate in terms of being acceptable and delivering specific feedback?

Sources: Ladan Nikravan, "Performance Reviews Don't Meet Expectations," *Talent Management*, October 2013, pp. 16–19; Jeri Darling, "Reframing Performance Reviews for Greater Impact: An Interview with Accretive Health Chief People Officer, Caroline Stockdale," *People and Strategy*, June 2013, Business Insights: Global, http://bi.galegroup.com; Jena McGregor, "The Corporate Kabuki of Performance Reviews," *Washington Post*, February 14, 2013, http://www.washingtonpost.com.

Making Comparisons

The performance appraisal method may require the rater to compare one individual's performance with that of others. This method involves some form of ranking, in which some employees are best, some are average, and others are worst. The usual techniques for making comparisons are simple ranking, forced distribution, and paired comparison.

Simple ranking requires managers to rank employees in their group from the highest performer to the poorest performer. In a variation of this approach, *alternation ranking*, the manager works from a list of employees. First, the manager decides which employee is best and crosses that person's name off the list. From the remaining names, the manager selects the worst employee and crosses off that name. The process continues with the manager selecting the second best, second worst, third best, and so on, until all the employees have been ranked. The major downside of ranking involves validity. To state a performance measure as broadly as "best" or "worst" doesn't define

Simple Ranking
Method of performance measurement that requires managers to rank employees in their group from the highest performer to the poorest performer.

Table 10.1

Basic Approaches to Performance Measurement

		CRITERIA			
APPROACH	**FIT WITH STRATEGY**	**VALIDITY**	**RELIABILITY**	**ACCEPTABILITY**	**SPECIFICITY**
Comparative	Poor, unless manager takes time to make link	Can be high if ratings are done carefully	Depends on rater, but usually no measure of agreement used	Moderate; easy to develop and use but resistant to normative standard	Very low
Attribute	Usually low; requires manager to make link	Usually low; can be fine if developed carefully	Usually low; can be improved by specific definitions of attributes	High; easy to develop and use	Very low
Behavioral	Can be quite high	Usually high; minimizes contamination and deficiency	Usually high	Moderate; difficult to develop, but accepted well for use	Very high
Results	Very high	Usually high; can be both contaminated and deficient	High; main problem can be test–retest—depends on timing of measure	High; usually developed with input from those to be evaluated	High regarding results, but low regarding behaviors necessary to achieve them
Quality	Very high	High, but can be both contaminated and deficient	High	High; usually developed with input from those to be evaluated	High regarding results, but low regarding behaviors necessary to achieve them

what exactly is good or bad about the person's contribution to the organization. Ranking therefore raises questions about fairness.

Another way to compare employees' performance is with the **forced-distribution method.** This type of performance measurement assigns a certain percentage of employees to each category in a set of categories. For example, the organization might establish the following percentages and categories:

- Exceptional—5%
- Exceeds standards—25%
- Meets standards—55%
- Room for improvement—10%
- Not acceptable—5%

The manager completing the performance appraisal would rate 5% of his or her employees as exceptional, 25% as exceeding standards, and so on. A forced-distribution approach works best if the members of a group really do vary this much in terms of their performance. It overcomes the temptation to rate everyone high in order to avoid conflict. Research simulating some features of forced rankings found that they improved performance when combined with goals and rewards, especially in the first few years, when the system eliminated the poorest performers.[5] However, a manager

Forced-Distribution Method
Method of performance measurement that assigns a certain percentage of employees to each category in a set of categories.

who does very well at selecting, motivating, and training employees will have a group of high performers. This manager would have difficulty assigning employees to the bottom categories. In that situation, saying that some employees require improvement or are "not acceptable" not only will be inaccurate, but will hurt morale.

Paired-Comparison Method
Method of performance measurement that compares each employee with each other employee to establish rankings.

Another variation on rankings is the **paired-comparison method.** This approach involves comparing each employee with each other employee to establish rankings. Suppose a manager has five employees, Allen, Barbara, Caitlin, David, and Edgar. The manager compares Allen's performance to Barbara's and assigns one point to whichever employee is the higher performer. Then the manager compares Allen's performance to Caitlin's, then to David's, and finally to Edgar's. The manager repeats this process with Barbara, comparing her performance to Caitlin's, David's, and Edgar's. When the manager has compared every pair of employees, the manager counts the number of points for each employee. The employee with the most points is considered the top-ranked employee. Clearly, this method is time consuming if a group has more than a handful of employees. For a group of 15, the manager must make 105 comparisons.

In spite of the drawbacks, ranking employees offers some benefits. It counteracts the tendency to avoid controversy by rating everyone favorably or near the center of the scale. Also, if some managers tend to evaluate behavior more strictly (or more leniently) than others, a ranking system can erase that tendency from performance scores. Therefore, ranking systems can be useful for supporting decisions about how to distribute pay raises or layoffs. Some ranking systems are easy to use, which makes them acceptable to the managers who use them. A major drawback of rankings is that they often are not linked to the organization's goals. Also, a simple ranking system leaves the basis for the ranking open to interpretation. In that case, the rankings are not helpful for employee development and may hurt morale or result in legal challenges.

Rating Individuals

Instead of focusing on arranging a group of employees from best to worst, performance measurement can look at each employee's performance relative to a uniform set of standards. The measurement may evaluate employees in terms of attributes (characteristics or traits) believed desirable. Or the measurements may identify whether employees have *behaved* in desirable ways, such as closing sales or completing assignments. For both approaches, the performance management system must identify the desired attributes or behaviors, then provide a form on which the manager can rate the employee in terms of those attributes or behaviors. Typically, the form includes a rating scale, such as a scale from 1 to 5, where 1 is the worst performance and 5 is the best. The "Did You Know?" box shows some commonly used performance measures.

Graphic Rating Scale
Method of performance measurement that lists traits and provides a rating scale for each trait; the employer uses the scale to indicate the extent to which an employee displays each trait.

Rating Attributes   The most widely used method for rating attributes is the **graphic rating scale**. This method lists traits and provides a rating scale for each trait. The employer uses the scale to indicate the extent to which the employee being rated displays the traits. The rating scale may provide points to circle (as on a scale going from 1 for poor to 5 for excellent), or it may provide a line representing a range of scores, with the manager marking a place along the line. Figure 10.3 shows an example of a graphic rating scale that uses a set of ratings from 1 to 5. A drawback of this approach is that it leaves to the particular manager the decisions about what is "excellent knowledge" or "commendable judgment" or "poor interpersonal skills." The result is low reliability because managers are likely to arrive at different judgments.

Did You Know?

Popular Performance Measures

Most companies conduct performance appraisals, and the measure used most often is quality of work, according to an annual survey by Business & Legal Resources. Over two recent years, the same five measures were most common. More broadly, in both years, slightly more than half of companies said they measure goal achievement, and less than half said they measure individuals' attributes.

Question

Of the five measurements shown, which would you describe as *attributes*, and which would you describe as *traits*? Why?

Sources: Business and Legal Resources, "Results: 2014 Performance Management Survey," *Compensation Management News*, June 9, 2014, http://compensation.blr.com; Stephen Bruce, "Performance Management Survey Results In: How Do You Compare?" *HR Daily Advisor*, June 13, 2013, http://hrdailyadvisor.blr.com.

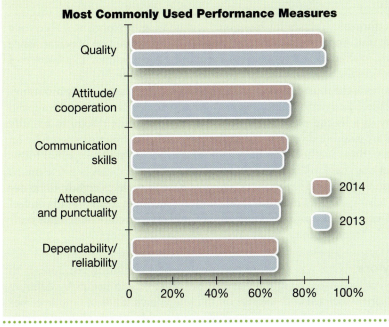

Most Commonly Used Performance Measures

Figure 10.3

Example of a Graphic Rating Scale

The following areas of performance are significant to most positions. Indicate your assessment of performance on each dimension by circling the appropriate rating.

PERFORMANCE DIMENSION	RATING				
	DISTINGUISHED	EXCELLENT	COMMENDABLE	ADEQUATE	POOR
Knowledge	5	4	3	2	1
Communication	5	4	3	2	1
Judgment	5	4	3	2	1
Managerial skill	5	4	3	2	1
Quality performance	5	4	3	2	1
Teamwork	5	4	3	2	1
Interpersonal skills	5	4	3	2	1
Initiative	5	4	3	2	1
Creativity	5	4	3	2	1
Problem solving	5	4	3	2	1

Mixed-Standard Scales
Method of performance measurement that uses several statements describing each trait to produce a final score for that trait.

To get around this problem, some organizations use **mixed-standard scales,** which use several statements describing each trait to produce a final score for that trait. The manager scores the employee in terms of how the employee compares to each statement. Consider the sample mixed-standard scale in Figure 10.4. To create this scale, the organization determined that the relevant traits are initiative, intelligence, and relations with others. For each trait, sentences were written to describe a person having a high level of that trait, a medium level, and a low level. The sentences for the traits were rearranged so that the nine statements about the three traits are mixed together. The manager who uses this scale reads each sentence, then indicates whether the employee performs above (+), at (0), or below (−) the level described. The key in the middle section of Figure 10.4 tells how to use the pluses, zeros, and minuses to score performance. Someone who excels at every level of performance (pluses for high, medium, and low performance) receives a score of 7 for that trait. Someone who fails to live up to every description of performance (minuses for high, medium, and low) receives a score of 1 for that trait. The bottom of Figure 10.4 calculates the scores for the ratings used in this example.

Rating attributes is the most popular way to measure performance in organizations. In general, attribute-based performance methods are easy to develop and can be applied to a wide variety of jobs and organizations. If the organization is careful to identify which attributes are associated with high performance, and to define them carefully on the appraisal form, these methods can be reliable and valid. However, appraisal forms often fail to meet this standard. In addition, measurement of attributes is rarely linked to the organization's strategy. Furthermore, employees tend perhaps rightly to be defensive about receiving a mere numerical rating on some attribute. How would you feel if you were told you scored 2 on a 5-point scale of initiative or communication skill? The number might seem arbitrary, and it doesn't tell you how to improve.

Rating Behaviors   One way to overcome the drawbacks of rating attributes is to measure employees' behavior. To rate behaviors, the organization begins by defining which behaviors are associated with success on the job. Which kinds of employee behavior help the organization achieve its goals? The appraisal form asks the manager to rate an employee in terms of each of the identified behaviors.

Critical-Incident Method
Method of performance measurement based on managers' records of specific examples of the employee acting in ways that are either effective or ineffective.

One way to rate behaviors is with the **critical-incident method**. This approach requires managers to keep a record of specific examples of the employee acting in ways that are either effective or ineffective. Here's an example of a critical incident in the performance evaluation of an appliance repairperson:

> A customer called in about a refrigerator that was not cooling and was making a clicking noise every few minutes. The technician prediagnosed the cause of the problem and checked his truck for the necessary parts. When he found he did not have them, he checked the parts out from inventory so that the customer's refrigerator would be repaired on his first visit and the customer would be satisfied promptly.

Behaviorally Anchored Rating Scale (BARS)
Method of performance measurement that rates behavior in terms of a scale showing specific statements of behavior that describe different levels of performance.

This incident provides evidence of the employee's knowledge of refrigerator repair and concern for efficiency and customer satisfaction. Evaluating performance in this specific way gives employees feedback about what they do well and what they do poorly. The manager can also relate the incidents to how the employee is helping the company achieve its goals. Keeping a daily or weekly log of critical incidents requires significant effort, however, and managers may resist this requirement. Also, critical incidents may be unique, so they may not support comparisons among employees.

A **behaviorally anchored rating scale (BARS)** builds on the critical-incidents approach. The BARS method is intended to define performance dimensions

Figure 10.4

Example of a Mixed-Standard Scale

Three traits being assessed:	Levels of performance in statements:
Initiative (INTV)	High (H)
Intelligence (INTG)	Medium (M)
Relations with others (RWO)	Low (L)

Instructions: Please indicate next to each statement whether the employee's performance is above (+), equal to (0), or below (−) the statement.

INTV	H	1. This employee is a real self-starter. The employee always takes the initiative and his/her superior never has to prod this individual.	+
INTG	M	2. While perhaps this employee is not a genius, s/he is a lot more intelligent than many people I know.	+
RWO	L	3. This employee has a tendency to get into unnecessary conflicts with other people.	0
INTV	M	4. While generally this employee shows initiative, occasionally his/her superior must prod him/her to complete work.	±
INTG	L	5. Although this employee is slower than some in understanding things, and may take a bit longer in learning new things, s/he is of average intelligence.	+
RWO	H	6. This employee is on good terms with everyone. S/he can get along with people even when s/he does not agree with them.	−
INTV	L	7. This employee has a bit of a tendency to sit around and wait for directions.	+
INTG	H	8. This employee is extremely intelligent, and s/he learns very rapidly.	−
RWO	M	9. This employee gets along with most people. Only very occasionally does s/he have conflicts with others on the job, and these are likely to be minor.	−

Scoring Key:

STATEMENTS			SCORE
HIGH	MEDIUM	LOW	
+	+	+	7
0	+	+	6
−	+	+	5
−	0	+	4
−	−	+	3
−	−	0	2
−	−	−	1

Example score from preceding ratings:

	STATEMENTS			SCORE
	HIGH	MEDIUM	LOW	
Initiative	+	+	+	7
Intelligence	0	+	+	6
Relations with others	−	−	0	2

specifically using statements of behavior that describe different levels of performance.[6] (The statements are "anchors" of the performance levels.) For example, consider the various levels of behavior associated with a patrol officer preparing for duty. The highest rating on the 7-point scale could include the following behaviors: early to work; gathers all necessary equipment needed for work; and previews previous shift's activities and any news/updates before roll call. The lowest statement on the scale (rating 1) describes behavior associated with poor performance (e.g. late for roll call; does not check equipment; and not prepared for shift activities). These statements are based on data about past performance. The organization gathers many critical incidents representing effective and ineffective performance, then classifies them from most to least effective. When experts about the job agree the statements clearly represent levels of performance, they are used as anchors to guide the rater. Although BARS can improve interrater reliability, this method can bias the manager's memory. The statements used as anchors can help managers remember similar behaviors, at the expense of other critical incidents.[7]

Behavioral Observation Scale (BOS)
A variation of a BARS which uses all behaviors necessary for effective performance to rate performance at a task.

A **behavioral observation scale (BOS)** is a variation of a BARS. Like a BARS, a BOS is developed from critical incidents.[8] However, while a BARS discards many examples in creating the rating scale, a BOS uses many of them to define all behaviors necessary for effective performance (or behaviors that signal ineffective performance). As a result, a BOS may use 15 behaviors to define levels of performance. Also, a BOS asks the manager to rate the frequency with which the employee has exhibited the behavior during the rating period. These ratings are averaged to compute an overall performance rating. Figure 10.5 provides a simplified example of a BOS for measuring the behavior "overcoming resistance to change."

A major drawback of this method is the amount of information required. A BOS can have 80 or more behaviors, and the manager must remember how often the employee

Figure 10.5

Example of a Behavioral Observation Scale

Overcoming Resistance to Change

Directions: Rate the frequency of each behavior from 1 (Almost Never) to 5 (Almost Always).

	Almost Never				Almost Always
1. Describes the details of the change to employees.	1	2	3	4	5
2. Explains why the change is necessary.	1	2	3	4	5
3. Discusses how the change will affect the employee.	1	2	3	4	5
4. Listens to the employee's concerns.	1	2	3	4	5
5. Asks the employee for help in making the change work.	1	2	3	4	5
6. If necessary, specifies the date for a follow-up meeting to respond to the employee's concerns.	1	2	3	4	5

Score: Total number of points = _____

Performance

Points	Performance Rating
6–10	Below adequate
11–15	Adequate
16–20	Full
21–25	Excellent
26–30	Superior

Scores are set by management.

exhibited each behavior in a 6- to 12-month rating period. This is taxing enough for one employee, but managers often must rate 10 or more employees. Even so, compared to BARS and graphic rating scales, managers and employees have said they prefer BOS for ease of use, providing feedback, maintaining objectivity, and suggesting training needs.[9]

Another approach to assessment builds directly on a branch of psychology called *behaviorism*, which holds that individuals' future behavior is determined by their past experiences—specifically, the ways in which past behaviors have been reinforced. People tend to repeat behaviors that have been rewarded in the past. Providing feedback and reinforcement can therefore modify individuals' future behavior. Applied to behavior in organizations, **organizational behavior modification (OBM)** is a plan for managing the behavior of employees through a formal system of feedback and reinforcement. Specific OBM techniques vary, but most have four components[10]:

1. Define a set of key behaviors necessary for job performance.
2. Use a measurement system to assess whether the employee exhibits the key behaviors.
3. Inform employees of the key behaviors, perhaps in terms of goals for how often to exhibit the behaviors.
4. Provide feedback and reinforcement based on employees' behavior.

> **Organizational Behavior Modification (OBM)**
> A plan for managing the behavior of employees through a formal system of feedback and reinforcement.

OBM techniques have been used in a variety of settings. For example, a community mental health agency used OBM to increase the rates and timeliness of critical job behaviors by showing employees the connection between job behaviors and the agency's accomplishments.[11] This process identified job behaviors related to administration, record keeping, and service provided to clients. Feedback and reinforcement improved staff performance. OBM also increased the frequency of safety behaviors in a processing plant.[12]

Behavioral approaches such as organizational behavior modification and rating scales can be very effective. These methods can link the company's goals to the specific behavior required to achieve those goals. Behavioral methods also can generate specific feedback, along with guidance in areas requiring improvements. As a result, these methods tend to be valid. The people to be measured often help in developing the measures, so acceptance tends to be high as well. When raters are well trained, reliability also tends to be high. However, behavioral methods do not work as well for complex jobs in which it is difficult to see a link between behavior and results or there is more than one good way to achieve success.[13]

Measuring Results

Performance measurement can focus on managing the objective, measurable results of a job or work group. Results might include sales, costs, or productivity (output per worker or per dollar spent on production), among many possible measures. Two of the most popular methods for measuring results are measurement of productivity and management by objectives.

Productivity is an important measure of success because getting more done with a smaller amount of resources (money or people) increases the company's profits. Productivity usually refers to the output of production workers, but it can be used more generally as a performance measure. To do this, the organization identifies the products—set of activities or objectives—it expects a group or individual to accomplish.

At a repair shop, for instance, a product might be something like "quality of repair." The next step is to define how to measure production of these products. For quality of repair, the repair shop could track the percentage of items returned because they still do not work after a repair and the percentage of quality-control inspections passed. For each measure, the organization decides what level of performance is desired. Finally, the organization sets up a system for tracking these measures and giving employees feedback about their performance in terms of these measures. This type of performance measurement can be time consuming to set up, but research suggests it can improve productivity.[14]

Management by Objectives (MBO)
A system in which people at each level of the organization set goals in a process that flows from top to bottom, so employees at all levels are contributing to the organization's overall goals; these goals become the standards for evaluating each employee's performance.

Management by objectives (MBO) is a system in which people at each level of the organization set goals in a process that flows from top to bottom, so employees at all levels are contributing to the organization's overall goals. These goals become the standards for evaluating each employee's performance. An MBO system has three components[15]:

1. Goals are specific, difficult, and objective. The goals listed in the second column of Table 10.2 provide two examples for a bank.
2. Managers and their employees work together to set the goals.
3. The manager gives objective feedback through the rating period to monitor progress toward the goals. The two right-hand columns in Table 10.2 are examples of feedback given after one year.

MBO can have a very positive effect on an organization's performance. In 70 studies of MBO's performance, 68 showed that productivity improved.[16] The productivity gains tended to be greatest when top management was highly committed to MBO. Also, because staff members are involved in setting goals, it is likely that MBO systems effectively link individual employees' performance with the organization's overall goals.

In general, evaluation of results can be less subjective than other kinds of performance measurement. This makes measuring results highly acceptable to employees and managers alike. Results-oriented performance measurement is also relatively easy to link to the organization's goals. However, measuring results has problems with validity because results may be affected by circumstances beyond each employee's performance. Also, if the organization measures only final results, it may fail to measure significant aspects of performance that are not directly related to those results. If individuals focus only on aspects of performance that are measured, they may neglect significant skills or behaviors. For example, one company measured how well employees in the purchasing department kept costs down and how efficiently people in the manufacturing department made its products.

Table 10.2

Management by Objectives: Two Objectives for a Bank

KEY RESULT AREA	OBJECTIVE	% COMPLETE	ACTUAL PERFORMANCE
Loan portfolio management	Increase portfolio value by 10% over the next 12 months	90	Increased portfolio value by 9% over the past 12 months
Sales	Generate fee income of $30,000 over the next 12 months	150	Generated fee income of $45,000 over the past 12 months

When the purchasing department kept its costs under control by ordering cheap materials, production slowed down, making overall costs higher—but the purchasing manager earned a bonus for high performance.[17] A final limitation of evaluation based on results is that these measures do not provide guidance on how to improve.

Total Quality Management

The principles of *total quality management*, introduced in Chapter 2, provide methods for performance measurement and management. Total quality management (TQM) differs from traditional performance measurement in that it assesses both individual performance and the system within which the individual works. This assessment is a process through which employees and their customers work together to set standards and measure performance, with the overall goal being to improve customer satisfaction. In this sense, an employee's customers may be inside or outside the organization; a "customer" is whoever uses the goods or services produced by the employee. The feedback aims at helping employees continuously improve the satisfaction of their customers. The focus on continuously improving customer satisfaction is intended to avoid the pitfall of rating individuals on outcomes, such as sales or profits, over which they do not have complete control.

With TQM, performance measurement essentially combines measurements of attributes and results. The feedback in TQM is of two kinds: (1) subjective feedback

A TQM approach to performance measurement involves employees and their internal and external customers working together to improve overall customer satisfaction.

from managers, peers, and customers about the employee's personal qualities such as cooperation and initiative; and (2) objective feedback based on the work process. The second kind of feedback comes from a variety of methods called *statistical quality control*. These methods use charts to detail causes of problems, measures of performance, or relationships between work-related variables. Employees are responsible for tracking these measures to identify areas where they can avoid or correct problems. Because of the focus on systems, this feedback may result in changes to a work process, rather than assuming that a performance problem is the fault of an employee. The TQM system's focus has practical benefits, but it does not serve as well to support decisions about work assignments, training, or compensation.

LO 10-5 Describe major sources of performance information in terms of their advantages and disadvantages.

Sources of Performance Information

All the methods of performance measurement require decisions about who will collect and analyze the performance information. To qualify for this task, a person should have an understanding of the job requirements and the opportunity to see the employee doing the job. The traditional approach is for managers to gather information about their employees' performances and arrive at performance ratings. However, many sources are possible. In fact, many employees welcome feedback from multiple sources.[18] Possibilities of information sources include managers, peers, subordinates, self, and customers.

Using just one person as a source of information poses certain problems. People tend to like some people more than others, and those feelings can bias how an employee's efforts are perceived. Also, one person is likely to see an employee in a limited number of situations. A supervisor, for example, cannot see how an employee behaves when the supervisor is not watching—for example, when a service technician is at the customer's facility. To get as complete an assessment as possible, some organizations combine information from most or all of the possible sources, in what is called a **360-degree performance appraisal**.

360-Degree Performance Appraisal
Performance measurement that combines information from the employee's managers, peers, subordinates, self, and customers.

Managers

The most-used source of performance information is the employee's manager. It is usually safe for organizations to assume that supervisors have extensive knowledge of the job requirements and that they have enough opportunity to observe their employees. In other words, managers possess the basic qualifications for this responsibility. Another advantage of using managers to evaluate performance is that they have an incentive to provide accurate and helpful feedback because their own success depends so much on their employees' performance.[19] Finally, when managers try to observe employee behavior or discuss performance issues in the feedback session, their feedback can improve performance, and employees tend to perceive the appraisal as accurate.[20]

Still, in some situations, problems can occur with using supervisors as the source of performance information. For employees in some jobs, the supervisor does not have enough opportunity to observe the employee performing job duties. A sales manager with many outside salespeople cannot be with the salespeople on many visits to customers. Even if the sales manager does make a point of traveling with salespeople for a few days, they are likely to be on their best behavior while the manager is there. The manager cannot observe how they perform at other times.

Peers

Another source of performance information is the employee's peers or co-workers. Peers are an excellent source of information about performance in a job where the supervisor does not often observe the employee. Examples include law enforcement and sales. For these and other jobs, peers may have the most opportunity to observe the employee in day-to-day activities. Peers have expert knowledge of job requirements. They also bring a different perspective to the evaluation and can provide extremely valid assessments of performance.[21]

Peer evaluations obviously have some potential disadvantages. Friendships (or rivalries) have the potential to bias ratings. Research, however, has provided little evidence that this is a problem.[22] Another disadvantage is that when the evaluations are done to support administrative decisions, peers are uncomfortable with rating employees for decisions that may affect themselves. Generally, peers are more favorable toward participating in reviews to be used for employee development.[23]

Performance management is critical for executing a talent management system and involves one-on-one contact with managers to ensure that proper training and development are taking place.

Subordinates

For evaluating the performance of managers, subordinates are an especially valuable source of information. Subordinates—the people reporting to the manager—often have the best chance to see how well a manager treats employees. At HCL Technologies, for example, managers not only receive reviews from their employees but are expected to publish the reports on the company's internal website to create a climate that values open communication and personal development. Sanjeev Nikore, a vice president who did this, learned that his employees found him resistant to delegating. He acknowledged he needed to improve his people skills, made some changes, and earned a key promotion.[24]

Subordinate evaluations have some potential problems because of the power relationships involved. Subordinates are reluctant to say negative things about the person to whom they report; they prefer to provide feedback anonymously. Managers, however, have a more positive reaction to this type of feedback when the subordinates are identified. When feedback forms require that the subordinates identify themselves, they tend to give the manager higher ratings.[25] Another problem is that when managers receive ratings from their subordinates, the employees have more power, so managers tend to emphasize employee satisfaction, even at the expense of productivity. This issue arises primarily when the evaluations are used for administrative decisions. Therefore, as with peer evaluations, subordinate evaluations are most appropriate for developmental purposes. To protect employees, the process should be anonymous and use at least three employees to rate each manager.

Despite these challenges, subordinate ratings of managers could become even more widespread for the simple reason that individuals are growing used to the experience of using social media to publish online ratings of everything from movies and restaurants to professors and doctors. For more on this phenomenon and how it might affect performance management, see the "HRM Social" box.

Crowdsourcing Performance Reviews

The collaborative tools of social media can allow individuals to work together by contributing small pieces to a bigger project. Especially when this is done on a large scale, it is known as *crowdsourcing.* An employer might conduct a research project quickly by inviting many people to complete small portions of it simultaneously. Or a travel website might invite travelers to post reviews of hotels and airlines to create an online travel guide.

With regard to performance management, crowdsourcing can apply to gathering and using data from all of an employee's coworkers or all of a manager's employees to develop an appraisal. One attraction of this approach is that the information will be more complete. Employees might therefore consider the resulting appraisal to be fairer than if it were based on one or a few people's observations.

Gathering performance data through an online application could further improve the accuracy and completeness of information by inviting employees to post performance information whenever they observe it. The company might even open up the submission of feedback to the whole organization. Suppose a salesperson is trying to

solve a customer problem and gets valuable help from one of the engineers; the salesperson could visit the appraisal site and post an appreciative comment describing the situation. Assuming that employees can read the feedback about themselves as it is posted, this type of information gathering also provides positive recognition—or in the case of negative comments, early warning of problems to correct.

A growing number of companies are attracted to the potential and beginning to use some form of crowdsourced appraisals. However, the approach does raise some concerns. One is that employees may not be motivated to provide careful feedback about their coworkers. They might, for example, find it easier to rate employees based on likability. Another is that bringing everyone into the appraisal process can interfere with legal requirements. As described later in the chapter, performance appraisals are used as evidence to show that employment decisions have not been discriminatory. If courts see appraisals as too subjective, employers defending a discrimination claim could run into trouble.

Still, the idea that more voices add more information, and more

information will increase accuracy continues to attract favorable attention. Employers are motivated to overcome the concerns about fairness and legal requirements, so crowdsourcing may indeed be the future of appraisals.

Questions

1. Suppose you work for a company that is crowdsourcing its appraisals. Would you consider the feedback fairer if your supervisor's feedback were combined with the crowdsourced feedback or if it were presented separately? Why?

2. Do you think the advantages of crowdsourcing appraisals outweigh the disadvantages? Why or why not?

Sources: Adam Vaccaro, "Quick Fix for Performance Reviews: Crowdsource 'Em," *Inc.*, February 4, 2014, http://www.inc.com; Eric Mosley, "The Power of the Crowdsourced Performance Review," *Compensation and Benefits Review* 45, no. 6 (November/December 2013): 320–323; Anne Fisher, "Should Performance Reviews Be Crowdsourced?" *Fortune*, October 8, 2013, http://fortune.com; Eric Mosley, "Crowdsource Your Performance Reviews," *Harvard Business Review*, June 15, 2012, http://blogs.hbr.org.

Self

No one has a greater chance to observe the employee's behavior on the job than does the employee himself or herself. Self-ratings are rarely used alone, but they can contribute valuable information. A common approach is to have employees evaluate their own performance before the feedback session. This activity gets employees thinking about their performance. Areas of disagreement between the self-appraisal and other evaluations can be fruitful topics for the feedback session. At an Australia-based software company called Atlassian, self-appraisals are part of weekly performance feedback. Employees use an online app that displays performance-related questions such as, "How often have you stretched yourself?" and lets employees move a dot along a scale with a range of possible answers. The responses then serve as a catalyst for discussion in meetings between each employee and his or her supervisor.[26]

The obvious problem with self-ratings is that individuals have a tendency to inflate assessments of their performance. Especially if the ratings will be used for administrative decisions, exaggerating one's contributions has practical benefits. Also, social psychologists have found that, in general, people tend to blame outside circumstances for their failures while taking a large part of the credit for their successes. Supervisors can soften this tendency by providing frequent feedback, but because people tend to perceive situations this way, self-appraisals are not appropriate as the basis for administrative decisions.[27]

Customer feedback is one source of information used in performance appraisals. Other sources include managers, peers, subordinates, and employees themselves.

Customers

Services are often produced and consumed on the spot, so the customer is often the only person who directly observes the service performance and may be the best source of performance information. Many companies in service industries have introduced customer evaluations of employee performance. Marriott Corporation provides a customer satisfaction card in every room and mails surveys to a random sample of its hotel customers. Whirlpool's Consumer Services Division conducts mail and telephone surveys of customers after factory technicians have serviced their appliances. These surveys allow the company to evaluate an individual technician's customer-service behaviors while in the customer's home.

Using customer evaluations of employee performance is appropriate in two situations.[28] The first is when an employee's job requires direct service to the customer or linking the customer to other services within the organization. Second, customer evaluations are appropriate when the organization is interested in gathering information to determine what products and services the customer wants. That is, customer evaluations contribute to the organization's goals by enabling HRM to support the organization's marketing activities. In this regard, customer evaluations are useful both for evaluating an employee's performance and for helping to determine whether the organization can improve customer service by making changes in HRM activities such as training or compensation.

The weakness of customer surveys for performance measurement is their expense. The expenses of a traditional survey can add up to hundreds of dollars to evaluate one individual. Many organizations therefore limit the information gathering to short periods once a year.

Errors in Performance Measurement

As we noted in the previous section, one reason for gathering information from several sources is that performance measurements are not completely objective and errors can occur. People observe behavior, and they have no practical way of knowing all the circumstances, intentions, and outcomes related to that behavior, so they interpret what they see. In doing so, observers make a number of judgment calls and in some situations may even distort information on purpose. Therefore, fairness in rating performance and interpreting performance appraisals requires that managers understand the kinds of distortions that commonly occur.

LO 10-6 Define types of rating errors, and explain how to minimize them.

Types of Rating Errors

Several kinds of errors and biases commonly influence performance measurements:

- People often tend to give a higher evaluation to people they consider similar to themselves. Most of us think of ourselves as effective, so if others are like us, they must be effective, too. Research has demonstrated that this effect is strong. Unfortunately, it is sometimes wrong, and when similarity is based on characteristics such as race or sex, the decisions may be discriminatory.[29]
- If the rater compares an individual, not against an objective standard, but against other employees, *contrast errors* occur. A competent performer who works with exceptional people may be rated lower than competent simply because of the contrast.
- Raters make *distributional errors* when they tend to use only one part of a rating scale. The error is called *leniency* when the reviewer rates everyone near the top, *strictness* when the rater favors lower rankings, and *central tendency* when the rater puts everyone near the middle of the scale. Distributional errors make it difficult to compare employees rated by the same person. Also, if different raters make different kinds of distributional errors, scores by these raters cannot be compared.
- Raters often let their opinion of one quality color their opinion of others. For example, someone who speaks well might be seen as helpful or talented in other areas simply because of the overall good impression created by this one quality. Or someone who is occasionally tardy might be seen as lacking in motivation. When the bias is in a favorable direction, this is called the *halo error*. When it involves negative ratings, it is called the *horns error*. Halo error can mistakenly tell employees they don't need to improve in any area, while horns error can cause employees to feel frustrated and defensive.

Ways to Reduce Errors

Usually people make these errors unintentionally, especially when the criteria for measuring performance are not very specific. Raters can be trained how to avoid rating errors.[30] Prospective raters watch videos whose scripts or storylines are designed to lead them to make specific rating errors. After rating the fictional employees in the videos, raters discuss their rating decisions and how such errors affected their rating decisions. Training programs offer tips for avoiding the errors in the future.

Another training method for raters focuses on the complex nature of employee performance.[31] Raters learn to look at many aspects of performance that deserve their attention. Actual examples of performance are studied to bring out various performance dimensions and the standards for those dimensions. This training aims to help raters evaluate employees' performance more thoroughly and accurately.

Political Behavior in Performance Appraisals

Unintentional errors are not the only cause of inaccurate performance measurement. Sometimes the people rating performance distort an evaluation on purpose to advance their personal goals. This kind of appraisal politics is unhealthy especially because the resulting feedback does not focus on helping employees contribute to the organization's goals. High-performing employees who are rated unfairly will become frustrated, and low-performing employees who are overrated will be rewarded rather than encouraged to improve. Therefore, organizations try to identify and discourage appraisal politics.

Several characteristics of appraisal systems and company culture tend to encourage appraisal politics. Appraisal politics are most likely to occur when raters are accountable to the employee being rated, the goals of rating are not compatible with one another, performance appraisal is directly linked to highly desirable rewards, top executives tolerate or ignore distorted ratings, and senior employees tell newcomers company "folklore" that includes stories about distorted ratings.

Political behavior occurs in every organization. Organizations can minimize appraisal politics by establishing an appraisal system that is fair. One technique is to hold a **calibration meeting,** a gathering at which managers discuss employee performance ratings and provide evidence supporting their ratings with the goal of eliminating the influence of rating errors. As they discuss ratings and the ways they arrive at ratings, managers may identify undervalued employees, notice whether they are much harsher or more lenient than other managers, and help each other focus on how well ratings are associated with relevant performance outcomes. Surveys have found a majority of organizations holding calibration meetings, with changes to evaluations being a common result. In a survey by the Society for Human Resource Management, the biggest reasons for a change were that managers discovered they weren't rating their employees consistently or learned new information about employees.[32] The organization can also help managers give accurate and fair appraisals by training them to use the appraisal process, encouraging them to recognize accomplishments that the employees themselves have not identified, and fostering a climate of openness in which employees feel they can be honest about their weaknesses.[33]

Calibration Meeting
Meeting at which managers discuss employee performance ratings and provide evidence supporting their ratings with the goal of eliminating the influence of rating errors.

Giving Performance Feedback

LO 10-7 Explain how to provide performance feedback effectively.

Once the manager and others have measured an employee's performance, this information must be given to the employee. Only after the employee has received feedback can he or she begin to plan how to correct any shortcomings. Although the feedback stage of performance management is essential, it is uncomfortable to managers and employees. Delivering feedback feels to the manager as if he or she is standing in judgment of others—a role few people enjoy. Receiving criticism feels even worse. Fortunately, managers can do much to smooth the feedback process and make it effective.

Scheduling Performance Feedback

Performance feedback should be a regular, expected management activity. The custom or policy at many organizations is to give formal performance feedback once a year. But annual feedback is not enough. One reason is that managers are responsible for correcting performance deficiencies as soon as they occur. If the manager notices a problem with an employee's behavior in June, but the annual appraisal is scheduled for November, the employee will miss months of opportunities for improvement.

Another reason for frequent performance feedback is that feedback is most effective when the

When giving performance feedback, do it in an appropriate meeting place. Meet in a setting that is neutral and free of distractions. What other factors are important for a feedback session?

information does not surprise the employee. If an employee has to wait for up to a year to learn what the manager thinks of his work, the employee will wonder whether he is meeting expectations. Employees should instead receive feedback so often that they know what the manager will say during their annual performance review.

Finally, employees have indicated that they are motivated and directed by regular feedback; they want to know if they are on the right track. Managers have found that young employees in particular are looking for frequent and candid performance feedback from their managers. Across the generations, according to consultant Don MacPherson, employees are more engaged when they receive recognition for their accomplishments, identify opportunities for career advancement, and see a future role for themselves in the company—all of which a manager can address in the context of delivering feedback. MacPherson also sees frequent feedback as an opportunity for strengthening a relationship of trust between the manager and the employee.[34]

Preparing for a Feedback Session

Managers should be well prepared for each formal feedback session. The manager should create the right context for the meeting. The location should be neutral. If the manager's office is the site of unpleasant conversations, a conference room may be more appropriate. In announcing the meeting to an employee, the manager should describe it as a chance to discuss the role of the employee, the role of the manager, and the relationship between them. Managers should also say (and believe) that they would like the meeting to be an open dialogue. The content of the feedback session and the type of language used can determine the success of this meeting.

Managers should also enable the employee to be well prepared. The manager should ask the employee to complete a self-assessment ahead of time. The self-assessment requires employees to think about their performance over the past rating period and to be aware of their strengths and weaknesses so they can participate more fully in the discussion. Even though employees may tend to overstate their accomplishments, the self-assessment can help the manager and employee identify areas for discussion. When the purpose of the assessment is to define areas for development, employees may actually understate their performance. Also, differences between the manager's and the employee's rating may be fruitful areas for discussion.

Conducting the Feedback Session

During the feedback session, managers can take any of three approaches. In the "tell-and-sell" approach, managers tell the employees their ratings and then justify those ratings. In the "tell-and-listen" approach, managers tell employees their ratings and then let the employees explain their side of the story. In the "problem-solving" approach, managers and employees work together to solve performance problems in an atmosphere of respect and encouragement. Not surprisingly, research demonstrates that the problem-solving approach is superior. Perhaps surprisingly, most managers rely on the tell-and-sell approach.[35] Managers can improve employee satisfaction with the feedback process by letting employees voice their opinions and discuss performance goals.[36]

The content of the feedback should emphasize behavior, not personalities. For example, "You did not meet the deadline" can open a conversation about what needs to change, but "You're not motivated" may make the employee feel defensive and angry. The feedback session should end with goal setting and a decision about when to follow up. The "HR How To" box provides additional guidance on delivering performance feedback.

HR How To

Discussing Employee Performance

Employees and managers often dread feedback sessions, because they expect some level of criticism, and criticism feels uncomfortable. However, there are ways to structure communication about employee performance so that it feels more constructive. Here are some ideas for talking about employee performance in a way that comes across as clear, honest, and fair:

- **Use specific, concrete examples.** Statements about "attitude" or "commitment" require some mind-reading, and employees may feel misunderstood. In contrast, references to specific accomplishments and examples of behavior are more neutral. Even if the supervisor is concerned about attitude, talking about behaviors can open a discussion of the real changes that might be needed: "Several customers commented that you seemed angry when you spoke to them. Let's talk about what's happening in those conversations so you can find a way to come across to customers as pleasant."

- **Listen as well as talk.** Especially when the reviewer is nervous, the instinct is to fill up the interview time with comments. However, this interview is a valuable opportunity for the supervisor to learn

about the employee's expectations and hopes for learning and advancement. Also, ahead of the meeting, invite the employee to bring a list of his or her proudest moments. Open the meeting by inviting the employee to talk about the items on the list.

- **Be honest.** If performance is not acceptable, don't pretend that it is. Pretending is disrespectful of the employee and could get the organization in legal trouble if the employee is later let go and believes the company discriminated. If the employee asks a question and the supervisor is unsure of the answer, honesty is again the wisest course. Guessing at an answer related to an employee's future is another way to create problems for the organization, as well as for the supervisor's relationship with the employee.

- **Be positive.** Within the limits of honesty, express yourself as positively as you can. Instead of negative expressions like "You shouldn't," use positive language such as "What if we tried." Make eye contact, and use a pleasant tone of voice. Also, recognize that most employers expect their employees to handle heavy workloads. Especially if employees are

shouldering extra duties, take time to thank them.

- **Prepare for success.** Look forward to the future as well as backward at past performance. For areas where you expect a change in performance, help the employee arrive at a plan for how to make that change. Furthermore, either take time to discuss goals for career development or plan a time to do so.

Questions

1. Why would a feedback session be more effective if a manager followed these guidelines?

2. If you were conducting a feedback session with an employee who reports to you, which of these guidelines would require you to prepare ahead of time? Which are skills you already have?

Sources: Scott Halford, "Five Steps for Giving Productive Feedback," *Entrepreneur*, http://www.entrepreneur.com, accessed June 20, 2014; Bureau of National Affairs, "For Better Reviews, Discuss Money First, Avoid 'Compliment Sandwiches,'" *HR Focus*, June 2013, pp. 8–9; Andrea Murad, "How to Deliver Feedback to Employees without Squashing Morale," *Fox Business*, May 24, 2013, http://www.foxbusiness.com; Eric Jackson, "Ten Biggest Mistakes Bosses Make in Performance Reviews," *Forbes*, January 9, 2012, http://www.forbes.com.

Finding Solutions to Performance Problems

LO 10-8 Summarize ways to produce improvement in unsatisfactory performance.

When performance evaluation indicates that an employee's performance is below standard, the feedback process should launch an effort to correct the problem. Even when the employee is meeting current standards, the feedback session may identify areas in which the employee can improve in order to contribute more to the organization in a current or future job. In sum, the final feedback stage of performance management involves identifying areas for improvement and ways to improve performance in those areas.

The most effective way to improve performance varies according to the employee's ability and motivation. In general, when employees have high levels of ability and motivation, they perform at or above standards. But when they lack ability, motivation, or both, corrective action is needed. The type of action called for depends on what the employee lacks:

- *Lack of ability*—When a motivated employee lacks knowledge, skills, or abilities in some area, the manager may offer coaching, training, and more detailed feedback. Sometimes it is appropriate to restructure the job so the employee can handle it.
- *Lack of motivation*—Managers with an unmotivated employee can explore ways to demonstrate that the employee is being treated fairly and rewarded adequately. The solution may be as simple as more positive feedback (praise). Employees may need a referral for counseling or help with stress management.
- *Lack of both*—Performance may improve if the manager directs the employee's attention to the significance of the problem by withholding rewards or providing specific feedback. If the employee does not respond, the manager may have to demote or terminate the employee.

As a rule, employees who combine high ability with high motivation are solid performers. However, managers should by no means ignore these employees on the grounds of leaving well enough alone. Rather, such employees are likely to appreciate opportunities for further development. Rewards and direct feedback help to maintain these employees' high motivation levels.

LO 10-9 Discuss legal and ethical issues that affect performance management.

Legal and Ethical Issues in Performance Management

In developing and using performance management systems, human resource professionals need to ensure that these systems meet legal requirements, such as the avoidance of discrimination. In addition, performance management systems should meet ethical standards, such as protection of employees' privacy.

Legal Requirements for Performance Management

Because performance measures play a central role in decisions about pay, promotions, and discipline, employment-related lawsuits often challenge an organization's performance management system. Lawsuits related to performance management usually involve charges of discrimination or unjust dismissal.

Discrimination claims often allege that the performance management system discriminated against employees on the basis of their race or sex. Many performance measures are subjective, and measurement errors, such as those described earlier in the chapter, can easily occur. The Supreme Court has held that the selection guidelines in the federal government's *Uniform Guidelines on Employee Selection Procedures* also apply to performance measurement.[37] In general, these guidelines (discussed in Chapters 3 and 6) require that organizations avoid using criteria such as race and age as a basis for employment decisions. This requires overcoming widespread rating errors. A substantial body of evidence has shown that white and black raters tend to give higher ratings to members of their own racial group, even after rater training.[38] In addition, evidence suggests that this tendency is strongest when one group is only a small percentage of the total work group. When the vast majority of the group is male, females receive lower ratings; when the minority is male, males receive lower ratings.[39]

With regard to lawsuits filed on the grounds of unjust dismissal, the usual claim is that the person was dismissed for reasons besides the ones that the employer states. Suppose an employee who works for a defense contractor discloses that the company defrauded the government. If the company fires the employee, the employee might argue that the firing was a way to punish the employee for blowing the whistle. In this type of situation, courts generally focus on the employer's performance management system, looking to see whether the firing could have been based on poor performance. To defend itself, the employer would need a performance management system that provides evidence to support its employment decisions.

To protect against both kinds of lawsuits, it is important to have a legally defensible performance management system.[40] Such a system would be based on valid job analyses, as described in Chapter 4, with the requirements for job success clearly communicated to employees. Performance measurement should evaluate behaviors or results rather than traits. The organization should use multiple raters (including self-appraisals) and train raters in how to use the system. The organization should provide for a review of all performance ratings by upper-level managers and set up a system for employees to appeal when they believe they were evaluated unfairly. Along with feedback, the system should include a process for coaching or training employees to help them improve, rather than simply dismissing poor performers.

Electronic Monitoring and Employee Privacy

Computer technology now supports many performance management systems. Organizations often store records of employees' performance ratings, disciplinary actions, and work-rule violations in electronic databases. Many companies use computers to monitor productivity and other performance measures electronically. A company called E22 Alloy has developed a service that collects data about employees' activities on their computers, smartphones, and other devices and stores the data in the "cloud" (using computer servers accessed online). Employees can visit the service to review the data collected about themselves and delete any data they believe to be inaccurate or irrelevant. Employers can review the data—including information about what data were erased and by whom—to identify employees' activities. They can combine this information with data on business results (say, projects completed or sales closed) to inform decisions about which employees are delivering the most value.[41]

Although electronic monitoring can improve productivity, it also generates privacy concerns. Critics point out that an employer should not monitor employees when it has no reason to believe anything is wrong. They complain that monitoring systems threaten to make the workplace an electronic sweatshop in which employees are treated as robots, robbing them of dignity. Some note that employees' performances should be measured by accomplishments, not just time spent at a desks or workbenches. Electronic systems should not be a substitute for careful management. When monitoring is necessary, managers should communicate the reasons for using it. Monitoring may be used more positively to gather information for coaching employees and helping them develop their skills. Finally, organizations must protect the privacy of performance measurements, as they must do with other employee records.

THINKING ETHICALLY

HOW FAIR ARE FORCED RANKINGS?

Opinions are strong and divided about the practice of using forced rankings for identifying the top performers to reward and the bottom performers to let go. When Jack Welch was CEO of General Electric, he was famous for using a system that rated employees 1 if they ranked in the top 15%, 2 in the middle 75%, and 3 in the bottom 10%. Unless the 3s improved, they were asked to leave, so Welch's system acquired the nickname "rank and yank."

That term expresses the feelings of those who criticize forced rankings. Critics question whether organizations are really managing performance if a set percentage of people each year perform below the standards needed to stay at the company. They especially criticize performance management systems that establish a forced distribution defining what percentage of employees must fall into each level. If the forced distribution doesn't match the actual distribution of performance levels, then managers must assign employees to categories based on something other than whether they are meeting or exceeding standards.

Not surprisingly, Welch disagrees. He and others who favor forced rankings say the system is fair because it is transparent. People know where they stand and what they must achieve to improve in the rankings. Advocates of these systems also point to another kind of fairness: by defining which employees are delivering the top performance, organizations can direct the greatest rewards to the people who contribute the most. Those in favor of forced rankings also note that these systems benefit the employer by encouraging the lowest performers to leave, which opens up those positions to new employees who might perform better.

Some companies seek the advantages of forced rankings but modify the system to make it fairer. Some require rankings without establishing a forced distribution. Or a forced distribution can place most employees into one middle group, separating out only small percentages (say, 10%) at the top and bottom who need to be treated differently. Stroll, an online marketer of educational products, uses a forced distribution with three performance levels. To keep the ratings fair, the company ties each measure to one of the company's core values, and it defines each measure in terms of specific behaviors and results. Stroll also gathers self-ratings and ties feedback to planning for improvement.

Questions

1. Suppose you are an employee who exceeds every goal set for you, and you work on a team where most people seem not to try very hard and often fall short. Would a forced-ranking system seem to you like a fair way to measure and reward performance? Why or why not?

2. Suppose you are an employee who exceeds every goal set for you, and your employer has challenged you to develop by placing you on a team with brilliant, extraordinary people who not only meet goals but lead the company into great new opportunities. In this new situation, would a forced-ranking system seem to you like a fair way to measure and reward performance? Why or why not?

Sources: Laurie Harley, "The Forced Ranking Controversy," *HR and Talent Management*, November 23, 2013, http://www.hrtalentmanagement.com; Kristin Cifolelli, "Forced Rankings in Performance Reviews: Good or Bad for Business?" *EverythingPeople* (American Society of Employers), November 20, 2013, http://www.aseonline.org; Stroll, "Forced Ranking: Doing It Right, Doing It Wrong," *Hypergrowth* (Stroll blog), February 22, 2013, http://blog.stroll.com; Peter Wright, "Some Practical Thoughts on Annual Performance Management Process," *People and Strategy* 36, no. 2 (2013): 54–57.

SUMMARY

LO 10-1   Identify the activities involved in performance management.

- Performance management is the process through which managers ensure that employees' activities and outputs contribute to the organization's goals.
- First, the organization specifies which aspects of performance are relevant to the organization.
- Next, the organization measures the relevant aspects of performance through performance appraisal.

- Finally, in performance feedback sessions, managers provide employees with information about their performance so they can adjust their behavior to meet the organization's goals. Feedback includes efforts to identify and solve problems.

LO 10-2   Discuss the purposes of performance management systems.

- Organizations establish performance management systems to meet three broad purposes.

- The *strategic purpose* is aimed at meeting business objectives. The system does this by helping to link employees' behavior with the organization's goals.
- The *administrative purpose* of performance management is to provide information for day-to-day decisions about salary, benefits, recognition, and retention or termination.
- The *developmental purpose* of performance management is using the system as a basis for developing employees' knowledge and skills.

LO 10-3   Define five criteria for measuring the effectiveness of a performance management system.

- Performance measures should be *strategic*—fitting with the organization's strategy by supporting its goals and culture.
- Performance measures should be *valid*, so they measure all the relevant aspects of performance and do not measure irrelevant aspects of performance.
- These measures should also provide interrater and test-retest *reliability*, so that appraisals are consistent among raters and over time.
- Performance measurement systems should be *acceptable* to the people who use them or receive feedback from them.
- A performance measure should be *specific*, telling employees what is expected of them and how they can meet those expectations.

LO 10-4   Compare the major methods for measuring performance.

- Performance measurement may use *ranking* systems such as simple ranking, forced distribution, or paired comparisons to compare one individual's performance with that of other employees.
- These methods may be time consuming, and they will be seen as unfair if actual performance is not distributed in the same way as the ranking system requires.
- However, ranking counteracts some forms of rater bias and helps distinguish employees for administrative decisions.
- Other approaches involve *rating* employees' attributes, behaviors, or outcomes.
- Rating attributes is relatively simple but not always valid, unless attributes are specifically defined.
- Rating behaviors requires a great deal of information, but these methods can be very effective. They can link behaviors to goals, and ratings by trained raters may be highly reliable. Rating results, such as productivity or achievement of objectives, tends to be less subjective than other kinds of rating, making this approach highly acceptable.
- Validity may be a problem because of factors outside the employee's control. This method also

tends not to provide much basis for determining how to improve.
- Focusing on quality can provide practical benefits, but is not as useful for administrative and developmental decisions.

LO 10-5   Describe major sources of performance information in terms of their advantages and disadvantages.

- Performance information may come from an employee's self-appraisal and from appraisals by the employee's supervisor, employees, peers, and customers.
- Using only one source makes the appraisal more subjective. Organizations may combine many sources into a 360-degree performance appraisal.
- Gathering information from each employee's manager may produce accurate information, unless the supervisor has little opportunity to observe the employee.
- Peers are an excellent source of information about performance in a job where the supervisor does not often observe the employee. Disadvantages are that friendships (or rivalries) may bias ratings and peers may be uncomfortable with the role of rating a friend.
- Subordinates often have the best chance to see how a manager treats employees. Employees may be reluctant to contribute honest opinions about a supervisor unless they can provide information anonymously.
- Self-appraisals may be biased, but they do come from the person with the most knowledge of the employee's behavior on the job, and they provide a basis for discussion in feedback sessions, opening up fruitful comparisons and areas of disagreement between the self-appraisal and other appraisals.
- Customers may be an excellent source of performance information, although obtaining customer feedback tends to be expensive.

LO 10-6   Define types of rating errors, and explain how to minimize them.

- People observe behavior often without a practical way of knowing all the relevant circumstances and outcomes, so they necessarily interpret what they see.
- A common tendency is to give higher evaluations to people we consider similar to ourselves.
- Other errors involve using only part of the rating scale: Giving all employees ratings at the high end of the scale is called leniency error. Rating everyone at the low end of the scale is called strictness error. Rating all employees at or near the middle is called central tendency.
- The halo error refers to rating employees positively in all areas because of strong performance observed in one area.

- The horns error is rating employees negatively in all areas because of weak performance observed in one area.
- Ways to reduce rater error are training raters to be aware of their tendencies to make rating errors and training them to be sensitive to the complex nature of employee performance so they will consider many aspects of performance in greater depth.
- Politics also may influence ratings. Organizations can minimize appraisal politics by establishing a fair appraisal system and bringing managers together to discuss ratings in calibration meetings.

LO 10-7   Explain how to provide performance feedback effectively.

- Performance feedback should be a regular, scheduled management activity so that employees can correct problems as soon as they occur.
- Managers should prepare by establishing a neutral location, emphasizing that the feedback session will be a chance for discussion, and asking the employee to prepare a self-assessment.
- During the feedback session, managers should strive for a problem-solving approach and encourage employees to voice their opinions and discuss performance goals.
- The manager should look for opportunities to praise and should limit criticism.
- The discussion should focus on behavior and results rather than on personalities.

LO 10-8   Summarize ways to produce improvement in unsatisfactory performance.

- For an employee who is motivated but lacks ability, the manager should provide coaching and training, give detailed feedback about performance, and consider restructuring the job.
- For an employee who has ability but lacks motivation, the manager should investigate whether outside problems are a distraction and, if so, refer the employee for help. If the problem has to do with the employee's not feeling appreciated or

rewarded, the manager should try to deliver more praise and evaluate whether additional pay and other rewards are appropriate.
- For an employee lacking both ability and motivation, the manager should consider whether the employee is a good fit for the position. Specific feedback or withholding rewards may spur improvement, or the employee may have to be demoted or terminated.
- Solid employees who are high in ability and motivation will continue so and may be able to contribute even more if the manager provides appropriate direct feedback, rewards, and opportunities for development.

LO 10-9   Discuss legal and ethical issues that affect performance management.

- Lawsuits related to performance management usually involve charges of discrimination or unjust dismissal. Managers must make sure that performance management systems and decisions treat employees equally, without regard to their race, sex, or other protected status.
- Organizations can do this by establishing and using valid performance measures and by training raters to evaluate performance accurately. A system is more likely to be legally defensible if it is based on behaviors and results, rather than on traits, and if multiple raters evaluate each person's performance.
- The system should include a process for coaching or training employees to help them improve, rather than simply dismissing poor performers.
- An ethical issue of performance management is the use of electronic monitoring. This type of performance measurement provides detailed, accurate information, but employees may find it demoralizing, degrading, and stressful.
- Employees are more likely to accept electronic monitoring if the organization explains its purpose, links it to help in improving performance, and keeps the performance data private.

KEY TERMS

performance management, 299
simple ranking, 304
forced-distribution method, 305
paired-comparison method, 306
graphic rating scale, 306
mixed-standard scales, 308

critical-incident method, 308
behaviorally anchored rating scale (BARS), 308
behavioral observation scale (BOS), 310
organizational behavior modification (OBM), 311

management by objectives (MBO), 312
360-degree performance appraisal, 314
calibration meeting, 319

REVIEW AND DISCUSSION QUESTIONS

1. How does a complete performance management system differ from the use of annual performance appraisals? *(LO 10-1)*
2. Give two examples of an administrative decision that would be based on performance management information. Give two examples of developmental decisions based on this type of information. *(LO 10-2)*
3. How can involving employees in the creation of performance standards improve the effectiveness of a performance management system? (Consider the criteria for effectiveness listed in the chapter.) *(LO 10-3)*
4. Consider how you might rate the performance of three instructors from whom you are currently taking a course. (If you are currently taking only one or two courses, consider this course and two you recently completed.) *(LO 10-4)*
   a. Would it be harder to *rate* the instructors' performance or to *rank* their performance? Why?
   b. Write three items to use in rating the instructors—one each to rate them in terms of an attribute, a behavior, and an outcome.
   c. Which measure in (*b*) do you think is most valid? Most reliable? Why?
   d. Many colleges use questionnaires to gather data from students about their instructors' performance. Would it be appropriate to use the data for administrative decisions? Developmental decisions? Other decisions? Why or why not?
5. Imagine that a pet supply store is establishing a new performance management system to help employees provide better customer service. Management needs to decide who should participate in measuring the performance of each of the store's salespeople. From what sources should the store gather information? Why? *(LO 10-5)*
6. Would the same sources be appropriate if the store in Question 5 used the performance appraisals to support decisions about which employees to promote? Explain. *(LO 10-6)*
7. Suppose you were recently promoted to a supervisory job in a company where you have worked for two years. You genuinely like almost all your co-workers, who now report to you. The only exception is one employee, who dresses more formally than the others and frequently tells jokes that embarrass you and the other workers. Given your preexisting feelings for the employees, how can you measure their performance fairly and effectively? *(LO 10-7)*
8. Continuing the example in Question 7, imagine that you are preparing for your first performance feedback session. You want the feedback to be effective—that is, you want the feedback to result in improved performance. List five or six steps you can take to achieve your goal. *(LO 10-7)*
9. Besides giving employees feedback, what steps can a manager take to improve employees' performance? *(LO 10-8)*
10. Suppose you are a human resource professional helping to improve the performance management system of a company that sells and services office equipment. The company operates a call center that takes calls from customers who are having problems with their equipment. Call center employees are supposed to verify that the problem is not one the customer can easily handle (for example, equipment that will not operate because it has come unplugged). Then, if the problem is not resolved over the phone, the employees arrange for service technicians to visit the customer. The company can charge the customer only if a service technician visits, so performance management of the call center employees focuses on productivity—how quickly they can complete a call and move on to the next caller. To measure this performance efficiently and accurately, the company uses electronic monitoring. *(LO 10-9)*
    a. How would you expect the employees to react to the electronic monitoring? How might the organization address the employees' concerns?
    b. Besides productivity in terms of number of calls, what other performance measures should the performance management system include?
    c. How should the organization gather information about the other performance measures?

TAKING RESPONSIBILITY

REI's Purpose Drives Its Performance Management

REI (the letters stand for Recreational Equipment Inc.) is not your typical business. The company, which designs and sells equipment for outdoor recreation, is a consumer cooperative rather than a publicly traded corporation. Anyone can buy from REI, but consumers who want to can pay $20 to become lifetime members of the co-op. This makes them part-owners, who are eligible for a share of the profits and other membership benefits, along with REI's other 5 million active members.

REI is also distinctive in being driven by its mission. The co-op was started in 1938 by 23 friends who shared a love of hiking. Continuing the founders' passion, REI today states its mission as "inspiring, educating and outfitting its members and the community for a lifetime of outdoor adventure and stewardship." The resulting culture is casual, fun, and nontraditional—but also intensely concerned with high performance.

In that context, says Michelle Clements, REI's senior vice president of human resources, executives went on a retreat where they were challenged to identify "three dead ideas in three minutes." One of Clements's ideas was to abolish the organization's annual performance appraisals. It drew a standing ovation. With that response, Clements couldn't back down. She interviewed employees and managers, studied alternatives that other companies were trying, and evaluated the risks and rewards of various ideas.

Based on that work, Clements and her team developed a new program they call Real Talk, Real Results. Instead of emphasizing annual reviews, the new system focuses on training managers to give meaningful performance feedback. To support that development effort, the team defined "anchor points," using the analogy to rock climbing, where anchor points help climbers move to the next level. Online training helps managers attain such anchor points as mentoring their employees and having difficult conversations. As far as the feedback process, it no longer involves annual ratings of employees. Instead, managers are supposed to give ongoing feedback and they meet for twice-a-year calibration sessions at which they categorize employees as leading performers, solid performers, or still developing. The categories affect compensation decisions. In addition, teams are responsible for meeting team-level performance targets.

A few years since the launch of that new system, REI's company-level performance appears healthy. In 2013, REI reported annual sales of $2.0 billion, a record high. On those earnings, it generated income of more than $153 million, most of which it distributed to the active members of the co-op. In addition, more than 840,000 people became members—and that means hundreds of thousands more people participating in the mission to inspire, educate, and outfit people for outdoor adventures.

Questions

1. How did REI address the strategic, administrative, and developmental purposes of performance management?
2. If REI asked you to evaluate the effectiveness of its performance management, what criteria would you apply?

Sources: REI, "REI Overview," http://www.rei.com, accessed June 20, 2014; "REI Sales Top $2 Billion in 2013," *PR Newswire*, March 17, 2014, Business Insights: Global, http://bi.galegroup.com; Amy Armitage and Donna Parrey, "Reinventing Performance Management: Creating Purpose-Driven Practices," *People and Strategy* 36, no. 2 (2013): 26–33.

MANAGING TALENT

Adobe Systems Asks Managers to Check-In

Most people know Adobe Systems for its Photoshop software and the Acrobat and Adobe Reader programs for creating and viewing its portable document format (PDF) files. Recently, Adobe has been shifting its focus from packaged software programs to online software. During that transition, Adobe's senior vice president of people resources, Donna Morris, wondered whether its HR systems—particularly performance management—also needed a new strategy.

Evidence signaled a need for change at the 11,500-employee company. Adobe was using a process of annual reviews that ranked employees. Morris's team calculated that Adobe's managers spent 80,000 hours per year on the process, equivalent to the time of 40 full-time employees. Was the effort improving performance? Probably not. Every year, immediately following the feedback sessions, voluntary departures by employees spiked. On the corporate blog, Morris wrote a piece about her desire to eliminate formal performance appraisals. It became one of Adobe's most popular blog posts, and comments poured in from employees who were delighted with the idea and disappointed in managers' apparent lack of recognition of their accomplishments and failure to support their career development.

Morris determined that she had to act. She announced that Adobe would go forward with abolishing performance appraisals, along with related schedules and forms. Instead, the company would prepare managers to carry out a practice called the Check-In, through which they provide ongoing feedback and coaching. The timing of the feedback is up to the managers, consistent with Adobe's strategy of encouraging managers to act as "business owners" of the group they lead. Managers were trained to focus on goals, objectives, and career development. Instead of tying pay increases to rankings, managers relate them to employee achievement of their goals.

Instituting a less formal system poses some challenges. For example, without a schedule for conducting performance reviews, Adobe needs a way to ensure that managers are engaging in performance-related discussions. For this, Adobe has employees meet with managers two levels above (their boss's boss) to discuss whether they have the support they need for their team to meet its goals. The HR department emphasizes training managers in the skills needed for providing feedback.

Reactions to the changes have been overwhelmingly positive. In annual surveys, employees say the Check-ins are easier and more effective than the old system, and that their managers are getting better at helping them improve. Also telling are the rates at which employees leave. *Involuntary* departures are more common, suggesting that managers are having franker conversations with employees who do not improve. *Voluntary* departures have dropped by 30%, and a larger share of these are what Adobe calls "non-regrettable" departures.

Questions

1. How can managers at Adobe ensure that the feedback they provide during check-ins is effective?
2. In terms of the criteria for effective performance management, what advantages does Adobe gain and lose by shifting its methods from rating individuals to measuring results?

Sources: Adobe Systems, "Just Checking In," *Adobe Life* (corporate blog), http://blogs.adobe.com, accessed June 20, 2014; Bob Sutton, "How Adobe Got Rid of Traditional Performance Reviews," LinkedIn, February 6, 2014, http://www.linkedin.com; Peter Cohan, "Adobe's Stock Up 68% since It Dumped Stack Ranking, Will Microsoft's Follow?" *Forbes*, November 29, 2013, http://www.forbes.com; Julie Cook Ramirez, "Rethinking the Review," *HRE Online*, July 24, 2013, http://www.hreonline.com; Amy Armitage and Donna Parrey, "Reinventing Performance Management: Creating Purpose-Driven Practices," *People and Strategy* 36, no. 2 (2013): 26–33.

HR IN SMALL BUSINESS

Appraisals Matter at Meadow Hills Veterinary Center

Brian Conrad, the practice manager of Meadow Hills Veterinary Center, makes a claim that sounds a lot like statements you often hear in management and HR circles: "The staff is my number one asset in this hospital." Sometimes statements like that are puffery, but in Conrad's case, he puts the claim into action in the way he handles performance management at his two Washington State facilities.

Because the organization is small, appraisal interviews are handled at the highest level: each employee being evaluated meets with Conrad and the owners of the practice. Conrad wants them to be full participants in the process, not nervous subjects under a microscope, so he tries to put them at ease by giving employees a few months to look over evaluation forms ahead of time so they can see what measures will be evaluated. He also keeps the meetings regular and predictable by scheduling a meeting with each employee twice a year.

Conrad also tries to dial down the tension by separating compensation discussions from performance evaluations. In his experience, employees don't listen well to feedback if they're busy calculating whether the review will qualify them for a raise. Instead, Conrad meets twice a year with the owners to go over the budget and all the employees' contributions. Raises and bonuses are determined in those meetings and awarded to employees in meetings separate from the appraisal interviews. This keeps the appraisals focused on what is getting in the way of top performance and how employees can improve.

Conrad also tries to keep appraisal interviews positive by not waiting for appraisal time to address performance problems. His understanding of his position is that he is responsible for addressing performance problems as they arise. When a situation can't be resolved by a few words from a supervisor, Conrad invites the employee and his or her supervisor to join him for lunch away from the workplace. There they discuss the issue and look for a solution.

Conrad doesn't limit communication and feedback to problems. He tries to know employees and their work situations better by looking for informal opportunities for two-way communication. If he needs to run an errand or attend a community event, he invites one of the employees to accompany him and uses that time to ask about their career goals and how they feel about their work. Often, he uncovers opportunities for employees to develop and use untapped skills. In one case, a part-time administrative employee indicated she was interested in full-time work. Over lunch, Conrad and the employee mapped out possible career paths, and she decided to get involved in treatment of the animals. She continued to apply her administrative skills by coordinating surgeries and dentistry, and she enrolled in continuing-education classes so she could assist in the treatment area.

This approach to performance management is part of a larger objective at Meadow Hills. Conrad says he promised employees, "No team member will leave the practice feeling unchallenged, concede to a lack of direction, or have professional growth hindered." Keeping that promise requires a combination of careful hiring, ongoing training, and honest review of any mistakes that are made. When employees don't perform up to expectations, managers evaluate whether changes are needed in training or hiring. Conrad expects that employees will keep their part of the bargain by showing a willingness to try new opportunities and participate in problem solving. If employees aren't willing to buy into this culture, Conrad won't keep them on board. But apparently not many want to leave. While the rate of employee turnover for the veterinary industry is about 30%, turnover of Meadow Hills has fallen from 25% several years ago to just 10% soon after Conrad made his promise to employees.

Questions

1. Based on the information given, discuss how well the performance management at Meadow Hills

Veterinary Center meets its strategic, administrative, and developmental purposes.
2. What methods for measuring employee performance do you think would be most beneficial for Meadow Hills? Why?
3. Evaluate Brian Conrad's approach to appraisal interviews. Write a paragraph or two summarizing what Conrad is doing well and how he might further improve the effort.

Sources: "Four Ways to Add Value to Employee Evaluations," *Veterinary Economics,* January 2010, Business & Company Resource Center, http:// galenet.galegroup.com; "Help Me to Help You," *Veterinary Economics,* August 2008, Business & Company Resource Center, http://galenet.galegroup.com; Brian Conrad, "Make the Promise: Keep Your Team," *Veterinary Economics,* May 2008, Business & Company Resource Center, http://galenet.galegroup.com.

NOTES

1. Stephen Miller, "'Stack Ranking' Ends at Microsoft, Generating Heated Debate," HR Disciplines (Society for Human Resource Management), November 20, 2013, http://www.shrm.org; Elizabeth G. Olson, "Microsoft, GE, and the Futility of Ranking Employees," *Fortune,* November 18, 2013, http://fortune.com; Tom Waren, "Microsoft Axes Its Controversial Employee-Ranking System," *The Verge,* November 12, 2013, http://www.theverge.com; Shira Ovide and Rachel Feintzeig, "Microsoft Abandons 'Stack Ranking' of Employees," *The Wall Street Journal,* November 12, 2013, http://online.wsj.com.
2. Discussion based on E. Pulakos, *Performance Management* (Oxford, England: Wiley-Blackwell, 2009); H. Aguinis, "An Expanded View of Performance Management," in J. W. Smith and M. London (eds.), *Performance Management* (San Francisco: Jossey-Bass, 2009), pp. 1–43; J. Russell and L. Russell, "Talk Me Through It: The Next Level of Performance Management," *T + D,* April 2010, pp. 42–48.
3. E. Krell, "All for Incentives, Incentives for All," *HR Magazine,* January 2011, pp. 35–38.
4. Matt Schur, "Upon Further Review," *PM Network,* March 2014, pp. 38–43; Bureau of National Affairs, "Turning Mediocre Employees Great Requires Two-Way Conversation," *HR Focus,* September 2013, pp. 9–10.
5. S. Scullen, P. Bergey, and L. Aiman-Smith, "Forced Choice Distribution Systems and the Improvement of Workforce Potential: A Baseline Simulation," *Personnel Psychology* 58 (2005), pp. 1–32.
6. P. Smith and L. Kendall, "Retranslation of Expectations: An Approach to the Construction of Unambiguous Anchors for Rating Scales," *Journal of Applied Psychology* 47 (1963), pp. 149–55.
7. K. Murphy and J. Constans, "Behavioral Anchors as a Source of Bias in Rating," *Journal of Applied Psychology* 72 (1987), pp. 573–77; M. Piotrowski, J. Barnes-Farrel, and F. Estig, "Behaviorally Anchored Bias: A Replication and Extension of Murphy and Constans," *Journal of Applied Psychology* 74 (1989), pp. 823–26; R. Harvey, "Job Analysis," in *Handbook of Industrial and Organizational Psychology,* 2nd ed. (Palo Alto, CA: Consulting Psychologists Press, 1991).
8. G. Latham and K. Wexley, *Increasing Productivity through Performance Appraisal* (Boston: Addison-Wesley, 1981).
9. U. Wiersma and G. Latham, "The Practicality of Behavioral Observation Scales, Behavioral Expectation Scales, and Trait Scales," *Personnel Psychology* 39 (1986), pp. 619–28.
10. D. C. Anderson, C. Crowell, J. Sucec, K. Gilligan, and M. Wikoff, "Behavior Management of Client Contacts in a Real Estate Brokerage: Getting Agents to Sell More," *Journal of Organizational Behavior Management* 4 (2001), pp. 580–90; F. Luthans and R. Kreitner, *Organizational Behavior Modification and Beyond* (Glenview, IL: Scott-Foresman, 1975).
11. K. L. Langeland, C. M. Jones, and T. C. Mawhinney, "Improving Staff Performance in a Community Mental Health Setting: Job Analysis, Training, Goal Setting, Feedback, and Years of Data," *Journal of Organizational Behavior Management* 18 (1998), pp. 21–43.
12. J. Komaki, R. Collins, and P. Penn, "The Role of Performance Antecedents and Consequences in Work Motivation," *Journal of Applied Psychology* 67 (1982), pp. 334–40.
13. S. Snell, "Control Theory in Strategic Human Resource Management: The Mediating Effect of Administrative Information," *Academy of Management Journal* 35 (1992), pp. 292–327.
14. R. Pritchard, S. Jones, P. Roth, K. Stuebing, and S. Ekeberg, "The Evaluation of an Integrated Approach to Measuring Organizational Productivity," *Personnel Psychology* 42 (1989), pp. 69–115.
15. G. Odiorne, *MOBII: A System of Managerial Leadership for the 80s* (Belmont, CA: Pitman, 1986).
16. R. Rodgers and J. Hunter, "Impact of Management by Objectives on Organizational Productivity," *Journal of Applied Psychology* 76 (1991), pp. 322–26.
17. P. Wright, J. George, S. Farnsworth, and G. McMahan, "Productivity and Extra-role Behavior: The Effects of Goals and Incentives on Spontaneous Helping," *Journal of Applied Psychology* 78, no. 3 (1993), pp. 374–81; Mike Ledyard and Joseph Tillman, "Do Your Metrics Measure Up?" *Material Handling and Logistics,* December 2013, pp. 27–29.

18. "U.S. Employees Desire More Sources of Feedback for Performance Reviews," *T + D*, February 2012, p. 18; Cornerstone OnDemand, "Stopping the Exodus: Findings from the Cornerstone OnDemand/Harris Employee Performance Management Study," news release, December 6, 2011, http://www.cornerstoneondemand.com.

19. R. Heneman, K. Wexley, and M. Moore, "Performance Rating Accuracy: A Critical Review," *Journal of Business Research* 15 (1987), pp. 431–48.

20. T. Becker and R. Klimoski, "A Field Study of the Relationship between the Organizational Feedback Environment and Performance," *Personnel Psychology* 42 (1989), pp. 343–58; H. M. Findley, W. F. Giles, and K. W. Mossholder, "Performance Appraisal and Systems Facets: Relationships with Contextual Performance," *Journal of Applied Psychology* 85 (2000), pp. 634–40.

21. K. Wexley and R. Klimoski, "Performance Appraisal: An Update," in *Research in Personnel and Human Resource Management*, vol. 2, ed. K. Rowland and G. Ferris (Greenwich, CT: JAI Press, 1984).

22. F. Landy and J. Farr, *The Measurement of Work Performance: Methods, Theory, and Applications* (New York: Academic Press, 1983).

23. G. McEvoy and P. Buller, "User Acceptance of Peer Appraisals in an Industrial Setting," *Personnel Psychology* 40 (1987), pp. 785–97.

24. Joann S. Lublin, "Transparency Pays Off in 360-Degree Reviews," *The Wall Street Journal*, December 8, 2011, http://online.wsj.com.

25. D. Antonioni, "The Effects of Feedback Accountability on Upward Appraisal Ratings," *Personnel Psychology* 47 (1994), pp. 349–56.

26. Rachel Emma Silverman, "Performance Reviews Lose Steam," *The Wall Street Journal*, December 19, 2011, http://online.wsj.com.

27. H. Heidemeier and K. Moser, "Self-Other Agreement in Job Performance Rating: A Meta-Analytic Test of a Process Model," *Journal of Applied Psychology* 94 (2008), pp. 353–70.

28. J. Bernardin, C. Hagan, J. Kane, and P. Villanova, "Effective Performance Management: A Focus on Precision, Customers, and Situational Constraints," in *Performance Appraisal: State of the Art in Practice*, ed. J. W. Smither (San Francisco: Jossey-Bass, 1998), pp. 3–48.

29. K. Wexley and W. Nemeroff, "Effects of Racial Prejudice, Race of Applicant, and Biographical Similarity on Interviewer Evaluations of Job Applicants," *Journal of Social and Behavioral Sciences* 20 (1974), pp. 66–78.

30. D. Smith, "Training Programs for Performance Appraisal: A Review," *Academy of Management Review* 11 (1986), pp. 22–40; G. Latham, K. Wexley, and E. Pursell, "Training Managers to Minimize Rating Errors in the Observation of Behavior," *Journal of Applied Psychology* 60 (1975), pp. 550–55.

31. E. Pulakos, "A Comparison of Rater Training Programs: Error Training and Accuracy Training," *Journal of Applied Psychology* 69 (1984), pp. 581–88.

32. Claudine Kapel, "Addressing Consistency in Performance Reviews," *HR Reporter*, March 5, 2012, http://www.hrreporter.com; Ovide and Feintzeig, "Microsoft Abandons 'Stack Ranking' of Employees"; Olson, "Microsoft, GE, and the Futility of Ranking Employees."

33. S. W. J. Kozlowski, G. T. Chao, and R. F. Morrison, "Games Raters Play: Politics, Strategies, and Impression Management in Performance Appraisal," in *Performance Appraisal: State of the Art in Practice*, pp. 163–205; C. Rosen, P. Levy, and R. Hall, "Placing Perceptions of Politics in the Context of the Feedback Environment, Employee Attitudes, and Job Performance," *Journal of Applied Psychology* 91 (2006), pp. 211–20.

34. Bureau of National Affairs, "Consultants Explain How to Revamp Performance Appraisals," *Report on Salary Surveys*, April 2014, pp. 10–11.

35. K. Wexley, V. Singh, and G. Yukl, "Subordinate Participation in Three Types of Appraisal Interviews," *Journal of Applied Psychology* 58 (1973), pp. 54–57; K. Wexley, "Appraisal Interview," in *Performance Assessment*, ed. R. A. Berk (Baltimore: Johns Hopkins University Press, 1986), pp. 167–85; B. D. Cawley, L. M. Keeping, and P. E. Levy, "Participation in the Performance Appraisal Process and Employee Reactions: A Meta-analytic Review of Field Investigations," *Journal of Applied Psychology* 83, no. 3 (1998), pp. 615–63; H. Aguinis, *Performance Management* (Upper Saddle River, NJ: Pearson Prentice-Hall, 2007); C. Lee, "Feedback, Not Appraisal," *HR Magazine*, November 2006, pp. 111–14.

36. D. Cederblom, "The Performance Appraisal Interview: A Review, Implications, and Suggestions," *Academy of Management Review* 7 (1982), pp. 219–27; B. D. Cawley, L. M. Keeping, and P. E. Levy, "Participation in the Performance Appraisal Process and Employee Reactions: A Meta-analytic Review of Field Investigations," *Journal of Applied Psychology* 83, no. 3 (1998), pp. 615–63; W. Giles and K. Mossholder, "Employee Reactions to Contextual and Session Components of Performance Appraisal," *Journal of Applied Psychology* 75 (1990), pp. 371–77.

37. *Brito v. Zia Co.*, 478 F.2d 1200 (10th Cir. 1973).

38. K. Kraiger and J. Ford, "A Meta-Analysis of Ratee Race Effects in Performance Rating," *Journal of Applied Psychology* 70 (1985), pp. 56–65.

39. P. Sackett, C. DuBois, and A. Noe, "Tokenism in Performance Evaluation: The Effects of Work Group Representation on Male-Female and White-Black Differences in Performance Ratings," *Journal of Applied Psychology* 76 (1991), pp. 263–67.

40. G. Barrett and M. Kernan, "Performance Appraisal and Terminations: A Review of Court Decisions since *Brito v. Zia* with Implications for Personnel Practices," *Personnel Psychology* 40 (1987), pp. 489–503; H. Feild and W. Holley, "The Relationship of Performance Appraisal System Characteristics to Verdicts in Selected Employment Discrimination Cases," *Academy of Management Journal* 25 (1982), pp. 392–406; J. M. Werner and M. C. Bolino, "Explaining U.S. Courts of Appeals Decisions Involving Performance Appraisal: Accuracy, Fairness, and Validation," *Personnel Psychology* 50 (1997), pp. 1–24; J. Segal, "Performance Management Blunders," *HR Magazine*, November 2010, pp. 75–77; Janove, "Reviews—Good for Anything?"

41. Michael Hugos, "Monitoring Employee Performance in Real Time," *CIO*, February 29, 2012, http://blogs.cio.com.

11

Separating and Retaining Employees

What Do I Need to Know?

After reading this chapter, you should be able to:

LO 11-1 Distinguish between involuntary and voluntary turnover, and describe their effects on an organization.

LO 11-2 Discuss how employees determine whether the organization treats them fairly.

LO 11-3 Identify legal requirements for employee discipline.

LO 11-4 Summarize ways in which organizations can fairly discipline employees.

LO 11-5 Explain how job dissatisfaction affects employee behavior.

LO 11-6 Describe how organizations contribute to employees' job satisfaction and retain key employees.

Introduction

If you follow news about public schools in the United States, you might assume teachers are unhappy and even want to change jobs. Common complaints are that standards are rigid, students fail to meet standards, and schools must constantly restructure because they fail to improve performance adequately—all while governments are cutting funds. These reports, combined with the claim that teacher pay is low relative to job requirements, sound like a recipe for employee dissatisfaction. Yet according to a survey by the Center for American Progress (CAP), teachers' job satisfaction has been rising, and turnover has been falling. One reason is wide latitude in decision making: 90% of surveyed teachers said they have "a good or great deal of control" over teaching methods, and a majority said they have freedom to adapt the curriculum to their classroom. Similarly, in a survey by the Organization for Economic Cooperation and Development, roughly 90% of U.S. teachers reported being highly satisfied with their work, despite challenges such as difficulty in motivating students, a heavy workload, lack of incentives, and high expenses. And in a Gallup poll of Americans' well-being, teachers ranked second after physicians for overall well-being—reporting stress but also happiness and a chance to use their personal strengths at work. Unsurprisingly then, in the CAP study, two-thirds of first-year teachers said they would want to keep teaching even if they had a chance to switch careers.[1]

Teachers' love of teaching is good news for communities that want to keep effective teachers. But teachers are not all equally effective, so school administrators

also manage those who underperform. Their options are limited in many cases by the practice of granting tenure: after a set number of years on the job, a teacher may not be fired except for just cause. Establishing just cause is difficult and expensive. Therefore, if a teacher is not performing well, administrators either focus on helping the teacher improve or accept the poor performance.[2]

Although there are specific issues of management in the public sector, such as in a school district, every organization must meet the challenges of managing high-performing and low-performing employees. Organizations want to keep their high-performing employees. Research provides evidence that retaining employees helps retain customers and increase sales.[3] Organizations with low turnover and satisfied employees tend to perform better.[4] On the other side of the coin, organizations have to act when an employee's performance consistently falls short. Sometimes terminating a poor performer is the only way to show fairness, ensure quality, and maintain customer satisfaction.

This chapter explores the dual challenges of separating and retaining employees. We begin by distinguishing involuntary and voluntary turnover, describing how each affects the organization. Next we explore the separation process, including ways to manage this process fairly. Finally, we discuss measures the organization can take to encourage employees to stay. These topics provide a transition between Parts 3 and 4. The previous chapters considered how to assess and improve performance, and this chapter describes measures to take depending on whether performance is high or low. Part 4 discusses pay and benefits, both of which play an important role in employee retention.

Managing Voluntary and Involuntary Turnover

Organizations must try to ensure that good performers want to stay with the organization and that employees whose performance is chronically low are encouraged—or forced—to leave. Both of these challenges involve *employee turnover*, that is, employees leaving the organization. When the organization initiates the turnover (often with employees who would prefer to stay), the result is **involuntary turnover**. Examples include terminating an employee for drug use or laying off employees during a downturn. Most organizations use the word *termination* to refer only to a discharge related to a discipline problem, but some organizations call any involuntary turnover a termination. When the employees initiate the turnover (often when the organization would prefer to keep them), it is **voluntary turnover**. Employees may leave to retire or to take a job with a different organization. Typically, the employees who leave voluntarily are either the organization's worst performers, who quit before they are fired, or its best performers, who can most easily find attractive new opportunities.[5]

In general, organizations try to avoid the need for involuntary turnover and to minimize voluntary turnover, especially among top performers. Both kinds of turnover are costly, as summarized in Table 11.1. Replacing workers is expensive, and new employees need time to learn their jobs and build teamwork skills.[6] Employees who leave voluntarily out of anger and frustration may not be shy about generating unfavorable publicity. People who leave involuntarily are sometimes ready to sue a former employer if they feel they were unfairly discharged. The prospect of workplace violence also raises the risk associated with discharging employees. Effective human resource management can help the organization minimize both kinds of turnover, as well as carry it out effectively when necessary. Despite a company's best efforts at personnel selection, training, and compensation, some employees will fail to meet

LO 11-1 Distinguish between involuntary and voluntary turnover, and describe their effects on an organization.

Involuntary Turnover
Turnover initiated by an employer (often with employees who would prefer to stay).

Voluntary Turnover
Turnover initiated by employees (often when the organization would prefer to keep them).

Table 11.1

Costs Associated with Turnover

INVOLUNTARY TURNOVER	VOLUNTARY TURNOVER
Recruiting, selecting, and training replacements	Recruiting, selecting, and training replacements
Lost productivity	Lost productivity
Lawsuits	Loss of talented employees
Workplace violence	

performance requirements or will violate company policies. When this happens, organizations need to apply a discipline program that could ultimately lead to discharging the individual.

For a number of reasons, discharging employees can be very difficult. First, the decision has legal aspects that can affect the organization. Historically, if the organization and employee do not have a specific employment contract, the employer or employee may end the employment relationship at any time. This is the *employment-at-will doctrine*, described in Chapter 5. This doctrine has eroded significantly, however. Employees who have been terminated sometimes sue their employers for wrongful discharge. Some judges have considered that employment at will is limited where managers make statements that amount to an implied contract; a discharge also can be found illegal if it violates a law (such as antidiscrimination laws) or public policy (for example, firing an employee for refusing to do something illegal).[7] In a typical lawsuit for wrongful discharge, the former employee tries to establish that the discharge violated either an implied agreement or public policy. Most employers settle these claims out of court. Even though few former employees win wrongful-discharge suits, and employers usually win when they appeal, the cost of defending the lawsuit can be hundreds of thousands of dollars.[8]

Along with the financial risks of dismissing an employee, there are issues of personal safety. Distressing as it is that some former employees go to the courts, far worse are the employees who react to a termination decision with violence. Violence in the workplace has become a major organizational problem. Although any number of organizational actions or decisions may incite violence among employees, the "nothing else to lose" aspect of an employee's dismissal makes the situation dangerous, especially when the nature of the work adds other risk factors.[9]

Retaining top performers is not always easy either, and recent trends have made this more difficult than ever. Today's psychological contract, in which workers feel responsibility for their own careers rather than loyalty to a particular employer, makes voluntary turnover more likely. Also, competing organizations are constantly looking at each other's top performers. For high-demand positions, such as software engineers, "poaching talent" from other companies has become the norm.

Employee Separation

Because of the critical financial and personal risks associated with employee dismissal, it is easy to see why organizations must develop a standardized, systematic approach to discipline and discharge. These decisions

Competition for qualified, motivated workers in the STEM (scientific, technology, engineering, and medical) fields is intense. Retaining these employees is especially critical to an organization's overall success.

should not be left solely to the discretion of individual managers or supervisors. Policies that can lead to employee separation should be based on principles of justice and law, and they should allow for various ways to intervene.

Principles of Justice

The sensitivity of a system for disciplining and possibly terminating employees is obvious, and it is critical that the system be seen as fair. Employees form conclusions about the system's fairness based on the system's outcomes and procedures and the way managers treat employees when carrying out those procedures. Figure 11.1 summarizes these principles as outcome fairness, procedural justice, and interactional justice. Outcome fairness involves the ends of a discipline process, while procedural and interactional justice focus on the means to those ends. Not only is behavior ethical that is in accord with these principles, but research has also linked the last two categories of justice with employee satisfaction and productivity.[10] In considering these principles, however, keep in mind that individuals differ in how strongly they react to perceived injustice.[11]

People's perception of **outcome fairness** depends on their judgment that the consequences of a decision to employees are just. As shown in Figure 11.1, one employee's consequences should be consistent with other employees' consequences. Suppose several employees went out to lunch, returned drunk, and were reprimanded. A few weeks later, another employee was fired for being drunk at work. Employees might well conclude that outcomes are not fair because they are inconsistent. Another basis for outcome fairness is that everyone should know what to expect. Organizations promote outcome fairness when they clearly communicate policies regarding the consequences of inappropriate behavior. Finally, the outcome should be proportionate to the behavior. Terminating an employee for being late to work, especially if this is the first time the employee is late, would seem out of proportion to the offense in most situations. Employees' sense of outcome fairness usually would reserve loss of a job for the most serious offenses.

People's perception of **procedural justice** is their judgment that fair methods were used to determine the consequences an employee receives. Figure 11.1 shows

LO 11-2 Discuss how employees determine whether the organization treats them fairly.

Outcome Fairness
A judgment that the consequences given to employees are just.

Procedural Justice
A judgment that fair methods were used to determine the consequences an employee receives.

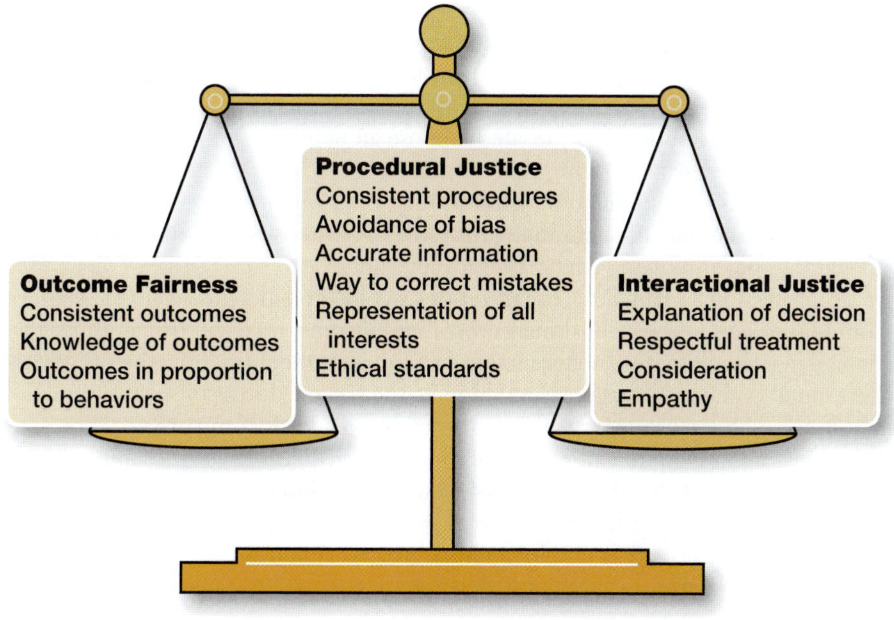

Figure 11.1
Principles of Justice

Outcome Fairness
Consistent outcomes
Knowledge of outcomes
Outcomes in proportion
  to behaviors

Procedural Justice
Consistent procedures
Avoidance of bias
Accurate information
Way to correct mistakes
Representation of all
  interests
Ethical standards

Interactional Justice
Explanation of decision
Respectful treatment
Consideration
Empathy

six principles that determine whether people perceive procedures as fair. The procedures should be consistent from one person to another, and the manager using them should suppress any personal biases. The procedures should be based on accurate information, not rumors or falsehoods. The procedures should also be correctable, meaning the system includes safeguards, such as channels for appealing a decision or correcting errors. The procedures should take into account the concerns of all the groups affected—for example, by gathering information from employees, customers, and managers. Finally, the procedures should be consistent with prevailing ethical standards, such as concerns for privacy and honesty.

Interactional Justice
A judgment that the organization carried out its actions in a way that took the employee's feelings into account.

A perception of **interactional justice** is a judgment that the organization carried out its actions in a way that took the employee's feelings into account. It is a judgment about the ways that managers interact with their employees. A disciplinary action meets the standards of interactional justice if the manager explains to the employee how the action is procedurally just. The manager should listen to the employee. The manager should also treat the employee with dignity and respect and should empathize with the employee's feelings. Even when a manager discharges an employee for doing something wrong, the manager can speak politely and state the reasons for the action. These efforts to achieve interactional justice are especially important when managing an employee who has a high level of hostility and is at greater risk of responding with violence.[12]

LO 11-3 Identify legal requirements for employee discipline.

Legal Requirements

The law gives employers wide latitude in hiring and firing, but employers must meet certain requirements. They must avoid wrongful discharge and illegal discrimination. They also must meet standards related to employees' privacy and adequate notice of layoffs.

Wrongful Discharge   As we noted earlier in the chapter, discipline practices must avoid the charge of wrongful discharge. First, this means the discharge may not violate an implied agreement. Terminating an employee may violate an implied agreement if the employer had promised the employee job security or if the action is inconsistent with company policies. An example might be that an organization has stated that an employee with an unexcused absence will receive a warning for the first violation, but an angry supervisor fires an employee for being absent on the day of an important meeting.

Another reason a discharge may be considered wrongful is that it violates public policy. Violations of public policy include terminating the employee for refusing to do something illegal, unethical, or unsafe. Suppose an employee refuses to dump chemicals into the sewer system; firing that employee could be a violation of public policy. It is also a violation of public policy to terminate an employee for doing what the law requires—for example, cooperating with a government investigation, reporting illegal behavior by the employer, or reporting for jury duty.

HR professionals can help organizations avoid (and defend against) charges of wrongful discharge by establishing and communicating policies for handling misbehavior. They should define unacceptable behaviors and identify how the organization will respond to them. Managers should follow these procedures consistently and document precisely the reasons for disciplinary action. In addition, the organization should train managers to avoid making promises that imply job security (for example, "As long as you keep up that level of performance, you'll have a job with us"). Finally, in writing and reviewing employee handbooks, HR professionals should avoid any statements that could be interpreted as employment contracts. When there is any doubt about a statement, the organization should seek legal advice.

Discrimination Another benefit of a formal discipline policy is that it helps the organization comply with equal employment opportunity requirements. As in other employment matters, employers must make decisions without regard to individuals' age, sex, race, or other protected status. If two employees steal from the employer but one is disciplined more harshly than the other, the employee who receives the harsher punishment could look for the cause in his or her being of a particular race, country of origin, or some other group. Evenhanded, carefully documented discipline can avoid such claims.

Employees' Privacy The courts also have long protected individuals' privacy in many situations. At the same time, employers have legitimate reasons for learning about some personal matters, especially when behavior outside the workplace can affect productivity, workplace safety, and employee morale. Employers therefore need to ensure that the information they gather and use is relevant to these matters. For example, safety and security make it legitimate to require drug testing of all employees holding jobs such as police officer, firefighter, and airline flight crew.[13] (Governments at the federal, state, and local levels have many laws affecting drug-testing programs, so it is wise to get legal advice before planning such tests.) The use of social media is another area where employers have considered employees' personal activities to be relevant; for more on this, see the "HRM Social" box.

Privacy issues also surface when employers wish to search or monitor employees on the job. An employer that suspects theft, drug use, or other misdeeds on the job may wish to search employees for evidence. In general, random searches of areas such as desks, lockers, toolboxes, and communications such as e-mails are permissible, so long as the employer can justify that there is probable cause for the search and the organization has work rules that provide for searches.[14] Employers can act fairly and minimize the likelihood of a lawsuit by publicizing the search policy, applying it consistently, asking for the employee's consent before the search begins, and conducting the search discreetly. Also, when a search is a random check, it is important to clarify that no one has been accused of misdeeds.[15]

No matter how sensitively the organization gathers information leading to disciplinary actions, it should also consider privacy issues when deciding who will see the information.[16] In general, it is advisable to share the information only with people who have a business need to see it—for example, the employee's supervisor, union officials, and in some cases, co-workers. Letting outsiders know the reasons for terminating an employee can embarrass the employee, who might file a defamation lawsuit. HR professionals can help organizations avoid such lawsuits by working with managers to determine fact-based explanations and to decide who needs to see these explanations.

Table 11.2 summarizes these measures for protecting employees' privacy.

Ensure that information is relevant.
Publicize information-gathering policies and consequences.
Request consent before gathering information.
Treat employees consistently.
Conduct searches discreetly.
Share information only with those who need it.

Table 11.2

Measures for Protecting Employees' Privacy

Employees' Privacy vs. Employer's Reputation

For the most part, what employees post on Facebook and Pinterest or share with their followers on Twitter relates only to their personal lives and relationships. Occasionally, however, an employee shares information that should have been confidential or expresses an opinion that could damage the employer's reputation. This possibility leaves employers wondering how far they should go in monitoring what employees share on social media.

The chief argument in favor of monitoring is that employees have occasionally done real damage to a company by posting nasty statements about customers or harassing their co-workers. If this kind of behavior goes far enough, it can damage the company's reputation and even provoke a lawsuit. Hospitals have discovered that their employees discussed patients on Facebook, which is illegal as well as unethical.

The major argument against monitoring is that unless an employer has a reason to be suspicious of particular employees, it is an invasive overreaction. According to this viewpoint, most employees' social-media activities are unrelated to work, so employers should respect their privacy. In a company that makes a habit out of tracking employees' personal use of social media, it too easily becomes possible to weigh every photo and statement, looking for supposedly offensive behavior until employees are penalized for behavior that has nothing to do with the employer's well-being. Beyond the justice issue is the practical question of whether it is even possible to monitor all of employees' social-media activity, given that most applications have privacy settings.

There is another way to think about employees' use of social media: it can also be an asset for the employer. At a company where people are highly satisfied with their jobs and engaged in their work, employees are likely to say positive things about work, thereby enhancing the company's reputation. Some even go so far as to become "employee activists," who defend their company against critics, promote it as a great place to work, and generally advocate for it online.

Questions

1. Under what conditions do you think an employer should monitor employees' personal use of social media?
2. Aside from legal requirements, how should the principles of justice shape any efforts by employers to monitor employees' personal use of social media?

Sources: "Should Companies Monitor Their Employees' Social Media?" *The Wall Street Journal*, May 11, 2014, http://online.wsj.com; Karen Higginbottom, "Social Media Ignites Employee Activism," *Forbes*, April 14, 2014, http://www.forbes.com; Suzanne Lucas, "Yes, Your Employees Use Social Media. Now Stop Spying on Them," *Inc.*, September 26, 2013, http://www.inc.com.

LO 11-4 Summarize ways in which organizations can discipline employees fairly.

Notification of Layoffs Sometimes terminations are necessary not because of individuals' misdeeds, but because the organization determines that for economic reasons it must close a facility. An organization that plans such broad-scale layoffs may be subject to the Workers' Adjustment Retraining and Notification Act. This federal law requires that organizations with more than 100 employees give 60 days' notice before any closing or layoff that will affect at least 50 full-time employees. If employers covered by this law do not give notice to the employees (and their union, if applicable), they may have to provide back pay and fringe benefits and pay penalties as well. Several states and cities have similar laws, and the federal law contains a number of exemptions. Therefore, it is important to seek legal advice before implementing a plant closing.

Hot-Stove Rule
Principle of discipline that says discipline should be like a hot stove, giving clear warning and following up with consistent, objective, immediate consequences.

Progressive Discipline

Organizations look for methods of handling problem behavior that are fair, legal, and effective. A popular principle for responding effectively is the **hot-stove rule**. According to this principle, discipline should be like a hot stove: The glowing or burning stove gives warning not to touch. Anyone who ignores the warning will be burned. The stove has no feelings to influence which people it burns, and it delivers the same burn to any touch. Finally, the burn is immediate. Like the hot stove, an organization's discipline should give warning and have consequences that are consistent, objective, and immediate.

The principles of justice suggest that the organization prepare for problems by establishing a formal discipline process in which the consequences become more serious if the employee repeats the offense. Such a system is called **progressive discipline**. A typical progressive discipline system identifies and communicates unacceptable behaviors and responds to a series of offenses with the actions shown in Figure 11.2—spoken and then written warnings, temporary suspension, and finally, termination. This process fulfills the purpose of discipline by teaching employees what is expected of them and creating a situation in which employees must try to do what is expected. It seeks to prevent misbehavior (by publishing rules) and to correct, rather than merely punish, misbehavior.

Such procedures may seem exasperatingly slow, especially when the employee's misdeeds hurt the team's performance. In the end, however, if an employee must be discharged, careful use of the procedure increases other employees' belief that the organization is fair and reduces the likelihood that the problem employee will sue (or at least that the employee will win in court). For situations in which misbehavior is dangerous, the organization may establish a stricter policy, even terminating an employee for the first offense. In that case, it is especially important to communicate the procedure—not only to ensure fairness but also to prevent the dangerous misbehavior.

Creating a formal discipline process is a primary responsibility of the human resource department. The HR professional should consult with supervisors and managers to identify unacceptable behaviors and establish rules and consequences for violating the rules. The rules should cover disciplinary problems such as the following behaviors encountered in many organizations:

- Tardiness
- Absenteeism
- Unsafe work practices
- Poor quantity or quality of work
- Sexual harassment of co-workers
- Coming to work impaired by alcohol or drugs
- Theft of company property
- Cyberslacking (conducting personal business online during work hours)

For each infraction, the HR professional would identify a series of responses, such as those in Figure 11.2. In addition, the organization must communicate these rules and consequences in writing to every employee. Ways of publishing rules include

Progressive Discipline
A formal discipline process in which the consequences become more serious if the employee repeats the offense.

Figure 11.2
Progressive Discipline Responses

| Unofficial spoken warning | Official written warning | 2nd written warning plus threat of temporary suspension | Temporary suspension plus written notice that this is a last chance to improve | Termination |

presenting them in an employee handbook, posting them on the company's intranet, and displaying them on a bulletin board. Supervisors should be familiar with the rules, so that they can discuss them with employees and apply them consistently.

Along with rules and a progression of consequences for violating the rules, a progressive discipline system should have requirements for documenting the rules, offenses, and responses. For issuing an unofficial warning about a less-serious offense, it may be enough to have a witness present. Even then, a written record would be helpful in case the employee repeats the offense in the future. The organization should provide a document for managers to file, recording the nature and date of the offense, the specific improvement expected, and the consequences of the offense. It is also helpful to indicate how the offense affects the performance of the individual employee, others in the group, or the organization as a whole. These documents are important for demonstrating to a problem employee why he or she has been suspended or terminated. They also back up the organization's actions if it should have to defend a lawsuit. Following the hot-stove rule, the supervisor should complete and discuss the documentation immediately after becoming aware of the offense. A copy of the records should be placed in the employee's personnel file. The organization may have a policy of removing records of warnings after a period such as six months, on the grounds that the employee has learned from the experience.

As we noted in the earlier discussion of procedural justice, the discipline system should provide an opportunity to hear every point of view and to correct errors, following a procedure that is consistent for all employees.[17] As soon as possible and before discussing and filing records of misbehavior, it is important for the supervisor to investigate the incident. The employee should be made aware of what he or she is said to have done wrong and should have an opportunity to present his or her version of events. Anyone who witnessed the alleged misdeed also should have an opportunity to present his or her version of what happened. All the statements should be recorded in writing, signed, and dated. In general, employees who belong to a union have a right to the presence of a union representative during a formal investigation interview if they request representation. Finally, employers can support the discipline system's fairness by using a performance management system that gathers objective performance data.

Besides developing these policies, HR professionals have a role in carrying out progressive discipline.[18] In meetings to announce disciplinary actions, it is wise to include two representatives of the organization. Usually, the employee's supervisor presents the information, and a representative from the HR department acts as a witness. This person can help the meeting stay on track and, if necessary, can later confirm what happened during the meeting. Especially at the termination stage of the process, the employee may be angry, so it is helpful to be straightforward but polite. The supervisor should state the reason for the meeting, the nature of the problem behavior, and the consequences. For more details on how to conduct the meeting, see "HR How To." When an employee is suspended or terminated, the organization should designate a person to escort the employee from the building to protect the organization's people and property.

Alternative Dispute Resolution

Sometimes problems are easier to solve when an impartial person helps create the solution. Therefore, at various points in the discipline process, the employee or organization might want to bring in someone to help with problem solving. Rather than turning to the courts every time an outsider is desired, more and more organizations

HR How To

Announcing a Disciplinary Action

No one likes delivering bad news, but a few principles help to make the process as fair and straightforward as possible:

- Plan what to say, and stick to the plan. If there is an awkward silence, be patient; don't fill it up with statements that stray from the planned message.
- Move quickly to the main message. Unfortunately, that is easily identified as the point that is the hardest to say—for example, "We are suspending you" or "We have to end your employment with us." Dancing around the point will only confuse the employee. Starting off with small talk will make delivering the main point even more awkward.

- Stay on the main point. Do not minimize the problem, which could imply that your decision is unfair. Do not imply you will reconsider a decision or get bogged down in arguments or explanations. Again, this just confuses the employee by suggesting that a final decision is actually up for negotiation.
- Speak firmly, making eye contact, but be compassionate. Even in the case of misbehavior, the employee is a human being.
- Listen to the employee with respect but without implying that a decision is up for negotiation.
- Keep the meeting short—no more than about 15 minutes. The employee should leave with information on how to contact

the HR department with any questions that come up later.

Questions

1. How do these guidelines meet the principles of justice?
2. How can managers respect an employee's privacy in applying these guidelines?

Sources: Amy DelPo, "What to Say When You Fire an Employee," *Nolo Legal Encyclopedia*, http://www.nolo.com, accessed June 25, 2014; Anne Fisher, "Four Steps to Delivering Really Bad News," *Fortune*, February 6, 2014, http://fortune.com; Rich Hein, "Eight Tips for How to Fire an Employee," *CIO*, January 22, 2013, http://www.cio.com.

---

are using **alternative dispute resolution (ADR)**. A variety of ADR techniques show promise for resolving disputes in a timely, constructive, cost-effective manner (see Figure 11.3):

1. **Open-door policy**—Based on the expectation that two people in conflict should first try to arrive at a settlement together, the organization has a policy of making managers available to hear complaints. Typically, the first "open door" is that of the employee's immediate supervisor, and if the employee does not get a

Alternative Dispute Resolution (ADR)
Methods of solving a problem by bringing in an impartial outsider but not using the court system.

Open-Door Policy
An organization's policy of making managers available to hear complaints.

Figure 11.3
Options for Alternative Dispute Resolution

Peer Review
Process for resolving disputes by taking them to a panel composed of representatives from the organization at the same levels as the people in the dispute.

Mediation
Nonbinding process in which a neutral party from outside the organization hears the case and tries to help the people in conflict arrive at a settlement.

Arbitration
Binding process in which a professional arbitrator from outside the organization (usually a lawyer or judge) hears the case and resolves it by making a decision.

Employee Assistance Program (EAP)
A referral service that employees can use to seek professional treatment for emotional problems or substance abuse.

resolution from that person, the employee may appeal to managers at higher levels. This policy works only to the degree that employees trust management and managers who hear complaints listen and are able to act.

2. **Peer review**—The people in conflict take their conflict to a panel composed of representatives from the organization at the same levels as the people in the dispute. The panel hears the case and tries to help the parties arrive at a settlement. To set up a panel to hear disputes as they arise, the organization may assign managers to positions on the panel and have employees elect nonmanagement panel members.

3. **Mediation**—A neutral party from outside the organization hears the case and tries to help the people in conflict arrive at a settlement. The process is not binding, meaning the mediator cannot force a solution.

4. **Arbitration**—A professional arbitrator from outside the organization hears the case and resolves it by making a decision. Most arbitrators are experienced employment lawyers or retired judges. The employee and employer both have to accept this person's decision.

Typically, an organization's ADR process begins with an open-door policy, which is the simplest, most direct, and least expensive way to settle a dispute. When the parties to a dispute cannot resolve it themselves, the organization can move the dispute to peer review, mediation, or arbitration. At some organizations, if mediation fails, the process moves to arbitration as a third and final option. Although arbitration is a formal process involving an outsider, it tends to be much faster, simpler, and more private than a lawsuit.[19]

Employee Assistance Programs

While ADR is effective in dealing with problems related to performance and disputes between people at work, many of the problems that lead an organization to want to terminate an employee involve drug or alcohol abuse. In these cases, the organization's discipline program should also incorporate an **employee assistance program (EAP)**. An EAP is a referral service that employees can use to seek professional treatment for emotional problems or substance abuse. EAPs began in the 1950s with a focus on treating alcoholism, and in the 1980s they expanded into drug treatment. Today, many are now fully integrated into employers' overall health benefits plans, where they refer employees to covered mental health services.

EAPs vary widely, but most share some basic elements. First, the programs are usually identified in official documents published by the employer, such as employee handbooks. Supervisors (and union representatives when workers belong to a union) are trained to use the referral service for employees whom they suspect of having health-related problems. The organization also trains employees to use the system to refer themselves when necessary. The organization regularly evaluates the costs and benefits of the program, usually once a year.

One source of variation in EAPs involves the options for delivering services. For example, some EAP providers offer certain services online. An EAP provider called Companion Benefit Alternatives has developed "Beating the Blues," an online program for coping with depression and anxiety. An employee using this program watches videos, maintains a diary, and fills out assessments that track his or her level of distress. The distress measures are displayed in a graph, so employees can see their progress and a nurse or social worker from the program can intervene if distress levels get too high. Studies of this program report improvement in a majority of participants, as well as faster recovery for patients found to need face-to-face therapy. Another option is telepsychiatry, in which the patient uses video conferencing equipment to participate in online meetings with a therapist.[20]

Outplacement Counseling

An employee who has been discharged is likely to feel angry and confused about what to do next. If the person feels there is nothing to lose and nowhere else to turn, the potential for violence or a lawsuit is greater than most organizations are willing to tolerate. This concern is one reason many organizations provide **outplacement counseling**, which tries to help dismissed employees manage the transition from one job to another. Organizations also may address ongoing poor performance with discussion about whether the employee is a good fit for the current job. Rather than simply firing the poor performer, the supervisor may encourage this person to think about leaving. In this situation, the availability of outplacement counseling may help the employee decide to look for another job. This approach may protect the dignity of the employee who leaves and promote a sense of fairness.

Some organizations have their own staff for conducting outplacement counseling. Other organizations have contracts with outside providers to help with individual cases. Either way, the goals for outplacement programs are to help the former employee address the psychological issues associated with losing a job—grief, depression, and fear—while at the same time helping the person find a new job.

The use of outplacement firms has become far more common since John Challenger witnessed IBM's first-ever round of major layoffs in 1993. Challenger's father, James, started the first outplacement firm in the United States, when downsizing was not yet a part of the business vocabulary. Today firms such as Challenger, Gray & Christmas, and Lee Hecht Harrison regularly dispatch counselors to help laid-off people recover from the shock of joblessness, polish their résumés, conduct job searches, and practice interviewing. Challenger's firm has even landed a contract to help with an increasingly common form of transition: moving from military service to employment in the civilian sector.[21]

Whatever the reason for downsizing, asking employees to leave is a setback for the employee and for the company. Retaining people who can contribute knowledge and talent is essential to business success. Therefore, the remainder of this chapter explores issues related to retaining employees.

Outplacement Counseling
A service in which professionals try to help dismissed employees manage the transition from one job to another.

Employee Engagement

Ideally, an organization does not merely want employees to come to work each day but rather wants employees to be fully engaged. As defined in Chapter 9, employee engagement is the degree to which employees are fully involved in their work and the strength of their commitment to their job and company. Employees who are engaged in their work and committed to the company they work for provide a clear competitive advantage to that firm, including higher productivity, better customer service, and lower turnover.[22] (For some supporting data, see the "Did You Know?" box.) Unfortunately, many companies have not given much attention to employee engagement in recent years, possibly due to the recession and slow recovery. Some survey results suggest that less than one-third of employees consider themselves as engaged. Still, some companies have managed to sustain and improve engagement levels during the recession by systematically gathering feedback from employees, analyzing their responses, and implementing changes. In these companies, engagement measures are considered as important as customer service or financial data.

Although the types of questions asked in employee engagement surveys may vary, some of the common themes generally measured include pride and satisfaction with

Did You Know?

Where Profits Are Growing, More Employees Are Engaged

Employees are more likely to be engaged at companies where profits are rising than at companies with flat or falling profits, according to research by Quantum Workplace. The same research found that in the companies with flat or falling profits, employees were less likely to feel valued, trust senior management, or see their work as aligned with corporate strategy.

Question

Based on the information given, how might the companies with falling profits address employee engagement? What effect would you expect this to have on future profits?

Sources: Bureau of National Affairs, "Studies Detail the Business Case for Employee Engagement," *Report on Salary Surveys*, November 2013, pp. 8–9; Hilary Wright, "Employee Engagement Continues to Improve: 2013 Trends," Quantum Workplace employee engagement blog, March 27, 2013, http://www.quantumworkplace.com; Quantum Workplace, "2013 Trends Report: The State of Employee Engagement," 2013, accessed at http://www.quantumworkplace.com.

Engaged Employees as a Percentage of Company Workforce

employer; opportunity to perform challenging work; recognition and positive feedback from contributions; personal support from supervisor; and understanding of the link between one's job and the company's overall mission. At Pitney Bowes, about 80% of its employees complete an engagement survey each year, which gives them a chance to share their feelings and perceptions and help the company address problems.[23] The survey is also used to determine if the company is doing enough to help employees reach their career goals. Based on survey results, the company is trying out a program that is designed to help managers improve their skills in listening, change management, and problem solving. Pitney-Bowes managers are held accountable for helping employees with their careers, and this program ensures they have the skills necessary for success.

Two other companies that have tackled employee engagement are London-based Aegis Media and Vi, which develops and manages retirement communities. Aegis Media matches each newly hired employee with a more experienced co-worker so that new employees have someone who can help them learn their way around. The HR team also checks with employees periodically to make sure they have the resources they need to succeed, and it conducts yearly surveys to measure employee engagement. Vi is especially concerned with engagement of nurses at its facilities, because employees in that profession can readily find jobs elsewhere. Its approach is to focus on training and leadership development, so that staying with Vi enables a rewarding career. In annual engagement surveys, nurses for Vi have rated their training and ability to achieve career goals higher than employees at other companies in the same industry, which bodes well for employee turnover.[24]

Job Withdrawal

A basic but important step on the path toward an engaged workforce is to prevent a broad negative condition called **job withdrawal**—or a set of behaviors with which employees try to avoid the work situation physically, mentally, or emotionally. Job withdrawal results when circumstances such as the nature of the job, supervisors and co-workers, pay levels, or the employee's own disposition cause the employee to become dissatisfied with the job. As shown in Figure 11.4, this job dissatisfaction produces job withdrawal. Job withdrawal may take the form of behavior change, physical job withdrawal, or psychological withdrawal. Some researchers believe employees engage in the three forms of withdrawal behavior in that order, while others think they select from these behaviors to address the particular sources of job dissatisfaction they experience.[25] Although the specifics of these models vary, the consensus is that withdrawal behaviors are related to one another and are at least partially caused by job dissatisfaction.[26]

Job Withdrawal
A set of behaviors with which employees try to avoid the work situation physically, mentally, or emotionally.

Job Dissatisfaction

Many aspects of people and organizations can cause job dissatisfaction, and managers and HR professionals need to be aware of them because correcting them can increase job satisfaction and prevent job withdrawal. Ideally, managers should catch and correct job dissatisfaction early because there is evidence linking changes in satisfaction levels to turnover: when satisfaction is falling, employees are far more likely to quit.[27] The causes of job dissatisfaction identified in Figure 11.4 fall into four categories: personal dispositions, tasks and roles, supervisors and co-workers, and pay and benefits.

LO 11-5 Explain how job dissatisfaction affects employee behavior.

Personal Dispositions Job dissatisfaction is a feeling experienced by individuals, so it is not surprising that many researchers have studied individual personality differences to see if some kinds of people are more disposed to be dissatisfied with their jobs. In general, job turnover (and presumably dissatisfaction leading up to it) is higher among employees who are low in emotional stability, conscientiousness, and agreeableness.[28] In addition, two other personal qualities associated with job satisfaction are negative affectivity and negative self-evaluations.

Negative affectivity means pervasive low levels of satisfaction with all aspects of life, compared with other people's feelings. People with negative affectivity experience

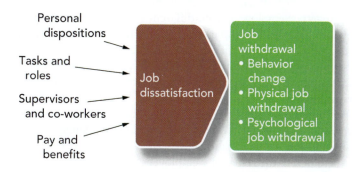

Figure 11.4

Job Withdrawal Process

Personal dispositions

Tasks and roles

Supervisors and co-workers

Pay and benefits

Job dissatisfaction

Job withdrawal
- Behavior change
- Physical job withdrawal
- Psychological job withdrawal

feelings such as anger, contempt, disgust, guilt, fear, and nervousness more than other people do, at work and away. They tend to focus on the negative aspects of themselves and others.[29] Not surprisingly, people with negative affectivity tend to be dissatisfied with their jobs, even after changing employers or occupations.[30]

Core self-evaluations are bottom-line opinions individuals have of themselves and may be positive or negative. People with a positive core self-evaluation have high self-esteem, believe in their ability to accomplish their goals, and are emotionally stable. They also tend to experience job satisfaction.[31] Part of the reason for their satisfaction is that they tend to seek out and obtain jobs with desirable characteristics, and when they are in a situation they dislike, they are more likely to seek change in socially acceptable ways.[32] In contrast, people with negative core self-evaluations tend to blame other people for their problems, including their dissatisfying jobs. They are less likely to work toward change; they either do nothing or act aggressively toward the people they blame.[33]

Tasks and Roles   As a predictor of job dissatisfaction, nothing surpasses the nature of the task itself.[34] Many aspects of a task have been linked to dissatisfaction. Of particular significance are the complexity of the task, the degree of physical strain and exertion required, and the value the employee places on the task.[35] In general, employees (especially women) are bored and dissatisfied with simple, repetitive jobs.[36] People also are more dissatisfied with jobs requiring a great deal of physical strain and exertion. Because automation has removed much of the physical strain associated with jobs, employers often overlook this consideration. Still, many jobs remain physically demanding. Finally, employees feel dissatisfied if their work is not related to something they value.

Employees not only perform specific tasks but also have roles within the organization.[37] A person's **role** consists of the set of behaviors that people expect of a person in that job. These expected behaviors include the formally defined duties of the job but also much more. Sometimes things get complicated or confusing. Co-workers, supervisors, and customers have expectations for how the employee should behave, often going far beyond a formal job description and having a large impact on the employee's work satisfaction. Several role-related sources of dissatisfaction are the following:

- **Role ambiguity** is uncertainty about what the organization and others expect from the employee in terms of what to do or how to do it. Employees suffer when they are unclear about work methods, scheduling, and performance criteria, perhaps because others hold different ideas about these. Employees particularly want to know how the organization will evaluate their performance. When they aren't sure, they become dissatisfied.[38]

- **Role conflict** is an employee's recognition that demands of the job are incompatible or contradictory; a person cannot meet all the demands. For example, a company might bring together employees from different functions to work on a team to develop a new product. Team members feel role conflict when they realize that their team leader and functional manager have conflicting expectations of them. Also, many employees may feel conflict between work roles and family roles. A role conflict may be triggered by an organization's request that an employee take an assignment overseas. Foreign assignments can be highly disruptive to family members, and the resulting role conflict is the top reason that people quit overseas assignments.[39]

- **Role overload** results when too many expectations or demands are placed on a person. (The opposite situation is *role underload*.) After an organization downsizes, it may expect so much of the remaining employees that they experience role overload.

Role
The set of behaviors that people expect of a person in a particular job.

Role Ambiguity
Uncertainty about what the organization expects from the employee in terms of what to do or how to do it.

Role Conflict
An employee's recognition that demands of the job are incompatible or contradictory.

Role Overload
A state in which too many expectations or demands are placed on a person.

Supervisors and Co-workers   Negative behavior by managers and peers in the workplace can produce tremendous dissatisfaction. Often much of the responsibility for positive relationships is placed on direct supervisors. For example, employees want their supervisors to define expectations clearly, measure progress fairly and accurately, and acknowledge their accomplishments.[40] Employees want supervisors to see them as individuals and help create the conditions in which they can succeed—for example, giving assignments suitable for their skills and providing access to the necessary resources. Employees want some evidence that the company's leaders care about them, so they are more likely to be dissatisfied if management is distant and unresponsive.

In other cases, conflicts between employees left unaddressed by management may cause job dissatisfaction severe enough to lead to withdrawal or departure. Research suggests that turnover is higher when employees do not feel that their values and beliefs fit with their work group's values and beliefs.[41] Furthermore uncivil behavior by co-workers generates unhappiness that manifests in a variety of ways, such as decreased commitment, effort, and performance.[42]

Pay and Benefits   For all the concern with positive relationships and interesting work, it is important to keep in mind that employees definitely care about their earnings. A job is the primary source of income and financial security for most people. Pay also is an indicator of status within the organization and in society at large, so it contributes to some people's self-worth. For all these reasons, satisfaction with pay is significant for retaining employees. Decisions about pay and benefits are so important and complex that the chapters of the next part of this book are devoted to this topic.

With regard to job satisfaction, the pay level—that is, the amount of income associated with each job—is especially important. Employers seeking to lure away another organization's employees often do so by offering higher pay. Benefits, such as insurance and vacation time, are also important, but employees often have difficulty measuring their worth. Therefore, although benefits influence job satisfaction, employees may not always consider them as much as pay itself.

Behavior Change

A reasonable expectation is that an employee's first response to dissatisfaction would be to try to change the conditions that generate the dissatisfaction. As the employee tries to bring about changes in policy or personnel, the efforts may involve confrontation and conflict with the employee's supervisor. In an organization where employees are represented by a union, as we will discuss in Chapter 15, more grievances may be filed.

Military reservists who are sent overseas often experience role conflict among *three* roles: soldier, family member, and civilian employee. Overseas assignments often intensify role conflicts.

From the manager's point of view, the complaints, confrontations, and grievances may feel threatening. On closer inspection, however, this is an opportunity for the manager to learn about and solve a potentially important problem. When a secure and supportive manager properly channels employees' expressions of dissatisfaction, the results can include greater employee engagement, lower turnover, and substantial improvements in the organization's performance.[43]

When employees cannot work with management to make changes, they may look for help from outside the organization. Some employees may engage in *whistle-blowing*, taking their charges to the media in the hope that if the public learns about the situation, the organization will be forced to change. From the organization's point of view, whistle-blowing is harmful because of the negative publicity.

Another way employees may go outside the organization for help is to file a lawsuit. This way to force change is available if the employee is disputing policies on the grounds that they violate state and federal laws, such as those forbidding employment discrimination or requiring safe working conditions. Defending a lawsuit is costly, both financially and in terms of the employer's image, whether the organization wins or loses. Most employers would prefer to avoid lawsuits and whistle-blowing. Keeping employees satisfied is one way to do this.

Physical Job Withdrawal

If behavior change has failed or seems impossible, a dissatisfied worker may physically withdraw from the job. Options for physically leaving a job range from arriving late to calling in sick, requesting a transfer, or leaving the organization altogether. Even while they are on the job, employees may withdraw by not actually working. All these options are costly to the employer. The problem is compounded when employees offer evasive explanations for their physical withdrawal, as described in the "HR Oops!" box.

Finding a new job is rarely easy and can take months, so employees often are cautious about quitting. Employees who would like to quit may be late for work. Tardiness is costly because late employees are not contributing for part of the day. Especially when work is done by teams, the tardiness creates difficulties that spill over and affect the entire team's ability to work. Absenteeism is even more of a problem. The U.S. Department of Labor has estimated that on the average workday, 3% to 5% of an employer's workforce is absent, costing the nation's employers perhaps $100 billion annually.[44]

An employee who is dissatisfied because of circumstances related to the specific job—for example, an unpleasant workplace or unfair supervisor—may be able to resolve that problem with a job transfer. If the source of the dissatisfaction is organizational policies or practices, such as low pay scales, the employee may leave the organization altogether. These forms of physical job withdrawal contribute to high turnover rates for the department or organization. As a result, the organization faces the costs of replacing the employees (often tens of thousands of dollars per employee), as well as lost productivity and sometimes lost sales until replacement employees learn the jobs.[45]

Organizations need to be concerned with their overall turnover rates as well as the nature of the turnover in terms of who is staying and who is leaving. For example, younger workers, who are less likely to be tied down by a mortgage or children in local schools, are more ready to quit their jobs when they become disengaged. Although the recent recession lowered the rate of quitting by limiting opportunities to find a different job,

that trend reverses when the labor market expands, and employers may soon discover that their young workers are eager to find jobs that better match their abilities and interests.[46] Also, among managers, women and minorities often have higher turnover rates. Many leave because they see little opportunity for promotions. Chapter 8 discussed how organizations are addressing this problem through career management and efforts to break the glass ceiling.

Psychological Withdrawal

Employees need not leave the company in order to withdraw from their jobs. Especially if they have been unable to find another job, they may psychologically remove themselves. They are physically at work, but their minds are elsewhere.

Psychological withdrawal can take several forms. If an employee is primarily dissatisfied with the job itself, the employee may display a very low level of job involvement. **Job involvement** is the degree to which people identify themselves with their jobs. People with a high level of job involvement consider their work an important part of their life. Doing well at work contributes to their sense of who they are (their *self-concept*). For a dissatisfied employee with low job involvement, performing well or poorly does not affect the person's self-concept.

When an employee is dissatisfied with the organization as a whole, the person's organizational commitment may be low. **Organizational commitment** is the degree to which an employee identifies with the organization and is willing to put forth effort on its behalf.[47] Employees with high organizational commitment will stretch themselves to help the organization through difficult times. Employees with low organizational commitment are likely to leave at the first opportunity for a better job. They have a strong intention to leave, so like employees with low job involvement, they are hard to motivate.

Job Involvement
The degree to which people identify themselves with their jobs.

Organizational Commitment
The degree to which an employee identifies with the organization and is willing to put forth effort on its behalf.

LO 11-6 Describe how organizations contribute to employees' job satisfaction and retain key employees.

Job Satisfaction
A pleasant feeling resulting from the perception that one's job fulfills or allows for the fulfillment of one's important job values.

Job Satisfaction

Clearly, organizations want to prevent withdrawal behaviors. As we saw in Figure 11.4, the driving force behind job withdrawal is dissatisfaction. To prevent job withdrawal, organizations therefore need to promote **job satisfaction**, a pleasant feeling resulting from the perception that one's job fulfills or allows for the fulfillment of one's important job values.[48] This definition has three components:

- Job satisfaction is related to a person's *values*, defined as "what a person consciously or unconsciously desires to obtain."
- Different employees have different views of which values are *important*, so the same circumstances can produce different levels of job satisfaction.
- Job satisfaction is based on *perception*, not always on an objective and complete measurement of the situation. Each person compares the job situation to his or her values, and people are likely to differ in what they perceive.

In sum, people will be satisfied with their jobs as long as they perceive that their jobs meet their important values. As shown in Figure 11.5, organizations can contribute to job satisfaction by addressing the four sources of job dissatisfaction we identified earlier: personal dispositions, job tasks and roles, supervisors and co-workers, and pay and benefits.

Personal Dispositions

In our discussion of job withdrawal, we noted that sometimes personal qualities of the employee, such as negative affectivity and negative core self-evaluation, are associated with job dissatisfaction. This linkage suggests employee selection in the first instance plays a role in raising overall levels of employee satisfaction. People making the

Figure 11.5
Increasing Job Satisfaction

Monitoring job satisfaction

| Hiring employees predisposed to being satisfied | Designing complex, meaningful jobs | Reinforcing shared values | Setting satisfactory pay levels |

Referring depressed employees for help

Establishing clear, appropriate roles

Encouraging social support

Communicating pay structure and policies

Helping employees pursue goals

selection decisions should look for evidence of whether employees are predisposed to being satisfied.[49] Interviews should explore employees' satisfaction with past jobs. If an applicant says he was dissatisfied with his past six jobs, what makes the employer think the person won't be dissatisfied with the organization's vacant position?

Psychologists have explored which personal qualities are associated with having a positive attitude about work.[50] One finding is that such people keep their failures in perspective by thinking of their career in terms of the big picture, not dwelling too much on one victory or disappointment. Also, their commitment to the purpose of their work overrides fear of failure, so they are determined to act, even in the face of uncertainty. They also express their interest in their work by sharing knowledge and developing less experienced employees.

Tasks and Roles

Organizations can improve job satisfaction by making jobs more complex and meaningful, as we discussed in Chapter 4. Some of the methods available for this approach to job design are job enrichment and job rotation. Organizations also can increase satisfaction by developing clear and appropriate job roles.

Job Complexity   Not only can job design add to enriching complexity, but employees themselves sometimes take measures to make their work more interesting. Some employees bring personal music players with headsets to work so they can listen to music or radio shows while they are working. Many supervisors disapprove, worrying that the headsets will interfere with the employees' ability to provide good customer service. However, in simple jobs with minimal customer contact (like processing paperwork or entering data into computers), research suggests that personal headsets can improve performance. One study examined the use of stereo headsets by workers in 32 jobs at a large retailing company. The stereo-using group outperformed the no-stereo group on simple jobs (like invoice processor), but performed worse than the stereo-free group on complex jobs (such as accountant).[51]

Meaningful Work   When it comes to generating satisfaction, the most important aspect of work is the degree to which it is meaningfully related to workers' core values. People sign on to help charitable causes for little or no pay simply because of the value they place on making a difference in the world. Royal DSM has shifted its business strategy from a focus on materials petrochemicals, plastics, and base chemicals—to emphasizing health-enhancing technologies and products such as nutritional supplements, pharmaceutical ingredients, and energy-efficient building materials. This sustainable strategy opens up opportunities for employees to use the organization's resources for good works. For example, Royal DSM partners with the World Food Programme to distribute vitamins and nutrient mixes free to poor people in Afghanistan, Bangladesh, Kenya, and Nepal. Furthering employee engagement, Royal DSM invites employees to nominate projects for the company to fund, and local managers include outreach and community engagement in their budgets.[52]

Appropriate tasks and roles include safety precautions, especially when work could involve risks to workers' health and safety.

A similar kind of motivation can drive activities directly related to doing business. When Jeffrey Scott owned a landscaping business, he taught his foremen how each crew's output was related to the company's productivity. He also gave them authority to make spending decisions up to a certain dollar level so they could take action on the job to satisfy customers who had quality concerns. And Scott authorized them to "fire" clients if that seemed the best course of action. As a result, the foremen could see connections between their decisions, the company's well-being, and the customers' satisfaction. They were no longer just completing projects; they were building a business and pleasing customers. Their crews began to deliver better quality, and customers were happier as well, so the company was retaining clients, not firing them.[53]

Role Analysis Technique
A process of formally identifying expectations associated with a role.

Clear and Appropriate Roles   Organizations can do much to avoid role-related sources of dissatisfaction. They can define roles, clearly spelling out work methods, schedules, and performance measures. They can be realistic about the number of hours required to complete job requirements. When jobs require overtime hours, the employer must be prepared to comply with laws requiring overtime pay, as well as to help employees manage the conflict between work and family roles.

To help employees manage role conflict, employers have turned to a number of family-friendly policies. These policies may include provisions for child care, elder care, flexible work schedules, job sharing, telecommuting, and extended parental leaves. Although these programs create some headaches for managers in terms of scheduling work and reporting requirements, they increase employees' satisfaction and commitment to the organization.[54] Organizations with family-friendly policies also have enjoyed improvements in performance, especially at companies that employ a large percentage of women.[55] Chapter 14 discusses such benefits in greater detail.

Because role problems rank just behind job problems in creating job dissatisfaction, some interventions aim directly at role elements. One of these is the **role analysis technique**, a process of formally identifying expectations associated with a role. The technique follows the steps shown in Figure 11.6. The *role occupant* (the person who fills a role) and each member of the person's *role set* (people who directly interact with this employee) each write down their expectations for the role. They meet to discuss their expectations and develop a preliminary list of the role's duties and behaviors, trying to resolve any conflicts among expectations. Next, the role occupant lists what he or she expects of others in the set, and the group meets again to reach a consensus on these expectations. Finally, the group modifies its preliminary list and reaches a consensus on the occupant's role. This process may uncover instances of overload and underload, and the group tries to trade off requirements to develop more balanced roles.

Members of role set write expectations for role

Members of role set discuss expectations

Preliminary list of role's duties and behaviors

Role occupant lists expectations for others in role set

Members of role set discuss expectations and reach consensus on occupant's role

Modified list of role's duties and behaviors

Figure 11.6
Steps in the Role Analysis Technique

Supervisors and Co-Workers

The two primary sets of people in an organization who affect job satisfaction are co-workers and supervisors. A person may be satisfied with these people for one of three reasons:

1. The people share the same values, attitudes, and philosophies. Most individuals find this very important, and many organizations try to foster a culture of shared values. Even when this does not occur across the whole organization, values shared between workers and their supervisor can increase satisfaction.[56]

Employees Are Quicken Loans' Most Valuable Asset

A lending company based in Detroit might not sound like a great place to work, but Quicken Loans, head-quartered in the Motor City, keeps landing on *Fortune*'s list of the Best Companies to Work For and *Computerworld*'s list of Best Places to Work in IT (information technology). Both honors say something good is happening with job satisfaction, because employee surveys play a large part in determining which companies earn the recognition.

One of the main sources of satisfaction at Quicken Loans is the supportive work relationships and the culture that promotes them. One of the company's principles for working together is "Yes before no," promoting an attitude of open-mindedness and helpfulness. Anne Way, the company's director of project management, says that although the culture is "fast-paced and intensive," employees "are genuinely open and available to each other." Application engineer Ian Kwiotek agrees, saying the best part of his job is working with smart people who are willing to help solve problems.

Another major source of satisfaction at Quicken Loans is

designing jobs and feedback so employees can see the importance of what they do. Employees see importance in the company's work to help customers buy a home, and they take pride in its commitment to help rebuild the troubled city where it is located. When Linglong He took over as chief information officer in 2010, she restructured IT work so that instead of everyone working together on the one function, IT workers are assigned to each business unit. That way they can stay on projects through the end and see their impact on the company. Lisa Phillip, who is the architect for the business intelligence team, says she "[gets] to see the value of what we provide every day." She also appreciates that even though her team's work is highly technical, Quicken Loans' CEO has taken time to praise the group's accomplishments.

CEO Bill Emerson sums up the company's practices by saying, "We win when our team members [employees] feel connected to the company." He contributes to that feeling by holding regular meetings with employees to talk about

whatever they believe can improve the company. His efforts have paid off in a high level of commitment; in a survey by the Great Place to Work Institute, 95% of Quicken Loans employees said they feel they are "all in it together."

Questions

1. What qualities of job relationships do Quicken Loans' employees value? How does the company promote such relationships?
2. How do tasks and roles contribute to job satisfaction at Quicken Loans?

Sources: Stephanie Wilkinson, "The No. 1 Large Place to Work in IT: Quicken Loans," *Computerworld*, June 23, 2014, http://www.computerworld.com; Michael Giardina, "Innovative Employers Abandon Outdated Management Structure," *Employee Benefit News*, May 2014, p. 25; Great Place to Work Institute, "Quicken Loans," *Great Place to Work Guide*, January 16, 2014, http://us.greatrated.com; "Best Companies to Work For 2014: Quicken Loans," *Fortune*, January 16, 2014, http://fortune.com/best-companies.

2. The co-workers and supervisor may provide social support, meaning they are sympathetic and caring. Social support greatly increases job satisfaction, whether the support comes from supervisors or co-workers.[57] Turnover is also lower among employees who experience support from other members of the organization.[58]
3. The co-workers or supervisor may help the person attain some valued outcome. For example, they can help a new employee figure out what goals to pursue and how to achieve them.[59]

For an example of an organization where these kinds of relationships contribute to satisfaction, see "Best Practices."

Because a supportive environment reduces dissatisfaction, many organizations foster team building both on and off the job (such as with softball or bowling leagues). The idea is that playing together as a team will strengthen ties among group members and develop relationships in which individuals feel supported by one another. DaVita Healthcare brought together 3,000 of its employees for a Village Service Day to reinforce their contributions to the company's strategic goals. Employees worked in teams of three to assemble prosthetic hands while developing skills in collaboration and communication. The employees appreciated the program all the more when they learned that the prostheses would be donated to international organizations serving amputees.[60] Organizations also create a supportive environment by developing their managers' mentoring skills and helping to set up these beneficial relationships.[61] (Mentoring was described in Chapter 8.)

Employees' own job satisfaction also interacts with the job satisfaction of co-workers. In a study of more than 5,000 employees in 150 businesses, employees with declining job satisfaction were more likely to stay on the job if co-workers' satisfaction was rising. For employees experienced rising satisfaction, the employees were more likely to quit if their co-workers were growing less satisfied. In effect, when employees were out of step with their co-workers, their likelihood of quitting was influenced by the co-workers' job satisfaction.[62]

Pay and Benefits

Organizations recognize the importance of pay in their negotiations with job candidates. HR professionals can support their organizations in this area by repeatedly monitoring pay levels in their industry and for the professions or trades they employ. As we noted in Chapter 5 and will discuss further in Chapter 12, organizations make decisions about whether to match or exceed the industry averages. Also, HR professionals can increase job satisfaction by communicating to employees the value of their benefits.

Two other aspects of pay satisfaction influence job satisfaction. One is satisfaction with pay structure—the way the organization assigns different pay levels to different levels and job categories. A manager of a sales force, for example, might be satisfied with her pay level until she discovers that some of the sales representatives she supervises are earning more than she is. The other important aspect of pay satisfaction is pay raises. People generally expect that their pay will increase over time. They will be satisfied if their expectations are met or dissatisfied if raises fall short of expectations. HR professionals can contribute to these sources of job satisfaction by helping to communicate the reasoning behind the organization's pay structure and pay raises. For example, sometimes economic conditions force an organization to limit pay raises. If employees understand the circumstances (and recognize that the same conditions are likely to be affecting other employers), they may feel less dissatisfied.

How can an organization measure whether efforts to have fun at work and build positive work relationships can actually translate to greater job satisfaction?

Monitoring Job Satisfaction

Employers can better retain employees if they are aware of satisfaction levels, so they can make changes if employees are dissatisfied. The usual way to measure job satisfaction is with some kind of survey. A systematic, ongoing program of employee surveys should be part of the organization's human resource strategy. This program allows the organization to monitor trends and prevent voluntary turnover. For example, if satisfaction with promotion opportunities has been falling over several years, the trend may signal a need for better career management (a topic of Chapter 8). An organizational change, such as a merger, also might have important consequences for job satisfaction. In addition, ongoing surveys give the organization a way to measure whether policies adopted to improve job satisfaction and employee retention are working.

Instructions: Think of your present work. What is it like most of the time? In the blank beside each word given below, write

__Y__   for "Yes" if it describes your work
__N__   for "No" if it does NOT describe your work
__?__   if you cannot decide

Work Itself	**Pay**	**Promotion Opportunities**
_____ Routine	_____ Less than I deserve	_____ Dead-end job
_____ Satisfying	_____ Highly paid	_____ Unfair policies
_____ Good	_____ Insecure	_____ Based on ability

Supervision	**Co-workers**
_____ Impolite	_____ Intelligent
_____ Praises good work	_____ Responsible
_____ Doesn't supervise enough	_____ Boring

Figure 11.7
Example of Job Descriptive Index (JDI)

Source: W. K. Balzar, D. C. Smith, D. E. Kravitz, S. E. Lovell, K. B. Paul, B. A. Reilly, and C. E. Reilly, *User's Manual for the Job Descriptive Index (JDI)* (Bowling Green, OH: Bowling Green State University, 1990).

Organizations can also compare results from different departments to identify groups with successful practices that may apply elsewhere in the organization. Another benefit is that some scales provide data that organizations can use to compare themselves to others in the same industry. This information will be valuable for creating and reviewing human resource policies that enable organizations to attract and retain employees in a competitive job market. Finally, conducting surveys gives employees a chance to be heard, so the practice itself can contribute to employee satisfaction.

To obtain a survey instrument, an excellent place to begin is with one of the many established scales. The validity and reliability of many satisfaction scales have been tested, so it is possible to compare the survey instruments. The main reason for the organization to create its own scale would be that it wants to measure satisfaction with aspects of work that are specific to the organization (such as satisfaction with a particular health plan).

A widely used measure of job satisfaction is the Job Descriptive Index (JDI). The JDI emphasizes specific aspects of satisfaction—pay, the work itself, supervision, coworkers, and promotions. Figure 11.7 shows several items from the JDI scale. Other scales measure general satisfaction, using broad questions such as "All in all, how satisfied are you with your job?"[63] Some scales avoid language altogether, relying on pictures. The faces scale in Figure 11.8 is an example of this type of measure. Other scales exist for measuring more specific aspects of satisfaction. For example, the Pay Satisfaction Questionnaire (PSQ) measures satisfaction with specific aspects of pay, such as pay levels, structure, and raises.[64]

Job Satisfaction from the Faces Scale
Consider all aspects of your job. Circle the face that best describes your feelings about your job in general.

Figure 11.8
Example of a Simplified, Nonverbal Measure of Job Satisfaction

Source: From R. B. Dunham and J. B. Herman, *Journal of Applied Psychology* 60 (1975), pp. 629–31. Reprinted with permission.

Along with administering surveys, more organizations are analyzing basic HR data to look for patterns in employee retention and turnover. The results may confirm expectations or generate surprises that merit further investigation. Either way, they can help HR departments and managers determine which efforts deliver the best return. Rosemont Center, a Columbus, Ohio, social-service agency, analyzed turnover rates after government funding cutbacks contributed to stress and soaring employee turnover. The industry average turnover is 50% to 60%, but Rosemont Center's rate shot up from 41% in 2007 to 72% three years later. The agency's HR director reviewed annual turnover rates, exit interviews, and employee satisfaction surveys and determined that Rosemont was failing to retain employees because of a lack of career development, below-average benefits and compensation, a need for better support of managers, poor communication, and lack of support for work-life balance. The HR director studied how other agencies in the area were handling similar challenges, and she interviewed employees to learn which of those actions they thought would help. By implementing ideas from this process, Rosemont Center brought employee turnover down to 48% in a single year—again below the industry average.[65]

Exit Interview
A meeting of a departing employee with the employee's supervisor and/or a human resource specialist to discuss the employee's reasons for leaving.

In spite of surveys and other efforts to retain employees, some employees inevitably will leave the organization. This presents another opportunity to gather information for retaining employees: the **exit interview**—a meeting of the departing employee with the employee's supervisor and/or a human resource specialist to discuss the employee's reasons for leaving. A well-conducted exit interview can uncover reasons why employees leave and perhaps set the stage for some of them to return. HR professionals can help make exit interviews more successful by arranging for the employee to talk to someone from the HR department (rather than the departing employee's supervisor) in a neutral location or over the phone.[66] Questions should start out open-ended and general, giving the employee a chance to name the source of the dissatisfaction or explain why leaving is attractive.

A recruiter armed with information about what caused a specific person to leave may be able to negotiate a return when the situation changes. And when several exiting employees give similar reasons for leaving, management should consider whether this indicates a need for change. In the war for talent, the best way to manage retention is to engage in a battle for every valued employee, even when it looks as if the battle has been lost.

THINKING ETHICALLY

IS IT ETHICAL TO FIRE BY E-MAIL AND TEXT?

In an interview, George Zimmer talked about his experience of learning that the board of directors of Men's Wearhouse had decided that he should no longer be the company's chief executive. He realized what was happening when he received an e-mail he described as "extremely harsh and mean-spirited."

Zimmer's public discussion of the termination sparked sympathy on social media, perhaps because so many people have experienced or known someone who has experienced receiving bad news in an impersonal way. Another example was the closing of Barducci's Italian Bistro in Winter Park, Florida. Employees said the restaurant's owner notified them they would no longer be needed by sending them a text message stating, "I have been forced to close Barducci's immediately" because "there were circumstances I was not able to address." The message wished each employee "all the best." More than a week later, employers were not sure whether they would receive their final paychecks.

Perhaps the employers that dismiss employees through e-mail and text messages believe they are sparing the employees an awkward conversation. However, employees who have had the experience say it is impersonal and hurtful.

Questions

1. How well does employment termination by e-mail or text message meet the principles of justice described in this chapter?

2. How well does it respect the basic human rights described in Chapter 1?

Sources: Bruce Weinstein, "You're Fired by E-mail?" *Huffington Post*, June 25, 2014, http://www.huffingtonpost.com; Dan Primack, "Exclusive: George Zimmer on Being Fired by Men's Wearhouse, and What's Next," *Fortune*, December 9, 2013, http://fortune.com; Alan Farnham, "Kicked to the Curb by Text: New, Awful Way to Be Fired," *ABC News*, July 16, 2013, http://abcnews.go.com.

SUMMARY

LO 11-1 Distinguish between involuntary and voluntary turnover, and describe their effects on an organization.

- Involuntary turnover occurs when the organization requires employees to leave, often when they would prefer to stay.
- Voluntary turnover occurs when employees initiate the turnover, often when the organization would prefer to keep them.
- Both are costly because of the need to recruit, hire, and train replacements. Involuntary turnover can also result in lawsuits and even violence.

LO 11-2 Discuss how employees determine whether the organization treats them fairly.

- Employees draw conclusions based on the outcomes of decisions regarding them, the procedures applied, and the way managers treat employees when carrying out those procedures.
- Outcome fairness is a judgment that the consequences are just. The consequences should be consistent, expected, and in proportion to the significance of the behavior.
- Procedural justice is a judgment that fair methods were used to determine the consequences. The procedures should be consistent, unbiased, based on accurate information, and correctable. They should take into account the viewpoints of everyone involved, and they should be consistent with prevailing ethical standards.
- Interactional justice is a judgment that the organization carried out its actions in a way that took the employee's feelings into account—for example, by listening to the employee and treating the employee with dignity.

LO 11-3 Identify legal requirements for employee discipline.

- Employee discipline should not result in wrongful discharge, such as a termination that violates an implied contract or public policy.
- Discipline should be administered evenhandedly, without discrimination.
- Discipline should respect individual employees' privacy. Searches and surveillance should be for a legitimate business purpose, and employees should know about and consent to them. Reasons behind disciplinary actions should be shared only with those who need to know them.
- When termination is part of a plant closing, employees should receive the legally required notice, if applicable.

LO 11-4 Summarize ways in which organizations can discipline employees fairly.

- Discipline should follow the principles of the hot-stove rule, meaning discipline should give warning and have consequences that are consistent, objective, and immediate.
- A system that can meet these requirements is called progressive discipline, in which rules are established and communicated, and increasingly severe consequences follow each violation of the rules. Usually, consequences range from a spoken warning through written warnings, suspension, and termination. These actions should be documented in writing.
- Organizations also may resolve problems through alternative dispute resolution, including an open-door policy, peer review, mediation, and arbitration.
- When performance problems seem to result from substance abuse or mental illness, the manager may refer the employee to an employee assistance program.
- When a manager terminates an employee or encourages an employee to leave, outplacement counseling may smooth the process.

LO 11-5 Explain how job dissatisfaction affects employee behavior.

- Circumstances involving the nature of a job, supervisors and co-workers, pay levels, or the employee's own disposition may produce job dissatisfaction.
- When employees become dissatisfied, they may engage in job withdrawal: behavior change, physical job withdrawal, or psychological job withdrawal.
- Behavior change means employees try to bring about changes in policy and personnel through inside action or through whistle-blowing or lawsuits.
- Physical job withdrawal may range from tardiness and absenteeism to job transfer or leaving the organization altogether.
- Psychological withdrawal involves displaying low levels of job involvement and organizational commitment. It is especially likely when employees cannot find another job.

LO 11-6 Describe how organizations contribute to employees' job satisfaction and retain key employees.

- Organizations can try to identify and select employees who have personal dispositions associated with job satisfaction.
- They can make jobs more complex and meaningful—for example, through job enrichment and job rotation.
- They can use methods such as the role analysis technique to make roles clear and appropriate.
- They can reinforce shared values and encourage social support among employees.
- They can try to establish satisfactory pay levels and communicate with employees about pay structure and pay raises.
- Monitoring job satisfaction helps organizations identify which of these actions are likely to be most beneficial.

KEY TERMS

involuntary turnover, 333
voluntary turnover, 333
outcome fairness, 335
procedural justice, 335
interactional justice, 336
hot-stove rule, 338
progressive discipline, 339
alternative dispute resolution (ADR), 341

open-door policy, 341
peer review, 342
mediation, 342
arbitration, 342
employee assistance program (EAP), 342
outplacement counseling, 343
job withdrawal, 345
role, 346

role ambiguity, 346
role conflict, 346
role overload, 346
job involvement, 349
organizational commitment, 349
job satisfaction, 350
role analysis technique, 352
exit interview, 356

REVIEW AND DISCUSSION QUESTIONS

1. Give an example of voluntary turnover and an example of involuntary turnover. Why should organizations try to reduce both kinds of turnover? (LO 11-1)
2. A member of a restaurant's serving staff is chronically late to work. From the organization's point of view, what fairness issues are involved in deciding how to handle this situation? In what ways might the employee's and other servers' ideas of fairness be different? (LO 11-2)
3. For the situation in Question 2, how would a formal discipline policy help the organization address issues of fairness? (LO 11-2)
4. In what type of situation would an employer have a legitimate reason for learning about an employee's personal matters outside the workplace? (LO 11-3)
5. The progressive discipline process described in this chapter is meant to be fair and understandable, but it tends to be slow. Try to think of two or three offenses that should result in immediate discharge, rather than follow all the steps of progressive discipline. Explain why you selected these offenses. If the dismissed employee sued, do you think the organization would be able to defend its action in court? (LO 11-4)

6. A risk of disciplining employees is that some employees retaliate. To avoid that risk, what organizational policies might encourage low-performing employees to leave while encouraging high-performing employees to stay? (Consider the sources of employee satisfaction and dissatisfaction discussed in this chapter.) *(LO 11-5)*

7. List forms of behavior that can signal job withdrawal. Choose one of the behaviors you listed, and describe how you would respond if an otherwise valuable employee whom you supervised engaged in this kind of behavior. *(LO 11-5)*

8. What are the four factors that influence an employee's job dissatisfaction (or satisfaction)? Which of these do you think an employer can most easily change? Which would be the most expensive to change? *(LO 11-5)*

9. Consider your current job or a job you recently held. Overall, were you satisfied or dissatisfied with that job? How did your level of satisfaction or dissatisfaction affect your behavior on the job?

Is your own experience consistent with this chapter's models of job withdrawal and job satisfaction? *(LO 11-5)*

10. Suppose you are an HR professional who convinced your company's management to conduct a survey of employee satisfaction. Your budget was limited, and you could not afford a test that went into great detail. Rather, you investigated overall job satisfaction and learned that it is low, especially among employees in three departments. You know that management is concerned about spending a lot for HR programs because sales are in a slump, but you want to address the issue of low job satisfaction. Suggest some ways you might begin to make a difference, even with a small budget. How will you convince management to try your ideas? *(LO 11-6)*

11. Why are exit interviews important? Should an organization care about the opinions of people who are leaving? How are those opinions relevant to employee separation and retention? *(LO 11-6)*

TAKING RESPONSIBILITY

General Motors Tries to Steer in a New Direction

General Motors drew attention when it chose Mary Barra as chief executive, because she is the first female CEO of a major automobile corporation. Barra, who has spent her entire career at GM, started as an engineering intern, rose through the ranks, and held executive positions as vice president of human resources and senior vice president for global product development. Despite her impressive career, Barra shifted the focus from the historic nature of her appointment, saying GM would remain committed to the profitability and sales goals defined by her predecessor.

However, it quickly became apparent that Barra would have to change direction. Months after her appointment, the company admitted that ignition switches on many GM cars were malfunctioning. A nudge on the switch would move the key into the off position, shutting down the engine—and the air bag system. Reports connected the problem to dozens of crashes and at least 13 deaths. Worse, GM allegedly knew about the problem for months or years without recalling the cars. GM launched an investigation, as did Congress and the National Highway Traffic Safety Administration.

Meanwhile, GM suspended (with pay) two engineers involved with the development of the ignition switch and the small-car line in which it is installed. Barra also replaced several executives who left the company, though she did not associate their departures

with the ignition switch. Among those who left was the vice president of global vehicle engineering, John Calabrese. Leading up to his retirement, Calabrese worked on a restructuring that included splitting his position into a head of vehicle development and a vice president of global product integrity, responsible for preventing safety problems. GM also more than doubled its safety investigator positions.

The results of the internal investigation indicated that employees throughout GM had failed to notice or act on evidence that the ignition switches had a potentially dangerous design flaw. One employee, an engineer handling the switch design, came in for the most criticism. Evidence showed him being aware that the switch failed to meet specifications, struggling to find a solution, and then signing off on the component. Later, when another engineer raised questions about the switch's performance, he started writing replies but never sent any. Several years later, he approved a design change without following a standard practice: changing the part number to create evidence that the design had changed and when. Therefore, it was extremely difficult to spot the existence of a problem and determine which cars contained which version of the switch. GM dismissed the engineer along with 14 other employees, the majority of them executives. Five other GM employees were disciplined but not terminated.

CEO Barra announced that these actions marked the beginning of an effort to replace a corporate culture tolerant of incompetence with one committed to taking responsibility.

Questions

1. Within months of Barra's appointment as CEO and during the time of the internal investigation, several executives departed the company. Does this suggest that GM was managing turnover effectively? Explain.
2. What disciplinary steps did GM say it took with regard to the engineer responsible for its ignition switch? How consistent are these steps with the principles of progressive discipline?

Sources: Neal E. Boudette and Mike Ramsey, "GM Report Slams Switch Engineer for Actions in Troubled Recall," *The Wall Street Journal*, June 5, 2014, http://online.wsj.com; Jeff Bennett and Mike Ramsey, "GM Fires 15 Employees over Recall Failures," *The Wall Street Journal*, June 5, 2014, http://online.wsj.com; Jeff Bennett and Katy Stech, "GM Engineering Chief to Depart," *Wall Street Journal*, April 22, 2014, http://online.wsj.com; Jeff Bennett, "GM CEO Shakes Up Senior Staff amid Recall," *The Wall Street Journal*, April 14, 2014, http://online.wsj.com; Nathan Bomey, "New GM CEO Mary Barra: No Time to Dwell on Historic Appointment," *Detroit Free Press*, January 23, 2014, http://www.freep.com; Jeff Bennett, "General Motors Names Mary Barra as CEO," *Wall Street Journal*, December 10, 2013, http://online.wsj.com.

MANAGING TALENT

What Makes Genentech So Great for Scientists?

For scientists, Genentech is a dream employer. The biotechnology company started in the 1970s to apply innovative technology for researching human genetics. Genentech's 12,000 employees use human genetic information to develop and make medicines for treating patients with serious and life-threatening conditions. Their accomplishments include more than 11,000 patents and creation of 35 medicines, with more in the pipeline.

Genentech's mission gives it an advantage in cultivating employee satisfaction and engagement. In *Science* magazine's annual survey, scientists at Genentech rank the company especially high for being an innovative leader in its industry, having a clear vision, and doing important, high-quality research. Employees are well aware that they are at the leading edge in their fields and that their efforts create drugs that improve health and save lives. One employee refers to a "proud legacy here of doing the right thing," and another speaks of being "seen to be at the forefront of innovative science." A third says, "We all recognize that these products change lives—and it could be someone in our own family or ourselves." Recently, when the Food and Drug Administration approved a drug Genentech had developed to fight breast cancer, employees in the distribution center cut short their celebration to get the drug shipped to three women at UCLA Medical Center, where they were waiting for the drug's approval.

Employees freely say that this ability to use science to make a difference is what keeps them committed. Paul Bezy, vice president of manufacturing at the South San Francisco facility, says, "The thing that really keeps me coming to work and coming to work happy is knowing that we're making a difference." He says a start-up company approached him about a position, and although he would be highly visible there, he wanted to stay with Genentech's "great people."

Human resource management contributes to maintaining this culture. To reinforce the sense of purposeful work, HR managers invite patients to visit and speak about how Genentech medications have helped them. Recognizing that staying at the forefront of innovation requires intense effort, they also plan fun activities, such as an annual Give Back concert and Friday-afternoon outings. Benefits include a sabbatical—six months of paid time off for employees to recharge after every six years of service.

In 2009, Genentech was acquired by the pharmaceutical giant Roche Group. Some employees worried that Genentech's innovative culture would be lost within the larger business. So far, however, employees continue to praise the meaningfulness of their work and vote Genentech onto lists of best companies to work for. Recently, more than 90% said they feel a sense of pride in their accomplishments and that their work has special meaning.

Questions

1. What contributors to job satisfaction does this case describe at Genentech?
2. How else could Genentech retain its qualified employees?

Sources: Genentech, "About Us," http://www.gene.com, accessed June 25, 2014; "Best Companies to Work For 2014," *Fortune*, http://fortune.com/best-companies, accessed June 25, 2014; Great Place to Work, "Genentech," *Great Rated!*, http://us.greatrated.com/genentech, accessed June 25, 2014; Richard Procter, "Genentech's Leadership Calls to Employees," *San Francisco Business Times*, April 11, 2014, http://www.bizjournals.com/sanfrancisco; Kendall Powell, "Top Employers Survey 2013: Top Firms Directed by Data, Led by Scientists," *Science Careers*, October 25, 2013, http://sciencecareers.sciencemag.org.

HR IN SMALL BUSINESS

Learning to Show Appreciation at Datotel

Datotel is a St. Louis company whose name explains what it does. The name combines the word *data* with the word *hotel*, and it uses its computers to safely store backups of its client companies' data. It's a fast-growing business, and for founder David Brown, one important challenge has been making sure employees know the company appreciates them even as everyone is scrambling to keep up with the demands of expanding a small business.

With about three dozen people to think about, Brown first tried a methodical approach: He created an employee-of-the-month program in which the lucky recipient would receive a thank-you e-mail message, a $25 gift card, and recognition for all employees to see on the company's intranet. Brown saw this program as one he could readily find the time to implement, and he hoped the reward and recognition would inspire high levels of job involvement and organizational commitment.

One advantage of a small company is that you can quickly see people's reactions to your efforts. Unfortunately, what Brown saw on people's faces and heard in their conversations was that recipients of the employee-of-the-month rewards were not exactly excited. The program was just too formulaic and impersonal. If Datotel was to keep employees engaged, it needed a different way to show that their efforts mattered.

So Brown tried a different approach, even though it requires more effort. He committed his eight managers to noticing and reporting employee accomplishments. To implement this, he sets aside part of regular management meetings—part of each daily phone meeting and 15 minutes of each weekly in-person meeting—to discuss employee accomplishments. Whenever a manager notes that an employee has done something extraordinary, Brown asks for one of the managers besides the person's direct supervisor to thank the employee in person. Brown has also made a personal commitment to write thank-you notes. In fact, with e-mail the norm at his technology company, he makes some of the notes stand out by writing them by hand and mailing them to the employees at home.

One employee who thinks the extra effort matters is engineer Stephanie Lewis. One day Lewis returned home to find a note from Brown, observing that he had heard during management meetings that Lewis had done exceptionally well in working with a customer. Brown thanked her for the effort. Lewis's reaction: "It made me feel important to get something so personal and unique" from her company's busy leader.

Just as communicating "thank you" has helped with motivation, going the extra mile to communicate has helped Datotel's managers stay connected with one another and the company's mission. As the company grew and jobs became more specialized, Brown recognized that he would have to bring people together formally to share information about what was happening. He began to call meetings once a quarter, and so that the environment will be positive, he establishes a theme he thinks will get employees thinking and generate some fun. When the theme was "Rumble in the Jungle," the company leaders dressed as boxers, and when the theme was "Top Gun," they dressed as aviators and met in an airplane hangar.

The effort to allow for fun is interwoven with the company's core values: passion, integrity, fun, teamwork, "superior business value," and "improving the community in which we work." These aim to unite the employees in a commitment to customer service that gives the company an edge in the industry. The values are also meant to be an advantage for recruiting and retaining the best people. On Datotel's website, the "Inside Datotel" page lists 10 reasons for wanting to work at the company, and the top reason is the core values: "Our Core Values represent everything that we stand for, and we take pride in them."

Questions

1. Based on the information given, which sources of job satisfaction has Datotel addressed? What other sources might the company address, and how?
2. Suggest several measures Datotel could use to evaluate the success of its employee retention efforts. Be sure these are practical for a company of a few dozen employees.
3. In a company as small as Datotel, losing even one employee can present real difficulties. Suppose one of Datotel's managers begins to have performance problems and seems unwilling or unable to improve. Suggest how you, as an HR consultant, could help David Brown resolve this problem in a way that is fair to everyone involved and that keeps the company moving forward.

Sources: Datotel corporate website, www.datotel.com, accessed July 6, 2014; Nadine Heintz, "Building a Culture of Employee Appreciation," Inc., September 2009, www.inc.com; Jeremy Nulik, "Never Stop Being a Student of Business," *Small Business Monthly (St. Louis)*, July 2009, www.sbmon.com; Christopher Boyce, "Engineer Finds Solution to Business Problem," *St. Louis Post-Dispatch*, June 12, 2009, Business & Company Resource Center, http://galenet.galegroup.com.

NOTES

1. Maureen Downey, "New Survey: U.S. Teachers Teach More Students in Poverty, with Special Needs," *Atlanta Journal-Constitution*, June 25, 2014, http://www.ajc.com; James Marshall Crotty, "Report Finds Rising Job Satisfaction and Autonomy among Teachers," *Forbes*, January 30, 2014, http://www.forbes.com; Motoko Rich, "Beleaguered? Not Teachers, a Poll on 'Well-Being' Finds," *The New York Times*, March 27, 2013, http://www.nytimes.com.

2. "Teacher Tenure Pros and Cons," ProCon.org, accessed June 25, 2014; "Teacher Tenure: *Brown v. Board*, the Sequel," *The Economist*, June 14, 2014, http://www.economist.com; Jesse Rothstein, "Taking On Teacher Tenure Backfires," *The New York Times*, June 12, 2014, http://www.nytimes.com.

3. J. D. Shaw, M. K. Duffy, J. L. Johnson, and D. E. Lockhart, "Turnover, Social Capital Losses, and Performance," *Academy of Management Journal* 48 (2005), pp. 594–606; R. Batt, "Managing Customer Services: Human Resource Practices, Quit Rates, and Sales Growth," *Academy of Management Journal* 45 (2002), pp. 587–97.

4. D. J. Koys, "The Effects of Employee Satisfaction, Organizational Citizenship Behavior, and Turnover on Organizational Effectiveness: A Unit-Level Longitudinal Study," *Personnel Psychology* 54 (2001), pp. 101–14; Batt, "Managing Customer Services"; T. Y. Park and J. D. Shaw, "Turnover Rates and Organizational Performance: A Meta-analysis," *Journal of Applied Psychology* 98 (2013): 268–309.

5. W. J. Becker and R. Cropanzano, "Dynamic Aspects of Voluntary Turnover: An Integrated Approach to Curvilinearity in the Performance–Turnover Relationship," *Journal of Applied Psychology* 96 (2011): 233–46.

6. K. M. Kacmer, M. C. Andrews, D. L. Van Rooy, R. C. Steilberg, and S. Cerrone, "Sure Everyone Can Be Replaced . . . but at What Cost? Turnover as a Predictor of Unit-Level Performance," *Academy of Management Journal* 49 (2006), pp. 133–44; J. D. Shaw, N. Gupta, and J. E. Delery, "Alternative Conceptualizations of the Relationship between Voluntary Turnover and Organizational Performance," *Academy of Management Journal* 48 (2005), pp. 50–68; J. Lublin, "Keeping Clients by Keeping Workers," *Wall Street Journal*, November 20, 2006, p. B1.

7. The Lorrie Willey, "The Public Policy Exception to Employment at Will: Balancing Employer's Right and the Public Interest," *Journal of Legal, Ethical and Regulatory Issues* 12, no. 1 (2009), pp. 55–72; Mitch Baker, "Commentary: 'At Will' Firing Shouldn't Lack a Reason," *Daily Journal of Commerce, Portland*, January 17, 2008, Business & Company Resource Center, http://galenet.galegroup.com.

8. Joel Brockner, "Why It's So Hard to Be Fair," *Harvard Business Review*, March 2006, http://hbr.org; Cynthia Barnes-Slater and John Ford, "Measuring Conflict: Both the Hidden Costs and Benefits of Conflict Management Interventions," *LawMemo*, http://www.lawmemo.com, accessed April 10, 2012.

9. M. M. Le Blanc and K. Kelloway, "Predictors and Outcomes of Workplace Violence and Aggression," *Journal of Applied Psychology*, 87, 2002, pp. 444–53.

10. B. J. Tepper, "Relationship among Supervisors' and Subordinates' Procedural Justice Perceptions and Organizational Citizenship Behaviors," *Academy of Management Journal* 46 (2003), pp. 97–105; T. Simons and Q. Roberson, "Why Managers Should Care about Fairness: The Effects of Aggregate Justice Perception on Organizational Outcomes," *Journal of Applied Psychology* 88 (2003), pp. 432–43; C. M. Holmvall and D. R. Bobocel, "What Fair Procedures Say about Me: Self-Construals and Reactions to Procedural Fairness," *Organizational Behavior and Human Decision Processes* 105 (2008), pp. 147–68.

11. E. C. Bianchi and J. Brockner, "In the Eyes of the Beholder: The Role of Dispositional Trust in Judgments of Procedural and Interactional Justice," *Organizational Behavior and Human Decision Processes* 118 (2012): 46–59.

12. T. A. Judge, B. A. Scott, and R. Ilies, "Hostility, Job Attitudes and Workplace Deviance: A Test of a Multilevel Model," *Journal of Applied Psychology* 91 (2006), pp. 126–38.

13. *Harmon v. Thornburgh*, CA, DC No. 88-5265 (July 30, 1989); *Treasury Employees Union v. Von Raab*, U.S. Sup. Ct. No. 86-18796 (March 21, 1989); *City of Annapolis v. United Food & Commercial Workers Local 400*, Md. Ct. App. No. 38 (November 6, 1989); *Skinner v. Railway Labor Executives Association*, U.S. Sup. Ct. No. 87-1555 (March 21, 1989); *Bluestein v. Skinner*, 908 F 451, 9th Cir. (1990).

14. D. J. Hoekstra, "Workplace Searches: A Legal Overview," *Labor Law Journal* 47, no. 2 (February 1996), pp. 127–38; "Workplace Searches and Interrogations," *FindLaw*, http://employment.findlaw.com, accessed April 6, 2012; "Workplace Searches: Dos and Don'ts," Nolo.com, http://www.nolo.com, accessed April 6, 2012.

15. G. Henshaw and K. Youmans, "Employee Privacy in the Workplace and an Employer's Right to Conduct Workplace Searches and Surveillance," *SHRM Legal Report*, Spring 1990, pp. 1–5; B. K. Repa, *Your Rights in the Workplace* (Berkeley, CA: Nolo Press, 1997).

16. M. Denis and J. Andes, "Defamation—Do You Tell Employees Why a Co-worker Was Discharged?" *Employee Relations Law Journal* 16, no. 4 (Spring 1991), pp. 469–79; R. S. Soderstrom and J. R. Murray, "Defamation in Employment: Suits by At-Will Employees," *FICC Quarterly*, Summer 1992, pp. 395–426; "Keeping Pandora's Box Closed: Best Practices in Maintaining Personnel Records," *Mondaq Business Briefing*, June 8, 2009, Business & Company Resource Center, http://galenet.galegroup.com. "Your Rights in the Workplace: Privacy Rights," Nolo.com, http://www.nolo.com, accessed April 6, 2012.

17. Business and Legal Resources, "Employee Discipline: Properly Document Complaints and Investigations," *HR.BLR.com*, December 8, 2011, http://hr.blr.com; Michael S. Lavenant, "The Art of Employee Discipline: How to Retain Control and Increase Production," *Nonprofit World*, July/August 2010, pp. 22–23.

18. K. Karl and C. Sutton, "A Review of Expert Advice on Employment Termination Practices: The Experts Don't Always Agree," in *Dysfunctional Behavior in Organizations*, eds. R. Griffin, A. O'Leary-Kelly, and J. Collins (Stanford, CT: JAI Press, 1998).

19. Resolution Systems Institute and Center for Conflict Resolution, "Why Do Courts Use ADR?" *Court ADR Pocket Guide*, http://courtadr.org, accessed April 6, 2012; Douglas Shontz, Fred Kipperman, and Vanessa Soma, *Business-to-Business Arbitration in the United States: Perceptions of Corporate Counsel* (Rand Institute for Civil Justice, 2011), http://www.rand.org.

20. Kathleen Koster, "Therapy Goes Digital," *Employee Benefit News*, October 2013, pp. 31–32.

21. Al Lewis, "Challenger Thrives in Challenging Economy," *Fox Business*, March 16, 2012, http://www.foxbusiness.com; Jim Doyle, "Five Questions: Getting Laid Off Workers Back on the Job," *St. Louis Post-Dispatch*, September 30, 2011, http://www.stltoday.com.

22. For examples see M. Huselid, "The Impact of Human Resource Management Practices on Turnover, Productivity, and Corporate Financial Performance," *Academy of Management Journal* 38 (1995), pp. 635–72; S. Payne and S. Webber, "Effects of Service Provider Attitudes and Employment Status on Citizenship Behaviors and Customers' Attitudes and Loyalty Behavior," *Journal of Applied Psychology* 91 (2006), pp. 365–68; J. Hartner, F. Schmidt, and T. Hayes, "Business-Unit Level Relationship between Employee Satisfaction, Employee Engagement, and Business Outcomes: A Meta-Analysis," *Journal of Applied Psychology* 87 (2002), pp. 268–79; I. Fulmer, B. Gerhart, and K. Scott, "Are the 100 Best Better? An Empirical Investigation of the Relationship between Being a 'Great Place to Work' and Firm Performance," *Performance Psychology* 56 (2003), pp. 965–93; "Working Today: Understanding What Drives Employee Engagement," *Towers Perrin Talent Report* (2003).

23. G. Kranz, "Losing Lifeblood," *Workforce Management*, June 2011, pp. 24–28; R. Vance, *Employee Engagement and Commitment* (Alexandria, VA: Society for Human Resource Management, 2006).

24. Margery Weinstein, "No More Revolving Door," *Training*, July 2013, http://www.trainingmag.com.

25. D. W. Baruch, "Why They Terminate," *Journal of Consulting Psychology* 8 (1944), pp. 35–46; J. G. Rosse, "Relations among Lateness, Absence and Turnover: Is There a Progression of Withdrawal?" *Human Relations* 41 (1988), pp. 517–31; C. Hulin, "Adaptation, Persistence and Commitment in Organizations," in *Handbook of Industrial & Organizational Psychology*, 2nd ed., eds. M. D. Dunnette and L. M. Hough (Palo Alto, CA: Consulting Psychologists Press, 1991), pp. 443–50; E. R. Burris, J. R. Detert, and D. S. Chiaburu, "Quitting before Leaving: The Mediating Effects of Psychological Attachment and Detachment on Voice," *Journal of Applied Psychology* 93 (2008), pp. 912–22.

26. D. A. Harrison, D. A. Newman, and P. L. Roth, "How Important Are Job Attitudes? Meta-analytic Comparisons of Integrative Behavioral Outcomes and Time Sequences," *Academy of Management Journal* 49 (2006), pp. 305–25.

27. G. Chen, R. E. Ployhart, H. C. Thomas, N. Anderson, and P. D. Bliese, "The Power of Momentum: A New Model of Dynamic Relationships between Job Satisfaction Change and Turnover Intentions," *Academy of Management Journal*, 54 (2011): 159–81.

28. R. D. Zimmerman, "Understanding the Impact of Personality Traits on Individuals' Turnover Decisions: A Meta-analysis," *Personnel Psychology* 61 (2008), pp. 309–48.

29. T. A. Judge, E. A. Locke, C. C. Durham, and A. N. Kluger, "Dispositional Effects on Job and Life Satisfaction: The Role of Core Evaluations," *Journal of Applied Psychology* 83 (1998), pp. 17–34.

30. B. M. Staw, N. E. Bell, and J. A. Clausen, "The Dispositional Approach to Job Attitudes: A Lifetime Longitudinal Test," *Administrative Science Quarterly* 31 (1986), pp. 56–78; B. M. Staw and J. Ross, "Stability in the Midst of Change: A Dispositional Approach to Job Attitudes," *Journal of Applied Psychology* 70 (1985), pp. 469–80; R. P. Steel and J. R. Rentsch, "The Dispositional Model of Job Attitudes Revisited: Findings of a 10-Year Study," *Journal of Applied Psychology* 82 (1997), pp. 873–79.

31. T. A. Judge and J. E. Bono, "Relationship of Core Self-Evaluation Traits—Self-Esteem, Generalized Self-Efficacy, Locus of Control, and Emotional Stability—with Job Satisfaction and Job Performance: A Meta-Analysis," *Journal of Applied Psychology* 86 (2001), pp. 80–92.

32. T. A. Judge, J. E. Bono, and E. A. Locke, "Personality and Job Satisfaction: The Mediating Role of Job Characteristics," *Journal of Applied Psychology* 85 (2000), pp. 237–49.

33. S. C. Douglas and M. J. Martinko, "Exploring the Role of Individual Differences in the Prediction of Workplace Aggression," *Journal of Applied Psychology* 86 (2001), pp. 547–59.

34. B. A. Gerhart, "How Important Are Dispositional Factors as Determinants of Job Satisfaction? Implications for Job Design and Other Personnel Programs," *Journal of Applied Psychology* 72 (1987), pp. 493–502.

35. E. F. Stone and H. G. Gueutal, "An Empirical Derivation of the Dimensions along Which Characteristics of Jobs Are Perceived," *Academy of Management Journal* 28 (1985), pp. 376–96.

36. L. W. Porter and R. M. Steers, "Organizational Work and Personal Factors in Employee Absenteeism and Turnover," *Psychological Bulletin* 80 (1973), pp. 151–76; S. Melamed, I. Ben-Avi, J. Luz, and M. S. Green, "Objective and Subjective Work Monotony: Effects on Job Satisfaction, Psychological Distress, and Absenteeism in Blue Collar Workers," *Journal of Applied Psychology* 80 (1995), pp. 29–42.

37. D. R. Ilgen and J. R. Hollenbeck, "The Structure of Work: Job Design and Roles," in *Handbook of Industrial & Organizational Psychology*, 2nd ed.

38. J. A. Breaugh and J. P. Colihan, "Measuring Facets of Job Ambiguity: Construct Validity Evidence," *Journal of Applied Psychology* 79 (1994), pp. 191–201.

39. M. A. Shaffer and D. A. Harrison, "Expatriates' Psychological Withdrawal from Interpersonal Assignments: Work, Nonwork, and Family Influences," *Personnel Psychology* 51 (1998), pp. 87–118.

40. Robert J. Keating, Stephen C. Harper, and David J. Glew, "Emotional Intelligence Dilutes the Toxins," *Industrial Engineer*, June 2013, 30–35; Mark C. Crowley, "Gallup's Workplace Jedi on How to Fix Our Employee Engagement Problem," *Fast Company*, June 4, 2013, http://www.fastcompany.com.

41. J. M. Sacco and N. Schmitt, "A Dynamic Multilevel Model of Demographic Diversity and Misfit Effects," *Journal of Applied Psychology* 90 (2005), pp. 203–31; R. E. Ployhart, J. A. Weekley, and K. Baughman, "The Structure and Function of Human Capital Emergence: A Multilevel Examination of the

Attraction–Selection–Attrition Model," *Academy of Management Journal* 49 (2006), pp. 661–77.

42. S. Lim, L. M. Cortina, and V. J. Magley, "Personal and Work-Group Incivility: Impact on Work and Health Outcomes," *Journal of Applied Psychology* 93 (2008), pp. 95–107.

43. E. J. McClean, E. R. Burris, and J. R. Detert, "When Does Voice Lead to Exit? It Depends on Leadership," *Academy of Management Review* 56 (2013), pp. 525–48.

44. Robert J. Grossman, "Gone but Not Forgotten," *HR Magazine*, September 2011, http://www.shrm.org.

45. Katherine Graham-Leviss, "The High Cost of Sales Team Turnover," *Entrepreneur*, September 15, 2011, http://www.entrepreneur.com; Gwen Moran, "The Hidden Costs of Employee Turnover," *Entrepreneur*, September 10, 2011, http://www.entrepreneur.com.

46. Economic Policy Institute, "Voluntary Quits Barely Budge: Critical Loss of Opportunities for Young Workers," news release, May 9, 2014, http://www.epi.org; B. Lynn Ware, "Stop the Gen Y Revolving Door," *T+D*, May 2014, pp. 58–63.

47. R. T. Mowday, R. M. Steers, and L. W. Porter, "The Measurement of Organizational Commitment," *Journal of Vocational Behavior* 14 (1979), pp. 224–47.

48. E. A. Locke, "The Nature and Causes of Job Dissatisfaction," in *The Handbook of Industrial & Organizational Psychology*, ed. M. D. Dunnette (Chicago: Rand McNally, 1976), pp. 901–69.

49. N. A. Bowling, T. A. Beehr, S. H. Wagner, and T. M. Libkuman, "Adaptation-Level Theory, Opponent Process Theory, and Dispositions: An Integrated Approach to the Stability of Job Satisfaction," *Journal of Applied Psychology* 90 (2005), pp. 1044–53.

50. For these and other examples, see David DiSalvo, "10 Reasons Why Some People Love What They Do," *Psychology Today*, May/June 2013, pp. 48–50.

51. G. R. Oldham, A. Cummings, L. J. Mischel, J. M. Schmidtke, and J. Zhou, "Listen While You Work? Quasi-experimental Relations between Personal-Stereo Headset Use and Employee Work Responses," *Journal of Applied Psychology* 80 (1995), pp. 547–64.

52. Alison Beard and Richard Hornik, "It's Hard to Be Good," *Harvard Business Review*, November 2011, pp. 88–96.

53. Jeffrey Scott, "Give Employees Ownership Thinking," *Landscape Management*, October 2011, EBSCOhost, http://web.ebscohost.com.

54. Mary Shapiro, Cynthia Ingols, Stacy Blake-Beard, and Regina O'Neill, "Canaries in the Mine Shaft: Women Signaling a New Career Model," Alison Greco, "Corporate Culture: Culture Key to Work-Life Programs," *Employee Benefit News*, February 2012, Business & Company Resource Center, http://galenet.galegroup.com.

55. J. E. Perry-Smith, "Work Family Human Resource Bundles and Perceived Organizational Performance," *Academy of Management Journal* 43 (2000), pp. 801–15; M. M. Arthur, "Share Price Reactions to Work-Family Initiatives: An Institutional Perspective," *Academy of Management Journal* 46 (2003), pp. 497–505.

56. B. M. Meglino, E. C. Ravlin, and C. L. Adkins, "A Work Values Approach to Corporate Culture: A Field Test of the Value Congruence Process and Its Relationship to Individual Outcomes," *Journal of Applied Psychology* 74 (1989), pp. 424–33.

57. G. C. Ganster, M. R. Fusilier, and B. T. Mayes, "Role of Social Support in the Experience of Stress at Work," *Journal of Applied Psychology* 71 (1986), pp. 102–11.

58. R. Eisenberger, F. Stinghamber, C. Vandenberghe, I. L. Sucharski, and L. Rhoades, "Perceived Supervisor Support: Contributions to Perceived Organizational Support and Employee Retention," *Journal of Applied Psychology* 87 (2002), pp. 565–73.

59. R. T. Keller, "A Test of the Path-Goal Theory of Leadership with Need for Clarity as a Moderator in Research and Development Organizations," *Journal of Applied Psychology* 74 (1989), pp. 208–12.

60. Bill John and Jennifer Colosimo, "Lending a Hand," *T+D*, December 2013, p. 72.

61. S. C. Payne and A. H. Huffman, "A Longitudinal Examination of the Influence of Mentoring on Organizational Commitment and Turnover," *Academy of Management Journal* 48 (2005), pp. 158–68.

62. D. Liu, T. R. Mitchell, T. W. Lee, B. C. Holtom, and T. R. Hinken, "When Employees Are Out of Step with Co-workers: How Job Satisfaction Trajectory and Dispersion Influence Individual and Unit-Level Voluntary Turnover," *Academy of Management Journal* 55 (2012): 1360–1380.

63. R. P. Quinn and G. L. Staines, *The 1977 Quality of Employment Survey* (Ann Arbor, MI: Survey Research Center, Institute for Social Research, University of Michigan, 1979).

64. T. Judge and T. Welbourne, "A Confirmatory Investigation of the Dimensionality of the Pay Satisfaction Questionnaire," *Journal of Applied Psychology* 79 (1994), pp. 461–66.

65. Sonya M. Latta, "Save Your Staff, Improve Your Business," *HR Magazine*, January 2012, pp. 30–32.

66. Patricia M. Buhler, "The Exit Interview: A Goldmine of Information," *Supervision*, August 2011, pp. 11–13; Chuck Schwartau, "Exit Interviews Matter: Feedback to Enhance the Work Environment," *Top Producer*, February 2012, Business & Company Resource Center, http://galenet.gale-group.com; Robert Half Legal, "Exit Interviews," http://www.roberthalflegal.com, accessed April 6, 2012.

Compensating Human Resources

PART FOUR

12 Establishing a Pay Structure

What Do I Need to Know?

After reading this chapter, you should be able to:

LO 12-1 Identify the kinds of decisions involved in establishing a pay structure.

LO 12-2 Summarize legal requirements for pay policies.

LO 12-3 Discuss how economic forces influence decisions about pay.

LO 12-4 Describe how employees evaluate the fairness of a pay structure.

LO 12-5 Explain how organizations design pay structures related to jobs.

LO 12-6 Describe alternatives to job-based pay.

LO 12-7 Summarize how to ensure that pay is actually in line with the pay structure.

LO 12-8 Discuss issues related to paying employees serving in the military and paying executives.

Introduction

As the United States continues its climb out of the Great Recession, people notice price increases and greater job opportunities. This creates pressure for higher pay. In the political environment affecting organizations, this plays out as efforts to raise the minimum wage required by federal, state, and local laws. For example, the Illinois legislature recently raised the minimum that employers must pay from $7.75 per hour to $8.25, and in California, the city of San Jose raised the minimum wage by 25% to $10.15.

As employers respond to this kind of change in the law, they have to consider how the wages they pay support the company's strategy and performance. Two White Castle restaurants on either side of the Illinois–Indiana state line charge the same prices because they serve the same set of consumers, but the Illinois minimum wage makes the Illinois restaurant more expensive to operate. The company has coped by not filling two positions after employees left. In San Jose, a Carl's Jr. franchise owner was able to keep the same level of profits with a modest price increase and a reduction in workers' hours. Another San Jose business, Philz Coffee, had already raised employees' wages to $11 an hour to attract a higher caliber of workers. The business has increased hiring and enjoys declining turnover, greater job satisfaction, and improved customer service.[1]

From the employer's point of view, pay is a powerful tool for meeting the organization's goals. Pay has a large impact on employee attitudes and behaviors. It influences which kinds of employees are attracted to (and remain with) the organization. By rewarding certain behaviors, it can align employees' interests with the organization's goals. Employees care about policies affecting earnings because the policies affect the employees' income and standard of living. Besides the level of pay, employees care about the fairness of pay compared with what others earn. Also, employees consider pay a sign of status and success. They attach great importance to pay decisions when they evaluate their relationship with their employer. For these reasons, organizations must carefully manage and communicate decisions about pay.

At the same time, pay is a major cost. Its share of total costs varies widely from one industry or company to another. At the low end, the wholesaling industry spends over 5% of revenues on payroll expenses. At the other extreme, transportation, entertainment, and health care companies spend more than 25% to almost 40% of revenues on payroll.[2] Managers have to keep this cost reasonable.

This chapter begins a three-chapter exploration of how companies compensate employees with pay and benefits. It describes how managers weigh the importance and costs of pay to arrive at a structure for compensation and levels of pay for different jobs. We first define the basic decisions in terms of pay structure and pay level. Next, we look at several considerations that influence these decisions: legal requirements related to pay, economic forces, the nature of the organization's jobs, and employees' judgments about the fairness of pay levels. We describe methods for evaluating jobs and market data to arrive at a pay structure. We then summarize alternatives to the usual focus on jobs. The chapter closes with a look at two issues of current importance—pay for employees on leave to serve in the military and pay for executives.

Decisions about Pay

Because pay is important both in its effect on employees and on account of its cost, organizations need to plan what they will pay employees in each job. An unplanned approach, in which each employee's pay is independently negotiated, will likely result in unfairness, dissatisfaction, and rates that are either overly expensive or so low that positions are hard to fill. Organizations therefore make decisions about two aspects of pay structure: job structure and pay level. **Job structure** consists of the relative pay for different jobs within the organization. It establishes relative pay among different functions and different levels of responsibility. For example, job structure defines the difference in pay between an entry-level accountant and an entry-level assembler, as well as the difference between an entry-level accountant, the accounting department manager, and the organization's comptroller. **Pay level** is the average amount (including wages, salaries, and bonuses) the organization pays for a particular job. Together, job structure and pay levels establish a **pay structure** that helps the organization achieve goals related to employee motivation, cost control, and the ability to attract and retain talented human resources.

The organization's job structure and pay levels are policies of the organization rather than the amount a particular employee earns. For example, an organization's pay structure could include the range of pay that a person may earn in the job of entry-level accountant. An individual accountant could be earning an amount anywhere within that range. Typically, the amount a person earns depends on the individual's qualifications, accomplishments, and experience. The individual's pay may also depend partly on how well the organization performs. This chapter focuses on the organization's decisions

LO 12-1 Identify the kinds of decisions involved in establishing a pay structure.

Job Structure
The relative pay for different jobs within the organization.

Pay Level
The average amount (including wages, salaries, and bonuses) the organization pays for a particular job.

Pay Structure
The pay policy resulting from job structure and pay-level decisions.

Figure 12.1

Issues in Developing a Pay Structure

Legal Requirements
- Equal pay for equal work
- Minimum wage
- Overtime pay
- Restrictions on child labor

Market Forces
- Product markets
- Labor markets

Organization's Goals
- High-quality workforce
- Cost control
- Equity and fairness
- Legal compliance

Pay Level Decision
Job Structure Decision
Pay Structure Decisions
- Pay rates
- Pay grades
- Pay ranges
- Pay differentials

about pay structure, and the next chapter will explore decisions that affect the amount of pay an individual earns.

Especially in an organization with hundreds or thousands of employees, it would be impractical for managers and the human resource department to make an entirely unique decision about each employee's pay. The decision would have to weigh so many factors that this approach would be expensive, difficult, and often unsatisfactory. Establishing a pay structure simplifies the process of making decisions about individual employees' pay by grouping together employees with similar jobs. As shown in Figure 12.1, human resource professionals develop this pay structure based on legal requirements, market forces, and the organization's goals, such as attracting a high-quality workforce and meeting principles of fairness.

Legal Requirements for Pay

LO 12-2 Summarize legal requirements for pay policies.

Pay policies and practices in the United States are subject to government laws and regulations. For example, just as competing businesses may not conspire to set prices, they may not conspire to set wage rates. In addition, government regulation affects pay structure in the areas of equal employment opportunity, minimum wages, pay for overtime, and prevailing wages for federal contractors. All of an organization's decisions about pay should comply with the applicable laws.

Equal Employment Opportunity

Under the laws governing equal employment opportunity, described in Chapter 3, employers may not base differences in pay on an employee's age, sex, race, or other protected status. Any differences in pay must instead be tied to such business-related considerations as job responsibilities or performance. The goal is for employers to provide *equal pay for equal work*. Job descriptions, job structures, and pay structures can help organizations demonstrate that they are upholding these laws.

These laws do not guarantee equal pay for men and women, whites and minorities, or any other groups, because so many legitimate factors, from education to choice of occupation, affect a person's earnings. In fact, numbers show that women and racial minorities in the United States tend to earn less than white men. Among full-time workers in 2012, women on average earned 73 cents for every dollar earned by men. Among male employees, black workers earned 76 cents for every dollar earned by white workers, and Hispanic workers earned just 67 cents (a racial gap among black and Hispanic female employees also exists, at 84 and 73 cents per dollar, respectively).[3] Even when these figures are adjusted to take into account education, experience, and occupation, the earnings gap does not completely close.[4] Among executives, one cause of lower pay for women appears to be that less of their pay is tied to performance (for example, bonuses and stock, described in the next chapter).[5]

Two employees who do the same job cannot be paid different wages because of gender, race, or age. It would be illegal to pay these two employees differently because one is male and the other is female. Only if there are differences in their experience, skills, seniority, or job performance are there legal reasons why their pay might be different.

One explanation for historical lower pay for women has been that employers have undervalued work performed by women—in particular, placing a lower value on occupations traditionally dominated by women. Some policy makers have proposed a remedy for this called equal pay for *comparable worth*. This policy uses job evaluation (described later in the chapter) to establish the worth of an organization's jobs in terms of such criteria as their difficulty and their importance to the organization. The employer then compares the evaluation points awarded to each job with the pay for each job. If jobs have the same number of evaluation points, they should be paid equally. If they are not, pay of the lower-paid job is raised to meet the goal of comparable worth.

Comparable-worth policies are controversial. From an economic standpoint, the obvious drawback of such a policy is that raising pay for some jobs places the employer at an economic disadvantage relative to employers that pay the market rate. In addition, a free-market economy assumes people will take differences in pay into account when they choose a career. The courts allow organizations to defend themselves against claims of discrimination by showing that they pay the going market rate.[6] Businesses are reluctant to place themselves at an economic disadvantage, but many state governments adjust pay to achieve equal pay for comparable worth. Also, at both private and government organizations, policies designed to shatter the "glass ceiling" (discussed in Chapter 8) can help to address the problem of unequal pay.

Employers considering how to address equal employment opportunity should bear in mind that the consequences of pay discrimination can be far reaching. The Lilly Ledbetter Fair Pay Act of 2009, described in Chapter 3, allows employees claiming discrimination to treat each receipt of a paycheck as an instance of discrimination for purposes of determining their eligibility to file a complaint.

Minimum Wage

In the United States, employers must pay at least the **minimum wage** established by law. (A *wage* is the rate of pay per hour.) At the federal level, the 1938 **Fair Labor Standards Act (FLSA)** establishes a minimum wage that is now $7.25 per hour. The FLSA also permits a lower "training wage," which employers may pay to workers under the age of 20 for a period of up to 90 days. This subminimum wage is approximately 85% of the minimum wage. Some states have laws specifying minimum wages; in these states, employers must pay whichever rate is higher.

Minimum Wage
The lowest amount that employers may pay under federal or state law, stated as an amount of pay per hour.

Fair Labor Standards Act (FLSA)
Federal law that establishes a minimum wage and requirements for overtime pay and child labor.

From the standpoint of social policy, an issue related to the minimum wage is that it tends to be lower than the earnings required for a full-time worker to rise above the poverty level. A number of cities have therefore passed laws requiring a so-called *living wage*, essentially a minimum wage based on the cost of living in a particular region.

Overtime Pay

Another requirement of the FLSA is that employers must pay higher wages for overtime, defined as hours worked beyond 40 hours per week. The overtime rate under the FLSA is one and a half times the employee's usual hourly rate, including any bonuses and piece-rate payments (amounts paid per item produced). The overtime rate applies to the hours worked beyond 40 in one week. Time worked includes not only hours spent on production or sales but also time on such activities as attending required classes, cleaning up the work site, or traveling between work sites. Figure 12.2 shows how this applies to an employee who works 50 hours to earn a base rate of $12 per hour plus a weekly bonus of $40. The overtime pay is based on the base pay ($480) plus the bonus ($40), for a rate of $13.00 per hour. For each of the 10 hours of overtime, the employee would earn $19.50, so the overtime pay is $195.00 ($19.50 times 10). When employees are paid per unit produced or when they receive a monthly or quarterly bonus, those payments must be converted into wages per hour, so that the employer can include these amounts when figuring the correct overtime rate.

Overtime pay is required, whether or not the employer specifically asked or expected the employee to work more than 40 hours. In other words, if the employer knows the employee is working overtime but does not pay time and a half, the employer may be violating the FLSA.

Not everyone is eligible for overtime pay. Under the FLSA, executive, professional, administrative, and highly compensated white-collar employees are considered **exempt employees**, meaning employers need not pay them one and a half times their regular pay for working more than 40 hours per week. Exempt status depends on the employee's job responsibilities, salary level (at least $455 per week), and "salary basis," meaning that the employee is paid a given amount regardless of the number of hours worked or

Exempt Employees
Managers, outside salespeople, and any other employees not covered by the FLSA requirement for overtime pay.

Figure 12.2
Computing Overtime Pay

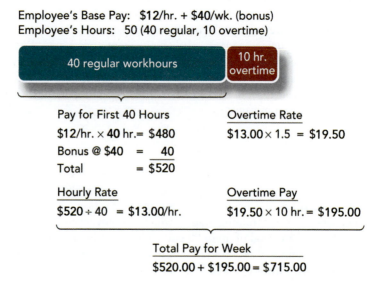

Employee's Base Pay:　$12/hr. + $40/wk. (bonus)
Employee's Hours:　50 (40 regular, 10 overtime)

| 40 regular workhours | 10 hr. overtime |

Pay for First 40 Hours	Overtime Rate
$12/hr. × 40 hr.= $480	$13.00 × 1.5 = $19.50
Bonus @ $40　=　40	
Total　= $520	

Hourly Rate	Overtime Pay
$520 ÷ 40　= $13.00/hr.	$19.50 × 10 hr.= $195.00

Total Pay for Week
$520.00 + $195.00 = $715.00

Overlooking Overtime

The Labor Department recently required two Texas companies to pay workers back wages for overtime. An investigation by the Wage and Hour Division found that a construction company had failed to account for all of its workers' hours in determining their eligibility to be paid at one and a half times their regular rates. The company was supposed to count all of workers' scheduled and unscheduled hours, including the time spent traveling to and from work sites, between the times they started and ended the workday. However, when unscheduled hours such as travel time exceeded the 40-hour workweek, the company did not count those hours and pay the workers at time and a half.

At a firm that provides maintenance and construction services to an oil and gas refinery, the problem was that the company told managers they would be paid a salary, but then the company actually paid the managers on an hourly basis, at least when it benefited the company. If a manager worked less than a 40-hour workweek, the company paid the manager at an hourly rate totaling less than the full-time salary. However, if a manager worked more than 50 hours, the company did not pay the manager for overtime. The managers could have qualified as exempt because they were performing managerial duties, but for the company to apply that classification legally, it had to pay them a flat rather than an hourly amount.

Questions

1. How could the construction company in the first example have met the legal requirements for overtime pay?

2. How could the services firm in the second example have met the requirements for overtime pay?

Sources: Adair Buckner, "Overtime Pay Mistakes Make DOL News Releases for Two Texas Panhandle Employers," Adair M. Buckner Attorney at Law Legal Blog, March 29, 2013, http://www.adairbuckner.com; U.S. Department of Labor Wage and Hour Division, "Austin Industrial Services LP in Borger, Texas, Pays More than $214,000 in Overtime Back Wages to 13 Employees following US Labor Department Investigation," news release, February 6, 2013, http://www.dol.gov; U.S. Department of Labor Wage and Hour Division, "Diversified Interiors of Amarillo, Texas, Pays 63 Employees More than $76,000 in Overtime Back Wages following US Department of Labor Investigation," news release, January 22, 2013, http://www.dol.gov.

---

quality of the work.[7] Paying an employee on a salary basis means the organization expects that this person can manage his or her own time to get the work done, so the employer may deduct from the employee's pay only in certain limited circumstances, such as disciplinary action or for unpaid leave for personal reasons. Additional exceptions apply to certain occupations, including outside salespersons, teachers, and computer professionals (if they earn at least $27.63 per hour). Thus, the standards are fairly complicated. For more details about the standards for exempt employees, contact the Labor Department's Wage and Hour Division or refer to its website at **www.dol.gov/whd**.

Any employee who is not in one of the exempt categories is called a **nonexempt employee**. Most workers paid on an hourly basis are nonexempt and therefore subject to the laws governing overtime pay. However, paying a salary does not necessarily mean a job is exempt. The "HR Oops!" describes some problems that have arisen when employers failed to properly identify and pay workers who should have been classified as nonexempt.

Nonexempt Employees
Employees covered by the FLSA requirements for overtime pay.

Child Labor

In the early years of the Industrial Revolution, employers could pay low wages by hiring children. The FLSA now sharply restricts the use of child labor, with the aim of protecting children's health, safety, and educational opportunities.[8] The restrictions apply to children younger than 18. Under the FLSA, children aged 16 and 17 may not be employed in hazardous occupations defined by the Department of Labor, such as mining, meatpacking, and certain kinds of manufacturing using heavy machinery. Children aged 14 and 15 may work only outside school hours in jobs defined as nonhazardous and for limited time periods. A child under age 14 may not be employed in any work associated with interstate commerce, except work performed in a nonhazardous job for a business entirely owned by the child's parent or guardian. A few additional exemptions from this ban include acting, babysitting, and delivering newspapers to consumers.

Besides the FLSA, state laws also restrict the use of child labor. Many states have laws requiring working papers or work permits for minors, and many states restrict the number of hours or times of day that minors aged 16 and older may work. Before hiring any workers under the age of 18, employers must ensure they are complying with the child labor laws of their state, as well as the FLSA requirements for their industry.

Prevailing Wages

Two additional federal laws, the Davis-Bacon Act of 1931 and the Walsh-Healy Public Contracts Act of 1936, govern pay policies of federal contractors. Under these laws, federal contractors must pay their employees at rates at least equal to the prevailing wages in the area. The calculation of prevailing rates must be based on 30% of the local labor force. Typically, the rates are based on relevant union contracts. Pay earned by union members tends to be higher than the pay of nonunion workers in similar jobs, so the effect of these laws is to raise the lower limit of pay an employer can offer.

These laws do not cover all companies. Davis-Bacon covers construction contractors that receive more than $2,000 in federal money. Walsh-Healy covers all government contractors receiving $10,000 or more in federal funds.

LO 12-3 Discuss how economic forces influence decisions about pay.

Economic Influences on Pay

An organization cannot make spending decisions independent of the economy. Organizations must keep costs low enough that they can sell their products profitably, yet they must be able to attract workers in a competitive labor market. Decisions about how to respond to the economic forces of product markets and labor markets limit an organization's choices about pay structure.

Product Markets

The organization's *product market* includes organizations that offer competing goods and services. In other words, the organizations in a product market are competing to serve the same customers. To succeed in their product markets, organizations must be able to sell their goods and services at a quantity and price that will bring them a sufficient profit. They may try to win customers by being superior in a number of areas, including quality, customer service, and price. An important influence on price is the cost to produce the goods and services for sale. As we mentioned earlier, the cost of labor is a significant part of an organization's costs.

If an organization's labor costs are higher than those of its competitors, it will be under pressure to charge more than competitors charge for similar products. If one company spends $50 in labor costs to make a product and its competitor spends only $35, the second company will be more profitable unless the first company can justify a higher price to customers. This is one reason U.S. automakers have had difficulty competing against Japanese companies. The labor-related expenses per vehicle for a U.S. company have been $700 higher than for Japanese carmakers operating in the United

States. Recently, U.S. automakers have been able to reduce labor costs, partly by hiring new workers at lower wages, down to an average of $58 per hour. This is still somewhat above Toyota and Honda's $52 per hour and far above the average $27 per hour that Volkswagen is paying workers to build Volkswagen Passats at its plant in Tennessee.[9]

Product markets place an upper limit on the pay an organization will offer. This upper limit is most important when labor costs are a large part of an organization's total costs and when the organization's customers place great importance on price. Organizations that want to lure top-quality employees by offering generous salaries therefore have to find ways to automate routine activities (so that labor is a smaller part of total costs) or to persuade customers that high quality is worth a premium price. Organizations under pressure to cut labor costs may respond by reducing staff levels, freezing pay levels, postponing hiring decisions, or requiring employees to bear more of the cost of benefits such as insurance premiums.

Labor Markets

Besides competing to sell their products, organizations must compete to obtain human resources in *labor markets*. In general, workers prefer higher-paying jobs and avoid employers that offer less money for the same type of job. In this way, competition for labor establishes the minimum an organization must pay to hire an employee for a particular job. If an organization pays less than the minimum, employees will look for jobs with other organizations.

An organization's competitors in labor markets typically include companies with similar products and companies in other industries that hire similar employees. For example, a truck transportation firm would want to know the pay earned by truck drivers at competing firms as well as truck drivers for manufacturers that do their own shipping, drivers for moving and storage companies, and drivers for stores that provide delivery services. In setting pay levels for its bookkeepers and administrative assistants, the company would probably define its labor market differently because bookkeepers and administrative assistants work for most kinds of businesses. The company would likely look for data on the earnings of bookkeepers and administrative assistants in the region. For all these jobs, the company wants to know what others are paying so that it will pay enough to attract and keep qualified employees. The "Did You Know?" box compares average pay levels for some broad occupational categories in the United States.

Another influence on labor markets is the *cost of living*—the cost of a household's typical expenses, such as house payments, groceries, medical care, and gasoline. In some parts of the country, the cost of living is higher than in others, so the local labor markets there will likely demand higher pay. Also, over time, the cost of living tends to rise. When the cost of living is rising rapidly, labor markets demand pay increases. The federal government tracks trends in the nation's cost of living with a measure called the Consumer Price Index (CPI). Following and studying changes in the CPI can help employers prepare for changes in the demands of the labor market.

There is a strong demand for nurses in the labor market. What this means for hospitals is that they have to pay competitive wages and other perks to attract and retain staff. How does this differ from the airline industry's current labor market?

Management, Professional, Computer Occupations Are the Highest Paid

Looking at broad occupational categories, the highest pay goes to managers, followed by experts in computers and mathematics. The lowest-paid occupational groups involve agriculture and services (personal care and food preparation and service).

The pay rates shown in the graph are for the *median* worker in each category (half the workers earn more, and half earn less). However, keep in mind that the range of earnings for an occupational category may be great. In sales, for example, median earnings range as low as $9.12 an hour for cashiers and as high as $45.14 for sales engineers. The overall median is low because there are many more cashiers than sales engineers.

Question

If a company were to hire a new human resource manager, would the $45.96 hourly figure shown here for management be an appropriate rate of pay? Why or why not?

Sources: Bureau of Labor Statistics, "Occupational Employment and Wages, May 2013," news release, April 1, 2014, http://www.bls.gov; Bureau of Labor Statistics, "May 2013 National Occupational Employment and Wage Estimates," Occupational Employment Statistics, http://data.bls.gov.

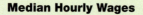

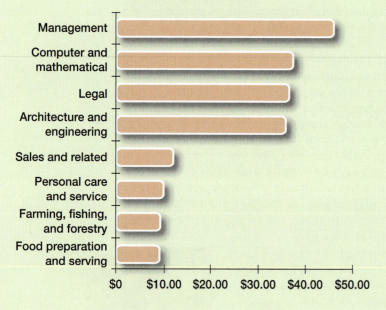

Pay Level: Deciding What to Pay

Although labor and product markets limit organizations' choices about pay levels, there is a range within which organizations can make decisions.[10] The size of this range depends on the details of the organization's competitive environment. If many workers are competing for a few jobs, employers will have more choice. Similarly, employers can be more flexible about pay policies if they use technology and work design to get better results from employees than their competitors do.

When organizations have a broad range in which to make decisions about pay, they can choose to pay at, above, or below the rate set by market forces. Economic theory holds that the most profitable level, all things being equal, would be at the market rate. Often, however, all things are not equal from one employer to another. For instance, an organization may gain an advantage by paying above the market rate if it uses the higher pay as one means to attract top talent and then uses these excellent employees' knowledge to be more innovative, produce higher quality, or work more efficiently. For example, in the highly competitive world of information technology, Google, Amazon, Microsoft, and Apple try to get and keep the best people by paying salaries far above market rates.[11] This pay policy leaves smaller high-tech companies with less cash to offer at a disadvantage in the competition for talent.

This approach is based on the view of employees as resources. Higher pay may be an investment in superior human resources. Having higher labor costs than your competitors is not necessarily bad if you also have the best and most effective workforce, which produces more products of better quality. Pay policies are one of the most important human resource tools for encouraging desired employee behaviors and discouraging undesired behaviors. Therefore, organizations must evaluate pay as more than a cost—it is an investment that can generate returns in attracting, retaining, and motivating a high-quality workforce. For this reason, paying above the going rate may be advantageous for an organization that empowers employees or that cannot closely watch employees (as with repair technicians who travel to customers). Those employers might use high pay to attract and retain top candidates and to motivate them to do their best because they want to keep their high-paying jobs.[12]

Gathering Information about Market Pay

To compete for talent, organizations use **benchmarking**, a procedure in which an organization compares its own practices against those of successful competitors. In terms of compensation, benchmarking involves the use of pay surveys. These provide information about the going rates of pay at competitors in the organization's product and labor markets. An organization can conduct its own surveys, but the federal government and other organizations make a great deal of data available already.

Benchmarking
A procedure in which an organization compares its own practices against those of successful competitors.

Pay surveys are available for many kinds of industries (product markets) and jobs (labor markets). The primary collector of this kind of data in the United States is the Bureau of Labor Statistics, which conducts an ongoing National Compensation Survey measuring wages, salaries, and benefits paid to the nation's employees. The "HR How To" box provides guidelines for using the BLS website as a source of wage data. Besides the BLS, the most widely used sources of compensation information include HR organizations such as WorldatWork and the Society for Human Resource Management.[13] In addition, many organizations, especially large ones, purchase data from consulting groups such as Mercer, Towers Watson, and Hewitt. Consulting firms charge for the service but can tailor data to their clients' needs. Employers also should investigate what compensation surveys are available from any industry or trade groups their company belongs to.

Human resource professionals need to determine whether to gather data focusing on particular industries or on job categories. Industry-specific data are especially relevant for jobs with skills that are specific to the type of product. For jobs with skills that can be transferred to companies in other industries, surveys of job classifications will be more relevant.

Employee Judgments about Pay Fairness

In developing a pay structure, it is important to keep in mind employees' opinions about fairness. After all, one of the purposes of pay is to motivate employees, and they will not be motivated by pay if they think it is unfair.

LO 12-4 Describe how employees evaluate the fairness of a pay structure.

Gathering Wage Data at the BLS Website

A convenient source of data on hourly wages is the Bureau of Labor Statistics (BLS). This federal agency makes data available at its website on an interactive basis. The data come from the BLS's National Compensation Survey. The user specifies the category of data desired, and the BLS provides tables of data almost instantly. Here's how to use the BLS system.

Visit the Data Tools page of the BLS website (**www.bls.gov/data/**), and click on the link to Pay and Benefits. Find the options offered for the National Compensation Survey (NCS). The multiscreen search asks you to specify one search category at a time, then click to open the next screen.

After you select Multi-Screen Data Search for NCS, the system presents you with a window in which to select either the entire United States or a single state. Click to highlight your choice and then click on Next Form. If you choose United States, your next choice is a Census region of the country; if you choose a state, the next option is a metropolitan region of the state.

On the next screen, select the occupation you wish to research. The survey data cover hundreds of occupations, grouped into more general categories. For example, at the most specific level, you could look at civil engineers. More broadly, you could look at all engineers, or at the larger grouping of architecture and engineering occupations. You should select the most specific grouping that covers the occupation you want to investigate.

After selecting an occupation, select a work level. This describes the level of such work features as knowledge required and the scope, complexity, and demands of the job. For instance, you could look only at data for entry-level or senior accountants, rather than all accountants. Some occupations, including artists, athletes, and announcers, are not classified by work level.

Click on the Retrieve Data link to submit the request to the BLS. The system immediately processes the request and presents the table (or tables) on your computer screen.

Questions

1. If you wanted to hire an accountant to work in New York City, would you search the database for wages in the New York City metropolitan area or for the whole state? Why?
2. Why might your employer decide to pay the accountant it hires a different amount than the median pay reported for accountants in the BLS database?

Source: Bureau of Labor Statistics, "Databases, Tables and Calculators by Subject," http://data.bls.gov, accessed July 1, 2014.

Judging Fairness

Employees evaluate their pay relative to the pay of other employees. Social scientists have studied this kind of comparison and developed *equity theory* to describe how people make judgments about fairness.[14] According to equity theory, people measure outcomes such as pay in terms of their inputs. For example, an employee might think of her pay in terms of her master's degree, her 12 years of experience, and her 60-hour workweeks. To decide whether a level of pay is equitable, the person compares her ratio of outcomes and inputs with other people's outcome/input ratios, as shown in Figure 12.3. The person in the previous example might notice that an employee with less education or experience is earning more than she is (unfair) or that an employee who works 80 hours a week is earning more (fair). In general, employees compare their pay and contributions against several yardsticks:

- What they think employees in other organizations earn for doing the same job.
- What they think other employees holding different jobs within the organization earn for doing work at the same or different levels.
- What they think other employees in the organization earn for doing the same job as theirs.

Equity: Pay Seems Fair

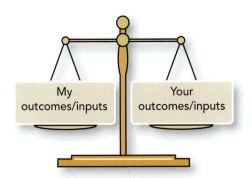

Inequity: Pay Seems Unfair

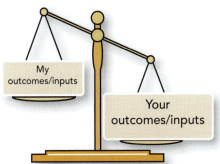

Figure 12.3
Opinions about
Fairness: Pay Equity

Employees' conclusions about equity depend on what they choose as a standard of comparison. The results can be surprising. For example, some organizations have set up two-tier wage systems as a way to cut labor costs without cutting employees' existing salaries. Typically, employers announce these programs as a way to avoid moving jobs out of the country or closing down altogether. In a two-tier wage system, existing employees continue on at their current (upper-tier) pay rate while new employees sign on for less pay (the lower tier). One might expect reaction among employees in the lower tier that the pay structure is unfair. But a study of these employees found that they were *more* satisfied than the top-tier employees.[15] The lower-tier employees were not comparing their pay with that of the upper-tier employees but with the other alternatives they saw for themselves: lower-paying jobs or unemployment.

The ways employees respond to their impressions about equity can have a great impact on the organization. Typically, if employees see their pay as equitable, their attitudes and behavior continue unchanged. If employees see themselves as receiving an advantage, they usually rethink the situation to see it as merely equitable. But if employees conclude that they are underrewarded, they are likely to make up the difference in one of three ways. They might put forth less effort (reducing their inputs), find a way to increase their outcomes (for example, stealing), or withdraw by leaving the organization or refusing to cooperate. Employees' beliefs about fairness also influence their willingness to accept transfers or promotions. For example, if a job change involves more work, employees will expect higher pay.

Communicating Fairness

Equity theory tells organizations that employees care about their pay relative to what others are earning and that these feelings are based on what the employees *perceive* (what they notice and form judgments about). An organization can do much to contribute to what employees know and, as a result, what they perceive. If the organization researches salary levels and concludes that it is paying its employees generously, it should communicate this. If the employees do not know what the organization learned from its research, they may reach an entirely different conclusion about their pay. Conversely, a female nurse who is satisfied with earning $50,000 a year—the average for a woman in nursing in 2011—might change her mind if she learns that a male coworker earns $60,000, the average for a male in the same position that year.[16] Employers should recognize that as work becomes more collaborative and the emphasis on knowledge sharing increases, it grows ever more likely that the shared knowledge

HRM Social

Salary Talk Is Trending

Young workers especially are used to the idea of sharing details about their lives on social media. For someone who has that comfort level with sharing, it makes no sense to keep quiet about earnings. Some people remain concerned that talking about money is impolite and can cause envy, but others have been revealing their pay. They get encouragement to do that—anonymously, for now—on job-reviewing websites such as Glassdoor.

Most employers prefer the long-standing taboo against discussing pay. Many point to concern that employees whose pay is at or below coworkers' earnings will become dissatisfied. Some think it strengthens their hand in negotiations with employees.

Despite these concerns, employers are limited in what they can do about the trend toward sharing pay information. Under the National Labor Relations Act, discussed in Chapter 15, employers may not forbid non-management employees from talking to each other about their earnings. That right does not extend to conversations with people outside the company. But as a practical matter, it is difficult and perhaps impossible or unethical to police everything employees post on their personal social networks.

Therefore, companies are tolerating the sharing of pay information. Some are even jumping on the transparency bandwagon. For example, SumAll, a New York firm that provides clients with data analytics services, freely discloses pay scales and individual salaries, on the grounds that it creates a more open, efficient culture. Another approach, of course, is to offer attractive levels of pay and enjoy the positive attention. For example, Glassdoor recently reported that Google and Costco employees rate their satisfaction with pay higher than employees at other companies. Although Google pays much more than Costco, both companies pay generously for their respective industry.

Questions

1. How would a trend toward sharing salary information on social media affect a company that has a below-market strategy for setting pay levels?
2. How would this trend affect a company that has a strategy of setting pay levels at the market rate?

Sources: Katie Roof, "Employees Satisfied with Pay at Google and Costco," *Fox Business*, May 23, 2014, http://www.fox-business.com; Lauren Weber and Rachel Emma Silverman, "Workers Share Their Salary Secrets," *The Wall Street Journal*, April 16, 2013, http://online.wsj.com; Rachel Cromidas, "The Thing We're Still Uncomfortable Sharing Online," *RedEye*, March 3, 2014, http://articles.redeyechicago.com; Jenny Tsay, "Legal to Prohibit Employees from Discussing Salary?" *Free Enterprise* (FindLaw blog), December 19, 2013, http://blogs.findlaw.com.

---

includes information about pay. The "HRM Social" box discusses how social media is contributing to this trend.

Employers must also recognize that employees know much more about what other employers pay now than they did before the Internet became popular. In the past, when gathering wage and salary data was expensive and difficult, employers had more leeway in negotiating with individual employees. Today's employees can go to websites like jobstar.org or salary.com to find hundreds of links to wage and salary data. For a fee, executive search firms such as Korn/Ferry provide data. Resources like these give employees information about what other workers are earning, along with the expectation that information will be shared. This means employers will face increased pressure to clearly explain their pay policies.

Managers play the most significant role in communication because they interact with their employees each day. The HR department should prepare them to explain why the organization's pay structure is designed as it is and to judge whether employee concerns about the structure indicate a need for change. A common issue is whether to reclassify a job because its content has changed. If an employee takes on more responsibility, the employee will often ask the manager for help in seeking more pay for the job.

Table 12.1

Job Evaluation of Three Jobs with Three Factors

JOB TITLE	COMPENSABLE FACTORS			
	EXPERIENCE	EDUCATION	COMPLEXITY	TOTAL
Computer operator	40	30	40	110
Computer programmer	40	50	65	155
Systems analyst	65	60	85	210

Job Structure: Relative Value of Jobs

Along with market forces and principles of fairness, organizations consider the relative contribution each job should make to the organization's overall performance. In general, an organization's top executives have a great impact on the organization's performance, so they tend to be paid much more than entry-level workers. Executives at the same level of the organization—for example, the vice president of marketing and the vice president of information systems—tend to be paid similar amounts. Creation of a pay structure requires that the organization develop an internal structure showing the relative contribution of its various jobs.

One typical way of doing this is with a **job evaluation**, an administrative procedure for measuring the relative worth of the organization's jobs. Usually, the organization does this by assembling and training a job evaluation committee, consisting of people familiar with the jobs to be evaluated. The committee often includes a human resource specialist and, if its budget permits, may hire an outside consultant.

To conduct a job evaluation, the committee identifies each job's *compensable factors*, meaning the characteristics of a job that the organization values and chooses to pay for. As shown in Table 12.1, an organization might value the experience and education of people performing computer-related jobs, as well as the complexity of those jobs. Other compensable factors might include working conditions and responsibility. Based on the job attributes defined by job analysis (discussed in Chapter 4), the jobs are rated for each factor. The rater assigns each factor a certain number of points, giving more points to factors when they are considered more important and when the job requires a high level of that factor. Often the number of points comes from one of the *point manuals* published by trade groups and management consultants. If necessary, the organization can adapt the scores in the point manual to the organization's situation or even develop its own point manual. As in the example in Table 12.1, the scores for each factor are totaled to arrive at an overall evaluation for each job.

Job evaluations provide the basis for decisions about relative internal worth. According to the sample assessments in Table 12.1, the job of systems analyst is worth almost twice as much to this organization as the job of computer operator. Therefore, the organization would be willing to pay almost twice as much for the work of a systems analyst as it would for the work of a computer operator.

The organization may limit its pay survey to jobs evaluated as *key jobs*. These are jobs that have relatively stable content and are common among many organizations, so it is possible to obtain survey data about what people earn in these jobs. Organizations

LO 12-5 Explain how organizations design pay structures related to jobs.

Job Evaluation
An administrative procedure for measuring the relative internal worth of the organization's jobs.

Popular actors, such as Leonardo DiCaprio, are evaluated by their impact on box office receipts and other revenues and then compensated based on these evaluations.

can make the process of creating a pay structure more practical by defining key jobs. Research for creating the pay structure is limited to the key jobs that play a significant role in the organization. Pay for the key jobs can be based on survey data, and pay for the organization's other jobs can be based on the organization's job structure. A job with a higher evaluation score than a particular key job would receive higher pay than that key job.

Pay Structure: Putting It All Together

Hourly Wage
Rate of pay for each hour worked.

Piecework Rate
Rate of pay for each unit produced.

Salary
Rate of pay for each week, month, or year worked.

As we described in the first section of this chapter, the pay structure reflects decisions about how much to pay (pay level) and the relative value of each job (job structure). The organization's pay structure should reflect what the organization knows about market forces, as well as its own unique goals and the relative contribution of each job to achieving the goals. By balancing this external and internal information, the organization's goal is to set levels of pay that employees will consider equitable and motivating.

Organizations typically apply the information by establishing some combination of pay rates, pay grades, and pay ranges. Within this structure, they may state the pay in terms of a rate per hour, commonly called an **hourly wage**; a rate of pay for each unit produced, known as a **piecework rate**; or a rate of pay per month or year, called a **salary**.

Pay Rates

Pay Policy Line
A graphed line showing the mathematical relationship between job evaluation points and pay rate.

If the organization's main concern is to match what people are earning in comparable jobs, the organization can base pay directly on market research of as many of its key jobs as possible. To do this, the organization looks for survey data for each job title. If it finds data from more than one survey, it must weight the results based on their quality and relevance. The final number represents what the competition pays. In light of that knowledge, the organization decides what it will pay for the job.

The next step is to determine salaries for the nonkey jobs, for which the organization has no survey data. Instead, the person developing the pay structure creates a graph like the one in Figure 12.4. The vertical axis shows a range of possible pay rates, and the horizontal axis measures the points from the job evaluation. The analyst plots points according to the job evaluation and pay rate for each key job. Finally, the analyst fits a line, called a **pay policy line**, to the points plotted. (This can be done statistically on a computer, using a procedure called regression analysis.) Mathematically, this line shows the relationship between job evaluation and rate of pay. Thus, the line slopes upward from left to right, and if higher-level jobs are especially valuable to the organization, the line may curve upward to indicate even greater pay for high-level jobs. Using this line, the analyst can estimate the market pay level for a given job evaluation. Looking at the graph will give approximate numbers, or the regression analysis will provide an equation for calculating the rate of pay. For example, using the pay policy line in Figure 12.4, a job with 315 evaluation points would have a predicted salary of $6,486 per month.

The pay policy line reflects the pay structure in the market, which does not always match rates in the organization (see key job F in Figure 12.4). Survey data may show that people in certain jobs are actually earning significantly more or less than the amount shown on the pay policy line. For example, some kinds of expertise are in short supply. People with that expertise can command higher salaries because they can easily

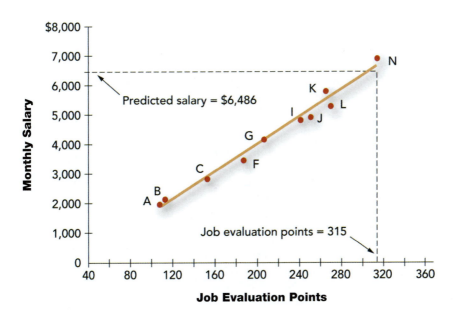

Figure 12.4
Pay Policy Lines

leave one employer to get higher pay somewhere else. Suppose, in contrast, that local businesses have laid off many warehouse employees. Because so many of these workers are looking for jobs, organizations may be able to pay them less than the rate that job evaluation points would suggest.

When job structure and market data conflict in these ways, organizations have to decide on a way to resolve the two. One approach is to stick to the job evaluations and pay according to the employees' worth to the organization. Organizations that do so will be paying more or less than they have to, so they will likely have more difficulty competing for customers or employees. A way to moderate this approach is to consider the importance of each position to the organization's goals.[17] If a position is critical for meeting the organization's goals, paying more than competitors pay may be worthwhile.

At the other extreme, the organization could base pay entirely on market forces. However, this approach also has some practical drawbacks. One is that employees may conclude that pay rates are unfair. Two vice presidents or two supervisors will expect to receive similar pay because their responsibilities are similar. If the differences between their pay are large, because of different market rates, the lower-paid employee will likely be dissatisfied. Also, if the organization's development plans include rotating managers through different assignments, the managers will be reluctant to participate if managers in some departments receive lower pay. Organizations therefore must weigh all the objectives of their pay structure to arrive at suitable rates. For an example of a company that balanced fairness and market forces in making pay decisions, see the "Best Practices" box.

Pay Grades

A large organization could have hundreds or even thousands of different jobs. Setting a pay rate for each job would be extremely complex. Therefore, many organizations group jobs into **pay grades**—sets of jobs having similar worth or content, grouped together to establish rates of pay. For example, the organization could establish five pay grades, with the same pay available to employees holding any job within the same grade.

Pay Grades
Sets of jobs having similar worth or content, grouped together to establish rates of pay.

Parkland Health Rethinks Entry-Level Pay Rates

Parkland Health and Hospital System, located in Dallas, has about 230 employees earning its lowest rate of pay. Most of these employees hold positions in dietary, environmental, and linen services. Until recently, they were earning $8.78 an hour, which is above the Texas minimum wage of $7.25 per hour (equal to the federal minimum wage).

Parkland Health has a new top-management team, which has been leading a turnaround since a management shakeup in response to federal government criticism of quality and safety at its facilities. As part of that effort, Parkland's leaders considered how they could improve employee morale. They identified entry-level wages as a place to start because $8.78 is less than a "living wage." The executives decided to raise the lowest pay rate to $10.25 per hour. Employees already earning more than $8.78 would see their wages boosted

so they continue making more than the lowest rate at Parkland.

Parkland estimated that the wage increase in the first year would cost $350,000. To find the money to cover this, the executive team looked at the funds budgeted for their bonuses, to be paid if they met specific goals. Parkland expected that in the next quarter, its top 60 executives would divide up $750,000 to $1.2 million among themselves. The executives agreed that the additional entry-level pay could be taken from those funds. They would accept smaller bonuses as a way to motivate their entry-level workers. Jim Dunn, Parkland's chief talent officer, said the decision is a way to "break down any gaps or anything between the top leaders and those who are closest to our patients," adding, "We feel like it's the right thing to do."

Questions

1. How do you predict these pay rate changes at Parkland Health will affect its performance?
2. Do you agree with Jim Dunn's assertion that these pay decisions were "the right thing to do"? Why or why not?

Sources: Bryce Covert, "Hospital Uses Executive Bonus Money to Give Its Workers a Raise," *Think Progress,* June 16, 2014, http://thinkprogress.org; Bob Herman, "Parkland Health to Boost Its Minimum Wage, Funded by Exec Bonus Pool," *Modern Healthcare*, June 12, 2014, http://www.modernhealthcare .com; Sherry Jacobson, "Parkland Officials Recommend Entry-Level Pay Boost to $10.25 an Hour," *Dallas News*, June 11, 2014, http://thecoopblog .dallasnews.com.

A drawback of pay grades is that grouping jobs will result in rates of pay for individual jobs that do not precisely match the levels specified by the market and the organization's job structure. Suppose, for example, that the organization groups together its senior accountants (with a job evaluation of 255 points) and its senior systems analysts (with a job evaluation of 270 points). Surveys might show that the market rate of pay for systems analysts is higher than that for accountants. In addition, the job evaluations give more points to systems analysts. Even so, for simplicity's sake, the organization pays the same rate for the two jobs because they are in the same pay grade. The organization would have to pay more than the market requires for accountants or pay less than the market rate for systems analysts (so it would probably have difficulty recruiting and retaining them).

Pay Range
A set of possible pay rates defined by a minimum, maximum, and midpoint of pay for employees holding a particular job or a job within a particular pay grade.

Pay Ranges

Usually, organizations want some flexibility in setting pay for individual jobs. They want to be able to pay the most valuable employees the highest amounts and to give rewards for performance, as described in the next chapter. Flexibility also helps the organization balance conflicting information from market surveys and job evaluations. Therefore, pay structure usually includes a **pay range** for each job or pay grade. In other words, the organization establishes a minimum, maximum, and midpoint of pay

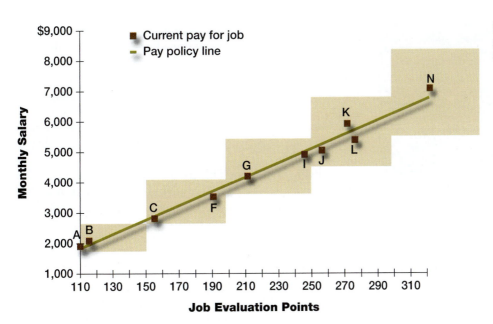

Figure 12.5
Sample Pay Grade
Structure

for employees holding a particular job or a job within a particular pay grade. Employees holding the same job may receive somewhat different pay, depending on where their pay falls within the range.

A typical approach is to use the market rate or the pay policy line as the midpoint of a range for the job or pay grade. The minimum and maximum values for the range may also be based on market surveys of those amounts. Pay ranges are most common for white-collar jobs and for jobs that are not covered by union contracts. Figure 12.5 shows an example of pay ranges based on the pay policy line in Figure 12.4. Notice that the jobs are grouped into five pay grades, each with its own pay range. In this example, the range is widest for employees who are at higher levels in terms of their job evaluation points. That is because the performance of these higher-level employees will likely have more effect on the organization's performance, so the organization needs more latitude to reward them. For instance, as discussed earlier, the organization may want to select a higher point in the range to attract an employee who is more critical to achieving the organization's goals.

Usually pay ranges overlap somewhat, so that the highest pay in one grade is somewhat higher than the lowest pay in the next grade. Overlapping ranges gives the organization more flexibility in transferring employees among jobs, because transfers need not always involve a change in pay. On the other hand, the less overlap, the more important it is to earn promotions in order to keep getting raises. Assuming the organization wants to motivate employees through promotions (and assuming enough opportunities for promotion are available), the organization will want to limit the overlap from one level to the next.

Pay Differentials

In some situations organizations adjust pay to reflect differences in working conditions or labor markets. For example, an organization may pay extra to employees who work the night shift because night hours are less desirable for most workers. Similarly, organizations may pay extra to employees in locations where living expenses are higher. These adjustments are called **pay differentials**.

Pay Differential
Adjustment to a pay rate to reflect differences in working conditions or labor markets.

Night hours are less desirable for most workers. There-fore, some companies pay a differential for night work to compensate them.

A survey of businesses in the United States found that almost three-quarters have a policy of providing pay differentials based on geographic location.[18] These differentials are intended as a way to treat employees fairly without regard to where they work. The most common approach is to move an employee higher in the pay structure to compensate for higher living costs. For instance, according to the Bureau of Labor Statistics, the average human resource manager earns $100,780 in Huntsville, Alabama, and $122,010 in the Boston area. One reason could be a higher cost of living in Boston. This pay policy can become expensive for organizations that must operate in high-cost locations. Also, organizations need to handle the delicate issue of how to pay employees transferred to lower-cost areas.

Alternatives to Job-Based Pay

LO 12-6 Describe alternatives to job-based pay.

The traditional and most widely used approach to developing a pay structure focuses on setting pay for jobs or groups of jobs.[19] This emphasis on jobs has some limitations. The precise definition of a job's responsibilities can contribute to an attitude that some activities "are not in my job description," at the expense of flexibility, innovation, quality, and customer service. Also, the job structure's focus on higher pay for higher status can work against an effort at empowerment. Organizations may avoid change because it requires repeating the time-consuming process of creating job descriptions and related paperwork. Another change-related problem is that when the organization needs a new set of knowledge, skills, and abilities, the existing pay structure may be rewarding the wrong behaviors. Finally, a pay structure that rewards employees for winning promotions may discourage them from gaining valuable experience through lateral career moves.

Delayering
Reducing the number of levels in the organization's job structure.

Organizations have responded to these problems with a number of alternatives to job-based pay structures. Some organizations have found greater flexibility through **delayering**, or reducing the number of levels in the organization's job structure. By combining more assignments into a single layer, organizations give managers more flexibility in making assignments and awarding pay increases. These broader groupings often are called *broad bands*. In the 1990s, IBM changed from a pay structure with 5,000 job titles and 24 salary grades to one with 1,200 jobs and 10 bands. When IBM began using broad bands, it replaced its point-factor job evaluation system with an approach based on matching jobs to descriptions. Job descriptions are assigned to the band whose characteristics best match those in the job description. Broad bands reduce the opportunities for promoting employees, so organizations that eliminate layers in their job descriptions must find other ways to reward employees.

Skill-Based Pay Systems
Pay structures that set pay according to the employees' levels of skill or knowledge and what they are capable of doing.

Another way organizations have responded to the limitations of job-based pay has been to move away from the link to jobs and toward pay structures that reward employees based on their knowledge and skills.[20] **Skill-based pay systems** are pay structures that set pay according to the employees' level of skill or knowledge and what they are capable of doing. Paying for skills makes sense at organizations where changing technology requires employees to continually widen and deepen their knowledge. For example, modern machinery often requires that operators know how to program and monitor computers to perform a variety of tasks. Skill-based pay also supports efforts to empower employees and enrich jobs because it encourages employees to add to their knowledge so they can make decisions in many areas. In this way, skill-based pay helps organizations become more flexible and innovative. More generally, skill-based pay can encourage a climate of learning and adaptability and give employees a broader view of how the organization functions. These changes should help employees use their knowledge and ideas more productively. A field study of a manufacturing plant found that changing to a skill-based pay structure led to better quality and lower labor costs.[21]

Of course, skill-based pay has its own disadvantages.[22] It rewards employees for acquiring skills but does not provide a way to ensure that employees can use their new skills. The result may be that the organization is paying employees more for learning skills that the employer is not benefiting from. The challenge for HRM is to design work so that the work design and pay structure support each other. Also, if employees learn skills very quickly, they may reach the maximum pay level so quickly that it will become difficult to reward them appropriately. Skill-based pay does not necessarily provide an alternative to the bureaucracy and paperwork of traditional pay structures because it requires records related to skills, training, and knowledge acquired. Finally, gathering market data about skill-based pay is difficult because most wage and salary surveys are job-based.

Pay Structure and Actual Pay

LO 12-7 Summarize how to ensure that pay is actually in line with the pay structure.

Usually, the human resource department is responsible for establishing the organization's pay structure. But building a structure is not the end of the organization's decisions about pay structure. The structure represents the organization's policy, but what the organization actually does may be different. As part of its management responsibility, the HR department therefore should compare actual pay to the pay structure, making sure that policies and practices match.

A common way to do this is to measure a *compa-ratio*, the ratio of average pay to the midpoint of the pay range. Figure 12.6 shows an example. Assuming the organization has pay grades, the organization would find a compa-ratio for each pay grade: the average paid to all employees in the pay grade divided by the midpoint for the pay grade. If the average equals the midpoint, the compa-ratio is 1. More often, the compa-ratio is somewhat above 1 (meaning the average pay is above the midpoint for the pay grade) or below 1 (meaning the average pay is below the midpoint).

Assuming that the pay structure is well planned to support the organization's goals, the compa-ratios should be close to 1. A compa-ratio greater than 1 suggests that the organization is paying more than planned for human resources and may have difficulty keeping costs under control. A compa-ratio less than 1 suggests that the organization is

Pay Grade: 1
Midpoint of Range: $2,175 per month

Salaries of Employees in Pay Grade
Employee 1 $2,306
Employee 2 $2,066
Employee 3 $2,523
Employee 4 $2,414

Compa-Ratio

$$\frac{\text{Average}}{\text{Midpoint}} = \frac{\$2,327.25}{\$2,175.00} = 1.07$$

Average Salary of Employees
$2,306 + $2,066 + $2,523 + $2,414 = $9,309
$9,309 ÷ 4 = $2,327.25

Figure 12.6

Finding a Compa-Ratio

underpaying for human resources relative to its target and may have difficulty attracting and keeping qualified employees. When compa-ratios are more or less than 1, the numbers signal a need for the HR department to work with managers to identify whether to adjust the pay structure or the organization's pay practices. The compa-ratios may indicate that the pay structure no longer reflects market rates of pay. Or maybe performance appraisals need to be more accurate, as discussed in Chapter 10.

Current Issues Involving Pay Structure

LO 12-8 Discuss issues related to paying employees serving in the military and paying executives.

An organization's policies regarding pay structure greatly influence employees' and even the general public's opinions about the organization. Issues affecting pay structure therefore can hurt or help the organization's reputation and ability to recruit, motivate, and keep employees. Recent issues related to pay structure include decisions about paying employees on active military duty and decisions about how much to pay the organization's top executives.

Pay during Military Duty

As we noted in Chapter 3, the Uniformed Services Employment and Reemployment Rights Act (USERRA) requires employers to make jobs available to their workers when they return after fulfilling military duties for up to five years. During the time these employees are performing their military service, the employer faces decisions related to paying these people. The armed services pay service members during their time of duty, but military pay often falls short of what they would earn in their civilian jobs. Some employers have chosen to support their employees by paying the difference between their military and civilian earnings for extended periods. Sears Holdings provides a pay differential for up to 60 months and also makes reservists on active duty eligible for annual raises and bonuses. In addition, these employees have the option to continue their medical, dental, and life insurance benefits while on duty.[23]

Policies to make up the difference between military pay and civilian pay are costly. The employer is paying employees while they are not working for the organization, and it may have to hire temporary employees as well. This challenge has posed a significant hardship on some employers since 2002, as hundreds of thousands of Reservists and National Guard members have been mobilized. Even so, as the nation copes with this challenge, hundreds of employers have decided that maintaining positive relations with employees—and the goodwill of the American public—makes the expense worthwhile.

Pay for Executives

The media have drawn public attention to the issue of executive pay. The issue attracts notice because of the very high pay that the top executives of major U.S. companies have received in recent years. For example, recent reviews of executive compensation at the largest publicly owned companies in the United States found that median compensation of chief executive offices has surpassed $9 million. However, most CEOs do not run a Fortune 500 or S&P 500 company, and broader studies have found more modest—though still high—executive pay. A study by Chief Executive Group found that CEOs at private companies received median compensation of $362,900.[24] Notice also that as shown in Figure 12.7, only a small share of the average compensation paid to CEOs is in the form of a salary. Most CEO compensation takes the form of

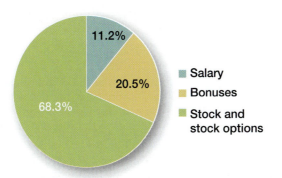

Source: Hay Group, "The Wall Street Journal/Hay Group CEO Compensation Study Finds Pay Levels Increased Slightly in 2012, as Companies Continue to Navigate Say-on-Pay Era," news release, May 16, 2013, http://www .haygroup.com.

Figure 12.7
Average CEO Pay at 300 Largest U.S. Companies

performance-related pay, such as bonuses and stock. This variable pay, discussed in the next chapter, causes the pay of executives to vary much more widely than other employees' earnings.

Although these high amounts apply to only a small proportion of the total workforce, the issue of executive pay is relevant to pay structure in terms of equity theory. As we discussed earlier in the chapter, employees draw conclusions about the fairness of pay by making comparisons among employees' inputs and outcomes. By many comparisons, U.S. CEOs' pay is high. Data from the Associated Press and Equilar compare average CEO compensation with the compensation of the average U.S. worker. According to the data, median CEO compensation in 2012 was at 257 times the pay of an average worker, up from 181 times in 2009. In a separate study by the Hay Group, CEO pay increased at a rate of 5.5%, compared with a 1.8% increase in private-sector workers' pay.[25] To assess the fairness of this ratio, equity theory would consider not only the size of executive pay relative to pay for other employees but also the amount the CEOs contribute. An organization's executives potentially have a much greater effect on the organization's performance than its lowest-paid employees have. But if they do not seem to contribute 257 times more, employees will see the compensation as unfair. Likewise, if CEOs in the United States don't contribute more to their organization than CEOs in other countries do, the difference would be perceived as unfair.

Top executives help to set the tone or culture of the organization, and employees at all levels are affected by behavior at the top. As a result, the equity of executive pay can affect more employees than, say, equity among warehouse workers or salesclerks. Recognizing this issue, Warren Buffett takes home a modest salary—for example, total compensation of $423,923 in 2012, when his company was valued at more than $288 billion. Some CEOs, including Google's Larry Page and Facebook's Mark Zuckerberg, have taken the symbolic compensation of just $1.[26] These executives are hardly poor, of course; most of their wealth comes from their stock holdings.

One study that investigated this issue compared the pay of rank-and-file employees and executives in various business units.[27] In business units where the difference in pay was greater, customer satisfaction was lower. The researchers speculated that employees thought pay was inequitable and adjusted their behavior to provide lower inputs by putting forth less effort to satisfy customers. To avoid this type of situation, organizations need to plan not only *how much* to pay managers and executives, but also *how* to pay them. In the next chapter, we will explore many of the options available.

THINKING ETHICALLY

IS PAY DISPARITY IN THE FAST-FOOD BUSINESS ETHICAL?

As you saw in this chapter's "Did You Know?" box, food preparation and service jobs are among the lowest-paid occupations in the United States. Many of these positions are entry-level jobs in fast-food restaurants. The concentration of low-paid occupations may explain why a study found that the fast-food industry has the greatest pay disparity, or difference between pay for the lowest- and highest-paid positions.

At the bottom end of the range are the workers who cook and serve the food in fast-food restaurants. The median wage for front-line workers in the fast-food industry is $8.69 an hour, and the mean is $9.09. At these rates, even some full-time employees are qualifying for government assistance. For example, a recent study found that more than half of fast-food workers enrolled themselves or their families for benefits such as SNAP (formerly called food stamps) and Medicaid, at a cost of about $7 billion.

At the other extreme are fast-food chief executives. Analysis of pay reported for executives of the large fast-food chains found that their compensation between 2000 and 2013 quadrupled. In 2013, total compensation (including bonuses and stock, as well as salary) was $7.7 million for the CEO of McDonald's, $13.8 million for Chipotle's CEO, and $22 million for the CEO of Yum, which owns KFC, Pizza Hut, and Taco Bell. On average, according to the public policy group Demos, the ratio of a fast-food CEO's pay to an average fast-food worker's pay exceeds a thousand to one.

Questions

1. Under what conditions, if any, is it ethical for an employer to pay employees a wage low enough that full-time workers are eligible for public assistance?
2. Under what conditions, if any, is it ethical for a CEO to make a thousand times more than a front-line worker in the same organization?

Sources: Allison Aubrey, "Fast-Food CEOs Earn Supersize Salaries; Workers Earn Small Potatoes," *The Salt* (NPR blog), April 22, 2014, http://www.npr.org; Catherine Ruetschlin, "Fast Food Failure: How CEO-to-Worker Pay Disparity Undermines the Industry and the Overall Economy," Demos, April 22, 2014, http://www.demos.org; Kathleen Maclay, "Low-Wage Fast-Food Jobs Leave Hefty Tax Bill, Report Says," news release, University of California at Berkeley, October 15, 2013, http://newscenter.berkeley.edu.

SUMMARY

LO 12-1   Identify the kinds of decisions involved in establishing a pay structure.

- A job structure establishes relative pay for different jobs within the organization.
- Organizations establish relative pay for different functions and different levels of responsibility for each function.
- They also must establish pay levels, or the average paid for the different jobs.
- These decisions are based on the organization's goals, market data, legal requirements, and principles of fairness.
- Together, job structure and pay level establish a pay structure policy.

LO 12-2   Summarize legal requirements for pay policies.

- To meet the standard of equal employment opportunity, employers must provide equal pay for equal work, regardless of an employee's age, race, sex, or other protected status. Differences in pay must relate to factors such as a person's qualifications or market levels of pay.
- Under the Fair Labor Standards Act (FLSA), the employer must pay at least the minimum wage established by law. Some state and local governments have established higher minimum wages.
- The FLSA also requires overtime pay—at one and a half times the employee's regular pay rate, including bonuses—for hours worked beyond 40 in each week. Managers, professionals, and outside salespersons are exempt from the overtime pay requirement.
- Employers must meet FLSA requirements concerning child labor.
- Federal contractors also must meet requirements to pay at least the prevailing wage in the area where their employees work.

LO 12-3   Discuss how economic forces influence decisions about pay.

- To remain competitive, employers must meet the demands of product and labor markets.

- Product markets seek to buy at the lowest price, so organizations must limit their costs as much as possible. In this way, product markets place an upper limit on the pay an employer can afford to offer.
- Labor markets consist of workers who want to earn as much as possible. To attract and keep workers, employers must pay at least the going rate in their labor markets.
- Organizations make decisions about whether to pay at, above, or below the pay rate set by these market forces.
- Paying above the market rate may make the organization less competitive in product markets but give it an advantage in labor markets. The organization benefits only if it can attract the best candidates and provide the systems that motivate and enable them to do their best work.
- Organizations that pay below the market rate need creative practices for recruiting and training workers so that they can find and keep enough qualified people.

LO 12-4 Describe how employees evaluate the fairness of a pay structure.

- According to equity theory, employees think of their pay relative to their inputs, such as training, experience, and effort. To decide whether their pay is equitable, they compare their outcome (pay)/input ratio with other people's outcome/input ratios.
- Employees make these comparisons with people doing the same job in other organizations and with people doing the same or different jobs in the same organization.
- If employees conclude that their outcome/input ratio is less than the comparison person's, they conclude that their pay is unfair and may engage in behaviors to create a situation they think is fair.

LO 12-5 Explain how organizations design pay structures related to jobs.

- Organizations typically begin with a job evaluation to measure the relative worth of their jobs. A job evaluation committee identifies each job's compensable factors and rates each factor.
- The committee may use a point manual to assign an appropriate number of points to each job.
- The committee can research market pay levels for key jobs and then identify appropriate rates of pay for other jobs based on their number of points relative to the key jobs. The organization can do this with a pay policy line, which plots a salary for each job.
- The organization can combine jobs into several groups, called pay grades.

- For each pay grade or job, the organization typically establishes a pay range, using the market rate or pay policy line as the midpoint.
- Differences in working conditions or labor markets sometimes call for the use of pay differentials to adjust pay levels.

LO 12-6 Describe alternatives to job-based pay.

- To obtain more flexibility, organizations may use delayering. They reduce the levels in the organization's job structure, creating broad bands of jobs with a pay range for each.
- Organizations may use skill-based pay. They reward employees according to their knowledge and skills by establishing skill-based pay systems. These are structures that set pay according to the employees' level of knowledge and capabilities.
- Skill-based pay encourages employees to be more flexible and adapt to changing technology. However, if the organization does not also provide systems in which employees can apply new skills, it may be paying them for skills they do not actually use.

LO 12-7 Summarize how to ensure that pay is actually in line with the pay structure.

- The human resource department should routinely compare actual pay with the pay structure to see that policies and practices match.
- A common way to do this is to measure a compa-ratio for each job or pay grade. The compa-ratio is the ratio of average pay to the midpoint of the pay range.
- Assuming the pay structure supports the organization's goals, the compa-ratios should be close to 1.
- When compa-ratios are more or less than 1, the HR department should work with managers to identify whether to adjust the pay structure or the organization's pay practices.

LO 12-8 Discuss issues related to paying employees serving in the military and paying executives.

- The Uniformed Services Employment and Reemployment Rights Act requires employers to make jobs available to any of their employees who leave to fulfill military duties for up to five years.
- While these employees are performing their military service, many are earning far less. To demonstrate their commitment to these employees and to earn the public's goodwill, many companies pay the difference between their military and civilian earnings, even though this policy is costly.
- Executive pay has drawn public scrutiny because top executive pay is much higher than average workers' pay.

- The great difference is an issue in terms of equity theory. Chief executive officers have an extremely large impact on the organization's performance, but critics complain that when performance falters, executive pay does not decline as fast as the organization's profits or stock price.

- Top executives help set the organization's tone or culture, and employees at all levels are affected by the behavior of the people at the top. Therefore, employees' opinions about the equity of executive pay can have a large effect on the organization's performance.

KEY TERMS

job structure, 367

pay level, 367

pay structure, 367

minimum wage, 369

Fair Labor Standards
    Act (FLSA), 369

exempt employees, 370

nonexempt employees, 371

benchmarking, 375

job evaluation, 379

hourly wage, 380

piecework rate, 380

salary, 380

pay policy line, 380

pay grades, 381

pay range, 382

pay differential, 383

delayering, 384

skill-based pay systems, 384

REVIEW AND DISCUSSION QUESTIONS

1. In setting up a pay structure, what legal requirements must an organization meet? Which of these do you think would be most challenging for a small start-up business? Why? *(LO 12-1)*

2. In gathering data for its pay policies, what product markets would a city's hospital want to use as a basis for comparison? What labor markets would be relevant? How might the labor markets for surgeons be different from the labor markets for nursing aides? *(LO 12-1)*

3. Why might an organization choose to pay employees more than the market rate? Why might it choose to pay less? What are the consequences of paying more or less than the market rate? *(LO 12-3)*

4. Suppose you work in the HR department of a manufacturing company that is planning to enrich jobs by having production workers work in teams and rotate through various jobs. The pay structure will have to be adjusted to fit this new work design. How would you expect the employees to evaluate the fairness of their pay in their redesigned jobs? In terms of equity theory, what comparisons would they be likely to make? *(LO 12-4)*

5. Summarize the way organizations use information about jobs as a basis for a pay structure. *(LO 12-5)*

6. Imagine that you manage human resources for a small business. You have recently prepared a report on the market rate of pay for salespeople, and the company's owner says the market rate is too high. The company cannot afford this level of pay, and furthermore, paying that much would cause salespeople to earn more than most of the company's managers. Suggest three possible measures the company might take to help resolve this conflict. *(LO 12-5)*

7. What are the advantages of establishing pay ranges, rather than specific pay levels, for each job? What are the drawbacks of this approach? *(LO 12-5)*

8. Suppose the company in Question 1 wants to establish a skills-based pay structure. What would be some advantages of this approach? List the issues the company should be prepared to address in setting up this system. Consider the kinds of information you will need and the ways employees may react to the new pay structure. *(LO 12-6)*

9. Why do some employers subsidize the pay of military reserve members called up to active duty? If the military instead paid these people the wage they command in the civilian market (that is, the salary they earn at their regular jobs), who would bear the cost? When neither the reserve members' employers nor the military pays reserve members their civilian wage, reserve members and their families bear the cost. In your opinion, who *should* bear this cost—employers, taxpayers, or service members (or someone else)? *(LO 12-8)*

10. Do you think U.S. companies pay their chief executives too much? Why or why not? *(LO 12-8)*

TAKING RESPONSIBILITY

IKEA Aims to Pay a Living Wage

Along with a legal requirement to pay at least the minimum wage, some employers also see a social responsibility requirement to pay workers at least a living wage—that is, enough to provide themselves and their families with the basics of daily life. Paying a living wage is one way to treat employees with dignity.

Sweden-based furniture and home furnishings retailer IKEA is among the companies that have committed to paying a living wage. IKEA recently announced that in the United States it would raise the lowest hourly wage it pays, going from $9.17 per hour to a nationwide average of $10.76. The change affects about half of the employees in its 38 existing stores and will apply to those hired at new locations.

The $10.76 figure is not a set amount that will apply nationwide, but an average across facilities. IKEA intends to calculate a minimum for each store based on the local cost of living. It uses the MIT Living Wage Calculator, which factors in the costs of food, housing, taxes, and transportation. IKEA's wages will be based on the amounts calculated for a single person without children. In Pittsburgh and West Chester, Ohio, the minimum will be just $8.69; at the other extreme, workers in Woodbridge, Virginia, will receive wages starting at $13.22 per hour. Thus, wages are influenced by employee needs, not solely based on market rates. IKEA also said it would review wages every year but did not commit to raising rates every time the calculator shows a higher cost of living.

Before the wage increase, IKEA already exceeded the federal minimum wage of $7.25. And even if the president can convince Congress to accept his idea of raising the minimum to $10.10 per hour, IKEA's minimum will continue exceeding the national requirement. IKEA also is generous relative to competitors. Gap, whose stores include Banana Republic and Old Navy, recently announced it would phase in an increase to $9 in 2014 and then to $10 in 2015. Following IKEA's announcement of the new $10.76 minimum wage, Walmart's Twitter account sent a tweet saying its "average hourly wage for full and part time associates is $11.81." However, Walmart did not draw a comparison with its hourly minimum.

IKEA sees the establishment of a living wage as supporting its mission of creating a better everyday life for people—in this case, its employees. Rob Olson, IKEA's chief financial officer, indicated that the company does not intend to raise prices to make up for the added expense of higher wages. Rather, it hopes that because the company "invests in" its employees, they in turn will invest more of themselves in the stores and their customers.

Questions

1. What are some risks and challenges that IKEA is likely to face as a result of basing its minimum pay on the living-wage formula, rather than just legal requirements and the market rate?
2. Given that IKEA's management considers the living wage to be consistent with the company's mission, what advice would you give the company for implementing it successfully?

Sources: Anna Prior, "IKEA to Raise Minimum Wage at U.S. Stores," *The Wall Street Journal*, June 26, 2014, http://online.wsj.com; Steven Greenhouse, "Ikea to Increase Minimum Hourly Pay," *The New York Times*, June 26, 2014, http://www.nytimes.com; Jena McGregor, "Ikea to Raise Workers' Pay to a 'Living Wage,'" *The Washington Post*, June 26, 2014, http://www.washingtonpost.com; Mark Lennihan, "IKEA Gets Flexible with Minimum Worker Pay," *Christian Science Monitor*, June 26, 2014, http://www.csmonitor.com.

MANAGING TALENT

Twitter Tries to Be an Employer You'd Tweet About

Twitter spent much of 2013 preparing for its November initial public offering, meaning it became a publicly traded company, selling stock to investors. That change had some big HRM implications. First, the influx of investment money enables a company to grow, and in the months leading up to the IPO, Twitter hired 300 employees, bringing its workforce to 2,300. Also, engineers and other employees who received shares of stock as part of their compensation could suddenly become rich if the stock value rose significantly, as expected. They could become millionaires, and if they did, would they stay with the company? The HR challenge would be to keep attracting and retaining hard-to-replace talent.

Pay levels have played an important part in meeting the challenge. Based on salaries employees share on the Glassdoor website, Twitter has been generous. Among companies where 50 or more software engineers told Glassdoor their salary, Twitter had the fifth-highest pay, averaging $124,863. At the top of the list was Juniper Networks, paying $159,990, followed by

LinkedIn, Yahoo, and Google. Other big names paid less; the average at Apple was $124,630, and Facebook paid $121,507. They still outspent the average of around $100,000 to $112,000 paid to software engineers in San Francisco, where Twitter is located.

Twitter is operating in an expensive labor market. Software engineers are in general a high-demand, high-pay occupation. The number of Bay Area start-ups and growing complexity of technology have been fueling demand. Also, according to Glassdoor's data, San Francisco is the high-paid location in the United States. That situation is unlikely to change as long as the cost of living in San Francisco remains high; that $124,000 salary buys very modest housing in the area.

Along with these challenges for paying software engineers, Twitter faces the struggle to find and keep top executives. It paid Christopher Fry, the senior vice president in charge of Twitter's engineers, $10.3 million in the year of its IPO, close to the earnings of CEO Dick Costolo. Most of that compensation was in the value of stock awards; Fry's salary was $145,513, and he received bonus pay of $100,000. Other high-level executives at Twitter received similar compensation. Chief financial officer Mike Gupta earned the most, receiving $24.6 million (including a salary of $250,000) for leading the organization through the IPO. For his part, Fry was considered invaluable because Twitter's survival requires that the site operate reliably, especially during this time of expansion.

Questions

1. Do you think the levels of pay described in this case contribute to Twitter's business success? Why or why not?
2. Suppose you work in Twitter's HR department, and the company's executives ask you to try reining in the spending on salaries. What would you recommend?

Sources: Yoree Koh, "In IPO Year, Twitter CEO Dick Costolo's Pay Plunged to $130,250," *The Wall Street Journal*, April 9, 2014, http://blogs .wsj.com; J. P. Mangalindan, "Twitter's Highest-Paid Starting Salaries," *Fortune*, November 8, 2013, http://fortune.com; Sarah Frier, "Twitter Ranks Fifth in Engineer Pay behind Google and Yahoo," *Bloomberg News*, October 17, 2013, http://go.bloomberg.com; Ray Hennessey, "Because Twitter Isn't a Bank, Big Pay Packages Are OK," *Entrepreneur*, October 14, 2013, http://www.entrepreneur.com; Sarah McBride, "Twitter Pays Engineer $10 Million as Silicon Valley Tussles for Talent," *Reuters*, October 13, 2013, http://www.reuters.com.

HR IN SMALL BUSINESS

Changing the Pay Level at Eight Crossings

Based in Sacramento, California, Eight Crossings provides medical transcription services for physicians and hospitals. Its employees also answer phones, edit documents, and transcribe legal documents. The company's 85 employees work either at the service center in Sacramento or in their homes, where they receive audio or text files via the Internet. In this way, Eight Crossings employees can work in their specialty as needed without tying up a doctor's or attorney's office space.

Initially, the ease of sending files electronically was an advantage that enabled Eight Crossings to grow at a tremendous pace. But it has also opened up the company to competition from similar services provided from low-wage locations such as India. In addition, as voice recognition software has improved, automation could take over some of the processes that have been handled by skilled, experienced transcribers.

In that situation, Eight Crossings CEO Patrick Maher felt the pressure when clients began to ask him for a lower rate. Most of the costs of running Eight Crossings are related to labor. Overhead and materials are minimal for this type of work. Consequently, for Maher to offer his clients a better price, he would have to cut what he paid employees or stop earning a profit.

The pay level at Eight Crossings had been about 5% above the average for the industry. Maher believed that this pay strategy gave his company an advantage in recruiting and keeping the best transcribers. Pay was calculated per line of text at a rate that varied according to the complexity of the material being transcribed. Depending on how many hours they worked and how complex the jobs they took, each transcriber earned between $20,000 and $70,000 a year.

In looking for ways to trim expenses, Maher considered that part of most documents included sections of boilerplate text. These are generated automatically by transcribers' software but were included in the number of lines for which the transcribers were paid. Maher concluded these amounted to a 5% bonus paid for each assignment. Maher decided he could cut transcribers' pay by 5% and in effect still pay them the same rate for what they were actually transcribing (but without the "bonus").

That pay cut would bring pay levels at Eight Crossings down to the market rate. Would that mean employees would leave for greener pastures? Maher guessed not, considering that his company was receiving résumés from experienced transcribers looking for work.

Maher's next challenge was how to communicate the pay cut to employees working in 22 locations, many working from home and communicating with the office electronically. He began by discussing the situation with the company's eight supervisors, who check the transcribers' work for quality. This prepared them to address employees' concerns. Next, he sent an e-mail to the transcribers, explaining the reasons for the change and inviting questions.

Maher's fears about the pay cut were not realized. Employees expressed understanding of the move and appreciation for his commitment to continue sending work to U.S. workers. And because Eight Crossings is paying the market rate, moving to another company would not offer employees an advantage in terms of pay.

Questions

1. How did the change in pay level at Eight Crossings affect its ability to attract and retain a high-quality workforce?
2. Do you think the company's pay structure was better suited to its objectives before or after the reduction in pay level? Why?
3. How would you evaluate the company's method of communicating the change in pay level? What improvements to that process can you suggest?

Sources: Darren Dahl, "Special Financial Report: Employee Compensation," *Inc.*, July 2009, www.inc.com; Eight Crossings, corporate website, www.eightcrossings.com, accessed July 8, 2014; "Company Profile: No. 609, Eight Crossings," Inc. 500/5000 (2000), www.inc.com.

NOTES

1. Julie Jargon and Eric Morath, "As Wage Debate Rages, Some Have Made the Shift," *The Wall Street Journal*, April 8, 2014, http://online.wsj.com.
2. U.S. Census Bureau, *Statistical Abstract of the United States: 2012*, Table 756, p. 499, accessed at https: www.census.gov.
3. Bureau of Labor Statistics, "Labor Force Characteristics by Race and Ethnicity, 2012," *BLS Reports*, Report 1044, October 2013, http://www.bls.gov.
4. B. Gerhart, "Gender Differences in Current and Starting Salaries: The Role of Performance, College Major, and Job Title," *Industrial and Labor Relations Review* 43 (1990), pp. 418–33; G. G. Cain, "The Economic Analysis of Labor Market Discrimination: A Survey," in *Handbook of Labor Economics*, eds. O. Ashenfelter and R. Layard (New York: North-Holland, 1986), pp. 694–785; F. D. Blau and L. M. Kahn, "The Gender Pay Gap: Have Women Gone as Far as They Can?" *Academy of Management Perspectives*, February 2007, pp. 7–23.
5. C. Kulich, G. Trojanowski, M. K. Ryan, S. A. Haslam, and L. R. R. Renneboog, "Who Gets the Carrot and Who Gets the Stick? Evidence of Gender Disparities in Executive Remuneration," *Strategic Management Journal* 32 (2011): 301–321; F. Muñoz-Bullón, "Gender-Level Differences among High-Level Executives," *Industrial Relations* 49 (2010): 346–70.
6. S. L. Rynes and G. T. Milkovich, "Wage Surveys: Dispelling Some Myths about the 'Market Wage,'" *Personnel Psychology* 39 (1986), pp. 71–90; G. T. Milkovich, J. M. Newman, and B. Gerhart, *Compensation*, 10th ed. (New York: McGraw-Hill/Irwin, 2010).
7. U.S. Department of Labor, Wage and Hour Division, "Exemption for Executive, Administrative, Professional, Computer and Outside Sales Employees under the Fair Labor Standards Act (FLSA)," Face Sheet 17A, http://www.dol.gov/whd, accessed July 1, 2014.
8. U.S. Department of Labor, Wage and Hour Division, "What Do I Need to Know about Workplace Hazards?" *Youth Rules*, http://www.youthrules.dol.gov, accessed July 1, 2014; U.S. Department of Labor, Wage and Hour Division, "Frequently Asked Questions," *Youth Rules*, http://www.youthrules.dol.gov, accessed July 1, 2014; U.S. Department of Labor, Wage

and Hour Division, "Basic Information," June 2012, http://www.dol.gov.
9. Mike Ramsey, "VW Chops Labor Costs in U.S.," *The Wall Street Journal*, May 23, 2011, http://online.wsj.com; Bill Poovey, "Volkswagen's New Passat Makes Hometown Debut," *Yahoo Finance*, January 13, 2011, http://finance.yahoo.com.
10. B. Gerhart and G. T. Milkovich, "Organizational Differences in Managerial Compensation and Financial Performance," *Academy of Management Journal* 33 (1990), pp. 663–91; E. L. Groshen, "Why Do Wages Vary among Employers?" *Economic Review* 24 (1988), pp. 19–38.
11. Nathan Eddy, "IT Management: Google, Intel, Microsoft among Top-Paying IT Firms," *eWeek*, June 9, 2011, http://www.eweek.com.
12. G. A. Akerlof, "Gift Exchange and Efficiency-Wage Theory: Four Views," *American Economic Review* 74 (1984), pp. 79–83; J. L. Yellen, "Efficiency Wage Models of Unemployment," *American Economic Review* 74 (1984), pp. 200–5; B. Klaas and J. A. McClendon, "To Lead, Lag, or Match: Estimating the Financial Impact of Pay Level Policies," *Personnel Psychology* 49 (1996): 121–141; S. C. Currall, A. J. Towler, T. A. Judge, and L. Kohn, "Pay Satisfaction and Organizational Outcomes," *Personnel Psychology* 58 (2005): 613–640; A. L. Heavey, J. A. Holwerda, and J. P. Hausknecht, "Causes and Consequences of Collective Turnover: A Meta-analytic Review," *Journal of Applied Psychology* 98 (2013): 412–453.
13. IOMA, "Salary Data Sources Critical to Compensation Planning," *Report on Salary Surveys*, January 2012, pp. 11–13.
14. J. S. Adams, "Inequity in Social Exchange," in *Advances in Experimental Social Psychology*, ed. L. Berkowitz (New York: Academic Press, 1965); P. S. Goodman, "An Examination of Referents Used in the Evaluation of Pay," *Organizational Behavior and Human Performance* 12 (1974), pp. 170–95; C. O. Trevor and D. L. Wazeter, "A Contingent View of Reactions to Objective Pay Conditions: Interdependence among Pay Structure Characteristics and Pay Relative to Internal and External Referents," *Journal of Applied Psychology* 91 (2006): 1260–75; M. M. Harris, F. Anseel, and F. Lievens, "Keeping Up with the Joneses: A Field Study of

the Relationships among Upward, Lateral, and Downward Comparisons and Pay Level Satisfaction," *Journal of Applied Psychology* 93, no. 3 (May 2008), pp. 665–73; Gordon D. A. Brown, Jonathan Gardner, Andrew J. Oswald, and Jing Qian, "Does Wage Rank Affect Employees' Well-Being?" *Industrial Relations* 47, no. 3 (July 2008), p. 355.

15. P. Capelli and P. D. Sherer, "Assessing Worker Attitudes under a Two-Tier Wage Plan," *Industrial and Labor Relations Review* 43 (1990), pp. 225–44.

16. B. Casselman, "Male Nurses Make More Money," *The Wall Street Journal*, February 25, 2013, http://online.wsj.com; R. E. Silverman, "Psst . . . This Is What Your Co-worker Is Paid," *The Wall Street Journal*, January 29, 2013, http://online.wsj.com.

17. J. P. Pfeffer and A. Davis-Blake, "Understanding Organizational Wage Structures: A Resource Dependence Approach," *Academy of Management Journal* 30 (1987), pp. 437–55.

18. Culpepper, "Geographic Pay Differentials: Practices in Managing Pay between Locations," *Culpepper eBulletin*, March 2011, http://www.culpepper.com; Bureau of Labor Statistics, Occupational Employment Statistics Query System, http://data.bls.gov, accessed July 1, 2014.

19. This section draws freely on B. Gerhart and R. D. Bretz, "Employee Compensation," in *Organization and Management of Advanced Manufacturing*, eds. W. Karwowski and G. Salvendy (New York: Wiley, 1994), pp. 81–101.

20. E. E. Lawler III, *Strategic Pay* (San Francisco: Jossey-Bass, 1990); G. E. Ledford, "Paying for the Skills, Knowledge, Competencies of Knowledge Workers," *Compensation and Benefits Review*, July–August 1995, p. 55; G. Ledford, "Factors Affecting the Long-Term Success of Skill-Based Pay," *WorldatWork Journal*, First Quarter 2008, pp. 6–18; E. C. Dierdorff and E. A. Surface, "If You Pay for Skills, Will They Learn? Skill Change and Maintenance under a Skill-Based Pay System," *Journal of Management* 34 (2008), pp. 721–43.

21. B. C. Murray and B. Gerhart, "An Empirical Analysis of a Skill-Based Pay Program and Plant Performance Outcomes," *Academy of Management Journal* 41, no. 1 (1998), pp. 68–78.

22. Ibid.; N. Gupta, D. Jenkins, and W. Curington, "Paying for Knowledge: Myths and Realities," *National Productivity Review*, Spring 1986, pp. 107–23; J. D. Shaw, N. Gupta, A. Mitra, and G. E. Ledford, "Success and Survival of Skill-Based Pay Plans," *Journal of Management* 31 (2005), pp. 28–49.

23. Sears Holdings Corporation, "Sears Holdings Increases Commitment to Providing Jobs and Support to Military Personnel," *PR Newswire*, December 1, 2011, http://www.prnewswire.com; Sears Holdings, "Community Relations: Military Support," http://www.searsholdings.com, accessed April 12, 2012.

24. Ken Sweet, "Median CEO Pay Crosses $10 Million in 2013," *Associated Press*, May 27, 2014, http://hosted.ap.org; Michael Bamberger, "How Much Does the Average CEO Really Earn?" *CEO Briefing*, November 16, 2012.

25. Sweet, "Median CEO Pay Crosses $10 Million"; Theo Francis and Joann S. Lublin, "CEO Pay Rises Moderately; a Few Reap Huge Rewards," *The Wall Street Journal*, May 27, 2014, http://online.wsj.com.

26. Bloomberg Best (and Worst): "Lowest Paid with Strong Stock Performance: CEOs," *Bloomberg*, last updated October 25, 2013, http://www.bloomberg.com; Juliette Garside, "Facebook Founder Mark Zuckerberg's Base Salary Falls to $1," *Guardian* (London), April 1, 2014, http://the guardian.com.

27. D. M. Cowherd and D. I. Levine, "Product Quality and Pay Equity between Lower-Level Employees and Top Management: An Investigation of Distributive Justice Theory," *Administrative Science Quarterly* 37 (1992), pp. 302–20.

13

Recognizing Employee Contributions with Pay

What Do I Need to Know?

After reading this chapter, you should be able to:

LO 13-1 Discuss the connection between incentive pay and employee performance.

LO 13-2 Describe how organizations recognize individual performance.

LO 13-3 Identify ways to recognize group performance.

LO 13-4 Explain how organizations link pay to their overall performance.

LO 13-5 Describe how organizations combine incentive plans in a "balanced scorecard."

LO 13-6 Summarize processes that can contribute to the success of incentive programs.

LO 13-7 Discuss issues related to performance-based pay for executives.

Introduction

Selling cars is a far different job today. Just a few years ago, salespeople would wander the dealership lot, pointing out features and using their inside knowledge of the industry to close profitable sales. Today's car buyers visit a dealership only after going online to compare models and makes, find the best prices, and determine whether the dealer has what they want. When they arrive, most have already made their purchase decision. That means most of a dealer's workday is now spent at a desk, looking for those online shoppers and answering questions.

With the changing style of work comes a changing method of paying salespeople. A dealership used to focus on what would motivate employees to close profitable deals in face-to-face negotiations. That usually meant paying a commission, that is, a percentage of the profit on each car sold. The way to make more money was to sell more cars at a higher profit. But in today's era of informed customers, there is little room for dealers to negotiate prices; buyers know they can find a dealer who will accept the best price shown online. Some will even stand in the showroom and call a competitor to compare prices. Spitzer Auto Group in Elyria, Ohio, now pays salespeople a flat amount for each car they sell plus bonuses twice a month if they achieve a goal for sales volume. The revised pay scheme rewards Spitzer's salespeople for connecting with prospects, delivering great service, and completing sales rather than focusing on price. Nissan of Manhattan dropped commissions altogether and pays its staff a salary. Many of its salespeople quit following that change; a salary means a limit on how much you can earn even with exceptional performance. The dealership had to bring in new salespeople, some from other lines of work. However, customers love the idea of no pressure from commissioned salespeople, and the dealership is closing more sales faster than under the old system.[1]

The auto dealerships changed the way they pay employees when they wanted to change the kinds of behavior they reward. In this chapter we focus on using pay to recognize and reward employees' contributions to the organization's success. Employees' pay does not depend solely on the jobs they hold. Instead, organizations vary the amount paid according to differences in performance of the individual, group, or whole organization, as well as differences in employee qualities such as seniority and skills.[2]

Incentive Pay

Forms of pay linked to an employee's performance as an individual, group member, or organization member.

In contrast to decisions about pay structure, organizations have wide discretion in setting performance-related pay, called **incentive pay.** Organizations can tie incentive pay to individual performance, profits, or many other measures of success. They select incentives based on their costs, expected influence on performance, and fit with the organization's broader HR and company policies and goals. These decisions are significant. A study of 150 organizations found that the way organizations paid employees was strongly associated with their level of profitability.[3]

This chapter explores the choices available to organizations with regard to incentive pay. First, the chapter describes the link between pay and employee performance. Next, we discuss ways organizations provide a variety of pay incentives to individuals. The following two sections describe pay related to group and organizational performance. We then explore the organization's processes that can support the use of incentive pay. Finally, we discuss incentive pay for the organization's executives.

LO 13-1 Discuss the connection between incentive pay and employee performance.

Incentive Pay

Along with wages and salaries, many organizations offer *incentive pay*—that is, pay specifically designed to energize, direct, or maintain employees' behavior. Incentive pay is influential because the amount paid is linked to certain predefined behaviors or outcomes. For example, as we will see in this chapter, an organization can pay a salesperson a *commission* for closing a sale, or the members of a production department can earn a *bonus* for meeting a monthly production goal. Usually, these payments are in addition to wages and salaries. Knowing they can earn extra money for closing sales or meeting departmental goals, the employees often try harder or get more creative than they might without the incentive pay. In addition, the policy of offering higher pay for higher performance may make an organization attractive to high performers when it is trying to recruit and retain these valuable employees.[4] For reasons such as these, the share of companies offering variable pay rose from 78% of employers in 2005 to 92% in 2011.[5]

For incentive pay to motivate employees to contribute to the organization's success, the pay plans must be well designed. In particular, effective plans meet the following requirements:

- Performance measures are linked to the organization's goals.
- Employees believe they can meet performance standards.
- The organization gives employees the resources they need to meet their goals.

- Employees value the rewards given.
- Employees believe the reward system is fair.
- The pay plan takes into account that employees may ignore any goals that are not rewarded.

Since incentive pay is linked to particular outcomes or behaviors, the organization is encouraging employees to demonstrate those chosen outcomes and behaviors. As obvious as that may sound, the implications are more complicated. If incentive pay is extremely rewarding, employees may focus on only the performance measures rewarded under the plan and ignore measures that are not rewarded. Suppose an organization pays managers a bonus when employees are satisfied; this policy may interfere with other management goals. A manager who doesn't quite know how to inspire employees to do their best might be tempted to fall back on overly positive performance appraisals, letting work slide to keep everyone happy. Similarly, many call centers pay employees based on how many calls they handle, as an incentive to work quickly and efficiently. However, speedy call handling does not necessarily foster good customer relationships. As we will see in this chapter, organizations may combine a number of incentives so employees do not focus on one measure to the exclusion of others.

Attitudes that influence the success of incentive pay include whether employees value the rewards and think the pay plan is fair. One idea for promoting a sense of fairness is to give employees a say in allocating incentives. Often, co-workers are in the best position to see individuals' performances. Four times a year, Coffee & Power, a San Francisco start-up company, gives each of its employees the authority to distribute stock options among their co-workers. Only a few restrictions apply: employees may not reward themselves or give the options to the company's founders. In one quarter, workers had 1,200 apiece to distribute. That quarter, the largest bonus was 2,530 shares, and the smallest was 855. One of the biggest rewards went to a developer who works in a remote location and devotes much of her time to helping her colleagues—someone the founders did not know well and might have neglected with a traditional reward system.[6]

Although most, if not all, employees value pay, it is important to remember that earning money is not the only reason people try to do a good job. As we discuss in other chapters (see Chapters 4, 10, and 14), people also want interesting work, appreciation for their efforts, flexibility, and a sense of belonging to the work group—not to mention the inner satisfaction of work well done. Therefore, a complete plan for motivating and compensating employees has many components, from pay to work design to developing managers so they can exercise positive leadership.

With regard to the fairness of incentive pay, the preceding chapter described equity theory, which explains how employees form judgments about the fairness of a pay structure. The same process applies to judgments about incentive pay. In general, employees compare their efforts and rewards with those of other employees, considering a plan to be fair when the rewards are distributed according to what the employees contribute.

The remainder of this chapter identifies elements of incentive pay systems. We consider each option's strengths

Paying call center workers based on the number of calls they handle rewards efficiency but does not necessarily promote great customer service.

Did You Know?

Employers Stress Merit Pay to Retain Workers

A majority of companies consider employee retention to be a major concern, according to a survey by PayScale, a specialist in compensation data and software. The way companies are using compensation to attract and retain high-performing employees is with merit-based pay.

Fewer are relying on bonuses (discretionary or nondiscretionary incentives) or grants of stock or stock options. Beside compensation, about one-third of companies said they are relying on training and development to attract and keep talent.

Question

If your goal is to keep and engage high-performing employees, would you expect incentive pay to be more effective than simply increasing pay equally for all workers? Why or why not?

Sources: Bureau of National Affairs, "Surveys Examine 2014 Compensation Trends in U.S., Globally," *Report on Salary Surveys*, April 2014, pp. 5–8; PayScale, "The Year of the Great Balancing Act," Compensation Best Practice Report 2014, http://resources.payscale .com; PayScale, "New PayScale Report Warns Businesses They May Lose Top Talent," news release, February 11, 2014, http://www.payscale.com.

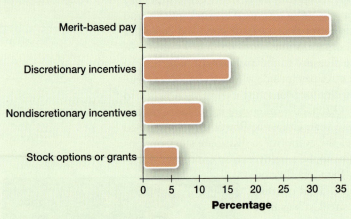

Compensation Plans for Attracting and Keeping Talent

and limitations with regard to these principles. The many kinds of incentive pay fall into three broad categories: incentives linked to individual, group, or organizational performance. Choices from these categories should consider not only their strengths and weaknesses, but also their fit with the organization's goals. The choice of incentive pay may affect not only the level of motivation but also the kinds of employees who are attracted to and stay with the organization. For example, there is some evidence that organizations with team-based rewards will tend to attract employees who are more team-oriented, while rewards tied to individual performance make an organization more attractive to those who think and act independently, as individuals.[7] Given the potential impact, organizations not only should weigh the strengths and weaknesses in selecting types of incentive pay but also should measure the results of these programs. For examples of what organizations are doing in practice, see the "Did You Know" box.

LO 13-2 Describe how organizations recognize individual performance.

Pay for Individual Performance

Organizations may reward individual performance with a variety of incentives:

- Piecework rates
- Standard hour plans
- Merit pay
- Individual bonuses
- Sales commissions

Piecework Rates

As an incentive to work efficiently, some organizations pay production workers a **piecework rate,** a wage based on the amount they produce. The amount paid per unit is set at a level that rewards employees for above-average production volume. For example, suppose that, on average, assemblers can finish 10 components in an hour. If the organization wants to pay its average assemblers $8 per hour, it can pay a piecework rate of $8/hour divided by 10 components/hour, or $.80 per component. An assembler who produces the average of 10 components per hour earns an amount equal to $8 per hour. An assembler who produces 12 components in an hour would earn $.80 × 12, or $9.60 each hour. This is an example of a **straight piecework plan** because the employer pays the same rate per piece no matter how much the worker produces.

A variation on straight piecework is **differential piece rates** (also called *rising* and *falling differentials*), in which the piece rate depends on the amount produced. If the worker produces more than the standard output, the piece rate is higher. If the worker produces at or below the standard, the amount paid per piece is lower. In the preceding example, the differential piece rate could be $1 per component for components exceeding 12 per hour and $.80 per component for up to 12 components per hour.

In one study, the use of piece rates increased production output by 30%—more than any other motivational device evaluated.[8] An obvious advantage of piece rates is the direct link between how much work the employee does and the amount the employee earns. This type of pay is easy to understand and seems fair to many people, if they think the production standard is reasonable. In spite of their advantages, piece rates are relatively rare for several reasons.[9] Most jobs, including those of managers, have no physical output, so it is hard to develop an appropriate performance measure. This type of incentive is most suited for very routine, standardized jobs with output that is easy to measure. For complex jobs or jobs with hard-to-measure outputs, piecework plans do not apply very well. Also, unless a plan is well designed to include performance standards, it may not reward employees for focusing on quality or customer satisfaction if it interferes with the day's output. In Figure 13.1, the employees quickly realize they can earn huge bonuses by writing software "bugs" and then fixing them, while writing bug-free software

Piecework Rate
A wage based on the amount workers produce.

Straight Piecework Plan
Incentive pay in which the employer pays the same rate per piece, no matter how much the worker produces.

Differential Piece Rates
Incentive pay in which the piece rate is higher when a greater amount is produced.

Figure 13.1
How Incentives Sometimes "Work"

affords no chance to earn bonuses. More seriously, a bonus based on number of faucets produced gives production workers no incentive to stop a manufacturing line to correct a quality-control problem. Production-oriented goals may do nothing to encourage employees to learn new skills or cooperate with others. Therefore, individual incentives such as these may be a poor incentive in an organization that wants to encourage teamwork. They may not be helpful in an organization with complex jobs, employee empowerment, and team-based problem solving.

Standard Hour Plans

Standard Hour Plan
An incentive plan that pays workers extra for work done in less than a preset "standard time."

Another quantity-oriented incentive for production workers is the **standard hour plan,** an incentive plan that pays workers extra for work done in less than a preset "standard time." The organization determines a standard time to complete a task, such as tuning up a car engine. If the mechanic completes the work in less than the standard time, the mechanic receives an amount of pay equal to the wage for the full standard time. Suppose the standard time for tuning up an engine is 2 hours. If the mechanic finishes a tune-up in 1½ hours, the mechanic earns 2 hours' worth of pay in 1½ hours. Working that fast over the course of a week could add significantly to the mechanic's pay.

In terms of their pros and cons, standard hour plans are much like piecework plans. They encourage employees to work as fast as they can, but not necessarily to care about quality or customer service. Also, they only succeed if employees want the extra money more than they want to work at a pace that feels comfortable.

Merit Pay

Merit Pay
A system of linking pay increases to ratings on performance appraisals.

Almost all organizations have established some program of **merit pay**—a system of linking pay increases to ratings on performance appraisals. (Chapter 10 described the content and use of performance appraisals.) To make the merit increases consistent, so they will be seen as fair, many merit pay programs use a *merit increase grid*, such as the sample in Table 13.1. As the table shows, the decisions about merit pay are based on two factors: the individual's performance rating and the individual's compa-ratio (pay relative to average pay, as defined in Chapter 12). This system gives the biggest pay increases to the best performers and to those whose pay is relatively low for their job. At the highest extreme, an exceptional employee earning 80% of the average pay for his job could receive a 7% merit raise. An employee rated as "below expectations" would receive a raise only if that employee was earning relatively low pay for the job (compa-ratio of 90% or less).

Organizations establish and revise merit increase grids in light of changing economic conditions. When organizations revise pay ranges, employees have new

Table 13.1

Sample Merit Increase Grid: Recommended Salary Increase

	COMPA-RATIO[a]		
PERFORMANCE RATING	80%–90%	91%–110%	111%–120%
Exceeds expectations	7%	5%	3%
Meets expectations	4%	3%	2%
Below expectations	2%	—	—

[a]Compa-ratio is the employee's salary divided by the midpoint of his or her salary range.

compa-ratios. A higher pay range would result in lower compa-ratios, causing employees to become eligible for bigger merit increases. An advantage of merit pay is therefore that it makes the reward more valuable by relating it to economic conditions.

A drawback is that conditions can shrink the available range of increases. During recent years, budgets for pay increases were about 2% to 4% of pay, so average performers could receive a 3% raise, and top performers perhaps as much as 5%. The 2-percentage-point difference, after taxes and other deductions, would amount to only a few dollars a week on a salary of $40,000 per year. Over an entire career, the bigger increases for top performers can grow into a major change, but viewed on a year-by-year basis, they are not much of an incentive to excel.[10] As Figure 13.2 shows, companies typically spread merit raises fairly evenly across all employees. However, experts advise making pay increases far greater for top performers than for average employees—and not rewarding the poor performers with a raise at all.[11] Imagine if the raises given to the bottom two categories in Figure 13.2 instead went toward 7% or greater raises for the one-quarter of employees who are high performers. This type of decision signals that excellence is rewarded. As the unemployment rate continues to fall, upward pressure on wages may increase the possible range for merit increases. If average pay rises by 4% or more, there are more dollars to distribute among high- and middle-performing employees.

Another advantage of merit pay is that it provides a method for rewarding performance in all of the dimensions measured in the organization's performance management system. If that system is appropriately designed to measure all the important job behaviors, then the merit pay is linked to the behaviors the organization desires. This link seems logical, although so far there is little research showing the effectiveness of merit pay.[12]

A drawback of merit pay, from the employer's standpoint, is that it can quickly become expensive. Managers at a majority of organizations rate most employees' performance in the top two categories (out of four or five).[13] Therefore, the majority of employees are eligible for the biggest merit increases, and their pay rises rapidly. This cost is one reason that some organizations have established guidelines about the percentage of employees that may receive the top rating, as discussed in Chapter 10.

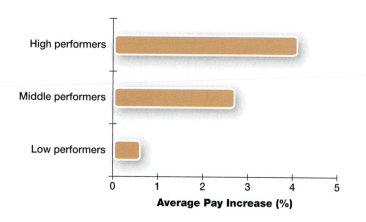

Figure 13.2

Ratings and Raises: Under-Rewarding the Best

Source: Bureau of National Affairs, "Salary Budgets for 2014 May Top 3 Percent, WorldatWork Survey Reports," *Report on Salary Surveys,* September 2013, pp. 1–4.

Another correction might be to use 360-degree performance feedback (discussed in Chapter 8), but so far, organizations have not used multisource data for pay decisions.[14]

Another drawback of merit pay is that it makes assumptions that may be misleading. Rewarding employees for superior performance ratings assumes that those ratings depend on employees' ability and motivation. But performance may actually depend on forces outside the employee's control, such as managers' rating biases, the level of cooperation from co-workers, or the degree to which the organization gives employees the authority, training, and resources they need. Under these conditions, employees will likely conclude that the merit pay system is unfair.

Quality guru W. Edwards Deming also criticizes merit pay for discouraging teamwork. In Deming's words, "Everyone propels himself forward, or tries to, for his own good, on his own life preserver. The organization is the loser."[15] For example, if employees in the purchasing department are evaluated based on the number or cost of contracts they negotiate, they may have little interest in the quality of the materials they buy, even when the manufacturing department is having quality problems. In reaction to such problems, Deming advocated the use of group incentives. Another alternative is for merit pay to include ratings of teamwork and cooperation. Some employers ask co-workers to provide such ratings.

Performance Bonuses

Like merit pay, performance bonuses reward individual performance, but bonuses are not rolled into base pay. The employee must re-earn them during each performance period. In some cases, the bonus is a one-time reward. Bonuses may also be linked to objective performance measures, rather than subjective ratings. In a recent survey, performance bonuses ranged from an average 3.3% paid to hourly wage earners to 6.9% for salaried workers exempt from overtime pay (top executives received much higher bonuses, as described later in the chapter).[16]

Bonuses for individual performance can be extremely effective and give the organization great flexibility in deciding what kinds of behavior to reward. In many cases, employees receive bonuses for meeting such routine targets as sales or production numbers. Airlines can reward good customer service with bonuses for meeting goals for on-time performance, and trucking firms can reward safe practices with bonuses for accident-free driving. Companies can award bonuses for learning, innovation, or any other behavior they associate with success. Savant Capital Management wanted its financial advisers to take more responsibility for bringing in new clients and helping to grow a firm that will remain strong after its founders retire. So the Rockford, Illinois, financial planning firm shifted part of advisers' pay from salary to a potentially larger set of bonuses. Each adviser may earn a bonus based on a percentage of revenue from each of his or her clients and additional bonuses for each new client brought in. Besides these individual bonuses, Savant pays bonuses linked to the firm's overall achievement of goals for profit, revenues, and new assets (clients' investments).[17]

All this flexibility makes it essential to be sure bonuses are tied to behavior that makes a difference to the organization's overall performance. Also, employees have to have some control over whether they can meet the bonus requirements. For an example of why these conditions are important, see the "HR Oops!" box.

Adding to the flexibility of annual or more frequent bonuses, organizations also may motivate employees with one-time bonuses. For example, when one organization acquires another, it usually wants to retain certain valuable employees in the organization it is buying. Therefore, it is common for organizations involved in an acquisition

Giving Arbitrary Bonuses to Employees

Josh Patrick is now a successful adviser to business owners, and many of his lessons are ones he learned from personal experience. He started his business career by building a food service and vending company. In that role, he wanted to reward his employees for doing their jobs well, so he set up a program for paying bonuses. At the beginning of this program, the company had about 40 employees, and Patrick tried to evaluate whether each employee had performed well enough to earn a bonus. However, the decisions were not always tied to an objective measurement or to the company's profitability. In some cases, employees were rewarded for individual successes that did not contribute to the company's overall success.

So Patrick decided to discard the individual bonus plan and start over. Initially, employees were upset about the change, but Patrick addressed their resistance through communication. He explained that the company would pay bonuses for group success, and he began to teach them about the company's finances. When employees understood how their actions contributed to profits, they began working together to build a stronger company.

Patrick's move toward group bonuses was a response to some problems that can arise with poorly constructed individual bonuses. Employees may not understand what they need to do to earn a bonus and why those goals matter. Further, employees who do not understand the bonus requirements may resent any occasion when their bonus is smaller than it has been previously.

Questions

1. What problems do you see in the way Patrick set up his original bonus program?
2. How might Patrick have improved his system for awarding individual bonuses without switching to awards for group performance? That is, how could he continue to reward individual performance but do it more effectively?

Sources: Purposeful Planning Institute, "Josh Patrick," collaborators, accessed July 9, 2014; Robert Moskowitz, "Using Group instead of Individual Bonuses to Reward Employees," *Intuit Small Business Blog*, April 8, 2013, http://blog .intuit.com; Josh Patrick, "Do You Pay Employees to Exist or to Produce?" *The New York Times*, March 14, 2013, http:// boss.blogs.nytimes.com.

to pay *retention bonuses*—one-time incentives paid in exchange for remaining with the company—to top managers, engineers, top-performing salespeople, and information technology specialists. When Cisco Systems acquired Sourcefire, it paid retention bonuses to the executives of that company, which specializes in cybersecurity. When Office Depot merged with OfficeMax, it paid top executives bonuses of up to $500,000 a year over a three-year period so they would stay through the transition.[18]

Sales Commissions

A variation on piece rates and bonuses is the payment of **commissions,** or pay calculated as a percentage of sales. For instance, a furniture salesperson might earn commissions equaling 6% times the price of the furniture the person sells during the period. Selling a $2,000 couch would add $120 to the salesperson's commissions for the period. Commission rates vary tremendously from one industry and company to another. Examples reported include an average rate between 5.0% and 5.5% for real estate, 15% to 20% of the annual premium for car insurance (paid to an independent insurance agent), and 22% to 30% of *profits* for auto sales.[19]

Some salespeople earn a commission in addition to a base salary; others earn only commissions—a pay arrangement called a *straight commission plan.* Straight commissions are common among insurance and real estate agents and car salespeople. Other salespeople earn no commissions at all, but a straight salary. Paying most or all of a salesperson's compensation in the form of salary frees the salesperson to focus on developing customer goodwill. Paying most or all of a salesperson's compensation in

Commissions
Incentive pay calculated as a percentage of sales.

Real estate agents typically earn a straight commission, meaning that 100% of their pay comes from commission instead of salary. What type of individual might enjoy a job like this?

the form of commissions encourages the salesperson to focus on closing sales. In this way, differences in salespeople's compensation directly influence how they spend their time, how they treat customers, and how much the organization sells.

The nature of salespeople's compensation also affects the kinds of people who will want to take and keep sales jobs with the organization. Hard-driving, ambitious, risk-taking salespeople might enjoy the potential rewards of a straight commission plan. An organization that wants salespeople to concentrate on listening to customers and building relationships might want to attract a different kind of salesperson by offering more of the pay in the form of a salary. Basing part or all of a salesperson's pay on commissions assumes that the organization wants to attract people with some willingness to take risks—probably a reasonable assumption about people whose job includes talking to strangers and encouraging them to spend money.

Pay for Group Performance

LO 13-3 Identify ways to recognize group performance.

Employers may address the drawbacks of individual incentives by including group incentives in the organization's compensation plan. To win group incentives, employees must cooperate and share knowledge so that the entire group can meet its performance targets. Common group incentives include gainsharing, bonuses, and team awards.

Gainsharing

Gainsharing
Group incentive program that measures improvements in productivity and effectiveness and distributes a portion of each gain to employees.

Organizations that want employees to focus on efficiency may adopt a **gainsharing** program, which measures increases in productivity and effectiveness and distributes a portion of each gain to employees. For example, if a factory enjoys a productivity gain worth $30,000, half the gain might be the company's share. The other $15,000 would be distributed among the employees in the factory. Knowing that they can enjoy a financial benefit from helping the company be more productive, employees supposedly will look for ways to work more efficiently and improve the way the factory operates.

Gainsharing addresses the challenge of identifying appropriate performance measures for complex jobs. For example, how would a hospital measure the production of its nurses—in terms of satisfying patients, keeping costs down, or completing a number of tasks? Each of these measures oversimplifies the complex responsibilities involved in nursing care. Even for simpler jobs, setting acceptable standards and measuring performance can be complicated. Gainsharing frees employees to determine how to improve their own and their group's performance. It also broadens employees' focus beyond their individual interests. But in contrast to profit sharing, discussed later, it keeps the performance measures within a range of activity that most employees believe they can influence. Organizations can enhance the likelihood of a gain by providing a means for employees to share knowledge and make suggestions, as we will discuss in the last section of this chapter.

Gainsharing is most likely to succeed when organizations provide the right conditions. Among the conditions identified, the following are among the most common[20]:

- Management commitment.
- Need for change or strong commitment to continuous improvement.
- Management acceptance and encouragement of employee input.

- High levels of cooperation and interaction.
- Employment security.
- Information sharing on productivity and costs.
- Goal setting.
- Commitment of all involved parties to the process of change and improvement.
- Performance standard and calculation that employees understand and consider fair and that is closely related to managerial objectives.
- Employees who value working in groups.

A popular form of gainsharing is the **Scanlon plan,** developed in the 1930s by Joseph N. Scanlon, president of a union local at Empire Steel and Tin Plant in Mansfield, Ohio. The Scanlon plan gives employees a bonus if the ratio of labor costs to the sales value of production is below a set standard. To keep this ratio low enough to earn the bonus, workers have to keep labor costs to a minimum and produce as much as possible with that amount of labor. Figure 13.3 provides an example. In this example, the standard is a ratio of 20/100, or 20% and the workers produced parts worth $1.2 million. To meet the standard, the labor costs should be less than 20% of $1.2 million, or $240,000. Since the actual labor costs were $210,000, the workers will get a gainsharing bonus based on the $30,000 difference between the $240,000 target and the actual cost.

Typically, an organization does not pay workers all of the gain immediately. First, the organization keeps a share of the gain to improve its own bottom line. A portion of the remainder goes into a reserve account. This account offsets losses in any months when the gain is negative (that is, when costs rise or production falls). At the end of the year, the organization closes out the account and distributes any remaining surplus. If there were a loss at the end of the year, the organization would absorb it.

Target Ratio: $\dfrac{\text{Labor Costs}}{\text{Sales Value of Production}} = \dfrac{20}{100}$

Sales Value of Production: $1,200,000

Goal: $\dfrac{20}{100} \times \$1,200,000 = \$240,000$

Actual: $210,000

Gain: $240,000 − $210,000 = $30,000

Figure 13.3

Finding the Gain in a Scanlon Plan

Source: Example adapted from B. Graham-Moore and Timothy L. Ross, *Gainsharing: Plans for Improving Performance* (Washington, DC: Bureau of National Affairs, 1990), p. 57.

Scanlon Plan

A gainsharing program in which employees receive a bonus if the ratio of labor costs to the sales value of production is below a set standard.

Group Bonuses and Team Awards

In contrast to gainsharing plans, which typically reward the performance of all employees at a facility, bonuses for group performance tend to be for smaller work groups.[21] These bonuses reward the members of a group for attaining a specific goal, usually measured in terms of physical output. Team awards are similar to group bonuses, but they are more likely to use a broad range of performance measures, such as cost savings, successful completion of a project, or even meeting deadlines.

Both types of incentives have the advantage that they encourage group or team members to cooperate so that they can achieve their goal. However, depending on the reward system, competition among individuals may be replaced by competition among groups. Competition may be healthy in some situations, as when groups try to outdo one another in satisfying customers. On the downside, competition may also prevent necessary cooperation among groups. To avoid this, the organization should carefully set the performance goals for these incentives so that concern for costs or sales does not obscure other objectives, such as quality, customer service, and ethical behavior.

Group members that meet a sales goal or a product development team that meets a deadline or successfully launches a product may be rewarded with a bonus for group performance. What are some advantages and disadvantages of group bonuses?

LO 13-4 Explain how organizations link pay to their overall performance.

Pay for Organizational Performance

Two important ways organizations measure their performance are in terms of their profits and their stock price. In a competitive marketplace, profits result when an organization is efficiently providing products that customers want at a price they are willing to pay. Stock is the owners' investment in a corporation; when the stock price is rising, the value of that investment is growing. Rather than trying to figure out what performance measures will motivate employees to do the things that generate high profits and a rising stock price, many organizations offer incentive pay tied to those organizational performance measures. The expectation is that employees will focus on what is best for the organization.

These organization-level incentives can motivate employees to align their activities with the organization's goals. At the same time, linking incentives to the organization's profits or stock price exposes employees to a high degree of risk. Profits and stock price can soar very high very fast, but they can also fall. The result is a great deal of uncertainty about the amount of incentive pay each employee will receive in each period. Therefore, these kinds of incentive pay are likely to be most effective in organizations that emphasize growth and innovation, which tend to need employees who thrive in a risk-taking environment.[22]

Profit Sharing

Profit Sharing
Incentive pay in which payments are a percentage of the organization's profits and do not become part of the employees' base salary.

Under **profit sharing,** payments are a percentage of the organization's profits and do not become part of the employees' base salary. For example, General Motors provides for profit sharing in its contract with its workers' union, the United Auto Workers. Depending on how large GM's profits are in relation to its total sales for the year, at least 6% of the company's profits are divided among the workers according to how many hours they worked during the year.[23] The formula for computing and dividing the profit-sharing bonus is included in the union contract.

Organizations use profit sharing for a number of reasons. It may encourage employees to think more like owners, taking a broad view of what they need to do in order to make the organization more effective. They are more likely to cooperate and less likely to focus on narrow self-interests. Also, profit sharing has the practical advantage of costing less when the organization is experiencing financial difficulties. If the organization has little or no profit, this incentive pay is small or nonexistent, so employers may not need to rely as much on layoffs to reduce costs.[24]

Does profit sharing help organizations perform better? The evidence is not yet clear. Although research supports a link between profit-sharing payments and profits, researchers have questioned which of these causes the other.[25] For example, Ford, Chrysler, and GM have similar profit-sharing plans in their contracts with the United Auto Workers, but the payouts are not always similar. In one year, the average worker received $4,000 from Ford, $550 from GM, and $8,000 from Chrysler. Since the plans are similar, something other than the profit sharing must have made Ford and Chrysler more profitable than GM.

Differences in payouts, as in the preceding example, raise questions not only about the effectiveness of the plans, but about equity. Assuming workers at Ford, Chrysler, and GM have similar jobs, they would expect to receive similar profit-sharing checks. In the year of this example, GM workers might have seen their incentive pay as highly inequitable unless GM could show how Chrysler workers did more to earn their big checks. Employees also may feel that small profit-sharing checks are unfair because they have little control over profits. If profit sharing is offered to all employees but most employees think only management decisions about products, price, and marketing have much impact on profits, they will conclude that there is little connection between their actions and their rewards. In that case, profit-sharing plans will have little impact on employee behavior. This problem is even greater when employees have to wait months before profits are distributed. The time lag between high-performance behavior and financial rewards is simply too long to be motivating.

Adequate communication is essential for addressing issues related to equity, especially since profits can shrivel for reasons beyond employees' control. At Jim's Formal Wear, a tuxedo wholesaler, workers at each warehouse split 3% of the facility's profits in the second, third, and fourth quarter of each year. Employees also can earn up to $1,200 per year in bonuses if the company meets goals for customer satisfaction. Every month, managers at each warehouse review the facility's business performance, comparing the current year with the previous year and with the year's goals. Every week, employees gather in team meetings to discuss ways to improve the next week's performance, such as reducing costs or errors.[26] The weekly and monthly meetings provide opportunities to educate employees and involve them in decision making. For another example of a profit-sharing plan that met expectations, see the "Best Practices" box.

Given the limitations of profit-sharing plans, one strategy is to use them as a component of a pay system that includes other kinds of pay more directly linked to individual behavior. This increases employees' commitment to organizational goals while addressing concerns about fairness.

Stock Ownership

While profit-sharing plans are intended to encourage employees to "think like owners," a stock ownership plan actually makes employees part owners of the organization. Like profit sharing, employee ownership is intended as a way to encourage employees to focus on the success of the organization as a whole. The drawbacks of stock ownership as a form of incentive pay are similar to those of profit sharing. Specifically, it may not have a strong effect on individuals' motivation. Employees may not see a strong link between their actions and the company's stock price, especially in larger organizations. The link between pay and performance is even harder to appreciate because the financial benefits mostly come when the stock is sold—typically when the employee leaves the organization.

Ownership programs usually take the form of *stock options* or *employee stock ownership plans.* These are illustrated in Figure 13.4.

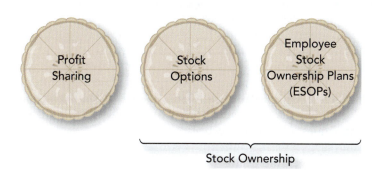

Figure 13.4
Types of Pay for Organizational Performance

Profit Sharing at Paul Downs Cabinetmakers

Paul Downs Cabinetmakers is a customer furniture shop specializing in large conference and boardroom tables. Its skilled craftspeople work in a facility in Bridgeport, Pennsylvania. The company's owner, Paul Downs, was concerned that the business did not always operate profitably. Orders were growing faster than production output. The greater efficiency needed to generate stronger profits might involve changes that would be unwelcome to employees more interested in craftsmanship. To encourage them to care more about the business impact of their work, Downs introduced a profit-sharing plan.

Downs assembled his 17 workers and explained the plan. In any profitable quarter, 15% of the company's profits would be divided among all the workers. If they also met that month's target for dollar volume shipped, another 15% of the profits would be divided among them. The workers were unenthusiastic

until the final month of the quarter, when Downs realized they had the potential to earn a solid profit. He explained to the workers what they had to do to earn bonuses of more than $1,000 each, and the workers pushed hard to meet the goals.

In the following year, it appeared that the incentive was working. Out of four quarters, the company reported profits and paid bonuses in three, totaling $3,122 per worker. During the one unprofitable quarter, employees were not upset because ongoing communication showed them that shipments were behind and would take place in the following quarter. Revenues for the first year of the profit-sharing program were up more than 43% over the previous year, and profits rose substantially. All this growth came without a price increase, so Downs concluded that his production workers had chosen to operate more efficiently.

Questions

1. What evidence suggests that profit sharing was successful at Paul Downs Cabinetmakers?
2. Do you think the workers are likely to see this profit-sharing program as equitable? Why or why not?

Sources: Paul Downs Cabinetmakers, "About Paul Downs," http://www.custom-conference-tables.com, accessed July 7, 2014; Paul Downs, "Assessing the Impact of a Profit-Sharing Plan," *The New York Times*, April 21, 2014, http://boss.blogs.nytimes.com; Paul Downs, "Debating the Merits of a Profit-Sharing Plan," *The New York Times*, September 17, 2013, http://boss.blogs.nytimes.com; Paul Downs, "Here's What Happened When I Introduced Profit Sharing," *The New York Times*, September 9, 2013, http://boss.blogs.nytimes.com.

Stock Options
Rights to buy a certain number of shares of stock at a specified price.

Stock Options   One way to distribute stock to employees is to grant them **stock options**—the right to buy a certain number of shares of stock at a specified price. (Purchasing the stock is called *exercising* the option.) Suppose that in 2012 a company's employees received options to purchase the company's stock at $10 per share. The employees will benefit if the stock price rises above $10 per share because they can pay $10 for something (a share of stock) that is worth more than $10. If in 2017 the stock is worth $30, they can exercise their options and buy stock for $10 a share. If they want to, they can sell their stock for the market price of $30, receiving a gain of $20 for each share of stock. Of course, stock prices can also fall. If the 2017 stock price is only $8, the employees would not bother to exercise the options.

Traditionally, organizations have granted stock options to their executives. During the 1990s, many organizations pushed eligibility for options further down in the organization's structure. Walmart and PepsiCo are among the large companies that have granted stock options to employees at all levels. Stock values were rising so fast during the 1990s that options were extremely rewarding for a time.

Some studies suggest that organizations perform better when a large percentage of top and middle managers are eligible for long-term incentives such as stock options.

This evidence is consistent with the idea of encouraging employees to think like own-ers.[27] It is not clear whether these findings would hold up for lower-level employees. They may see much less opportunity to influence the company's performance in the stock market.

Recent scandals have drawn attention to another challenge of using stock op-tions as incentive pay. As with other performance measures, employees may focus so much on stock price that they lose sight of other goals, including ethical behav-ior. Ideally, managers would bring about an increase in stock price by adding value in terms of efficiency, innovation, and customer satisfaction. But there are other, unethical ways to increase stock price by tricking investors into thinking the orga-nization is more valuable and more profitable than it actually is. Hiding losses and inflating the recorded value of revenues are just two of the ways some companies have boosted stock prices, enriching managers until these misdeeds come to light. Several years ago, when stock prices tended to be high, some companies "back-dated" options, meaning they changed the date or price in the option agreement so that the option holder could buy shares at a bargain price (this practice may be illegal if done secretly).

Employee Stock Ownership Plans   While stock options are most often used with top management, a broader arrangement is the **employee stock ownership plan (ESOP).** In an ESOP, the organization distributes shares of stock to its employ-ees by placing the stock into a trust managed on the employees' behalf. Employees receive regular reports on the value of their stock, and when they leave the organiza-tion, they may sell the stock to the organization or (if it is a publicly traded company) on the open market.

ESOPs are the most common form of employee ownership, with the number of employees in such plans increasing from approximately 250,000 in 1975 to more than 10 million active participants (those who are currently employed and earning ben-efits).[28] The number of participants has grown even while the number of companies offering ESOPs has shrunk somewhat, as shown in Figure 13.5.

> **Employee Stock Ownership Plan (ESOP)**
> An arrangement in which the organization dis-tributes shares of stock to all its employees by placing it in a trust.

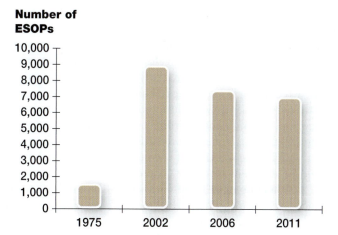

Figure 13.5
Number of Companies with ESOPs

Number of ESOPs

Source: National Center for Employee Ownership, "A Statistical Profile of Employee Ownership," updated June 2014, http://www.nceo.org.

ESOPs raise a number of issues. On the negative side, they carry a significant risk for employees. By law, an ESOP must invest at least 51% of its assets in the company's own stock (in contrast to other kinds of stock funds that hold a wide diversity of companies). Problems with the company's performance therefore can take away significant value from the ESOP. Many companies set up ESOPs to hold retirement funds, so these risks directly affect employees' retirement income. Adding to the risk, funds in an ESOP are not guaranteed by the Pension Benefit Guarantee Corporation (described in Chapter 14). Sometimes employees use an ESOP to buy their company when it is experiencing financial problems; this is a highly risky investment.

Still, ESOPs can be attractive to employers. Along with tax and financing advantages, ESOPs give employers a way to build pride in and commitment to the organization. Employees have a right to participate in votes by shareholders (if the stock is registered on a national exchange, such as the New York Stock Exchange).[29] This means employees participate somewhat in corporate-level decision making. Still, the overall level of participation in decisions appears to vary significantly among organizations with ESOPs. Some research suggests that the benefits of ESOPs are greatest when employee participation is greatest.[30]

Balanced Scorecard

LO 13-5 Describe how organizations combine incentive plans in a "balanced scorecard."

As the preceding descriptions indicate, any form of incentive pay has advantages and disadvantages. For example, relying exclusively on merit pay or other individual incentives may produce a workforce that cares greatly about meeting those objectives but competes to achieve them at the expense of cooperating to achieve organizational goals. Relying heavily on profit sharing or stock ownership may increase cooperation but do little to motivate day-to-day effort or to attract and retain top individual performers. Because of this, many organizations design a mix of pay programs. The aim is to balance the disadvantages of one type of incentive pay with the advantages of another type.

Balanced Scorecard
A combination of performance measures directed toward the company's long- and short-term goals and used as the basis for awarding incentive pay.

One way of accomplishing this goal is to design a **balanced scorecard**—a combination of performance measures directed toward the company's long- and short-term goals and used as the basis for awarding incentive pay. A corporation would have financial goals to satisfy its stockholders (owners), quality- and price-related goals to satisfy its customers, efficiency goals to ensure better operations, and goals related to acquiring skills and knowledge for the future to fully tap into employees' potential. Different jobs would contribute to those goals in different ways. For example, an engineer could develop products that better meet customer needs and can be produced more efficiently. The engineer could also develop knowledge of new technologies in order to contribute more to the organization in the future. A salesperson's goals would include measures related to sales volume, customer service, and learning about product markets and customer needs. Organizations customize their balanced scorecards according to their markets, products, and objectives. The scorecards of a company that is emphasizing low costs and prices would be different from the scorecards of a company emphasizing innovative use of new technology. Table 13.2 shows the kinds of information that go into a balanced scorecard. The "HRM Social" box explores another kind of information that could be added to balanced scorecards in the information age.

Not only does the balanced scorecard combine the advantages of different incentive-pay plans, it helps employees understand the organization's goals. By

Table 13.2

Sample Balanced Scorecard for an Electric Cooperative

PERFORMANCE CATEGORY	CRITICAL SUCCESS FACTORS	GOALS		
		BASE (2%)	TARGET (3%)	STRETCH (5%)
Member service (40% of incentive pay)	Reliability (average interruption duration)	140 min.	130 min.	120 min.
	Customer satisfaction (index from quarterly survey)	9.0	9.1	9.2
Financial performance (25% of incentive pay)	Total operating expenses (¢/kilowatt-hour)	4.03¢	3.99¢	3.95¢
	Cash flow (% of investment)	75%	80%	85%
Internal processes (20% of incentive pay)	Safety (safety index based on injury rate and severity)	4.6	3.6	2.6
Innovation and learning (15% of incentive pay)	Member value (revenue/kWh sold)	Budget	−10% state median	−13% state median
	Efficiency and effectiveness (total margins/no. employees)	$534,400	$37,200	$40,000

Source: Adapted from Tim Sullivan and Henry Cano, "Introducing a Balanced Scorecard for Electric Cooperatives: A Tool for Measuring and Improving Results," *Management Quarterly,* Winter 2009, Business & Company Resource Center, http://galenet.galegroup.com.

communicating the balanced scorecard to employees, the organization shows employees information about what its goals are and what it expects employees to accomplish. At ConocoPhillips, top executives have a scorecard that includes costs, health and safety, production, and resource replacement. In addition, the energy company has developed scorecards for operations-level activities such as safety measures.[31] In Table 13.2, the organization indicates not only that the manager should meet the four performance objectives but also that it is especially concerned with the financial target because half the incentive is based on this one target.

Processes That Make Incentives Work

As we explained in Chapter 12, communication and employee participation can contribute to a belief that the organization's pay structure is fair. In the same way, the process by which the organization creates and administers incentive pay can help it use incentives to achieve the goal of motivating employees. The monetary rewards of gainsharing, for example, can substantially improve productivity,[32] but the organization can set up the process to be even more effective. In a study of an automotive parts plant, productivity rose when the gainsharing plan added employee participation in the form of monthly meetings with managers to discuss the gainsharing plan and ways to increase productivity. A related study asked employees what motivated them to participate actively in the plan (for example, by making suggestions for improvement). According to employees, other factors besides the pay itself were important—especially the ability to influence and control the way their work was done.[33] Considerations

LO 13-6 Summarize processes that can contribute to the success of incentive programs.

Scoring Social Influence

A social-media service may shine a light on the future of balanced scorecards. Klout tracks social-media activity to compute a user's influence in terms of the number of people reached and the user's reputation as trustworthy and expert in some area. For example, many retweets of a person's Twitter posts would suggest that the person is influential. For a time, Klout scores drew attention as a way to compare famous individuals. Then some results (for example, pop star Justin Bieber being more influential than the president of the United States) drew scorn, and the idea that Klout will definitely measure influence may have faded.

Despite Klout's limitations, it suggests an interesting social measure for organizations. Employees are especially valuable if they work effectively in a network of colleagues who share knowledge and influence one another constructively. Organizations are already investigating ways to measure social influence among employees. In a few cases, companies have reportedly used Klout scores to select influential people for jobs that involve promoting the company to the general public. They also could use something like a Klout score to direct incentive pay toward their most influential people.

In practice, this could be part of a balanced scorecard. Along with contributing to financial and quality goals, an employee could have a target for influence, perhaps listed among other skills the employer values. Employees who score higher on influence could earn a larger bonus.

Questions

1. Suppose a manufacturing firm decided to add social influence to a balanced scorecard for its engineers and marketing staff. What percentage of the total incentive pay do you think should be based on the influence score? Why?

2. How fair do you think it would be to use social influence as a basis for incentive pay?

Sources: Jon Nathanson, "How Klout Finally Matters," *Slate*, May 1, 2014, http://www.slate.com; Jeanne Meister, "2014: The Year Social HR Matters," *Forbes*, January 6, 2014, http://www.forbes.com; Sharon Horrigan, "Is Social Media Clout a New Job Criteria?" *Society for Human Resource Management*, April 24, 2013, http://www.shrm.org; Will Oremus, "Could Your Crummy Klout Score Keep You from Getting a Job?" *Slate*, October 3, 2012, http://www.slate.com.

such as these are especially important in today's economic environment, where compensation budgets tend to be limited (see "HR How To").

Participation in Decisions

Employee participation in pay-related decisions can be part of a general move toward employee empowerment. If employees are involved in decisions about incentive pay plans and employees' eligibility for incentives, the process of creating and administering these plans can be more complex.[34] There is also a risk that employees will make decisions that are in their interests at the expense of the organization's interests. However, employees have hands-on knowledge about the kinds of behavior that can help the organization perform well, and they can see whether individuals are displaying that behavior.[35] Therefore, in spite of the potential risks, employee participation can contribute to the success of an incentive plan. This is especially true when monetary incentives encourage the monitoring of performance and when the organization fosters a spirit of trust and cooperation.

Communication

Along with empowerment, communicating with employees is important. It demonstrates to employees that the pay plan is fair. Also, when employees understand the requirements of the incentive pay plan, the plan is more likely to influence their behavior as desired.

HR How To

Getting the Most from a Limited Compensation Budget

You want to reward good performance, but there's hardly any money in the budget for raises and bonuses. That's the situation facing many HR managers in today's business climate. Here are some suggestions for making the most of whatever you can spend:

- Make sure that merit pay is truly related to performance gains. Raises are expensive and widely used, so high-performing employees expect to earn significantly more than average. Therefore, it is essential to be sure that performance measures used as the basis for raises are tied to business success and that the organization measures performance accurately.
- Offer modest but frequent incentives as quick rewards for accomplishments. An unexpected $100 one-time award for delighting a customer can have more impact than a $100 per month raise, at a lower cost.
- Implement other strategies to reward performance that can also serve as employee incentives, such as flexible schedules, interesting and unique projects, and formal recognition. These are particularly useful for companies that don't have large budgets to

provide meaningful year-end or spot bonuses.
- If the organization cannot afford to give everyone—or even all the above-average performers—a raise, it should target pay increases to the best of the best. Explain that merit pay is for doing something exceptional, not just performing one's job. When expressed clearly, this message actually can strengthen employees' understanding of the connection between performance and incentive pay.
- Set and communicate clear, measurable targets for earning incentive pay. Employees want to understand what they have to do to be eligible for a raise or bonus. They also appreciate knowing the size of the incentive they are eligible to earn.
- Accept that employees who do not achieve the requirements for earning incentive pay may leave. If the system is working properly, the employees who leave should be the ones who contribute the least. If good performers also are leaving, make sure the organization is providing employees with the resources they need—including training and empowerment—for meeting performance targets.

Questions

1. Suppose employees complain to HR managers that bonuses are meaningless because no one understands how to earn them. What measures should the company take to make incentive pay more effective?
2. Suppose a manager has enough money to give one employee a 4% raise and another employee no raise, or else the manager can give both employees a 2% raise. What would you recommend to the manager, and why?

Sources: Juan Pablo Gonzalez, Kate Richardson, and Hemali Desai, "Get More Bang for Your Comp Program Buck Despite Stagnant Salary Budget Increases," *Compensation Focus* (WorldatWork), October 2013, http://www.worldatwork.org; Radek Knesl, Sal DiFonzo, and Philip E. Warner, "Incentive Compensation Effectiveness Study: The 2013 U.S. Construction Industry Incentive Compensation Survey," FMI Corp., 2013, http://www.forconstructionpros.com; Bureau of National Affairs, "Consultant Details Advantages of Pay for Performance," *Report on Salary Surveys*, October 2013, pp. 8–9; Bloomberg BNA, "Pay for Performance to Retain and Engage, Speaker Says," *Report on Salary Surveys*, March 1, 2013, http://news.bna.com.

It is particularly important to communicate with employees when changing the plan. Employees tend to feel concerned about changes. Pay is a frequent topic of rumors and assumptions based on incomplete information, partly because of pay's importance to employees. When making any changes, the human resource department should determine the best ways to communicate the reasons for the change. Some organizations rely heavily on videos, played at meetings or posted on the company's intranet (internal website). The company can also publish descriptions and scenarios in brochures or post them on its intranet. Most pay-related communications, however, come through individual discussions between employees and their supervisor.[36]

LO 13-7 Discuss issues related to performance-based pay for executives.

Incentive Pay for Executives

Because executives have a much stronger influence over the organization's performance than other employees do, incentive pay for executives warrants special attention. Assuming that incentives influence performance, decisions about incentives for executives should have a great impact on how well the executives and the organization perform. Along with overall pay levels for executives (discussed in Chapter 12), organizations need to create incentive plans for this small but important group of employees.

To encourage executives to develop a commitment to the organization's long-term success, executive compensation often combines short-term and long-term incentives. *Short-term incentives* include bonuses based on the year's profits, return on investment, or other measures related to the organization's goals. Sometimes, to gain tax advantages, the actual payment of the bonus is deferred (for example, by making it part of a retirement plan). *Long-term incentives* include stock options and stock purchase plans. The rationale for these long-term incentives is that executives will want to do what is best for the organization because that will cause the value of their stock to grow.

Researchers have tried in vain to find a link between the size of CEOs' incentive pay and companies' performance in terms of profits or other financial measures.[37] In an analysis of CEO pay at 300 large U.S.-traded companies, none of the 10 top-paid CEOs worked for companies that attained the top 10% in terms of performance, even though their pay far exceeded the median. And in a study that compared historical CEO pay with the companies' performance over the following three years, CEOs who earned in the top 10% saw their companies do increasingly *worse* than others over the three years that followed. Of course, incentive pay is generally tied to one's past accomplishments, not (formally) to expectations. However, the highly paid executives in the study took more risks that did not pay off, so if the incentives made them overconfident, this type of pay was not meeting long-range objectives.

A corporation's shareholders—its owners—want the corporation to encourage managers to act in the owners' best interests. They want managers to care about the company's profits and stock price, and incentive pay can encourage this interest. One study has found that relying on such long-term incentives is associated with greater profitability.[38]

Performance Measures for Executives

The balanced-scorecard approach is useful in designing executive pay. Merck, for example, has used a balanced scorecard that combines measures of whether the organization is delivering value to shareholders, customers, and employees. These measures are listed in Table 13.3. Rewarding achievement of a variety of goals in a balanced scorecard reduces the temptation to win bonuses by manipulating financial data.

Regulators and shareholders have pressured companies to do a better job of linking executive pay and performance. The Securities and Exchange Commission (SEC) has required companies to more clearly report executive compensation levels and the company's performance relative to that of competitors. These reporting requirements shine a light on situations where executives of poorly performing companies receive high pay, so companies feel more pressure to link pay to performance. The Dodd-Frank Wall Street Reform and Consumer Protection Act, passed in 2010, requires that public companies report the ratio of median compensation of all its employees to the CEO's total compensation. Dodd-Frank also gives shareholders a "say on pay," meaning shareholders may vote to indicate their approval or disapproval of the company's executive pay plans.

PERFORMANCE MEASURE	TARGET POINTS
Financial	60
Revenue	
Earnings per share	
Value of growth (e.g., return on investment)	
Customer	14
Percent of orders delivered on time	
Customer survey score	
Key Business Drivers	16
Operating expense	
Revenue growth (high-priority areas)	
Culture (High Performance, Sustainable)	10
Employee survey score	
Total	100

Table 13.3

Balanced Scorecard for Merck Executives

Source: Merck & Co., Proxy Statement, April 15, 2013, http://www.merck.com, accessed May 14, 2013.

Ethical Issues

Incentive pay for executives lays the groundwork for significant ethical issues. When an organization links pay to its stock performance, executives need the ethical backbone to be honest about their company's performance even when dishonesty or clever shading of the truth offers the tempting potential for large earnings. As scandals involving WorldCom, Enron, Global Crossing, and other companies have shown, the results can be disastrous when unethical behavior comes to light.

Among these issues is one we have already touched on in this chapter: the difficulty of setting performance measures that encourage precisely the behavior desired. In the case of incentives tied to stock performance, executives may be tempted to inflate the stock price in order to enjoy bonuses and valuable stock options. The intent is for the executive to boost stock value through efficient operations, technological innovation, effective leadership, and so on. Unfortunately, individuals at some companies determined that they could obtain faster results through accounting practices that stretched the norms in order to present the company's performance in the best light. When such practices are discovered to be misleading, stock prices plunge and the company's reputation is damaged, sometimes beyond repair.

A related issue when executive pay includes stock or stock options is insider trading. When executives are stockholders, they have a dual role as owners and managers. This places them at an advantage over others who want to invest in the company. An individual, a pension fund, or other investors have less information about the company than its managers do—for example, whether product development is proceeding on schedule, whether a financing deal is in the works, and so on. An executive who knows about these activities could therefore reap a windfall in the stock market by buying or selling stock based on knowledge about the company's future. The SEC places strict limits on this "insider trading," but some executives have violated these limits. In the worst

Whole Foods Markets limits cash salary and bonuses for top executives to 19 times the average pay of its full-time workers.

cases executives have sold stock, secretly knowing their company was failing, before the stock price collapsed. The losers are the employees, retirees, and other investors who hold the now-worthless stock.

As recent news stories have reminded us, linking pay to stock price can reward unethical behavior, at least in the short term and at least in the minds of a handful of executives. Yet, given the motivational power of incentive pay, organizations cannot afford to abandon incentives for their executives. These temptations are among the reasons that executive positions demand individuals who maintain the highest ethical standards.

THINKING ETHICALLY

CAN INCENTIVES PROMOTE ETHICS?

In recent years, the federal government has investigated allegations that Walmart had engaged in bribery in Mexico, China, and Brazil. Walmart reacted with changes aimed at promoting legal, ethical conduct—efforts costing hundreds of millions of dollars. It launched an internal investigation and linked a portion of executives' pay to meeting standards for compliance with legal requirements. The expectation for the compliance-related incentive pay was that if corporate executives are rewarded for the company behaving ethically, they will be more careful to ensure that it does so.

In 2014, Walmart issued a Global Compliance Program Report. According to the report, the compliance objectives fall into three categories: people, policies and processes, and systems. The people objective includes a company reorganization that brings together employees responsible for ethics and the law into one group reporting to a global chief compliance officer, increasing the number of employees charged with monitoring compliance, and training employees in ethical standards. The policies and processes objective focuses on establishing clear standards of conduct that apply globally. The systems objective is a plan for using technology to support efforts at maintaining compliance.

At the end of the year, the corporate audit committee determined that Walmart had "achieved substantial progress" on these objectives. Corporate executives were able to receive their bonuses without any compliance-related cuts.

Questions

1. Do you think Walmart's compliance-related performance standards, as described here, would ensure ethical conduct? Why or why not?
2. Review the principles for incentive pay described in the first section of this chapter. How, if at all, could Walmart apply these principles to strengthen its effort to promote compliance with legal and ethical standards?

Sources: Walmart, "Global Compliance Program Report on Fiscal Year 2014," http://corporate.walmart.com, accessed July 7, 2014; Paul Hodgson, "Wal-Mart: Have Any Executives Been Penalized for Recent Scandals?" *Fortune*, May 15, 2014, http://fortune.com; Emily Chasan and Joel Schectman, "Wal-Mart Set to Reveal How Compliance Moved Executives' Pay," *The Wall Street Journal*, April 22, 2014, http://blogs.wsj.com; Susan Berfield, "Wal-Mart Pays—and Pays—in Response to the Bribery Probe," *Bloomberg Businessweek*, April 25, 2014, http://www.businessweek.com.

SUMMARY

LO 13-1 Discuss the connection between incentive pay and employee performance.

- Incentive pay is pay tied to individual performance, profits, or other measures of success.
- Organizations select forms of incentive pay to energize, direct, or control employees' behavior.

- It is influential because the amount paid is linked to predefined behaviors or outcomes.
- To be effective, incentive pay should encourage the kinds of behavior that are most needed, and employees must believe they have the ability to meet the performance standards. Employees must

value the rewards, have the resources they need to meet the standards, and believe the pay plan is fair.

LO 13-2 Describe how organizations recognize individual performance.

- Organizations may recognize individual performance through such incentives as piecework rates, standard hour plans, merit pay, sales commissions, and bonuses for meeting individual performance objectives.
- Piecework rates pay employees according to the amount they produce.
- Standard hour plans pay workers extra for work done in less than a preset "standard time."
- Merit pay links increases in wages or salaries to ratings on performance appraisals.
- Bonuses are similar to merit pay, because they are paid for meeting individual goals, but they are not rolled into base pay, and they usually are based on achieving a specific output rather than subjective performance ratings.
- A sales commission is incentive pay calculated as a percentage of sales closed by a salesperson.

LO 13-3 Identify ways to recognize group performance.

- Common group incentives include gainsharing, bonuses, and team awards.
- Gainsharing programs, such as Scanlon plans, measure increases in productivity and distribute a portion of each gain to employees.
- Group bonuses reward the members of a group for attaining a specific goal, usually measured in terms of physical output.
- Team awards are more likely to use a broad range of performance measures, such as cost savings, successful completion of a project, or meeting a deadline.

LO 13-4 Explain how organizations link pay to their overall performance.

- Incentives for meeting organizational objectives include profit sharing and stock ownership.
- Profit-sharing plans pay workers a percentage of the organization's profits; these payments do not become part of the employees' base salary.
- Stock ownership incentives may take the form of stock options or employee stock ownership plans.
- A stock option is the right to buy a certain number of shares at a specified price. The employee benefits by exercising the option at a price lower than the market price, so the employee benefits when the company's stock price rises.
- An employee stock ownership plan (ESOP) is an arrangement in which the organization distributes shares of its stock to employees by placing the stock in a trust managed on the employees' behalf. When employees leave the organization, they may sell their shares of the stock.

LO 13-5 Describe how organizations combine incentive plans in a "balanced scorecard."

- A balanced scorecard is a combination of performance measures directed toward the company's long- and short-term goals and used as the basis for awarding incentive pay.
- Typically, it includes financial goals to satisfy stockholders, quality- and price-related goals for customer satisfaction, efficiency goals for improved operations, and goals related to acquiring skills and knowledge for the future.
- The mix of pay programs is intended to balance the disadvantages of one type of incentive with the advantages of another type.
- The balanced scorecard also helps employees to understand and care about the organization's goals.

LO 13-6 Summarize processes that can contribute to the success of incentive programs.

- Communication and participation in decisions can contribute to employees' feeling that the organization's incentive pay plans are fair.
- Employee participation in pay-related decisions can be part of a general move toward employee empowerment. Employees may put their own interests first in developing the plan, but they also have firsthand insight into the kinds of behavior that can contribute to organizational goals.
- Communicating with employees is important because it demonstrates that the pay plan is fair and helps them understand what is expected of them. Communication is especially important when the organization is changing its pay plan.

LO 13-7 Discuss issues related to performance-based pay for executives.

- Because executives have such a strong influence over the organization's performance, incentive pay for them receives special attention.
- Executive pay usually combines long-term and short-term incentives. By motivating executives, these incentives can significantly affect the organization's performance.
- The size of incentives should be motivating but also meet standards for equity.
- Performance measures should encourage behavior that is in the organization's best interests, including ethical behavior. Executives need ethical standards that keep them from insider trading or deceptive practices designed to manipulate the organization's stock price.

KEY TERMS

incentive pay, 396	merit pay, 400	stock options, 408
piecework rate, 399	commissions, 403	employee stock ownership plan
straight piecework plan, 399	gainsharing, 404	(ESOP), 409
differential piece rates, 399	Scanlon plan, 405	balanced scoreboard, 410
standard hour plan, 400	profit sharing, 406	

REVIEW AND DISCUSSION QUESTIONS

1. With some organizations and jobs, pay is primarily wages or salaries, and with others, incentive pay is more important. For each of the following jobs, state whether you think the pay should emphasize base pay (wages and salaries) or incentive pay (bonuses, profit sharing, and so on). Give a reason for each. *(LO 13-1)*
   a. An accountant at a manufacturing company.
   b. A salesperson for a software company.
   c. A chief executive officer.
   d. A physician in a health clinic.
2. Consider your current job or a job that you have recently held. Would you be most motivated in response to incentives based on your individual performance, your group's performance, or the organization's overall performance (profits or stock price)? Why? *(LO 13-2)*
3. What are the pros and cons of linking incentive pay to individual performance? How can organizations address the negatives? *(LO 13-2)*
4. Suppose you are a human resource professional at a company that is setting up work teams for production and sales. What group incentives would you recommend to support this new work arrangement? *(LO 13-3)*
5. Why do some organizations link incentive pay to the organization's overall performance? Is it appropriate to use stock performance as an incentive for employees at all levels? Why or why not? *(LO 13-4)*
6. Stock options have been called the pay program that "built Silicon Valley" because of their key role as incentive pay for employees in high-tech companies. They were popular during the 1990s, when

the stock market was rising rapidly. Since then, stock prices have fallen. *(LO 13-4)*
   a. How would you expect this change to affect employees' attitudes toward stock options as incentive pay?
   b. How would you expect this change to affect the effectiveness of stock options as an incentive?
7. Based on the balanced scorecard in Table 13.2, find the incentive pay for an employee earning a salary of $4,000 a month in each of the following situations. *(LO 13-5)*
   a. The company met all of its target goals for the year. (Multiply the percentage at the top of the table by the employee's salary.)
   b. The company met only its target goals for financial performance (25% of the total incentive pay) but none of the other goals.
   c. The company met its stretch goals for financial performance and its base goals in the other areas. (For each category of goals, multiply the percentages by the employee's salary, and then add the amounts together.)
8. Why might a balanced scorecard like the one in Question 7 be more effective than simply using merit pay for a manager? *(LO 13-5)*
9. How can the way an organization creates and carries out its incentive plan improve the effectiveness of that plan? *(LO 13-6)*
10. In a typical large corporation, the majority of the chief executive's pay is tied to the company's stock price. What are some benefits of this pay strategy? Some risks? How can organizations address the risks? *(LO 13-7)*

TAKING RESPONSIBILITY

At Rhino Foods, Incentive Pay Is an Expression of Respect

Rhino Foods, which operates a production facility and warehouse in Burlington, Vermont, is a small business with big ideas for how to treat employees. The company

produces handmade ice-cream sandwiches, and its bakery turns out cheesecakes, brownies, and cake pieces. It also developed the cookie dough used as a mix-in for

Ben & Jerry's ice cream. Rhino's two production shifts make products to order, with product lines changing from day to day, so workers have to be flexible. Rhino cross-trains its employees to handle baking, ice-cream processing, and cookie dough extrusion.

Management at Rhino Foods is focused on goals. When workers arrive each day, they pass by a bulletin board displaying the day's key performance indicators—measurements identified as important to business success that day. These performance indicators might include costs, sales volume, safety measures, or adherence to the schedule. Ted Castle, Rhino's founder and president, has observed that employees work on the areas of performance the company highlights. For example, when the company introduced safety targets, the number of injuries fell from triple the industry average to less than average.

This manner of operating is based on Rhino Foods' purpose and principles, which are posted on the company's website and in its lobby. Its purpose is "to impact the manner in which business is done." That impact comes from living up to principles in four categories: finances, employees, customers and suppliers, and community. The Employee Principle at Rhino Foods says, "We establish relationships with our employees and their families founded upon a climate of mutual trust and respect within an environment for listening and personal expression. We provide a vehicle for our people to develop and achieve their personal and professional aspirations."

That high-minded language is behind the company's use of goals and rewards. Posting business goals as key performance indicators treats employees with respect by being transparent about the connection between what they do each day and how well the business succeeds. Management practices open-book management and teaches employees to understand the financial measures of the company's success. By focusing on one to three critical measures at a time, the company makes financial literacy more achievable. The effort equips employees to contribute more at work and gives them financial skills they can transfer to their personal lives as well as to broader roles in their community.

Employees receive daily, weekly, and monthly reports of their progress. When the company meets its goals, employees receive a bonus. Use of bonuses in conjunction with open-book management has led to increases in production efficiency, customer service, and product quality. It also has lowered costs associated with workplace injuries, prompted innovation, and developed employees' leadership skills.

Questions

1. What form of incentive pay is described in this case? What are the pros and cons of this kind of incentive?
2. What additional types of incentive pay, if any, would you recommend for Rhino Foods?

Sources: Rhino Foods, "The Rhino Way," http://www.rhinofoods.com, accessed July 7, 2014; B Corporation, "Rhino Foods," http://www.bcorporation.net, accessed July 7, 2014; Rhino Foods, "Open Book Management/ Bonus on Goals at Rhino Foods," May 2013, http://www.rhinofoods.com; Ted Castle, "Be the Best at Asset Management," *Dairy Foods*, April 2013, p. 94; Jim Carper, "Made to Measure," *Dairy Foods*, February 2013, pp. 54–56.

MANAGING TALENT

Making Hilcorp Energy's Employees Feel (and Act) like Owners

Hilcorp Energy Company's vision is to be "America's premier private energy company." Founded by Jeffrey Hildebrand in 1989, Hilcorp already ranks as one of the biggest privately held oil and natural gas exploration and production companies in the United States. The company is based in Houston and operates in Texas, Louisiana, Alaska, and the northeastern United States. It has grown mainly by purchasing energy fields from bigger companies and then using new technology to make them profitable.

Hilcorp attributes its success to living out five core values. The first, ownership, means employees approach their jobs with the attitude that they own the company— that is, they are committed to its success. The second value, urgency, is a bias toward action. Alignment means working together as a team, because individual success is associated with the company's success. The final two values, innovation and integrity, are self-explanatory.

These values have created a culture of ownership and high performance. The culture is expressed in the transparency with which management shares financial information with its employees. Employees meet once a month to review performance and discuss concerns such as safety and training. The meetings also cover forecasts of the numbers the company needs to meet—for example, production volume, revenues, and net income, as well as division-specific numbers such as labor hours. During the meeting, employees learn how performance on these measures contributes to the company's profitability, so everyone understands the goals. Hilcorp then keeps the employees abreast of their progress by providing daily updates.

Hilcorp rewards high performance with annual and five-year bonuses. The annual bonus for meeting targets has averaged 35% of employees' base pay. Perhaps the most unusual incentive pay at Hilcorp is its Double

Drive bonus. The company gave employees five years to double the company's value, production rate, and reserves by 2010. If the company met those targets, they would all earn their choice of $35,000 or a new SUV. The company did—and spent more than $31 million to award those bonuses to the nearly 700 employees then working at Hilcorp. Now the second Double Drive bonus period is under way, with higher stakes. If the company against doubles in size, its 1,100 employees will be eligible for $100,000 bonuses.

Creating a sense of ownership is a remarkable accomplishment at a company with only one shareholder, Jeffrey Hildebrand. However, Hildebrand has accomplished this with his willingness to share information through open-book management and to share profits through the bonus programs. In addition, Hilcorp gives employees an allowance to invest in their choice of particular Hilcorp projects. With these investments, employees experience firsthand how success on a project translates into greater wealth for the investor.

Questions

1. How well would individual incentives align with Hilcorp's core values?
2. What advice would you give Hilcorp's management for adding merit pay (an individual incentive) to its current forms of incentive pay?

Sources: Hilcorp Energy Company, "About Us," http://www.hilcorp.com, accessed July 7, 2014; "Top Workplaces 2013: Hilcorp," *Houston Chronicle*, accessed at http://www.topworkplaces.com, July 7, 2014; Great Game of Business, "Playing the Game at Hilcorp Energy Company," January 21, 2014, http://www.greatgame.com; Erika Fry, "100 Best Companies to Work For: Hilcorp Energy," *Fortune*, August 12, 2013, EBSCOhost, http://web.a.ebscohost.com; Christopher Helman, "Secretive Oil Billionaire Scores New $550M Payday," *Forbes*, September 17, 2012, http://www.forbes.com.

HR IN SMALL BUSINESS

Employees Own Bob's Red Mill

Headquartered in Portland, Oregon, Bob's Red Mill Natural Foods sells a variety of whole-grain flours and mixes, specializing in gluten-free products. The "Bob" of the company's name is Bob Moore, the founder and president. In 2010, more than 30 years after he started the business, Moore called his 200 employees together and announced that he was giving them the company. As a retirement plan for them, he had set up an employee stock ownership plan, placing the company's stock in a trust fund. All employees who had been with the company at least three years were immediately fully vested in the plan. As employees retire, they will receive cash for their shares.

Watching the company's stock rise in their retirement plan is not the only financial incentive for employees of Bob's Red Mill. Fifteen years ago, the company established a profit-sharing plan. Chief financial officer John Wagner gives employees a weekly sales update, which they can use to estimate profits and determine their share.

The numbers have been mostly good during the past two decades. When Wagner joined the company in 1993, there were just 28 employees generating sales of $3.2 million. Under Wagner's guidance, the company began participating in trade shows, attracting the interest of health food stores, food distributors, and later on, supermarket chains. The company's market expanded from a few states to cover North America and some international markets. The company reports that its revenues have grown at rates between 20% and 30% in the years since 2004.

Along the way, Moore and his employees have been unwavering in their dedication to the company and its mission of providing foods that make America healthier. Ten years after the business started, a fire caused by arson destroyed the mill, but Moore had it rebuilt, and the company now runs a 15-acre production facility, operating in three shifts, six days a week.

Why did Moore give his company to his employees on his 81st birthday rather than selling it to one of the many parties who have expressed an interest in buying? For Moore, the answer is all about his employees and their commitment to the company. He told a reporter, "These people are far too good at their jobs for me to just sell [the business]." Employees return the praise. For example, Bo Thomas, maintenance superintendent, said, "It just shows how much faith and trust Bob has in us. For all of us, it's more than just a job."

Questions

1. Which types of incentive pay are described in this case? Are these based on individual, group, or company performance?
2. Would you expect the motivational impact of stock ownership or profit sharing to be different at a small company like Bob's Red Mill than in a large corporation? Explain.
3. Suppose Bob's Red Mill brought you in as a consultant to review the company's total compensation. Explain why you would or would not recommend that the company add other forms of incentive pay,

and identify any additional forms of compensation you would recommend for the company's employees.

Sources: Karen E. Klein, "ESOPs on the Rise among Small Businesses," *Bloomberg Businessweek*, April 26, 2010, www.businessweek.com; Dana Tims, "Founder of Bob's Red Mill Natural Foods Transfers Business to Employees," *Oregon Live*, February 16, 2010, http://blog.oregonlive.com; Christine Brozyna, "American Heart: Owner of Multi-Million Dollar Company Hands Over Business to Employees," *ABC News*, February 18, 2010, http://abcnews.go.com.

NOTES

1. Christina Rogers, "Say Goodbye to the Car Salesman," *The Wall Street Journal*, November 20, 2013, http://online.wsj.com.

2. This chapter draws freely on several literature reviews: B. Gerhart and G. T. Milkovich, "Employee Compensation: Research and Practice," in *Handbook of Industrial and Organizational Psychology*, 2nd ed., eds. M. D. Dunnette and L. M. Hough (Palo Alto, CA: Consulting Psychologists Press, 1992), vol. 3; B. Gerhart and S. L. Rynes, *Compensation: Theory, Evidence, and Strategic Implications* (Thousand Oaks, CA: Sage, 2003); B. Gerhart, "Compensation Strategy and Organization Performance," in *Compensation in Organizations: Current Research and Practice*, eds. S. L. Rynes and B. Gerhart (San Francisco: Jossey-Bass, 2000), pp. 151–94; B. Gerhart, S. L. Rynes, and I. S. Fulmer, "Compensation," *Academy of Management Annals* 3 (2009); Barry Gerhart and Meiyu Fang, "Pay for (Individual) Performance: Issues, Claims, Evidence and the Role of Sorting Effects," *Human Resource Management Review* 24 (2014): 41–52.

3. B. Gerhart and G. T. Milkovich, "Organizational Differences in Managerial Compensation and Financial Performance," *Academy of Management Journal* 33 (1990), pp. 663–91.

4. G. T. Milkovich and A. K. Wigdor, *Pay for Performance* (Washington, DC: National Academy Press, 1991); Gerhart and Milkovich, "Employee Compensation"; Gerhart and Rynes, *Compensation*; A. Nyberg, "Retaining Your High Performers: Moderators of the Performance–Job Satisfaction–Voluntary Turnover Relationship," *Journal of Applied Psychology* 95, no. 3 (2010): 440–53; C. O. Trevor, G. Reilly, and B. Gerhart, "Reconsidering Pay Dispersion's Effect on the Performance of Interdependent Work: Reconciling Sorting and Pay Inequality," *Academy of Management Journal* (forthcoming).

5. Aon Corporation, "Salary Increases Stay Consistent with Recent Trends, as the Focus Remains on Variable Pay, according to Aon Hewitt," news release, September 1, 2011, http://aon.mediaroom .com.

6. Rachel Emma Silverman, "My Colleague, My Paymaster," *The Wall Street Journal*, April 3, 2012, http://online.wsj.com.

7. R. D. Bretz, R. A. Ash, and G. F. Dreher, "Do People Make the Place? An Examination of the Attraction-Selection-Attrition Hypothesis," Personnel Psychology 42 (1989), pp. 561–81; T. A. Judge and R. D. Bretz, "Effect of Values on Job Choice Decisions," *Journal of Applied Psychology* 77 (1992), pp. 261–71; D. M. Cable and T. A. Judge, "Pay Performance and Job Search Decisions: A Person-Organization Fit Perspective," *Personnel Psychology* 47 (1994), pp. 317–48.

8. E. A. Locke, D. B. Feren, V. M. McCaleb, K. N. Shaw, and A. T. Denny, "The Relative Effectiveness of Four Methods of Motivating Employee Performance," in *Changes in Working Life*, eds. K. D. Duncan, M. M. Gruenberg, and D. Wallis (New York: Wiley, 1980), pp. 363–88.

9. Gerhart and Milkovich, "Employee Compensation."

10. E. E. Lawler III, "Pay for Performance: A Strategic Analysis," in *Compensation and Benefits*, ed. L. R. Gomez-Mejia (Washington, DC: Bureau of National Affairs, 1989); Bureau of National Affairs, "Salary Budgets for 2014 May Top 3 Percent, WorldatWork Survey Reports," *Report on Salary Surveys*, September 2013, pp. 1–4; Steve Goldstein, "Will Wage Growth Accelearte? Economists Are Divided," *MarketWatch*, June 10, 2014, http://blogs.marketwatch.com; Bloomberg BNA, "WTI Continues to Signal Pickup in Wage Growth," Wage Trend Indicator, June 17, 2014, http://www.bna.com/wage-trend-indicator; Marilyn Geewax, "Hiring Looks Good Now, but Wage Growth Lags," NPR, July 3, 2014, http://www.npr.org.

11. Lyle Leritz, "Principles of Merit Pay," Economic Research Institute, 2012, http://www.erieri.com; Joanne Dahm and Pete Sanborn, "Addressing Talent and Rewards in 'The New Normal,'" Aon Hewitt, 2010, http://aonhewitt.com; Stephen Miller, "Pay for Performance: Make It More than a Catchphrase," *SHRM Online* Compensation Discipline, May 30, 2011, http://www.shrm.org.

12. R. D. Bretz, G. T. Milkovich, and W. Read, "The Current State of Performance Appraisal Research and Practice," *Journal of Management* 18 (1992), pp. 321–52; R. L. Heneman, "Merit Pay Research," Research in *Personnel and Human Resource Management* 8 (1990), pp. 203–63; Milkovich and Wigdor, *Pay for Performance*.

13. Bretz et al., "Current State of Performance Appraisal Research."

14. S. L. Rynes, B. Gerhart, and L. Parks, "Personnel Psychology: Performance Evaluation and Compensation," *Annual Review of Psychology* (2005).

15. W. E. Deming, *Out of the Crisis* (Cambridge, MA: Center for Advanced Engineering Study, Massachusetts Institute of Technology, 1986), p. 110.

16. Gerhart and Fang, "Pay for (Individual) Performance"; WorldatWork, "Compensation Programs and Practices 2012," Scottsdale, AZ, October 2012.

17. Charles Paikert, "How Advisors Get Paid Now," *Financial Planning*, March 2014, pp. 46–53.

18. Marcia Heroux, "Office Depot Execs Get Bonuses to Stay," *Sun Sentinel (Fort Lauderdale, FL)*, March 26, 2014, http://articles.sun-sentinel.com; Gwen Moran, "When Are

Pay-to-Stay Bonuses a Good Idea?" *Entrepreneur*, July 23, 2013, http://www.entrepreneur.com.

19. U.S. Department of Justice, Antitrust Division, "Competition and Real Estate: Home Prices and Commissions over Time," http://www.justice.gov, accessed April 19, 2012; Leslie Scism, "Insurance Fees, Revealed," *The Wall Street Journal*, March 30, 2012, http://online.wsj.com; Anonymous, "Confessions of a Car Salesman," *Popular Mechanics*, May 4, 2011, http://www.popularmechanics.com.

20. T. L. Ross and R. A. Ross, "Gainsharing: Sharing Improved Performance," in *The Compensation Handbook*, 3rd ed., eds. M. L. Rock and L. A. Berger (New York: McGraw-Hill, 1991).

21. T. M. Welbourne and L. R. Gomez-Mejia, "Team Incentives in the Workplace," in *The Compensation Handbook*, 3rd ed.

22. L. R. Gomez-Mejia and D. B. Balkin, *Compensation, Organizational Strategy, and Firm Performance* (Cincinnati: South-Western, 1992).

23. J. A. Fossum, *Labor Relations* (New York: McGraw-Hill, 2002).

24. This idea has been referred to as the "share economy." See M. L. Weitzman, "The Simple Macroeconomics of Profit Sharing," *American Economic Review* 75 (1985), pp. 937–53. For supportive research, see the following studies: J. Chelius and R. S. Smith, "Profit Sharing and Employment Stability," *Industrial and Labor Relations Review* 43 (1990), pp. 256S–73S; B. Gerhart and L. O. Trevor, "Employment Stability under Different Managerial Compensation Systems," working paper (Cornell University Center for Advanced Human Resource Studies, 1995); D. L. Kruse, "Profit Sharing and Employment Variability: Microeconomic Evidence on the Weitzman Theory," *Industrial and Labor Relations Review* 44 (1991), pp. 437–53.

25. Gerhart and Milkovich, "Employee Compensation"; M. L. Weitzman and D. L. Kruse, "Profit Sharing and Productivity," in *Paying for Productivity*, ed. A. S. Blinder (Washington, DC: Brookings Institution, 1990); D. L. Kruse, *Profit Sharing: Does It Make a Difference?* (Kalamazoo, MI: Upjohn Institute, 1993); M. Magnan and S. St.-Onge, "The Impact of Profit Sharing on the Performance of Financial Services Firms," *Journal of Management Studies* 42 (2005), pp. 761–91.

26. Dori Meinert, "An Open Book," *HR Magazine*, April 2013, http://www.shrm.org.

27. Gerhart and Milkovich, "Organizational Differences in Managerial Compensation."

28. National Center for Employee Ownership, "A Statistical Profile of Employee Ownership," updated June 2014, http://www.nceo.org.

29. M. A. Conte and J. Svejnar, "The Performance Effects of Employee Ownership Plans," in *Paying for Productivity*, pp. 245–94.

30. Ibid.; T. H. Hammer, "New Developments in Profit Sharing, Gainsharing, and Employee Ownership," in *Productivity in Organizations*, eds. J. P. Campbell, R. J. Campbell, et al. (San Francisco: Jossey-Bass, 1988); K. J. Klein, "Employee Stock Ownership and Employee Attitudes: A Test of Three Models," *Journal of Applied Psychology* 72 (1987), pp. 319–32.

31. SAS Institute, "SAS Helps ConocoPhillips Norway Fucus on Performance and Control Costs," Customer Success, http://www.sas.com, accessed April 24, 2012.

32. R. T. Kaufman, "The Effects of Improshare on Productivity," *Industrial and Labor Relations Review* 45 (1992), pp. 311–22; M. H. Schuster, "The Scanlon Plan: A Longitudinal Analysis," *Journal of Applied Behavioral Science* 20 (1984), pp. 23–28; J. A. Wagner III, P. Rubin, and T. J. Callahan, "Incentive Payment and Nonmanagerial Productivity: An Interrupted Time Series Analysis of Magnitude and Trend," *Organizational Behavior and Human Decision Processes* 42 (1988), pp. 47–74.

33. C. R. Gowen III and S. A. Jennings, "The Effects of Changes in Participation and Group Size on Gainsharing Success: A Case Study," *Journal of Organizational Behavior Management* 11 (1991), pp. 147–69.

34. D. I. Levine and L. D. Tyson, "Participation, Productivity, and the Firm's Environment," in *Paying for Productivity*.

35. T. Welbourne, D. Balkin, and L. Gomez-Mejia, "Gainsharing and Mutual Monitoring: A Combined Agency–Organizational Justice Interpretation," *Academy of Management Journal* 38 (1995), pp. 881–99.

36. WorldatWork, "Compensation Programs and Practices 2012."

37. Theo Francis and Joann S. Lublin, "CEO Pay Rises Moderately; A Few Reap Huge Rewards," *The Wall Street Journal*, May 27, 2014, http://online.wsj.com; Michael J. Cooper, Huseyin Gulen, and P. Raghavendra Rau, "Performance for Pay? The Relation between CEO Incentive Compensation and Future Stock Price Performance" (January 30, 2013), available at Social Science Research Network, http://ssrn.com.

38. Gerhart and Milkovich, "Organizational Differences in Managerial Compensation"; B. Gerhart, S. L. Rynes, and I. S. Fulmer, "Pay and Performance: Individuals, Groups, and Executives," *Academy of Management Annals* 3 (2009), pp. 251–315.

14

Providing Employee Benefits

What Do I Need to Know?

After reading this chapter, you should be able to:

LO 14-1 Discuss the importance of benefits as a part of employee compensation.

LO 14-2 Summarize the types of employee benefits required by law.

LO 14-3 Describe the most common forms of paid leave.

LO 14-4 Identify the kinds of insurance benefits offered by employers.

LO 14-5 Define the types of retirement plans offered by employers.

LO 14-6 Describe how organizations use other benefits to match employees' wants and needs.

LO 14-7 Explain how to choose the contents of an employee benefits package.

LO 14-8 Summarize the regulations affecting how employers design and administer benefits programs.

LO 14-9 Discuss the importance of effectively communicating the nature and value of benefits to employees.

Introduction

Recently, the Connecticut legislature passed a law requiring organizations with more than 50 employees to provide an hour of paid sick leave for every 40 hours they work. For up to five days a year, employees—unless they are temporary workers or employed by a manufacturer—can call in sick and be paid for the time off. Some managers worried about the expense, but not Tom McDonald, president of NSI, a provider of information technology services. To McDonald, paying employees to stay home when sick is a way to "do what's right for your employees," which is simply "good business." At NSI, employees earn between 15 and 25 days off with pay each year, and they can use the time to recover from an illness, take a vacation, or do whatever they prefer. When his business reaches the 50-employee mark, McDonald will not have to change his time-off policy, because he already meets the legal requirements. He is not alone in that regard; a survey of Connecticut businesses found that only a tenth of them saw their compensation costs rise by more than 3% when sick leave became mandatory.

Other state and local governments have addressed whether to require paid sick leave. Wisconsin and Florida have forbidden their cities from requiring it.

In contrast, Jersey City, New Jersey, requires employers with at least 10 workers to provide employees with up to five paid sick days each year. There, Karen Davis-Farage, co-owner of a go-kart racing business, sees the law as harmful to her company. Most of her employees are part-timers—students earning minimum wage. She suspects they are not "loyal" enough to limit their use of sick days. If they abuse the benefit, she might reduce the money spent on quarterly bonuses so she can afford to pay for workers to come in when others call in sick.[1]

Whether or not the law requires it, many companies offer employees some paid time off. Employees earn this privilege along with their pay. It is a part of the employees' total compensation package, which includes some combination of wages or salary, incentive pay, and benefits. The term for compensation in forms other than cash is **employee benefits**. Along with paid sick leave, examples of benefits include employer-paid health insurance, retirement savings plans, and paid vacations, among a wide range of possibilities.

Employee Benefits
Compensation in forms other than cash.

This chapter describes the contents of an employee benefits package and the way organizations administer employee benefits. We begin by discussing the important role of benefits as a part of employee compensation. The following sections define major types of employee benefits: benefits required by law, paid leave, insurance policies, retirement plans, and other benefits. We then discuss how to choose which of these alternatives to include in an employee benefits package so that it contributes to meeting the organization's goals. The next section summarizes the regulations affecting how employers design and administer benefits programs. Finally, we explain why and how organizations should effectively communicate with employees about their benefits.

The Role of Employee Benefits

LO 14-1 Discuss the importance of benefits as a part of employee compensation.

As a part of the total compensation paid to employees, benefits serve functions similar to pay. Benefits contribute to attracting, retaining, and motivating employees. The variety of possible benefits also helps employers tailor their compensation to the kinds of employees they need. Different employees look for different types of benefits. Employers need to examine their benefits package regularly to see whether they meet the needs of today. At the same time, benefits packages are more complex than pay structures, so benefits are harder for employees to understand and appreciate. Even if employers spend large sums on benefits, if employees do not understand how to use them or why they are valuable, the cost of the benefits will be largely wasted.[2] Employers need to communicate effectively so that the benefits succeed in motivating employees.

Employees have come to expect that benefits will help them maintain economic security. Social Security contributions, pensions, and retirement savings plans help employees prepare for their retirement. Insurance plans help to protect employees from unexpected costs such as hospital bills. This important role of benefits is one reason that benefits are subject to government regulation. Some benefits, such as Social Security, are required by law. Other regulations establish requirements that benefits must meet to obtain the most favorable tax treatment. Later in the chapter, we will describe some of the most significant regulations affecting benefits.

Even though many kinds of benefits are not required by law, they have become so common that today's employees expect them. Many employers find that attracting

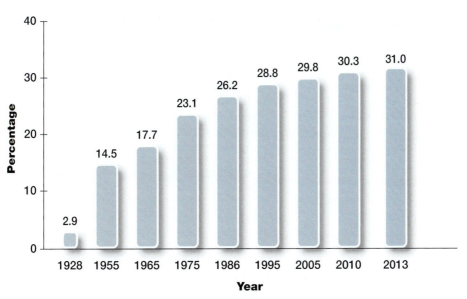

Source: Bureau of Labor Statistics, "Employer Costs for Employee Compensation," http://data.bls.gov, accessed July 11, 2014.

Figure 14.1

Benefits as a Percentage of Total Compensation

qualified workers requires them to provide medical and retirement benefits of some sort. A large employer without such benefits would be highly unusual and would have difficulty competing in the labor market. Still, the nature of the benefits package changes over time, as we will discuss at various points throughout the chapter.

Like other forms of compensation, benefits impose significant costs. On average, out of every dollar spent on compensation, more than 30 cents goes to benefits. As Figure 14.1 shows, this share has grown over the past decades. These numbers indicate that an organization managing its labor costs must pay careful attention to the cost of its employee benefits.

Why do organizations pay a growing share of compensation in the form of benefits? It would be simpler to pay all compensation in cash and let employees buy their own insurance and contribute to their own savings plans. That arrangement would also give employees greater control over what their compensation buys. However, several forces have made benefits a significant part of compensation packages. One is that laws require employers to provide certain benefits, such as contributions to Social Security and unemployment insurance. Also, tax laws can make benefits favorable to employees. For example, employees do not pay income taxes on most benefits they receive, but they pay income taxes on cash compensation. Therefore, an employee who receives a $1,000 raise "takes home" less than the full $1,000, but an employee who receives an additional $1,000 worth of benefits receives the full benefits. Another cost advantage of paying benefits is that employers, especially large ones, often can get a better deal on insurance or other programs than employees can obtain on their own. Finally, some employers assemble creative benefits packages that set them apart in the competition for talent. For example, Netflix lets people take off as much time as they want and doesn't keep track. This policy is in keeping with its HR strategy of "hiring adults"— experts who already have a history of success, love movies, and can manage their time. Since the company's success comes from people driven by a passion for what they do and what they can accomplish, offering freedom as a benefit contributes to attracting and keeping the right talent.[3]

Table 14.1

Benefits Required by Law

BENEFIT	EMPLOYER REQUIREMENT
Social Security	Flat payroll tax on employees and employers
Unemployment insurance	Payroll tax on employers that depends on state requirements and experience rating
Workers' compensation insurance	Provide coverage according to state requirements Premiums depend on experience rating
Family and medical leave	Up to 12 weeks of unpaid leave for childbirth, adoption, or serious illness
Health care	For employers with at least 50 employees, payment of a fee to the federal government if the employer does not meet conditions for providing health insurance benefits

LO 14-2 Summarize the types of employee benefits required by law.

Benefits Required by Law

The federal and state governments require various forms of social insurance to protect workers from the financial hardships of being out of work. In general, Social Security provides support for retired workers, unemployment insurance assists laid-off workers, and workers' compensation insurance provides benefits and services to workers injured on the job. Employers must also provide unpaid leave for certain family and medical needs. Because these benefits are required by law, employers cannot gain an advantage in the labor market by offering them, nor can they design the nature of these benefits. Rather, the emphasis must be on complying with the details of the law. Table 14.1 summarizes legally required benefits.

Social Security

In 1935 the federal Social Security Act established old-age insurance and unemployment insurance. Congress later amended the act to add survivor's insurance (1939), disability insurance (1956), hospital insurance (Medicare Part A, 1965), and supplementary medical insurance (Medicare Part B, 1965) for the elderly. Together, the law and its amendments created what is now the Old Age, Survivors, Disability, and Health Insurance (OASDHI) program, informally known as **Social Security.** This program covers over 90% of U.S. employees. The main exceptions are railroad and federal, state, and local government employees, who often have their own plans.

Workers who meet eligibility requirements receive the retirement benefits according to their age and earnings history. If they elect to begin receiving benefits at full retirement age, they can receive full benefits, or if they elect to begin receiving benefits at age 62, they receive benefits at a permanently reduced level. The full retirement age rises with birth year: a person born in 1940 reaches full retirement age at 65 years and 6 months, and a person born in 1960 or later reaches full retirement age at 67. The benefit amount rises with the person's past earnings, but the level goes up very little after a certain level. In 2014, the maximum benefit for a worker who retires at age 65 is more than $2,400, and it is above $3,400 for a worker who delays retirement until age 70. The government increases the payments each year according to the growth in the consumer price index. Also, spouses of covered earners receive benefits, even if they have no covered earnings. They receive either the benefit associated with their own earnings or one-half of the amount received by the covered earner, whichever is greater.

Benefits may be reduced if the worker is still earning wages above a maximum, called the *exempt amount*. In 2014, the exempt amount was $15,480 for beneficiaries under the full

Social Security
The federal Old Age, Survivors, Disability, and Health Insurance (OASDHI) program, which combines old age (retirement) insurance, survivor's insurance, disability insurance, hospital insurance (Medicare Part A), and supplementary medical insurance (Medicare Part B) for the elderly.

retirement age. A beneficiary in that age range who earns more than the exempt amount sees a reduction in his or her benefit. The amount of the reduction is $1 for every $2 the person earns above the exempt amount. For example a 63-year-old who earned $17,480 would have earned $2,000 above the exempt amount, so the person's Social Security benefits would be reduced by $1,000. During the year a worker reaches full retirement age, the maximum untaxed earnings are $41,400 (in 2014) and benefits are reduced $1 for every $3 in earnings. Beginning in the month they reach full retirement age, workers face no reduction in benefits for earning above the exempt amount. For workers below that age, the penalty increases the incentive to retire or at least reduce the number of hours worked. Adding to this incentive, Social Security benefits are free from federal income taxes and free from state taxes in about half the states.

Employers and employees share the cost of Social Security through a payroll tax. The percentage is set by law and has changed from time to time. In 2014, employers and employees each paid a tax of 7.65% on the first $117,000 of the employee's earnings. Of that, the majority goes to OASDI, and 2.9% of earnings go to Medicare (Part A). For earnings above $117,000, only the 2.9% for Medicare is assessed, with half paid by the employer and half paid by the employee. For earnings above $200,000, the employer must withhold an additional Medicare tax of 0.9% from the employee's pay.

Unemployment Insurance

Along with OASDHI, the Social Security Act of 1935 established a program of **unemployment insurance.** This program has four objectives related to minimizing the hardships of unemployment. It provides payments to offset lost income during involuntary unemployment, and it helps unemployed workers find new jobs. The payment of unemployment insurance taxes gives employers an incentive to stabilize employment. And providing workers with income during short-term layoffs preserves investments in worker skills because workers can afford to wait to return to their employer, rather than start over with another organization. Technically, the federal government left it to each state's discretion to establish an unemployment insurance program. At the same time, the Social Security Act created a tax incentive structure that quickly led every state to establish the program.

Most of the funding for unemployment insurance comes from federal and state taxes on employers. Employers who pay their state taxes currently pay a federal tax that after tax credits generally equals 0.6% of the first $7,000 of each employee's wages. The state tax rate varies from less than 1% to more than 15%, and the taxable wage base ranges from $7,000 to $41,300, so the amount paid depends a great deal on where the company is located.[4] Also, some states charge new employers whatever rate is the average for their industry, so the amount of tax paid in those states also depends on the type of business. In the severe recession of 2008–2009, layoffs were so widespread that unemployment insurance funds were drained and many states dramatically hiked premiums for unemployment insurance. Companies have therefore redoubled efforts to improve their experience ratings and control future costs for unemployment insurance. For example, helping laid-off workers find a new job can shorten the time in which they are receiving benefits. Some states allow short-time compensation, also called work sharing, in which companies reduce wages and hours, and employees receive partial unemployment benefits, rather than laying off workers.[5]

No state imposes the same tax rate on every employer in the state. The size of the unemployment insurance tax imposed on each employer depends on the employer's

Unemployment Insurance
A federally mandated program to minimize the hardships of unemployment through payments to unemployed workers, help in finding new jobs, and incentives to stabilize employment.

Experience Rating
The number of employees a company has laid off in the past and the cost of providing them with unemployment benefits.

experience rating—the number of employees the company laid off in the past and the cost of providing them with unemployment benefits. Employers with a history of laying off a large share of their workforces pay higher taxes than those with few layoffs. In some states, an employer with very few layoffs may pay no state tax. In contrast, an employer with a poor experience rating could pay a tax as high as 5.4% to 15.4%, depending on the state. The use of experience ratings gives employers some control over the cost of unemployment insurance. Careful human resource planning can minimize layoffs and keep their experience rating favorable.

To receive benefits, workers must meet four conditions:

1. They meet requirements demonstrating they had been employed (often 52 weeks or four quarters of work at a minimum level of pay).
2. They are available for work.
3. They are actively seeking work. This requirement includes registering at the local unemployment office.
4. They were not discharged for cause (such as willful misconduct), did not quit voluntarily, and are not out of work because of a labor dispute (such as a union member on strike).

Workers who meet these conditions receive benefits at the level set by the state—typically about half the person's previous earnings—for a period of 26 weeks. States with a sustained unemployment rate above a particular threshold or significantly above recent levels also offer extended benefits for up to 13 weeks. Sometimes Congress funds emergency extended benefits. All states have minimum and maximum weekly benefit levels.

Workers' Compensation

Decades ago, workers who suffered work-related injury or illness had to bear the cost unless they won a lawsuit against their employer. Those who sued often lost the case because of the defenses available to employers. Today, the states have passed **workers' compensation** laws, which help workers with the expenses resulting from job-related accidents and illnesses.[6] These laws operate under a principle of *no-fault liability*, meaning that an employee does not need to show that the employer was grossly negligent in order to receive compensation, and the employer is protected from lawsuits. The employer loses this protection if it intentionally contributes to a dangerous workplace. Employees are not eligible if their injuries are self-inflicted or if they result from intoxication or "willful disregard of safety rules."[7]

Workers' Compensation
State programs that provide benefits to workers who suffer work-related injuries or illnesses, or to their survivors.

About 9 out of 10 U.S. workers are covered by state workers' compensation laws, with the level of coverage varying from state to state. The benefits fall into four major categories: (1) disability income, (2) medical care, (3) death benefits, and (4) rehabilitative services. The amount of income varies from state to state but is typically two-thirds of the worker's earnings before the disability. The benefits are tax free.

The states differ in terms of how they fund workers' compensation insurance. Some states have a single state fund. Most states allow employers to purchase coverage from private insurance companies. Most also permit self-funding by employers. The cost of the workers' compensation insurance depends on the kinds of occupations involved, the state where the company is located, and the employer's experience rating. Premiums for low-risk occupations may be less than 1% of payroll. For some of the most hazardous occupations, the cost may be as high as 100% of payroll. Costs also vary from state to state, so that one state's program requires higher premiums than another state's program. As with unemployment insurance, unfavorable experience ratings lead to higher premiums. Organizations can minimize the cost of this benefit by keeping workplaces safe and making employees and their managers conscious of safety issues, as discussed in Chapter 3.

Unpaid Family and Medical Leave

In the United States, unpaid leave is required by law for certain family needs. Specifically, the **Family and Medical Leave Act (FMLA)** of 1993 requires organizations with 50 or more employees within a 75-mile radius to provide as much as 12 weeks of unpaid leave after childbirth or adoption; to care for a seriously ill child, spouse, or parent, for an employee's own serious illness; or to take care of urgent needs that arise when a spouse, child, or parent in the National Guard or Reserve is called to active duty. In addition, if a family member (child, spouse, parent, or next of kin) is injured while serving on active military duty, the employee may take up to 26 weeks of unpaid leave under FMLA. Employers must also guarantee these employees the same or a comparable job when they return to work. The law does not cover employees who have less than one year of service, work fewer than 25 hours per week, or are among the organization's 10% highest paid. The 12 weeks of unpaid leave amount to a smaller benefit than is typical of Japan and most countries in Western Europe. Japan and West European nations typically require paid family leave.

The Family and Medical Leave Act requires companies with 50 or more employees to provide up to 12 weeks of unpaid leave after childbirth or adoption.

Experience with the Family and Medical Leave Act suggests that a majority of those opting for this benefit fail to take the full 12 weeks. According to one report, about half took 10 days or fewer, and 80% took no more than 40 days of leave. The most common reason for taking a leave was the employee's own serious illness.[8] An obvious reason for not taking the full 12 weeks is that not everyone can afford three months without pay, especially when responsible for the expenses that accompany childbirth, adoption, or serious illness. Nevertheless, employers do need to keep track of leave requests to prevent abuse of the policy. In a recent case, the court upheld a Ford Motor Company decision to fire an employee for excessive absences. Ford had approved 68 workdays of medical leave, but on 10 occasions, the employee failed to meet the company's stated policies for providing documentation of her need for time off.[9]

When employees experience pregnancy and childbirth, employers must also comply with the Pregnancy Discrimination Act, described in Chapter 3. If an employee is temporarily unable to perform her job due to pregnancy, the employer must treat her in the same way as any other temporarily disabled employee. For example, the employer may provide modified tasks, alternative assignments, disability leave, or leave without pay.

Health Care Benefits

In 2010, Congress passed the **Patient Protection and Affordable Care Act,** a complex package of changes in how health care is to be paid for, including requirements for insurance companies, incentives and penalties for employers providing health insurance as a benefit, expansion of public funding, and creation of health insurance

Family and Medical Leave Act (FMLA)
Federal law requiring organizations with 50 or more employees to provide up to 12 weeks of unpaid leave after childbirth or adoption; to care for a seriously ill family member or for an employee's own serious illness; or to take care of urgent needs that arise when a spouse, child, or parent in the National Guard or Reserve is called to active duty.

Patient Protection and Affordable Care Act
Health care reform law passed in 2010 that includes incentives and penalties for employers providing health insurance as a benefit.

Complying with the Affordable Care Act

For employers, most of the requirements under the Affordable Care Act (ACA) involve either providing insurance that meets minimum standards or else paying the Employer Shared Responsibility Payment. Here are some guidelines for getting started:

- Keep track of the requirements on the HealthCare.gov website, especially its Small Business page. The site provides updates as regulations are developed and various requirements are phased in. It also offers links to information about tax credits, insurance exchanges, and other resources aimed at helping small businesses afford this benefit.

- Determine the number of full-time employees. Employers with fewer than 50 full-time workers are exempt from paying the Employer Shared Responsibility Payment, and employers with 50 to 99 employees may face less-stringent requirements. If some employees work part-time, count their hours to find the fraction equivalent to a full-time employee. Do not count volunteers (for example, at a non-profit) or seasonal workers who work up to 120 days or only during holiday seasons. Workers in educational institutions who are off during the summer are not considered seasonal workers.

- Compare the cost of health insurance (taking into account any tax credits) with the cost of the penalty. Basically, the annual penalty is $2,000 times the number of full-time employees after the first 30. So for an employer with 60 full-time employees, the penalty would be $2,000 times 30 (that is 60 minus 30), or $60,000. If offering health insurance would cost more than the penalty, some employers are considering that paying the penalty would be better for business than raising prices, accepting lower profits, or cutting other costs to afford adding or continuing health insurance benefits.

- Consider the purpose of offering health insurance. For some employers, health insurance is an important part of a compensation strategy; others emphasize costs. Decisions about this employee benefit should support the organization's strategy. This may explain why, in spite of predictions that employers would shift work to part-time jobs to avoid the 50-employee threshold, the trend has been toward more full-time workers as the economy strengthens.

Questions

1. A company has 120 employees, but they all work half time. Does this company meet the threshold of employing 50 full-time workers? Why or why not?

2. Why might an employer offer employees health insurance even if paying the Employer Shared Responsibility Payment would cost less?

Sources: "How Small-Business Owners Are Coping with the Health Law (So Far)," *The Wall Street Journal*, May 7, 2014, http://online.wsj.com; Employee Benefit Research Institute, "Trends in Health Coverage for Part-Time Workers, 1999–2012," *EBRI Notes*, May 2014, pp. 2–9; Sarah E. Needleman and Angus Loten, "Small Businesses Find Benefits, Costs as They Navigate Affordable Care Act," *The Wall Street Journal*, April 23, 2014, http://online.wsj.com; Bureau of National Affairs, "Final ACA Shared-Responsibility Rules Offer Transitional Relief, Clarification," *Payroll Manager's Report*, March 2014, pp. 1–2.

---

exchanges as an option for the sale of health insurance. The law does not require companies to offer health insurance benefits, but it does require medium-sized and large companies to choose between offering health insurance that meets its standards or paying a penalty, beginning in 2015. It also includes requirements for providing information to employees.

Whether an organization must make the choice to cover employees or pay a penalty depends on the number of full-time employees. In general, to avoid a penalty, an organization with at least 50 full-time employees (or full- and part-time employees equivalent to 50 or more) must offer affordable health care coverage of at least minimum value. For organizations with 50 to 99 full-time employees, this requirement takes effect in 2016. Organizations with at least 100 full-time employees must provide this coverage to at least 70% of full-time employees in 2015 and at least 95% starting in 2016. Organizations with at least 50 employees that do not meet these requirements must pay an Employer Shared Responsibility Payment; generally, the payment for a year is $2,000 times the number of full-time employees after the first 30.

Employers with fewer than 50 employees are not subject to the Employer Shared Responsibility Payment. However, the Affordable Care Act tries to encourage these small employers to offer health coverage. They may buy health insurance at the Small Business Health Options Program (SHOP) Marketplace (https://www.healthcare.gov /small-businesses/), state-level exchanges where employers may select a level of coverage or allow employees to choose from a set of options. In addition, organizations with fewer than 25 employees may qualify for tax credits. If they buy insurance through the SHOP Marketplace, they may be eligible for a credit of up to 50% of the insurance premiums.

Employers that provide health coverage to at least 250 employees must also meet reporting requirements. On the W-2 forms that report employees' earnings, they must indicate the value of the health benefits in terms of the cost paid by employer and employee. Organizations with fewer employees also may report this information—and may want to, as a way to show employees the value of the benefits they receive.

Because the law is complex, HR professionals must continue to educate themselves about the requirements and communicate often with employees, many of whom may be worried about how the law affects their health care benefits. A useful source of information continues to be the government's website at **www.healthcare.gov**. For more guidance on complying with the Affordable Care Act, see "HR How To."

Optional Benefits Programs

Other types of benefits are optional. These include various kinds of insurance, retirement plans, and paid leave. Figure 14.2 shows the percentage of full-time workers having access to the most common employee benefits. (Part-time workers often have access to

Type of Benefit

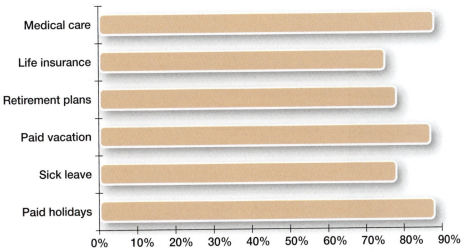

Figure 14.2

Percentage of Full-Time Workers with Access to Selected Benefit Programs

Source: Bureau of Labor Statistics, "Employee Benefits in the United States, March 2013," news release, July 17, 2013, http://www.bls.gov.

and receive fewer benefits.) The most widely offered benefits are paid leave for vacations and holidays, life and medical insurance, and retirement plans. In general, benefits packages at smaller companies tend to be more limited than at larger companies.

Benefits such as health insurance often extend to employees' dependents. Traditionally, these benefits have covered employees, their spouses, and dependent children. Today, many employers also cover *domestic partners*, defined either by local law or by the companies themselves. Typically, a domestic partner is an adult nonrelative who lives with the employee in a relationship defined as permanent and financially interdependent. Some local governments provide for registration of domestic partners. Organizations offering coverage to domestic partners generally require that the partners sign a document stating they meet the requirements for a domestic partnership. Benefits provided to domestic partners do not have the same tax advantages as benefits provided to spouses. The partner's benefits are taxed as wages of the employee receiving the benefits.

LO 14-3 Describe the most common forms of paid leave.

Paid Leave

The major categories of paid leave are vacations, holidays, and sick leave. Employers also should establish policies for other situations that may require time off. Organizations often provide for paid leave for jury duty, funerals of family members, and military duty. Some organizations provide for other paid leave, such as time off to vote or to donate blood. Establishing policies communicates the organization's values, clarifies what employees can expect, and prevents situations in which unequal treatment leads to claims of unfairness.

At first blush, paid vacation, holidays, sick leave, and other paid leave may not seem to make economic sense. The employer pays the employee for time spent not working, so the employer receives nothing in return for the pay. Some employers may see little direct advantage. This may be the reason that Western European countries require a minimum number of paid vacation days, with new employees receiving 30 days off in many countries. The United States, in contrast, has no such legal requirement. It is up to U.S. employers to decide whether paid leave has a payoff in recruiting and retaining employees. At U.S. companies, paid vacation is typically two weeks or less a year for the first few years. To receive as much vacation as European employees, U.S. workers must typically stay with an employer for 15 or 20 years.[10]

Paid holidays are time off on specified days in addition to vacation time. In Western Europe and the United States, employees typically have about 10 paid holidays each year, regardless of length of service. The most common paid holidays in the United States are New Year's Day, Memorial Day, Independence Day, Labor Day, Thanksgiving Day, and Christmas Day.

Sick leave programs pay employees for days not worked because of illness. The amount of sick leave is often based on length of service, so that it accumulates over time—for example, one day added to sick leave for each month of service. Employers must decide how many sick days to grant and whether to let them continue accumulating year after year. If sick days accumulate without limit, employees can "save" them in case of disability. If an employee becomes disabled, the employee can use up the accumulated sick days, receiving full pay rather than smaller payments from disability insurance, discussed later. Some employers let

Paid time off is a way for employees to enjoy time with their families and to refresh their bodies and spirits. Is paid time off an important factor for you when accepting a position?

sick days accumulate for only a year, and unused sick days "disappear" at year-end. This may provide an unintended incentive to use up sick days. Some healthy employees may call in sick near the end of the year so that they can obtain the benefit of the paid leave before it disappears. Employers may counter this tendency by paying employees for some or all of their unused sick days at year-end or when the employees retire or resign.

An organization's policies for time off may include other forms of paid and unpaid leave. For a workforce that values flexibility, the organization may offer paid *personal days*, days off that employees may schedule according to their personal needs, with the supervisor's approval. Typically, organizations offer a few personal days in addition to sick leave. *Floating holidays* are paid holidays that vary from year to year. The organization may schedule floating holidays so that they extend a Tuesday or Thursday holiday into a long weekend. Organizations may also give employees discretion over the scheduling of floating holidays.

The most flexible approach to time off is to grant each employee a bank of *paid time off*, in which the employer pools personal days, sick days, and vacation days for employees to use as the need or desire arises. This flexibility is especially attractive to younger workers, who tend to rate work/life balance as one of the most important sources of job satisfaction. The flexibility also fits with the U.S. trend toward more frequent but shorter vacations. With these advantages, paid time off has become available at a sizable share of companies, according to a recent survey.[11]

Employers should also establish policies for leaves without pay—for example, leaves of absence to pursue nonwork goals or to meet family needs. Unpaid leave is an employee benefit because the employee usually retains seniority and benefits during the leave.

Group Insurance

As we noted earlier, rates for group insurance are typically lower than for individual policies. Also, insurance benefits are not subject to income tax, unlike wages and salaries. When employees receive insurance as a benefit, rather than higher pay so they can buy their own insurance, employees can get more for their money. Because of this, most employees value group insurance. The most common types of insurance offered as employee benefits are medical, life, and disability insurance. As noted in the earlier discussion of benefits required under law, the U.S. government will require medium-sized and large businesses to offer health insurance or pay a penalty beginning in 2014. But until then, medical insurance is an optional benefit, and businesses continue to have many choices in the types of coverage they offer.

Medical Insurance   Although few employees fully appreciate what health insurance costs the employer, most value this benefit and look for it when they are contemplating a job offer.[12] As Figure 14.2 shows, almost 90% of full-time employees receive medical benefits. The policies typically cover three basic types of medical expenses: hospital expenses, surgical expenses, and visits to physicians. Some employers offer additional coverage, such as dental care, vision care, birthing centers, and prescription drug programs. Under the Mental Health Parity and Addiction Equity Act of 2008, if health insurance plans for employees include coverage for mental health care, that care must include the same scope of financial and treatment coverage as treatment for other illnesses. That means deductibles, copayments, coinsurance, and the number of covered days for hospitalization must be the same for treating mental illness and other illnesses. This law exempts

LO 14-4 Identify the kinds of insurance benefits offered by employers.

companies with fewer than 50 employees. Companies in states with stricter requirements must also meet the state requirements. In the past, many health insurance policies limited payments for treating mental illness, so the law could have the effect of making health insurance a more expensive benefit. However, a recent survey of employers found that most companies providing health insurance included coverage for mental illness.[13]

Consolidated Omnibus Budget Reconciliation Act (COBRA)

Federal law that requires employers to permit employees or their dependents to extend their health insurance coverage at group rates for up to 36 months following a qualifying event, such as a layoff, reduction in hours, or the employee's death.

Employers that offer medical insurance must meet the requirements of the **Consolidated Omnibus Budget Reconciliation Act (COBRA)** of 1985. This federal law requires employers to permit employees to extend their health insurance coverage at group rates for up to 36 months following a "qualifying event." Qualifying events include termination (except for gross misconduct), a reduction in hours that leads to loss of health insurance, and the employee's death (in which case the surviving spouse or dependent child would extend the coverage). To extend the coverage, the employee or the surviving spouse or dependent must pay for the insurance, but the payments are at the group rate. These employees and their families must have access to the same services as those who did not lose their health insurance.

As we will discuss later in the chapter, health insurance is a significant and fast-growing share of benefits costs at U.S. organizations, far outpacing the inflation rate.[14] Figure 14.3 shows that the United States spends much more of its total wealth on health care than other countries do. Most Western European countries have nationalized health systems, but the majority of Americans with coverage for health care expenses get it through their own or a family member's employer. Growth in the number of employees who lacked insurance because their employers could not afford this benefit was a major reason cited for passage of the Patient Protection and Affordable Care Act.

Figure 14.3

Health Care Costs in Various Countries

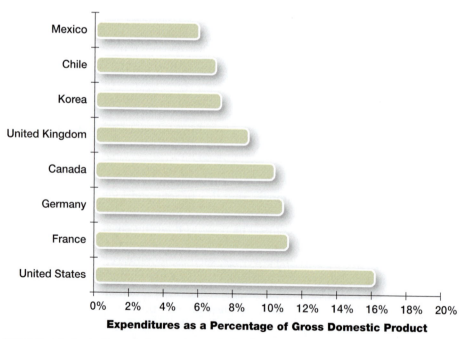

Expenditures as a Percentage of Gross Domestic Product

Source: Organisation for Economic Co-operation and Development, "Health Expenditures and Financing," *OECD StatExtracts,* http://stats.oecd.org, accessed July 11, 2014.

Employers have looked for ways to control the cost of health care coverage while keeping this valuable benefit. They have used variations of managed care, employee-driven savings, and promotion of employee wellness:

- With *managed care*, the insurer plays a role in decisions about health care, aimed at avoiding unnecessary procedures. The insurer may conduct claims review, studying claims to determine whether procedures are effective for the type of illness or injury. Patients may be required to obtain approval before hospital admissions, and the insurer may require alternatives to hospital stays—for example, outpatient surgery or home health care.

- A **health maintenance organization (HMO)** is a health care plan that requires patients to receive their medical care from the HMO's health care professionals, who are often paid a flat salary, and provides all services on a prepaid basis. In other words, the premiums paid for the HMO cover all the patient's visits and procedures, without an additional payment from the patient. By paying physicians a salary, rather than a fee for each service, the HMO hopes to remove any incentive to provide more services than the patients really need. HMO coverage tends to cost less than traditional health insurance. The downside is that employees sometimes complain cost-control incentives work so well that they are denied access to services they actually need.

- A **preferred provider organization (PPO)** is a health care plan that contracts with health care professionals to provide services at a reduced fee. Often, the PPO does not require employees to use providers in the network, but it pays a larger share of the cost of services from PPO providers. For example, the employee might pay 10% of the cost of a test by an in-network provider and 20% if the employee goes out of the PPO network. PPOs have quickly grown to become the most widely used health plan among U.S. employers. A recent survey by the Kaiser Family Foundation found that 57% of workers were enrolled in PPOs, compared with just 14% in HMOs, down from a peak of 31% in 1996.[15]

- With a **flexible spending account,** employees set aside a portion of pretax earnings to pay for eligible expenses. In particular, a *medical savings account* lets employees use their pretax savings to pay for qualified health care expenses (for example, payment of premiums). To avoid taxation, the money in the account must meet IRS requirements. Contributions to this account may not exceed $5,000 per year and must be designated in advance. The money in the account may be spent on health care expenses of the employee and employee's dependents during the plan year. At the end of the year, any remaining funds in the account revert to the employer. The major advantage of flexible spending accounts is that the money in the account is not taxed, so employees will have more take-home pay. But if they do not use all the money in the flexible spending account, they lose the amount they do not spend. Therefore, employees are most likely to benefit from a flexible spending account if they have predictable health care expenses, such as insurance premiums.

- *Consumer-driven health plans* (CDHPs) are intended to provide health coverage in a way that gets employees involved as consumers making decisions to lower costs. A CDHP typically brings together three elements: insurance with a high deductible, a medical savings account in which the employer contributes to employee-controlled accounts for paying expenses below the deductible, and health education aimed at helping employees improve their health and thus lower their need for health

Health Maintenance Organization (HMO)
A health care plan that requires patients to receive their medical care from the HMO's health care professionals, who are often paid a flat salary, and provides all services on a prepaid basis.

Preferred Provider Organization (PPO)
A health care plan that contracts with health care professionals to provide services at a reduced fee and gives patients financial incentives to use network providers.

Flexible Spending Account
Employee-controlled pretax earnings set aside to pay for certain eligible expenses, such as health care expenses, during the same year.

Tom Johnson runs on a treadmill at the Western & Southern Financial Group headquarters building in Cincinnati. The company is encouraging employees to reduce their health risks as insurance costs climb. Can you think of firms that offer other unique benefits to reduce health risks?

Employee Wellness Program (EWP)
A set of communications, activities, and facilities designed to change health-related behaviors in ways that reduce health risks.

care. Surveys of insured workers have found slow but steady growth in the share of employees who enroll in these plans. Compared with employees who have traditional insurance coverage, CDHP enrollees are more likely to be unmarried, to have a college education, and to rate their health as excellent or very good.[16] Perhaps these workers feel more confident in their ability to limit their own health care costs.

• An **employee wellness program (EWP)** is a set of communications, activities, and facilities designed to change health-related behaviors in ways that reduce health risks. Typically, an EWP aims at specific health risks, such as high blood pressure, high cholesterol levels, smoking, and obesity, by encouraging preventive measures such as exercise and good nutrition. *Passive* programs provide information and services, but no formal support or motivation to use the program. Examples include health education (such as lunchtime courses) and fitness facilities. *Active* wellness programs assume that behavior change requires support and reinforcement along with awareness and opportunity. Such a program may include counselors who tailor programs to individual employees' needs, take baseline measurements (for example, blood pressure and weight), and take follow-up measures for comparison to the baseline. The "HRM Social" box describes how social-media tools can help EWPs succeed. In general, passive health education programs cost less than fitness facilities and active wellness programs.[17] All these variations have had success in reducing risk factors associated with cardiovascular disease (obesity, high blood pressure, smoking, lack of exercise), but the follow-up method is most successful.

Life Insurance   Employers may provide life insurance to employees or offer the opportunity to buy coverage at low group rates. With a *term life insurance* policy, if the employee dies during the term of the policy, the employee's beneficiaries receive a payment called the death benefit. In policies purchased as an employee benefit, the usual death benefit is twice the employee's yearly pay. The policies may provide additional benefits for accidental death and dismemberment (loss of a body part such as a hand or foot). Along with a basic policy, the employer may give employees the option of purchasing additional coverage, usually at a nominal cost.

Short-Term Disability Insurance
Insurance that pays a percentage of a disabled employee's salary as benefits to the employee for six months or less.

Long-Term Disability Insurance
Insurance that pays a percentage of a disabled employee's salary after an initial period and potentially for the rest of the employee's life.

Disability Insurance   Employees risk losing their incomes if a disability makes them unable to work. Disability insurance provides protection against this loss of income. Typically, **short-term disability insurance** provides benefits for six months or less. **Long-term disability insurance** provides benefits after that initial period, potentially for the rest of the disabled employee's life. Disability payments are a percentage of the employee's salary—typically 50% to 70%. Payments under short-term plans may be higher. Often the policy sets a maximum amount that may be paid each month. Because its limits make it more affordable, short-term disability coverage is offered by more employers. Fewer than half of employers offer long-term plans.

In planning an employee benefits package, the organization should keep in mind that Social Security includes some long-term disability benefits. To manage benefits costs, the employer should ensure that the disability insurance is coordinated with Social Security and any other programs that help workers who become disabled.

Social Support for Getting Healthy

One of the big challenges with a wellness program is motivation—especially motivating employees who would benefit the most. Typically, many employees never complete the health assessment used for entering these programs and then even fewer sign up for activities that would improve the health issues identified in the assessment. An important consideration is that wellness programs work best when they are part of an integrated strategy that combines realistic goals with incentives, clear communication, and a supportive culture.

Some of that education and support can come through social-media tools. The knowledge-sharing function of social media readily lends itself to educating employees about health. For example, the site could feature low-fat and low-carb items on the cafeteria menu each week or a page to share ideas for managing stress or working exercise into one's daily routine.

In the area of support, just as employees might use the company's computer network to find colleagues with knowledge, the company could set up Web pages or a Twitter feed for groups with health-related interests such as a group that walks during lunch breaks or a weight-loss challenge group. While the company cannot disclose personal health information, it could reward team successes. For example, employees could form teams and see which team walks the most miles during a challenge period. (For such activities, employers must be sure to offer alternative activities to accommodate employees with disabilities.)

Questions

1. Would you expect participation in wellness programs to be greater if they have a social-media component? Why or why not?
2. How might the ideas described here be applied to a stop-smoking program for an organization's employees?

Sources: Rhonda Willingham, "Using Incentives within the New Regulatory World of the ACA to Improve Employee Wellness and Productivity," *Employee Benefit Plan Review*, October 2013, pp. 7–11; Barb Hendrickson, "Increasing Employee Participation in Corporate Wellness Programs," *Occupational Health and Safety*, September 1, 2013, http://ohsonline.com; David Roddenberry, "Six Keys to Maximize the Value of Wellness Incentive Programs," *EHS Today*, February 2013, pp. 37–38.

Long-Term Care Insurance   The cost of long-term care, such as care in a nursing home, can be devastating. Today, with more people living to an advanced age, many people are concerned about affording long-term care. Some employers address this concern by offering long-term care insurance. These policies provide benefits toward the cost of long-term care and related medical expenses.

Retirement Plans

Despite the image of retired people living on their Social Security checks, Figure 14.4 shows that those checks amount to less than half of a retired person's income. Among persons over age 65, pensions and retirement savings provided a significant share of income in 2012. Employers have no obligation to offer retirement plans beyond the protection of Social Security, but most offer some form of pension or retirement savings plan. About half of employees working for private businesses (that is, nongovernment jobs) have employer-sponsored retirement plans. These plans are most common for higher-earning employees. Among employees earning the top one-fourth of incomes, 80% participate in a retirement plan, and less than one out of four employees in the bottom one-fourth have such plans.[18] Retirement plans may be **contributory plans,** meaning they are funded by contributions from the employer and employee, or **noncontributory plans,** meaning all the contributions come from the employer.

LO 14-5 Define the types of retirement plans offered by employers.

Contributory Plan
Retirement plan funded by contributions from the employer and employee.

Noncontributory Plan
Retirement plan funded entirely by contributions from the employer.

Figure 14.4

Sources of Income for Persons 65 and Older

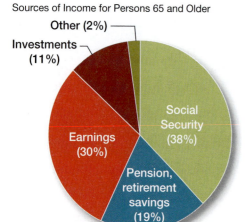

Source: Ke Bin Wu, "Sources of Income for Older Americans, 2012," AARP Public Policy Institute, fact sheet 296, December 2013, accessed at http://www.aarp.org.

Defined-Benefit Plan
Pension plan that guarantees a specified level of retirement income.

Employee Retirement Income Security Act (ERISA)
Federal law that increased the responsibility of pension plan trustees to protect retirees, established certain rights related to vesting and portability, and created the Pension Benefit Guarantee Corporation.

Pension Benefit Guarantee Corporation (PBGC)
Federal agency that insures retirement benefits and guarantees retirees a basic benefit if the employer experiences financial difficulties.

Defined-Contribution Plan
Retirement plan in which the employer sets up an individual account for each employee and specifies the size of the investment into that account.

Defined-Benefit Plans   Employers have a choice of using retirement plans that define the amount to be paid out after retirement or plans that define the amount the employer will invest each year. A **defined-benefit plan** guarantees a specified level of retirement income. Usually the amount of this defined benefit is calculated for each employee based on the employee's years of service, age, and earnings level (for example, the average of the employee's five highest-earnings years). Using years of service as part of the basis for calculating benefits gives employees an incentive to stay with the organization as long as they can, so it can help to reduce voluntary turnover.

Defined-benefit plans must meet the funding requirements of the **Employee Retirement Income Security Act (ERISA)** of 1974. This law increased the responsibility of pension plan trustees to protect retirees, established certain rights related to vesting (earning a right to receive the pension) and *portability* (being able to move retirement savings when changing employers), and created the **Pension Benefit Guarantee Corporation (PBGC).** The PBGC is the federal agency that insures retirement benefits and guarantees retirees a basic benefit if the employer experiences financial difficulties. To fund the PBGC, employers must make annual contributions of $35 per fund participant. Plans that are *underfunded—* meaning the employer does not contribute enough to the plan each year to meet future obligations—must pay an additional premium tied to the amount by which the plan is underfunded.[19] The PBGC's protection applies to the pensions of more than 44 million workers.

With a defined-benefit plan, the employer sets up a pension fund to invest the contributions. As required by ERISA, the employer must contribute enough for the plan to cover all the benefits to be paid out to retirees. If the pension fund earns less than expected, the employer makes up the difference from other sources. If the employer experiences financial difficulties so that it must end or reduce employee pension benefits, the PBGC provides a basic benefit, which does not necessarily cover the full amount promised by the employer's pension plan.

Defined-Contribution Plans   An alternative to defined benefits is a **defined-contribution plan,** which sets up an individual account for each employee and specifies the size of the investment into that account, rather than the amount to be paid out upon retirement. The amount the retiree receives will depend on the account's performance. Many kinds of defined-contribution plans are available, including the following:

- *Money purchase plan*—The employer specifies a level of annual contributions (for example, 10% of salary). The contributions are invested, and when the employee retires, he or she is entitled to receive the amount of the contributions plus the investment earnings. ("Money purchase" refers to the fact that when employees retire, they often buy an annuity with the money, rather than taking it as a lump sum.)
- *Profit-sharing and employee stock ownership plans*—As we saw in Chapter 13, incentive pay may take the form of profit sharing and employee stock ownership plans

(ESOPs). These payments may be set up so that the money goes into retirement plans. By defining its contributions in terms of stock or a share of profits, the organization has more flexibility to contribute less dollar value in lean years and more in good years.

- *Section 401(k) plans*—Employees contribute a percentage of their earnings, and employers may make matching contributions. The amount employees contribute is not taxed as part of their income until they receive it from the plan. The federal government limits the amount that may be contributed each year. The limit is $17,500 in 2014 and is subject to cost-of-living increases in years after 2014. The contribution limits are higher for persons 50 and older.[20]

These plans free employers from the risks that investments will not perform as well as expected. They put the responsibility for wise investing squarely on the shoulders of each employee (see the "HR Oops!" box). A defined-contribution plan is also easier to administer. The employer need not calculate payments based on age and service, and payments to the PBGC are not required. Considering the advantages to employers, it is not surprising that a growing share of retirement plans are defined-contribution plans. Since the 1980s, the share of employees participating in defined-benefit plans has been steadily falling, and the share participating in defined-contribution plans has risen. By 2012, just 21% of workers with a retirement plan had defined-benefit plans, while 78% percent of workers with a retirement plan participated in defined-contribution plans.[21]

When retirement plans make individual employees responsible for investment decisions, the employees need information about retirement planning. Retirement savings plans often give employees much control over decisions about when and how much to invest. Many employees do not appreciate the importance of beginning to save early in their careers. As Figure 14.5 shows, an employee who invests $3,000 a year ($250 a month) between the ages of 21 and 29 will have far more at age 65 than an employee who invests the same amount between ages 31 and 39. Another important lesson is to diversify investments. Based on investment performance between 1928 and 2012, stocks earned an average of 9.31% per year, bonds earned 5.11%, and low-risk (cash) investments earned less than 4%. But in any given year, one of these types of investments might outperform the other. And within the categories of stocks and bonds, it is important to invest in a wide variety of companies. If one company performs poorly, the investments in other companies might perform better. However, studies of investment decisions by employees have found that few employees have followed basic guidelines for diversifying investments among stocks, bonds, and savings accounts according to their age and investment needs.[22] To help employees handle such risks, some organizations provide financial planning as a separate benefit, offer an option to have a professional invest the funds in a 401(k) plan, or direct funds into default investments called

Figure 14.5

Value of Retirement Savings Invested at Different Ages

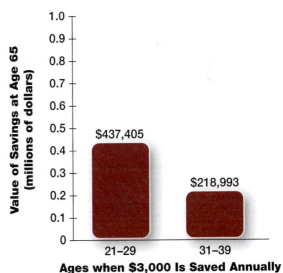

Note: Investment portfolio consists of 60% stocks, 30% bonds, and 10% cash (e.g., money-market funds, bank savings accounts), assuming average rates of return based on historical rates from 1928 to 2012.

Source: Data from Aswath Damodaran, "Annual Returns on Stocks, T. Bonds and T. Bills: 1928–Current," http://people.stern.nyu.edu /adamodar/New_Home_Page/datafile/histretSP.html, accessed May 20, 2014.

401(k) Plans Are a Missed Opportunity for Many

At organizations that offer employees a chance to save for retirement with a 401(k) plan, about three out of every ten employees do not participate. Even those who do participate typically contribute less than the amount their employer will match. That means employees are leaving money on the table, and employers are not getting the full motivational potential out of their compensation package.

Employers can address the enrollment problem by setting up a plan that automatically enrolls employees unless they opt out. Studies suggest that automatic enrollment can cut in half the share of employees who do not participate. With automatic enrollment, the employer must notify eligible employees about their benefits and rights, communicating before the automatic enrollment and once a year afterwards.

Even with automatic enrollment, employees fail to make the most of 401(k) plans. One study found that when enrollment was automatic, the average employee saved a smaller percentage of his or her income.

Logically, employees who make an effort to enroll would also prioritize saving more for retirement. Furthermore, organizations with automatic enrollment match on average a smaller percentage of workers' contributions than other employers offering 401(k) plans. Automatic enrollment evidently boosts overall participation at the expense of participants' individual retirement savings. Thus, to prepare for their eventual retirement, employees need information and motivation to save, not just access to a plan.

Another way employers are addressing low enrollment rates is by offering the benefit without the permitted waiting period. Employers may require employees to work for a set period—typically six months, but up to a year is allowed—before enrolling in a 401(k) plan. This saves the cost of administering plans for high-turnover workers, but it also makes saving enough more difficult and lowers enrollment rates. Employees seem to forget about enrolling after they join a company, sign

up for other benefits, and get busy with their jobs. Some employers, including Massachusetts Mutual Life Insurance and Biogen Idec, therefore let employees enroll immediately, saying it helps them attract and keep talent.

Questions

1. Why should an employer be concerned if enrollment in 401(k) plans is low?
2. How might an HR department encourage higher rates of enrollment and saving?

Sources: U.S. Department of Labor, Employee Benefits Security Administration, "Automatic Enrollment 401(k) Plans for Small Businesses," http://www.dol.gov, accessed July 14, 2014; Emily Brandon, "The Downside of 401(k) Automatic Enrollment," *U.S. News and World Report*, November 18, 2013, http://money.usnews.com; Beth Healy, "Waiting Periods on 401(k) Plans Can Be Costly for Workers," *Boston Globe*, March 30, 2013, http://www.boston.com.

target date funds (TDFs), which are geared toward the needs of employees at different life stages. Also, under the Pension Protection Act of 2006, defined-contribution plans that hold publicly traded securities must give employees the option to sell stock in the company they work for and must offer them at least three investment options other than the company's own stock. The law also allows employers to promote retirement saving by enrolling workers automatically and having their contributions automatically increase along with wages (employees can opt out). Since the law was enacted, automatic enrollment has become widespread.

In spite of these challenges, defined-contribution plans also offer an advantage to employees in today's highly mobile workforce. They do not penalize employees for changing jobs. With these plans, retirement earnings are less related to the number of years an employee stays with a company.

Cash Balance Plans An increasingly popular way to combine the advantages of defined-benefit plans and defined-contribution plans is to use a **cash balance plan.** This type of retirement plan consists of individual accounts, as in a 401(k) plan. But in

Cash Balance Plan
Retirement plan in which the employer sets up an individual account for each employee and contributes a percentage of the employee's salary; the account earns interest at a predefined rate.

contrast to a 401(k), all the contributions come from the employer. Usually, the employer contributes a percentage of the employee's salary, say, 4% or 5%. The money in the cash balance plan earns interest according to a predetermined rate, such as the rate paid on U.S. Treasury bills. Employers guarantee this rate as in a defined-benefit plan. This arrangement helps employers plan their contributions and helps employees predict their retirement benefits. If employees change jobs, they generally can roll over the balance into an individual retirement account.

A switch from traditional defined-benefit plans to cash balance plans, like any major change, requires employers to consider the effects on employees as well as on the organization's bottom line. Defined-benefit plans are most generous to older employees with many years of service, and cash balance plans are most generous to young employees who will have many years ahead in which to earn interest. For an organization with many experienced employees, switching from a defined-benefit plan can produce great savings in pension benefits. In that case, the older workers are the greatest losers, unless the organization adjusts the program to retain their benefits. After IBM switched to a cash-benefit plan, a group of employees filed an age discrimination lawsuit. IBM won the lawsuit on appeal, and the Pension Protection Act of 2006 seeks to clarify the legal requirements of such plans. As a result, some companies may renew their interest in cash balance plans, but IBM has decided to focus on its 401(k) plan.

Government Requirements for Vesting and Communication

Along with requirements for funding defined-benefit plans, ERISA specifies a number of requirements related to eligibility for benefits and communication with employees. ERISA guarantees employees that when they become participants in a pension plan and work a specified number of years, they earn a right to a pension upon retirement. These rights are called **vesting rights.** Employees whose contributions are *vested* have met the requirements (enrolling and length of service) to receive a pension at retirement age, regardless of whether they remained with the employer until that time. Employees' own contributions to their pension plans are always completely vested. In most cases, the vesting of employer-funded pension benefits must take place under one of two schedules selected by the employer:

> **Vesting Rights**
> Guarantee that when employees become participants in a pension plan and work a specified number of years, they will receive a pension at retirement age, regardless of whether they remained with the employer.

1. The employer may vest employees after five years and may provide zero vesting until that time.
2. The employer may vest employees over a three- to seven-year period, with at least 20% vesting in the third year and at least an additional 20% in each year after the third year.

These two schedules represent minimum requirements. Employers may vest employees more quickly if they wish. Two less common situations have different vesting requirements. One is a "top-heavy" pension plan, meaning pension benefits for *key employees* (such as highly paid top managers) exceed a government-specified share of total pension benefits. A top-heavy plan requires faster vesting for nonkey employees. Another exception from the usual schedule involves multi-employer pension plans. These plans need not provide vesting until after 10 years of employment.

The intent of vesting requirements is to protect employees by preventing employers from terminating them before they meet retirement age in order to avoid paying pension benefits. In addition, it is illegal for employers to transfer or lay off employees as a way to avoid pension obligations, even if these changes are motivated partly by business need.[23] One way employers may legally try to minimize pension costs is in choosing a vesting schedule. For example, if many employees leave after three or four years of employment, the five-year vesting schedule would minimize pension costs.

ERISA's reporting and disclosure requirements involve the Internal Revenue Service, the Department of Labor, and employees.[24] Within 90 days after employees enter a plan, they must receive a **summary plan description (SPD),** a report that describes the plan's funding, eligibility requirements, risks, and other details. If the employee requests one, the employer must also make available an individual benefit statement, which describes the employee's vested and unvested benefits. Many employers provide such information regularly, without waiting for employee requests. This type of communication helps employees understand and value their retirement benefits.

Summary Plan Description (SPD)
Report that describes a pension plan's funding, eligibility requirements, risks, and other details.

LO 14-6 Describe how organizations use other benefits to match employees' wants and needs.

"Family-Friendly" Benefits

As employers have recognized the significance of employees' need to manage conflicts between their work and family roles, many have added "family-friendly" benefits to their employee benefits. These benefits include family leave policies and child care. The programs discussed here apply directly to the subset of employees with family responsibilities. However, family-friendly benefits often have spillover effects in the form of loyalty because employees see the benefits as evidence that the organization cares about its people.[25] The following types of benefits are typical:

- *Family leave*—Family or parental leave grants employees time off to care for children and other dependents. As discussed earlier in the chapter, federal law requires 12 weeks of unpaid leave. Companies may choose to offer more generous leave policies, and California requires 6 weeks of leave at up to 55% of pay. Recent data from the Census Bureau show only 12% of workers having paid family leave, so employees wanting paid time off to care for a child most often have to make do with paid vacation or sick days. In contrast, most industrialized nations provide paid maternal leave and often paternal leave as well. Companies offering paternity as well as maternity leave include Yahoo, Bank of America, and Ernst and Young. However, fathers tend to take short leaves of no more than a week or two, perhaps out of fear that they will seem less dedicated to their jobs.[26]
- *Child care*—Child care benefits may take several forms, requiring different levels of organizational involvement. The lowest level of involvement is for the organization to supply and help employees collect information about the cost and quality of available child care. At the next level, organizations provide vouchers or discounts for employees to use at existing child care facilities. At the highest level of involvement, the employer provides child care at or near the work site. Staffing a child care facility is costly and involves important liability concerns. At the same time, the results of this type of benefit, in terms of reducing absenteeism and enhancing productivity, have been mixed.[27] In a recent survey of employers by the Families and Work Institute, the most common form of child-care benefits (offered by 61%) was a dependent care assistance plan, which lets employees set aside pretax income to pay for child care. A resource and referral program was the second most common benefit, offered by 37%.[28]

- *College savings*—As workers' children grow up, their needs shift from maternity leave and child care to college tuition. Some organizations have supported this concern by sponsoring tax-favored *529 savings plans*. These plans, named after the section of the Internal Revenue Code that regulates them, let parents and other family members defer taxes on the earnings of their deposits into the 529 account. Some states also provide a (limited) tax deduction for these contributions. As an employee benefit, organizations can arrange with a broker to offer direct deposit of a portion of employees' paychecks into their accounts. Besides offering the convenience of direct deposit, employers can negotiate lower management fees. At Johns Hopkins Bayview Medical Center, all employees are eligible to participate in a college savings plan that deducts contributions from employees' paychecks. This benefit is part of a compensation package designed to promote employees' personal and professional growth; related benefits include tuition reimbursement for employees (up to full tuition) and their dependent children (up to 50% reimbursement).[29]

- *Elder care*—As the population of the nation's elderly grows, so do the demands on adult children to care for elderly parents, aunts, and uncles. When these people become ill or disabled, they rely on family or professional caregivers. Responsibilities such as providing assistance, paying for professional caregivers, and locating services can be expensive, time consuming, and exhausting, often distracting employees from their work roles. In response, many employers have added elder care benefits. These programs often started by offering employees information and referrals; today these resources are often made available online.

More recent enhancements of elder care benefits include referrals to decision support from experts in geriatric care, insurance, and the law, as well as flexible hours and paid time off. Employees at Johnson & Johnson have free use of a service that assesses elderly relatives' needs, helps the employee plan and coordinate services, reviews care facilities, helps employees select caregivers, assists with paperwork, and provides referrals to community services.[30] Even companies that cannot afford to offer counseling or referral services can use intranets to provide links to helpful websites such as the National Alliance for Caregiving (**www.caregiving.org**), the National Council on Aging (**www.benefitscheckup.org**), and the federal government's benefits information site (**www.benefits.gov**).

Other Benefits

The scope of possible employee benefits is limited only by the imagination of the organization's decision makers. Organizations have developed a wide variety of benefits to meet the needs of employees and to attract and keep the kinds of workers who will be of value to the organization. Traditional extras include subsidized cafeterias, on-site health care for minor injuries or illnesses, and moving expenses for newly hired or relocating employees. Stores and manufacturers may offer employee discounts on their products.

In order to provide a relaxed environment for their employees, some companies allow employees to bring their pets to work. What other unique benefits do companies offer their employees?

To encourage learning and attract the kinds of employees who wish to develop their knowledge and skills, many organizations offer *tuition reimbursement* programs. A typical program covers tuition and related expenses for courses that are relevant to the employee's current job or future career at the organization. Employees are reimbursed for these expenses after they demonstrate they have completed an approved course.

Especially for demanding, high-stress jobs, organizations may look for benefits that help employees put in the necessary long hours and alleviate stress. Recreational activities such as on-site basketball courts or company-sponsored softball teams provide for social interaction as well as physical activity. Employers may reward hard-working groups or individuals with a trip for a weekend, a meal, or any activity employees are likely to enjoy. Employees at Yelp, which runs the user review website of the same name, can visit the company's pub, and at Etsy, which runs an online marketplace, employees get special weekly meals created from locally sourced ingredients. Busy employees of S. C. Johnson can take advantage of a concierge service, which will run errands for them.[31]

LO 14-7 Explain how to choose the contents of an employee benefits package.

Selecting Employee Benefits

Although the government requires certain benefits, employers have wide latitude in creating the total benefits package they offer employees.[32] Decisions about which benefits to include should take into account the organization's goals, its budget, and the expectations of the organization's current employees and those it wishes to recruit in the future. Employees have come to expect certain things from employers. An organization that does not offer the expected benefits will have more difficulty attracting and keeping talented workers. Also, if employees believe their employer feels no commitment to their welfare, they are less likely to feel committed to their employer.

The Organization's Objectives

A logical place to begin selecting employee benefits is to establish objectives for the benefits package. This helps an organization select the most effective benefits and monitor whether the benefits are doing what they should. Table 14.2 is an example of one organization's benefits objectives. Unfortunately, research suggests that most organizations do not have written benefits objectives.

Among companies that do set goals, common objectives include controlling the cost of health care benefits and retaining employees.[33] The first goal explains the growing use of wellness programs and consumer-directed health plans. For the second goal, employees do say that valued benefits keep them from walking away, but employers need to learn what employees care about. To find out what its young, predominately male workforce values, British mobile-phone service Three got its staff involved in designing the benefits package. The result was a set of flexible benefits that is heavy on communication and personal control. Employees can "buy" or "sell" time off if the basic package is too little or too much, and they can buy into health benefits over and above those provided through the government. An online pension calculator shows them how their retirement savings are expected to grow, given their current or possible rates of contribution to the plan.[34]

Employees' Expectations and Values

Employees expect to receive benefits that are legally required and widely available, and they value benefits they are likely to use. To meet employee expectations about

Table 14.2

**An Organization's
Benefits Objectives**

- To establish and maintain an employee benefit program that is based primarily on the employees' needs for leisure time and on protection against the risks of old age, loss of health, and loss of life.
- To establish and maintain an employee benefit program that complements the efforts of employees on their own behalf.
- To evaluate the employee benefit plan annually for its effect on employee morale and productivity, giving consideration to turnover, unfilled positions, attendance, employees' complaints, and employees' opinions.
- To compare the employee benefit plan annually with that of other leading companies in the same field and to maintain a benefit plan with an overall level of benefits based on cost per employee that falls within the second quintile of these companies.
- To maintain a level of benefits for nonunion employees that represents the same level of expenditures per employee as for union employees.
- To determine annually the costs of new, changed, and existing programs as percentages of salaries and wages and to maintain these percentages as much as possible.
- To self-fund benefits to the extent that a long-run cost savings can be expected for the firm and catastrophic losses can be avoided.
- To coordinate all benefits with social insurance programs to which the company makes payments.
- To provide benefits on a noncontributory basis except for dependent coverage, for which employees should pay a portion of the cost.
- To maintain continual communications with all employees concerning benefit programs.

Source: Adapted from B. T. Beam Jr. and J. J. McFadden, *Employee Benefits,* 3rd ed. Copyright © 1992 by Dearborn Financial Publishing, Inc. Published by Dearborn Financial Publishing, Inc., Chicago. All rights reserved.

benefits, it can be helpful to see what other organizations offer. Employers can purchase survey information about benefits packages from private consultants. In addition, the Bureau of Labor Statistics gathers benefits data. The BLS website (**www.bls.gov**) is therefore a good place to check for free information about employee benefits in the United States. With regard to value, medical insurance is a high-value benefit because employees usually realize that surgery or a major illness can be financially devastating. Vision and dental care tend to be much less expensive, but many employees appreciate this type of coverage because so many people receive dental or vision care in the course of a year. Therefore, employers tend to try to maintain basic health insurance coverage, and if they must cut benefits to save money, they more often eliminate long-term care insurance and health coverage for retirees.[35]

Employers should also consider that the value employees place on various benefits is likely to differ from one employee to another. At a broad level, basic demographic factors such as age and sex can influence the kinds of benefits employees want. An older workforce is more likely to be concerned about (and use) medical coverage, life insurance, and pensions. A workforce with a high percentage of women of childbearing age may care more about disability or family leave. Young, unmarried men and women often place more value on pay than on benefits. However, these are only general observations; organizations should check which considerations apply to their own employees and identify more specific needs and differences. One approach is to use surveys to ask employees about the kinds of benefits they value. The survey should be carefully worded so as not to raise employees' expectations by seeming to promise all the benefits asked about at no cost to the employee.

The choice of benefits may influence current employees' satisfaction and may also affect the organization's recruiting, in terms of both the ease of recruiting and the kinds of employees attracted to the organization. For example, a benefits package that has strong medical benefits and pensions may be particularly attractive to older people or to those with many dependents. Such benefits may attract people with extensive experience and those who wish to make a long-term commitment to the organization. This strategy may be especially beneficial when turnover costs are very high. On the other hand, offering generous health care benefits may attract and retain people with high health care costs. Thus, organizations need to consider the signals sent by their benefits package as they set goals for benefits and select benefits to offer.

Organizations can address differences in employees' needs and empower their employees by offering flexible benefits plans in place of a single benefits package for all employees. These plans, often called **cafeteria-style plans,** offer employees a set of alternatives from which they can choose the types and amounts of benefits they want. The plans vary. Some impose minimum levels for certain benefits, such as health care coverage; some allow better employees to receive money in exchange for choosing a "light" package; and some let employees pay extra for the privilege of receiving more benefits. For example, some plans let employees give up vacation days for more pay or to purchase extra vacation days in exchange for a reduction in pay.

Cafeteria-style plans have a number of advantages.[36] The selection process can make employees more aware of the value of the benefits, particularly when the plan assigns each employee a sum of money to allocate to benefits. Also, the individual choice in a cafeteria plan enables each employee to match his or her needs to the company's benefits, increasing the plan's actual value to the employee. And because employees would not select benefits they don't want, the company avoids the cost of providing employees with benefits they don't value. Another way to control costs is to give employees incentives to choose lower-cost options. For example, the employee's deductible on a higher-cost health plan could be larger than on a relatively low-cost HMO.

A drawback of cafeteria-style plans is that they have a higher administrative cost, especially in the design and start-up stages. Organizations can avoid some of the higher cost, however, by using software packages and standardized plans that have been developed for employers wishing to offer cafeteria-style benefits. Another possible drawback is that employee selection of benefits will increase rather than decrease costs because employees will select the kinds of benefits they expect to need the most. For example, an employee expecting to need a lot of dental work is more likely to sign up for a dental plan. The heavy use of the dental coverage would then drive up the employer's premiums for that coverage. Costs can also be difficult to estimate when employees select their benefits.

Benefits' Costs

Employers also need to consider benefits costs. One place to start is with general information about the average costs of various benefits types. Widely used sources of cost data include the Bureau of Labor Statistics (BLS), Employee Benefit Research Institute, and U.S. Chamber of Commerce. Annual surveys by the Chamber of Commerce state the cost of benefits as a percentage of total payroll costs and in dollar terms. In addition, the ability to process "big data" is enabling more employers to identify specific areas where they can rein in benefits costs without reducing the value of their compensation packages to employees. See the "Best Practices" box for an example.

Employers can use data about costs to help them select the kinds of benefits to offer. But in balancing these decisions against organizational goals and employee benefits, the organization may decide to offer certain high-cost benefits while also looking for ways to control the cost of those benefits. The highest-cost items tend to offer the

---

Cafeteria-Style Plan
A benefits plan that offers employees a set of alternatives from which they can choose the types and amounts of benefits they want.

Big Data Looks Like a Sure Bet for Caesars Entertainment

Companies have much more data available to them than they used to. If used properly, this "big data" can be a path to better spending on employee benefits. More and more managers are improving decisions by basing them on data instead of HIPPO (the highest-paid person's opinion) or intuition alone.

Caesars Entertainment is an example of a company using big data to improve its spending on health insurance. The company analyzes patterns in its employees' health insurance claims. They track variables such as the usage of particular medical services, the degree to which employees and their dependents use name-brand instead of generic drugs, and the number of emergency room visits (especially costly, at an average $1,200 for an outpatient visit).

Of course, sometimes an expensive procedure is necessary to protect a patient's health or life. But in the case of emergency rooms, patients sometimes use these facilities for nonemergency conditions that could be treated elsewhere at a far lower cost. A visit to an urgent-care center, for example, costs around $100 to $200. So when Caesars' analysis showed that employees of its Harrah's property in Philadelphia were far more likely to visit hospital emergency rooms than employees company-wide, it investigated.

The data showed that the Philadelphia workers and dependents sought immediate care at urgent-care centers only 11% of the time, versus 34% company-wide. The cost of that care would be far less if more of those Harrah's workers would choose urgent-care centers instead of emergency rooms. So Harrah's conducted an information campaign to remind employees of the high cost of ER visits and to provide them with a list of alternative facilities. Two years later, the use of urgent-care facilities had risen from 11% of emergencies to 17%, and employees were less likely to make multiple trips to the emergency room. Overall, since Caesars started monitoring the data about emergency room use, it has reduced the number of visits by 10,000, and the use of less expensive facilities has cut health care spending by $4.5 million. That kind of savings should translate into lower premiums for health benefits.

Questions

1. Given that the insurance company and employees are the ones paying the bills for emergency room visits, how does encouraging employees to use lower-cost facilities help Caesars reduce its costs?

2. How can a company such as Caesars benefit from using big data about health care spending without violating individual employees' privacy?

Sources: Steven Rosenbush and Michael Totty, "How Big Data Is Changing the Whole Equation for Business," *The Wall Street Journal*, March 8, 2013, http://online.wsj.com; Sarah Kliff, "An Average ER Visit Costs More Than the Average Month's Rent," *Washington Post*, March 2, 2013, http://www.washingtonpost.com; Anna Wilde Mathews, "Same Doctor Visit, Double the Cost," *The Wall Street Journal*, August 27, 2012, http://online.wsj.com.

most room for savings, but only if the items permit choice or negotiation. Also, as we noted earlier, organizations can control certain costs such as workers' compensation by improving their experience ratings. Cost control is especially important—and difficult—when economic growth slows or declines.

In recent years, benefits related to health care have attracted particular attention because these costs have risen very rapidly and because employers have a number of options. Concern over costs has prompted many employers to shift from traditional health insurance to PPOs and CDHPs. Some employers shift more of the cost to employees. They may lower the employer's payments by increasing the amounts employees pay for deductibles and coinsurance (the employee's share of the payment for services). Or they may require employees to pay some or all of the difference in cost between traditional insurance and a lower-cost plan. Excluding or limiting coverage for certain types of claims also can slow the increase in health insurance costs. Employee wellness programs, especially when they are targeted to employees with risk factors and include follow-up and encouragement, can reduce risk factors for disease.[37]

LO 14-8 Summarize the regulations affecting how employers design and administer benefits programs.

Legal Requirements for Employee Benefits

As we discussed earlier in this chapter, some benefits are required by law. This requirement adds to the cost of compensating employees. Organizations looking for ways to control staffing costs may look for ways to structure the workforce so as to minimize the expense of benefits. They may require overtime rather than adding new employees, hire part-time rather than full-time workers (because part-time employees generally receive much smaller benefits packages), and use independent contractors rather than hire employees. Some of these choices are limited by legal requirements, however. For example, the Fair Labor Standards Act requires overtime pay for nonexempt workers, as discussed in Chapter 12. Also, the Internal Revenue Service strictly limits the definition of "independent contractors," so that employers cannot avoid legal obligations by classifying workers as self-employed when the organization receives the benefits of a permanent employee. Other legal requirements involve tax treatment of benefits, antidiscrimination laws, and accounting for benefits.

Tax Treatment of Benefits

The IRS provides more favorable tax treatment of benefits classified as *qualified plans*. The details vary from one type of benefit to another. In the case of retirement plans, the advantages include the ability for employees to immediately take a tax deduction for the funds they contribute to the plans, no immediate tax on employees for the amount the employer contributes, and tax-free earnings on the money in the retirement fund.[38]

To obtain status as a qualified plan, a benefit plan must meet certain requirements.[39] In the case of pensions, these involve vesting and nondiscrimination rules. The nondiscrimination rules provide tax benefits to plans that do not discriminate in favor of the organization's "highly compensated employees." To receive the benefits, the organization cannot set up a retirement plan that provides benefits exclusively to the organization's owners and top managers. The requirements encourage employers to provide important benefits such as pensions to a broad spectrum of employees. Before offering pension plans and other benefits, organizations should have them reviewed by an expert who can advise on whether the benefits are qualified plans.

Antidiscrimination Laws

As we discussed in Chapter 3, a number of laws are intended to provide equal employment opportunity without regard to race, sex, age, disability, and several other protected categories. Some of these laws apply to the organization's benefits policies.

Legal treatment of men and women includes equal access to benefits, so the organization may not use the employee's gender as the basis for providing more limited benefits. That is the rationale for the Pregnancy Discrimination Act, which requires that employers treat pregnancy as it treats any disability. If an employee needs time off for conditions related to pregnancy or childbirth, the employee would receive whatever disability benefits the organization offers to employees who take disability leave for other reasons. Another area of concern in the treatment of male and female employees is pension benefits. On average, women live longer than men, so on average, pension benefits for female employees are more expensive (because the organization pays the pension longer), other things being equal. Some organizations have used this difference as a basis for requiring that female employees contribute more than male employees to defined benefit plans. The Supreme Court in 1978 determined that such a requirement is illegal.[40] According to the Supreme Court, the law is intended to protect individuals, and when women are considered on an individual basis (not as averages), not every woman outlives every man.

Age discrimination is also relevant to benefits policies. Two major issues have received attention under the Age Discrimination in Employment Act (ADEA) and amendments. First, employers must take care not to discriminate against workers over age 40 in providing pay or benefits. For example, employers may not set an age at which retirement benefits stop growing as a way to pressure older workers to retire.[41] Also, early-retirement incentive programs need to meet certain standards. The programs may not coerce employees to retire, they must provide accurate information about the options available, and they must give employees enough time to make a decision. In effect, employees must really have a choice about whether they retire.

When employers offer early retirement, they often ask employees to sign waivers saying they will not pursue claims under the ADEA. The Older Workers Benefit Protection Act of 1990 set guidelines for using these waivers. The waivers must be voluntary and understandable to the employee and employer, and they must spell out the employee's rights under the ADEA. Also, in exchange for signing the waiver, the employee must receive "compensation," that is, greater benefits than he or she would otherwise receive upon retirement. The employer must inform employees that they may consult a lawyer before signing, and employees must have time to make a decision about signing—21 days before signing plus 7 days afterward in which they can revoke the agreement.

The Americans with Disabilities Act imposes requirements related to health insurance. Under the ADA, employees with disabilities must have "equal access to whatever health insurance coverage the employer provides other employees." Even so, the terms and conditions of health insurance may be based on risk factors—as long as the employer does not use this basis as a way to escape offering health insurance to someone with a disability. From the standpoint of avoiding legal challenges, an employer who has risk-based insurance and then hires an employee with a disability is in a stronger position than an employer who switches to a risk-based policy after hiring a disabled employee.[42]

Accounting Requirements

Companies' financial statements must meet the many requirements of the Financial Accounting Standards Board (FASB). These accounting requirements are intended to ensure that financial statements are a true picture of the company's financial status and that outsiders, including potential lenders and investors, can understand and compare financial statements. Under FASB standards, employers must set aside the funds they expect to need for benefits to be paid after retirement, rather than funding those benefits on a pay-as-you-go basis. On financial statements, those funds must appear as future cost obligations. For companies with substantial retirement benefits, reporting those benefits as future cost obligations greatly lowers income each year. Along with rising benefits costs, this reporting requirement has encouraged many companies to scale back benefits to retirees.

Did You Know?

Employees Say Benefits Matter

In employee satisfaction surveys conducted since 2002, the Society of Human Resource Management has found that benefits ranked in the top five contributors to job satisfaction every year except 2012. Among the aspects of benefits that employees consider important or very important, paid time off and health insurance take the top spots. At the same time, the HR managers surveyed were more likely than the employees to say employees are satisfied with each aspect of the benefits.

Question

How do the data shown here support an argument that HR managers should actively communicate with employees about their benefits?

Sources: Society for Human Resource Management, "Employee Job Satisfaction and Engagement: The Road to Economic Recovery," research report, May 2014, http://www.shrm.org; Debra Cohen, "Employee Engagement," *People and Strategy* 36, no. 4 (2014): 13–14; Frank Giancola, "How Important Are Benefit Plans to Your Employees and How Satisfied Are They with Your Offerings?" *Employee Benefit Plan Review*, July 2013, pp. 27–30.

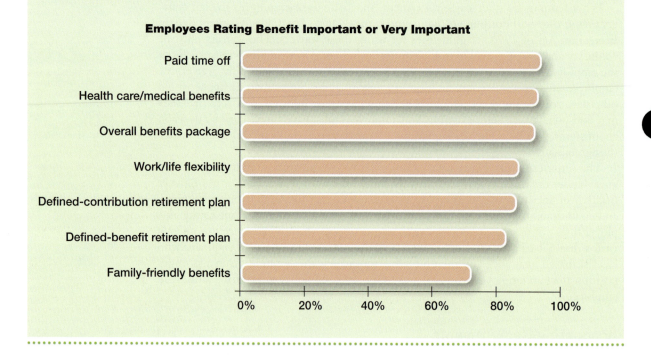

Employees Rating Benefit Important or Very Important

LO 14-9 Discuss the importance of effectively communicating the nature and value of benefits to employees.

Communicating Benefits to Employees

Organizations must communicate benefits information to employees so that they will appreciate the value of their benefits. This is essential so that benefits can achieve their objective of attracting, motivating, and retaining employees. Employees are interested in their benefits, as detailed in the "Did You Know?" box. Also, they need a great deal of detailed information to take advantage of benefits such as health insurance and 401(k) plans. It follows that electronic technology such as the Internet and supporting databases can play a significant role in modern benefit systems.

In actuality, employees and job applicants often have a poor idea of what benefits they have and what the market value of their benefits is. Research asking employees about their benefits has shown that employees significantly underestimate the cost and value of their benefits.[43] Probably a major reason for their lack of knowledge is a lack of communications from employers. Employees don't know what employers are spending for benefits, so many of them doubt employers' complaints about soaring costs and their impact on the company's future.[44] In one study, employees said their company neglected to tell them how to be better consumers of health care, and they would be willing to make changes in their lifestyle if they had a financial incentive to do so. Such research suggests to employers that better communication, coupled with well-designed benefits plans, will pay off in practical terms.

Employers have many options for communicating information about benefits. To increase the likelihood that employees will receive and understand the messages, employers can combine several media, such as brochures, question-and-answer meetings, intranet pages, memos, and e-mail. Some other possible media include paycheck inserts, retirement or health coaching, training programs, and benefits fairs. An investment of creativity in communications to employees can reap great returns in the form of committed, satisfied employees.

THINKING ETHICALLY

SHOULD ALL EMPLOYEES PAY THE SAME AMOUNT FOR HEALTH INSURANCE?

With health care costs rising faster than inflation, employers look for ways to cut the cost or at least slow the increase. Employees with unhealthy lifestyles need more health care, so coverage for an unhealthy workforce costs more. Therefore, and perhaps also out of concern for employees' well-being, employers want to motivate employees to take better care of their health.

One idea is to offer discounts or penalties on the employee's share of health insurance premiums. Michelin North America tried awarding a $600 credit to employees who completed a health assessment or participated in creating an action plan to improve wellness. Health costs rose anyway, so Michelin limits the credit to employees who meet health standards in three or more categories, such as blood pressure, cholesterol levels, and waist size. Employees who do not qualify may earn a smaller credit by signing up for health coaching.

The Affordable Care Act encourages employers to reward health-promoting behavior. Rewards and penalties may not exceed 30% of the employee's costs for the health insurance (50% for participation in a stop-smoking program). The typical amount of the incentives is 5% to 10% of an employee's share of the premium.

To avoid discrimination under the Americans with Disabilities Act, employers must reward behaviors employees are able to do and must provide alternatives to accommodate people with disabilities. Thus, instead of having a goal to walk a given number of miles, employees might wear a fitness tracking device such as Fitbit or Jawbone Up and measure their progress toward individual goals or measure a group's overall progress toward a shared goal. Also, a doctor can exempt an employee from a program; you would not, for example, want employees with anorexia or bulimia to enroll in a weight-loss rewards program.

Even when a company's incentives meet legal requirements, people question whether they are fair and respect employees' privacy. Some question whether employees will actually change their behavior—and improve their health—in exchange for a few hundred dollars. Perhaps the programs will simply reward people who are already taking good care of their health. Others feel it is unkind or unfair to penalize less healthy people, who already have higher bills for health care because they need more services. On the privacy question, CVS and other companies using incentives say they do not see individuals' health information. Rather, their insurance companies see the data and may report the overall costs and benefits of the program.

Questions

1. Suppose an employer gives employees an insurance discount based on number of hours of physical fitness activities. Who benefits from the program? Who is harmed? Is this ethical?
2. Suppose an employer charges all employees the same premium, regardless of their health habits. Who benefits? Who is harmed? Is this ethical?

Sources: Parmy Olson, "Wearable Tech Is Plugging into Health Insurance," *Forbes*, June 19, 2014, http://www.forbes.com; Rhonda Willingham, "Using Incentives within the New Regulatory World of the ACA to Improve Employee Wellness and Productivity," *Employee Benefit Plan Review*, October 2013, pp. 7–11; Leslie Kwoh, "When Your Boss Makes You Pay for Being Fat," *The Wall Street Journal*, April 5, 2013, http://online.wsj.com; Katie Thomas, "Companies Get Strict on Health of Workers," *The New York Times*, March 25, 2013, http://www.nytimes.com.

SUMMARY

LO 14-1 Discuss the importance of benefits as a part of employee compensation.

- Compensation includes wages and salaries, incentive pay, and benefits.
- Like other forms of compensation, benefits help employers attract, retain, and motivate employees.
- The variety of possible benefits helps employers tailor compensation packages to attract the right kinds of employees.
- Employees expect at least a minimum level of benefits, and providing more than the minimum helps an organization compete in the labor market.
- Benefits are also a significant expense.
- Employers provide benefits because employees value them, and many benefits are required by law.

LO 14-2 Summarize the types of employee benefits required by law.

- Employers must contribute to the Old Age, Survivors, Disability, and Health Insurance program known as Social Security through a payroll tax shared by employers and employees.
- Employers must pay federal and state taxes for unemployment insurance, based on each employer's experience rating, or percentage of employees a company has laid off in the past.
- State laws require that employers purchase workers' compensation insurance.
- Under the Family and Medical Leave Act, employees who need to care for a baby following birth or adoption or for an ill family member must be granted unpaid leave of up to 12 weeks.
- Under the Patient Protection and Affordable Care Act, organizations with 50 or more employees must choose between providing employees with health insurance or paying an Employer Shared Responsibility Payment.

LO 14-3 Describe the most common forms of paid leave.

- The major categories of paid leave are vacations, holidays, and sick leave.

- At large U.S. companies, paid vacation is typically 10 days—much less than is common in Western Europe.
- The typical number of paid holidays is 10 in both Western Europe and the United States.
- Sick leave programs often provide full salary replacement for a limited period of time, with the amount of sick leave usually based on length of service. Policies are needed to determine how the organization will handle unused sick days at the end of each year. Some organizations let employees roll over some or all of the unused sick days into the next year, and others let unused days expire at the end of the year.
- Other forms of paid leave include personal days and floating holidays.

LO 14-4 Identify the kinds of insurance benefits offered by employers.

- Medical insurance is one of the most valued employee benefits. Such policies typically cover hospital expenses, surgical expenses, and visits to physicians. Some employers offer additional coverage, such as dental care, vision care, birthing centers, and prescription drug programs.
- Under the Consolidated Omnibus Budget Reconciliation Act of 1985, employees must be permitted to extend their health insurance coverage at group rates for up to 36 months after they leave the organization.
- To manage the costs of health insurance, many organizations offer coverage through a health maintenance organization or preferred provider organization, or they may offer flexible spending accounts. Some encourage healthy behaviors through an employee wellness program.
- Life insurance usually takes the form of group term life insurance, with the usual benefit being two times the employee's yearly pay.
- Employers may also offer short-term and/or long-term disability insurance, with disability payments being a percentage of the employee's salary.

- Some employers provide long-term care insurance to pay the costs associated with long-term care such as nursing home care.

LO 14-5 Define the types of retirement plans offered by employers.

- Retirement plans may be contributory, meaning funded by contributions from employer and employee, or noncontributory, meaning funded only by the employer.
- These plans may be defined-benefit plans or defined-contribution plans.
- Defined-benefit plans guarantee a specified level of retirement income, usually based on the employee's years of service, age, and earnings level. Benefits under these plans are protected by the Pension Benefit Guarantee Corporation.
- In a defined-contribution plan, such as a 401(k) plan, the employer sets up an individual account for each employee and guarantees the size of the investment into that account, rather than the amount to be paid out on retirement. Because employees have control over investment decisions, the organization may also offer financial planning services as an employee benefit.
- A cash balance plan combines some advantages of defined-benefit plans and defined-contribution plans. The employer sets up individual accounts and contributes a percentage of each employee's salary. The account earns interest at a predetermined rate, so the contributions and benefits are easier to predict.

LO 14-6 Describe how organizations use other benefits to match employees' wants and needs.

- Employers have responded to work-family role conflicts by offering family-friendly benefits, including paid family leave, child care services or referrals, college savings plans, and elder care information and support.
- Other employee benefits have traditionally included subsidized cafeterias, on-site health clinics, and reimbursement of moving expenses.
- Stores and manufacturers may offer discounts on their products.
- Tuition reimbursement encourages employees to continue learning.
- Recreational services and employee outings provide social interaction as well as stress relief.

LO 14-7 Explain how to choose the contents of an employee benefits package.

- A logical place to begin is to establish organizational objectives and select benefits that support those objectives.

- Organizations should also consider employees' expectations and values. At a minimum, organizations offer the benefits employees have come to view as basic; some organizations go so far as to match extra benefits to individual employees' needs and interests.
- Cafeteria-style plans are an intermediate step that gives employees control over the benefits they receive.
- Employers must also weigh the costs of benefits, which are significant.

LO 14-8 Summarize the regulations affecting how employers design and administer benefits programs.

- Employers must provide the benefits that are required by law, and they may not improperly classify employees as "independent contractors" to avoid paying benefits.
- Tax treatment of qualified plans is favorable, so organizations need to learn the requirements for setting up benefits as qualified plans—for example, ensuring that pension plans do not discriminate in favor of the organization's highly compensated employees.
- Employers may not use employees' gender as the basis for discriminating against anyone, as in pension benefits on the basis that women as a group may live longer. Nor may employers discriminate against workers over age 40 in providing pay or benefits, such as pressuring older workers to retire by limiting retirement benefits.
- When employers offer early retirement, they must meet the requirements of the Older Workers Benefit Protection Act of 1990.
- Under the Americans with Disabilities Act, employers must give disabled employees equal access to health insurance.
- To meet the requirements of the Financial Accounting Standards Board, employers must set aside the funds they expect to need for retirement benefits ahead of time, rather than funding the benefits on a pay-as-you-go basis.

LO 14-9 Discuss the importance of effectively communicating the nature and value of benefits to employees.

- Communicating information about benefits is important so that employees will appreciate the value of their benefits.
- Communicating their value is the main way benefits attract, motivate, and retain employees.
- Employers have many options for communicating information about benefits, such as brochures, meetings, intranets, memos, and e-mail. Using a combination of such methods increases employees' understanding.

KEY TERMS

employee benefits, 424
Social Security, 426
unemployment insurance, 427
experience rating, 428
workers' compensation, 428
Family and Medical Leave Act (FMLA), 429
Patient Protection and Affordable Care Act, 429
Consolidated Omnibus Budget Reconciliation Act (COBRA), 434

health maintenance organization (HMO), 435
preferred provider organization (PPO), 435
flexible spending account, 435
employee wellness program (EWP), 436
short-term disability insurance, 436
long-term disability insurance, 436
contributory plan, 437
noncontributory plan, 437

defined-benefit plan, 438
Employee Retirement Income Security Act (ERISA), 438
Pension Benefit Guarantee Corporation (PBGC), 438
defined-contribution plan, 438
cash balance plan, 440
vesting rights, 441
summary plan description (SPD), 442
cafeteria-style plan, 446

REVIEW AND DISCUSSION QUESTIONS

1. Why do employers provide employee benefits, rather than providing all compensation in the form of pay and letting employees buy the services they want? *(LO 14-1)*
2. Of the benefits discussed in this chapter, list the ones you consider essential—that is, the benefits you would require in any job offer. Why are these benefits important to you? *(LO 14-1)*
3. Define the types of benefits required by law. How can organizations minimize the cost of these benefits while complying with the relevant laws? *(LO 14-2)*
4. What are some advantages of offering a generous package of insurance benefits? What are some drawbacks of generous insurance benefits? *(LO 14-3)*
5. Imagine that you are the human resource manager of a small architectural firm. You learn that the monthly premiums for the company's existing health insurance policy will rise by 15% next year. What can you suggest to help your company manage this rising cost? *(LO 14-4)*
6. In principle, health insurance would be most attractive to employees with large medical expenses, and

retirement benefits would be most attractive to older employees. What else might a company include in its benefits package to appeal to young, healthy employees? How might the company structure its benefits so these employees can take advantage of the benefits they care about most? *(LO 14-6)*
7. What issues should an organization consider in selecting a package of employee benefits? How should an employer manage the trade-offs among these considerations? *(LO 14-7)*
8. How do tax laws and accounting regulations affect benefits packages? *(LO 14-8)*
9. What legal requirements might apply to a family leave policy? Suggest how this type of policy should be set up to meet those requirements. *(LO 14-8)*
10. Why is it important to communicate information about employee benefits? Suppose you work in the HR department of a company that has decided to add new benefits—dental and vision insurance plus an additional two days of paid time off for "personal days." How would you recommend communicating this change? What information should your messages include? *(LO 14-9)*

TAKING RESPONSIBILITY

The Starbucks Way to Get an Education

Starbucks recently made headlines by announcing a program for helping employees earn college degrees. Starbucks employees who work at least 20 hours a week and enroll in Arizona State University's online bachelor's degree program are eligible for partial tuition reimbursements during their freshman and sophomore years.

During their junior and senior years, Starbucks will pay full tuition. Employees can choose from among ASU's degree programs; courses need not be job related, and employees need not stay at the company after graduating.

This employee benefit may be costly. Tuition for ASU's online program can run from $3,000 to $10,000.

Starbucks estimates that of its 135,000 part-time and full-time employees in the United States, about 70% are enrolled in college or want to pursue a degree. (Another one-fourth already have a degree.) Before the announcement, Starbucks had offered eligible employees about $1,000 a year in tuition assistance.

Starbucks believes the expense is worthwhile because this benefit supports a strategy of employee retention. The greater value of the benefit in the third and fourth years of school entices employees to stay, and the company hopes that even graduates who move to jobs elsewhere will promote Starbucks as a great place to work. The benefit differentiates Starbucks from its competitors. In a recent survey by the Society of Human Resource Management, just 54% of employers offer undergraduate tuition assistance. Furthermore, many of those programs require that employees take job-related courses. Retaining good employees is practical, potentially saving more than Starbucks spends on tuition reimbursement, but it may also reflect a sense of social responsibility. CEO Howard Schultz has expressed concern about "the fracturing of the American dream" and positioned tuition reimbursement as a way of taking action.

Reactions to the program included praise for a benefit that is both important and flexible in that employees can fit online courses around their work schedules. Some note that completion rates for online courses are not very high, but Starbucks's arrangement with ASU includes access to coaches, academic advisers, and financial-aid counselors. One downside is that ASU's online tuition is high relative to national averages for in-state college tuition. Employees, at least in the first two years, might be better off skipping this benefit and attending a community college.

Tuition reimbursement is just one component of Starbucks' benefits package designed to build employee loyalty. After three months, employees become eligible to enroll in health insurance, dental and vision plans, and a 401(k) retirement plan. Hourly workers start earning paid vacation after a year of continuous employment. More unusual benefits include free beverages during breaks, a pound of coffee beans (or the equivalent in other beverages) to take home each week, and annual stock options.

Questions

1. Discuss how well you think Starbucks's tuition reimbursement program meets the criteria for selecting employee benefits (organizational objectives, employees' expectations and values, and benefit costs).
2. If you had been advising Starbucks, would you have recommended that it introduce the tuition reimbursement plan or instead use the same budget to raise hourly workers' wages? Why?

Sources: Starbucks, "Working at Starbucks," http://www.starbucks.com, accessed July 11, 2014; Julie Jargon and Douglas Belkin, "Starbucks to Subsidize Workers' College Degrees," *The Wall Street Journal*, June 16, 2014, http://online.wsj.com; Victor Luckerson, "These Are All the Awesome Benefits Starbucks Baristas Get," *Time*, June 16, 2014, http://time.com; Ángel González, "Starbucks Will Pay Tuition for Many Employees to Finish College," *Seattle Times*, June 15, 2014 (modified June 19, 2014), http://seattletimes.com; Jena McGregor, "What Makes the Starbucks Tuition Perk Unusual among Companies," *Washington Post*, June 16, 2014, http://www.washingtonpost.com; Richard Feloni, "How the Starbucks Free College Plan Could Save It Millions of Dollars per Year," *Business Insider*, June 16, 2014, http://www.businessinsider.com; Quentin Fottrell, "The Venti Problem with Starbucks's Education Plan," *MarketWatch*, June 16, 2014, http://www.marketwatch.com.

MANAGING TALENT

Sodexo's Stumble on Benefits for Workers at Colleges

Sodexo USA provides food, health, and other services to client organizations. A school or hospital's cashiers and cafeteria workers may work for Sodexo under a contract with the institution. Sodexo needs dedicated workers but has to keep an eye on costs so it can win business from organizations watching their own bottom lines.

Cost is therefore among Sodexo's considerations in complying with the Patient Protection and Affordable Care Act (ACA). Sodexo must determine which workers are considered full-time, because full-time workers must receive health insurance benefits if the employer wants to avoid paying a fine. The ACA definition of "full-time" means the employee works on average at least 30 hours a week; the employer has some latitude in deciding the period over which it calculates the average.

In the past, Sodexo considered an employee full-time if he or she worked at least 30 hours a week for six or more weeks out of a quarter (12 weeks). In 2013, the company announced it would begin determining full-time status by averaging employees' hours over a one-year period.

Some employees who met the quarterly requirement no longer qualified as full-time and lost their eligibility for health insurance and other benefits available to full-time workers, such as disability insurance and paid vacation and sick time. Employees in schools were hit particularly hard. Some worked full-time or more during the academic year but little during the summer. The ACA requires that employers count only the academic year in figuring the full-time status of teachers, but the rule does not mention contract workers. According to

Sodexo, about 4,000 employees who had company-provided insurance lost it under the new formula.

Julie Peterson, Sodexo's vice president of compensation and benefits, explained that in planning its benefits package, Sodexo must balance "the most economically feasible model" against concern for employees' needs. She pointed out that part-time employees could "get access to benefits on the public [health insurance] exchanges in ways they couldn't have before." Peterson also noted that because the ACA requires individuals to have insurance, more employees were signing up for Sodexo's health insurance options, driving up total benefits costs.

Despite these explanations, Sodexo's decision caused a backlash. Backed by the Unite Here union, Sodexo workers launched protests and generated negative publicity. One school, Earlham College, insisted that its contract with Sodexo specify its workers be considered full-time. Peterson later announced that in a regular review, Sodexo had decided to revise its policy again. For school workers, its formula will use workers' average hours during the academic year as their hours for the summer months. Most workers who had lost benefits coverage would regain it. Peterson said Sodexo could make the change and "remain competitive in the market."

Questions

1. Which method of calculating full-time status do you think best supports Sodexo's strategy? Why?
2. What else could Sodexo do to promote employee satisfaction while managing benefits costs?

Sources: Sodexo, careers page, http://sodexousa.com, accessed July 14, 2014; Ricardo Alonso-Zaldivar, "Sodexo Cafeteria Workers Regain Health Coverage," *Associated Press*, June 26, 2014, http://bigstory.ap.org; Unite Here, "Sodexo Workers Demand Closure of Obamacare Loophole," June 12, 2014, http://unitehere.org; Lauren Weber, "Odd-Hour Workers Face Loss of Employer Health Plans," *The Wall Street Journal*, April 13, 2014, http://online.wsj.com.

HR IN SMALL BUSINESS

Babies Welcomed at T3

T3 is an independent advertising agency launched by Gay Warren Gaddis in Austin, Texas, in 1989. It has grown rapidly, thanks to Gaddis's ability to stay in front of tumultuous change in the advertising and marketing industry. Traditional agencies have approached their work by thinking about ads to be placed on the air or in newspapers and magazines. In contrast, Gaddis and her staff have specialized in developing integrated campaigns that harness all the ways to communicate about a brand, including communication via the Internet.

Innovation continues to be a company value. The company's careers web page says T3 looks for "Great thinkers. Individuals with curious, open minds. Relentless problem-solvers constantly looking for new, often uncon-ventional, solutions." The company is structured without the boundaries that have traditionally separated functions in the advertising world, so that employees can bring their perspectives together to solve client problems.

That innovative spirit hasn't been limited to advertising. Gaddis also thinks creatively about managing her firm's human resources. Six years after starting T3, Gaddis observed that four of her key employees were all pregnant at about the same time. If they all proceeded in the traditional way, taking a few months' leave, Gaddis would be scrambling to keep her agency running without them. So Gaddis decided to try something unusual: she told the four employees they were welcome to bring their babies to work. While some big companies establish on-site day care, Gaddis simply counted on the employees to work flexibly in the presence of their children.

Many people would assume that babies at work would create a distracting environment, but in fact, the new program was a success. T3 kept the policy in place and even gave it a name: T3 and Under. So far, 80 babies have come to work at one point or another. Gaddis says parents are so appreciative that they try extra hard to make the arrangement work. One such parent, Emily Dalton, feels reassured by being able to just swivel her chair when she wants to check on her baby: "You're not worrying," she told a newspaper reporter, "You're being spit up on, but you're not . . . calling somewhere to check on your child." She admits that she has to be extra flexible when her baby, Annie, is awake but adds, "I powerhouse when she sleeps." When the babies reach nine months or start to crawl, the parents are expected to make arrangements for day care.

Bringing babies to work is, of course, only one employee benefit. T3, which now has offices in New York and San Francisco as well as the one in Austin, offers medical, dental, and vision insurance; various life insurance policies; disability insurance; a 401(k) plan; paid time for vacations, holidays, and sick leave; and discounts on gym memberships and cell phone plans. There are also some other unusual benefits: breakfast on Mondays, candy on Fridays, a book club, and a "bring your dog to work" policy. As for this last policy, the T3 website comments, "While we don't have hard metrics on what [dogs] do for our creativity or productivity, we do believe they play a part in adding balance to what can be a very unbalanced business."

Advertising may be an "unbalanced" business, but so far, T3 seems to be coping well enough. And T3's fearless leader, Gay Warren Gaddis, was recently named Ernst and Young's Entrepreneur of the Year for central Texas.

Questions

1. Of the employee benefits mentioned in this case, which of them do you think are important for keeping a creative workforce engaged at T3?
2. What are some of the advantages of the agency's T3 and Under policy? What are some of the risks? How can the company address those risks?
3. At what other kinds of companies, if any, do you think a "bring your baby to work" policy might be effective as an employee benefit? Why?

Sources: Josh Spiro, "Where Every Day Is Take Your Baby to Work Day," *Inc.*, December 9, 2009, www.inc.com; Eric Aasen, "Babies-at-Work Programs Let New Parents Stay Close to Their Kids," *Dallas Morning News*, March 26, 2008, Business & Company Resource Center, http://galenet.galegroup.com; T3, "Careers" and "Company," corporate website, www.t-3.com, accessed July 21, 2014.

NOTES

1. Angus Loten and Sarah E. Needleman, "Laws on Paid Sick Leave Divide Businesses," *The Wall Street Journal*, February 5, 2014, http://online.wsj.com.
2. B. Gerhart and G. T. Milkovich, "Employee Compensation: Research and Practice," in *Handbook of Industrial and Organizational Psychology*, 2nd ed., eds. M. D. Dunnette and L. M. Hough (Palo Alto, CA: Consulting Psychologists Press, 1992), vol. 3; J. Swist, "Benefits Communications: Measuring Impact and Values," *Employee Benefit Plan Review*, September 2002, pp. 24–26.
3. Erik Sherman, "Four Perks Employees Love," *Inc.*, April 11, 2012, http://www.inc.com; Robert J. Grossman, "Tough Love at Netflix," *HR Magazine*, April 2010, http://www.shrm.org.
4. U.S. Department of Labor, Employment and Training Administration, "Comparison of State Unemployment Laws," chapter 2, http://workforcesecurity.doleta.gov, last updated June 23, 2014.
5. Julie M. Whittaker, "Expediting the Return to Work: Approaches in the Unemployment Compensation Program," Congressional Research Service Report for Congress, May 1, 2013, http://www.crs.gov.
6. J. V. Nackley, *Primer on Workers' Compensation* (Washington, DC: Bureau of National Affairs, 1989); T. Thomason, T. P. Schmidle, and J. F. Burton, *Workers' Compensation* (Kalamazoo, MI: Upjohn Institute, 2001).
7. B. T. Beam Jr. and J. J. McFadden, *Employee Benefits*, 6th ed. (Chicago: Dearborn Financial Publishing, 2000).
8. AAUW, "The Family and Medical Leave Act: Facts and Statistics," http://www.aauw.org, accessed April 27, 2012.
9. Scott M. Wich, "With FMLA Leave Claims, Attention to Detail—Not Timing—Counts," *HR Magazine*, February 2012, p. 77.
10. A. Pawlowski, "Why Is America the 'No-Vacation Nation'?" *CNNTravel*, May 23, 2011, http://articles.cnn.com.
11. "Survey: Formal Paid Time-Off Programs Gaining Steam," *Talent Management*, July 6, 2011, http://talentmgt.com.
12. Employee Benefit Research Institute, "The Most Valued Benefit Is . . . ," *Fast Facts* no. 256, November 21, 2013, http://www.ebri.org.
13. U.S. Government Accountability Office, "Mental Health and Substance Abuse: Employers' Insurance Coverage Maintained or Enhanced Since Parity Act," *Medical Benefits*, January 15, 2012, pp. 6, 8; National Conference of State Legislatures, "State Laws Mandating or Regulating Mental Health Benefits," Issues and Research: Health, updated December 2011, http://www.ncsl.org.
14. Reed Abelson, "Health Insurance Costs Rising Sharply This Year, Study Shows," *The New York Times*, September 27, 2011, http://www.nytimes.com; Deborah Brunswick, "Health Insurance Costs to Rise Again Next Year," *CNNMoney*, September 22, 2011, http://money.cnn.com.
15. Kaiser Family Foundation and Health Research and Educational Trust, "Summary of Findings," *2013 Employer Health Benefits Survey*, August 20, 2013, accessed at http://kff.org.
16. Paul Fronstin, "Characteristics of the Population with Consumer-Driven and High-Deductible Health Plans, 2005–2011," *Notes* (Employee Benefit Research Institute), April 2012, pp. 2–9.
17. J. C. Erfurt, A. Foote, and M. A. Heirich, "The Cost-Effectiveness of Worksite Wellness Programs for Hypertension Control, Weight Loss, Smoking Cessation and Exercise," *Personnel Psychology* 45 (1992), pp. 5–27.
18. Bureau of Labor Statistics, "Employee Benefits in the United States, March 2013," news release, July 17, 2013, http://www.bls.gov.
19. Pension Benefit Guaranty Corporation, "Pension Insurance Premiums Fact Sheet," Resources: Fact Sheets, http://www.pbgc.gov, accessed April 26, 2012.
20. Stephen Miller, "For 2014, IRS Issues 401(k) and Pension Plan Limits," HR Topics and Strategy: Benefits, November 1, 2013, http://www.shrm.org.
21. Employee Benefit Research Institute, "Retirement Plan Participation: Survey of Income and Program Participation (SIPP) Data, 2012," *EBRI Notes*, August 2013, pp. 2–13; Employee Benefit Research Institute, "FAQs about Benefits: Retirement Issues," http://www.ebri.org, accessed July 11, 2014.

22. BNA, "Employers Offer Too Much Information, Too Little Guidance about 401(k) Options," *Managing 401(k) Plans*, December 2011, pp. 1–4; Janet Levaux, "Target-Date Funds Dominate 401(k) Plans," *Research*, April 25, 2012, http://www.advisorone.com; Plan Sponsor Council of America, "PSCA's 55th Annual Survey," http://www.psca.org, accessed July 15, 2014.

23. "Supreme Court Lets Stand Third Circuit Ruling That Pension Avoidance Scheme Is ERISA Violation," *Daily Labor Report*, no. 234 (December 8, 1987), p. A-14, summarizing *Continental Can Company v. Gavalik*.

24. Beam and McFadden, *Employee Benefits*.

25. S. L. Grover and K. J. Crooker, "Who Appreciates Family Responsive Human Resource Policies: The Impact of Family-Friendly Policies on the Organizational Attachment of Parents and Non-parents," *Personnel Psychology* 48 (1995), pp. 271–88; M. A. Arthur, "Share Price Reactions to Work-Family Initiatives: An Institutional Perspective," *Academy of Management Journal* 46 (2003), p. 497; J. E. Perry-Smith and T. Blum, "Work-Family Human Resource Bundles and Perceived Organizational Performance," *Academy of Management Journal* 43 (2000), pp. 1107–17.

26. Kasia Klimasinska and Sandrine Rastello, "Moms in 'Survival Mode' as U.S. Trails World on Benefits," *Bloomberg News*, January 15, 2014, http://www.bloomberg.com; Lauren Weber, "Why Dads Don't Take Paternity Leave," *The Wall Street Journal*, June 12, 2013, http://online.wsj.com.

27. E. E. Kossek, "Diversity in Child Care Assistance Needs: Employee Problems, Preferences, and Work-Related Outcomes," *Personnel Psychology* 43 (1990), pp. 769–91.

28. Kenneth Matos and Ellen Galinsky, "2014 National Study of Employers," Families and Work Institute, 2014, http://www.familiesandwork.org.

29. Johns Hopkins Medicine, "Employee Benefits: Tuition Reimbursement/College Savings Plan," Bayview Jobs, http://www.bayviewjobs.org, accessed April 27, 2012.

30. National Alliance for Caregiving, *Best Practices in Workplace Eldercare*, March 2012, http://www.caregiving.org.

31. Colleen Kane, "Outrageous Workplace Perks," CNBC.com, August 4, 2011, http://www.cnbc.com; Sherman, "Four Perks Employees Love."

32. R. Broderick and B. Gerhart, "Nonwage Compensation," in *The Human Resource Management Handbook*, eds. D. Lewin, D. J. B. Mitchell, and M. A. Zadi (San Francisco: JAI Press, 1996).

33. Lauren Weber, "Benefits Matter," *The Wall Street Journal*, April 3, 2012, http://online.wsj.com.

34. Tynan Barton, "Sociable Network," *Employee Benefits*, September 2011, pp. 50–53.

35. "SHRM Report Says Economy Forced Benefit Cuts."

36. Beam and McFadden, *Employee Benefits*.

37. D. A. Harrison and L. Z. Liska, "Promoting Regular Exercise in Organizational Fitness Programs: Health-Related Differences in Motivational Building Blocks," *Personnel Psychology* 47 (1994), pp. 47–71; Erfurt et al., "The Cost-Effectiveness of Worksite Wellness Programs."

38. Beam and McFadden, *Employee Benefits*, p. 359.

39. For a description of these rules, see M. M. Sarli, "Nondiscrimination Rules for Qualified Plans: The General Test," *Compensation and Benefits Review* 23, no. 5 (September–October 1991), pp. 56–67.

40. *Los Angeles Department of Water & Power v. Manhart*, 435 U.S. S. Ct. 702 (1978), 16 E.P.D. 8250.

41. S. K. Hoffman, "Discrimination Litigation Relating to Employee Benefits," *Labor Law Journal*, June 1992, pp. 362–81.

42. Ibid., p. 375.

43. M. Wilson, G. B. Northcraft, and M. A. Neale, "The Perceived Value of Fringe Benefits," *Personnel Psychology* 38 (1985), pp. 309–20; H. W. Hennessey, P. L. Perrewe, and W. A. Hochwarter, "Impact of Benefit Awareness on Employee and Organizational Outcomes: A Longitudinal Field Experiment," *Benefits Quarterly* 8, no. 2 (1992), pp. 90–96; MetLife, *Employee Benefits Benchmarking Report*, www.metlife.com, accessed June 24, 2007.

44. M. C. Giallourakis and G. S. Taylor, "An Evaluation of Benefit Communication Strategy," *Employee Benefits Journal* 15, no. 4 (1991), pp. 14–18; Employee Benefit Research Institute, "How Readable Are Summary Plan Descriptions for Health Care Plans?" *EBRI Notes*, October 2006, www.ebri.org.

Meeting Other HR Goals

PART FIVE

15

Collective Bargaining and Labor Relations

What Do I Need to Know?

After reading this chapter, you should be able to:

LO 15-1 Define unions and labor relations and their role in organizations.

LO 15-2 Identify the labor relations goals of management, labor unions, and society.

LO 15-3 Summarize laws and regulations that affect labor relations.

LO 15-4 Describe the union organizing process.

LO 15-5 Explain how management and unions negotiate contracts.

LO 15-6 Summarize the practice of contract administration.

LO 15-7 Describe new approaches to labor-management relations.

Introduction

Recently, the football players at Northwestern University participated in a different kind of contest: one between their school and the College Athletes Players Association, which has financial backing from the United Steelworkers union. Some of the players had insisted that because the school granted them scholarships, it was in effect paying them for training and playing on Northwestern's football team. As employees, they said, they wanted the right to form a union. The school disputed the argument, but the National Labor Relations Board (NLRB) ruled that 76 football players did have the status of employees and could proceed with a vote on whether to form a union.

Northwestern continued to insist that the players were students first, not primarily employees, but it had to allow the election to go forward. In the days leading up to the vote, the administration continued to discourage the idea of forming a players' union. Northwestern gave all the players new iPads, and a coach told them that a union would interfere with relationships between players and their coaches. School officials also e-mailed players' parents, encouraging them to speak to their sons about the disadvantages of a union. Meanwhile, the players who wanted a union talked about how it could protect them from the consequences of being injured during games. These players wanted more power in obtaining coverage of sports-related medical bills, stricter rules to protect them from brain injuries, and a requirement that scholarships continue after players were injured on the field. The players voted for or against the union, but the election results were then sealed while the NLRB reviewed the university's request to overturn the decision.[1]

As in the case of the football players at Northwestern University, concerns about financial security and physical safety are common reasons for trying to form a union. When workers succeed and unions become a presence in an organization, human resource management must direct more attention to the interests of employees as a group. In general, employees and employers share the same interests. They both benefit when the organization is strong and growing, providing employees with jobs and employers with profits. But although the interests of employers and employees overlap, they obviously are not identical. In the case of pay, workers benefit from higher pay, but high pay cuts into the organization's profits, unless pay increases are associated with higher productivity or better customer service. Workers may negotiate differences with their employers individually, or they may form unions to negotiate on their behalf. This chapter explores human resource activities in organizations where employees belong to unions or where employees are seeking to organize unions.

We begin by formally defining unions and labor relations, and then describe the scope and impact of union activity. We next summarize government laws and regulations affecting unions and labor relations. The following three sections detail types of activities involving unions: union organizing, contract negotiation, and contract administration. Finally, we identify ways in which unions and management are working together in arrangements that are more cooperative than the traditional labor-management relationship.

Role of Unions and Labor Relations

In the United States today, most workers act as individuals to select jobs that are acceptable to them and to negotiate pay, benefits, flexible hours, and other work conditions. Especially when there is stiff competition for labor and employees have hard-to-replace skills, this arrangement produces satisfactory results for most employees. At times, however, workers have believed their needs and interests do not receive enough consideration from management. One response by workers is to act collectively by forming and joining labor **unions,** organizations formed for the purpose of representing their members' interests and resolving conflicts with employers.

Unions have a role because some degree of conflict is inevitable between workers and management.[2] As we commented earlier, for example, managers can increase profits by lowering workers' pay, but workers benefit in the short term if lower profits result because their pay is higher. Still, this type of conflict is more complex than a simple trade-off, such as wages versus profits. Rising profits can help employees by driving up profit sharing or other benefits, and falling profits can result in layoffs and a lack of investment. Although employers can use programs like profit sharing to help align employee interests with their own, some remaining divergence of interests is inevitable. Labor unions represent worker interests and the collective bargaining process provides a way to manage the conflict. In other words, through systems for hearing complaints and negotiating labor contracts, unions and managers resolve conflicts between employers and employees.

As unionization of workers became more common, universities developed training in how to manage union-management interactions. This specialty, called **labor relations,** emphasizes skills that managers and union leaders can use to foster effective labor-management cooperation, minimize costly forms of conflict (such as strikes), and seek win-win solutions to disagreements. Labor relations involves three levels of decisions[3]:

LO 15-1 Define unions and labor relations and their role in organizations.

Unions
Organizations formed for the purpose of representing their members' interests in dealing with employers.

Labor Relations
Field that emphasizes skills that managers and union leaders can use to minimize costly forms of conflict (such as strikes) and seek win-win solutions to disagreements.

The largest union in the United States is the National Education Association with 3 million members.

1. *Labor relations strategy*—For management, the decision involves whether the organization will work with unions or develop (or maintain) nonunion operations. This decision is influenced by outside forces such as public opinion and competition. For unions, the decision involves whether to fight changes in how unions relate to the organization or accept new kinds of labor-management relationships.

2. *Negotiating contracts*—As we will describe later in the chapter, contract negotiations in a union setting involve decisions about pay structure, job security, work rules, workplace safety, and many other issues. These decisions affect workers' and the employer's situation for the term of the contract.

3. *Administering contracts*—These decisions involve day-to-day activities in which union members and the organization's managers may have disagreements. Issues include complaints of work rules being violated or workers being treated unfairly in particular situations. A formal grievance procedure is typically used to resolve these issues.

Later sections in this chapter describe how managers and unions carry out the activities connected with these levels of decisions, as well as the goals and legal constraints affecting these activities.

National and International Unions

Most union members belong to a national or international union. In the United States, the largest unions are the National Education Association and the Service Employees International Union, each with several million members. Globally, even the largest U.S. unions are dwarfed by the All-China Federation of Trade Unions, a state-controlled union with more than 200 million members.[4]

Craft Union
Labor union whose members all have a particular skill or occupation.

Labor unions may be either craft or industrial unions. The members of a **craft union** all have a particular skill or occupation. Examples include the International Brotherhood of Electrical Workers for electricians and the National Education Association for teachers. Craft unions are often responsible for training their members through apprenticeships and for supplying craft workers to employers. For example, an employer would send requests for carpenters to the union hiring hall, which would decide which carpenters to send out. In this way, craft workers may work for many employers over time but have a constant link to the union. A craft union's bargaining power depends greatly on its control over the supply of its workers.

Industrial Union
Labor union whose members are linked by their work in a particular industry.

In contrast, **industrial unions** consist of members who are linked by their work in a particular industry. Examples include the Communication Workers of America and the American Federation of State, County, and Municipal Employees. Typically, an industrial union represents many different occupations. Membership in the union is the result of working for a particular employer in the industry. Changing employers is less common than it is among craft workers, and employees who change employers remain members of the same union only if they happen to move to other employers covered by that union. Another difference is that whereas a craft union may restrict the number of skilled craftsmen—say, carpenters—to maintain higher wages, industrial unions try to organize as many employees in as wide a range of skills as possible.

Most national unions in the United States are affiliated with the **American Federation of Labor and Congress of Industrial Organizations (AFL-CIO).** The AFL-CIO is not a labor union but an association that seeks to advance the shared interests of its member unions at the national level, much as the Chamber of Commerce and the National Association of Manufacturers do for their member employers. Approximately 55 national and international unions are affiliated with the AFL-CIO. An important responsibility of the AFL-CIO is to represent labor's interests in public policy issues, such as labor law, economic policy, and occupational safety and health. The organization also provides information and analysis that member unions can use in their activities. In 2005, several unions broke away from the AFL-CIO to form an alliance called Change to Win, which is focused on innovative organizing campaigns. This group includes four unions representing a membership of more than 5 million workers.

American Federation of Labor and Congress of Industrial Organizations (AFL-CIO)
An association that seeks to advance the shared interests of its member unions at the national level.

Local Unions

Most national unions consist of multiple local units. Even when a national union plays the most critical role in negotiating the terms of a collective bargaining contract, negotiation occurs at the local level for work rules and other issues that are locally determined. In addition, administration of the contract largely takes place at the local union level. As a result, most day-to-day interaction between labor and management involves the local union.

Membership in the local union depends on the type of union. For an industrial union, the local may correspond to a single large facility or to a number of small facilities. In a craft union, the local may cover a city or a region.

Typically, the local union elects officers, such as president, vice president, and treasurer. The officers may be responsible for contract negotiation, or the local may form a bargaining committee for that purpose. When the union is engaged in bargaining, the national union provides help, including background data about other settlements, technical advice, and the leadership of a representative from the national office.

Individual members participate in local unions in various ways. At meetings of the local union, they elect officials and vote on resolutions to strike. Most of workers' contact is with the **union steward,** an employee elected by union members to represent them in ensuring that the terms of the contract are enforced. The union steward helps investigate complaints and represents employees to supervisors and other managers when employees file grievances alleging contract violations.[5] When the union deals with several employers, as in the case of a craft union, a *business representative* performs some of the same functions as a union steward. Because of union stewards' and business representatives' close involvement with employees, it is to management's advantage to cultivate positive working relationships with them.

Union Steward
An employee elected by union members to represent them in ensuring that the terms of the labor contract are enforced.

Trends in Union Membership

Union membership in the United States peaked in the 1950s, reaching over one-third of employees. Since then, the share of employees who belong to unions has fallen. It now stands at 11.3% overall and 6.7% of private-sector employment.[6] As Figure 15.1 indicates, union membership has fallen steadily since the 1980s. The decline has been driven by falling union membership in the private sector, while the share of government workers in unions has mostly held steady.

The decline in union membership has been attributed to several factors[7]:

- *Change in the structure of the economy*—Much recent job growth has occurred in the service sector of the economy, while union strength has traditionally been among

Figure 15.1

Union Membership Density among U.S. Wage and Salary Workers, 1973–2013

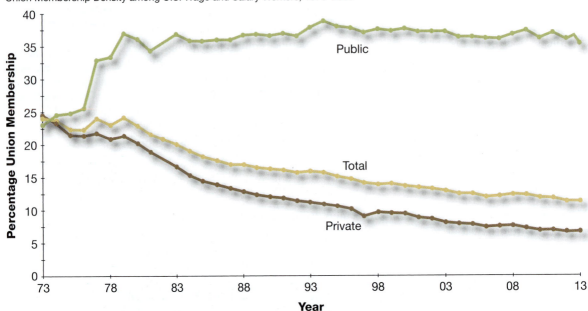

ª Percentage of total, private-sector, and public-sector wage and salary workers who are union members. Beginning in 1977, workers belonging to "an employee association similar to a union" are included as members.

Source: Data for 1973–2001 from B. T. Hirsch and D. A. MacPherson, *Union Membership and Earnings Data Book 2001* (Washington, DC: Bureau of National Affairs, 2002), using data from U.S. Current Population Surveys. Data for 2002 through 2013 from Bureau of Labor Statistics, "Union Affiliation Data from the Current Population Survey," http://data.bls.gov, accessed July 21, 2014.

urban blue-collar workers. Services industries such as finance, insurance, and real estate have lower union representation than manufacturing. Also, much business growth has been in the South, where workers are less likely to join unions.

- *Management efforts to control costs*—On average, unionized workers receive higher pay than their nonunionized counterparts, and the pressure is greater because of international competition. In the past, union membership across an industry such as automobiles or steel resulted in similar wages and work requirements for all competitors. Today, U.S. producers must compete with companies that have entirely different pay scales and work rules, often placing the U.S. companies at a disadvantage.
- *Human resource practices*—Competition for scarce human resources can lead employers to offer much of what employees traditionally sought through union membership.
- *Government regulation*—Stricter regulation in such areas as workplace safety and equal employment opportunity leaves fewer areas in which unions can show an advantage over what employers must already offer.

As Figure 15.2 indicates, the percentage of U.S. workers who belong to unions is lower than in many other countries. More dramatic is the difference in "coverage"—the percentage of employees whose terms and conditions of employment are governed by a union contract, whether or not the employees are technically union members. In Western Europe, it is common to have coverage rates of 80% to 90%, so the influence of labor unions far outstrips what membership levels would imply.[8] Also, employees in Western

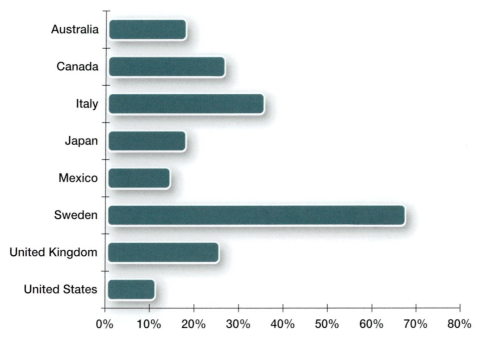

Figure 15.2
Union Membership
Rates in Selected
Countries

Note: Data for 2011.

Source: Organisation for Economic Co-operation and Development, StatExtracts, http://stats.oecd.org, accessed July 21, 2014.

Europe tend to have a larger formal role in decision making than in the United States. This role, including worker representatives on boards of directors, is often mandated by the government. But as markets become more and more global, pressure to cut labor costs and increase productivity is likely to be stronger in every country. Unless unions can help companies improve productivity or organize new production facilities opened in lower-wage countries, union influence may decline in countries where it is now strong.

Although union members are a smaller share of the U.S. workforce, they are a significant part of many industries' labor markets. Along with strength in numbers, large unions have strength in dollars. Union retirement funds, taken together, are huge. Unions try to use their investment decisions in ways that influence businesses. The "Did You Know?" box presents some statistics on union members.

Unions in Government

Unlike union membership for workers in businesses, union membership among government workers has remained strong. Union membership in the public sector grew during the 1960s and 1970s and has remained steady ever since. Over one-third of government employees are union members, and a larger share are covered by collective bargaining agreements. Among them are nurses, park rangers, school librarians, corrections officers, and many workers in clerical and other white-collar occupations. One reason for this strength is that government regulations and laws support the right of government workers to organize. In 1962 Executive Order 10988 established collective bargaining rights for federal employees. By the end of the 1960s, most states had passed similar laws.

Labor relations with government workers are different in some respects, such as regarding the right to strike. Strikes are illegal for federal workers and for state workers in most states. At the local level, all states prohibit strikes by police (Hawaii being

Did You Know?

Profile of a Typical Union Worker

In the United States today, a worker 55 or older is far more likely to be a union member than a young worker is. Men are slightly more likely to be union members than women. Workers in education and protective services jobs—that is, teachers, police officers, and firefighters—are most likely to be in a union. In contrast, only 2.9% of salespeople are members of unions.

Question

What trend shown in Figure 15.1 helps to explain why jobs in education and protective services have the highest rates of unionization?

Source: Bureau of Labor Statistics, "Union Members, 2013," news release, January 24, 2014, http://www.bls.gov.

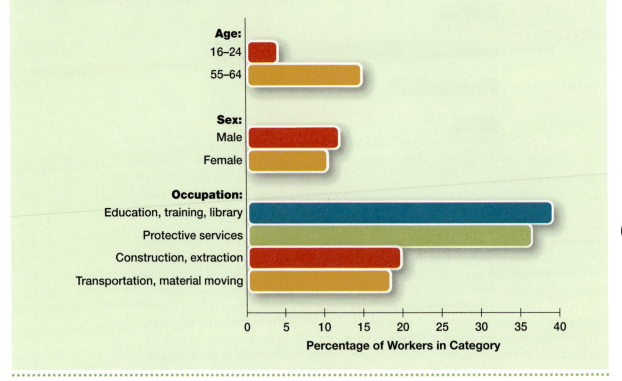

a partial exception) and firefighters (Idaho being the exception). Teachers and state employees are somewhat more likely to have the right to strike, depending on the state.

Impact of Unions on Company Performance

Organizations are concerned about whether union organizing and bargaining will hurt their performance, in particular, unions' impact on productivity, profits, and stock performance. Researchers have studied the general relationship between unionization and these performance measures. Through skillful labor relations, organizations can positively influence outcomes.

There has been much debate regarding the effects of unions on productivity.[9] One view is that unions decrease productivity because of work rules and limits on workloads set by union contracts and production lost to such union actions as strikes and work slowdowns. At the same time, unions can have positive effects on productivity.[10] They can reduce turnover by giving employees a route for resolving problems.[11] Unions emphasize pay systems based on seniority, which remove incentives for employees to compete rather than cooperate. The introduction of a union also may force an employer to improve its management practices and pay greater attention to employee ideas.

Although there is evidence that unions have both positive and negative effects on productivity, most studies have found that union workers are more productive than nonunion workers. Still, questions remain. Are highly productive workers more likely to form unions, or does a union make workers more productive? The answer is unclear. In theory, if unions caused greater productivity, we would expect union membership to be rising, not falling as it has been.[12]

Even if unions do raise productivity, a company's profits and stock performance may still suffer if unions raise wage and benefits costs by more than the productivity gain. On average, union members receive higher wages and more generous benefits than nonunion workers, and evidence shows that unions have a large negative effect on profits. Also, union coverage tends to decline faster in companies with a lower return to shareholders.[13] In summary, companies wishing to become more competitive must continually monitor their labor relations strategy.

Harley-Davidson and the International Association of Machinists and Aerospace Workers have cooperated to produce good results. In general, though, companies wishing to become more competitive need to continually monitor their labor relations strategies.

The studies tend to look at the average effects of unions, not at individual companies or innovative labor relations. Some organizations excel at labor relations, and some have worked with unions to meet business needs. For example, even when the economy has slowed in recent years, manufacturers have reported that it is difficult to find enough skilled labor. Many companies depend on unions to recruit and train new workers through apprenticeship programs. In Alaska, more than half of the registered apprenticeship programs are partnerships between employers and unions or employee associations. For example, construction businesses, unions, and government organizations banded together to form the Construction Education Foundation, which sponsors training programs that prepare workers to enter the construction industry.[14]

Goals of Management, Labor Unions, and Society

LO 15-2 Identify the labor relations goals of management, labor unions, and society.

Resolving conflicts in a positive way is usually easiest when the parties involved understand each other's goals. Although individual cases vary, we can draw some general conclusions about the goals of labor unions and management. Society, too, has goals for labor and business, given form in the laws regulating labor relations.

Management Goals

Management goals are to increase the organization's profits. Managers tend to prefer options that lower costs and raise output. When deciding whether to discourage employees from forming a union, a concern is that a union will create higher costs in wages and benefits, as well as raise the risk of work stoppages. Managers may also fear that a union will make managers and workers into adversaries or limit management's discretion in making business and employment decisions.

When an employer has recognized a union, management's goals continue to emphasize restraining costs and improving output. Managers continue to prefer to keep the organization's operations flexible, so they can adjust activities to meet competitive challenges and customer demands. Therefore, in their labor relations managers prefer to limit increases in wages and benefits and to retain as much control as they can over work rules and schedules.

Labor Union Goals

In general, labor unions have the goals of obtaining pay and working conditions that satisfy their members and of giving members a voice in decisions that affect them. Traditionally, they obtain these goals by gaining power in numbers. The more workers who belong to a union, the greater the union's power. More members translates into greater ability to halt or disrupt production. Larger unions also have greater financial resources for continuing a strike; the union can help to make up for the wages the workers lose during a strike. The threat of a long strike—stated or implied—can make an employer more willing to meet the union's demands.

As we noted earlier, union membership is indeed linked to better compensation. In 2013, private-sector unionized workers received, on average, wages 21% higher than nonunion workers.[15] Benefits packages also tend to be more generous for union members. However, union goals related to compensation have become more complex since globalization's downward pressure on wages. Especially in manufacturing, some unions have accepted two-tier wage systems in which existing workers' wage rates are protected while new workers are hired at a lower tier. The United Auto Workers' recently elected president, Dennis Williams, has said that one of his goals is to end the two-tier system, which causes some resentment among the newer, younger workers.[16]

As in the case of two-tier wage structures, unions typically want to influence the *way* pay and promotions are determined. Unlike management, which tries to consider employees as individuals so that pay and promotion decisions relate to performance differences, unions try to build group solidarity and avoid possible arbitrary treatment of employees. To do so, unions focus on equal pay for equal work. They try to have any pay differences based on seniority, on the grounds that this measure is more objective than performance evaluations. As a result, where workers are represented by a union, it is common for all employees in a particular job classification to be paid at the same rate.

Along with compensation, union members often are concerned about working conditions. For example, unsafe conditions are one motivation to form a union. Unions may conduct safety training for their members. They may partner with management to identify ways of getting work done more efficiently as well as more safely. For an example of this partnership approach, see the "Best Practices" box.

The survival and security of a union depend on its ability to ensure a regular flow of new members and member dues to support the services it provides. Therefore, unions typically place high priority on negotiating two types of contract provisions with an employer that are critical to a union's security and viability: checkoff provisions and provisions relating to union membership or contribution.

Under a **checkoff provision,** the employer, on behalf of the union, automatically deducts union dues from employees' paychecks. Security provisions related to union membership are *closed shop, union shop, agency shop,* and *maintenance of membership*.

The strongest union security arrangement is a **closed shop,** under which a person must be a union member before being hired. Under the National Labor Relations Act, discussed later in this chapter, closed shops are illegal. A legal membership arrangement that supports the goals of labor unions is the **union shop,** an arrangement that requires an employee to join the union within a certain time (30 days) after beginning employment. A similar alternative is the **agency shop,** which requires the payment of union dues but not union membership. **Maintenance of membership** rules do not require union member-

---

Checkoff Provision
Contract provision under which the employer, on behalf of the union, automatically deducts union dues from employees' paychecks.

Closed Shop
Union security arrangement under which a person must be a union member before being hired; illegal for those covered by the National Labor Relations Act.

Union Shop
Union security arrangement that requires employees to join the union within a certain amount of time (30 days) after beginning employment.

Agency Shop
Union security arrangement that requires the payment of union dues but not union membership.

Maintenance of Membership
Union security rules not requiring union membership but requiring that employees who join the union remain members for a certain period of time.

Best Practices

Machinists and Steelworkers Unions Help Harley-Davidson Get Lean

For years, Harley-Davidson got by without worrying too much about efficiency at its factory in York, Pennsylvania. High rates of absenteeism and a slow pace didn't matter much when customers were willing to wait months for their motorcycle and pay a premium for the brand. But when the Great Recession hit, sales slumped, and the company's stock price plunged from $75 to $8 per share. Management realized the company had to change, or it wouldn't survive.

Many businesses in this situation have closed their unionized factories and moved production overseas or to southern states where unions are unpopular. Harley's managers investigated new locations for a more efficient plant and selected Shelbyville, Kentucky. Then they notified the unions representing the workers in York—the International Association of Machinists and the United Steelworkers. Management explained that the plant would close unless the union workers would make concessions so the company would be more efficient. The workers voted to make the changes.

Harley tore down the old factory and built a more efficient one in York. The machinists' union agreed to layoffs of 1,000 plant workers and a pay freeze for several years to save the jobs of the remaining workers. The result was that when Harley opened its new factory, it had dedicated, experienced workers who skillfully work in teams of five or six to build each motorcycle. The union workers agreed to a more flexible arrangement, which replaced more than 60 job classifications with just five classifications involving broader responsibilities.

Furthermore, 150 workers are charged with monitoring an area of production with the aim of continuously improving quality and efficiency. For example, one such worker noticed that it took a few extra seconds to tap in a plastic piece that didn't fit exactly. Multiplied by all the motorcycles using that part, the extra time would cost millions of dollars in lost production. The worker identified an adjustment to the part's design that would eliminate the problem. He and others making improvements have helped to increase quality while bringing down costs at the York facility by $100 million.

Harley's production workers say they understand the need for a change. They have to work at a faster pace, but the jobs offer more variety. Some also see more respect between workers and management.

Questions

1. In this example, what were management's goals?
2. What were the union's goals?

Sources: Kenneth Quinnell, "How Union Members Saved Harley-Davidson," AFL-CIO blog, February 4, 2014, http://www.aflcio.org; Adam Davidson, "The Reward for Working with Unions," *The New York Times,* February 1, 2014, Business Insights: Global, http://bi.galegroup.com; Adam Davidson, "Building a Harley Faster," *The New York Times,* January 28, 2014, www.nytimes.com; Ginger Christ-Martin, "Driving a Future of Excellence," *Industry Week,* January 2014, pp. 17–18; James R. Hagerty, "Harley Goes Lean to Build Hogs," *The Wall Street Journal,* September 21, 2012, http://online.wsj.com.

ship but do require that employees who join the union remain members for a certain period of time, such as the length of the contract. As we will discuss later in the chapter, some states forbid union shops, agency shops, and maintenance of membership.

All these provisions are ways to address unions' concern about "free riders"—employees who benefit from union activities without belonging to a union. By law, all members of a bargaining unit, whether union members or not, must be represented by the union. If the union must offer services to all bargaining unit members but some of them are not dues-paying union members, the union may not have enough financial resources to operate successfully.

Societal Goals

The activities of unions and management take place within the context of society, with society's values driving the laws and regulations that affect labor relations. As long ago as the late 1800s and early 1900s, industrial relations scholars saw unions as a way to make up for individual employees' limited bargaining power.[17] At that time, clashes between workers and management could be violent, and many people hoped that unions would replace the violence with negotiation. Since then, observers have expressed concern that unions in certain industries have become too strong, achieving their goals at the expense of employers' ability to compete or meet other objectives. But even former Senator Orrin Hatch, described by *BusinessWeek* as "labor's archrival on Capitol Hill," has spoken of a need for unions:

> There are always going to be people who take advantage of workers. Unions even that out, to their credit. We need them to level the field between labor and management. If you didn't have unions, it would be very difficult for even enlightened employers not to take advantage of workers on wages and working conditions, because of [competition from less-enlightened] rivals. I'm among the first to say I believe in unions.[18]

Senator Hatch's statement implies that society's goal for unions is to ensure that workers have a voice in how they are treated by their employers. As we will see in the next section, this view has produced a set of laws and regulations intended to give workers the right to join unions if they so wish.

LO 15-3 Summarize laws and regulations that affect labor relations.

Laws and Regulations Affecting Labor Relations

The laws and regulations pertaining to labor relations affect unions' size and bargaining power, so they significantly affect the degree to which unions, management, and society achieve their varied goals. These laws and regulations set limits on union structure and administration and the ways in which unions and management interact.

National Labor Relations Act (NLRA)

National Labor Relations Act (NLRA)
Federal law that supports collective bargaining and sets out the rights of employees to form unions.

Perhaps the most dramatic example of labor laws' influence is the 1935 passage of the Wagner Act (also known as the **National Labor Relations Act,** or **NLRA**), which actively supported collective bargaining. After Congress passed the NLRA, union membership in the United States nearly tripled, from 3 million in 1933 to 8.8 million (19.2% of employment) in 1939.[19]

Before the 1930s, the U.S. legal system was generally hostile to unions. The courts tended to view unions as coercive organizations that hindered free trade. Unions' focus on collective voice and collective action (such as strikes and boycotts) did not fit well with the U.S. emphasis on capitalism, individualism, freedom of contract, and property rights.[20] Then the Great Depression of the 1930s shifted public attitudes toward business and the free-enterprise system. Unemployment rates as high as 25% and a steep fall in production between 1929 and 1933 focused attention on employee rights and the shortcomings of the economic system of the time. The nation was in crisis, and President Franklin Roosevelt responded dramatically with the New Deal. On the labor front, the 1935 NLRA ushered in an era of public policy for labor unions, enshrining collective bargaining as the preferred way to settle labor-management disputes.

Section 7 of the NLRA sets out the rights of employees, including the "right to self-organization, to form, join, or assist labor organizations, to bargain collectively through representatives of their own choosing, and to engage in other concerted activities for the purpose of collective bargaining."[21] Employees also have the right to refrain from these activities, unless union membership is a condition of employment. The following activities are among those protected under the NLRA:

- Union organizing.
- Joining a union, whether recognized by the employer or not.
- Going out on strike to secure better working conditions.
- Refraining from activity on behalf of the union.

Most employees in the private sector are covered by the NLRA. However, workers employed under the following conditions are not covered[22]:

- Employed as a supervisor.
- Employed by a parent or spouse.
- Employed as an independent contractor.
- Employed in the domestic service of any person or family in a home.
- Employed as agricultural laborers.
- Employed by an employer subject to the Railway Labor Act.
- Employed by a federal, state, or local government.
- Employed by any other person who is not an employer as defined in the NLRA.

State or local laws may provide additional coverage. For example, California's 1975 Agricultural Labor Relations Act covers agricultural workers in that state.

In Section 8(a), the NLRA prohibits certain activities by employers as unfair labor practices. In general, employers may not interfere with, restrain, or coerce employees in exercising their rights to join or assist a labor organization or to refrain from such activities. Employers may not dominate or interfere with the formation or activities of a labor union. They may not discriminate in any aspect of employment that attempts to encourage or discourage union activity, nor may they discriminate against employees for providing testimony related to enforcement of the NLRA. Finally, employers may not refuse to bargain collectively with a labor organization that has standing under the act. For more guidance in complying with the NLRA, see the examples in the "HR How To" box.

When employers or unions violate the NLRA, remedies typically include ordering that unfair labor practices stop. Employers may be required to rehire workers, with or without back pay. The NLRA is not a criminal law, and violators may not be assigned punitive damages (fines to punish rather than merely make up for the harm done).

Laws Amending the NLRA

Originally, the NLRA did not list any unfair labor practices by unions. In later amendments to the NLRA—the Taft-Hartley Act of 1947 and the Landrum-Griffin Act of 1959—Congress established some restrictions on union practices deemed unfair to employers and union members.

Under the Taft-Hartley Act, unions may not restrain employers through actions such as the following[23]:

- Mass picketing in such numbers that nonstriking employees physically cannot enter the workplace.
- Engaging in violent acts in connection with a strike.
- Threatening employees with physical injury or job loss if they do not support union activities.

HR How To

Avoiding Unfair Labor Practices

The National Labor Relations Act prohibits employers and unions from engaging in unfair labor practices. For employers, this means they must not interfere with employees' decisions about whether to join a union and engage in union-related activities. Employers may not discriminate against employees for being involved in union activities or testifying in court about actions under the NLRA. Here are some specific examples of unfair labor practices that *employers must avoid:*

- Threatening employees with loss of their jobs or benefits if they join or vote for a union.
- Threatening to close down a plant if it is organized by a union.
- Questioning employees about their union membership or activities in a way that restrains or coerces them.
- Taking an active part in organizing a union or committee to represent employees.

- Discharging employees for urging other employees to join a union.
- Promising benefits, such as a holiday or better working conditions, to employees if they don't support a union.
- Asking employees or job applicants about any union-organizing activities they might have engaged in.
- Preventing employees from promoting a union—for example, distributing literature—during breaks and other nonworking hours.
- Discouraging employees from conversations or other activities aimed at improving working conditions.
- Spying on employee activities to determine workers' views about a union.
- Forbidding employees from wearing union logos on shirts or jackets.
- Failing to bargain about the effects of a decision to close one of the employer's facilities.

Questions

1. Suppose you are an HR manager. You walk into the company lunchroom and notice several employees talking quietly but intensely. You think you hear the words "safety" and "organize," and you are concerned. What should you do?
2. A supervisor notices an employee distributing union literature during working hours. What should the supervisor do?

Sources: National Labor Relations Board, "Employer/Union Rights and Obligations," Rights We Protect, http://www.nlrb.gov, accessed July 22, 2014; National Labor Relations Board, "Protected Concerted Activity," Rights We Protect, http://www.nlrb.gov, accessed July 22, 2014; HR Specialist, "Unions in t he Spotlight: What Employers Can and Can't Do," white paper, http://www.thehrspecialist.com, accessed July 22, 2014; Gary S. Fealk, "NLRA Covers Nonunion Employers, Too," *HR Hero,* December 4, 2013, http://www.hrhero.com.

- During contract negotiations, insisting on illegal provisions, provisions that the employer may hire only workers who are union members or "satisfactory" to the union, or working conditions to be determined by a group to which the employer does not belong.
- Terminating an existing contract and striking for a new one without notifying the employer, the Federal Mediation and Conciliation Service, and the state mediation service (where one exists).

Right-to-Work Laws
State laws that make union shops, maintenance of membership, and agency shops illegal.

The Taft-Hartley Act also allows the states to pass so-called **right-to-work laws,** which make union shops, maintenance of membership, and agency shops illegal. The idea behind such laws is that requiring union membership or the payment of union dues restricts the employees' right to freedom of association. In other words, employees should be free to choose whether they join a union or other group. Of course, unions have a different point of view. The union perspective is that unions provide services to all members of a bargaining unit (such as all of a company's workers), and all members who receive the benefits of a union

Figure 15.3

States with Right-to-Work Laws

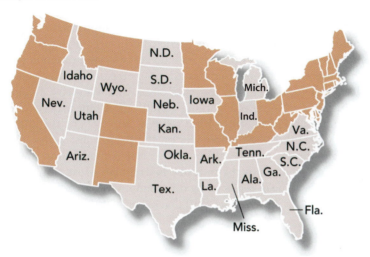

Source: National Right to Work Legal Defense Foundation, "Right to Work States," http://nrtw.org, accessed July 21, 2014.

should pay union dues. Figure 15.3 indicates which states currently have right-to-work laws.

The Landrum-Griffin Act regulates unions' actions with regard to their members, including financial disclosure and the conduct of elections. This law establishes and protects rights of union members. These include the right to nominate candidates for union office, participate in union meetings and secret-ballot elections, and examine unions' financial records.

National Labor Relations Board (NLRB)

Enforcement of the NLRA rests with the **National Labor Relations Board (NLRB).** This federal government agency consists of a five-member board, the general counsel, and 52 regional and other field offices. Because the NLRB is a federal agency, its enforcement actions are limited to companies that have an impact on interstate commerce, but as a practical matter, this extends to all but purely local businesses. For federal government workers under the Civil Service Reform Act of 1978, Title VII, the Federal Labor Relations Authority has a role similar to that of the NLRB. Many states have similar agencies to administer their laws governing state and local government workers.

The NLRB has two major functions: to conduct and certify representation elections and to prevent unfair labor practices. It does not initiate either of these actions but responds to requests for action.

Representation Elections   The NLRB is responsible for ensuring that the organizing process follows certain steps, described in the next section. Depending on the response to organizing efforts, the NLRB conducts elections. When a majority of

National Labor Relations Board (NLRB)
Federal government agency that enforces the NLRA by conducting and certifying representation elections and investigating unfair labor practices.

workers vote in favor of a union, the NLRB certifies it as the exclusive representative of a group of employees. The NLRB also conducts elections to decertify unions, following the same process as for representation elections.

The NLRB is also responsible for determining the appropriate bargaining unit and the employees who are eligible to participate in organizing activities. As we stated earlier, bargaining units may not include certain types of employees, such as agricultural laborers, independent contractors, supervisors, and managers. Beyond this, the NLRB attempts to group together employees who have a community of interest in their wages, hours, and working conditions. A unit may cover employees in one facility or multiple facilities within a single employer, or the unit may cover multiple employers. In general, employees on the payroll just before the ordering of an election are eligible to vote, although this rule is modified in some cases, for example, when employment in the industry is irregular. Most employees who are on strike and who have been replaced by other employees are eligible to vote in an election (such as a decertification election) that occurs within 12 months of the onset of the strike.

Prevention of Unfair Labor Practices The NLRB prevents unfair labor practices by educating employers and employees about their rights and responsibilities under the National Labor Relations Act and by responding to complaints. The handling of complaints regarding unfair labor practices begins when someone files a charge. The deadline for filing a charge is six months after the alleged unfair practice. All parties must be served with a copy of the charge. (Registered mail is recommended.) The charge is investigated by a regional office. If, after investigating, the NLRB finds the charge has merit and issues a complaint, two actions are possible. The NLRB may defer to a grievance procedure agreed on by the employer and the union; grievances are discussed later in this chapter. Or a hearing may be held before an administrative law judge. The judge makes a recommendation, which either party may appeal. For example, the "HRM Social" box describes rulings related to employees' activities on social media.

The NLRB has the authority to issue cease-and-desist orders to halt unfair labor practices. It also can order the employer to reinstate workers, with or without back pay. The NLRB can set aside the results of an election if it believes either the union or the employer has created "an atmosphere of confusion or fear of reprisals."[24] If an employer or union refuses to comply with an NLRB order, the board has the authority to petition the U.S. Court of Appeals. The court may enforce the order, recommend it to the NLRB for modification, change the order itself, or set it aside altogether.

Union Organizing

LO 15-4 Describe the union organizing process.

Unions begin their involvement with an organization's employees by conducting an organizing campaign. To meet its objectives, a union needs to convince a majority of workers that they should receive better pay or other employment conditions and that the union will help them do so. The employer's objectives will depend on its strategy—whether it seeks to work with a union or convince employees that they are better off without union representation.

Protected Social Activity

In recent years, employees have complained to the National Labor Relations Board that employers have penalized them for engaging in concerted activity on social media. And increasingly, the NLRB is agreeing with them.

The issue is when employees' postings about work amount to concerted action, protected by the National Labor Relations Act. In one case, for example, an employee of Hispanics United of Buffalo grumbled on Facebook about a co-worker who criticized her efforts at work. The original post asked "my fellow co-workers" for their opinions, and four of them provided comments referring to the employee and working conditions. When the employee who was the subject of the original post saw the comments, she complained to the supervisor, and the supervisor fired all of the co-workers involved on the grounds that they had been harassing that employee. An administrative law judge held that the supervisor had wrongfully terminated the employees, and the NLRB agreed. The NLRB's ruling was based on the interpretation that the original Facebook post was soliciting co-workers' views and the others were "making common cause with her," and that the posts could be seen as steps toward taking a group action to protect themselves if the employee complained about them to management. The NLRB required the employer to pay the employees back wages and let them return to work.

Some principles emerge from the ruling. First, an employee who merely posts a negative statement concerning matters that affect only him- or herself is not seen as engaged in concerted activity and therefore is not protected by the NLRA. However, posts that imply an objective of group action aimed at mutual aid or protection may be treated as concerted activity. Because the interpretation of whether social-media posts are aimed at encouraging some kind of group action and mutual aid is subjective, employers have to tread carefully.

Despite this, employers can continue to set certain kinds of limits on employees' social-media conduct. For example, they can ask employees not to disclose confidential information. However, social-media policies must be specific enough that employees do not feel forbidden from taking the kinds of actions protected by the NLRA.

Questions

1. Would an employee who posts, "I hate my job!" be protected, according to the principles cited here? Why or why not?
2. How would you have advised the supervisor at Hispanics United of Buffalo to handle the situation in the case described?

Sources: Martin Berman-Gorvine, "Employer Ability to Silence Employee Speech May Be Narrowing," *HR Focus,* July 2014, Business Insights: Global, http://bi.galegroup.com; Andrew O. Metcalf, "'Concert' or Solo Gig? Where the NLRB Went Wrong When It Linked in to Social Networks," *Washington University Law Review,* July 2013, Business Insights: Global, http://bi.galegroup.com; Josh Eidelson, "Go Ahead, Complain about Your Job on Facebook," *Slate,* January 3, 2013, http://www.slate.com.

The Process of Organizing

The organizing process begins when union representatives make contact with employees, present their message about the union, and invite them to sign an authorization card. For the organization process to continue, at least 30% of the employees must sign an authorization card.

If over half the employees sign an authorization card, the union may request that the employer voluntarily recognize the union. If the employer agrees, the NLRB certifies the union as the exclusive representative of employees. If the employer refuses, or if only 30% to 50% of employees signed cards, the NLRB conducts a secret-ballot election. The arrangements are made in one of two ways:

1. For a *consent election*, the employer and the union seeking representation arrive at an agreement stating the time and place of the election, the choices included on the ballot, and a way to determine who is eligible to vote.

The services sector, including janitorial workers, continues to be an area in which unions are actively organizing. Here union members march in support of contracted janitors who might lose their jobs due to budget cutbacks in Boston.

2.   For a *stipulation election*, the parties cannot agree on all of these terms, so the NLRB dictates the time and place, ballot choices, and method of determining eligibility.

On the ballot, workers vote for or against union representation, and they may also have a choice from among more than one union. If the union (or one of the unions on the ballot) wins a majority of votes, the NLRB certifies the union. If the ballot includes more than one union and neither gains a simple majority, the NLRB holds a runoff election.

As noted earlier, if the NLRB finds the election was not conducted fairly, it may set aside the results and call for a new election. Conduct that may lead to an election result's being set aside includes the following examples[25]:

- Threats of loss of jobs or benefits by an employer or union to influence votes or organizing activities.
- A grant of benefits or a promise of benefits as a means of influencing votes or organizing activities.
- Campaign speeches by management or union representatives to assembled groups of employees on company time less than 24 hours before an election.
- The actual use or threat of physical force or violence to influence votes or organizing activities.

The "HR Oops!" box describes another situation in which a union has contested election results.

After certification, there are limits on future elections. Once the NLRB has certified a union as the exclusive representative of a group of employees, it will not permit additional elections for one year. Also, after the union and employer have finished negotiating a contract, an election cannot be held for the time of the contract period or for three years, whichever comes first. The parties to the contract may agree not to hold an election for longer than three years, but an outside party (another union) cannot be barred for more than three years. Note that both union certifications and union elections can be conducted online.

Management Strategies

Sometimes an employer will recognize a union after a majority of employees have signed authorization cards. More often, there is a hotly contested election campaign. During the campaign, unions try to persuade employees that their wages, benefits, treatment by employers, and chances to influence workplace decisions are too poor or small and that the union will be able to obtain improvements in these areas. Management typically responds with its own messages providing an opposite point of view. Management messages say the organization has provided a valuable package of wages and benefits and has treated employees well. Management also argues that the union will not be able to keep its promises but will instead create costs for employees, such as union dues and lost income during strikes.

Employers use a variety of methods to oppose unions in organizing campaigns.[26] Their efforts range from hiring consultants to distributing leaflets and letters to presenting the

HR Oops!

Did Too Many Voters Spoil the Election?

Art handlers are typically highly educated artists with a deep appreciation for the chance to work with valuable art pieces. They work for auction houses and art-handling services, carefully packing items and transporting them to museums, homes, businesses, and auction houses. Customers may pay hundreds of dollars for a shipment. However, the art handlers' work is not necessarily well paid. A worker at Terry Dowd, Chicago's largest art-handling company, said he earns $14 an hour with variable hours—not enough to pay back his student loans and barely enough to pay his other bills.

With these conditions, the Teamsters saw an opportunity to organize art handlers. In 2011, they negotiated higher starting salaries for workers at Christie's auction house. In 2012, they successfully organized the art handlers for Sotheby's and negotiated a contract that provides for higher starting salaries, annual raises,

and continuance of the existing benefits package. With these victories behind them, the Teamsters turned to organizing workers at Terry Dowd.

The art handlers at Terry Dowd recently voted on whether to be represented by Teamsters Local 705. The initial count was close, and the Teamsters challenged the vote on the grounds that five management employees of Terry Dowd had voted in the election. Managers are not eligible to vote for union representation. Terry Dowd agreed to remove two of the ballots as ineligible, and the National Labor Relations Board must now consider the eligibility of the other three challenged votes. Ahead of their decision, the outcome is close: 14 voting yes and 12 voting no.

Questions

1. If the NLRB rules that the three remaining contested votes are eligible, how many of these must be "no" votes for

the union organizing effort to lose its majority and lose the election?
2. What can the NLRB do if it finds that the election at Terry Dowd was not conducted fairly?

Sources: Terry Dowd, website, http://www.terrydowd.com, accessed July 21, 2014; Matt Morris, "News: Vote for Art Handler Unionization Still Undecided," *Newcity Art,* June 13, 2014, http://art.newcity.com; Henry Kaye, "Chicago Art Handlers and Teamsters Fight over Results of Unionization Vote," *Art F City,* June 3, 2014, http://artfcity.com; Alejandra Cancino, "Art Handlers to Vote on Joining Teamsters," *Chicago Tribune,* April 25, 2014, http://articles.chicago-tribune.com; Teamsters Joint Council 25, "Chicago Art Handlers Bidding to Become Teamsters," news release, April 15, 2014, http://www.teamstersjc25.com; Daniel Massey, "Sotheby's, Teamsters Hammer Out a Deal," *Crain's New York Business,* May 31, 2012, http://www.crainsnewyork.com.

company's viewpoint at meetings of employees. Some management efforts go beyond what the law permits, especially in the eyes of union organizers. Why would employers break the law? One explanation is that the consequences, such as reinstating workers with back pay, are small compared to the benefits.[27] If coercing workers away from joining a union saves the company the higher wages, benefits, and other costs of a unionized workforce, management may feel an incentive to accept costs like back pay.

Supervisors have the most direct contact with employees. Thus, as Table 15.1 indicates, it is critical that they establish good relationships with employees even before there is any attempt at union organizing. Supervisors also must know what *not* to do if a union drive takes place. They should be trained in the legal principles discussed earlier in this chapter.

Union Strategies

The traditional union organizing strategy has been for organizers to call or visit employees at home, when possible, to talk about issues like pay and job security. Local 130 UA of the Chicago Journeymen Plumbers Association forms a committee of volunteers to comb through lists of journeyman plumbers within the local's jurisdiction. The committee members cross off the names of union members to create a list of plumbers

Table 15.1

What Supervisors Should and Should Not Do to Discourage Unions

WHAT TO DO:
Report any direct or indirect signs of union activity to a core management group.
Deal with employees by carefully stating the company's response to pro-union arguments. These responses should be coordinated by the company to maintain consistency and to avoid threats or promises. Take away union issues by following effective management practices all the time:

    Deliver recognition and appreciation.

    Solve employee problems.

    Protect employees from harassment or humiliation.

    Provide business-related information.

    Be consistent in treatment of different employees.

    Accommodate special circumstances where appropriate.

    Ensure due process in performance management.

    Treat all employees with dignity and respect.

WHAT TO AVOID:
Threatening employees with harsher terms and conditions of employment or employment loss if they engage in union activity.
Interrogating employees about pro-union or anti-union sentiments that they or others may have or reviewing union authorization cards or pro-union petitions.
Promising employees that they will receive favorable terms or conditions of employment if they forgo union activity.
Spying on employees known to be, or suspected of being, engaged in pro-union activities.

Source: Excerpted from J. A. Segal, "Unshackle Your Supervisors to Stay Union Free," in *HR Magazine*, June 1998. Copyright © 1998, Society for Human Resource Management, Alexandria, VA. Used with permission. All rights reserved.

who are not represented by a union. The local mails organizing kits to these individuals, and then the volunteers follow up to arrange visits with interested individuals in their homes.[28]

Beyond encouraging workers to sign authorization cards and vote for the union, organizers use some creative alternatives to traditional organizing activities. They sometimes offer workers **associate union membership,** which is not linked to an employee's workplace and does not provide representation in collective bargaining. Rather, an associate member receives other services, such as discounts on health and life insurance or credit cards.[29] In return for these benefits, the union receives membership dues and a broader base of support for its activities. Associate membership may be attractive to employees who wish to join a union but cannot because their workplace is not organized by a union.

Associate Union Membership
Alternative form of union membership in which members receive discounts on insurance and credit cards rather than representation in collective bargaining.

Corporate Campaigns
Bringing public, financial, or political pressure on employers during union organization and contract negotiation.

Another alternative to traditional organizing is to conduct **corporate campaigns**—bringing public, financial, or political pressure on employers during union organization and contract negotiation.[30] The Amalgamated Clothing and Textile Workers Union (ACTWU) corporate campaign against textile maker J. P. Stevens during the late 1970s was one of the first successful corporate campaigns and served as a model for those that followed. The ACTWU organized a boycott of J. P. Stevens products and threatened to withdraw its pension funds from financial institutions where J. P. Stevens officers acted as directors. The company eventually agreed to a contract with ACTWU.[31]

Another winning union organizing strategy is to negotiate employer neutrality and card-check provisions into a contract. Under a *neutrality provision*, the employer pledges not to oppose organizing attempts elsewhere in the company. A *card-check provision* is an agreement that if a certain percentage—by law, at least a majority—of employees sign an authorization card, the employer will recognize their union representation. An impartial outside agency, such as the American Arbitration Association, counts the cards. Evidence suggests that this strategy can be very effective for unions.[32]

Decertifying a Union

The Taft-Hartley Act expanded union members' right to be represented by leaders of their own choosing to include the right to vote out an existing union. This action is called *decertifying* the union. Decertification follows the same process as a representation election. An election to decertify a union may not take place when a contract is in effect.

The number of decertification elections has increased from about 5% of all elections in the 1950s and 1960s to more than double that rate in recent years. In fiscal year 2013, the NLRB reported that 13% of elections were decertification elections.[33]

Collective Bargaining

When the NLRB has certified a union, that union represents employees during contract negotiations. In **collective bargaining,** a union negotiates on behalf of its members with management representatives to arrive at a contract defining conditions of employment for the term of the contract and to resolve differences in the way they interpret the contract. Typical contracts include provisions for pay, benefits, work rules, and resolution of workers' grievances. Table 15.2 shows typical provisions negotiated in collective bargaining contracts.

Collective bargaining differs from one situation to another in terms of *bargaining structure*—that is, the range of employees and employers covered by the contract. A contract may involve a narrow group of employees in a craft union or a broad group in an industrial union. Contracts may cover one or several facilities of the same employer, or the bargaining structure may involve several employers. Many more interests must be considered in collective bargaining for an industrial union with a bargaining structure that includes several employers than in collective bargaining for a craft union in a single facility.

The majority of contract negotiations take place between unions and employers that have been through the process before. In the typical situation, management has come to accept the union as an organization it must work with. The situation can be very different when a union has just been certified and is negotiating its first contract. In over one-fourth of negotiations for a first contract, the parties are unable to reach an agreement.[34]

Bargaining over New Contracts

Clearly, the outcome of contract negotiations can have important consequences for labor costs, productivity, and the organization's ability to compete. Therefore, unions and management need to prepare carefully for collective bargaining. Preparation includes establishing objectives for the contract, reviewing the old contract, gathering data (such as compensation paid by competitors and the company's ability to survive a strike), predicting the likely demands to be made, and establishing the cost of meeting the demands.[35] This preparation can help negotiators develop a plan for how to negotiate.

LO 15-5 Explain how management and unions negotiate contracts.

Collective Bargaining
Negotiation between union representatives and management representatives to arrive at a contract defining conditions of employment for the term of the contract and to administer that contract.

Table 15.2

Typical Provisions in Collective Bargaining Contracts

Establishment and administration of the agreement	Contract duration and reopening and renegotiation provisions
	Grievance procedures
	Arbitration and mediation
	Strikes and lockouts
	Contract enforcement
Functions, rights, and responsibilities	Management rights clauses
	Subcontracting
	Union activities on company time and premises
	Union–management cooperation
	Regulation of technological change
	Advance notice and consultation
Wage determination and administration	Rate structure and wage differentials
	Incentive systems and production bonus plans
	Production standards and time studies
	Job classification and job evaluation
	Wage adjustments—individual and general
Job or income security	Hiring and transfer arrangements
	Employment and income guarantees
	Supplemental unemployment benefit plans
	Regulation of overtime, shift work, etc.
	Reduction of hours to forestall layoffs
	Layoff procedures; seniority; recall
	Promotion practices
	Training and retraining
	Relocation allowances
	Severance pay and layoff benefit plans
Plant operations	Work and shop rules
	Rest periods and other in-plant time allowances
	Safety and health
	Hours of work and premium pay practices
	Shift operations
	Hazardous work
	Discipline and discharge
Paid and unpaid leave	Vacations holidays, sick leave
	Funeral and personal leave
	Military leave and jury duty
Employee benefit plans	Health and insurance plans
	Pension plans
	Profit-sharing, stock purchase, and thrift plans
	Bonus plans
Special groups	Apprentices and learners
	Workers with disabilities
	Veterans
	Union representatives

Source: Adapted from T. A. Kochan, *Collective Bargaining and Industrial Relations* (Homewood, IL: Richard D. Irwin, 1980), p. 29. Original data from J. W. Bloch, "Union Contracts—A New Series of Studies," *Monthly Labor Review 87* (October 1964), pp. 1184–85.

Negotiations go through various stages.[36] In the earliest stages, many more people are often present than in later stages. On the union side, this may give all the various internal interest groups a chance to participate and voice their goals. Their input helps communicate to management what will satisfy union members and may help the union achieve greater solidarity. At this stage, union negotiators often present a long list of proposals, partly to satisfy members and partly to introduce enough issues that they will have flexibility later in the process. Management may or may not present proposals of its own. Sometimes management prefers to react to the union's proposals.

During the middle stages of the process, each side must make a series of decisions, even though the outcome is uncertain. How important is each issue to the other side? How likely is it that disagreement on particular issues will result in a strike? When and to what extent should one side signal its willingness to compromise?

In the final stage of negotiations, pressure for an agreement increases. Public negotiations may be only part of the process. Negotiators from each side may hold one-on-one meetings or small-group meetings where they escape some public relations pressures. A neutral third party may act as a go-between or facilitator. In some cases, bargaining breaks down as the two sides find they cannot reach a mutually acceptable agreement. The outcome depends partly on the relative bargaining power of each party. That power, in turn, depends on each party's ability to withstand a strike, which costs the workers their pay during the strike and costs the employer lost production and possibly lost customers.

When Bargaining Breaks Down

The intended outcome of collective bargaining is a contract with terms acceptable to both parties. If one or both sides determine that negotiation alone will not produce such an agreement, bargaining breaks down. To bring this impasse to an end, work may stop, or the parties may bring in outside help to resolve their differences.

Work Stoppages In the past, a breakdown in bargaining often led union members to stop working, a practice called a strike. Management also can initiate a type of work stoppage known as a lockout. However, the number of work stoppages (strikes and lockouts) has plunged since the 1950s, as shown in Figure 15.4.

A **strike** is a collective decision of the union members not to work until certain demands or conditions are met. The union members vote, and if the majority favors a strike, they all go on strike at that time or when union leaders believe the time is right. Strikes are typically accompanied by *picketing*—the union stations members near the worksite with signs indicating the union is on strike. During the strike, the union members do not receive pay from their employer, but the union may be able to make up for some of the lost pay. The employer loses production unless it can hire replacement workers, and even then, productivity may be reduced. Often, other unions support striking workers by refusing to cross their picket line—for example, refusing to make deliveries to a company during a strike.

A primary reason strikes are rare is that a strike is seldom in the best interests of either party. Not only do workers lose wages and employers lose production, but the negative experience of a strike can make future interactions more difficult. When strikes do occur, the conduct of each party during the strike can do lasting harm to labor-management relations. Violence by either side or threats of job loss or actual job loss because jobs went to replacement workers can make future relations difficult. Finally, many government employees do not have a right to strike, and their

Strike
A collective decision by union members not to work until certain demands or conditions are met.

Figure 15.4

Work Stoppages Involving 1,000 or More Workers

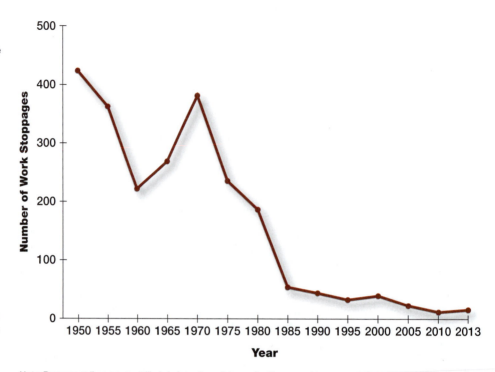

Note: Because strikes are most likely in large bargaining units, these numbers represent most lost working time in the United States.

Source: Bureau of Labor Statistics, "Work Stoppage Data," http://data.bls.gov, accessed July 21, 2014.

Lockout

An employer's exclusion of workers from a workplace until they meet certain conditions.

Mediation

Conflict resolution procedure in which a mediator hears the views of both sides and facilitates the negotiation process but has no formal authority to dictate a resolution.

percentage among unionized employees overall has risen in recent decades, as we discussed earlier.

In a **lockout,** the employer excludes workers from the workplace until they meet certain conditions. During the 1990s and 2000s, lockouts accounted for less than 5% of work stoppages, but they have become a larger share, mainly because unions are much more reluctant to strike. In other words, the rate of lockouts has been falling, but the rate of strikes has been falling faster.[37] Some of the most widely noticed lockouts are those involving sports leagues, including the National Hockey League and National Football League. During a lockout, an employer may hire replacement workers, which makes the tactic powerful in bargaining with a union.

Alternatives to Work Stoppages   Because work stoppages are so costly and risky, unions and employers generally prefer other methods for resolving conflicts. Three common alternatives rely on a neutral third party, usually provided by the Federal Mediation and Conciliation Service (FMCS):

Lockouts are not limited to workers in the manufacturing and construction trades. Recently, the Metropolitan Opera in New York City threatened to lock out the musicians' unions if agreements couldn't be reached on new contracts.

• **Mediation** is the least formal and most widely used of these procedures. A mediator hears the views of both sides and facilitates the negotiation process. The mediator has no formal authority to dictate a resolution, so a strike remains a possibility. In a survey studying negotiations between unions and large businesses, mediation was used in almost 4 out of 10 negotiation efforts.[38]

- A **fact finder,** most often used for negotiations with governmental bodies, typically reports on the reasons for the dispute, the views and arguments of both sides, and (sometimes) a recommended settlement, which the parties may decline. The public nature of these recommendations may pressure the parties to settle. Even if they do not accept the fact finder's recommended settlement, the fact finder may identify or frame issues in a way that makes agreement easier.

- Under **arbitration,** the most formal type of outside intervention, an arbitrator or arbitration board determines a settlement that is *binding*, meaning the parties have to accept it. In conventional arbitration, the arbitrator fashions the solution. In "final-offer arbitration," the arbitrator must choose either management's or the union's final offer for each issue or for the contract as a whole. "Rights arbitration" focuses on enforcing or interpreting contract terms. Arbitration in the writing of contracts or setting of contract terms has traditionally been reserved for special circumstances such as negotiations between unions and government agencies, where strikes may be illegal or especially costly.

Fact Finder
Third party to collective bargaining who reports the reasons for a dispute, the views and arguments of both sides, and possibly a recommended settlement, which the parties may decline.

Arbitration
Conflict resolution procedure in which an arbitrator or arbitration board determines a binding settlement.

Contract Administration

LO 15-6 Summarize the practice of contract administration.

Although the process of negotiating a labor agreement (including the occasional strike) receives the most publicity, other union-management activities occur far more often. Bargaining over a new contract typically occurs only about every three years, but administering labor contracts goes on day after day, year after year. The two activities are linked, of course. Vague or inconsistent language in the contract can make administering the contract more difficult. The difficulties can create conflict that spills over into the next round of negotiations.[39] Events during negotiations—strikes, the use of replacement workers, or violence by either side—also can lead to difficulties in working successfully under a conflict.

Contract administration includes carrying out the terms of the agreement and resolving conflicts over interpretation or violation of the agreement. Under a labor contract, the process for resolving these conflicts is called a **grievance procedure.** This procedure has a key influence on success in contract administration. A grievance procedure may be started by an employee or discharged employee who believes the employer violated the contract or by a union representative on behalf of a group of workers or union representatives.

For grievances launched by an employee, a typical grievance procedure follows the steps shown in Figure 15.5. The grievance may be settled during any of the four steps. In the first step, the employee talks to his or her supervisor about the problem. If this conversation is unsatisfactory, the employee may involve the union steward in further discussion. The union steward and employee decide whether the problem has been resolved and, if not, whether it is a contract violation. If the problem was not resolved and does seem to be a contract violation, the union moves to step 2, putting the grievance in writing and submitting it to a line manager. The union steward meets with a management representative to try to resolve the problem. Management consults with the industrial relations staff and puts its response in writing too at this second stage. If step 2 fails to resolve the problem, the union appeals the grievance to top line management and representatives of the

Grievance Procedure
The process for resolving union-management conflicts over interpretation or violation of a collective bargaining agreement.

Figure 15.5

Steps in an Employee-Initiated Grievance Procedure

Step 1

- Employee (and union steward) discusses problem with supervisor.
- Union steward and employee decide whether problem was resolved.
- Union steward and employee decide whether contract was violated.

Step 2

- Written grievance is submitted to production superintendent, another line manager, or industrial relations representative.
- Steward and manager discuss grievance.
- Management puts response in writing.

Step 3

- Union appeals grievance to top line management and senior industrial relations staff.
- Additional local or international union officers may be involved.
- Decision resulting from appeal is put into writing.

Step 4

- Union decides whether to appeal unresolved grievance to arbitration.
- Union appeals grievance to arbitration for binding decision.

Sources: Adapted from T. A. Kochan, *Collective Bargaining and Industrial Relations* (Homewood, IL: Richard D. Irwin, 1980), p. 395; and J. A. Fossum, *Labor Relations* (Boston: McGraw-Hill/Irwin, 2002), pp. 448–52.

industrial relations staff. The union may involve more local or international officers in discussions at this stage (see step 3 in Figure 15.5). The decision resulting from the appeal is put into writing. If the grievance is still not resolved, the union may decide (step 4) to appeal the grievance to an arbitrator. If the grievance involves a discharged employee, the process may begin at step 2 or 3, however, and the time limits between steps may be shorter. Grievances filed by the union on behalf of a group may begin at step 1 or step 2.

The majority of grievances are settled during the earlier steps of the process. This reduces delays and avoids the costs of arbitration. If a grievance does reach arbitration, the arbitrator makes the final ruling in the matter. Based on a series of Supreme Court decisions, courts generally avoid reviewing arbitrators' decisions and focus only on whether the grievance involved an issue that is subject to arbitration under the contract.[40]

Employers can judge a grievance procedure in terms of various criteria.[41] One consideration is effectiveness: how well the procedure resolves day-to-day contract questions. A second basic consideration is efficiency: whether it resolves issues at a reasonable cost and without major delays. The company also should consider how well the grievance procedure adapts to changing circumstances. For example, if sales drop off and the company needs to cut costs, how clear are the provisions related to layoffs and subcontracting of work? In the case of contracts covering multiple business units, the procedure should allow for resolving local contract issues, such as work rules at a particular facility. Companies also should consider whether the grievance procedure is fair—whether it treats employees equitably and gives them a voice in the process.

From the point of view of employees, the grievance procedure is an important means of getting fair treatment in the workplace. Its success depends on whether it provides for all the kinds of problems that are likely to arise (such as how to handle a business slowdown), whether employees feel they can file a grievance without being punished for it, and whether employees believe their union representatives will follow through. Under the National Labor Relations Act, the union has a *duty of fair representation*, which means the union must give equal representation to all members of the bargaining unit, whether or not they actually belong to the union.

New Approaches to Labor Relations

LO 15-7 Describe new approaches to labor-management relations.

The growing role of employee empowerment and the shrinking size of union membership have helped to establish new approaches to labor relations. Among these developments are an emphasis on cooperation between unions and management and the use of nonunion systems for employee representation.

Labor-Management Cooperation

The traditional understanding of union-management relations is that the two parties are adversaries, meaning each side is competing to win at the expense of the other. There have always been exceptions to this approach. And since at least the 1980s, there seems to be wider acceptance of the view that greater cooperation can increase employee commitment and motivation while making the workplace more flexible.[42] Also, evidence suggests that employees who worked under traditional labor relations systems and then under the new, more cooperative systems prefer the cooperative approach.[43]

Cooperation between labor and management may feature employee involvement in decision making, self-managing employee teams, labor-management problem-solving teams, broadly defined jobs, and sharing of financial gains and business information with employees.[44] The search for a win-win solution requires that unions and their members understand the limits on what an employer can afford in a competitive marketplace.

Without the union's support, efforts at employee empowerment are less likely to survive and less likely to be effective if they do survive.[45] Unions have often resisted employee empowerment programs, precisely because the programs try to change workplace relations and the role that unions play. Union leaders have feared that such programs will weaken unions' role as independent representatives of employee interests. Indeed, the National Labor Relations Act makes it an unfair labor practice for an employer to "dominate or interfere with the formation or administration of any labor organization or contribute financial or other support to it."

Although employers must be careful to meet legal requirements, the NLRB has clearly supported employee involvement in work teams and decision making. For example, in a 2001 ruling, the NLRB found that employee participation committees at Crown Cork & Seal's aluminum-can factory did not violate federal labor law.[46] Those committees make and carry out decisions regarding a wide range of issues, including production, quality, training, safety, and certain types of discipline. The NLRB determined that the committees were not employer dominated. Instead of "dealing with" management, where employees make proposals for management to accept or reject, the committees exercise authority within boundaries set by management, similar to the authority of a first-line supervisor.

In spite of the legal concerns, cooperative approaches to labor relations likely contribute to an organization's success.[47] Southwest Airlines' management would agree with that view. The airline's management training incorporates lessons and experience in working constructively with union representatives. With the highest share of union employees in the airline industry (85%), Southwest has among the fewest grievances per employee and has avoided many of the financial woes that have plagued the industry.[48]

Nonunion Representation Systems

Given that only about 11% of workers are now represented by unions, what recourse do the other 89% have if they want someone to represent their interests to management? Employees want some form of representation, which often involves "substitutes" for unions. A recent survey of hundreds of U.S. workers found that 17% were covered by a collective bargaining agreement, and another 28% said they had some form of management-established system to represent them.[49] The management-established system involved representatives of the employees meeting with management to discuss working conditions including wages and benefits. Both groups of workers were equally likely to say the employee representatives could be "counted on to stand up for workers." It is important to note that these "substitutes" may violate the NLRA. However, they exist because the legal guidelines covering these systems are ambiguous. It is difficult for unions to make the case that a company illegally organizes its employees into "company unions" unless the union has previously tried to organize the employees. Moreover, the punishments that companies can receive from the NLRB for these types of violations are limited.

Another nonunion approach is the *worker center*, a nonprofit organization offering its members services such as training, legal advice, lobbying, and worker advocacy.[50] For example, the Coalition of Immokalee Workers in Florida provides services to immigrant laborers who harvest tomatoes. A few worker centers are affiliated with unions; for example, Justice for Janitors is part of the Service Employees International Union. Most are not part of unions, so they are not constrained by some of the requirements on unions. For example, they can engage in secondary boycotts (boycotting one company so it will pressure another to make a change), and they do not have to win an election before they can confront management on behalf of workers. Instead of negotiating contracts with management, worker centers pressure employers through publicity campaigns, and they lobby legislators to pass laws favorable to their members. They may lack the financial resources of a major union, but they can be a powerful force when they rally community support around a cause such as wages, workplace safety, and fair treatment of workers.

THINKING ETHICALLY

FREE RIDE OR FREE SPEECH?

As the chapter explains, union goals include security provisions, such as agency shops, to ensure a regular flow of union dues. Right-to-work states forbid these provisions, but in Illinois (which is not a right-to-work state), personal care assistants providing services through the state-run programs serving people with disabilities or in rehabilitation were required to pay union dues, whether or not they wanted to join the union. A majority of the personal care assistants had voted to make the Service Employees International Union (SEIU) their representative in 2003. The collective bargaining agreement included a "fair share" provision that required nonmembers of the union to pay not the full amount of dues, but a proportionate share of union costs for collective bargaining and contract administration.

Several of the personal care assistants sued the state government, saying the "fair share" provision violated their rights to freedom of speech and freedom of association. They lost the case in district court and in the appellate court, but the U.S. Supreme Court disagreed in a 5–4 vote. According to the majority, the concern that workers should not get a free ride does not override concern for workers' First Amendment rights. Their ruling applied to the particular case of "quasi-public" workers who are paid by but not directly supervised by the government. When a person's employer is a government entity, the union's stance in bargaining with that government could conflict with a worker's political views. The court saw the requirement to support the union by paying dues as potentially forcing people to support the union's political message over the workers' own views. The dissenting view emphasized the fairness and protection provided by a system in which a single body representing workers' interests bargains with the government entity and no workers can take advantage of the resulting benefits for free.

According to the SEIU, it could lose up to one-third of the revenue from the affected personal care workers. Given that these workers can continue to enjoy any benefits that the SEIU negotiates on their behalf without paying (their wages have almost doubled since the SEIU started representing them), the union anticipates that it will have many free riders. Some union workers believe that organizing is actually easier without an agency shop, because organizers can point out that no one will be forced to join the union or pay dues. The SEIU's challenge now is to persuade these workers that union dues are worth the cost.

Questions

1. What issues of fairness and equity come into play in this case?
2. How well does the outcome of this case represent respect for basic human rights? How well does it do the greatest good for the greatest number?

Sources: Oyez Project, *"Harris v. Quinn,"* IIT Chicago–Kent College of Law, July 19, 2014, http://www.oyez.org; Cynthia Estlund and William E. Forbath, "The War on Workers," *The New York Times,* July 2, 2014, http://www.nytimes.com; Lydia DePillis, "Why *Harris v. Quinn* Isn't as Bad for Workers as It Sounds," *Washington Post,* July 1, 2014, http://www.washingtonpost.com; Daniel Fisher, "Public-Sector Unions Survive Supreme Court Review, Barely," *Forbes,* June 30, 2014, http://www.forbes.com.

SUMMARY

LO 15-1 Define unions and labor relations and their role in organizations.

- A union is an organization formed for the purpose of representing its members in resolving conflicts with employers.
- Labor relations is the management specialty emphasizing skills that managers and union leaders can use to minimize costly forms of conflict and to seek win-win solutions to disagreements.
- Unions—often locals belonging to national and international organizations—engage in organizing, collective bargaining, and contract administration with businesses and government organizations.
- In the United States, union membership has been declining among businesses but has held steady with government employees.
- Unionization is associated with more generous compensation and higher productivity but lower profits. Unions may reduce a business's flexibility and economic performance, but some companies rely on union expertise—for example, to train skilled workers.

LO 15-2 Identify the labor relations goals of management, labor unions, and society.

- Management goals are to increase the organization's profits. Managers generally expect that unions will make these goals harder to achieve.
- Labor unions have the goal of obtaining pay and working conditions that satisfy their members. They obtain these results by gaining power in numbers.
- Society's values have included the hope that the existence of unions will replace conflict or violence between workers and employers with fruitful negotiation.

LO 15-3 Summarize laws and regulations that affect labor relations.

- The National Labor Relations Act supports the use of collective bargaining and sets out the rights of employees, including the right to organize, join a union, and go on strike. The NLRA prohibits unfair labor practices by employers, including interference with efforts to form a labor union and discrimination against employees who engage in union activities.
- The Taft-Hartley Act and Landrum-Griffin Act establish restrictions on union practices that restrain workers, such as their preventing employees from working during a strike or determining whom an employer may hire.
- The Taft-Hartley Act also permits state right-to-work laws.

LO 15-4 Describe the union organizing process.

- Organizing begins when union representatives contact employees and invite them to sign an authorization card.
- If over half the employees sign a card, the union may request that the employer voluntarily recognize the union.
- If the employer refuses or if 30% to 50% of employees signed authorization cards, the NLRB conducts a secret-ballot election.
- If the union wins, the NLRB certifies the union.
- If the union loses but the NLRB finds that the election was not conducted fairly, it may set aside the results and call a new election.

LO 15-5 Explain how management and unions negotiate contracts.

- Negotiations take place between representatives of the union and the management bargaining unit. The majority of negotiations involve parties that have been through the process before.
- The process begins with preparation, including research into the other side's strengths and demands. In the early stages of negotiation, many more people are present than at later stages.
- The union presents its demands, and management sometimes presents demands as well.
- Then the sides evaluate the demands and the likelihood of a strike.
- In the final stages, pressure for an agreement increases and a neutral third party may be called on to help reach a resolution.
- If bargaining breaks down, the impasse may be broken with a strike, lockout, mediation, fact finder, or arbitration.

LO 15-6 Summarize the practice of contract administration.

- Contract administration is a daily activity under the labor agreement. It includes carrying out the terms of the agreement and resolving conflicts over interpretation or violation of the contract.
- Conflicts are resolved through a grievance procedure. Typically, the grievance procedure begins with an employee talking to his or her supervisor about the problem and possibly involving the union steward in the discussion.
- If this does not resolve the conflict, the union files a written grievance with a line manager, and union and management representatives meet to discuss the problem.
- If this effort fails, the union appeals the grievance to top line management and the industrial relations staff.
- If the appeal fails, the union may appeal the grievance to an arbitrator.

LO 15-7 Describe new approaches to labor-management relations.

- The growing role of employee empowerment and the shrinking size of union membership have helped to propel new approaches to labor relations, including an emphasis on cooperation between unions and management and the use of nonunion systems for employee representation.
- In contrast to the traditional view that labor and management are adversaries, some organizations and unions work more cooperatively. Cooperation may feature employee involvement in decision making, self-managing employee teams, labor-management problem-solving teams, broadly defined jobs, and sharing of financial gains and business information with employees.
- If such cooperation is tainted by attempts of the employer to dominate or interfere with labor organizations, however, such as by dealing with

wages, grievances, or working conditions, it may be illegal under the NLRA.

- In spite of such legal concerns, cooperative labor relations seem to contribute to an organization's success.
- In some organizations without a union, there is a management-established system to represent workers.
- Another nonunion approach is the worker center, a nonprofit organization offering its members services such as training, legal advice, lobbying, and worker advocacy.
- Most worker centers are not part of unions, so they are not constrained by some of the requirements on unions. Instead of negotiating contracts with management, worker centers pressure employers through publicity campaigns, and they lobby legislators to pass laws favorable to their members.

KEY TERMS

unions, 461
labor relations, 461
craft union, 462
industrial union, 462
American Federation of Labor and Congress of Industrial Organizations (AFL-CIO), 463
union steward, 463
checkoff provision, 468

closed shop, 468
union shop, 468
agency shop, 468
maintenance of membership, 468
National Labor Relations Act (NLRA), 470
right-to-work laws, 472
National Labor Relations Board (NLRB), 473

associate union membership, 478
corporate campaigns, 478
collective bargaining, 479
strike, 481
lockout, 482
mediation, 482
fact finder, 483
arbitration, 483
grievance procedure, 483

REVIEW AND DISCUSSION QUESTIONS

1. Why do employees join labor unions? Did you ever belong to a labor union? If you did, do you think union membership benefited you? If you did not, do you think a union would have benefited you? Why or why not? *(LO 15-1)*
2. Why do managers at most companies prefer that unions not represent their employees? Can unions provide benefits to an employer? Explain. *(LO 15-2)*
3. How has union membership in the United States changed over the past few decades? How does union membership in the United States compare with union membership in other countries? How might these patterns in union membership affect the HR decisions of an international company? *(LO 15-2)*
4. What legal responsibilities do employers have regarding unions? What are the legal requirements affecting unions? *(LO 15-3)*
5. Suppose you are the HR manager for a chain of clothing stores. You learn that union representatives have been encouraging the stores' employees to sign authorization cards. What events can follow in this process of organizing? Suggest some ways that you might respond in your role as HR manager. *(LO 15-4)*
6. If the parties negotiating a labor contract are unable to reach an agreement, what actions can resolve the situation? *(LO 15-5)*
7. Why are strikes uncommon? Under what conditions might management choose to accept a strike?
8. What are the usual steps in a grievance procedure? What are the advantages of resolving a grievance in the first step? What skills would a supervisor need so grievances can be resolved in the first step? *(LO 15-5)*
9. What can a company gain from union-management cooperation? What can workers gain? *(LO 15-7)*
10. What are the legal restrictions on labor-management cooperation? *(LO 15-7)*

TAKING RESPONSIBILITY

The SEIU's "Fight for 15" Campaign

An important way unions are making an impact is through shaping public opinion and lobbying for government action. Unions present issues as a matter of social responsibility, hoping legislators and managers will take the actions unions once sought through collective bargaining. The Fight for 15 campaign, supported by the Service Employees International Union (SEIU), is a case in point. The campaign seeks an increase in the minimum wage to $15 an hour. That would more than double the federal minimum, and it would be about two-thirds more than the $9 per hour earned by the average fast-food worker in the United States.

Fast-food workers are the face of the SEIU-backed campaign. Protesters have rallied in front of McDonald's headquarters in Oak Brook, Illinois, and at restaurants in more than 100 cities. As these protests have drawn media attention, the union has coordinated international protests by workers in 30 countries. Global pressure could be important, since international markets are important sources of corporate growth.

The SEIU's objectives in backing the campaign focus on fairness, not membership growth. Whereas fast-food restaurants once employed mainly young people, the Great Recession drove more adults to take those jobs. With more people trying to support families on fast-food pay, governments are spending billions of dollars on public assistance to working people. The SEIU's president, Mary Kay Henry, has expressed the issue in ethical terms: "Americans know that it's wrong that so many families have no financial security, no matter how hard they work." She also expresses a broader social benefit from raising the minimum wage: "more money in the pockets of workers" will help "get our economy moving again."

The fast-food industry as a whole is among the nation's largest and fastest-growing employers, with roughly 4 million workers, but it has been a difficult one for unions to organize. Most workers are not employed by large corporations but by franchisees serving local markets. The franchisees point out that their profit margins are so small that they cannot afford higher wages without major price increases. A $15 minimum wage would force them to replace workers with automation, slowing job growth in one of the few industries where it is strong.

With these obstacles, why is the SEIU bothering to rally fast-food workers? One reason is that it positions the union as relevant to today's workers. The SEIU has made a point of experimenting with new tactics, and at a time when overall union membership is falling, the SEIU's membership is growing. In addition, some collective bargaining agreements set wages relative to the minimum wage, so some members could see direct benefits from this activity. And a recent NLRB ruling that McDonald's could be treated as a joint employer with its franchisees in labor complaints could have huge implications for how restaurant companies deal with their employees in the future.

Questions

1. What are the goals of management, unions, and society in this situation?
2. How might fast-food companies and their franchisees approach the minimum-wage issue through union-management collaboration? Would you recommend this approach? Why or why not?

Sources: Julie Jargon, "McDonald's Ruling Sets Ominous Tone for Franchisers," *The Wall Street Journal*, July 29, 2014, http://online.wsj.com; Alejandra Cancino, "Union Spent at Least $2 Million Last Year on Fight for $15 Movement," *Chicago Tribune*, May 29, 2014, http://www.chicagotribune.com; Eric Morath, "Workers Try a New Tactic in Minimum-Wage Fight," *The Wall Street Journal*, May 20, 2014, http://online.wsj.com; Barbara Tasch, "Fast Food Workers to Protest Wages in 80 Cities across the World," *Time*, May 16, 2014, EBSCOhost, http://web.a.ebscohost.com; Service Employees International Union, "SEIU's Henry: Fast Food Strikers Fighting for Economy That Works for All of Us," news release, May 15, 2014, http://www.seiu.org; Susan Berfield, "Fast-Food Workers of the World, Unite!" *Bloomberg Businessweek*, December 9, 2013, pp. 20, 22; Claire Zillman, "Fast-Food Workers: Labor Movement's New Lease on Life," *Fortune*, December 6, 2013, EBSCOhost, http://web.a.ebscohost.com; Richard Berman, "Why Unions Like Minimum Wage," *Investor's Business Daily*, August 26, 2013, Business Insights: Global, http://bi.galegroup.com; Venessa Wong, "This Is What Would Happen If Fast-Food Workers Got Raises," *Bloomberg Businessweek*, August 2, 2013, http://www.businessweek.com.

MANAGING TALENT

Volkswagen wants the United Auto Workers

The United Auto Workers' failure in organizing the workers of Volkswagen's Chattanooga, Tennessee, plant was surprising because the election campaign had been so unusual. It is typical for management to discourage a union, but Volkswagen seemed to welcome the UAW to the plant, where 2,400 workers assemble Passat sedans. The union had partnered with the IG Metall union in Germany, where VW is headquartered and where union membership is an accepted part of business. There, VW and IG Metall had a cooperative relationship in which the workers served on a works council, a formal committee that negotiates with management about how to handle production issues. VW has similar arrangements in its other international facilities and hoped to set up a works council in Chattanooga. Management believed this would require that workers first belong to a union. In an unusual move, the company allowed UAW organizers to campaign inside the factory.

In spite of this favorable context, the workers voted 712 to 626 against the union in February 2014. While some workers were attracted to the idea of a works council, others worried that the UAW's presence would create conflict and divisions. Some said they disliked the union's support for political candidates whose views they disagreed with.

The UAW's initial response was to appeal the vote to the National Labor Relations Board, citing interference from outsiders. The governor had said he doubted the state would go ahead with plans to offer VW incentives for locating in Chattanooga if the plant became unionized. Senator Bob Corker had said he had information that VW would not build a second production line in Chattanooga if the union vote passed. Conservative political groups posted anti-union billboards around Chattanooga. Believing these actions made the vote unfair, the union asked the NLRB to order a new election.

But in another surprise, the UAW dropped the appeal two months later. The union's president at that time, Bob King, said he feared the appeal process "could drag on for months or even years." Ordering a new

election could take two years, whereas accepting the election's results would allow the union to campaign again in another year.

More surprises followed in July. The UAW announced that it had reached a consensus with Volkswagen. The company invited UAW Local 42 to sign up workers voluntarily, and the union would partner with management to set up a works council. Local 42 would prioritize ensuring the company's growth and developing a training program for employees. That same month, VW announced that it would expand the Chattanooga plant to build midsized SUVs, adding about 2,000 new jobs.

Questions

1. What objectives were Volkswagen managers trying to meet in allowing the UAW to organize its workforce in Chattanooga?
2. Assuming that Local 42 succeeds in signing up workers, do you expect that VW's management will need to prepare for problems in collective bargaining with the union? Why or why not?

Sources: Kathleen Foody, "Tenn. Leaders Downplay Union Debate at VW Plant," *ABC News*, July 15, 2014, http://abcnews.go.com; Justin Bachman, "As Union Moves In, Volkswagen Will Build Its SUV in Tennessee," *Bloomberg Businessweek*, July 14, 2014, http://www.businessweek.com; United Auto Workers, "UAW Charters Local 42 at Volkswagen in Chattanooga," news release, July 10, 2014, http://uaw.org; Steven Greenhouse, "UAW Drops Appeal of VW Vote in Tennessee," *The New York Times*, April 21, 2014, http://www.nytimes.com; Neal E. Boudette, "Union Suffers Big Loss at Tennessee VW Plant," *The Wall Street Journal*, February 15, 2014, http://online.wsj.com.

HR IN SMALL BUSINESS

Republic Gets Serious

When Serious Materials acquired Republic Windows and Doors, union–management relations got a much-needed breath of fresh air. Republic had nearly vanished amidst economic meltdown and accusations of mismanagement and corruption. Serious Materials, by contrast, is a firm with a high-minded business strategy and a commitment to fair-mindedness.

The problems became public when workers at Republic staged a six-day sit-in at the Chicago factory, which had been one of the largest window-glass factories in the United States. When orders from construction companies stopped coming in, management, after just three days' warning, closed the plant without granting workers any severance pay or giving the legally required 60 days' notice, and filed for bankruptcy. Bowing to public pressure, the company's lenders, including Bank of America, reached an agreement to give the workers $6,000 apiece in severance pay.

But that wasn't the end. The workers turned to the National Labor Relations Board with another complaint. They said Republic's owner, Richard Gillman, had secretly begun transferring the company's machinery to a (non-union) window-manufacturing facility he bought in Iowa just before closing the Chicago factory. In fact, all the equipment would have been gone, they said, except that their six-day occupation of the factory interfered with the plan—they wouldn't allow Gillman to enter. Employees also followed trucks carrying machinery to learn where it was being taken. The union demanded that the machinery be returned to the Chicago plant, so a new owner could operate it.

Meanwhile, a hero arrived on the scene: Kevin Surace, founder and chief executive of Serious Materials, a maker of eco-friendly building products, including energy-efficient windows. Surace saw acquisition of the Republic facility as a chance to expand into the Chicago region with a ready-made plant and equipment, not to mention trained people eager to work.

When he decided to make an offer, Surace did something unusual: instead of talking first to the firms' main creditors, he made his first visit to the employees' union, the United Electrical, Radio, and Machine Workers of America. He met with the union's president, Carl Rosen, as well as several Republic workers. Rosen recalled that Surace's reasoning was that for the deal to work, he needed a skilled workforce. The parties agreed that Serious Materials would make the facility a union shop, and employees would be paid their former salaries and receive credit for their seniority at Republic. Only then did Surace approach Bank of America. The bank initially wasn't interested, so Surace went to General Electric, owner of the lease on the equipment, and bought out the lease, a coup that convinced the bank to sell. Surace announced plans to reopen the plant and rehire all the 300 employees who had been laid off when Republic closed its doors. The resulting publicity quickly brought in inquiries and even some paying customers.

Since the acquisition, the Republic story may be nearing its end. County prosecutors brought charges against Gillman for looting the business and stealing machinery for the Iowa enterprise (which also failed, less than two months after it launched). Because Republic had been in bankruptcy, the equipment was not Gillman's but belonged to his creditor, GE. State's Attorney Anita Alvarez said, "Just two weeks before Christmas, in a dire economy, the company shut the doors of their business and deserted their workers and all of their families." Gillman denied the charges.

A sign of Surace's very different attitude toward his workforce came a few months after the acquisition by Serious Materials, when Vice President Joe Biden came to visit the Chicago facility. Biden was there to represent how the Obama administration's economic stimulus plan was supporting "green" initiatives. Surace noticed that onstage for the press conference were various dignitaries but no representatives of the workers. In spite of the Secret Service's reluctance to add last-minute guests, Surace insisted that workers have a face at the press conference. By the time the TV cameras were rolling, the cast of dignitaries included Armando Robles, a maintenance worker and the president of the employees' union.

Questions

1. Richard Gillman attempted to stay in business by transferring work to a nonunion facility, and Kevin Surace plans to make the operation profitable as a union shop. Do you think the decision to rely on union or non-union labor spells the difference between the success and failure of this enterprise? Why or why not?

2. How (if at all) do you think Kevin Surace's initial approach to the union when acquiring the company will influence the business success of the window factory?

3. Imagine that Serious Materials has hired you as an HR consultant for the Chicago window factory. Suggest how the company can build on its initial goodwill with workers to create positive labor relations and a highly motivated workforce for the long run.

Sources: Robert Mitchum, "Republic Workers File Labor Charges," *Chicago Tribune*, January 7, 2009, NewsBank, http://infoweb.newsbank.com; Robert Mitchum, "Former Republic Workers Find Hope," *Chicago Tribune*, January 15, 2009, NewsBank, http://infoweb.newsbank.com; Annie Sweeney and Matthew Walberg, "Tables Turn on Man Who Shut Republic Windows," *Chicago Tribune*, September 11, 2009, NewsBank, http://infoweb.newsbank.com; Leigh Buchanan, "Entrepreneur of the Year: Kevin Surace of Serious Materials," *Inc.*, December 2009, www.inc.com.

NOTES

1. Alan K. Cubbage, "Northwestern Asks National Labor Relations Board to Overturn Regional Director's Ruling on Football Players Unionization," Northwestern University news page, July 3, 2014, http://www.northwestern.edu; Ira Boudway, "With Union Ballots Cast by Northwestern Football Team, Real Contest Is Just Beginning," *Bloomberg Businessweek*, April 25, 2014, http://www.businessweek.com; Alejandra Cancino and Teddy Greenstein, "Northwestern Football Players Cast Ballots in Union Vote," *Chicago Tribune*, April 25, 2014, http://articles.chicagotribune.com; Melanie Trottman, "NLRB to Review Northwestern's Appeal of Student-Athletes' Union Decision," *The Wall Street Journal*, April 24, 2014, http://online.wsj.com.

2. J. T. Dunlop, *Industrial Relations Systems* (New York: Holt, 1958); C. Kerr, "Industrial Conflict and Its Mediation," *American Journal of Sociology* 60 (1954), pp. 230–45.

3. T. A. Kochan, *Collective Bargaining and Industrial Relations* (Homewood, IL: Richard D. Irwin, 1980), p. 25; H. C. Katz and T. A. Kochan, *An Introduction to Collective Bargaining and Industrial Relations*, 3rd ed. (New York: McGraw-Hill, 2004).

4. Tom Raum, "Unions Representing Government Workers Are Gaining," *Minneapolis Star Tribune*, July 4, 2014, http://www.startribune.com; Elias Groll, "The World's Most Powerful Labor Unions," *Foreign Policy*, September 2, 2013, http://www.foreignpolicy.com.

5. Whether the time the union steward spends on union business is paid for by the employer, the union, or a combination is a matter of negotiation between the employer and the union.

6. Bureau of Labor Statistics, "Union Members, 2013," news release, January 24, 2014, http://www.bls.gov.

7. Katz and Kochan, *An Introduction to Collective Bargaining*, building on J. Fiorito and C. L. Maranto, "The

Contemporary Decline of Union Strength," *Contemporary Policy Issues* 3 (1987), pp. 12–27; G. N. Chaison and J. Rose, "The Macrodeterminants of Union Growth and Decline," in *The State of the Unions*, ed. G. Strauss et al. (Madison, WI: Industrial Relations Research Association, 1991).

8. C. Brewster, "Levels of Analysis in Strategic HRM: Questions Raised by Comparative Research," Conference on Research and Theory in HRM, Cornell University, October 1997.

9. J. T. Addison and B. T. Hirsch, "Union Effects on Productivity, Profits, and Growth: Has the Long Run Arrived?" *Journal of Labor Economics* 7 (1989), pp. 72–105; R. B. Freeman and J. L. Medoff, "The Two Faces of Unionism," *Public Interest* 57 (Fall 1979), pp. 69–93.

10. L. Mishel and P. Voos, *Unions and Economic Competitiveness* (Armonk, NY: M. E. Sharpe, 1991); Freeman and Medoff, "Two Faces"; S. Slichter, J. Healy, and E. R. Livernash, *The Impact of Collective Bargaining on Management* (Washington, DC: Brookings Institution, 1960).

11. A. O. Hirschman, *Exit, Voice, and Loyalty* (Cambridge, MA: Harvard University Press, 1970); R. Batt, A. J. S. Colvin, and J. Keefe, "Employee Voice, Human Resource Practices, and Quit Rates: Evidence from the Telecommunications Industry," *Industrial and Labor Relations Review* 55 (1970), pp. 573–94.

12. R. B. Freeman and J. L. Medoff, *What Do Unions Do?* (New York: Basic Books, 1984); Addison and Hirsch, "Union Effects on Productivity"; M. Ash and J. A. Seago, "The Effect of Registered Nurses' Unions on Heart-Attack Mortality," *Industrial and Labor Relations Review* 57 (2004), p. 422; C. Doucouliagos and P. Laroche, "What Do Unions Do to Productivity? A Meta-Analysis," *Industrial Relations* 42 (2003), pp. 650–91.

13. B. E. Becker and C. A. Olson, "Unions and Firm Profits," *Industrial Relations* 31, no. 3 (1992), pp. 395–415; B. T. Hirsch and B. A. Morgan, "Shareholder Risks and Returns in Union and Nonunion Firms," *Industrial and Labor Relations Review* 47, no. 2 (1994), pp. 302–18; Hristos Doucouliagos and Patrice Laroche, "Unions and Profits: A Meta-Regression Analysis," *Industrial Relations* 48, no. 1 (January 2008), p. 146.

14. Nicole A. Bonham Colby, "Labor and Management: Working Together for a Stable Future," *Alaska Business Monthly*, October 2011, Business & Company Resource Center, http://galenet.galegroup.com.

15. Bureau of Labor Statistics, "Union Members, 2013."

16. Christina Rogers, "Next UAW Chief to Confront Wage Dispute," *The Wall Street Journal*, June 2, 2014, http://online.wsj.com. See also Bradford Wernle, "Why Mess with Two-Tier Wage Success?" *Automotive News*, May 26, 2014, http://www.autonews.com.

17. S. Webb and B. Webb, *Industrial Democracy* (London: Longmans, Green, 1897); J. R. Commons, *Institutional Economics* (New York: Macmillan, 1934).

18. "Why America Needs Unions, but Not the Kind It Has Now," *Bloomberg Businessweek*, May 23, 1994, p. 70.

19. E. E. Herman, J. L. Schwartz, and A. Kuhn, *Collective Bargaining and Labor Relations* (Englewood Cliffs, NJ: Prentice Hall, 1992).

20. Kochan, *Collective Bargaining and Industrial Relations*, p. 61.

21. National Labor Relations Board, *Basic Guide to the National Labor Relations Act* (Washington, DC: U.S. Government Printing Office, 1997).

22. National Labor Relations Board, "Who Is Covered by the National Labor Relations Act?" Frequently Asked Questions, http://www.nlrb.gov, accessed May 4, 2012; U.S. Department of Labor, Office of Labor-Management Standards, "Employee Rights under the National Labor Relations Act," poster, http://www.dol.gov/olms/, accessed May 8, 2012.

23. National Labor Relations Board, *Basic Guide*.

24. Ibid.

25. Ibid.

26. R. B. Freeman and M. M. Kleiner, "Employer Behavior in the Face of Union Organizing Drives," *Industrial and Labor Relations Review* 43, no. 4 (April 1990), pp. 351–65.

27. J. A. Fossum, *Labor Relations*, 8th ed. (New York: McGraw-Hill, 2002), p. 149.

28. Local Union 130 UA, Chicago Journeymen Plumbers, "Organizing," http://www.plumberslu130ua.org, accessed May 4, 2012.

29. Herman et al., *Collective Bargaining*; P. Jarley and J. Fiorito, "Associate Membership: Unionism or Consumerism?" *Industrial and Labor Relations Review* 43 (1990), pp. 209–24.

30. Katz and Kochan, *An Introduction to Collective Bargaining*.

31. Katz and Kochan, *An Introduction to Collective Bargaining*.

32. A. E. Eaton and J. Kriesky, "Union Organizing under Neutrality and Card Check Agreements," *Industrial and Labor Relations Review* 55 (2001), pp. 42–59.

33. National Labor Relations Board, "Election Data, FY 2011," Election Reports, http://www.nlrb.gov/election-reports, accessed May 7, 2012.

34. Chaison and Rose, "The Macrodeterminants of Union Growth and Decline."

35. Fossum, *Labor Relations*, p. 262.

36. C. M. Steven, *Strategy and Collective Bargaining Negotiations* (New York: McGraw-Hill, 1963); Katz and Kochan, *An Introduction to Collective Bargaining*.

37. Kochan, *Collective Bargaining and Industrial Relations*, p. 272.

38. Robert Combs, "Labor Stats and Facts: Lockout Rates Continue to Surge," *Bloomberg BNA*, October 17, 2012, http://www.bna.com.

39. Katz and Kochan, *An Introduction to Collective Bargaining*.

40. *United Steelworkers v. American Manufacturing Company*, 363 U.S. 564 (1960); *United Steelworkers v. Warrior Gulf and Navigation Company*, 363 U.S. 574 (1960); *United Steelworkers v. Enterprise Wheel and Car Corporation*, 363 U.S. 593 (1960).

41. Kochan, *Collective Bargaining and Industrial Relations*, p. 386; John W. Budd and Alexander J. S. Colvin, "Improved Metrics for Workplace Dispute Resolution Procedures: Efficiency, Equity, and Voice," *Industrial Relations* 47, no. 3 (July 2008), p. 460.

42. T. A. Kochan, H. C. Katz, and R. B. McKersie, *The Transformation of American Industrial Relations* (New York: Basic Books, 1986), chap. 6; E. Appelbaum, T. Bailey, and P. Berg, *Manufacturing Advantage: Why High-Performance Work Systems Pay Off* (Ithaca, NY: Cornell University Press, 2000).

43. L. W. Hunter, J. P. MacDuffie, and L. Doucet, "What Makes Teams Take? Employee Reactions to Work Reforms," *Industrial and Labor Relations Review* 55 (2002), pp. 448–72.

44. J. B. Arthur, "The Link between Business Strategy and Industrial Relations Systems in American Steel Minimills," *Industrial and Labor Relations Review* 45 (1992), pp. 488–506; M. Schuster, "Union Management Cooperation," in *Employee and Labor Relations*, ed. J. A. Fossum (Washington, DC: Bureau of National Affairs, 1990); E. Cohen-Rosenthal and C. Burton, *Mutual Gains: A Guide to Union-Management Cooperation*, 2nd ed. (Ithaca, NY: ILR Press, 1993); T. A. Kochan and P. Osterman, *The Mutual Gains Enterprise* (Boston: Harvard Business School Press, 1994); E. Applebaum and R. Batt, *The New American Workplace* (Ithaca, NY: ILR Press, 1994).

45. A. E. Eaton, "Factors Contributing to the Survival of Employee Participation Programs in Unionized Settings," *Industrial and Labor Relations Review* 47, no. 3 (1994), pp. 371–89.

46. "NLRB 4–0 Approves Crown Cork & Seal's Use of Seven Employee Participation Committees," *HR News*, September 3, 2001.

47. Kochan and Osterman, *The Mutual Gains Enterprise*; W. N. Cooke, "Employee Participation Programs, Group-Based Incentives, and Company Performance: A Union-Nonunion Comparison," *Industrial and Labor Relations Review* 47, no. 4 (1994), pp. 594–609; C. Doucouliagos, "Worker Participation and Productivity in Labor-Managed and Participatory Capitalist Firms: A Meta-Analysis," *Industrial and Labor Relations Review* 49, no. 1 (1995), pp. 58–77; S. J. Deery and R. D. Iverson, "Labor-Management Cooperation: Antecedents and Impact on Organizational Performance," *Industrial and Labor Relations Review* 58 (2005), pp. 588–609; James Combs, Yongmei Liu, Angela Hall, and David Ketchen, "How Much Do High-Performance Work Practices Matter? A Meta-analysis of Their Effects on Organizational Performance," *Personnel Psychology* 59, no. 3 (2006), pp. 501–28; Robert D. Mohr and Cindy Zoghi, "High-Involvement Work Design and Job Satisfaction," *Industrial and Labor Relations Review* 61, no. 3 (April 2008), pp. 275–96; T. Rabl, M. Jayasinghe, B. Gerhart, and T. M. Köhlmann, "How Much Does Country Matter? A Meta-analysis of the HPWP Systems–Business Performance Relationship," *Academy of Management Annual Meeting Proceedings*, August 2011.

48. Kate Everson, "Learning to Work with Unions," *Chief Learning Officer*, July 2014, pp. 26–29.

49. John Godard and Carola Frege, "Labor Unions, Alternative Forms of Representation, and the Exercise of Authority Relations in U.S. Workplaces," *Industrial and Labor Relations Review* 6 (2013): 142–168.

50. Robert J. Grossman, "Leading from Behind?" *HR Magazine*, December 2013, Business Insights: Global, http://bi.galegroup.com.

16

Managing Human Resources Globally

What Do I Need to Know?

After reading this chapter, you should be able to:

LO 16-1 Summarize how the growth in international business activity affects human resource management.

LO 16-2 Identify the factors that most strongly influence HRM in international markets.

LO 16-3 Discuss how differences among countries affect HR planning at organizations with international operations.

LO 16-4 Describe how companies select and train human resources in a global labor market.

LO 16-5 Discuss challenges related to managing performance and compensating employees from other countries.

LO 16-6 Explain how employers prepare managers for international assignments and for their return home.

Introduction

HR professionals in the United States are still trying to figure out the best ways to encourage their employees to be as healthy as possible. Some offer access to an onsite fitness center, and others offer financial incentives for joining a weight loss program, but the financial return on this spending is not always obvious. The choices become even more complex at organizations with operations in several countries. One reason is that the main health issues differ from one region to another. For example, in sub-Saharan Africa, infectious diseases are more of a problem even as chronic conditions such as diabetes are becoming more common. At the same time, cultural and economic issues come into play. In countries where HIV/AIDS is a major problem, there also may be a stigma attached to being HIV-positive. That makes it harder to set up a program for screening and education in managing the infection. Furthermore, employees in some parts of the world have little access to health care. In contrast, in the United Kingdom, a major concern is that such a program not seem to intrude into employees' personal lives.

One way around the complexity is for an employer to address issues of shared concern around the world. In particular, lifestyles that include physical activity and healthy eating will strengthen employees to prevent or cope with a wide variety of health problems. American Express offers a program

called Healthy Living in 16 of the 45 countries where it operates. The program has internationally relevant content: nutrition, exercise, health care, and emotional well-being. The company launched Healthy Living in the United States and then expanded it to employees in India, the United Kingdom, Mexico, and elsewhere. As it extends the program to each country, it sets objectives relevant to the country and tailors the program to each set of employees. In the United Kingdom, Healthy Living aims to boost employee engagement and productivity, while in India, it is meant to help attract and retain workers.[1]

Like American Express, many companies have operations in foreign countries. Therefore, human resource management truly takes place on an international scale. This chapter discusses the HR issues that organizations must address in a world of global competition. We begin by describing how the global nature of business is affecting human resource management in modern organizations. Next, we identify how global differences among countries affect the organization's decisions about human resources. In the following sections we explore HR planning, selection, training, and compensation practices in international settings. Finally, we examine guidelines for managing employees sent on international assignments.

HRM in a Global Environment

LO 16-1 Summarize how the growth in international business activity affects human resource management.

The environment in which organizations operate is rapidly becoming a global one. More and more companies are entering international markets by exporting their products, building facilities in other countries, and entering into alliances with foreign companies. At the same time, companies based in other countries are investing and setting up operations in the United States. Indeed, most organizations now function in the global economy.

What is behind the trend toward expansion into global markets? Foreign countries can provide a business with new markets in which there are millions or billions of new customers; developing countries often provide such markets, but developed countries do so as well. In addition, companies set up operations overseas because they can operate with lower labor costs—for example, video game developers that pay $12,000 to $15,000 per month for U.S. employees can hire Indian workers at monthly pay scales in the range of $4,000 to $5,000.[2] Finally, thanks to advances in telecommunications and information technology, companies can more easily spread work around the globe, wherever they find the right mix of labor costs and abilities. Teams with members in different time zones can keep projects moving around the clock, or projects can be assigned according to regions with particular areas of expertise. Once organizations have taken advantage of these opportunities, they sometimes find themselves locked into overseas arrangements. In the consumer electronics industry, for example, so much of the manufacturing has shifted to China and other low-wage countries that U.S. companies no longer would have suppliers nearby if they tried to build a factory in North America.[3]

Global activities are simplified and encouraged by trade agreements among nations. For example, most countries in Western Europe belong to the European Union and share a common currency, the euro. Canada, Mexico, and the United States have encouraged trade among themselves with the North American Free Trade Agreement (NAFTA). The World Trade Organization (WTO) resolves trade disputes among more than 100 participating nations.

As these trends and arrangements encourage international trade, they increase and change the demands on human resource management. Organizations with customers or suppliers in other countries need employees who understand those customers or suppliers. Organizations that operate facilities in foreign countries need to understand the laws and customs that apply to employees in those countries. They may have to prepare managers and other personnel to take international assignments. They have to adapt their human resource plans and policies to different settings. Even if some practices are the same worldwide, the company now has to communicate them to its international workforce. A variety of international activities require managers to understand HRM principles and practices prevalent in global markets.

Employees in an International Workforce

When organizations operate globally, their employees are very likely to be citizens of more than one country. Employees may come from the employer's parent country, a host country, or a third country. The **parent country** is the country in which the organization's headquarters is located. For example, the United States is the parent country of General Motors, because GM's headquarters is in Michigan. A GM employee who was born in the United States and works at GM's headquarters or one of its U.S. factories is therefore a *parent-country national.*

As companies in the United States and Britain cut software jobs and outsource to other countries in order to drive down costs, countries such as India continue to see employment rates rise.

A **host country** is a country (other than the parent country) in which an organization operates a facility. Great Britain is a host country of General Motors because GM has operations there. Any British workers hired to work at GM's British facility would be *host-country nationals,* that is, employees who are citizens of the host country.

A **third country** refers to a country that is neither the parent country nor the host country. (The organization may or may not have a facility in the third country.) In the example of GM's operations in Great Britain, the company could hire an Australian manager to work there. The Australian manager would be a *third-country national* because the manager is neither from the parent country (the United States) nor from the host country (Great Britain).

When organizations operate overseas, they must decide whether to hire parent-country nationals, host-country nationals, or third-country nationals for the overseas operations. Usually, they hire a combination of these. In general, employees assigned to work in another country are called **expatriates.** In the GM example, the U.S. and Australian managers working in Great Britain would be expatriates during those assignments.

The extent to which organizations use parent-country, host-country, or third-country nationals varies. Until recently, Western companies tended to use parent company nationals to manage operations in China, where employers found a shortage of management skills. Today, however, those skills are more widely available, and at multinational

Parent Country
The country in which an organization's headquarters is located.

Host Country
A country (other than the parent country) in which an organization operates a facility.

Third Country
A country that is neither the parent country nor the host country of an employer.

Expatriates
Employees assigned to work in another country.

companies, three-fourths of senior executives are now host country nationals. Employers prefer these leaders because they understand the culture of their customers, governments, and business partners. Competition is stiffest for hiring Asian managers who lived in the host country but were educated in the United States or Europe. An example is Mei-Wei Cheng, who was born in China and educated at Cornell University. Siemens, based in Germany, hired Cheng to lead its Chinese operations, formerly headed by a European executive.[4]

Employers in the Global Marketplace

Just as there are different ways for employees to participate in international business—as parent-country, host-country, or third-county nationals—so there are different ways for employers to do business globally, ranging from simply shipping products to customers in other countries to transforming the organization into a truly global one, with operations, employees, and customers in many countries. Figure 16.1 shows the major levels of global participation.

Most organizations begin by serving customers and clients within a domestic marketplace. Typically, a company's founder has an idea for serving a local, regional, or national market. The business must recruit, hire, train, and compensate employees to produce the product, and these people usually come from the business owner's local labor market. Selection and training focus on employees' technical abilities and, to some extent, on interpersonal skills. Pay levels reflect local labor conditions. If the product succeeds, the company might expand operations to other domestic locations, and HRM decisions become more complex as the organization draws from a larger labor market and needs systems for training and motivating employees in several locations. As the employer's workforce grows, it is also likely to become more diverse. Even in small domestic organizations, a significant share of workers may be immigrants. In this way, even domestic companies are affected by issues related to the global economy.

As organizations grow, they often begin to meet demand from customers in other countries. The usual way that a company begins to enter foreign markets is by *exporting*, or shipping domestically produced items to other countries to be sold there. Eventually, it may become economically desirable to set up operations in one or more

Figure 16.1
Levels of Global Participation

CHAPTER 16 Managing Human Resources Globally **499**

foreign countries. An organization that does so becomes an **international organization.** The decision to participate in international activities raises a host of HR issues, including the basic question of whether a particular location provides an environment where the organization can successfully acquire and manage human resources.

While international companies build one or a few facilities in another country, **multinational companies** go overseas on a broader scale. They build facilities in a number of different countries as a way to keep production and distribution costs to a minimum. In general, when organizations become multinationals, they move production facilities from relatively high-cost locations to lower-cost locations. The lower-cost locations may have lower average wage rates, or they may reduce distribution costs by being nearer to customers. The HRM challenges faced by a multinational company are similar to but larger than those of an international organization because more countries are involved. More than ever, the organization needs to hire managers who can function in a variety of settings, give them necessary training, and provide flexible compensation systems that take into account the different pay rates, tax systems, and costs of living from one country to another.

At the highest level of involvement in the global marketplace are **global organizations.** These flexible organizations compete by offering top products tailored to segments of the market while keeping costs as low as possible. A global organization locates each facility based on the ability to effectively, efficiently, and flexibly produce a product or service, using cultural differences as an advantage. Rather than treating differences in other countries as a challenge to overcome, a global organization treats different cultures as equals. It may have multiple headquarters spread across the globe, so decisions are more decentralized. This type of organization needs HRM practices that encourage flexibility and are based on an in-depth knowledge of differences among countries. Global organizations must be able to recruit, develop, retain, and use managers who can get results across national boundaries.

A global organization needs a **transnational HRM system**[5] that features decision making from a global perspective, managers from many countries, and ideas contributed by people from a variety of cultures. Decisions that are the outcome of a transnational HRM system balance uniformity (for fairness) with flexibility (to account for cultural and legal differences). This balance and the variety of perspectives should work together to improve the quality of decision making. The participants from various countries and cultures contribute ideas from a position of equality, rather than the parent country's culture dominating.

International Organization
An organization that sets up one or a few facilities in one or a few foreign countries.

Multinational Company
An organization that builds facilities in a number of different countries in an effort to minimize production and distribution costs.

Global Organization
An organization that chooses to locate a facility based on the ability to effectively, efficiently, and flexibly produce a product or service, using cultural differences as an advantage.

Transnational HRM System
Type of HRM system that makes decisions from a global perspective, includes managers from many countries, and is based on ideas contributed by people representing a variety of cultures.

Factors Affecting HRM in International Markets

Whatever their level of global participation, organizations that operate in more than one country must recognize that the countries are not identical and differ in terms of many factors. To simplify this discussion, we focus on four major factors:

- Culture
- Education
- Economic systems
- Political-legal systems

LO 16-2 Identify the factors that most strongly influence HRM in international markets.

Culture

By far the most important influence on international HRM is the culture of the country in which a facility is located. *Culture* is a community's set of shared assumptions

In Taiwan, a country that is high in collectivism, co-workers consider themselves more as group members instead of individuals.

about how the world works and what ideals are worth striving for.[6] Cultural influences may be expressed through customs, languages, religions, and so on.

Culture is important to HRM for two reasons. First, it often determines the other three international influences. Culture can greatly affect a country's laws because laws often are based on the culture's definitions of right and wrong. Culture also influences what people value, so it affects people's economic systems and efforts to invest in education.

Even more important for understanding human resource management, culture often determines the effectiveness of various HRM practices. Practices that are effective in the United States, for example, may fail or even backfire in a country with different beliefs and values.[7] Consider the five dimensions of culture that Geert Hofstede identified in his classic study of culture[8]:

1. *Individualism/collectivism* describes the strength of the relation between an individual and other individuals in the society. In cultures that are high in individualism, such as the United States, Great Britain, and the Netherlands, people tend to think and act as individuals rather than as members of a group. People in these countries are expected to stand on their own two feet, rather than be protected by the group. In cultures that are high in collectivism, such as Colombia, Pakistan, and Taiwan, people think of themselves mainly as group members. They are expected to devote themselves to the interests of the community, and the community is expected to protect them when they are in trouble.

2. *Power distance* concerns the way the culture deals with unequal distribution of power and defines the amount of inequality that is normal. In countries with large power distances, including India and the Philippines, the culture defines it as normal to maintain large differences in power. In countries with small power distances, such as Denmark and Israel, people try to eliminate inequalities. One way to see differences in power distance is in the way people talk to one another. In the high-power-distance countries of Mexico and Japan, people address one another with titles (Señor Smith, Smith-san). At the other extreme, in the United States, in most situations people use one another's first names—behavior that would be disrespectful in other cultures.

3. *Uncertainty avoidance* describes how cultures handle the fact that the future is unpredictable. High uncertainty avoidance refers to a strong cultural preference for structured situations. In countries such as Greece and Portugal, people tend to rely heavily on religion, law, and technology to give them a degree of security and clear rules about how to behave. In countries with low uncertainty avoidance, including Singapore and Jamaica, people seem to take each day as it comes.

4. *Masculinity/femininity* is the emphasis a culture places on practices or qualities that have traditionally been considered masculine or feminine. A "masculine" culture is a culture that values achievement, money making, assertiveness, and competition. A "feminine" culture is one that places a high value on relationships, service, care for the weak, and preserving the environment. In this model, Germany and Japan are examples of masculine cultures, and Sweden and Norway are examples of feminine cultures.

5. *Long-term/short-term orientation* suggests whether the focus of cultural values is on the future (long term) or the past and present (short term). Cultures with a long-term orientation value saving and persistence, which tend to pay off in the future. Many Asian countries, including Japan and China, have a long-term orientation. Short-term orientations, as in the cultures of the United States, Russia, and West Africa, promote respect for past tradition and for fulfilling social obligations in the present.

Such cultural characteristics as these influence the ways members of an organization behave toward one another, as well as their attitudes toward various HRM practices. For instance, cultures differ strongly in their opinions about how managers should lead, how decisions should be handled, and what motivates employees. In Germany, managers achieve their status by demonstrating technical skills, and employees look to managers to assign tasks and resolve technical problems. In the Netherlands, managers focus on seeking agreement, exchanging views, and balancing the interests of the people affected by a decision.[9] Clearly, differences like these would affect how an organization selects and trains its managers and measures their performance.

Cultures strongly influence the appropriateness of HRM practices. For example, the extent to which a culture is individualist or collectivist will affect the success of a compensation program. Compensation tied to individual performance may be seen as fairer and more motivating by members of an individualist culture; a culture favoring individualism will be more accepting of great differences in pay between the organization's highest- and lowest-paid employees. Collectivist cultures tend to have much flatter pay structures.

The success of HRM decisions related to job design, benefits, performance management, and other systems related to employee motivation also will be shaped by culture. In an interesting study comparing call center workers in India (a collectivist culture) and the United States (an individualistic culture), researchers found that in the United States, employee turnover depended more on person–job fit than on person–organization fit. In the United States, employees were less likely to quit if they felt that they had the right skills, resources, and personality to succeed on the job. In India, what mattered more was for employees to feel they fit in well with the organization and were well connected to the organization and the community.[10] In some organizations, managers stumble on the way to learning how to apply HRM decisions in another culture. For examples, see the "HR Oops!" box.

Finally, cultural differences can affect how people communicate and how they coordinate their activities. In collectivist cultures, people tend to value group decision making, as in the previous example. When a person raised in an individualistic culture must work closely with people from a collectivist culture, communication problems and conflicts often occur. People from the collectivist culture tend to collaborate heavily and may evaluate the individualistic person as unwilling to cooperate and share information with them. Cultural differences in communication affected the way a North American agricultural company embarked on employee empowerment at its facilities in the United States and Brazil.[11] Empowerment requires information sharing, but in Brazil, high power distance leads employees to expect managers to make decisions, so they do not desire information that is appropriately held by managers. Empowering the Brazilian employees required involving managers directly in giving and sharing information to show that this practice was in keeping with the traditional chain of command. Also, because uncertainty avoidance is another aspect of Brazilian culture,

HR Oops!

Cross-Cultural Management Mishaps

When Andrew Pickup left his home country of the United Kingdom to take a management position in Singapore, he did not expect to have to adjust his style of gathering performance information. As Pickup analyzed the situation, he was traveling to a former British colony, where people spoke English and had grown used to British ways of doing business. He assumed his direct style of getting and sharing information would work well. Instead, when he invited feedback, employees were startled and were quiet. In Singapore, people consider it polite to be subtle. Pickup learned to take his time and develop relationships, and eventually he was better able to get the information he needed.

Debbie Nicol, an Australian, has a job that involves training others. When she arrived in Dubai for a six-year assignment, she experienced an embarrassment in the middle of a training session. One of the attendees suddenly stood up and headed for the door, and she felt she had failed to hold his interest in the subject. She asked why he was leaving. He said he was going to pray. After that, Nicol learned to build prayer breaks into training schedules at the appropriate times of the day.

Pickup and Nicol quickly learned from their experiences. Managers and employees can succeed in cross-cultural situations if they are flexible. Like Nicol, they may change their practices to suit an important cultural norm. Or like Pickup, they may persevere in demonstrating their own practices when these are most beneficial. Either way, it is important to behave respectfully and with an effort at genuine understanding. Success also is more likely for a person who is aware of and honest about his or her own cultural norms and values.

Questions

1. Based on the information given, how respectfully and effectively did Andrew Pickup handle his mistake in seeking feedback?
2. How respectfully and effectively did Debbie Nicol handle her mistake in the training schedule?

Sources: Culture Crossing, "Singapore: Culture, Customs and Etiquette," http://www.culturecrossing.net, accessed July 28, 2014; Andrea Murad, "Expat Angst: Four Expats Reveal Cultural Surprises," BBC, September 4, 2013, http://www.bbc.com; Paula Caligiuri, "Develop Your Cultural Agility," *T+D,* March 2013, pp. 70–72.

managers explained that greater information sharing would reduce uncertainty about their work. At the same time, greater collectivism in Brazil made employees comfortable with the day-to-day communication of teamwork. The individualistic U.S. employees needed to be sold more on this aspect of empowerment.

Because of these challenges, organizations must prepare managers to recognize and handle cultural differences. They may recruit managers with knowledge of other cultures or provide training, as described later in the chapter. For expatriate assignments, organizations may need to conduct an extensive selection process to identify individuals who can adapt to new environments. At the same time, it is important to be wary of stereotypes and avoid exaggerating the importance of cultural differences. Recent research that examined Hofstede's model of cultural differences found that differences among organizations within a particular culture were sometimes larger than differences from country to country.[12] This finding suggests that it is important for an organization to match its HR practices to its values; individuals who share those values are likely to be interested in working for the organization. When Sony Corporation wanted to reinvigorate innovation, it shifted away from Japan's traditional hiring practices for entry-level positions. Instead of administering formulaic interviews to a stream of college students attired in suits and prepared with rehearsed answers, Sony announced that it was looking for individuality and had set up a selection process that included more natural conversations in discussion groups.[13]

Education and Skill Levels

Countries also differ in the degree to which their labor markets include people with education and skills of value to employers. As discussed in Chapter 1, the United States suffers from a shortage of skilled workers in many occupations, and the problem is expected to increase. For example, the need for knowledge workers (engineers, teachers, scientists, health care workers) is expected to grow almost twice as fast as the overall rate of job growth in the United States.[14] On the other hand, the labor markets in many countries are very attractive because they offer high skills and low wages.

Educational opportunities also vary from one country to another. In general, spending on education is greater per pupil in high-income countries than in poorer countries.[15] Poverty, diseases such as AIDS, and political turmoil keep children away from school in some areas. A concerted international effort to provide universal access to primary education has dramatically reduced the number and proportion of children without access to schooling. However, progress stalled during the global recesssion, and the problem persists in sub-Saharan Africa.[16]

Companies with foreign operations locate in countries where they can find suitable employees. The education and skill levels of a country's labor force affect how and the extent to which companies want to operate there. In countries with a poorly educated population, companies will limit their activities to low-skill, low-wage jobs. In contrast, India's large pool of well-trained technical workers is one reason that the country has become a popular location for outsourcing computer programming jobs.

Economic System

A country's economic system, whether capitalist or socialist, as well as the government's involvement in the economy through taxes or compensation, price controls, and other activities, influences human resource management practices in a number of ways.

As with all aspects of a region's or country's life, the economic system and culture are likely to be closely tied, providing many of the incentives or disincentives for developing the value of the labor force. Socialist economic systems provide ample opportunities for educational development because the education system is free to students. At the same time, socialism may not provide economic rewards (higher pay) for increasing one's education. In capitalist systems, students bear more of the cost of their education, but employers reward those who invest in education.

The health of an economic system affects human resource management. In developed countries with great wealth, labor costs are relatively high. Such differences show up in compensation systems and in recruiting and selection decisions.

In general, socialist systems take a higher percentage of each worker's income as the worker's income increases. Capitalist systems tend to let workers keep more of their earnings. In this way, socialism

Students at the University of Warsaw in Poland are provided with a government-supported education. In general, former Soviet bloc countries tend to be generous in funding education, so they tend to have highly educated and skilled labor forces. Capitalist countries such as the United States generally leave higher education up to individual students to pay for, but the labor market rewards students who earn a college degree.

redistributes wealth from high earners to the poor, while capitalism apparently rewards individual accomplishments. In any case, since the amount of take-home pay a worker receives after taxes may thus differ from country to country, in an organization that pays two managers in two countries $100,000 each, the manager in one country might take home more than the manager in the other country. Such differences make pay structures more complicated when they cross national boundaries, and they can affect recruiting of candidates from more than one country.

Political-Legal System

A country's political-legal system—its government, laws, and regulations—strongly impinges on human resource management. The country's laws often dictate the requirements for certain HRM practices, such as training, compensation, hiring, firing, and layoffs. As we noted in the discussion of culture, the political-legal system arises to a large degree from the culture in which it exists, so laws and regulations reflect cultural values.

For example, the United States has led the world in eliminating discrimination in the workplace. Because this value is important in U.S. culture, the nation has legal safeguards such as the equal employment opportunity laws discussed in Chapter 3, which affect hiring and other HRM decisions. As a society, the United States also has strong beliefs regarding the fairness of pay systems. Thus, the Fair Labor Standards Act (discussed in Chapter 12), among other laws and regulations, sets a minimum wage for a variety of jobs. Other laws and regulations dictate much of the process of negotiation between unions and management. All these are examples of laws and regulations that affect the practice of HRM in the United States.

Similarly, laws and regulations in other countries reflect the norms of their cultures. In Western Europe, where many countries have had strong socialist parties, some laws have been aimed at protecting the rights and benefits of workers. The European Union has agreed that employers in member nations must respect certain rights of workers, including workplace health and safety; equal opportunities for men and women; protection against discrimination based on sex, race, religion, age, disability, and sexual orientation; and labor laws that set standards for work hours and other conditions of work. In Canada, the province of Quebec has an action plan for promoting gender equality. Montreal's McGill University has participated by reviewing its pay structure to ensure that pay for female-dominated occupations does not fall short of pay for equally important occupations dominated by men. The process required extensive job analysis and pay raises for some occupations.[17]

An organization that expands internationally must gain expertise in the host country's legal requirements and ways of dealing with its legal system, often leading organizations to hire one or more host-country nationals to help in the process. Some countries have laws requiring that a certain percentage of the employees of any foreign-owned subsidiary be host-country nationals, and in the context of our discussion here, this legal challenge to an organization's HRM may hold an advantage if handled creatively.

LO 16-3 Discuss how differences among countries affect HR planning at organizations with international operations.

Human Resource Planning in a Global Economy

As economic and technological change creates a global environment for organizations, human resource planning is involved in decisions about participating as an exporter or as an international, multinational, or global company. Even purely domestic companies may draw talent from the international labor market. As organizations consider decisions about their level of international activity, HR professionals should provide information about the relevant human resource issues, such as local market pay rates

HR How To

Supporting a Multinational Strategy

When organizations are making decisions about where and how to operate, HR professionals should help to ensure that decisions about hiring, training, rewarding, and so on are aligned with their organization's strategy. Here are some ideas for managing global human resources:

- Develop a "global mind-set." Learn about the global business environment, including the legal, economic, and cultural issues affecting the various locations where the organization operates or may decide to operate. Practice empathy and diplomacy, and think of differences as something interesting to explore.
- Build an HR department that reflects the organization's global diversity. Ensure that the people in HR represent the people in the organization.
- Build a network of relationships with co-workers in other

locations. Use the resources available, such as the corporate intranet, company meetings, and if possible, travel to other facilities.
- Learn what the HR best practices are in other countries. Instead of assuming that HR practices used in headquarters will work as well in all locations, weigh the pros and cons of different approaches in each context.
- Be sure training and development programs address talent needs globally. Identify and develop high-potential employees in all the locations where the organization operates. Review training materials to find and correct cultural assumptions that may not apply to all trainees or situations.
- Use company databases to create, analyze, and make available

information about employees' skills, including international experience and languages spoken, so the best individuals can be tapped as positions open up.

Questions

1. Do you think you already have a global mind-set, as described in the first bullet point? Why or why not?
2. How might a global mind-set help an HR manager follow the other guidelines listed?

Sources: David Gartside and Colin Sloman, "Adapting to a Workforce without Borders," *T+D,* April 2014, pp. 37–40; Fernando Sanchez-Arias, Hannelore Calmeyn, Ger Driesen, and Evert Pruis, "Human Capital Realities Pose Challenges across the Globe," *T+D,* February 2013, pp. 32–35; Mansour Javidan, Jennie L. Walker, and Amanda Bullough, "Behind the Global Curve," *People & Strategy* 36, no. 3 (2013): 42–47.

and labor laws. When organizations decide to operate internationally or globally, human resource planning involves decisions about where and how many employees are needed for each international facility. For guidelines on how to conduct this planning strategically, see "HR How To."

Decisions about where to locate include HR considerations such as the cost and availability of qualified workers. In addition, HR specialists must work with other members of the organization to weigh these considerations against financial and operational requirements. As discussed earlier, India and China have been popular locations because of low labor costs. But as the job creation has driven up living standards and demand for labor, it has driven up the price of labor in those countries. Cost-oriented call centers are looking to locations such as the Philippines and Eastern Europe. In response, Indian contractors have started up companies that offer more specialized skills, such as engineering, biotechnology, and computer animation. In China, where pay for factory workers has risen considerably, the reasons for operating there today have less to do with pay and more to do with the country's vast number of consumers and network of now-skilled suppliers.[18]

Other location decisions involve outsourcing, described in Chapter 2. Many companies have boosted efficiency by arranging to have specific functions performed by outside contractors. Many—but not all—of these arrangements involve workers outside the United States in lower-wage countries.

In Chapter 5, we saw that human resource planning includes decisions to hire and lay off workers to prepare for the organization's expected needs. Compared with other countries, the United States allows employers wide latitude in reducing their workforce, giving U.S. employers the option of hiring for peak needs, then laying off employees if needs decline. Other governments place more emphasis on protecting workers' jobs. European countries, and France in particular, tend to be very strict in this regard.

LO 16-4 Describe how companies select and train human resources in a global labor market.

Selecting Employees in a Global Labor Market

Many companies such as Microsoft have headquarters in the United States plus facilities in locations around the world. To be effective, employees in the Microsoft Mexico operations in Mexico City must understand that region's business and social culture. Organizations often meet this need by hiring host-country nationals to fill most of their foreign positions. A key reason is that a host-country national can more easily understand the values and customs of the local workforce than someone from another part of the world can. Also, training for and transporting families to foreign assignments is more expensive than hiring people in the foreign country. Employees may be reluctant to take a foreign assignment because of the difficulty of moving overseas. Sometimes the move requires the employee's spouse to quit a job, and some countries will not allow the employee's spouse to seek work, even if jobs might be available.

Even so, organizations fill many key foreign positions with parent-country or third-country nationals. Sometimes a person's technical and human relations skills outweigh the advantages of hiring locally. In other situations, the local labor market simply does not offer enough qualified people. For example, seafood processors and farmers in Alabama have reported difficulty in finding people willing to do demanding physical labor for long hours to gut catfish and pick tomatoes. Whether the problem is that Americans aren't willing to work that hard or that they expect higher pay and generous benefits in exchange for their efforts, these employers have for years turned to immigrant labor to fill the positions.[19] In recent years, immigrant workers in the United States have been most common in jobs where the demand for labor is highest—in the nation's fastest-growing occupations, both those at the low end of the pay scale, such as agriculture and food services, and in jobs requiring a technical education, such as high-tech manufacturing and information technology.[20] The ability to tap this labor supply is limited by government paperwork and delays. An international survey of HR professionals found that the United States ranked among the most challenging destinations for expatriate assignments, and respondents most often blamed the legal requirements for immigration.[21] In addition, as described in Chapter 6, U.S. employers must take care to hire employees who are eligible to work in the United States.

Whether the organization is hiring immigrants or selecting parent-country or third-country nationals for foreign assignments, some basic principles of selection apply. Selection of employees for foreign assignments should reflect criteria that have been associated with success in working overseas:

- Competency in the employee's area of expertise.
- Ability to communicate verbally and nonverbally in the foreign country.

Qualities associated with success in foreign assignments are the ability to communicate in the foreign country, flexibility, enjoying a challenging situation, and support from family members. What would persuade you to take a foreign assignment?

Figure 16.2
Emotional Stages Associated with a Foreign Assignment

Sources: Deborah de Cerff, "Returning from an Overseas Assignment? There's No Place Like Home," *HC Online,* October 28, 2013, http://www.hcmag.com; Delia Flanja, "Culture Shock in Intercultural Communication," *Studia Europaea* (October 2009), Business & Company Resource Center, http://galenet.galegroup.com.

- Flexibility, tolerance of ambiguity, and sensitivity to cultural differences.
- Motivation to succeed and enjoyment of challenges.
- Willingness to learn about the foreign country's culture, language, and customs.
- Support from family members.[22]

In research conducted a number of years ago, the factor most strongly influencing whether an employee completed a foreign assignment was the comfort of the employee's spouse and family.[23] Personality may also be important. Research has found successful completion of overseas assignments to be most likely among employees who are extroverted (outgoing), agreeable (cooperative and tolerant), and conscientious (dependable and achievement oriented).[24]

Qualities of flexibility, motivation, agreeableness, and conscientiousness are so important because of the challenges involved in entering another culture. The emotions that accompany an overseas assignment tend to follow stages like those in Figure 16.2.[25] For a month or so after arriving, the foreign worker enjoys a "honeymoon" of fascination and euphoria as the employee enjoys the novelty of the new culture and compares its interesting similarities to or differences from the employee's own culture. Before long, the employee's mood declines as he or she notices more unpleasant differences and experiences feelings of isolation, criticism, stereotyping, and even hostility. As the mood reaches bottom, the employee is experiencing **culture shock,** the disillusionment and discomfort that occur during the process of adjusting to a new culture and its norms, values, and perspectives. Eventually, if employees persist and continue learning about their host country's culture, they begin to recover from culture shock as they develop a greater understanding and a support network. As the employee's language skills and comfort increase, the employee's mood should improve as well. Eventually, the employee reaches a stage of adjustment in which he or she accepts and enjoys the host country's culture.

Culture Shock
Disillusionment and discomfort that occur during the process of adjusting to a new culture.

Training and Developing a Global Workforce

In an organization whose employees come from more than one country, some special challenges arise with regard to training and development: (1) Training and development programs should be effective for all participating employees, regardless of their country of origin; and (2) When organizations hire employees to work in a foreign country or transfer them to another country, the employer needs to provide the employees with training in how to handle the challenges associated with working in the foreign country.

Training Programs for an International Workforce

Developers of effective training programs for an international workforce must ask certain questions.[26] The first is to establish the objectives for the training and its content. Decisions about the training should support those objectives. The developers should next ask what training techniques, strategies, and media to use. Some will be more effective than others, depending on the learners' language and culture, as well as the content of the training. For example, in preparation U.S. employees might expect to discuss and ask questions about the training content, whereas employees from other cultures might consider this level of participation to be disrespectful, so for them some additional support might be called for. Language differences will require translations and perhaps a translator at training activities. Next, the developers should identify any other interventions and conditions that must be in place for the training to meet its objectives. For example, training is more likely to meet its objectives if it is linked to performance management and has the full support of management. Finally, the developers of a training program should identify who in the organization should be involved in reviewing and approving the training program.

The plan for the training program must consider international differences among trainees. For example, economic and educational differences might influence employees' access to and ability to use web-based training. Cultural differences may influence whether they will consider it appropriate to ask questions and whether they expect the trainer to spend time becoming acquainted with employees or to get down to business immediately. Table 16.1 provides examples of how cultural characteristics can affect training design.

Cross-Cultural Preparation

Cross-Cultural Preparation
Training to prepare employees and their family members for an assignment in a foreign country.

When an organization selects an employee for a position in a foreign country, it must prepare the employee for the foreign assignment. This kind of training is called **cross-cultural preparation,** preparing employees to work across national and cultural boundaries, and it often includes family members who will accompany the employee on the assignment. The training is necessary for all three phases of an international assignment:

1. Preparation for *departure*—language instruction and an orientation to the foreign country's culture.
2. The *assignment* itself—some combination of a formal program and mentoring relationship to provide ongoing further information about the foreign country's culture.

Table 16.1

Effects of Culture on Training Design

CULTURAL DIMENSION	IMPACT ON TRAINING
Individualism	Culture high in individualism expects participation in exercises and questioning to be determined by status in the company or culture.
Uncertainty avoidance	Culture high in uncertainty avoidance expects formal instructional environments. There is less tolerance for impromptu style.
Masculinity	Culture low in masculinity values relationships with fellow trainees. Female trainers are less likely to be resisted in low-masculinity cultures.
Power distance	Culture high in power distance expects trainers to be experts. Trainers are expected to be authoritarian and controlling of session.
Time orientation	Culture with a long-term orientation will have trainees who are likely to accept development plans and assignments.

Source: Based on B. Filipczak, "Think Locally, Act Globally," *Training,* January 1997, pp. 41–48.

Standard Chartered Bank Invests in Its Expatriates

With branches in 70 countries and nine-tenths of its income coming from Africa, Asia, and the Middle East, London-based Standard Chartered Bank often uses expatriates. When it needs someone to start up a new line of business or fill an opening on a project, the bank evaluates the existing skills throughout the organization. It has a workforce of 86,000 people of more than 130 nationalities, so Standard Chartered often can fill a need through internal recruitment.

At this point, the bank's staff responsible for talent acquisition, international mobility (relocation), and training and development work together closely. If the best candidate will have to relocate to another country, the international mobility team goes to work on estimating costs, and the training and development team begins to identify needs.

For any international assignment, Standard Chartered plans for employee development and leadership skills, regardless of the employee's level in the organization. Throughout the assignment, the expatriate employee stays connected with the bank's international talent deployment and talent acquisition group at a single location. Standard Chartered evaluates and coaches expatriates not only in whether they are adjusting to the new culture but also in how well expatriate managers are developing local talent to fill future roles. HR staffers participate in discussions about how each assignment will contribute to possible career paths for the expatriate. These discussions are particularly important in the last months of an assignment, so that returning employees see they are valued and are more likely to stay with Standard Chartered.

In India, the focus on training and development has been valuable as a way for Standard Chartered to compete in a tough labor market. Growth in the Indian economy has made retention of talented employees more difficult. The chance to take on interesting and important international assignments has been attractive to India's educated workers. Ensuring that these employees are well supported and developed means they can succeed at meeting the challenges of those assignments and thus build a career with the bank.

Questions

1. How might careful preparation for departure help Standard Chartered develop and retain talented employees?
2. How might thorough planning for the return home help Standard Chartered retain talent?

Sources: Standard Chartered Bank, "About Us," https://www.sc.com, accessed July 28, 2014; Charlene Solomon, "The Passport to Better Expatriate Experiences," *Chief Learning Officer*, March 2014, pp. 26, 28, 32; Anita Bhoir, "Banks Like Standard Chartered, JP Morgan and Others Offering Foreign Postings to Retain Staff," *The Economic Times*, March 25, 2013, http://articles.economictimes.indiatimes.com.

3. Preparation for the *return* home—providing information about the employee's community and home-country workplace (from company newsletters, local newspapers, and so on).

For an example of an organization that takes this broad approach to preparation, see "Best Practices."

Methods for providing this training may range from lectures for employees and their families to visits to culturally diverse communities.[27] Employees and their families may also spend time visiting a local family from the country where they will be working. In the later section on managing expatriates, we provide more detail about cross-cultural preparation.

Despite the importance of preparation, the 2014 Global Mobility Trends Survey found that only 39% of companies offer it for all expatriate assignments. Another 45% offer training for some assignments, based on considerations such as the challenges of the host location, the employee's familiarity with the location, and the type of assignment.[28] However, most of the companies offered repatriation discussions for returning employees. It is important for employers to remember that returning home is also a challenge when employees have been away for months or years. Returning employees often find that life at home seems boring, relative to the excitement of learning a new culture, and family members and colleagues at home may find it hard to relate to their recent experiences. Employers should be ready for employees who want to share what they learned and put their recently acquired skills to work in new assignments.[29]

Global Employee Development

At global organizations, international assignments are a part of many career paths. The organization benefits most if it applies the principles of employee development in deciding which employees should be offered jobs in other countries. Career development helps expatriate and inpatriate employees make the transitions to and from their assignments and helps the organization apply the knowledge the employees obtain from these assignments.

LO 16-5 Discuss challenges related to managing performance and compensating employees from other countries.

Performance Management across National Boundaries

The general principles of performance management may apply in most countries, but the specific methods that work in one country may fail in another. Therefore, organizations have to consider legal requirements, local business practices, and national cultures when they establish performance management methods in other countries. Differences may include which behaviors are rated, how and the extent to which performance is measured, who performs the rating, and how feedback is provided.[30]

For example, National Rental Car uses a behaviorally based rating scale for customer service representatives. To measure the extent to which customer service representatives' behaviors contribute to the company's goal of improving customer service, the scale measures behaviors such as smiling, making eye contact, greeting customers, and solving customer problems. Depending on the country, different behaviors may be appropriate. In Japan, culturally defined standards for polite behavior include the angle of bowing as well as proper back alignment and eye contact. In Ghana and many other African nations, appropriate measures would include behaviors that reflect loyalty and repaying of obligations as well as behaviors related to following regulations and procedures.

The extent to which managers measure performance may also vary from one country to another. In rapidly changing regions, such as Southeast Asia, the organization may have to update its performance plans more often than once a year.

Feedback is another area in which differences can occur. Employees around the world appreciate positive feedback, but U.S. employees are much more used to direct feedback than are employees in other countries. In Mexico managers are expected to provide positive feedback before focusing the discussion on behaviors the employee needs to improve.[31] At the Thai office of Singapore Airlines, managers resisted giving negative feedback to employees because they feared this would cause them to have bad karma, contributing to their reincarnation at a lower level in their next life.[32] The airlines therefore allowed the managers to adapt their feedback process to fit local cultures.

Compensating an International Workforce

The chapters in Part 4 explained that compensation includes decisions about pay structure, incentive pay, and employee benefits. All these decisions become more complex when an organization has an international workforce. Johnson & Johnson meets the challenge by

Managing Human Resources Globally

creating a global compensation strategy for its 250 pharmaceutical, consumer, and medical-device businesses with employees in 70 countries. J&J developed the strategy at its U.S. headquarters because compensation expertise at the company varied from one region to another. However, it had representatives from each region serve on the project teams so the company would be familiar with local issues, such as the need for frequent salary reviews in Venezuela and Argentina, where high inflation rates take a toll on buying power.[33]

Pay Structure

As Figure 16.3 shows, market pay structures can differ substantially across countries in terms of both pay level and the relative worth of jobs. For example, compared with the labor market in Germany, the market in Mexico provides much lower pay levels overall. In Germany, the pay differences between jobs are less dramatic than in South Korea; for example, the relative pay of teachers is much higher in South Korea. One reason for big pay differences in some countries is a shortage of talent in local labor markets. In Brazil, for example, companies have trouble finding enough managers with technical expertise, because big construction projects and oil drilling are driving heavy demand for those positions. In addition, the fast-growing Brazilian economy has drawn many multinationals to locate facilities in Brazil, further increasing the demand for managers there. Finally, Brazilian managers tend to be loyal employees, so recruiters need to offer especially tempting compensation packages to lure them away.[34]

Figure 16.3

Earnings in Selected Occupations in Three Countries

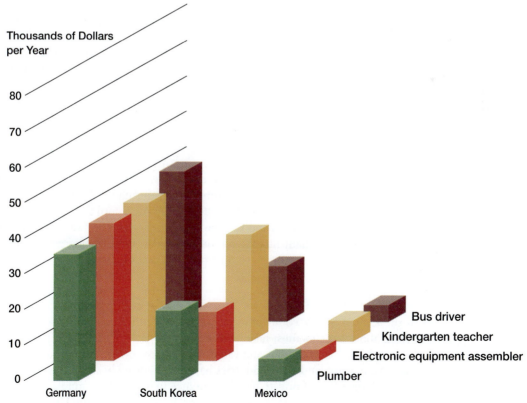

Source: Wage and hour data from International Labour Organization, LABORSTA Internet, http://laborsta.ilo.org, accessed July, 28, 2014.

Differences such as these create a dilemma for global companies: Should pay levels and differences reflect what workers are used to in their own countries? Or should they reflect the earnings of colleagues in the country of the facility, or earnings at the company headquarters? For example, should a German engineer posted to Mumbai be paid according to the standard in Frankfurt or the standard in Mumbai? If the standard is Frankfurt, the engineers in Mumbai will likely see the German engineer's pay as unfair. If the standard is Mumbai, the company will likely find it impossible to persuade a German engineer to take an assignment in Mumbai. Dilemmas such as these make a global compensation strategy important as a way to show employees that the pay structure is designed to be fair and related to the value that employees bring to the organization.

These decisions affect a company's costs and ability to compete. The average hourly labor costs in industrialized countries such as the United States, Germany, and Japan are far higher than these costs in newly industrialized countries such as Mexico, Brazil, and the Philippines.[35] As a result, we often hear that U.S. labor costs are too high to allow U.S. companies to compete effectively unless the companies shift operations to low-cost foreign subsidiaries. That conclusion oversimplifies the situation for many companies. Merely comparing wages ignores differences in education, skills, and productivity.[36] If an organization gets more or higher-quality output from a higher-wage workforce, the higher wages may be worth the cost. Besides this, if the organization has many positions requiring highly skilled workers, it may need to operate in (or hire immigrants from) a country with a strong educational system, regardless of labor costs. Finally, labor costs may be outweighed by other factors, such as transportation costs or access to resources or customers. When a production process is highly automated, differences in labor costs may not be significant.

Cultural and legal differences also can affect pay structure. Some countries, including Colombia, Greece, and Malaysia, require that companies provide salary increases to employees earning minimum wage. In Venezuela, employers must provide employees with a meal allowance. In Mexico and Puerto Rico, employers must pay holiday bonuses. Organizations with a global pay strategy must adjust the strategy to account for local requirements and determine how pay decisions for optional practices will affect their competitive standing in local labor markets.[37]

Incentive Pay

Besides setting a pay structure, the organization must make decisions with regard to incentive pay, such as bonuses and stock options. Although stock options became a common form of incentive pay in the United States during the 1990s, European businesses did not begin to embrace this type of compensation until the end of that decade.

However, the United States and Europe differ in the way they award stock options. European companies usually link the options to specific performance goals, such as the increase in a company's share price compared with that of its competitors.

Employee Benefits

As in the United States, compensation packages in other countries include benefits. Decisions about benefits must take into account the laws of each country involved, as well as employees' expectations and values in those countries. Some countries require paid maternity leave, and some countries have nationalized health care systems, which would affect the value of private health insurance in a compensation package. Pension plans are more widespread in parts of Western Europe than in the United States and

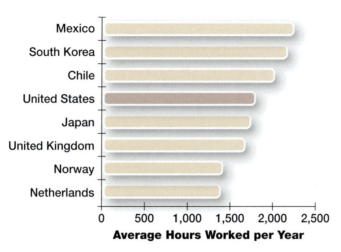

Figure 16.4
Average Hours Worked
in Selected Countries

Source: Organisation for Economic Co-operation and Development, "Average Annual Hours Actually Worked per Worker," OECD StatExtracts, http://stats.oecd.org, accessed July 28, 2014.

Japan. Over 90% of workers in Switzerland have pension plans, as do all workers in France. Among workers with pension plans, U.S. workers are significantly less likely to have defined benefit plans than workers in Japan or Germany.

Paid vacation, discussed in Chapter 14, tends to be more generous in Western Europe than in the United States. Figure 16.4 compares the number of hours the average employee works in various countries. Of these countries, only in Mexico, South Korea, and Chile do workers put in more hours than U.S. workers. In the other countries, the norm is to work fewer hours than a U.S. worker over the course of a year.

International Labor Relations

Companies that operate across national boundaries often need to work with unions in more than one country. Organizations establish policies and goals for labor relations, for overseeing labor agreements, and for monitoring labor performance (for example, output and productivity).[38] The day-to-day decisions about labor relations are usually handled by each foreign subsidiary. The reason is that labor relations on an international scale involve differences in laws, attitudes, and economic systems, as well as differences in negotiation styles.

At least in comparison with European organizations, U.S. organizations exert more centralized control over labor relations in the various countries where they operate.[39] U.S. management therefore must recognize differences in how various countries understand and regulate labor relations. For example, in the United States, collective bargaining usually involves negotiations between a union local and an organization's management, but in Sweden and Germany, collective bargaining generally involves negotiations between an employer's organization and a union representing an entire industry's employees.[40] China's only legal labor union—and the world's largest union—is the All-China Federation of Trade Unions (ACFTU), which is controlled by the government. The Chinese government limits the workers' rights to collective bargaining and striking, and it appoints leaders of the ACFTU. At some companies in recent years, workers have begun to conduct strikes and protests seeking greater rights.[41]

Legal differences range from who may form a union to how much latitude an organization is allowed in laying off workers. In some situations, governments get involved to protect workers. After an eight-story factory collapsed in Dhaka, Bangladesh, killing more than 1,100 people, the government of Bangladesh relaxed rules that had made it difficult for the country's workers to unionize. Until then, workers had to obtain permission from factory owners before forming trade unions.[42]

International labor relations must also take into account that negotiations between labor and management take place in a different social context, not just different economic and legal contexts. Cultural differences that affect other interactions come into play in labor negotiations as well. Negotiators will approach the process differently depending on whether the culture views the process as primarily cooperative or competitive and whether it is local practice to negotiate a deal by starting with the specifics or agreeing on overall principles.[43] Working with host-country nationals can help organizations navigate such differences in negotiation style.

Managing Expatriates

At some point, most international and global organizations assign managers to foreign posts. These assignments give rise to significant human resource challenges, from selecting managers for these assignments to preparing them, compensating them, and helping them adjust to a return home. The same kinds of HRM principles that apply to domestic positions can help organizations avoid mistakes in managing expatriates: planning and goal setting, selection aimed at achieving the HR goals, and performance management that includes evaluation of whether the overseas assignment delivered value relative to the costs involved.[44] Employers also can increase the likelihood of a successful assignment by ensuring that employees and their families have the resources they need. The "HRM Social" box offers examples of one kind of support.

Selecting Expatriate Managers

The challenge of managing expatriate managers begins with determining which individuals in the organization are most capable of handling an assignment in another country. Expatriate managers need technical competence in the area of operations, in part to help them earn the respect of subordinates. Of course, many other skills are also necessary for success in any management job, especially one that involves working overseas. Depending on the nature of the assignment and the culture where it is located, the organization should consider each candidate's skills, learning style, and approach to problem solving. Each of these should be related to achievement of the organization's goals, such as solving a particular problem, transferring knowledge to host-country employees, or developing future leaders for the organization.[45]

A successful expatriate manager must be sensitive to the host country's cultural norms, flexible enough to adapt to those norms, and strong enough to survive the culture shock of living in another culture. In addition, if the manager has a family, the family members must be able to adapt to a new culture. Adaptation requires three kinds of skills[46]:

1. Ability to maintain a positive self-image and feeling of well-being.
2. Ability to foster relationships with the host-country nationals.
3. Ability to perceive and evaluate the host country's environment accurately.

In a study that drew on the experience of people holding international assignments, expatriates told researchers that the most important qualities for an expatriate manager

Online Communities to Support Expatriates' Spouses

A common reason cited for the failure of an international assignment is that the expatriate's spouse was dissatisfied. The role of an accompanying spouse is difficult. Often, this person is not legally allowed to work in the host country, so it is more difficult for him or her to find new friends and meaningful activities.

Employers can help the accompanying spouse make connections. An employer, especially one with a lot of expatriate employees, might set up its own spouses' network. In The Netherlands, Eindhoven University of Technology recruits one-third of its employees from other countries but found that many left after a short period because spouses were unhappy there. It began offering spouses a "Get in Touch" program of weekly meetings to exchange information and visit places of interest. Between meetings, the spouses can keep in contact by joining the group's Facebook community. After the three-month program ended, many of the participants didn't want to stop participating, so the university added a Stay in Touch program.

Another approach is to provide information about non-company-related social networks for expatriate spouses. Spouses may appreciate the chance to build their own circle of friends. One example is the Trailing Spouse Network, a LinkedIn group where people can share ideas, advice, and support. The Trailing Spouse Network also has a page on Facebook.

Increasingly often, the accompanying spouse is a husband. Some men have had an especially hard time making connections, because support services have been geared to women. These spouses might especially welcome information about social networks for men. In Belgium, for instance, a group of men set up a group called STUDS (for Spouses Trailing under Duress Successfully), which offers activities and keeps members connected online with a blog. Even after leaving Belgium, friends who met in STUDS can keep in touch by posting news and questions on the blog's website.

Questions

1. What pros and cons do you see in having an organization set up its own social network for accompanying spouses?
2. What pros and cons do you see in referring an accompanying spouse to an outside social network?

Sources: Brookfield Global Relocation Services, *2014 Global Mobility Trends Survey*, 2014, http://knowledge.brookfieldgrs.com; Willem G. van Hoorn and Carola L. Eijsenring, "Setting Up a Social Support Program for Accompanying Spouses of International Knowledge Workers," *People & Strategy* 36, no. 4 (2014): 60–61, 64; Kendra Mirasol, "Following Her Job to Tokyo? Challenges Facing the Expat Male Trailing Spouse," IOR Global Services, http://www.iorworld.com, accessed July 28, 2014; Portable Career Network, "Trailing Spouse Network," http://www.portablecareer.net, accessed July 28, 2014; "STUDS (Spouses Trailing under Duress Successfully)," *(A)way Magazine*, http://www.awaymagazine.be, accessed July 28, 2014.

are, in order of importance, family situation, flexibility and adaptability, job knowledge and motivation, relational skills, and openness to other cultures.[47] To assess candidates' ability to adapt to a new environment, interviews should address topics such as the ones listed in Table 16.2. The interviewer should be certain to give candidates a clear and complete preview of the assignment and the host-country culture. This helps the candidate evaluate the assignment and consider it in terms of his or her family situation, so the employer does not violate the employee's privacy.[48]

Preparing Expatriates

LO 16-6 Explain how employers prepare managers for international assignments and for their return home.

Once the organization has selected a manager for an overseas assignment, it is necessary to prepare that person through training and development. Because expatriate success depends so much on the entire family's adjustment, the employee's spouse should be included in the preparation activities. Employees selected for expatriate assignments already have job-related skills, so preparation for expatriate assignments often focuses on cross-cultural training—that is, training in what to expect from the host country's culture. The general purpose of cross-cultural training is to create an appreciation of

Table 16.2

Selected Topics for Assessing Candidates for Overseas Assignments

Motivation
- What are the candidate's reasons and degree of interest in wanting an overseas assignment?
- Does the candidate have a realistic understanding of what is required in working and living overseas?
- What is the spouse's attitude toward an overseas assignment?

Health
- Are there any health issues with the candidate or family members that might impact the success of the overseas assignment?

Language ability
- Does the candidate have the potential to learn a new language?
- Does the candidate's spouse have the ability to learn a new language?

Family considerations
- How many moves has the family made among different cities or parts of the United States? What problems were encountered?
- What is the spouse's goal in this move overseas?
- How many children are in the family and what are their ages? Will all the children move as part of the overseas assignment?
- Has divorce or its potential, or the death of a family member had a negative effect on the family's cohesiveness?
- Are there any adjustment problems the candidate would expect should the family move overseas?

Resourcefulness and initiative
- Is the candidate independent and capable of standing by his or her decisions?
- Is the candidate able to meet objectives and produce positive results with whatever human resources and facilities are available regardless of challenges that might arise in a foreign business environment?
- Can the candidate operate without a clear definition of responsibility and authority?
- Will the candidate be able to explain the goals of the company and its mission to local managers and workers?
- Does the candidate possess sufficient self-discipline and self-confidence to handle complex problems?
- Can the candidate operate effectively in a foreign country without normal communications and supporting services?

Adaptability
- Is the candidate cooperative, open to the opinions of others, and able to compromise?
- How does the candidate react to new situations and efforts to understand and appreciate cultural differences?
- How does the candidate react to criticism, constructive or otherwise?
- Will the candidate be able to make and develop contacts with peers in a foreign country?
- Does the candidate demonstrate patience when dealing with problems? Is he or she resilient and able to move forward after setbacks?

Career planning
- Does the candidate consider the assignment more than a temporary overseas trip?
- Is the overseas assignment consistent with the candidate's career development and one that was planned by the company?
- What is the candidate's overall attitude toward the company?
- Is there any history or indication of interpersonal problems with this candidate?

Financial
- Are there any current financial and/or legal considerations that might affect the assignment (e.g., house or car purchase, college expenses)?
- Will undue financial pressures be put upon the candidate and his or her family as a result of an overseas assignment?

Sources: P. Caligiuri, *Cultural Agility: Building a Pipeline of Successful Global Professionals* (San Francisco: Jossey-Bass, 2012); P. Caligiuri, D. Lepak, and J. Bonache, *Managing the Global Workforce* (West Sussex, United Kingdom: John Wiley & Sons, 2010); M. Shaffer, D. Harrison, H. Gregersen, S. Black, and L. Ferzandi, "You Can Take It with You: Individual Differences and Expatriate Effectiveness," *Journal of Applied Psychology* 91(2006): 109–125; P. Caligiuri, "Developing Global Leaders," *Human Resource Management Review* 16 (2006): 219–228; P. Caligiuri, M. Hyland, A. Joshi, and A. Bross, "Testing a Theoretical Model for Examining the Relationship between Family Adjustment and Expatriates' Work Adjustment," *Journal of Applied Psychology* 83(1998): 598–614; David M. Noer, *Multinational People Management: A Guide for Organizations and Employees* (Arlington, VA: Bureau of National Affairs, 1975).

Figure 16.5

Impressions of Americans: Comments by Visitors to the United States

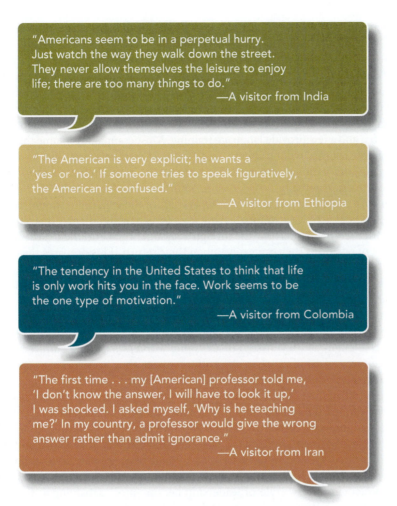

"Americans seem to be in a perpetual hurry. Just watch the way they walk down the street. They never allow themselves the leisure to enjoy life; there are too many things to do."
—A visitor from India

"The American is very explicit; he wants a 'yes' or 'no.' If someone tries to speak figuratively, the American is confused."
—A visitor from Ethiopia

"The tendency in the United States to think that life is only work hits you in the face. Work seems to be the one type of motivation."
—A visitor from Colombia

"The first time . . . my [American] professor told me, 'I don't know the answer, I will have to look it up,' I was shocked. I asked myself, 'Why is he teaching me?' In my country, a professor would give the wrong answer rather than admit ignorance."
—A visitor from Iran

Source: J. Feig and G. Blair, *There Is a Difference,* 2nd ed. (Washington, DC: Meridian House International, 1980), cited in N. Adler, *International Dimensions of Organizational Behavior,* 2nd ed. (Boston: PWS-Kent, 1991).

the host country's culture so expatriates can behave appropriately.[49] Paradoxically, this requires developing a greater awareness of one's own culture so that the expatriate manager can recognize differences and similarities between the cultures and, perhaps, home-culture biases. Consider, for example, the statements in Figure 16.5, which are comments made by visitors to the United States. Do you think these observations accurately describe U.S. culture?

On a more specific level, cross-cultural training for foreign assignments includes the details of how to behave in business settings in another country—the ways people behave in meetings, how employees expect managers to treat them, and so on. As an example, Germans value promptness for meetings to a much greater extent than do Latin Americans—and so on. How should one behave when first meeting one's business counterparts in another culture? The "outgoing" personality style so valued in the United States may seem quite rude in other parts of the world.[50] Ideally, the company also provides training for an expatriate manager's team in the host country, so that manager and employees can all learn about one another's cultural practices and values.[51]

Employees preparing for a foreign assignment also need information about such practical matters as housing, schools, recreation, shopping, and health care facilities in the country where they will be living. This is a crucial part of the preparation.

Communication in another country often requires a determined attempt to learn a new language. Some employers try to select managers who speak the language of the host country, and a few provide language training. Most companies assume that employees in the host country will be able to speak the host country's language. Even if this is true, host country nationals are not likely to be fluent in the home country's language, so language barriers remain.

Along with cross-cultural training, preparation of the expatriate should include career development activities. Before leaving for a foreign assignment, expatriates should discuss with their managers how the foreign assignment fits into their career plans and what types of positions they can expect upon their return. This prepares the expatriate to develop valuable skills during the overseas assignment and eases the return home when the assignment is complete. Coaching during the assignment also can improve the likelihood that the expatriate will succeed.

When the employee leaves for the assignment, the preparation process should continue. Expatriate colleagues, coaches, and mentors can help the employee learn to navigate challenges as they arise. For example, workers in a new culture sometimes experience internal conflict when the culture where they are working expects them to behave in a way that conflicts with values they learned from their own culture. For example, an Italian manager had difficulty motivating an Indian workforce because the employees were used to authoritarian leadership, and the manager felt as if that style was harsh and disempowering. By talking over the problem with experienced expatriates, the manager came to understand why the situation was so awkward and frustrating. He identified specific ways in which he could be more assertive without losing his temper, so that his Indian employees would better understand what was expected of them. Practicing a new style of leadership became more satisfying as the manager realized that the employees valued his style and that he was becoming a more capable cross-cultural leader.[52]

Managing Expatriates' Performance

Performance management of expatriates requires clear goals for the overseas assignment and frequent evaluation of whether the expatriate employee is on track to meet those goals. Communication technology including e-mail and teleconferencing provides a variety of ways for expats' managers to keep in touch with these employees to discuss and diagnose issues before they can interfere with performance. In addition, before employees leave for an overseas assignment, HR should work with managers to develop criteria measuring the success of the assignment.[53] Measures such as productivity should take into account any local factors that could make expected performance different in the host country than in the company's home country. For example, a country's labor laws or the reliability of the electrical supply could affect the facility's output and efficiency.

Compensating Expatriates

One of the greatest challenges of managing expatriates is determining the compensation package. Most organizations use a *balance sheet approach* to determine the total

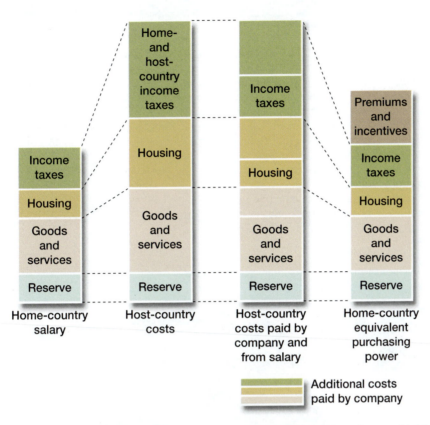

Figure 16.6

The Balance Sheet for Determining Expatriate Compensation

Home-country salary

Host-country costs

Host-country costs paid by company and from salary

Home-country equivalent purchasing power

Additional costs paid by company

Source: From C. Reynolds, "Compensation of Overseas Personnel," in *Handbook of Human Resource Administration,* 2nd ed., ed. by J. J. Famularo, McGraw-Hill, 1986, p. 51. Reprinted with permission of The McGraw-Hill Companies, Inc.

amount of the package. This approach adjusts the manager's compensation so that it gives the manager the same standard of living as in the home country plus extra pay for the inconvenience of locating overseas. As shown in Figure 16.6, the balance sheet approach begins by determining the purchasing power of compensation for the same type of job in the manager's own country—that is, how much a person can buy, after taxes, in terms of housing, goods and services, and a reserve for savings. Next, this amount is compared with the cost (in dollars, for a U.S. company) of these same expenses in the foreign country. In Figure 16.6, the greater size of the second column means the costs for a similar standard of living in the foreign country are much higher in every category except the reserve amount. This situation would be likely in one of the cities identified in the "Did You Know?" box. For the expatriate in this situation, the employer would pay the additional costs, as shown by the third column. Finally, the expatriate receives additional purchasing power from premiums and incentives. Because of these added incentives, the expatriate's purchasing power is more than what the manager could buy at home with the salary for an equivalent job. (Compare the fourth column with the first.) Expatriates sent to expensive destinations such as Singapore and Hong Kong can receive $200,000 a year in subsidies to cover the expenses of housing, transportation, and schools for their children—plus an additional $100,000 to cover the cost of taxes on these benefits. Adding in the costs to relocate the employee and his or her family can send the total bill for the assignment up to $1 million.[54] That

Priciest Cities Are Spread over Three Continents

Expatriates spend more for housing, transportation, food, clothing, and other living expenses in Luanda, Angola, than in any other major city, according to a survey by Mercer Human Resources Consulting. The capital cities of Angola and Chad are in the two top spots because they are rich sources of oil, so they are drawing in a stream of oil companies and their employees, increasing the demand for safe local housing and imported goods.

Rankings are influenced by the relative value of national currencies, as well as by political strife and natural disasters. The least expensive city among those studied was Karachi, Pakistan, where security concerns have reduced the demand for housing.

The only U.S. city in Mercer's top 50 is New York, which ranks 16th. Other U.S. cities are in the top 100: Los Angeles (62), San Francisco (74), Honolulu (97), and Miami (98).

Question

Why might an organization choose to locate a facility in one of the most expensive cities, in spite of the higher costs?

Sources: Roff Smith, "Move Over Tokyo: The World's Priciest Cities Are in Angola and Chad," KPBS, July 16, 2014, http://www.kpbs.org; Mercer, "2014 Cost of Living Rankings," news release, July 10, 2014, http://www.mercer.com; Ruth Holmes, "Housing Puts African Cities Top of Expat Cost-of-Living League," *Relocate*, July 10, 2014, http://www.relocatemagazine.com.

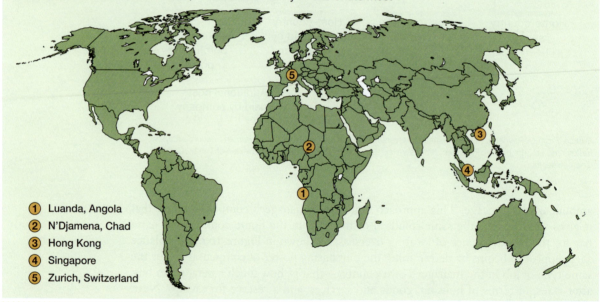

1. Luanda, Angola
2. N'Djamena, Chad
3. Hong Kong
4. Singapore
5. Zurich, Switzerland

high cost is one of the reasons employers are investing more in recruiting and training local talent.

After setting the total pay, the organization divides this amount into the four components of a total pay package:

1. *Base salary*—Determining the base salary is complex because different countries use different currencies (dollars, yen, euros, and so on). The exchange rate—the rate at which one currency may be exchanged for another—constantly shifts in response to a host of economic forces, so the real value of a salary in terms of dollars is constantly changing. Also, as discussed earlier, the base salary may be comparable to the pay of other managers at headquarters or comparable to other managers at the foreign subsidiary. Because many organizations pay a salary premium as an

incentive to accept an overseas assignment, expatriates' salaries are often higher than pay for staying at headquarters.

2. *Tax equalization allowance*—Companies have different systems for taxing income, and in many countries, tax rates are much higher than in the United States. Usually, the employer of an expatriate withholds the amount of tax to be paid in the parent country, then pays all of the taxes due in the country where the expatriate is working.

3. *Benefits*—Most benefits issues have to do with whether an employee can use the same benefits in the foreign country. For example, if an expatriate has been contributing to a pension plan in the United States, does this person have a new pension in the foreign country? Or can the expatriate continue to contribute to the U.S. pension plan? Similarly, health benefits may involve receiving care at certain health facilities. While the person is abroad, does the same health plan cover services received in the foreign country? In one case, flying a manager back to the United States for certain procedures actually would have cost less than having the procedures done in the country where the person was working. But the company's health plans did not permit this alternative. An employer may offer expatriates additional benefits to address the problem of uprooting the spouse when assigning an employee overseas.

4. *Allowances to make a foreign assignment more attractive*—Cost-of-living allowances make up the differences in expenses for day-to-day needs. Housing allowances ensure that the expatriate can maintain the same standard of living as in the United States. Education allowances reimburse expatriates who pay tuition for their children to attend private English-speaking schools. Relocation allowances cover the expenses of making the move to the foreign country, including transportation, shipping or storage of possessions, and expenses for temporary housing until the employee can rent or purchase a home.

Figure 16.7 is an example of a summary sheet for an expatriate manager's compensation package, showing a variety of allowances.

Helping Expatriates Return Home

As the expatriate's assignment nears its end, the human resource department faces a final challenge: helping the expatriate make the transition back to his or her home country. The process of preparing expatriates to return home from a foreign assignment is called **repatriation.** Reentry is not as simple as it might sound. Culture shock takes place in reverse. The experience has changed the expatriate, and the company's and expatriate's home cultures have changed as well. Also, because of differences in economies and compensation levels, a returning expatriate may experience a decline in living standards. The standard of living for an expatriate in many countries includes maid service, a limousine, private schools, and clubs.

Companies are increasingly making efforts to help expatriates through this transition. Two activities help the process along: communication and validation.[55] Communication refers to the expatriate receiving information and recognizing changes while abroad. The more the organization keeps in contact with the expatriate, the more effective and satisfied the person will be upon return. The expatriate plays a role in this process as well. Expatriates should work at maintaining important contacts in the company and industry. Communication related to career development before and during the overseas assignment also should help the employee return to a position that is

Repatriation
The process of preparing expatriates to return home from a foreign assignment.

Figure 16.7

International Assignment
Allowance Form

		Old	New
Name	John H. Doe		
Effective date	1 October 2015		
Location of assignment	Singapore		
Title	Manager, SLS./Serv. AP/ME		
Home base	Houston, Texas		
Emp. no.	1234		
LCA code	202		
Tax code	202		
Reason for Change:	International Assignment		
		Old	**New**
Monthly base salary			$5,000.00
Living cost allowance			$1,291.00
Foreign service premium			$ 750.00
Area allowance			-0-
Gross monthly salary			$7,041.00
Housing deduction			$ 500.00
Hypothetical tax			$ 570.00
Other			
Net monthly salary			$5,971.00

Prepared by   **Date**

Vice President, Human Resources   **Date**

challenging and interesting. Validation means giving the expatriate recognition for the overseas service when this person returns home. Expatriates who receive praise and recognition from colleagues and top managers for their overseas service and future contribution have fewer troubles with reentry than those whose contributions are disregarded. Validation should also include planning for how the returning employee will contribute to the organization. What skills will this person bring back? What position will he or she fill?

Guardian Industries, a glass manufacturer based in Auburn Hills, Michigan, treats its returning expatriates as valuable employees who have made a sacrifice for the company. They are therefore placed first in line for key assignments. After Dana Partridge worked for Guardian in Saudi Arabia and Thailand for a total of 13 years, the company couldn't immediately give him the job he was prepared for, plant manager, but as soon as a position became available, Partridge was selected.[56]

THINKING ETHICALLY

CAN OFFSHORING BE DONE MORE ETHICALLY?

As we saw in Chapter 5, human resource planning involves several options to meet an organization's needs for talent. One option is to outsource activities that can be performed more effectively and efficiently by a contractor. In today's global marketplace, outsourcing decisions frequently involve offshoring activities to companies in lower-wage locations. However, the reasons why labor costs are lower in another country include lower standards for working conditions—even conditions that would be considered unethical in the parent country.

This kind of decision can open up a company to criticism and may conflict with its own values related to social responsibility—a set of problems that Nike has been wrestling with for two decades. When the company was founded, in 1964, the idea of importing shoes from low-wage countries was an innovation. By the 1990s, reports of working conditions put Nike on the defensive, and it argued that it didn't own the factories, so it wasn't responsible. However, as negative publicity mounted, Nike began to share information openly and engage directly with factories to improve working conditions. In 2004, the company appointed Hannah Jones, a former reporter, to serve as its head of sustainable business.

Jones was especially concerned about working conditions in Bangladesh, but managers in the production division were drawn to the opportunity to buy shoes made at the lowest available cost. They believed that if they negotiated safety standards as part of their contracts, the suppliers would comply, but Jones had her doubts. To gather information and reach an agreement, Jones and the production managers visited one of the company's suppliers in Bangladesh. They saw safety hazards throughout the building and decided to stop buying from that supplier, even though the decision contributed to shrinking profit margins.

At Nike, decisions such as these have mostly eliminated purchases from suppliers that use certain hazardous materials and where workers have died. Still, organizations that investigate working conditions have found abuse of workers and violations of overtime and minimum-wage requirements at companies that sell to Nike. The company continues to set and monitor social responsibility goals such as buying from companies that have eliminated excessive overtime and that protect worker health and safety.

Questions

1. In deciding whether to outsource functions, does an organization such as Nike have an ethical obligation to consider how workers will be treated by the contractor that hires those workers? Why or why not?
2. What ethical standards for human resource management do you think a company should require from all its operations worldwide? In what areas of HRM, if any, should ethical standards be relaxed to match the prevailing norms of a particular country?

Sources: Shelly Banjo, "Inside Nike's Struggle to Balance Cost and Worker Safety in Bangladesh," *The Wall Street Journal,* April 21, 2014, http://online.wsj.com; Nike, *Sustainable Business Performance Summary,* FY 2012–2013, http://www.nikeresponsibility.com; Scott Cendrowski, "Can Outsourcing Be Improved?" *Fortune,* June 10, 2013, EBSCOhost, http://web.a.ebscohost.com.

SUMMARY

LO 16-1 Summarize how the growth in international business activity affects human resource management.

- More and more companies are entering international markets by exporting and operating foreign facilities.
- Organizations therefore need employees who understand customers and suppliers in other countries. They need to understand local laws and customs and be able to adapt their plans to local situations.
- Organizations may hire a combination of parent-country, host-country, and third-country nationals.

- They may operate on the scale of an exporter or an international, global, or multinational organization.
- A global organization needs a transnational HRM system, which makes decisions from a global perspective, includes managers from many countries, and is based on ideas contributed by people representing a variety of cultures.

LO1 6-2 Identify the factors that most strongly influence HRM in international markets.

- Culture is by far the most important influence. Each market's culture is its set of shared assumptions about how the world works and what ideals are worth striving for.
- A culture has the dimensions of individualism/collectivism, high or low power distance, high or low uncertainty avoidance, masculinity/femininity, and long-term or short-term orientation.
- Education is a second influence. Countries differ in the degree to which their labor markets include people with education and skills of value to employers.
- Another influence is the foreign country's political-legal system—its government, laws, and regulations.
- A final influence is a country's economic system. The system may be capitalist or socialist. The government's involvement in the country's economy, such as through taxes and price controls, is a strong factor determining HRM practices.

LO 16-3 Discuss how differences among countries affect HR planning at organizations with international operations.

- As organizations consider decisions about their level of international activity, HR professionals should provide information about the relevant human resource issues.
- When organizations decide to operate internationally or globally, HR planning involves decisions about where and how many employees are needed for each international facility.
- Some countries limit employers' ability to lay off workers, so organizations would be less likely to staff for peak periods. Other countries allow employers more flexibility in meeting human resource needs. HRM professionals need to be conversant with such differences.

LO 16-4 Describe how companies select and train human resources in a global labor market.

- Many organizations with foreign operations fill most positions with host-country nationals. These employees can more easily understand the values and customs of the local workforce, and hiring locally tends to be less expensive than moving employees to new locations.
- Organizations also fill foreign positions with parent-country and third-country nationals who have human relations skills associated with success in foreign assignments.
- When sending employees on foreign assignments, organizations prepare the employees (and often their families) through cross-cultural training.

- Before the assignment, the training provides instruction in the foreign country's language and culture.
- During the assignment, there is communication with the home country and mentoring.
- For the return home, the employer provides further training and development to aid retention.

LO 16-5 Discuss challenges related to managing performance and compensating employees from other countries.

- Pay structures can differ substantially among countries in terms of pay level and the relative worth of jobs.
- Organizations must decide whether to set pay levels and differences in terms of what workers are used to in their own countries or in terms of what employees' colleagues earn at headquarters. Typically, companies have resolved this dilemma by linking pay and benefits more closely to those of the employee's country, but this practice may be weakening so that it depends more on the nature and length of the foreign assignment.
- These decisions affect the organization's costs and ability to compete, so organizations consider local labor costs in their location decisions.
- Along with the basic pay structure, organizations must make decisions regarding incentive pay, such as bonuses and stock options.
- Laws may dictate differences in benefit packages, and the value of benefits will differ if a country requires them or makes them a government service.

LO 16-6 Explain how employers prepare managers for international assignments and for their return home.

- When an organization has selected a manager for an overseas assignment, it must prepare the person for the experience. In cross-cultural training, the soon-to-be expatriate learns about the foreign culture he or she is heading to, and studies her or his own home-country culture as well for insight. The trainee is given a detailed briefing on how to behave in business settings in the new country.
- Along with cross-cultural training, preparation of the expatriate should include career development activities to help the individual acquire valuable career skills during the foreign assignment and at the end of the assignment to handle repatriation successfully.
- Communication of changes at home and validation of a job well done abroad help the expatriate through the repatriation process.

KEY TERMS

parent country, 497
host country, 497
third country, 497
expatriates, 497

international organization, 499
multinational company, 499
global organization, 499
transnational HRM system, 499

culture shock, 507
cross-cultural preparation, 508
repatriation, 521

REVIEW AND DISCUSSION QUESTIONS

1. Identify the parent country, host country(ies), and third country(ies) in the following example: A global soft-drink company called Cold Cola has headquarters in Atlanta, Georgia. It operates production facilities in Athens, Greece, and in Jakarta, Indonesia. The company has assigned a manager from Boston to head the Athens facility and a manager from Hong Kong to manage the Jakarta facility. *(LO 16.1)*

2. What are some HRM challenges that arise when a U.S. company expands from domestic markets by exporting? When it changes from simply exporting to operating as an international company? When an international company becomes a global company? *(LO 16.2)*

3. In recent years, many U.S. companies have invested in Russia and sent U.S. managers there in an attempt to transplant U.S.-style management. According to Hofstede, U.S. culture has low power distance, uncertainty avoidance, and long-term orientation and high individuality and masculinity. Russia's culture has high power distance and uncertainty avoidance, low masculinity and long-term orientation, and moderate individuality. In light of what you know about cultural differences, how well do you think U.S. managers can succeed in each of the following U.S.-style HRM practices? (Explain your reasons.) *(LO 16.2)*
   a. Selection decisions based on extensive assessment of individual abilities.
   b. Appraisals based on individual performance.
   c. Systems for gathering suggestions from workers.
   d. Self-managing work teams.

4. Besides cultural differences, what other factors affect human resource management in an organization with international operations? *(LO 16.2)*

5. Suppose you work in the HR department of a company that is expanding into a country where the law and culture make it difficult to lay off employees. How should your knowledge of that difficulty affect human resource planning for the overseas operations? *(LO 16.3)*

6. Why do multinational organizations hire host-country nationals to fill most of their foreign positions, rather than sending expatriates for most jobs? *(LO 16.4)*

7. Suppose an organization decides to improve collaboration and knowledge sharing by developing an intranet to link its global workforce. It needs to train employees in several different countries to use this system. List the possible cultural issues you can think of that the training program should take into account. *(LO 16.4)*

8. For an organization with operations in three different countries, what are some advantages and disadvantages of setting compensation according to the labor markets in the countries where the employees live and work? What are some advantages and disadvantages of setting compensation according to the labor market in the company's headquarters? Would the best arrangement be different for the company's top executives and its production workers? Explain. *(LO 16.5)*

9. What abilities make a candidate more likely to succeed in an assignment as an expatriate? Which of these abilities do you have? How might a person acquire these abilities? *(LO 16.6)*

10. In the past, a large share of expatriate managers from the United States have returned home before successfully completing their foreign assignments. Suggest some possible reasons for the high failure rate. What can HR departments do to increase the success of expatriates? *(LO 16.6)*

TAKING RESPONSIBILITY

Coping with Pollution in Beijing

Beijing, China's capital city, has been plagued with serious air pollution. Of particular concern is a pollutant called fine particulate matter (PM), composed of a mix of solid and liquid particles, including sulfate, nitrates, ammonia, sodium chloride, carbon, mineral dust, and water. When people inhale PM that is 2.5 micrometers or smaller (called PM 2.5), it interferes with gas exchange in the lungs and contributes to development of lung cancer and cardiovascular and respiratory diseases. The standard of the World Health Organization is that PM 2.5 should not average more than 25 micrograms per cubic meter over a 24-hour period. But in a recent winter, PM 2.5 was measured at 755—a level at which people can see, feel, and taste the grit in the air. Along with increasing the risk of disease and premature death, that kind of pollution causes daily problems such as itchy throat and chronic cough.

Pollution that bad raises HRM challenges for organizations that operate in Beijing. A fundamental problem is that talented people in other countries do not want to relocate to the area. At BMW, several candidates for midlevel management positions withdrew their applications because of concerns about their families living in unhealthy conditions. A doctor at Beijing Family Hospital said he had heard from many expatriates that they intend not to renew their employment contracts to work in Beijing.

Some actions employers have taken involve making workers safer and more comfortable. Employers have purchased air purifiers and face masks for employees and have brought in experts to teach employees and their families how to stay healthy. They also have increased hardship allowances for employees working in the area.

Employers also can point to community efforts to make living in Beijing healthier. For example, international schools that teach the children of expatriates have taken actions to protect students. Dulwich College Beijing installed a huge dome over an outside play area, so students can leave the building to play basketball and other games when the PM 2.5 index is 250 or more.

The problem in Beijing also has become an opportunity for employers located away from the worst pollution. One Chinese company launched a "Blue Sky Recruitment" campaign in Beijing to lure young information technology engineers to the south of the country, where the air is better. The company's ads, posted in elevators, asked, "Do you dare to pursue a life with blue sky and white clouds?"

Questions

1. What would it take for you to accept an assignment in a location such as Beijing with extremely bad air pollution?
2. What should a socially responsible employer do to protect its employees in conditions such as these?

Sources: Laurie Burkitt and Brian Spegele, "Why Leave Job in Beijing? To Breathe," *The Wall Street Journal*, April 14, 2013; Jamil Anderlini and Leslie Hook, "Smog Dents Beijing's Expat Appeal," *Financial Times*, April 5, 2013; Peter Ford, "Beijing Is Booming, but Talent Is Leaving Due to Bad Air," *Christian Science Monitor*, April 4, 2013; Daryl Loo, "Beijing Air Akin to Living in Smoking Lounge: Chart of the Day," *Bloomberg News*, January 30, 2013, http://www.bloomberg.com; Jaime FlorCruz, "Living with Beijing's 'Air-pocalypse,'" CNN, January 19, 2013, http://www.cnn.com; World Health Organization, "Air Quality and Health," Media Center Fact Sheet 313, September 2011, http://www.who.int.

MANAGING TALENT

Global Mindset Gives Renault-Nissan a Strategic Edge

Carlos Ghosn's outlook is extraordinarily global. The chief executive of the Renault-Nissan Alliance was born in Brazil to Lebanese parents, spent most of his childhood in Lebanon, and earned engineering degrees in France. He went to work for Michelin, rose to management positions, led a turnaround of Michelin's South American division, and then moved again to head Michelin's North American division. His career caught the attention of French automaker Renault, which was looking for someone to lead a turnaround of Nissan after Renault had acquired a large stake in the struggling Japanese business. Ghosn returned Nissan to profitability and later became head of both automakers as well as the alliance they founded. He works in both Paris and Tokyo, also traveling to facilities in other countries.

Ghosn's global outlook has strengthened the alliance between Renault and Nissan, which has lasted longer than other such attempts in the industry. The companies share designs and hold ownership stakes in each other. Ghosn sees not only cultural barriers to overcome but also opportunities for applying each culture's strengths. For example, in Japan, Ghosn discovered a concept called *monozukuri*, which literally means making things but also implies a spirit of working together creatively over time to make improvements that result in excellent products. Ghosn found that *monozukuri* enables higher quality and lower costs by uniting employees across job categories in a common cause. So Renault-Nissan has taught the concept in its operations outside of Japan as a way to stimulate improvement.

Applying such lessons requires certain qualities. Two that Ghosn has identified include a thirst for learning and a humble attitude. These qualities promote learning from others. Another is what Ghosn calls "common" sense, by which he means a perspective that people share common ground, which helps them understand and listen to one another. Yet another important quality is mutual respect. According to Ghosn, the best way to acquire such skills and attitudes is to make a point of working with people from other cultures—say, by seeking out foreign assignments or collaborating with others from a position in one's home country. Nissan, for example, promotes this kind of communication by setting up leadership development programs in which employees from different countries participate in virtual classrooms online.

The global mindset remains important for Renault-Nissan's strategy of becoming one of the world's top three automakers. The alliance partners are deepening their relationship, with the goal of developing 70% of their vehicles jointly. The alliance also has set up a technology-sharing partnership with Daimler, based in Germany. Among other projects, they will produce luxury cars in Mexico. Daimler's Mercedes and Nissan's Infiniti will share engines and other parts with a common design.

Questions

1. Would you categorize the Renault-Nissan alliance as an international, multinational, or global organization? Why?
2. Suppose you work in the HR function at Nissan when it is identifying employees to work on the joint manufacturing project in Mexico. Briefly advise the company on how to prepare these employees to succeed as expatriates.

Sources: Eric Pfanner, "Nissan Reports Hefty Profit Rise," *The Wall Street Journal,* July 28, 2014, http://online.wsj.com; Lindsay Chappell, "Daimler and Nissan Hit the Gas; Partners to Build Luxury Vehicles, Engines, Parts," *Automotive News,* June 30, 2014, Business Insights: Global, http://bi.galegroup.com; Paul McVeigh and Bruce Gain, "How Ghosn Aims to Catch Toyota, GM, VW; Renault Rebound, Growth in China and Russia Are Keys," *Automotive News,* June 9, 2014, Business Insights: Global, http://bi.galegroup.com; Doron Levin, "Renault-Nissan Alliance Pushes Economies of Scale to New Level," *Fortune,* March 7, 2014, EBSCOhost, http://web.a.ebscohost.com; Günter K. Stahl, "Building Cross-Cultural Leadership Competence: An Interview with Carlos Ghosn," *Academy of Management Learning and Education* 12, no. 3 (2013): 494–502.

HR IN SMALL BUSINESS

Is Translating a Global Business?

One field in which small businesses have recently enjoyed rapid growth is in the business of providing translations. As barriers to international business continue to fall, more and more people are encountering language differences in the people they work with, sell to, and buy from. At the same time, advances in technology are providing avenues to deliver translations over the phone and over the Internet.

TransPerfect is one of the success stories. The company, based in New York, started out when founder Steve Iverson, a French teacher, began translating documents for clients. Satisfied customers returned, looking for translations of patents and annual reports—even for court reporting in foreign languages. The company now provides translations in over 170 languages. It has offices in more than 85 cities spread over six continents.

CETRA Language Solutions is headquartered in Elkins Park, Pennsylvania. It started with a lawsuit: while founder Jiri Stejskal was working on his doctorate degree in Slavic languages and literature, a Philadelphia law firm asked him to translate thousands of pages of documents related to a case. Stejskal brought in all the Czech translators he could find, and his company was born. Now CETRA's employees and hundreds of consultants serve the federal government plus companies involved in law, marketing research, and life sciences. The company's freelance translators and interpreters are located throughout the world.

LinguaLinx, based in Troy, New York, handles more than words. It converts documents, websites, and multimedia into almost 150 languages. The company not only has to find qualified translators, it needs experts in technology to make state-of-the-art presentations. To recruit employees, LinguaLinx emphasizes interesting work experiences, rather than fancy perks. The company's careers website describes opportunities to work with a diverse, multicultural group, including clients at leading corporations and nonprofit organizations.

Questions

1. What kinds of challenges would be involved in recruiting and selecting people to translate documents from Spanish, Polish, and French into English?
2. Would those challenges be easier to meet by recruiting within the United States or by looking for talent overseas? Explain.

3. Suppose a small translation business asked you to advise the company on how to overcome cultural barriers among a staff drawn from three countries. Suggest a few ways the company could use training and performance management to achieve this goal.

Sources: Tanisha A. Sykes, "Growth in Translation," *Inc.*, August 4, 2009, www.inc.com; Joel Dresang, "Iverson Language Associates Acquired by N.Y. Firm," *Milwaukee Journal Sentinel*, December 2, 2008, Business & Company Resource Center, http://galenet.galegroup.com; TransPerfect corporate website, www.transperfect.com, accessed August 5, 2014; CETRA Language Solutions corporate website, www.cetra.com, accessed August 5, 2014, and LinguaLinx corporate website, www.lingualinx.com, accessed August 5, 2014.

NOTES

1. Jennifer Paterson, "Is It Possible to Implement a Global Health and Wellbeing Programme?" *Employee Benefits*, September 3, 2013, EBSCOhost, http://web.a.ebscohost.com; Sloan Center on Aging and Work, Boston College, "The MetLife Study of Global Health and Wellness: A Look at How Multinational Companies Are Responding to the Need for a Healthier Workforce," MetLife, 2013, http://www.metlife.com.

2. Raju Gopalakrishnan, "Bangalore Software Industry Trying to Avoid an Ironic Fate," *Chicago Tribune*, April 17, 2012, sec. 2, p. 3.

3. "Moving Back to America," *The Economist*, May 14, 2011, EBSCOhost, http://web.ebscohost.com.

4. Kwoh, "Asia's Endangered Species."

5. N. Adler and S. Bartholomew, "Managing Globally Competent People," *The Executive* 6 (1992), pp. 52–65.

6. V. Sathe, *Culture and Related Corporate Realities* (Homewood, IL: Richard D. Irwin, 1985); M. Rokeach, *Beliefs, Attitudes, and Values* (San Francisco: Jossey-Bass, 1968).

7. N. Adler, *International Dimensions of Organizational Behavior*, 2nd ed. (Boston: PWS-Kent, 1991).

8. G. Hofstede, "Dimensions of National Cultures in Fifty Countries and Three Regions," in *Expectations in Cross-Cultural Psychology*, eds. J. Deregowski, S. Dziurawiec, and R. C. Annis (Lisse, Netherlands: Swets and Zeitlinger, 1983); G. Hofstede, "Cultural Constraints in Management Theories," *Academy of Management Executive* 7 (1993), pp. 81–90.

9. Hofstede, "Cultural Constraints in Management Theories."

10. A Ramesh and M. Gelfland, "Will They Stay or Will They Go? The Role of Job Embeddedness in Predicting Turnover in Individualistic and Collectivistic Cultures," *Journal of Applied Psychology* 95, no. 5 (2010), pp. 807–823.

11. W. A. Randolph and M. Sashkin, "Can Organizational Empowerment Work in Multinational Settings?" *Academy of Management Executive* 16, no. 1 (2002), pp. 102–15.

12. B. Gerhart and M. Fang, "National Culture and Human Resource Management: Assumptions and Evidence," *International Journal of Human Resource Management* 16, no. 6 (June 2005), pp. 971–86.

13. Yoree Koh, "Sony Throws Away Japan Recruitment Rulebook," *The Wall Street Journal*, January 7, 2012, http://blogs.wsj.com.

14. L. A. West Jr. and W. A. Bogumil Jr., "Foreign Knowledge Workers as a Strategic Staffing Option," *Academy of Management Executive* 14, no. 4 (2000), pp. 71–83.

15. Organization for Economic Co-operation and Development, "How Much Is Spent per Student?" in *Education at a Glance 2013: Highlights*, 2013, http://www.oecd.org.

16. World Bank, "The State of Education," Education Statistics, http://datatopics.worldbank.org, accessed July 29, 2014.

17. Sara Murray, "Mind the Gap: How One Employer Tackled Pay Equity," *The Wall Street Journal*, July 8, 2014, http://online.wsj.com.

18. Gopalakrishnan, "Bangalore Software Industry"; James T. Areddy and Tom Orlik, "Slower China Growth Signals Days of Miracles Are Waning," *The Wall Street Journal*, April 15, 2013, http://online.wsj.com; PricewaterhouseCoopers, "Going beyond Reshoring to Right-Shoring," September 2013, http://www.pwc.com.

19. Elizabeth Dwoskin, "Do You Want This Job?" *Bloomberg Businessweek*, November 14, 2011, EBSCOhost, http://web.ebscohost.com.

20. Brookings Institution, "Immigrant Workers in the U.S. Labor Force," research paper, March 15, 2012, http://www.brookings.edu.

21. Brookfield Global Relocation Services, *2014 Global Mobility Trends Survey*, 2014, http://knowledge.brookfieldgrs.com.

22. W. A. Arthur Jr. and W. Bennett Jr., "The International Assignee: The Relative Importance of Factors Perceived to Contribute to Success," *Personnel Psychology* 48 (1995), pp. 99–114; G. M. Spreitzer, M. W. McCall Jr., and J. D. Mahoney, "Early Identification of International Executive Potential," *Journal of Applied Psychology* 82 (1997), pp. 6–29.

23. J. S. Black and J. K. Stephens, "The Influence of the Spouse on American Expatriate Adjustment and Intent to Stay in Pacific Rim Overseas Assignments," *Journal of Management* 15 (1989), pp. 529–44.

24. P. Caligiuri, "The Big Five Personality Characteristics as Predictors of Expatriates' Desire to Terminate the Assignment and Supervisor-Rated Performance," *Personnel Psychology* 53 (2000), pp. 67–88.

25. Delia Flanja, "Culture Shock in Intercultural Communication," *Studia Europaea* (October 2009), Business & Company Resource Center, http://galenet.galegroup.com.

26. D. M. Gayeski, C. Sanchirico, and J. Anderson, "Designing Training for Global Environments: Knowing What

Questions to Ask," *Performance Improvement Quarterly* 15, no. 2 (2002), pp. 15–31.

27. J. S. Black and M. Mendenhall, "A Practical but Theory-Based Framework for Selecting Cross-Cultural Training Methods," in *Readings and Cases in International Human Resource Management*, eds. M. Mendenhall and G. Oddou (Boston: PWS-Kent, 1991), pp. 177–204.

28. Brookfield Global Relocation Services, 2014 Global Mobility Trends Survey.

29. Jordan Burchette, "Ultimate Checklist for Returning U.S. Expats," *CNNGo.com*, February 21, 2012, http://www.cnngo.com.

30. D. D. Davis, "International Performance Measurement and Management," in *Performance Appraisal: State of the Art in Practice*, ed. J. W. Smither (San Francisco: Jossey-Bass, 1998), pp. 95–131.

31. M. Gowan, S. Ibarreche, and C. Lackey, "Doing the Right Things in Mexico," *Academy of Management Executive* 10 (1996), pp. 74–81.

32. L. S. Chee, "Singapore Airlines: Strategic Human Resource Initiatives," in *International Human Resource Management: Think Globally, Act Locally*, ed. D. Torrington (Upper Saddle River, NJ: Prentice Hall, 1994), pp. 143–59.

33. "Johnson & Johnson Takes World View on Compensation," *Employee Benefits*, June 2011, p. 7.

34. "Top Whack: Big Country, Big Pay Cheques," *The Economist*, January 29, 2011, EBSCOhost, http://web.ebscohost.com.

35. Bureau of Labor Statistics, "International Comparisons of Hourly Compensation Costs in Manufacturing, 2012," August 9, 2013, http://www.bls.gov.

36. See, for example, A. E. Cobet and G. A. Wilson, "Comparing 50 Years of Labor Productivity in U.S. and Foreign Manufacturing," *Monthly Labor Review*, June 2002, pp. 51–63; Bureau of Labor Statistics, "International Comparisons of Manufacturing Productivity and Labor Cost Trends, 2008," news release, October 22, 2009, www.bls.gov; Daron Acemoglu and Melissa Dell, "Productivity Differences between and within Countries," *American Economic Journal: Macroeconomics 2010* 2, no. 1 (2010), pp. 169–88.

37. Stephen Miller, "Grasp Country Difference to Manage Global Pay," Compensation Discipline, March 30, 2010, http://www.shrm.org.

38. P. J. Dowling, D. E. Welch, and R. S. Schuler, *International Human Resource Management*, 3rd ed. (Cincinnati: South-Western, 1999), pp. 235–36.

39. Ibid.; J. La Palombara and S. Blank, *Multinational Corporations and National Elites: A Study of Tensions* (New York: Conference Board, 1976); A. B. Sim, "Decentralized Management of Subsidiaries and Their Performance: A Comparative Study of American, British and Japanese Subsidiaries in Malaysia," *Management International Review* 17, no. 2 (1977), pp. 45–51; Y. K. Shetty, "Managing the Multinational Corporation: European and American Styles," *Management International Review* 19, no. 3 (1979), pp. 39–48; J. Hamill, "Labor Relations Decision-Making within Multinational Corporations," *Industrial Relations Journal* 15, no. 2 (1984), pp. 30–34.

40. Dowling, Welch, and Schuler, *International Human Resource Management*, p. 231.

41. Bethany Allen-Ebrahimian, "The World's Largest Union: A 'Capitalist Running Dog,'" *Foreign Policy*, April 23, 2014, http://www.foreignpolicy.com; International Trade Union Confederation, "Internationally Recognised Core Labour Standards in the People's Republic of China," Report for the WTO General Council Review of the Trade Policies of the People's Republic of China (Geneva, May 10 and 12, 2010), http://www.ituc-csi.org.

42. Syed Zain Al-Mahmood and Tripti Lahri, "Bangladesh Opens Door to More Unions," *The Wall Street Journal*, May 13, 2013; Jason Burke, "Bangladesh Eases Trade Union Laws after Factory Building Collapse," *Guardian*, May 13, 2013.

43. J. K. Sebenius, "The Hidden Challenge of Cross-Border Negotiations," *Harvard Business Review*, March 2002, pp. 76–85.

44. E. Krell, "Evaluating Returns on Expatriates," *HRMagazine*, March 2005, downloaded from Infotrac at http://web5.infotrac.galegroup.com.

45. Ibid.; M. Harvey and M. M. Novicevic, "Selecting Expatriates for Increasingly Complex Global Assignments," *Career Development International* 6, no. 2 (2001), pp. 69–86.

46. M. Mendenhall and G. Oddou, "The Dimensions of Expatriate Acculturation," *Academy of Management Review* 10 (1985), pp. 39–47.

47. Arthur and Bennett , "The International Assignee."

48. J. I. Sanchez, P. E. Spector, and C. L. Cooper, "Adapting to a Boundaryless World: A Developmental Expatriate Model," *Academy of Management Executive* 14, no. 2 (2000), pp. 96–106.

49. P. Dowling and R. Schuler, *International Dimensions of Human Resource Management* (Boston: PWS-Kent, 1990).

50. Sanchez, Spector, and Cooper, "Adapting to a Boundaryless World."

51. Neal Goodman, "Helping Trainees Succeed Overseas," *Training*, March 2014, EBSCOhost, http://web.b.ebscohost.com.

52. Andrew L. Molinsky, "Code Switching between Cultures," *Harvard Business Review*, January–February 2012, pp. 140–41.

53. "How Can a Company Manage an Expatriate Employee's Performance?" *SHRM India*, www.shrmindia.org, accessed May 6, 2010.

54. Kwoh, "Asia's Endangered Species."

55. Adler, *International Dimensions of Organizational Behavior*.

56. Alice Andors, "Happy Returns," *HR Magazine*, March 2010, Business & Company Resource Center, http://galenet.galegroup.com.

Glossary

Achievement Tests: Tests that measure a person's existing knowledge and skills.

Action Learning: Training in which teams get an actual problem, work on solving it and commit to an action plan, and are accountable for carrying it out.

Adventure Learning: A teamwork and leadership training program based on the use of challenging, structured outdoor activities.

Affirmative Action: An organization's active effort to find opportunities to hire or promote people in a particular group.

Agency Shop: Union security arrangement that requires the payment of union dues but not union membership.

Alternative Dispute Resolution (ADR): Methods of solving a problem by bringing in an impartial outsider but not using the court system.

Alternative Work Arrangements: Methods of staffing other than the traditional hiring of full-time employees (for example, use of independent contractors, on-call workers, temporary workers, and contract company workers).

American Federation of Labor and Congress of Industrial Organizations (AFL-CIO): An association that seeks to advance the shared interests of its member unions at the national level.

Apprenticeship: A work-study training method that teaches job skills through a combination of on-the-job training and classroom training.

Aptitude Tests: Tests that assess how well a person can learn or acquire skills and abilities.

Arbitration: Conflict resolution procedure in which an arbitrator or arbitration board determines a binding settlement.

Assessment: Collecting information and providing feedback to employees about their behavior, communication style, or skills.

Assessment Center: A wide variety of specific selection programs that use multiple selection methods to rate applicants or job incumbents on their management potential.

Associate Union Membership: Alternative form of union membership in which members receive discounts on insurance and credit cards rather than representation in collective bargaining.

Avatars: Computer depictions of trainees, which the trainees manipulate in an online role-play.

Balanced Scorecard: A combination of performance measures directed toward the company's long- and short-term goals and used as the basis for awarding incentive pay.

Behavior Description Interview (BDI): A structured interview in which the interviewer asks the candidate to describe how he or she handled a type of situation in the past.

Behavioral Observation Scale (BOS): A variation of a BARS which uses all behaviors necessary for effective performance to rate performance at a task.

Behaviorally Anchored Rating Scale (BARS): Method of performance measurement that rates behavior in terms of a scale showing specific statements of behavior that describe different levels of performance.

Benchmarking: A procedure in which an organization compares its own practices against those of successful competitors.

Benchmarks: A measurement tool that gathers ratings of a manager's use of skills associated with success in managing.

Bona Fide Occupational Qualification (BFOQ): A necessary (not merely preferred) qualification for performing a job.

Brand Alignment: The process of ensuring that HR policies, practices, and programs support or are congruent with an organization's overall culture (or brand), products, and services.

Cafeteria-Style Plan: A benefits plan that offers employees a set of alternatives from which they can choose the types and amounts of benefits they want.

Calibration Meeting: Meeting at which managers discuss employee performance ratings and provide evidence supporting their ratings with the goal of eliminating the influence of rating errors.

Cash Balance Plan: Retirement plan in which the employer sets up an individual account for each employee and contributes a percentage of the employee's salary; the account earns interest at a predefined rate.

Checkoff Provision: Contract provision under which the employer, on behalf of the union, automatically deducts union dues from employees' paychecks.

Closed Shop: Union security arrangement under which a person must be a union member before being hired; illegal for those covered by the National Labor Relations Act.

Cloud Computing: The practice of using a network of remote servers hosted on the Internet to store, manage, and process data.

Coach: A peer or manager who works with an employee to motivate the employee, help him or her develop skills, and provide reinforcement and feedback.

Cognitive Ability Tests: Tests designed to measure such mental abilities as verbal skills, quantitative skills, and reasoning ability.

Collective Bargaining: Negotiation between union representatives and management representatives to arrive at a contract defining conditions of employment for the term of the contract and to administer that contract.

Commissions: Incentive pay calculated as a percentage of sales.

Communities of Practice: Groups of employees who work together, learn from each other, and develop a common understanding of how to get work accomplished.

Compensatory Model: Process of arriving at a selection decision in which a very high score on one type of assessment can make up for a low score on another.

Competency: An area of personal capability that enables employees to perform their work successfully.

Concurrent Validation: Research that consists of administering a test to people who currently hold a job, then comparing their scores to existing measures of job performance.

Consolidated Omnibus Budget Reconciliation Act (COBRA): Federal law that requires employers to permit employees or their dependents to extend their health insurance coverage at group rates for up to 36 months following a qualifying event, such as a layoff, reduction in hours, or the employee's death.

Construct Validity: Consistency between a high score on a test and high level of a construct such as intelligence or leadership ability, as well as between mastery of this construct and successful performance of the job.

Content Validity: Consistency between the test items or problems and the kinds of situations or problems that occur on the job.

Continuous Learning: Each employee's and each group's ongoing efforts to gather information and apply the information to their decisions in a learning organization.

Contributory Plan: Retirement plan funded by contributions from the employer and employee.

Coordination Training: Team training that teaches the team how to share information and make decisions to obtain the best team performance.

Core Competency: A set of knowledges and skills that make the organization superior to competitors and create value for customers.

Corporate Campaigns: Bringing public, financial, or political pressure on employers during union organization and contract negotiation.

Cost per Hire: The total amount of money spent to fill a vacancy. The number is computed by finding the cost of using a particular recruitment source and dividing that cost by the number of people hired to fill that type of vacancy.

Craft Union: Labor union whose members all have a particular skill or occupation.

Criterion-Related Validity: A measure of validity based on showing a substantial correlation between test scores and job performance scores.

Critical-Incident Method: Method of performance measurement based on managers' records of specific examples of the employee acting in ways that are either effective or ineffective.

Cross-Cultural Preparation: Training to prepare employees and their family members for an assignment in a foreign country.

Cross-Training: Team training in which team members understand and practice each other's skills so that they are prepared to step in and take another member's place.

Culture Shock: Disillusionment and discomfort that occur during the process of adjusting to a new culture.

Decision Support Systems: Computer software systems designed to help managers solve problems by showing how results vary when the manager alters assumptions or data.

Defined Benefit Plan: Pension plan that guarantees a specified level of retirement income.

Defined Contribution Plan: Retirement plan in which the employer sets up an individual account for each employee and specifies the size of the investment into that account.

Delayering: Reducing the number of levels in the organization's job structure.

Development: The acquisition of knowledge, skills, and behaviors that improve an employee's ability to meet changes in job requirements and in customer demands.

Differential Piece Rates: Incentive pay in which the piece rate is higher when a greater amount is produced.

Direct Applicants: People who apply for a vacancy without prompting from the organization.

Disability: Under the Americans with Disabilities Act, a physical or mental impairment that substantially limits one or more major life activities, a record of having such an impairment, or being regarded as having such an impairment.

DiSC: Brand of assessment tool that identifies individuals' behavioral patterns in terms of dominance, influence, steadiness, and conscientiousness.

Disparate Impact: A condition in which employment practices are seemingly neutral yet disproportionately exclude a protected group from employment opportunities.

Disparate Treatment: Differing treatment of individuals, where the differences are based on the individuals' race, color, religion, sex, national origin, age, or disability status.

Diversity Training: Training designed to change employee attitudes about diversity and/or develop skills needed to work with a diverse workforce.

Downsizing: The planned elimination of large numbers of personnel with the goal of enhancing the organization's competitiveness.

Downward Move: Assignment of an employee to a position with less responsibility and authority.

Due-Process Policies: Policies that formally lay out the steps an employee may take to appeal the employer's decision to terminate that employee.

EEO-1 Report: The EEOC's Employer Information Report, which details the number of women and minorities employed in nine different job categories.

E-Learning: Receiving training via the Internet or the organization's intranet.

Electronic Human Resource Management (e-HRM):   The processing and transmission of digitized HR information, especially using computer networking and the Internet.

Electronic Performance Support System (EPSS):   Computer application that provides access to skills training, information, and expert advice as needed.

Employee Assistance Program (EAP):   A referral service that employees can use to seek professional treatment for emotional problems or substance abuse.

Employee Benefits: Compensation in forms other than cash.

Employee Development: The combination of formal education, job experiences, relationships, and assessment of personality and abilities to help employees prepare for the future of their careers.

Employee Empowerment: Giving employees responsibility and authority to make decisions regarding all aspects of product development or customer service.

Employee Engagement: The degree to which employees are fully involved in their work and the strength of their job and company commitment.

Employee Retirement Income Security Act (ERISA):   Federal law that increased the responsibility of pension plan trustees to protect retirees, established certain rights related to vesting and portability, and created the Pension Benefit Guarantee Corporation.

Employee Stock Ownership Plan (ESOP):   An arrangement in which the organization distributes shares of stock to all its employees by placing it in a trust.

Employee Wellness Program (EWP):   A set of communications, activities, and facilities designed to change health-related behaviors in ways that reduce health risks.

Employment at Will: Employment principle that if there is no specific employment contract saying otherwise, the employer or employee may end an employment relationship at any time, regardless of cause.

Equal Employment Opportunity (EEO):   The condition in which all individuals have an equal chance for employment, regardless of their race, color, religion, sex, age, disability, or national origin.

Equal Employment Opportunity Commission (EEOC):   Agency of the Department of Justice charged with enforcing Title VII of the Civil Rights Act of 1964 and other antidiscrimination laws.

Ergonomics: The study of the interface between individuals' physiology and the characteristics of the physical work environment.

Ethics: The fundamental principles of right and wrong.

Evidence-Based HR: Collecting and using data to show that human resource practices have a positive influence on the company's bottom line or key stakeholders.

Exempt Employees: Managers, outside salespeople, and any other employees not covered by the FLSA requirement for overtime pay.

Exit Interview: A meeting of a departing employee with the employee's supervisor and/or a human resource specialist to discuss the employee's reasons for leaving.

Expatriates: Employees assigned to work in another country.

Experience Rating: The number of employees a company has laid off in the past and the cost of providing them with unemployment benefits.

Experiential Programs: Training programs in which participants learn concepts and apply them by simulating behaviors involved and analyzing the activity, connecting it with real-life situations.

Expert Systems: Computer systems that support decision making by incorporating the decision rules used by people who are considered to have expertise in a certain area.

External Labor Market: Individuals who are actively seeking employment.

Externship: Employee development through a full-time temporary position at another organization.

Fact Finder: Third party to collective bargaining who reports the reasons for a dispute, the views and arguments of both sides, and possibly a recommended settlement, which the parties may decline.

Fair Labor Standards Act (FLSA): Federal law that establishes a minimum wage and requirements for overtime pay and child labor.

Family and Medical Leave Act (FMLA): Federal law requiring organizations with 50 or more employees to provide up to 12 weeks of unpaid leave after childbirth or adoption, to care for a seriously ill family member, or for an employee's own serious illness.

Feedback: Information employers give employees about their skills and knowledge and where these assets fit into the organization's plans.

Fleishman Job Analysis System: Job analysis technique that asks subject-matter experts to evaluate a job in terms of the abilities required to perform the job.

Flexible Spending Account: Employee-controlled pretax earnings set aside to pay for certain eligible expenses, such as health care expenses, during the same year.

Flextime: A scheduling policy in which full-time employees may choose starting and ending times within guidelines specified by the organization.

Forced-Distribution Method: Method of performance measurement that assigns a certain percentage of employees to each category in a set of categories.

Forecasting: The attempts to determine the supply of and demand for various types of human resources to predict areas within the organization where there will be labor shortages or surpluses.

Four-Fifths Rule: Rule of thumb that provides (or shows) evidence of potential discrimination if an organization's hiring rate for a minority group is less than four-fifths the hiring rate for the majority group.

Gainsharing: Group incentive program that measures improvements in productivity and effectiveness objectives and distributes a portion of each gain to employees.

Generalizable: Valid in other contexts beyond the context in which the selection method was developed.

Glass Ceiling: Circumstances resembling an invisible barrier that keep most women and minorities from attaining the top jobs in organizations.

Global Organization: An organization that chooses to locate a facility based on the ability to effectively, efficiently, and flexibly produce a product or service, using cultural differences as an advantage.

Graphic Rating Scale: Method of performance measurement that lists traits and provides a rating scale for each trait; the employer uses the scale to indicate the extent to which an employee displays each trait.

Grievance Procedure: The process for resolving union-management conflicts over interpretation or violation of a collective bargaining agreement.

Health Maintenance Organization (HMO): A health care plan that requires patients to receive their medical care from the HMO's health care professionals, who are often paid a flat salary, and provides all services on a prepaid basis.

High-Performance Work System: An organization in which technology, organizational structure, people, and processes work together seamlessly to give an organization an advantage in the competitive environment.

Host Country: A country (other than the parent country) in which an organization operates a facility.

Hot-Stove Rule: Principle of discipline that says discipline should be like a hot stove, giving clear warning and following up with consistent, objective, immediate consequences.

Hourly Wage: Rate of pay for each hour worked.

HR Analytics: Type of assessment of HRM effectiveness that involves determining the impact of, or the financial cost and benefits of, a program or practice.

HR Dashboard: A display of a series of HR measures, showing the measure and progress toward meeting it.

HRM Audit: A formal review of the outcomes of HRM functions, based on identifying key HRM functions and measures of business performance.

Human Capital: An organization's employees, described in terms of their training, experience, judgment, intelligence, relationships, and insight.

Human Resource Information System (HRIS): A computer system used to acquire, store, manipulate, analyze, retrieve, and distribute information related to an organization's human resources.

Human Resource Management (HRM): The policies, practices, and systems that influence employees' behavior, attitudes, and performance.

Human Resource Planning: Identifying the numbers and types of employees the organization will require in order to meet its objectives.

Immigration Reform and Control Act of 1986: Federal law requiring employers to verify and maintain records on applicants' legal rights to work in the United States.

Incentive Pay: Forms of pay linked to an employee's performance as an individual, group member, or organization member.

Industrial Engineering: The study of jobs to find the simplest way to structure work in order to maximize efficiency.

Industrial Union: Labor union whose members are linked by their work in a particular industry.

Instructional Design: A process of systematically developing training to meet specified needs.

Interactional Justice: A judgment that the organization carried out its actions in a way that took the employee's feelings into account.

Internal Labor Force: An organization's workers (its employees and the people who have contracts to work at the organization).

International Organization: An organization that sets up one or a few facilities in one or a few foreign countries.

Internship: On-the-job learning sponsored by an educational institution as a component of an academic program.

Involuntary Turnover: Turnover initiated by an employer (often with employees who would prefer to stay).

Job: A set of related duties.

Job Analysis: The process of getting detailed information about jobs.

Job Description: A list of the tasks, duties, and responsibilities (TDRs) that a particular job entails.

Job Design: The process of defining how work will be performed and what tasks will be required in a given job.

Job Enlargement: Broadening the types of tasks performed in a job.

Job Enrichment: Empowering workers by adding more decision-making authority to jobs.

Job Evaluation: An administrative procedure for measuring the relative internal worth of the organization's jobs.

Job Experiences: The combination of relationships, problems, demands, tasks, and other features of an employee's job.

Job Extension: Enlarging jobs by combining several relatively simple jobs to form a job with a wider range of tasks.

Job Hazard Analysis Technique: Safety promotion technique that involves breaking down a job into basic elements, then rating each element for its potential for harm or injury.

Job Involvement: The degree to which people identify themselves with their jobs.

Job Posting: The process of communicating information about a job vacancy on company bulletin boards, in employee publications, on corporate intranets, and anywhere else the organization communicates with employees.

Job Rotation: Enlarging jobs by moving employees among several different jobs.

Job Satisfaction: A pleasant feeling resulting from the perception that one's job fulfills or allows for the fulfillment of one's important job values.

Job Sharing: A work option in which two part-time employees carry out the tasks associated with a single job.

Job Specification: A list of the knowledge, skills, abilities, and other characteristics (KSAOs) that an individual must have to perform a particular job.

Job Structure: The relative pay for different jobs within the organization.

Job Withdrawal: A set of behaviors with which employees try to avoid the work situation physically, mentally, or emotionally.

Knowledge Workers: Employees whose main contribution to the organization is specialized knowledge, such as knowledge of customers, a process, or a profession.

Labor Relations: Field that emphasizes skills that managers and union leaders can use to minimize costly forms of conflict (such as strikes) and seek win-win solutions to disagreements.

Leaderless Group Discussion: An assessment center exercise in which a team of five to seven employees is assigned a problem and must work together to solve it within a certain time period.

Leading Indicators: Objective measures that accurately predict future labor demand.

Learning Management System (LMS):   A computer application that automates the administration, development, and delivery of training programs.

Learning Organization: An organization that supports lifelong learning by enabling all employees to acquire and share knowledge.

Lockout: An employer's exclusion of workers from a workplace until they meet certain conditions.

Long-Term Disability Insurance: Insurance that pays a percentage of a disabled employee's salary after an initial period and potentially for the rest of the employee's life.

Maintenance of Membership: Union security rules not requiring union membership but requiring that employees who join the union remain members for a certain period of time.

Management by Objectives (MBO):   A system in which people at each level of the organization set goals in a process that flows from top to bottom, so employees at all levels are contributing to the organization's overall goals; these goals become the standards for evaluating each employee's performance.

Material Safety Data Sheets (MSDSs):   Forms on which chemical manufacturers and importers identify the hazards of their chemicals.

Mediation: Conflict resolution procedure in which a mediator hears the views of both sides and facilitates the negotiation process but has no formal authority to dictate a resolution.

Mentor: An experienced, productive senior employee who helps develop a less experienced employee (a protégé).

Merit Pay: A system of linking pay increases to ratings on performance appraisals.

Minimum Wage: The lowest amount that employers may pay under federal or state law, stated as an amount of pay per hour.

Mixed-Standard Scales: Method of performance measurement that uses several statements describing each trait to produce a final score for that trait.

Multinational Company: An organization that builds facilities in a number of different countries in an effort to minimize production and distribution costs.

Multiple-Hurdle Model: Process of arriving at a selection decision by eliminating some candidates at each stage of the selection process.

Myers-Briggs Type Indicator (MBTI):   Psychological inventory that identifies individuals' preferences for source of energy, means of information gathering, way of decision making, and lifestyle, providing information for team building and leadership development.

National Labor Relations Act (NLRA):   Federal law that supports collective bargaining and sets out the rights of employees to form unions.

National Labor Relations Board (NLRB):   Federal government agency that enforces the NLRA by conducting and certifying representation elections and investigating unfair labor practices.

Needs Assessment: The process of evaluating the organization, individual employees, and employees' tasks to determine what kinds of training, if any, are necessary.

Nepotism: The practice of hiring relatives.

Noncontributory Plan: Retirement plan funded entirely by contributions from the employer.

Nondirective Interview: A selection interview in which the interviewer has great discretion in choosing questions to ask each candidate.

Nonexempt Employees: Employees covered by the FLSA requirements for overtime pay.

Occupational Safety and Health Act (OSH Act):   U.S. law authorizing the federal government to establish and enforce occupational safety and health standards for all places of employment engaging in interstate commerce.

Occupational Safety and Health Administration (OSHA):   Labor Department agency responsible for inspecting employers, applying safety and health standards, and levying fines for violation.

Office of Federal Contract Compliance Programs (OFCCP):   The agency responsible for enforcing the executive orders that cover companies doing business with the federal government.

Offshoring: Moving operations from the country where a company is headquartered to a country where pay rates are lower but the necessary skills are available.

On-the-Job Training (OJT):   Training methods in which a person with job experience and skill guides trainees in practicing job skills at the workplace.

Open-Door Policy: An organization's policy of making managers available to hear complaints.

Organization Analysis: A process for determining the appropriateness of training by evaluating the characteristics of the organization.

Organizational Behavior Modification (OBM):   A plan for managing the behavior of employees through a formal system of feedback and reinforcement.

Organizational Commitment: The degree to which an employee identifies with the organization and is willing to put forth effort on its behalf.

Orientation: Training designed to prepare employees to perform their jobs effectively, learn about their organization, and establish work relationships.

Outcome Fairness: A judgment that the consequences given to employees are just.

Outplacement Counseling: A service in which professionals try to help dismissed employees manage the transition from one job to another.

Outsourcing: Contracting with another organization (vendor, third-party provider, or consultant) to provide services.

Paired-Comparison Method: Method of performance measurement that compares each employee with each other employee to establish rankings.

Panel Interview: Selection interview in which several members of the organization meet to interview each candidate.

Parent Country: The country in which an organization's headquarters is located.

Patient Protection and Affordable Care Act: Health care reform law passed in 2010 that includes incentives and penalties for employers providing health insurance as a benefit.

Pay Differential: Adjustment to a pay rate to reflect differences in working conditions or labor markets.

Pay Grades: Sets of jobs having similar worth or content, grouped together to establish rates of pay.

Pay Level: The average amount (including wages, salaries, and bonuses) the organization pays for a particular job.

Pay Policy Line: A graphed line showing the mathematical relationship between job evaluation points and pay rate.

Pay Ranges: A set of possible pay rates defined by a minimum, maximum, and midpoint of pay for employees holding a particular job or a job within a particular pay grade.

Pay Structure: The pay policy resulting from job structure and pay level decisions.

Peer Review: Process for resolving disputes by taking them to a panel composed of representatives from the organization at the same levels as the people in the dispute.

Pension Benefit Guarantee Corporation (PBGC):   Federal agency that insures retirement benefits and guarantees retirees a basic benefit if the employer experiences financial difficulties.

Performance Management: The process through which managers ensure that employees' activities and outputs contribute to the organization's goals.

Person Analysis: A process for determining individuals' needs and readiness for training.

Personnel Selection: The process through which organizations make decisions about who will or will not be allowed to join the organization.

Piecework Rate: Rate of pay for each unit produced.

Position: The set of duties (job) performed by a particular person.

Position Analysis Questionnaire (PAQ): A standardized job analysis questionnaire containing 194 questions about work behaviors, work conditions, and job characteristics that apply to a wide variety of jobs.

Predictive Validation: Research that uses the test scores of all applicants and looks for a relationship between the scores and future performance of the applicants who were hired.

Preferred Provider Organization (PPO): A health care plan that contracts with health care professionals to provide services at a reduced fee and gives patients financial incentives to use network providers.

Procedural Justice: A judgment that fair methods were used to determine the consequences an employee receives.

Profit Sharing: Incentive pay in which payments are a percentage of the organization's profits and do not become part of the employees' base salary.

Progressive Discipline: A formal discipline process in which the consequences become more serious if the employee repeats the offense.

Promotion: Assignment of an employee to a position with greater challenges, more responsibility, and more authority than in the previous job, usually accompanied by a pay increase.

Protean Career: A career that frequently changes based on changes in the person's interests, abilities, and values and in the work environment.

Psychological Contract: A description of what an employee expects to contribute in an employment relationship and what the employer will provide the employee in exchange for those contributions.

Readability: The difficulty level of written materials.

Readiness for Training: A combination of employee characteristics and positive work environment that permit training.

Realistic Job Preview: Background information about a job's positive and negative qualities.

Reasonable Accommodation: An employer's obligation to do something to enable an otherwise qualified person to perform a job.

Recruiting: Any activity carried on by the organization with the primary purpose of identifying and attracting potential employees.

Recruitment: The process through which the organization seeks applicants for potential employment.

Reengineering: A complete review of the organization's critical work processes to make them more efficient and able to deliver higher quality.

Referrals: People who apply for a vacancy because someone in the organization prompted them to do so.

Reliability: The extent to which a measurement is from random error.

Repatriation: The process of preparing expatriates to return home from a foreign assignment.

Right-to-Know Laws: State laws that require employers to provide employees with information about the health risks associated with exposure to substances considered hazardous.

Right-to-Work Laws: State laws that make union shops, maintenance of membership, and agency shops illegal.

Role: The set of behaviors that people expect of a person in a particular job.

Role Ambiguity: Uncertainty about what the organization expects from the employee in terms of what to do or how to do it.

Role Analysis Technique: A process of formally identifying expectations associated with a role.

Role Conflict: An employee's recognition that demands of the job are incompatible or contradictory.

Role Overload: A state in which too many expectations or demands are placed on a person.

Sabbatical: A leave of absence from an organization to renew or develop skills.

Salary: Rate of pay for each week, month, or year worked.

Scanlon Plan: A gainsharing program in which employees receive a bonus if the ratio of labor costs to the sales value of production is below a set standard.

Selection: The process by which the organization attempts to identify applicants with the necessary knowledge, skills, abilities, and other characteristics that will help the organization achieve its goals.

Self-Assessment: The use of information by employees to determine their career interests, values, aptitudes, and behavioral tendencies.

Self-Service: System in which employees have online access to information about HR issues and go online to enroll themselves in programs and provide feedback through surveys.

Sexual Harassment: Unwelcome sexual advances as defined by the EEOC.

Short-Term Disability Insurance: Insurance that pays a percentage of a disabled employee's salary as benefits to the employee for six months or less.

Simple Ranking: Method of performance measurement that requires managers to rank employees in their group from the highest performer to the poorest performer.

Simulation: A training method that represents a real-life situation, with trainees making decisions resulting in outcomes that mirror what would happen on the job.

Situational Interviews: A structured interview in which the interviewer describes a situation likely to arise on the job, then asks the candidate what he or she would do in that situation.

Skill-Based Pay Systems: Pay structures that set pay according to the employees' levels of skill or knowledge and what they are capable of doing.

Social Security: The federal Old Age, Survivors, Disability, and Health Insurance (OASDHI) program, which combines old age (retirement) insurance, survivor's insurance, disability insurance, hospital insurance (Medicare Part A), and supplementary medical insurance (Medicare Part B) for the elderly.

Stakeholders: The parties with an interest in the company's success (typically, shareholders, the community, customers, and employees).

Standard Hour Plan: An incentive plan that pays workers extra for work done in less than a preset "standard time."

Stock Options: Rights to buy a certain number of shares of stock at a specified price.

Straight Piecework Plan: Incentive pay in which the employer pays the same rate per piece, no matter how much the worker produces.

Strike: A collective decision by union members not to work until certain demands or conditions are met.

Structured Interview: A selection interview that consists of a predetermined set of questions for the interviewer to ask.

Succession Planning: The process of identifying and tracking high-potential employees who will be able to fill top management positions when they become vacant.

Summary Plan Description: Report that describes a pension plan's funding, eligibility requirements, risks, and other details.

Sustainability: An organization's ability to profit without depleting its resources, including employees, natural resources, and the support of the surrounding community.

Talent Management: A systematic, planned effort to attract, retain, develop, and motivate highly skilled employees and managers.

Task Analysis: The process of identifying and analyzing tasks to be trained for.

Team Leader Training: Training in the skills necessary for effectively leading the organization's teams.

Teamwork: The assignment of work to groups of employees with various skills who interact to assemble a product or provide a service.

Technic of Operations Review (TOR): Method of promoting safety by determining which specific element of a job led to a past accident.

Third Country: A country that is neither the parent country nor the host country of an employer.

360-Degree Performance Appraisal: Performance measurement that combines information from the employee's managers, peers, subordinates, self, and customers.

Total Quality Management (TQM): A company-wide effort to continuously improve the ways people, machines, and systems accomplish work.

Training: An organization's planned efforts to help employees acquire job-related knowledge, skills, abilities, and behaviors, with the goal of applying these on the job.

Transaction Processing: Computations and calculations involved in reviewing and documenting HRM decisions and practices.

Transfer: Assignment of an employee to a position in a different area of the company, usually in a lateral move.

Transfer of Training: On-the-job use of knowledge, skills, and behaviors learned in training.

Transitional Matrix: A chart that lists job categories held in one period and shows the proportion of employees in each of those job categories in a future period.

Transnational HRM System: Type of HRM system that makes decisions from a global perspective, includes managers from many countries, and is based on ideas contributed by people representing a variety of cultures.

Trend Analysis: Constructing and applying statistical models that predict labor demand for the next year, given relatively objective statistics from the previous year.

Unemployment Insurance: A federally mandated program to minimize the hardships of unemployment through payments to unemployed workers, help in finding new jobs, and incentives to stabilize employment.

Uniform Guidelines on Employee Selection Procedures: Guidelines issued by the EEOC and other agencies to identify how an organization should develop and administer its system for selecting employees so as not to violate antidiscrimination laws.

Union Shop: Union security arrangement that requires employees to join the union within a certain amount of time (30 days) after beginning employment.

Union Steward: An employee elected by union members to represent them in ensuring that the terms of the labor contract are enforced.

Unions: Organizations formed for the purpose of representing their members' interests in dealing with employers.

Utility: The extent to which something provides economic value greater than its cost.

Validity: The extent to which performance on a measure (such as a test score) is related to what the measure is designed to assess (such as job performance).

Vesting Rights: Guarantee that when employees become participants in a pension plan and work a specified number of years, they will receive a pension at retirement age, regardless of whether they remained with the employer.

Virtual Reality: A computer-based technology that provides an interactive, three-dimensional learning experience.

Voluntary Turnover: Turnover initiated by employees (often when the organization would prefer to keep them).

Work Flow Design: The process of analyzing the tasks necessary for the production of a product or service.

Workers' Compensation: State programs that provide benefits to workers who suffer work-related injuries or illnesses, or to their survivors.

Workforce Analytics: The use of quantitative tools and scientific methods to analyze data from human resource databases and other sources to make evidence-based decisions that support business goals.

Workforce Utilization Review: A comparison of the proportion of employees in protected groups with the proportion that each group represents in the relevant labor market.

Yield Ratio: A ratio that expresses the percentage of applicants who successfully move from one stage of the recruitment and selection process to the next.

Credits

Text Credits

Chapter 4

Figure 4.2: Union Pacific, "Union Pacific Careers: Train Crew," https://up.jobs/train-crew.html, accessed May 7, 2014. Used with permission; 4.3: Union Pacific, "Union Pacific Careers: Train Crew," https://up.jobs/train-crew.html, accessed May 7, 2014. Used with permission.

Chapter 9

Table 9.3: From Chapter 1.5, "Evaluating Human Resource Effectiveness," by Anne S. Tsui and Luis R. Gomez-Mejia from Human Resource Management: Evolving Roles & Responsibilities, edited by Lee Dyer, 1988. Copyright 1988, Society for Human Resource Management, Alexandria, VA. Used with permission. All rights reserved.

Chapter 11

Figure 11.7: Brodke, M. R., Sliter, M. T., Balzer, W. K., Gillespie, J. Z., Gillespie, M. A., Gopalkrishnan, P., Lake, C. J., Oyer, B., Withrow, S., & Yankelevich, M. (2009). The Job Descriptive Index and Job in General (2009 Revision): Quick Reference Guide. Bowling Green, OH: Bowling Green State University. Used with permission.

Chapter 13

Figure 13.1: DILBERT (c) 1995 Scott Adams. Used by permission of UNIVERSAL UCLICK. All rights reserved.

Chapter 15

Table 15.1: Excerpted from J. A. Segal, "Unshackle Your Supervisors to Stay Union Free," in HR Magazine, June 1998. Copyright © 1998, Society for Human Resource Management, Alexandria, VA. Used with permission. All rights reserved.

Chapter 16

Figure 16.6: From C. Reynolds, "Compensation of Overseas Personnel," in Handbook of Human Resource Administration, 2nd ed., ed. by J. J. Famularo, McGraw-Hill, 1986, p. 51. Reprinted with permission of The McGraw-Hill Companies, Inc.

Photo Credits

Chapter 1

Page 2: © John A Rizzo/Pixtal/SuperStock RF; **p. 5:** © Justin Sullivan/Getty Images; **p. 7:** © Lars A. Niki RF; **p. 10:** © PR NEWSWIRE/AP Images.

Chapter 2

Page 29: © Image Source, all rights reserved. RF; **p. 31:** © Jose Luis Pelaez, Inc./Corbis; **p. 39:** © Pixtal/AGE Fotostock RF; **p. 48:** © Comstock/PunchStock RF; **p. 53:** © Â© Redlink/Corbis RF.

Chapter 3

Page 62: © Associated Press; **p. 63:** Courtesy U. S. Department of Labor; **p. 71:** © AP Images/The Free-Lance Star, Mike Morones; **p. 84:** © Purestock/SuperStock RF; **p. 85:** Courtesy of OSHA/U.S. Department of Labor.

Chapter 4

Page 101: © Image Source, all rights reserved. RF; **p. 105:** © Stockbyte/Getty Images RF; **p. 109:** © Courtesy U.S. Department of Labor; **p. 118:** © AP Images/Elaine Thompson; **p. 123:** © Javier Pierini/Getty Images RF.

Chapter 5

Page 132: © Associated Press; **p. 135:** © Royalty-Free/Corbis RF; **p. 137:** Courtesy of Cold Stone Creamery; **p. 151:** © NetPhotos/Alamy; **p. 155:** © Neville Elder/Corbis.

Chapter 6

Page 167: © AP Images for U.S. Chamber of Commerce Foundation; **p. 169:** © Image Source/age fotostock RF; **p. 178:** © Brand X Pictures/PunchStock RF; **p. 184:** © AP Photo/Mark Lennihan; **p. 187:** © Phil Boorman/Cultura/Getty Images RF.

Chapter 7

Page 200: © Anton Vengo/Purestock/Superstock RF; **p. 204:** © Najlah Feanny/Corbis; **p. 215:** © Associated Press; **p. 217:** © David Pu'u/Corbis; **p. 226:** © Corbis.

Chapter 8

Page 236: © Press Association via AP Images; **p. 243:** © Karen Moskowitz/The Image Bank/Getty Images; **p. 248:** © Jacobs Stock Photography/Getty Images/RF; **p. 251:** © Jacobs Stock Photography/Getty Images/RF.

Chapter 9

Page 270: © Kali Nine LLC/Getty Images RF; **p. 273:** © Peter Beck/Corbis; **p. 275:** © Hero Images/Fancy/Corbis RF; **p. 284:** © B.O'Kane/Alamy; **p. 287:** © Lars Niki RF.

Chapter 10

Page 298: © iStockphoto.com/alynst RF; **p. 313:** © iStockphoto.com/dashadima RF; **p. 315:** © Ryan McVay/Photodisc/Getty Images RF; **p. 317:** © Ronnie Kaufman/Corbis; **p. 319:** © Ryan McVay/Getty Images RF.

Chapter 11

Page 332: © Image Source/Getty Images RF; **p. 334:** © Klaus Tiedge/Blend Images LLC RF; **p. 346:** © Sandy Huffaker/Getty Images; **p. 351:** © Kim Steele/Getty Images RF; **p. 354:** © Steve Chenn/Corbis.

Chapter 12

Page 366: © Bob Pardue—Signs/Alamy; **p. 369:** © Walter Hodges/Getty Images; **p. 373:** © Royalty-Free/Corbis RF; **p. 379:** © Jeff Vespa/Wire Images/Getty Images; **p. 384:** © John Boykin/PhotoEdit—All rights reserved.

Chapter 13

Page 395: Clerkenwell/Getty Images RF; **p. 397:** © Purestock/SuperStock RF; **p. 403:** © Ariel Skelley/Blend Images LLC RF; **p. 405:** © Kwame Zikomo/SuperStock; **p. 415:** © The McGraw-Hill Companies, Inc./Andrew Resek, photographer RF.

Chapter 14

Page 423: © Sergey Mironov/Alamy RF; **p. 429:** © Chris Ryan/age fotostock RF; **p. 432:** © Flying Colours Ltd/Getty Images RF; **p. 436:** © AP Images/Tom Uhlman; **p. 443:** © Stuart O'Sullivan/Getty Images.

Chapter 15

Page 460: © Associated Press; **p. 462:** © Tim Pannell/SuperStock RF; **p. 467:** © Steven Rubin/The Image Works; **p. 476:** © Boston Globe via Getty Images; **p. 482:** © AP Photo/John Minchillo.

Chapter 16

Page 495: © JGI/Blend Images LLC RF; **p. 497:** © Sherwin Crasto/Corbis; **p. 500:** © IMAGEMORE CO., LTD/Imagemore Co., Ltd./Corbis RF; **p. 503:** © Paul Alamy/Corbis; **p. 506:** © Rob Brimson/The Image Bank/Getty Images.

Name and Company Index

Subject Index